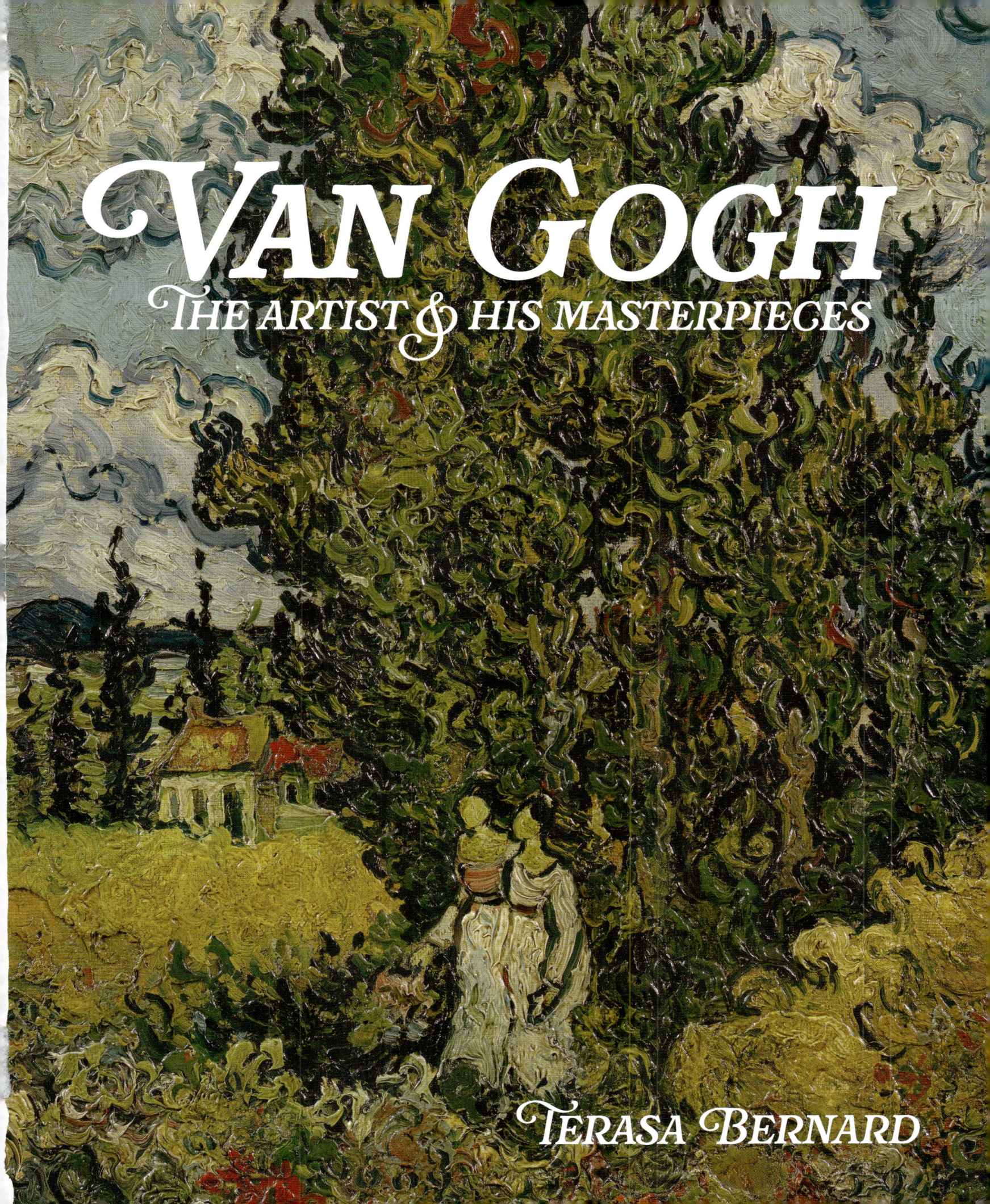

Van Gogh
The Artist & His Masterpieces

Terasa Bernard

CONTENTS

Hinkler Pty Ltd 2025
45–55 Fairchild Street
Heatherton Victoria 3202 Australia
www.hinkler.com

ISBN: 978-1-4889-7509-7

Printed in China

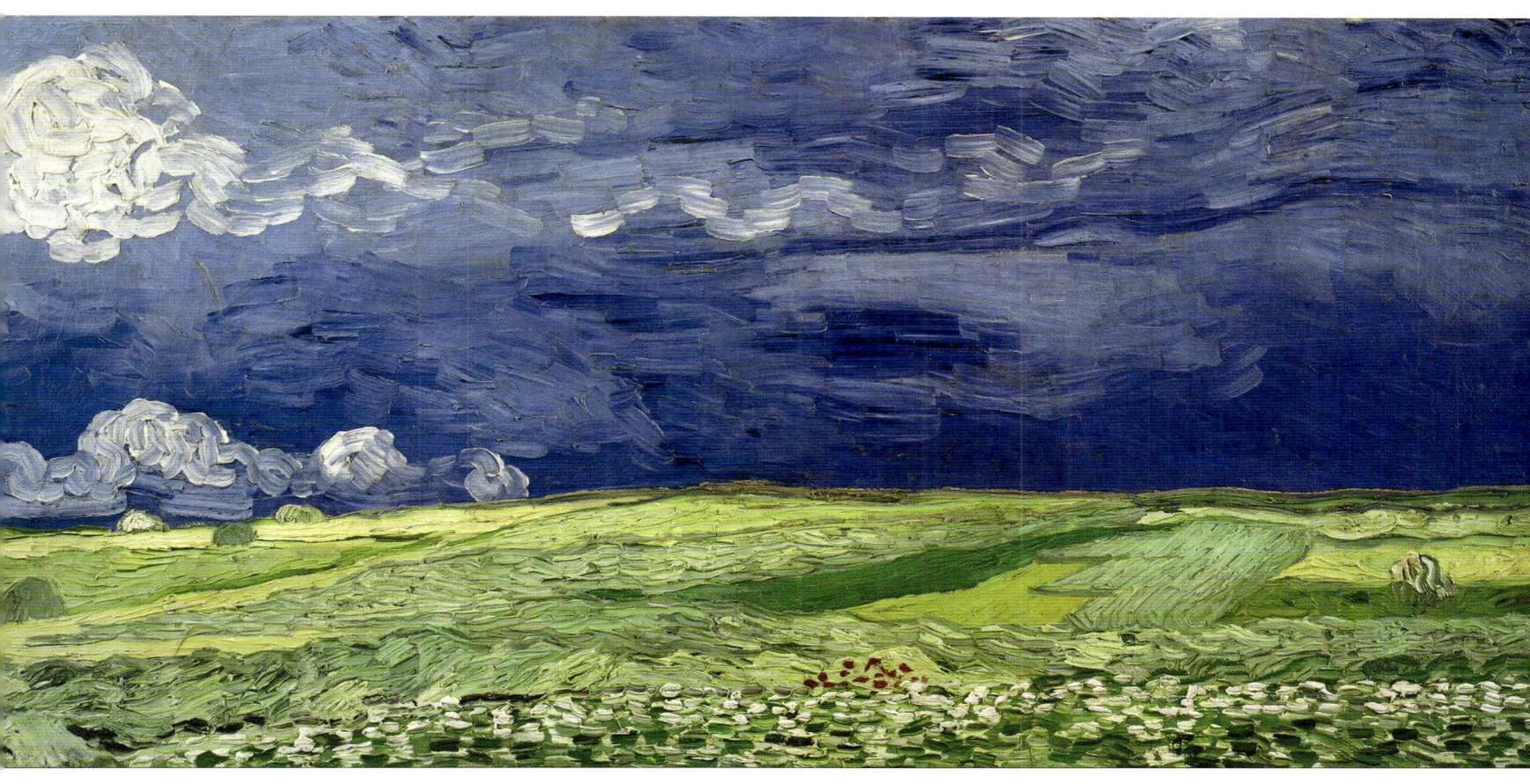

[ABOVE] *Wheatfield Under Thunderclouds* (July 1890). Oil on canvas. Van Gogh Museum, Amsterdam (Vincent van Gogh Foundation).

[TITLE PAGE] *Cypresses with Two Female Figures* (June 1889). Oil on canvas. Kröller-Müller Museum, Otterlo.

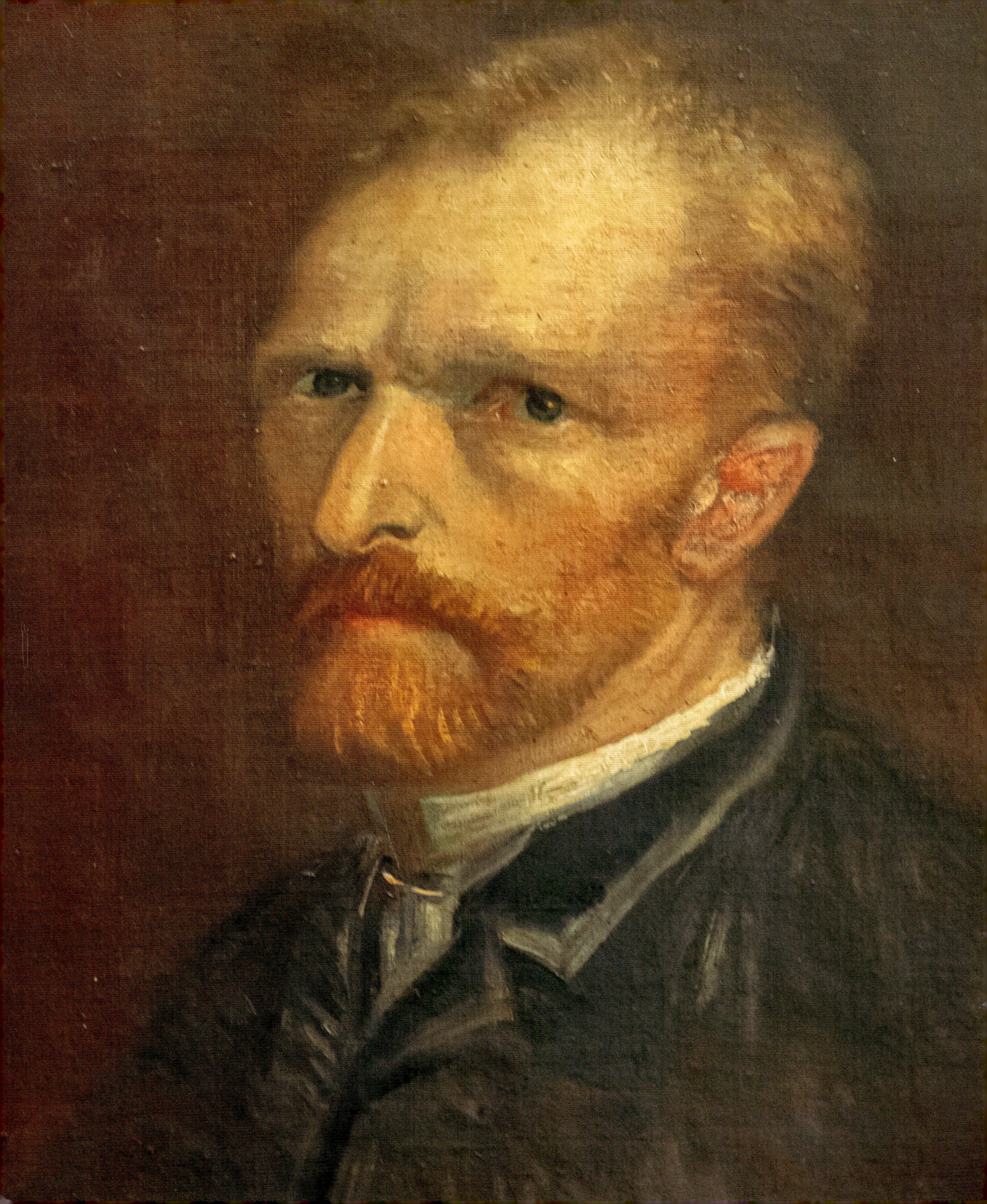

INTRODUCTION
WHO WAS VINCENT VAN GOGH?

VINCENT VAN GOGH is surely one of the most recognized names in the history of Western art. He was a prodigiously prolific artist: in just a decade, he created more than 2,000 works of art, including close to 900 oil paintings, most of which were made in the last two years of his life. Vincent, whose short life was filled with both exuberant creativity and unbridled tragedy, had the very soul of a tortured artist. Despite the astounding reputation his works garnered after his death, in his lifetime he never gained the success he deserved.

He was born Vincent Willem van Gogh on March 30, 1853, in Groot Zundert, North Brabant, Netherlands. His father, Theodorus van Gogh (1822–1885), was a minister of the Dutch Reformed Church, and his mother, Anna Cornelia Carbentus (1819–1907), came from a prosperous family in The Hague. Two of his uncles were art dealers, and he began his career at the age of 16, when his uncle Cent obtained a position for him at the art dealers Goupil & Cie in The Hague. It was during this stint as a salesman that he began the habit of writing letters to his devoted brother Theo, a habit that lasted his entire life and one that gives us so much insight into his thoughts and heart. From The Hague, Vincent was sent to a branch of the Goupil gallery in London, and then in 1875, to another branch in Paris. For Vincent, this was a happy period—he was absorbed in the vibrant life around him—but this happiness ended abruptly when his work was found unsatisfactory.

Once back in the Netherlands, he took a post as a missionary in 1879 and was eventually sent to Petit-Wasmes, in the poverty-stricken coal-mining district of Borinage in Belgium. He threw himself into this work, wanting to make a difference, but his overzealousness sparked his dismissal. He remained in Belgium to study art, now determined to give happiness to others by creating beauty. His first important work, *The Potato Eaters,* was painted in 1885. In 1886, he made the move to Paris, joining his brother Theo, who was a manager at Goupil's. Vincent went to study at the atelier of Fernand Cormon and met Camille Pissarro, Claude Monet, and Paul Gauguin. Here, he began to lighten his somber palette and to adopt the short brushstrokes of the Impressionists. This was a time of comparative contentment, but his volatile temperament made him a difficult companion. In addition, his physical health was suffering from the overextension of nighttime art discussions and daytime painting. He decided to travel south in the hopes of finding a more felicitous atmosphere for painting. He settled in Arles, a city on the Rhône River in Provence, and ever hopeful, he wished for his friends to join him there and help him to found an artistic community—a "Studio of the South." Gaugin did join him for a short time, but with disastrous results. After a row with Gauguin, Vincent, in the throes of a mental breakdown, cut off part of his own ear. For the rest of his life, he would alternate between fits of madness and more lucid periods. After a period of hospitalization in Arles, he left the city. Soon after leaving Arles, he committed himself to the asylum in Saint-Rémy de Provence, where he spent a year under treatment while also painting some of what would become his most famous works. By May 1890, he was deemed much better and was sent to Auvers-sur-Oise, near Paris, to be watched over by Dr. Gachet. Gachet had a good relationship with Vincent, and the work Vincent produced at Auvers is some of his best, yet his mental state sadly deteriorated. On a July day, he shot himself in the chest, dying two days later. But even at the very end, Vincent spoke of his love for humanity, telling Theo, "I did it for the good of all."

> " *Art is to console those who are broken by life.*"
>
> ~ VINCENT VAN GOGH

[OPPOSITE PAGE] *Self-Portrait* (Autumn 1886).
Oil on canvas. Kunstmuseum Den Haag, The Hague.

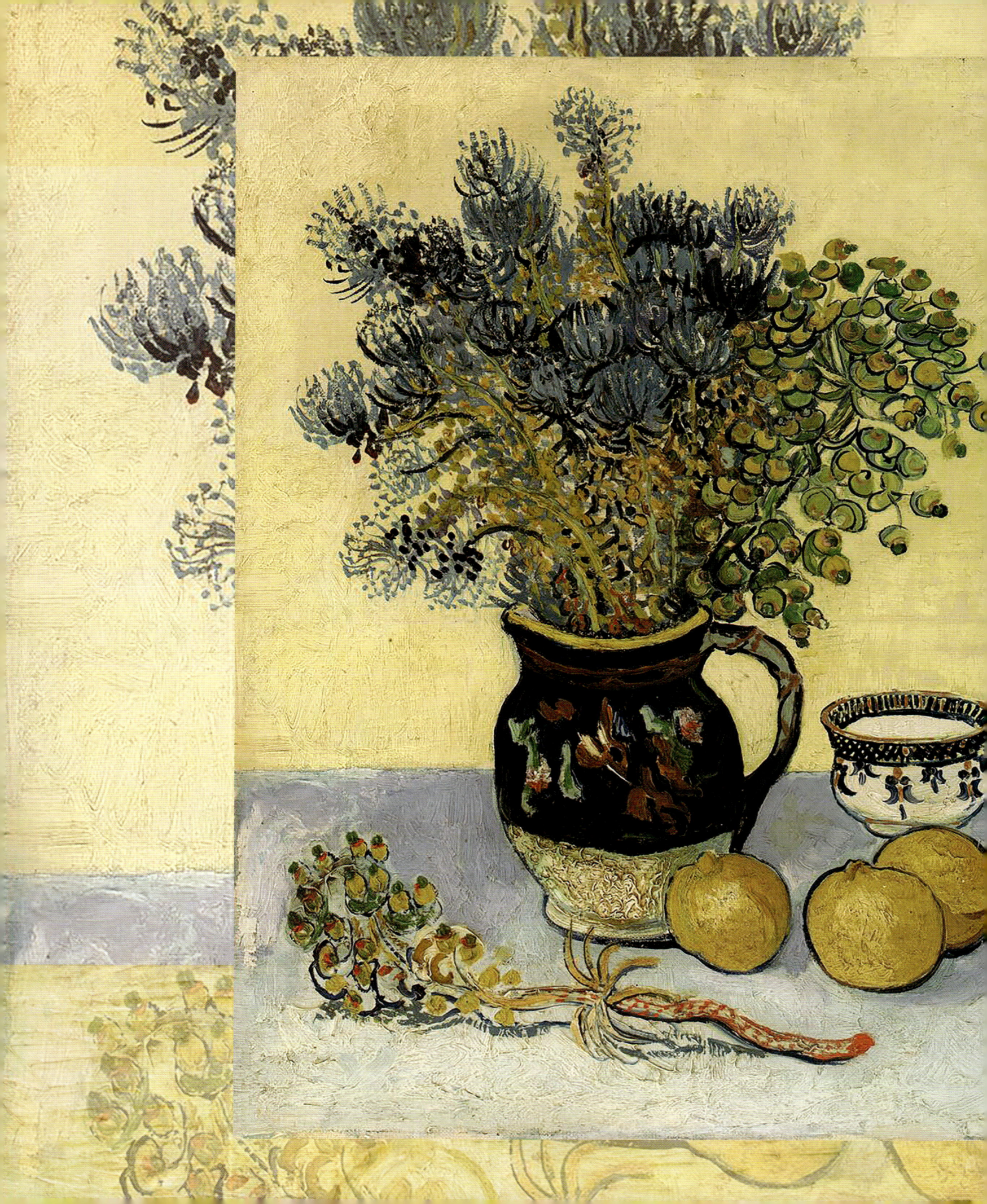

STILL LIFE & FLOWER PAINTINGS

STILL LIFE IS A GENRE Vincent periodically returned to during his artistic career. Of the estimated more than 900 paintings he created, roughly 170—about a fifth of his entire output—are still lifes, with images ranging from poppies, irises, and other flowers within vases to everyday objects like shoes, bottles, and fruit. Just as many young artists do during their training, he practiced this form in his early works to improve his technique, but it is the later works, particularly in the two famous *Sunflower* series, that he shows such a mastery of bold form and vibrant color executed with dynamic brushstrokes.

Still Life: Majolica with Wildflowers (May 1888).
Oil on canvas. The Barnes Foundation, Philadelphia.

EARLY STILL LIFES

Unlike many of the painters we now think of as masters of the art, Vincent received little formal training. In early November 1880, he did register for a course in drawing from antiquity at the Académie Royale des Beaux-Arts de Bruxelles, but his time there was short-lived. In 1881, he began a more informal study with artist Anton Mauve, the husband of his cousin Ariëtte (Jet) Carbentus. Mauve gave him instruction in painting with oils and watercolor, but they fell out, and Vincent was back on his own. The works he produced in these early years tend to be dark, with a more traditional brushwork technique than the bright, more dynamic method he developed over the course of his too-short career.

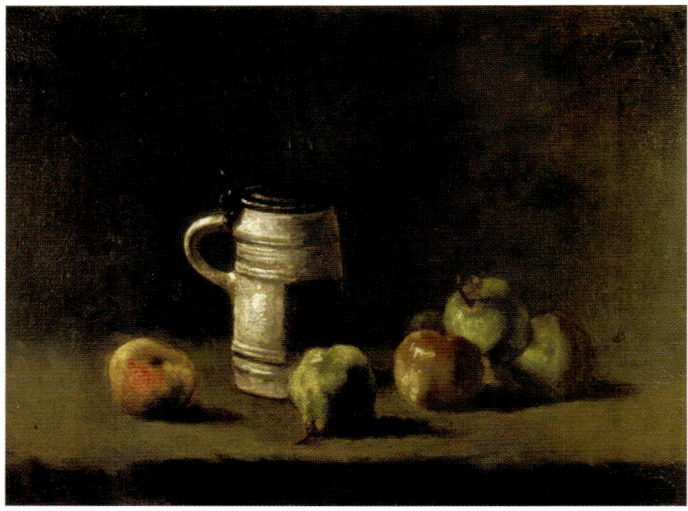

Still Life with Beer Mug and Fruit (December 1881). Oil on canvas. Von der Heydt Museum, Wuppertal.

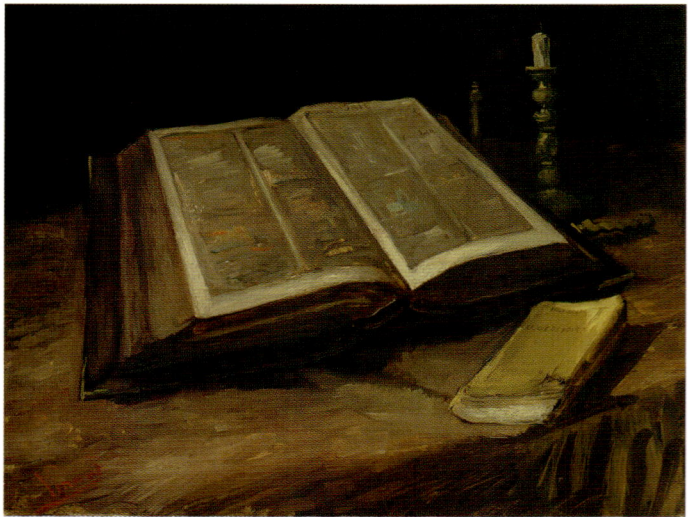

Still Life with Bible (October 1885). Oil on canvas. Van Gogh Museum, Amsterdam (Vincent van Gogh Foundation).

A few months after his father's death, Vincent chose to paint this hefty Bible, which had belonged to his father, who had been a Protestant minister.

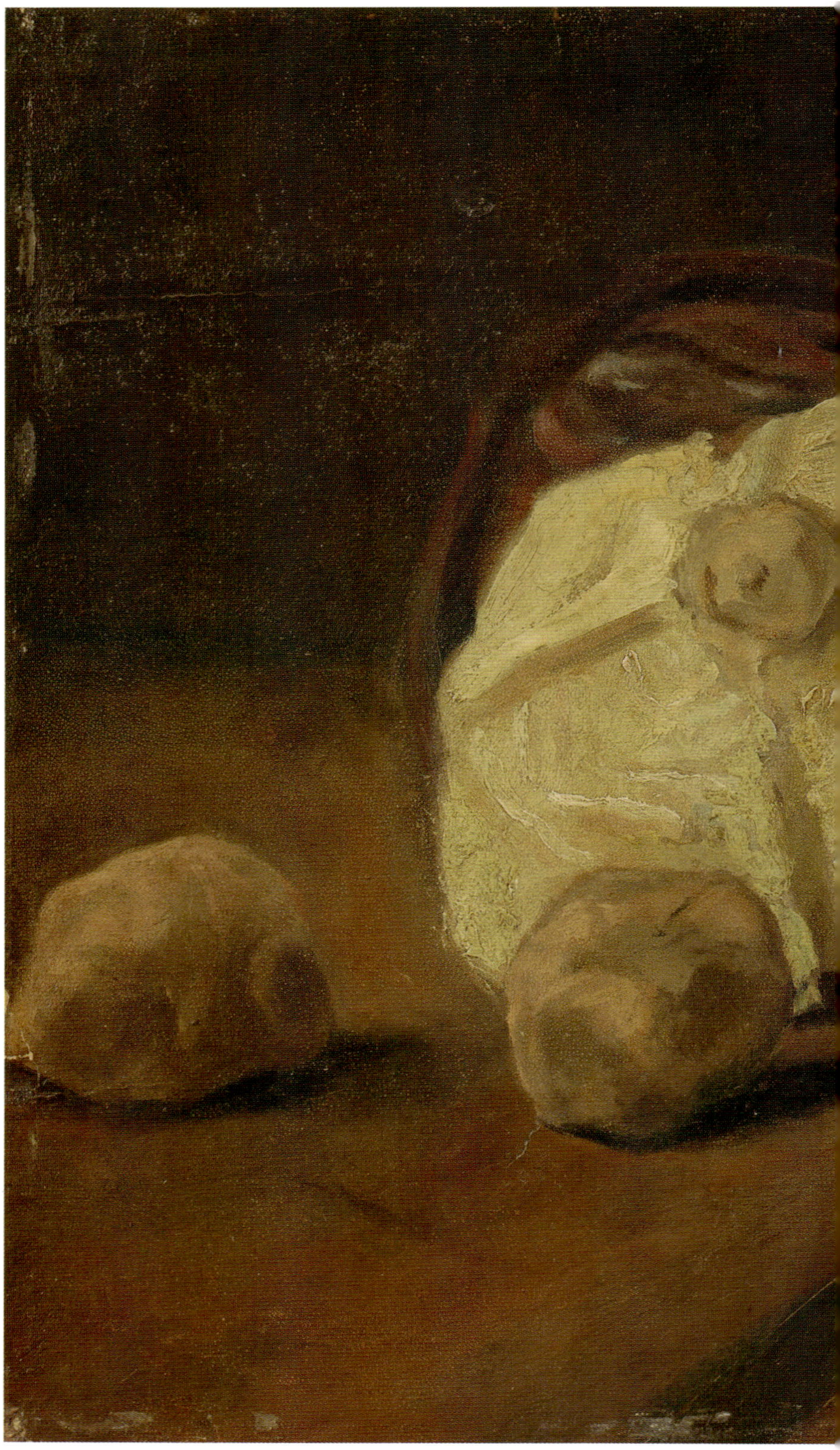

[ABOVE] *Still Life with Cabbage and Clogs* (November–December 1881). Oil on canvas. Van Gogh Museum, Amsterdam (Vincent van Gogh Foundation).

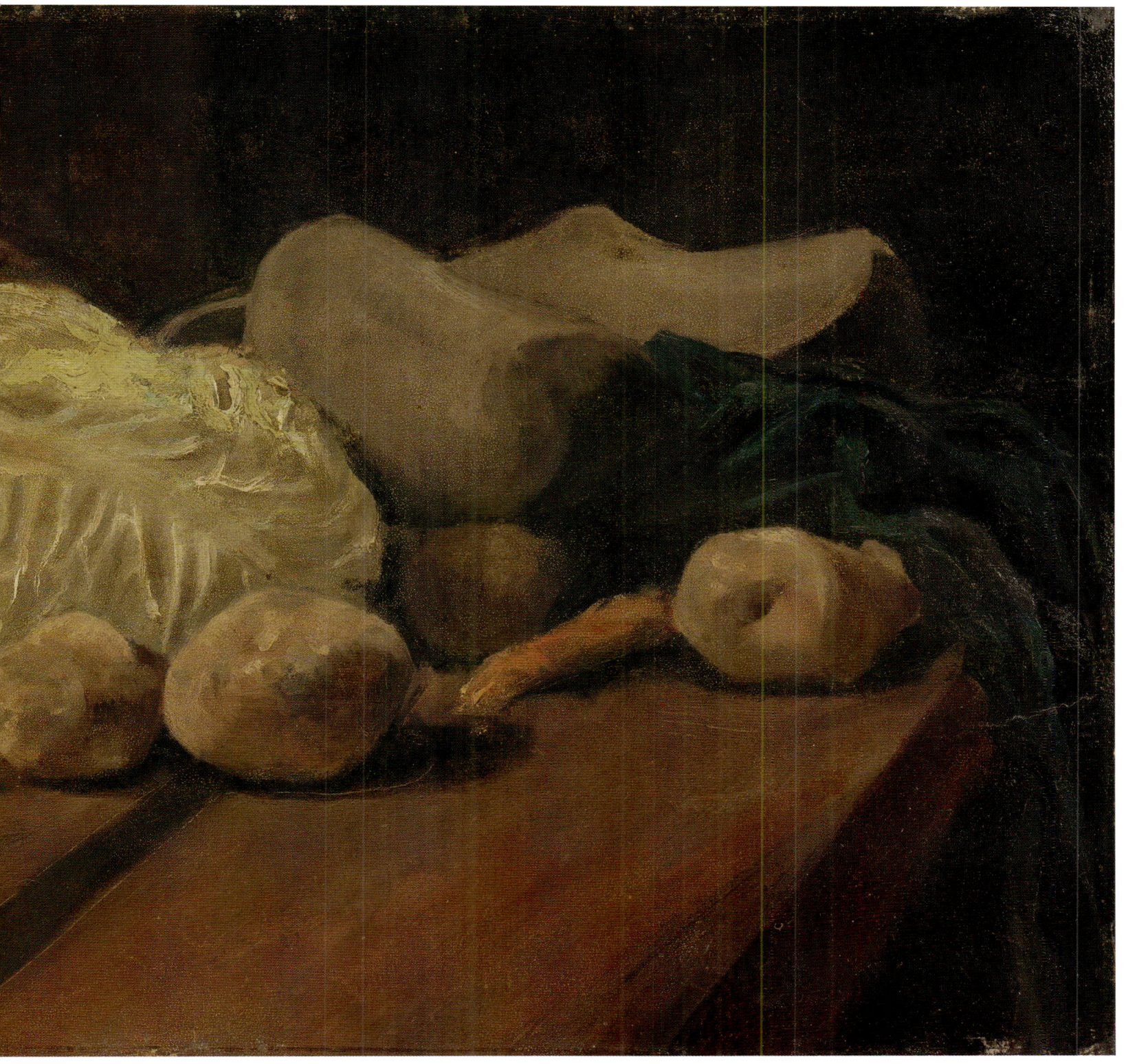

" *Well, Mauve immediately installed me in front of a still life consisting of a couple of old clogs and other objects, and so I could set to work."*

~ VINCENT TO THEO, ON HIS TRAINING UNDER
ANTON MAUVE, A FAMOUS ARTIST AND HIS COUSIN BY MARRIAGE

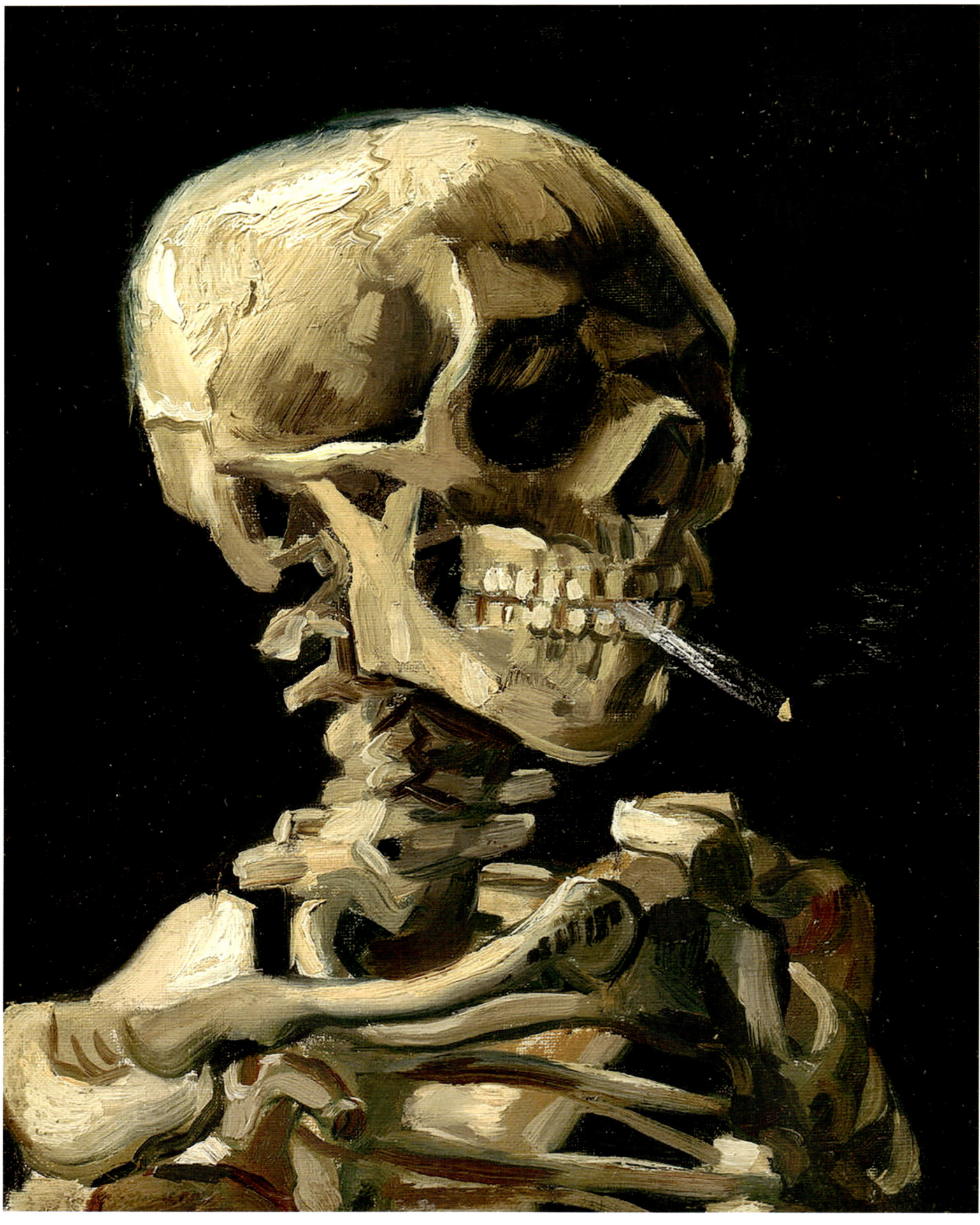

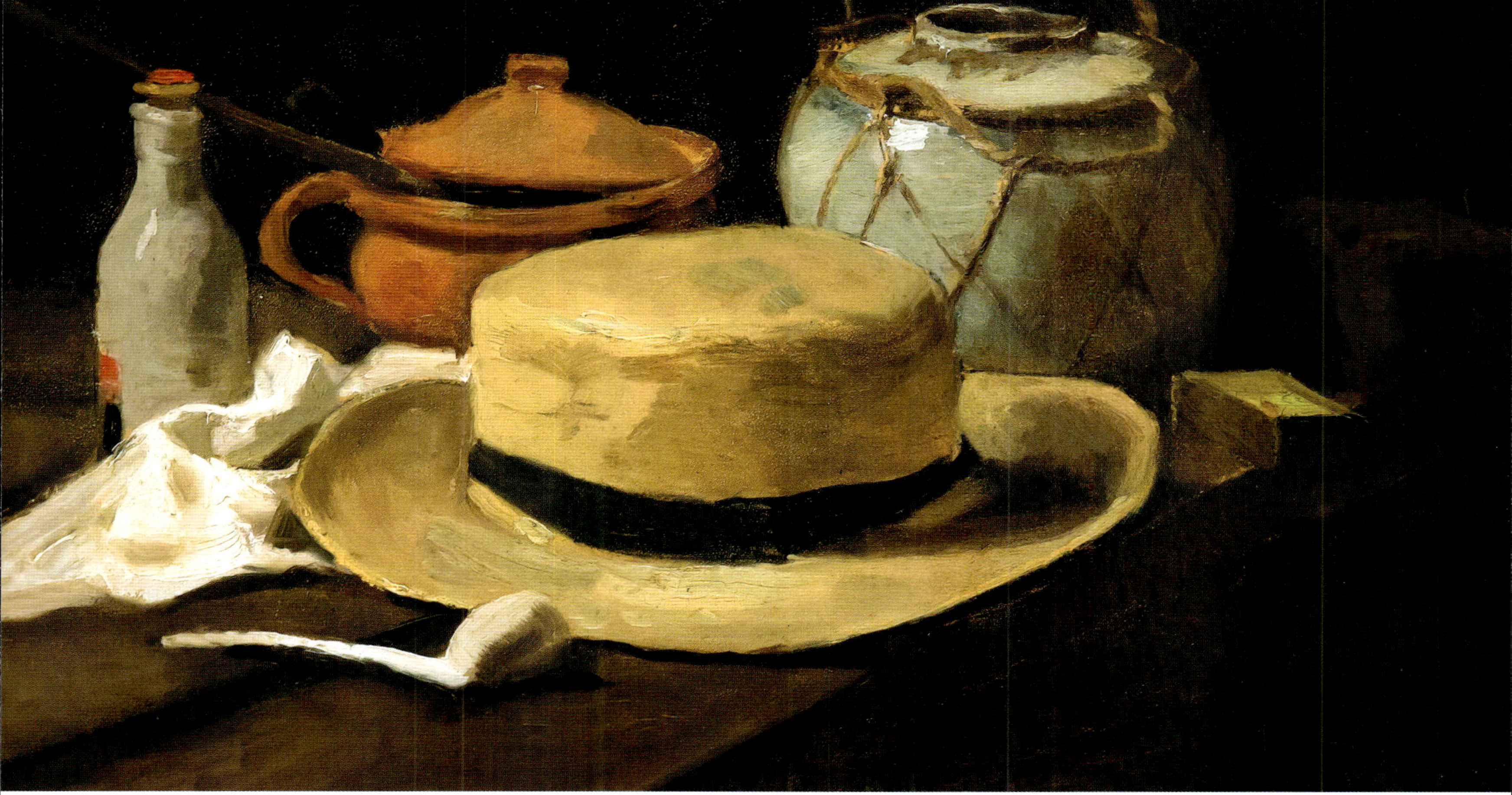

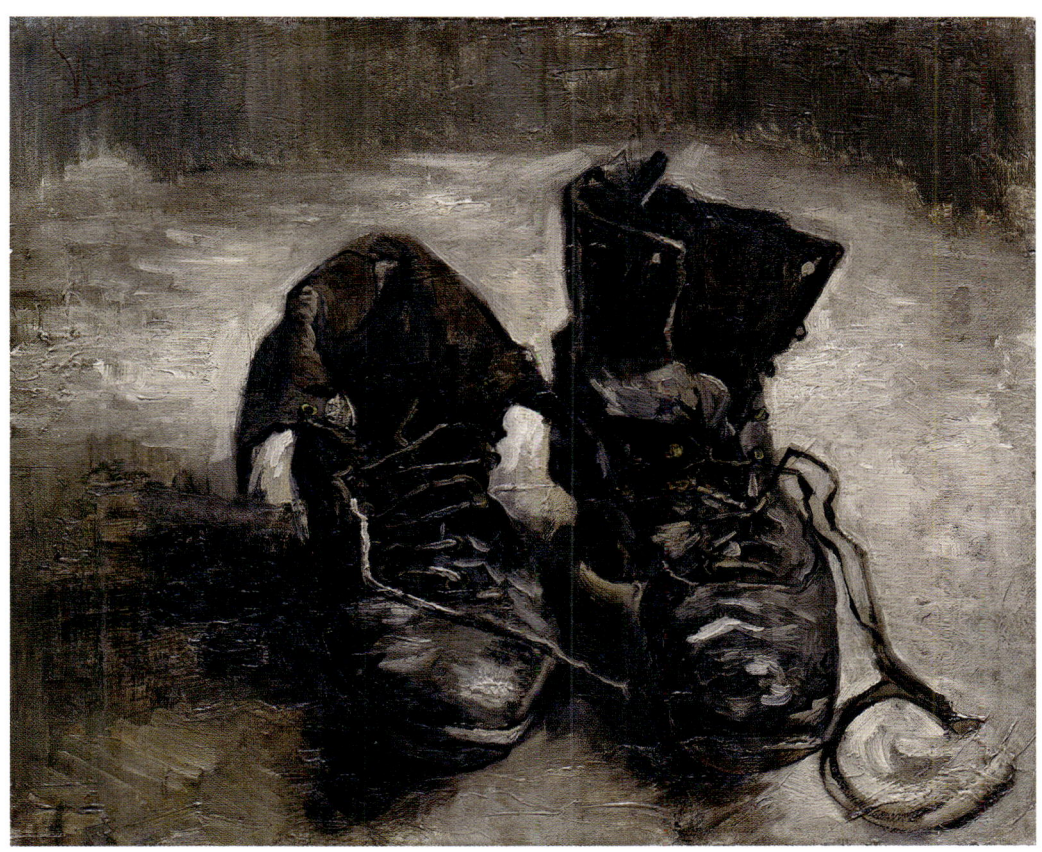

[ABOVE] ***Still Life with Straw Hat***
(c. late November–mid-December 1881
or 1885). Oil on paper mounted on canvas.
Kröller-Müller Museum, Otterlo.

[RIGHT] ***Shoes*** (September–November
1886). Oil on canvas. Van Gogh Museum,
Amsterdam (Vincent van Gogh Foundation).

*Worn-out shoes might be an unusual
choice for a still life subject, nonetheless,
Vincent made several of these paintings.*

[OPPOSITE PAGE] ***Skull of a Skeleton with
Burning Cigarette*** (c. 1886). Oil on canvas.
Van Gogh Museum, Amsterdam (Vincent
van Gogh Foundation).

*One of several paintings of skulls executed by
Vincent very early in his career, this version
is believed to have been painted as an art
student joke during his days studying art at
Antwerp's Royal Academy of Fine Arts.*

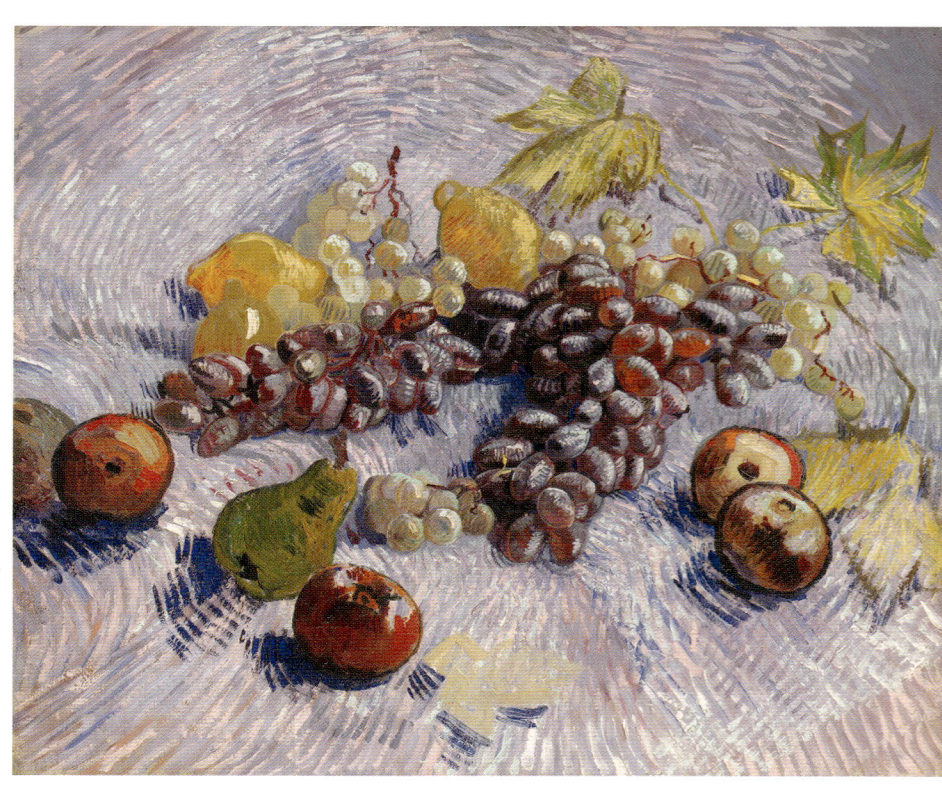

[RIGHT] *Still Life with Apples, Pears, Lemons and Grapes* (Autumn 1887). Oil on canvas. Art Institute of Chicago.

"*It is good to love many things, for therein lies the true strength.*"

~ VINCENT

[BELOW] *Apples* (September–October 1887). Oil on canvas. Van Gogh Museum, Amsterdam (Vincent van Gogh Foundation).

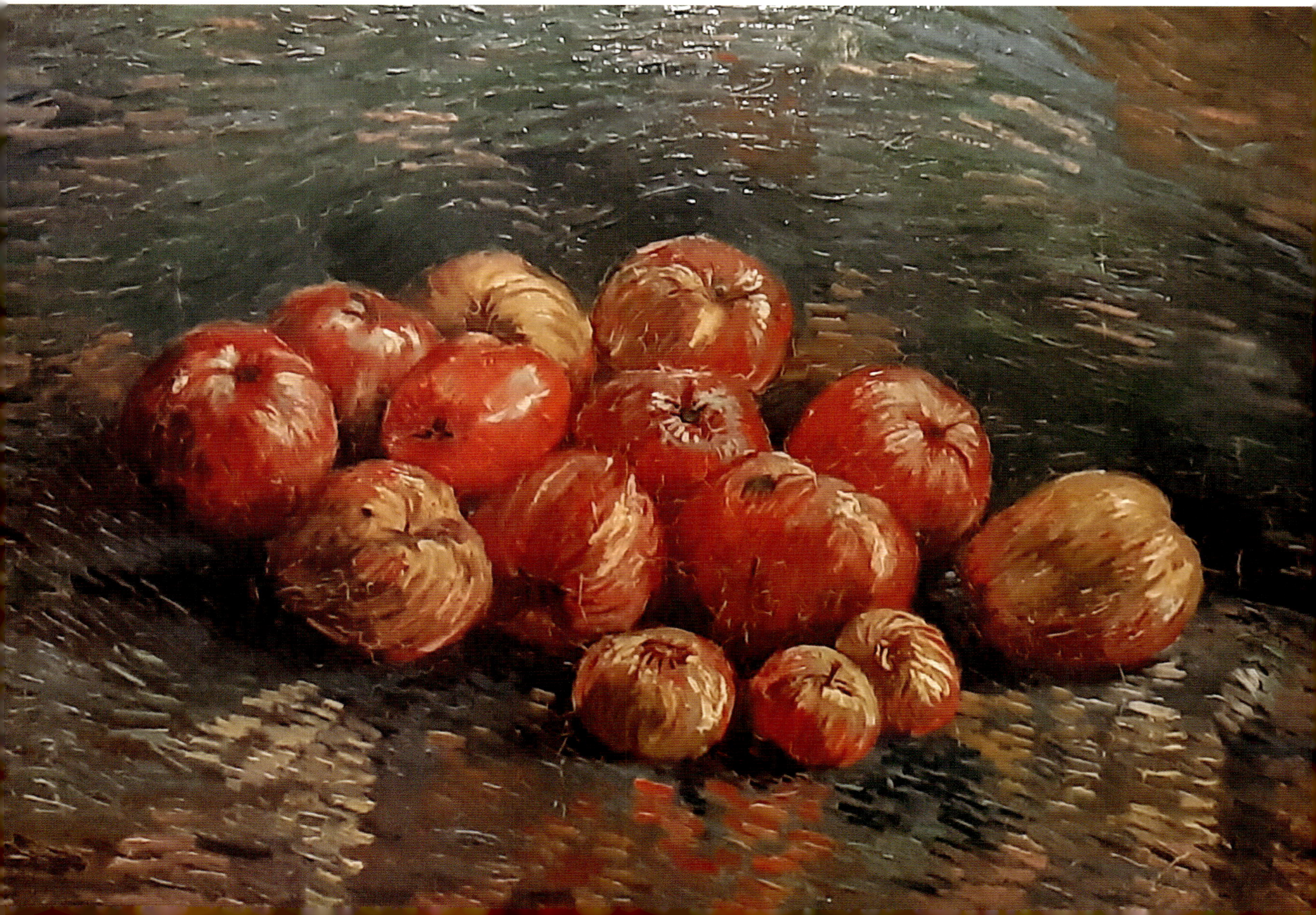

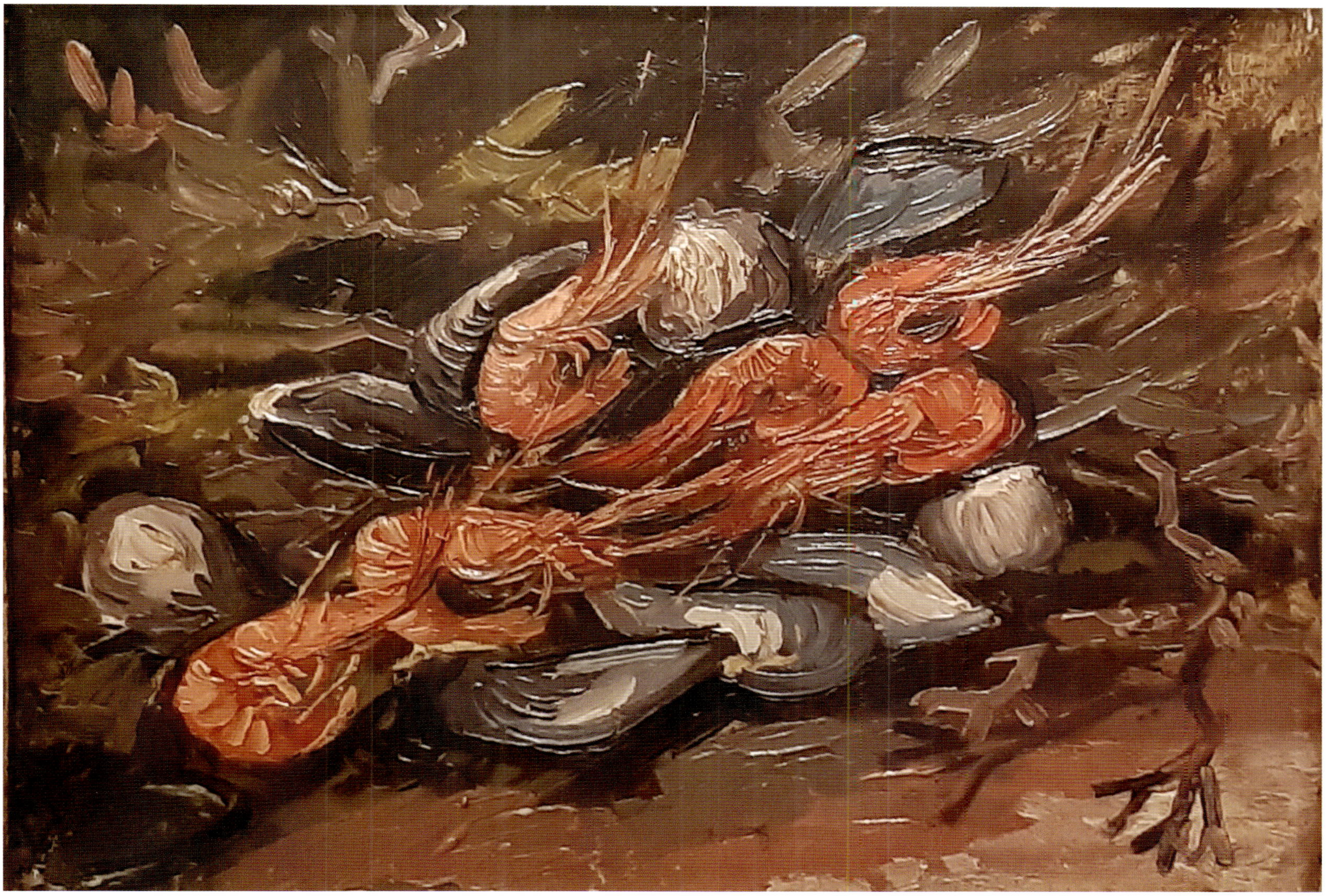

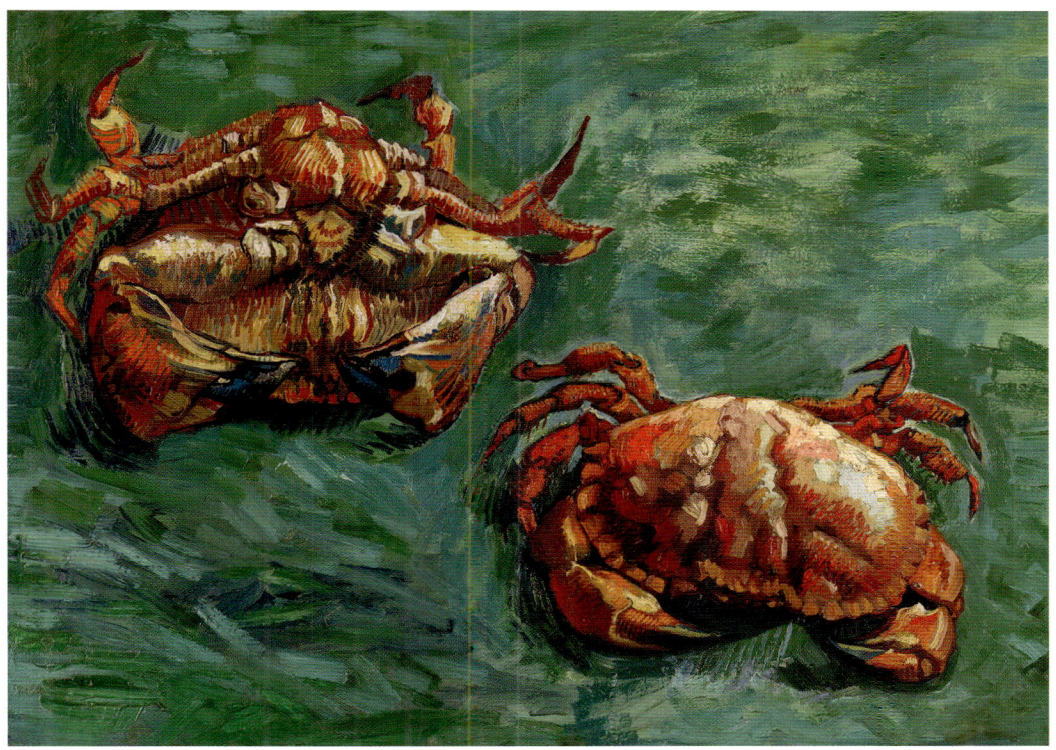

[ABOVE] *Prawns and Mussels* (September–November 1886). Oil on canvas. Van Gogh Museum, Amsterdam (Vincent van Gogh Foundation).

After serving as still life subjects, these prawns and mussels most likely served as Vincent's supper.

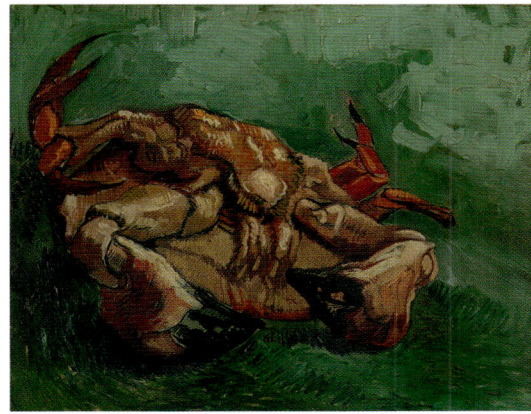

A Crab on Its Back (January 1889). Oil on canvas. Van Gogh Museum, Amsterdam (Vincent van Gogh Foundation).

Vincent returned to his portrayal of seafood after his release from the hospital in Arles in 1889.

Two Crabs (September–October 1889). Oil on canvas. National Gallery, London.

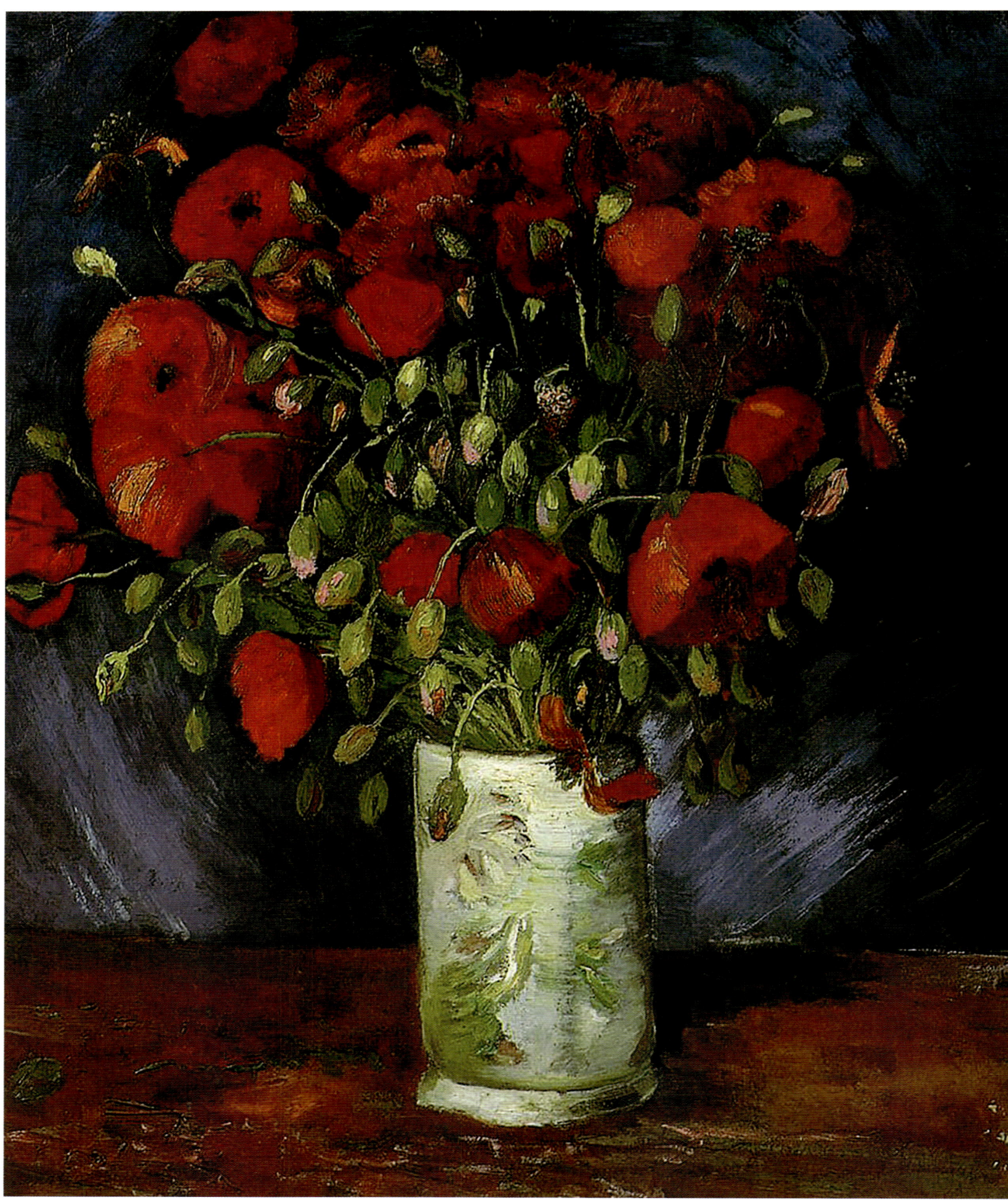

FLOWERS IN VASES

When Vincent turned his eye to flower arrangements as the subject of his still life paintings, his vibrant sense of color began to truly come to the fore. Vases filled with an assortment of floral species, from brilliant scarlet poppies and fritillaries to yellow and white daisies to creamy roses and his signature sunflowers, these canvases are drenched in saturated hues.

[OPPOSITE PAGE] *Vase with Poppies* (c. 1886). Oil on canvas. Wadsworth Atheneum Museum of Art, Hartford.

One of the paintings in a trove donated to the Wadsworth Atheneum Museum of Art in Hartford, Connecticut, in 1957, the authenticity of this work had been called into question by art historians in 1976 and 1990. It was then stashed in storage until Wadsworth Atheneum staff decided to take another look at it. A combination of advanced technology in its own lab and an analysis by the Van Gogh Museum in Amsterdam put to rest any questions about its creator. Once verified in 2019, it was returned to the walls of the Wadsworth Atheneum for display.

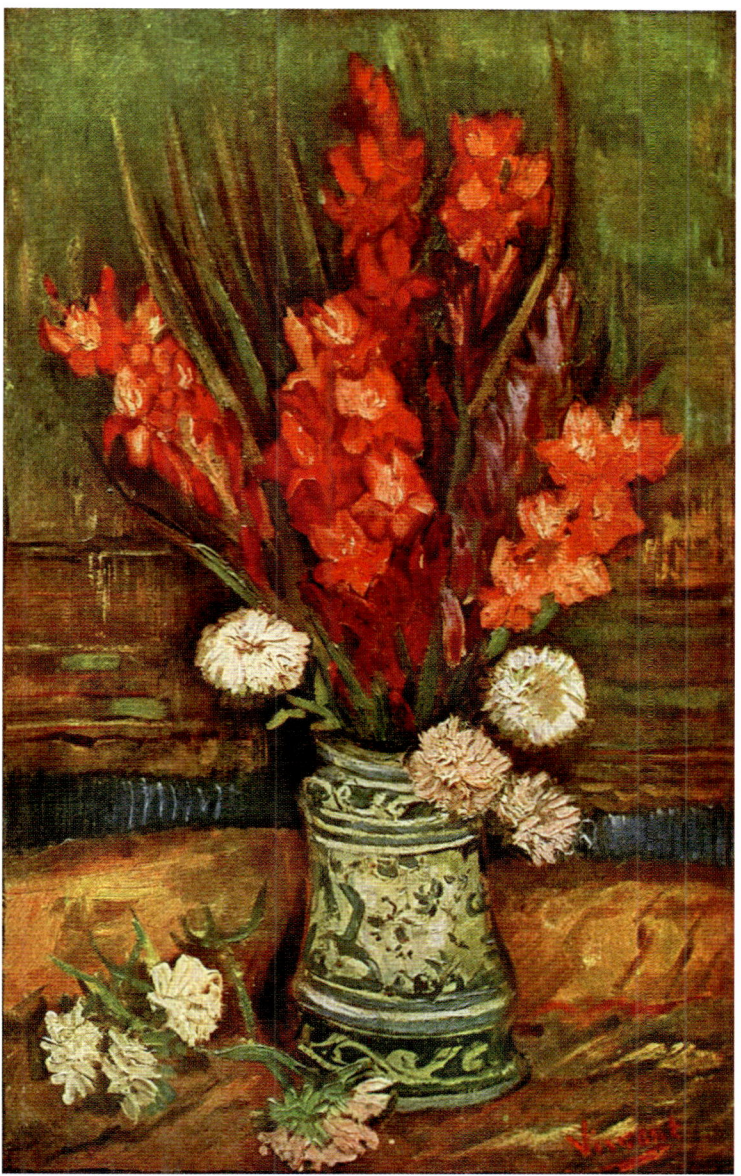

Vase with Red Gladioli (Summer, 1886). Oil on canvas. Private collection.

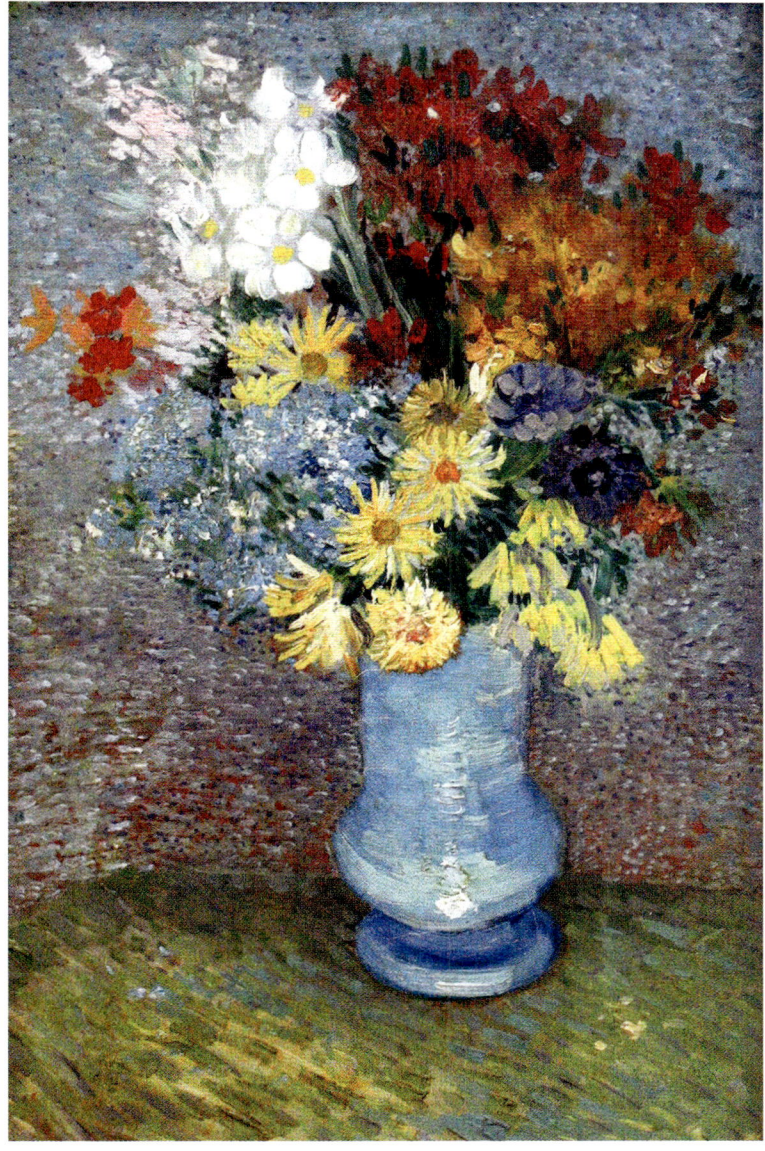

Flowers in a Blue Vase (June 1887). Oil on canvas. Kröller-Müller Museum, Otterlo.

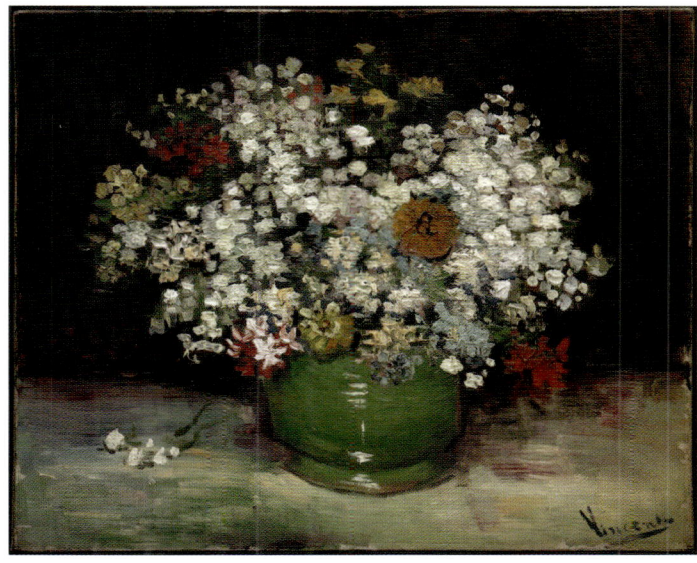

Bowl with Zinnias and Other Flowers (Summer, 1886). Oil on canvas. National Gallery of Canada, Ottawa.

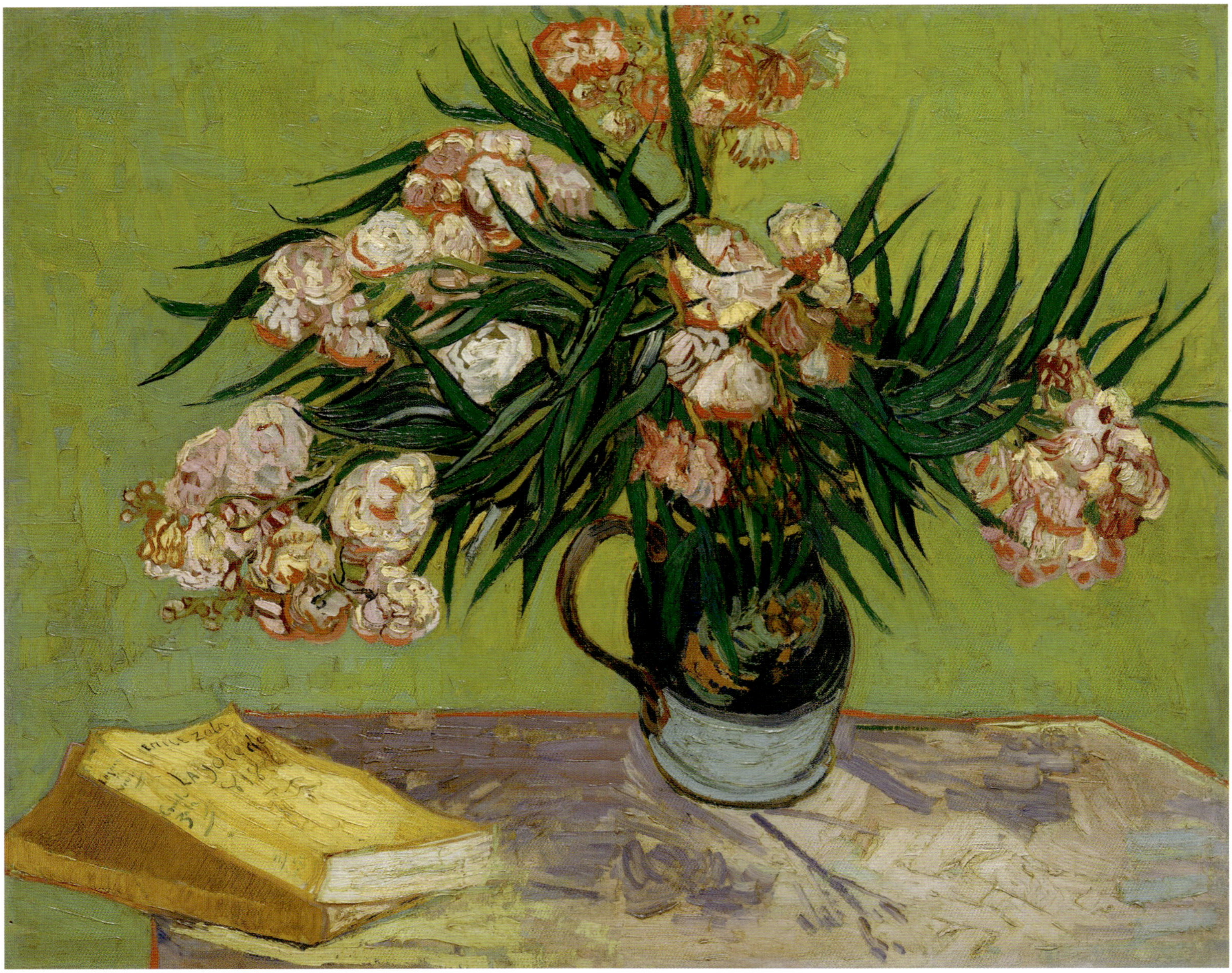

[ABOVE] *Oleanders* (1888).
Oil on canvas. Metropolitan
Museum of Art, New York.

[LEFT] *Vase with Gladioli and
Chinese Asters* (August–September
1886). Oil on canvas. Van Gogh
Museum, Amsterdam
(Vincent van Gogh Foundation).

[RIGHT] *Vase of Carnations* (1856).
Oil on canvas. Detroit Institute of Art.

[OPPOSITE PAGE] *Vase
with Cornflowers and Poppies*
(Summer 1887). Oil on canvas. National
Gallery of Victoria, Melbourne.

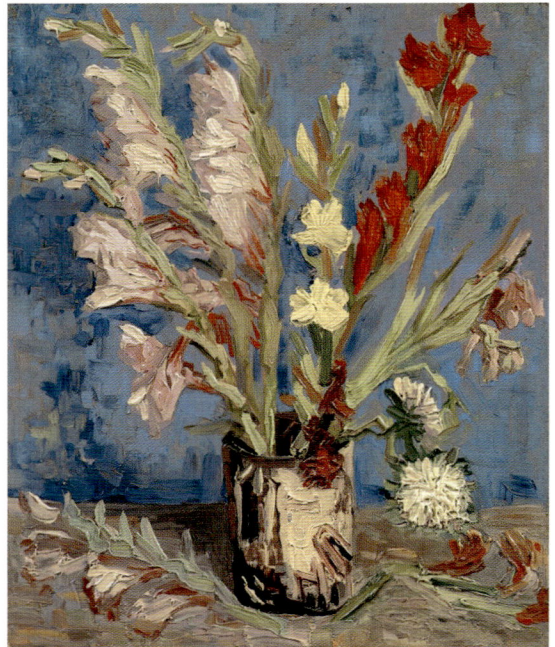

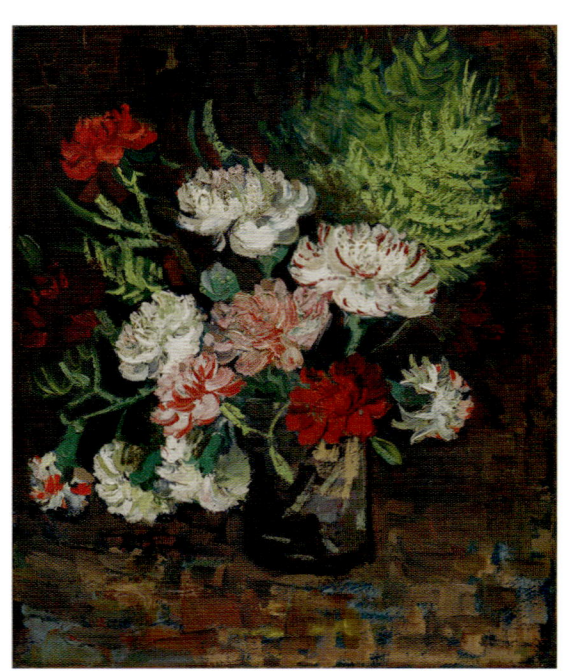

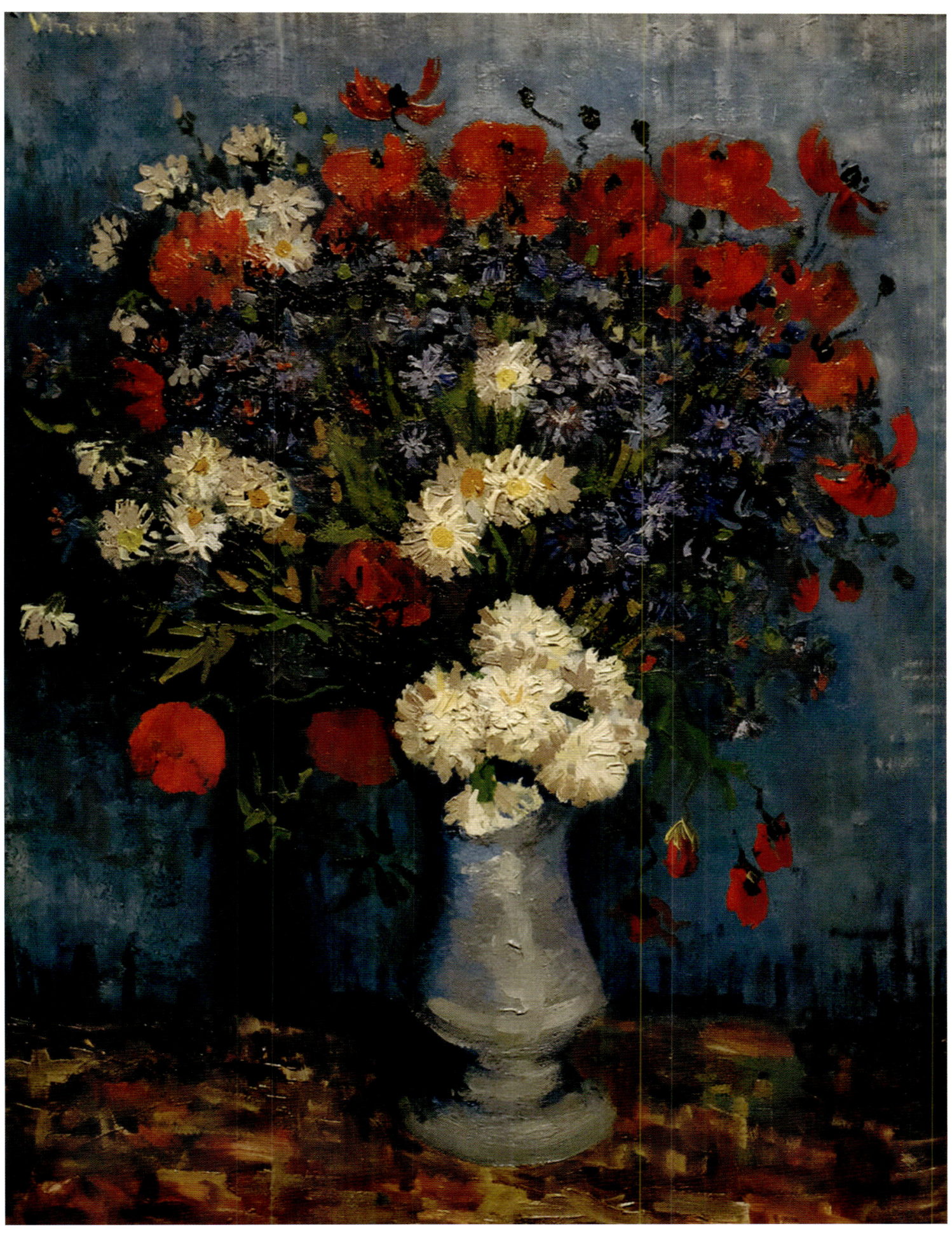

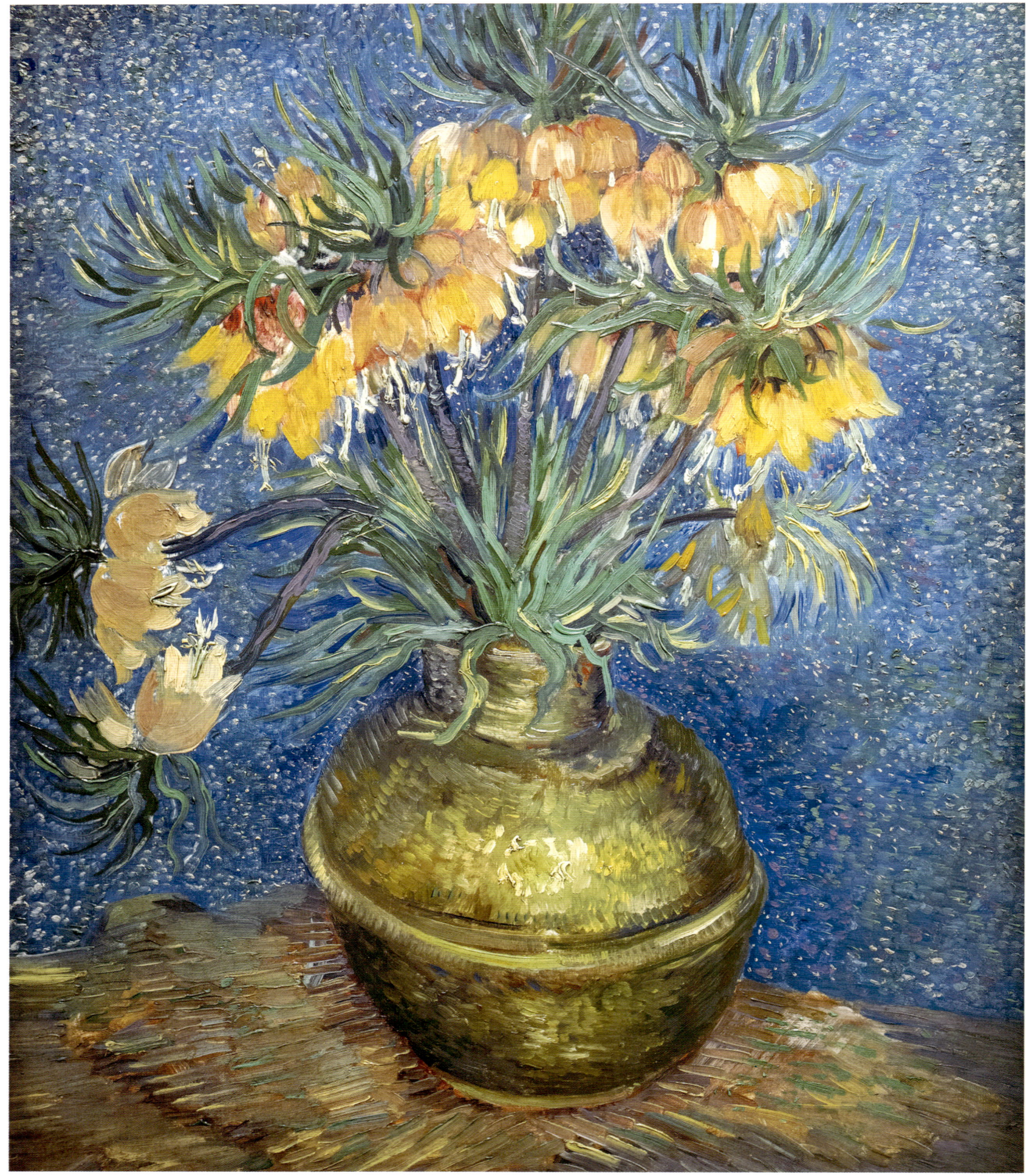

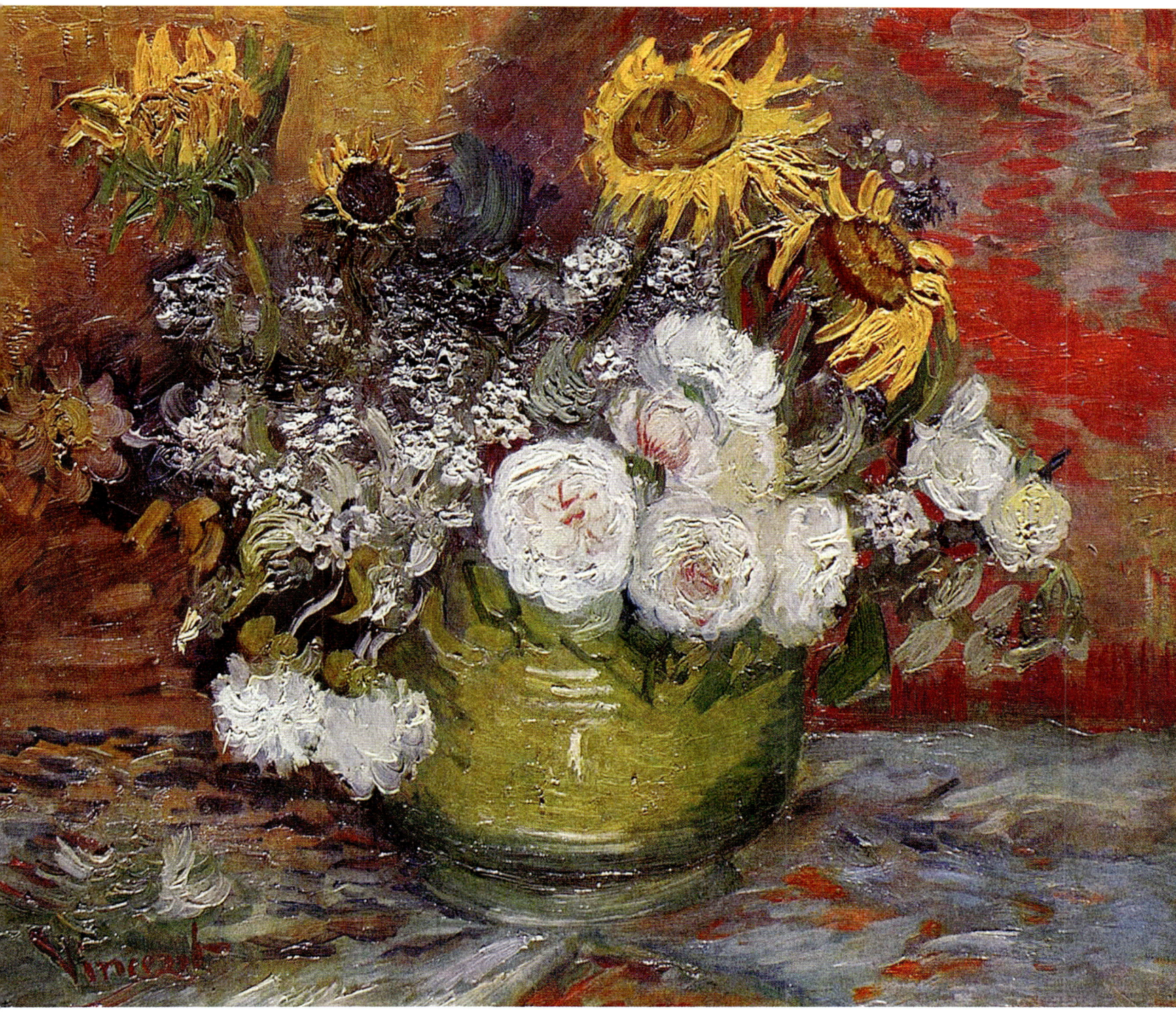

[ABOVE] *Still Life with Roses and Sunflowers* (1886).
Oil on canvas. Kunsthalle Mannheim, Mannheim.

"*Normality is a paved road:*

It's comfortable to walk,

but no flowers grow on it."

~ VINCENT

[OPPOSITE PAGE] *Imperial Fritillaries in a Copper Vase*
(April–May, 1887). Oil on canvas. Musée d'Orsay, Paris.

SUNFLOWERS

Inspired by the Impressionists, Vincent turned to floral still life to experiment with bright color. His initial forays show the use of quite traditional color choices, but as he progressed, he filled the canvas with bold, extreme contrasts. After depicting several flower varieties, he settled on the sunflower, a humble species that appealed to him for its coarseness. Sunflowers certainly inspired him—over a single week in August 1888, he painted four canvases at a speed that might have been driven by the need to capture them before they faded and wilted. *Sunflowers* is the title of two series of still life works. In the first, the Paris series executed in 1887, Vincent shows the flowers on the ground. In the second, completed in Arles, he gathers bouquets of the flowers in vases.

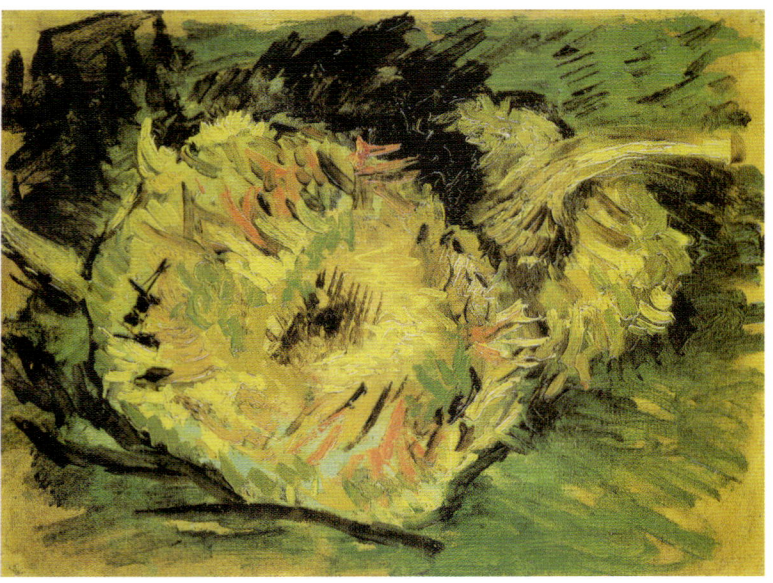

Two Cut Sunflowers (1887). Oil sketch. Van Gogh Museum, Amsterdam (Vincent van Gogh Foundation).

[OPPOSITE] *Still Life: Vase with Twelve Sunflowers*, third version: blue green background (August 1888). Oil on canvas. Neue Pinakothek, Munich.

[OVERLEAF] *Four Sunflowers Gone to Seed* (August–October 1887). Oil on canvas. Kröller-Müller Museum, Otterlo.

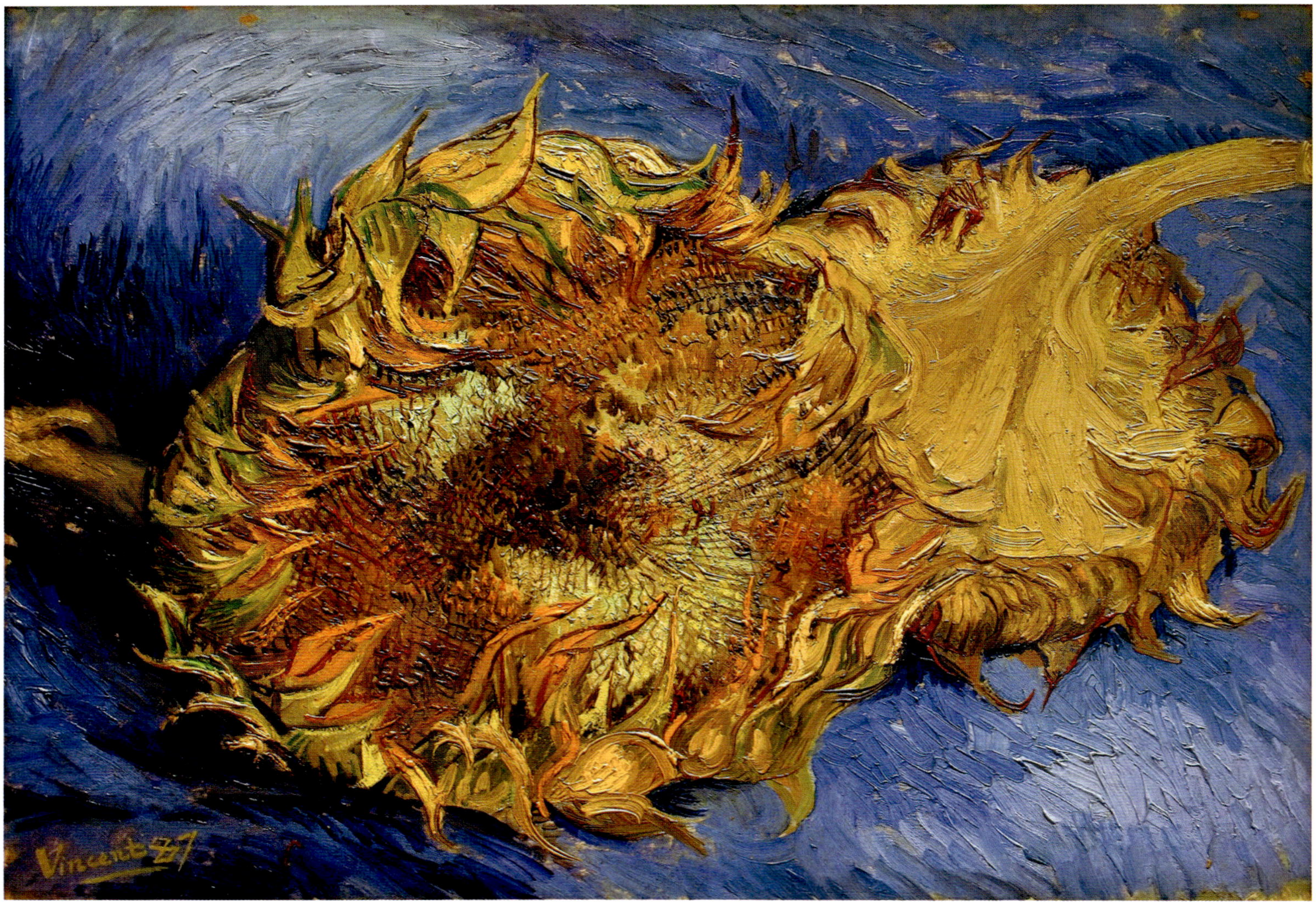

"*I'd like to do a decoration for the studio.*

Nothing but large sunflowers."

~ VINCENT, IN A LETTER TO THEO, AUGUST 1888

Two Cut Sunflowers (August–September, 1887). Oil on canvas. Metropolitan Museum of Art, New York.

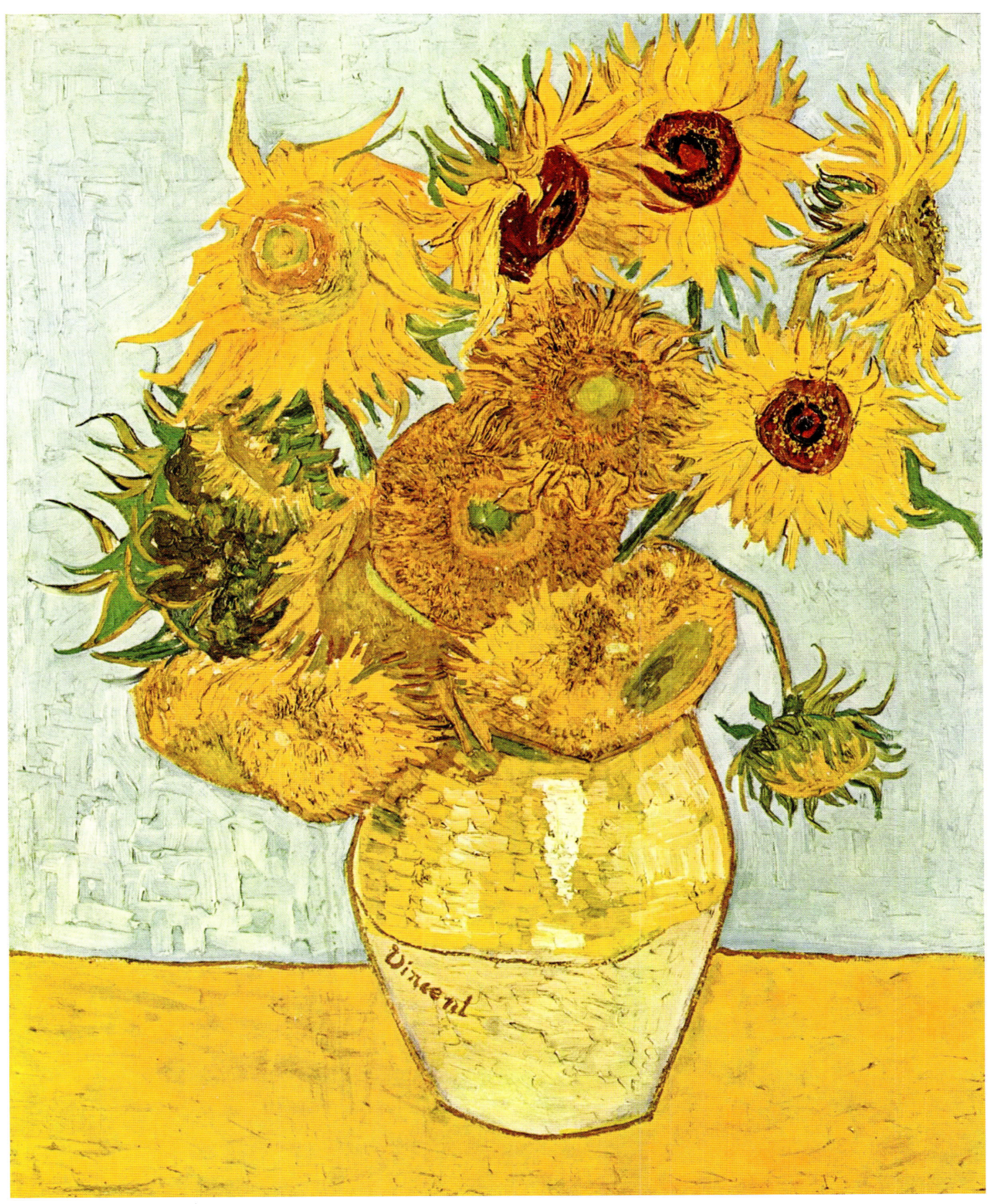

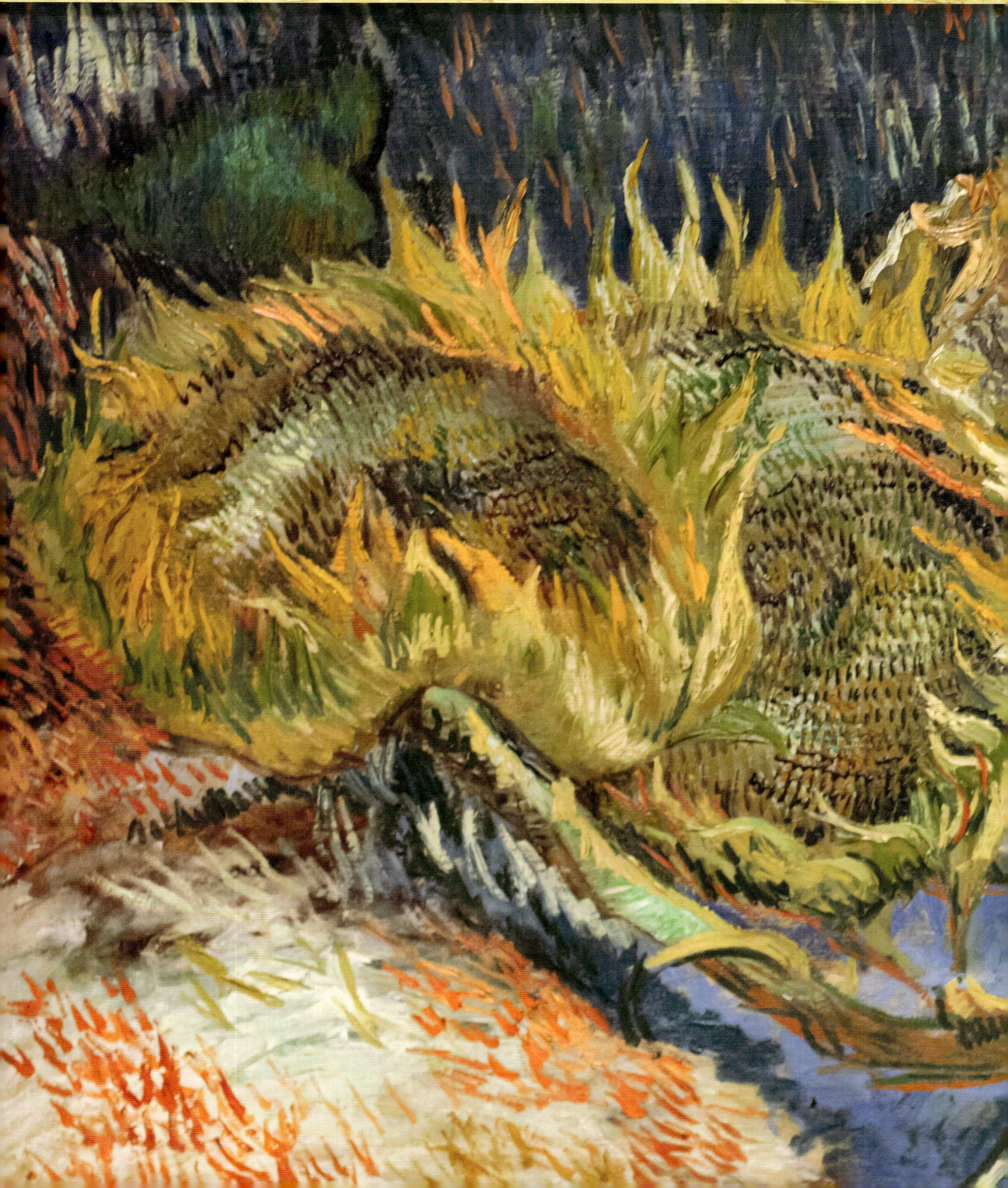

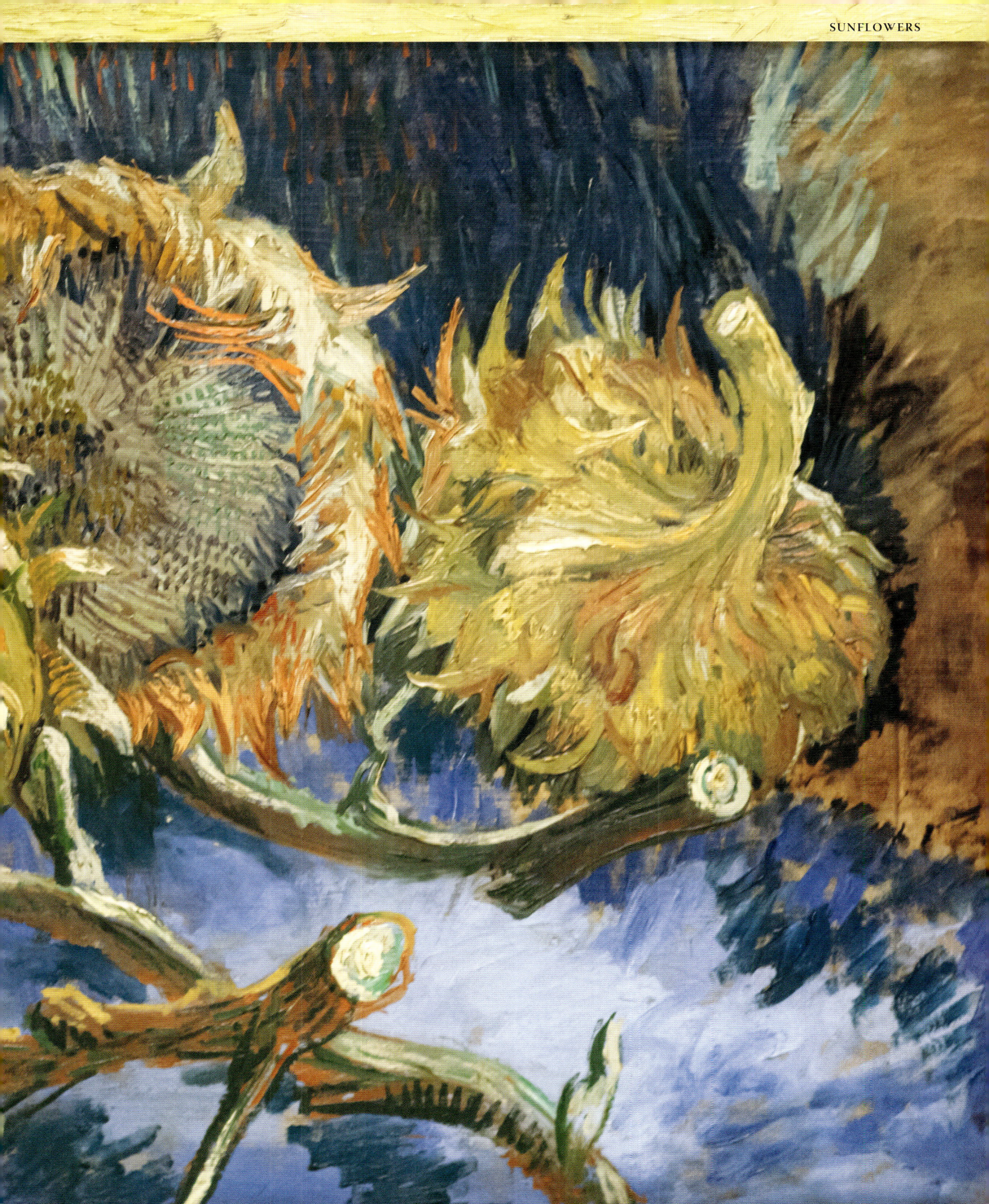

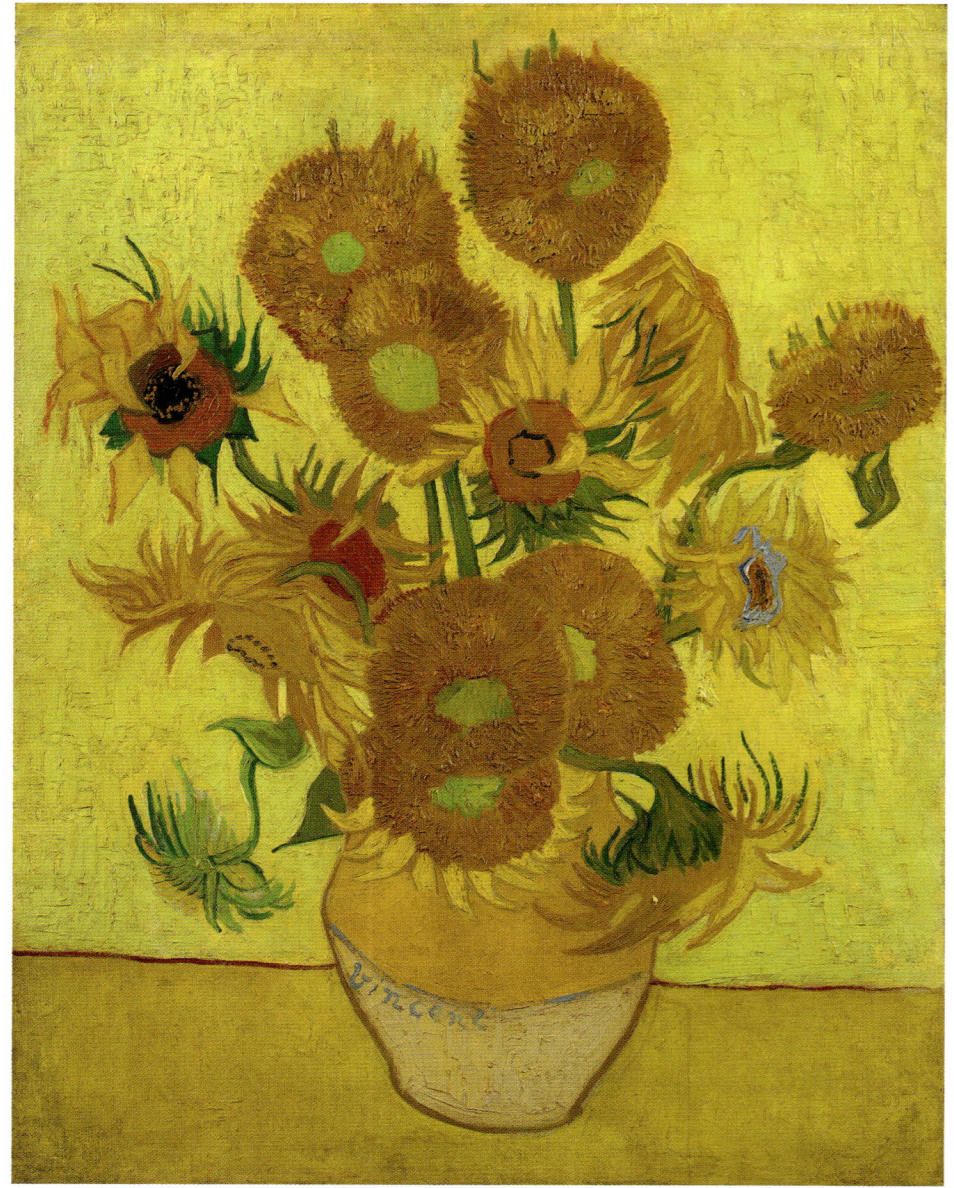

Vase with Fifteen Sunflowers (The Repetitions—replica of the 4th version) (January 1889). Oil sketch. Van Gogh Museum, Amsterdam (Vincent van Gogh Foundation).

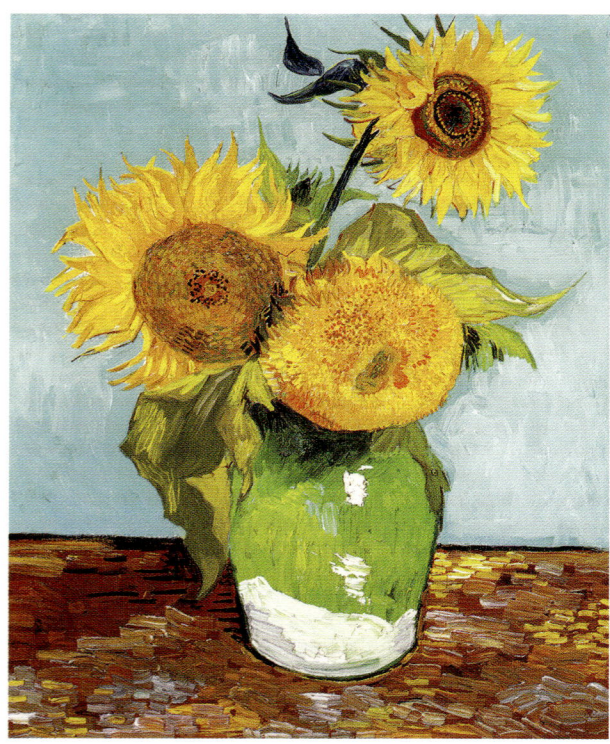

Three Sunflowers, first version: turquoise background (August 1888). Oil on canvas. Private collection.

Deemed the mysterious "Lausanne" Sunflowers, this painting has always been hidden away in private collections. In 1996, an unidentified collector purchased it from a New York dealer for an undisclosed sum. The last time it was exhibited in public was in 1948, in a one-month exhibition at the Cleveland Art Gallery.

[OPPOSITE PAGE] *Vase with Fifteen Sunflowers* (The Repetitions—replica of the 4th version) (January 1889). Oil on canvas. Sompo, Nipponkoa Museum, Tokyo.

"*It's a type of painting that changes its aspect a little, which grows in richness the more you look at it. Besides, you know that Gauguin likes them extraordinarily. He said to me about them, among other things: 'that — . . . that's . . . the flower.' You know that Jeannin has the peony, Quost has the hollyhock, but I have the sunflower, in a way.*"

~ VINCENT, IN A LETTER TO THEO, JANUARY 1889

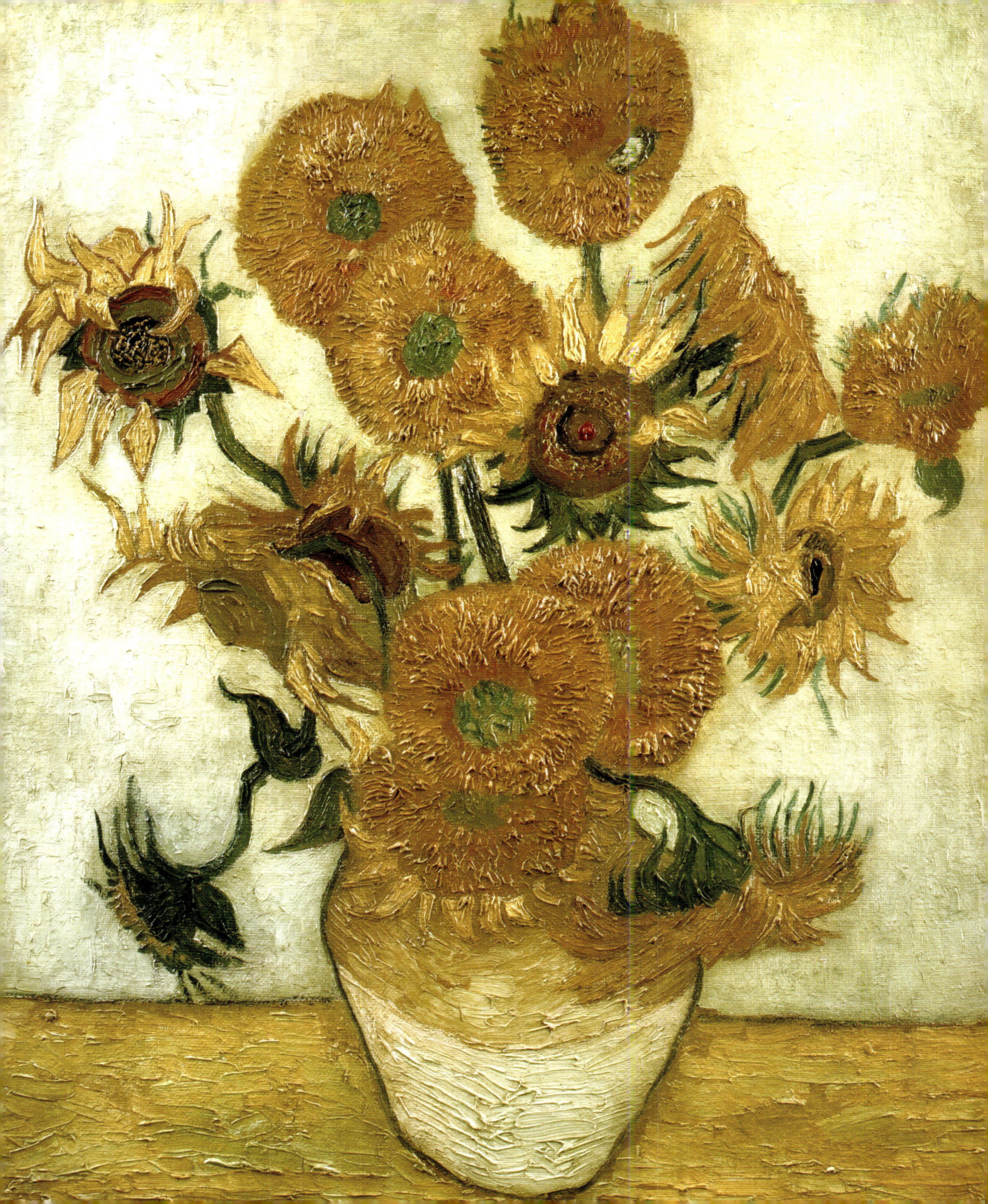

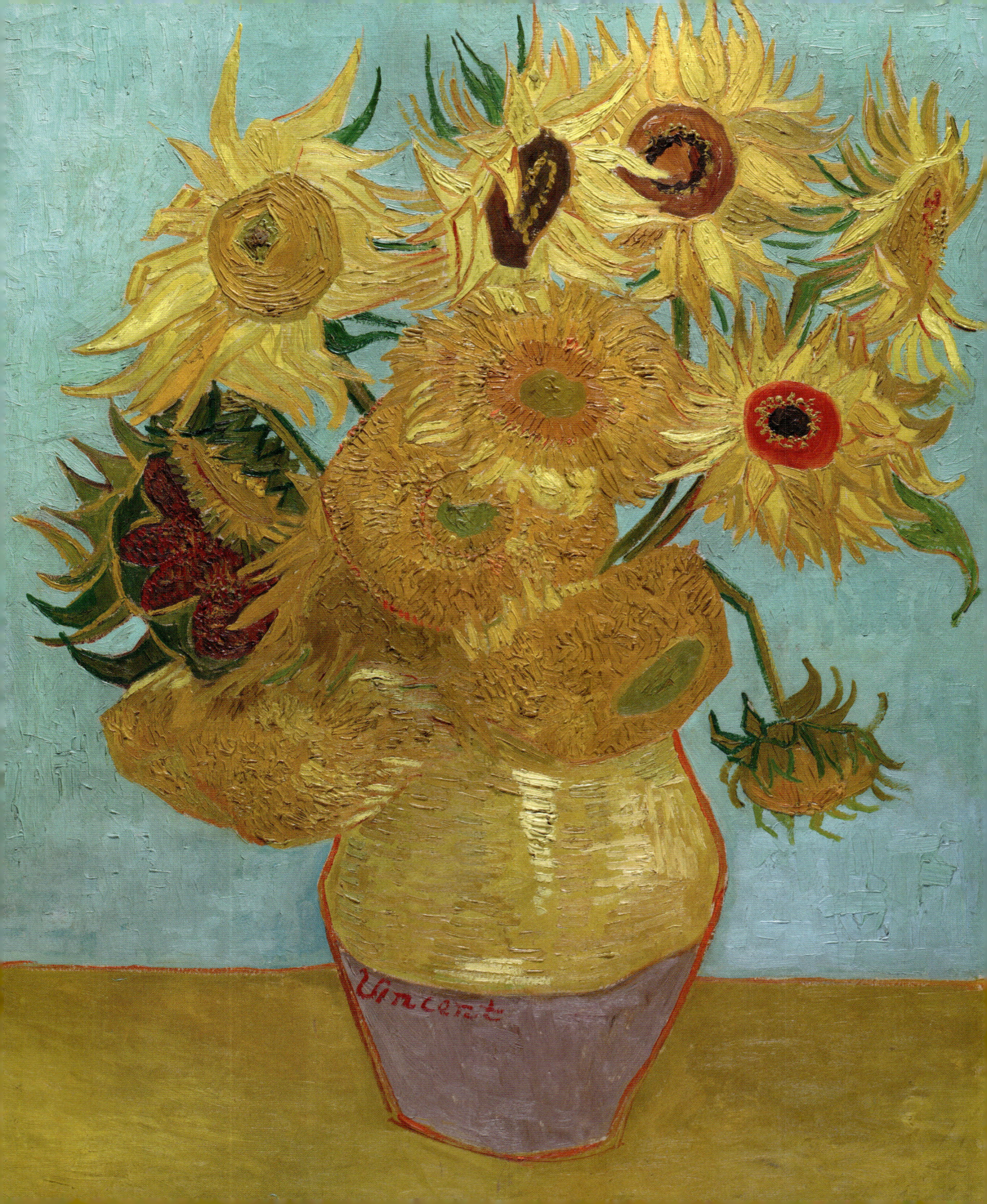

Vincent painted the second Sunflower series with thoughts of his friend Paul Gauguin—they represent hope and plans for a future. The were intended for his Décoration for the Yellow House project, an undertaking to fill his Arles studio with works to impress Gauguin and to adorn his bedroom there. It worked; Gauguin even became owner of three of them. The two artists would spend two months together at the Yellow House in the autumn of 1888. In November, just as things were heating up between these two tempestuous men, Gauguin painted Vincent in The Painter of Sunflowers. Vincent later wrote of this painting, "My face has lit up after all a lot since, but it was indeed me, extremely tired and charged with electricity as I was then."

> " *I am definitely keeping my sunflowers in question. He has two of them already, let that hold him. And if he is not satisfied with the exchange he has made with me, he can take back his little Martinique canvas, and his self-portrait sent me from Brittany, at the same time giving me back both my portrait and the two sunflower canvases which he has taken to Paris.*"

~ VINCENT, IN A LETTER
TO THEO, JANUARY 1889

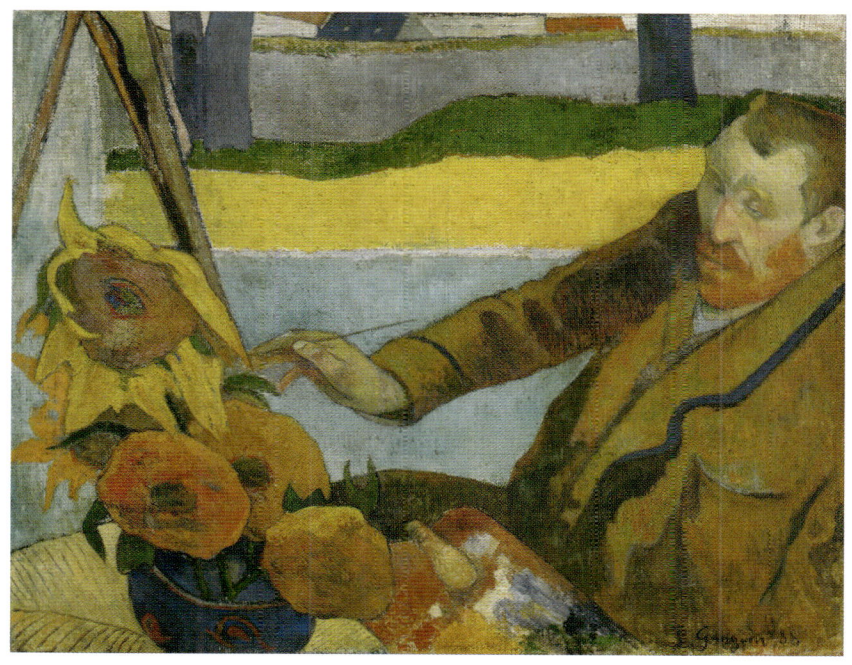

Paul Gauguin: *The Painter of Sunflowers* (1888).
Oil on canvas. Van Gogh Museum, Amsterdam
(Vincent van Gogh Foundation).

[ABOVE] *Excerpt from a letter from Vincent to his brother Theo.* (22 May 1889).

Vincent later intended for his Sunflowers to flank his five Berceuse paintings to form a triptych, telling Theo: "I picture to myself these same canvases between those of the sunflowers, which would thus form torches or candelabra beside them . . ."

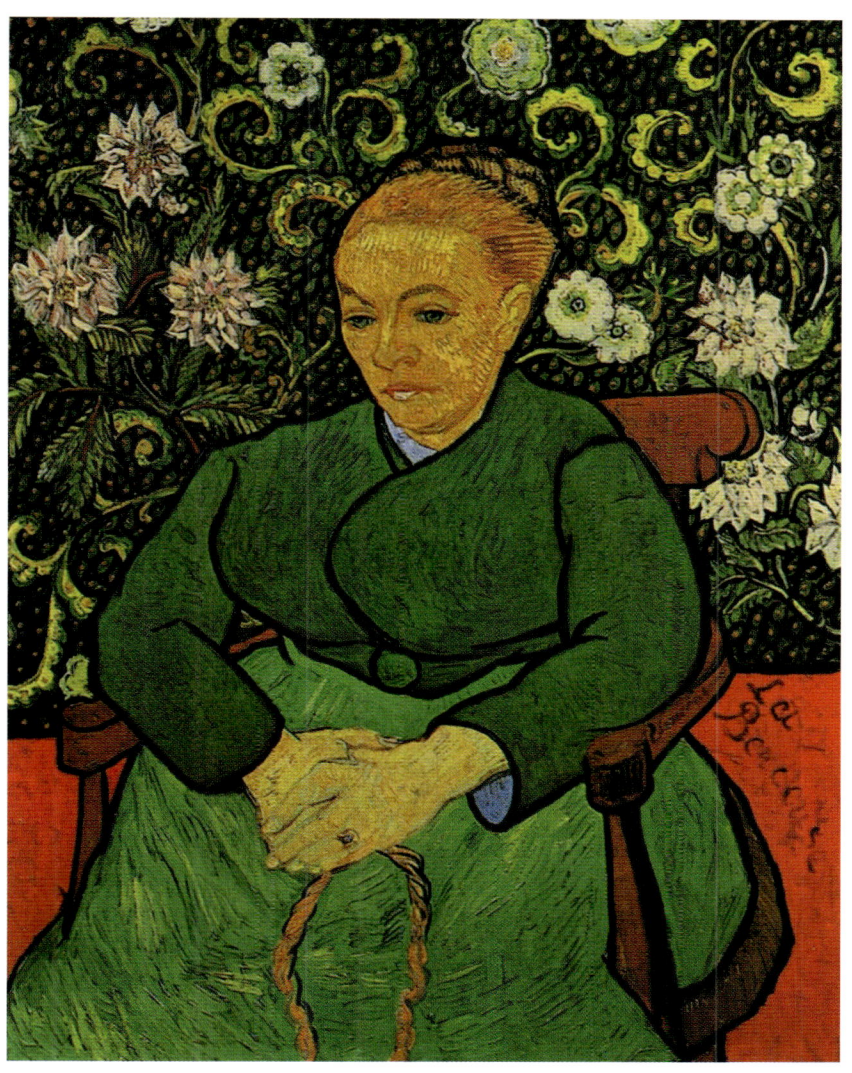

La Berceuse (Augustine Roulin) (December 1889).
Oil on canvas. Kröller-Müller Museum, Otterlo.

[OPPOSITE PAGE] *Sunflowers* (The Repetitions—replica of the 3rd version) (1889). Oil on canvas. Philadelphia Museum of Art.

ALMOND BLOSSOMS

Almond Blossoms is a series of paintings executed in 1888 and 1890 in Arles and Saint-Rémy. To Vincent, flowering trees represented awakening and hope. These works reflect the influence of French Impressionism, Divisionism, and Japanese woodcuts.

"*How glad I was when the news came. . . . I should have greatly preferred him to call the boy after Father . . . instead of after me; but seeing it has now been done, I started right away to make a picture for him, to hang in their bedroom, big branches of white almond blossom against a blue sky.*"

~ VINCENT, IN A LETTER TO HIS MOTHER ABOUT THE BIRTH OF HIS NAMESAKE

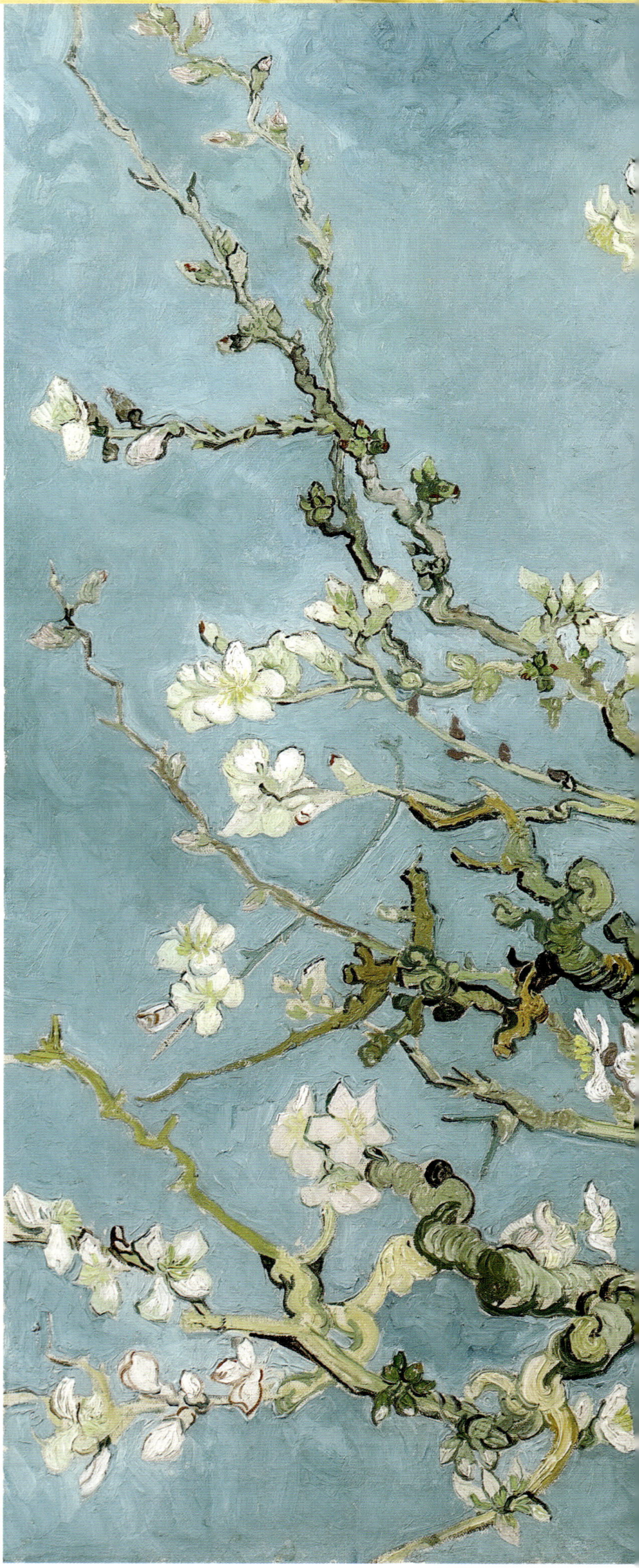

[RIGHT] ***Almond Blossoms*** (February 1890). Oil on canvas. Van Gogh Museum, Amsterdam (Vincent van Gogh Foundation).

Van Gogh painted Almond Blossoms *to celebrate the birth of his nephew and namesake, son of his brother Theo and sister-in-law Jo.*

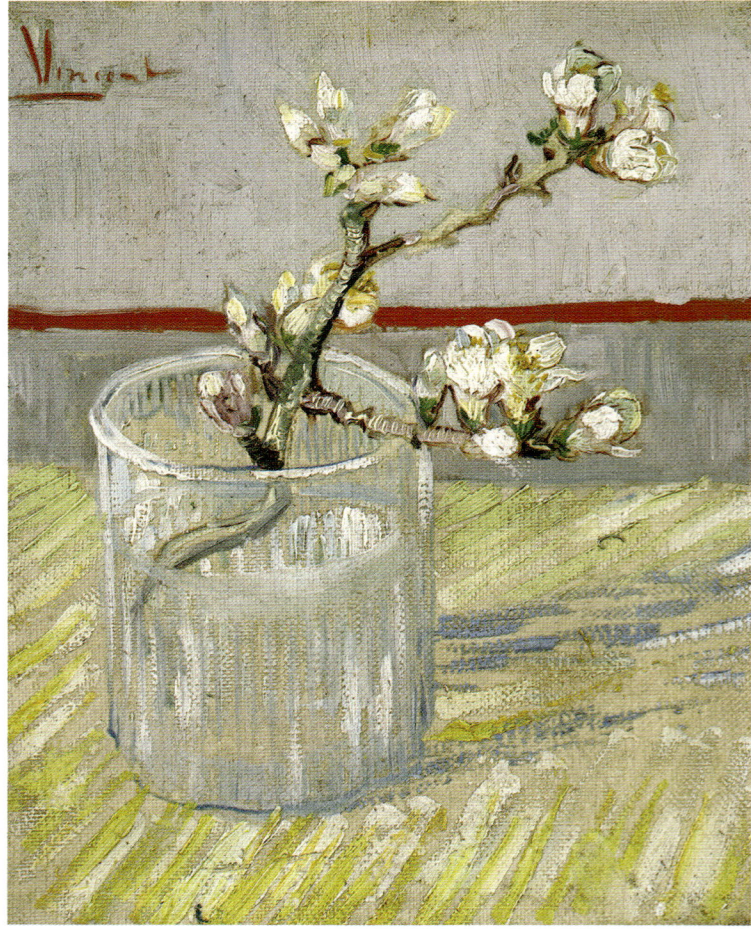

Blossoming Almond Branch in a Glass (March 1888). Oil on canvas. Van Gogh Museum, Amsterdam (Vincent van Gogh Foundation).

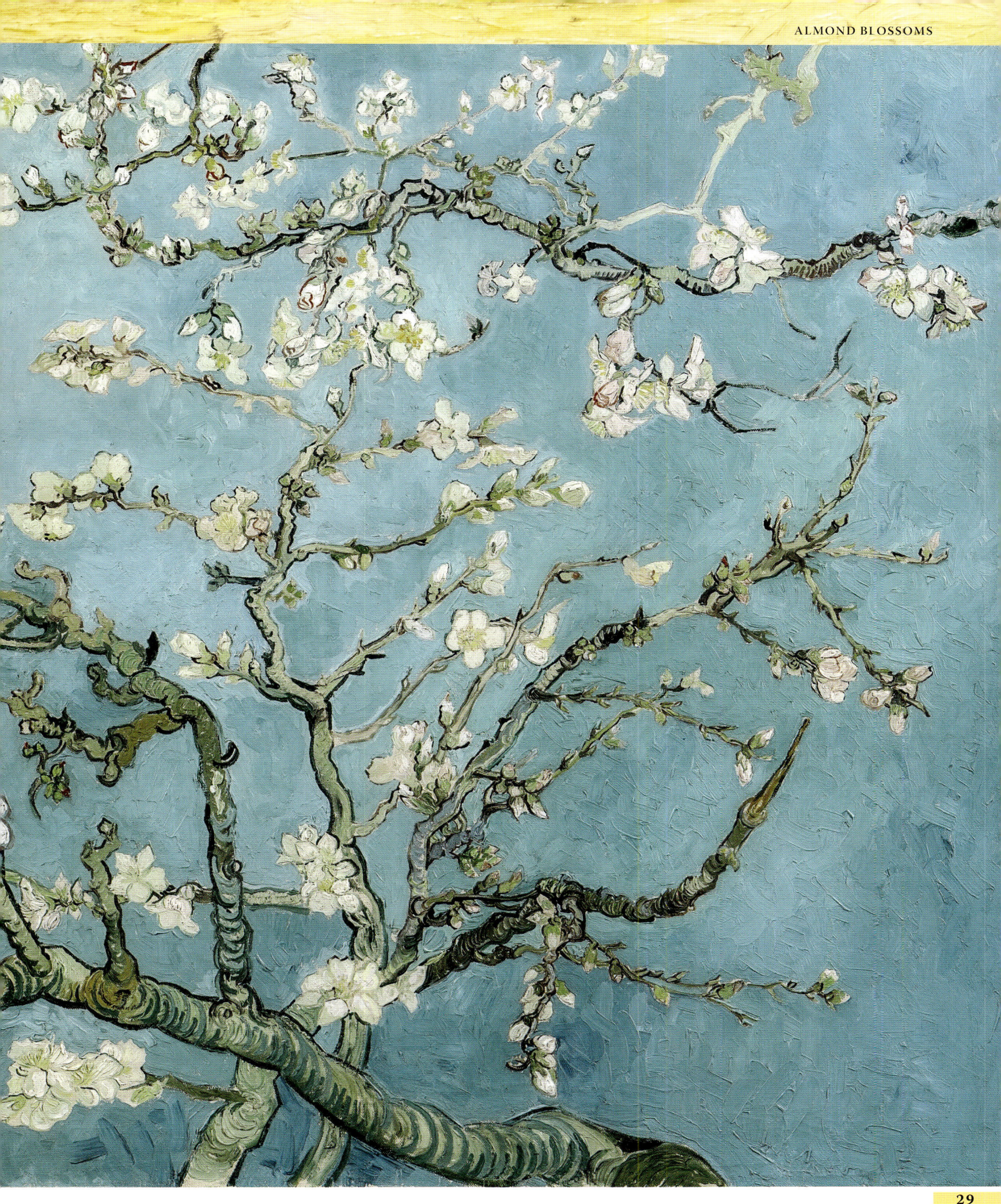

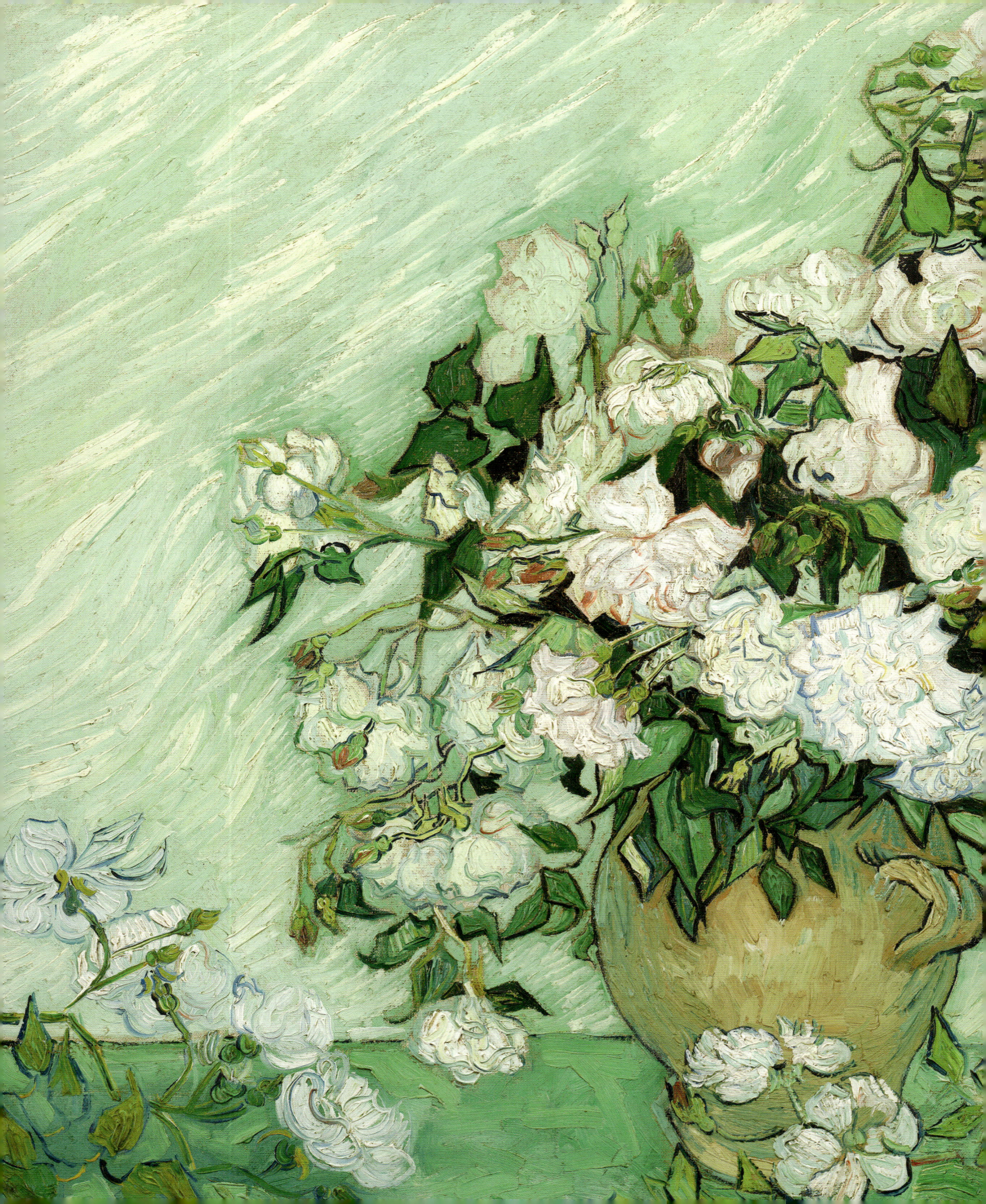

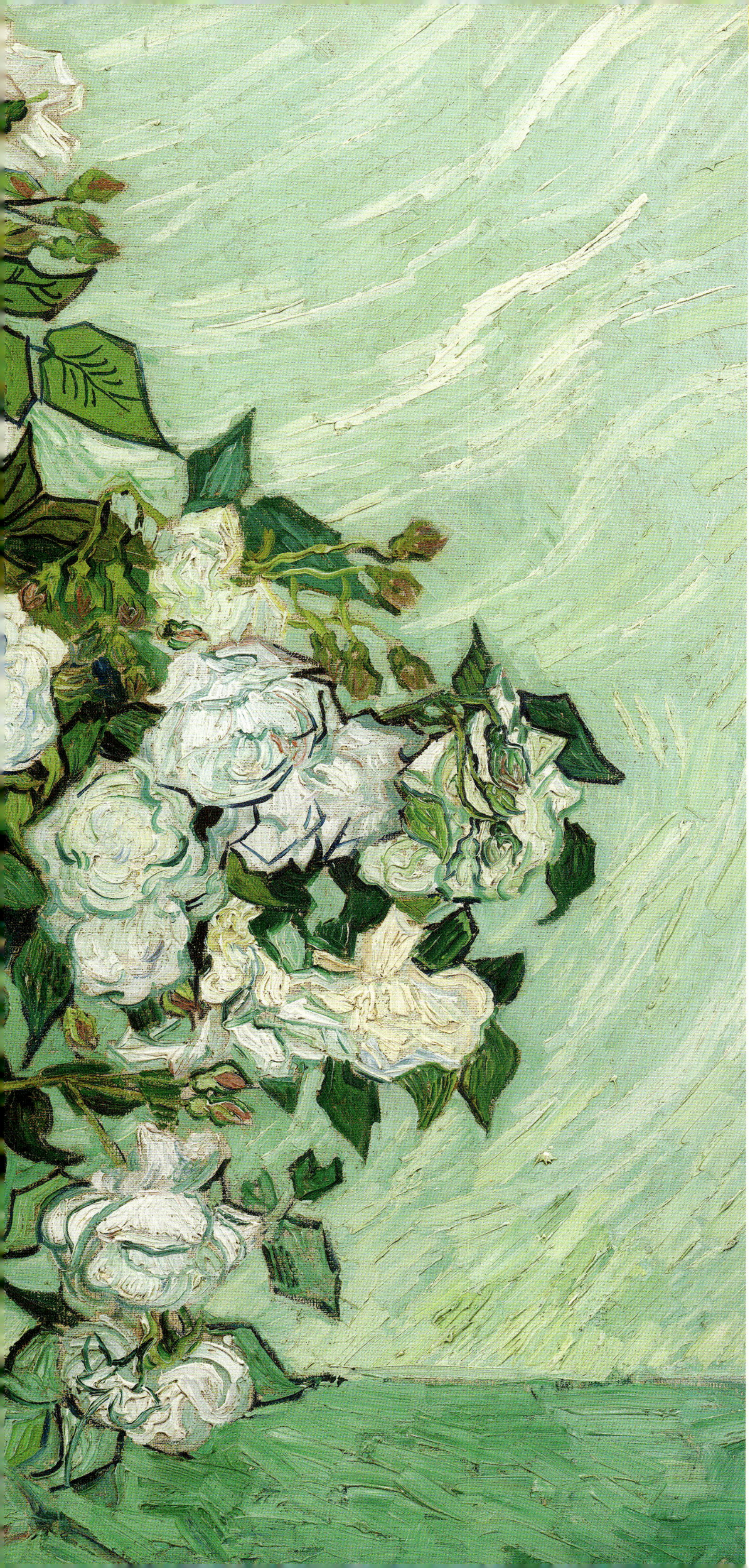

THE IRISES AND OTHER FLOWERS OF SAINT-RÉMY

During his stay at the Saint-Paul asylum in Saint-Rémy-de-Provence, Vincent produced a remarkable number of notable works. As his stay came to an end, he turned his focus to optimistic subjects and enthusiastically painted still lifes of exuberant floral arrangements. Among his Saint-Rémy flower paintings is the now-iconic series of irises.

[LEFT]
Roses (May 1890). Oil on canvas.
National Gallery of Art, Washington D.C.

[BELOW]
Still Life: Pink Roses in a Vase
(May, 1890). Oil on canvas.
Metropolitan Museum of Art, New York.

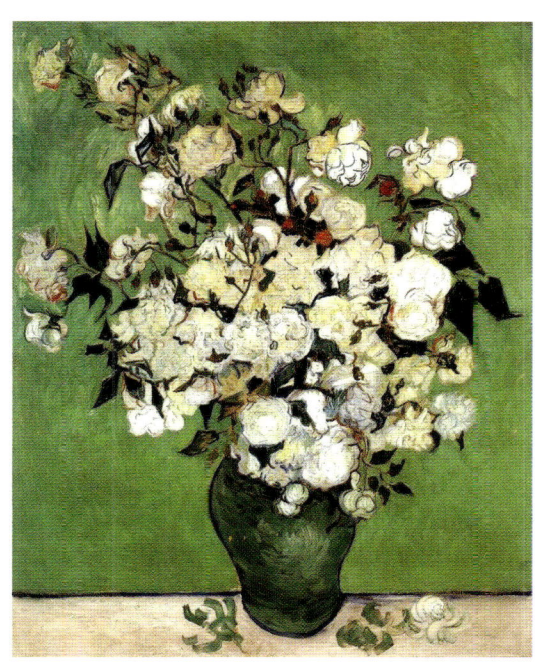

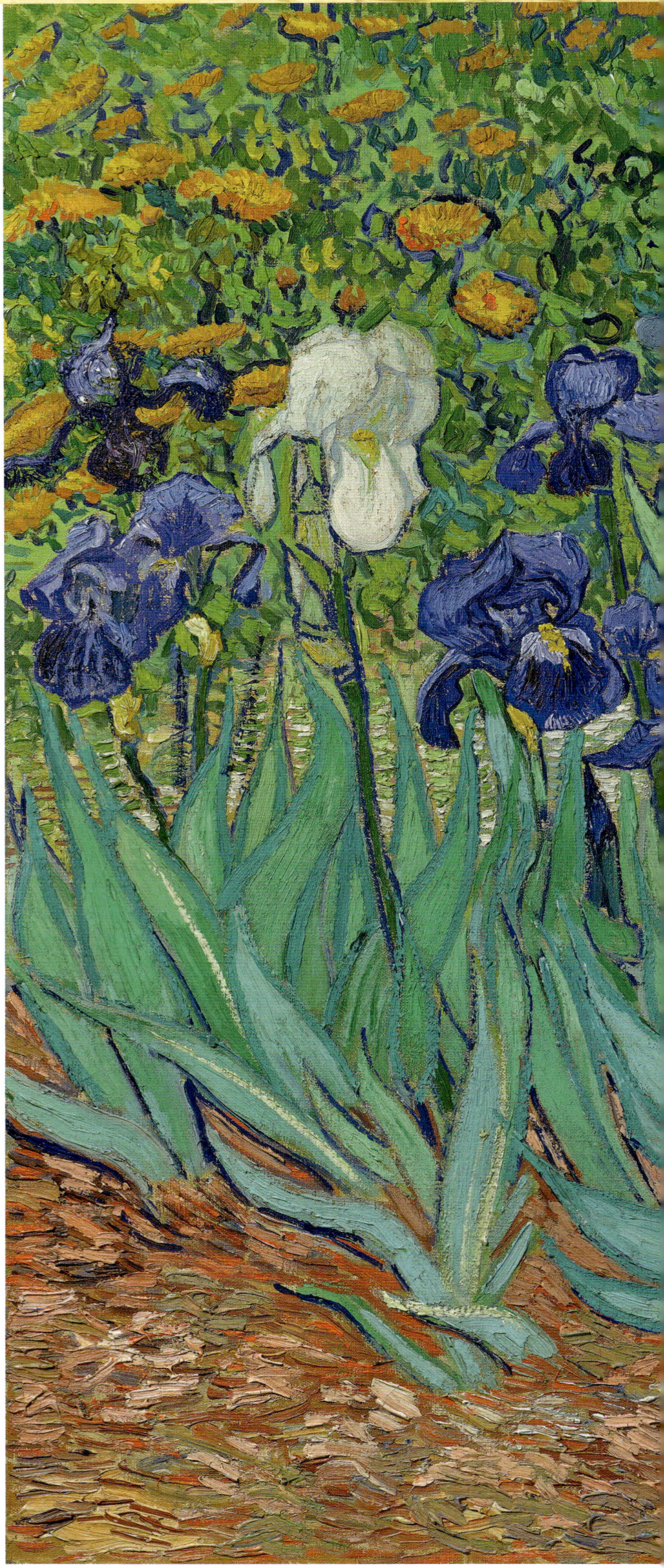

Irises (May 1890). Oil on canvas.
J. Paul Getty Museum, Los Angeles.

This famous version of Irises, *which captures the flowers growing in the small garden at Saint-Paul de Mausole, where Vincent was allowed to stroll and sit, was the first painting he started after arriving at the asylum. In 1987 it was sold for an impressive $53.9 million USD (around $100 million in the current economy).*

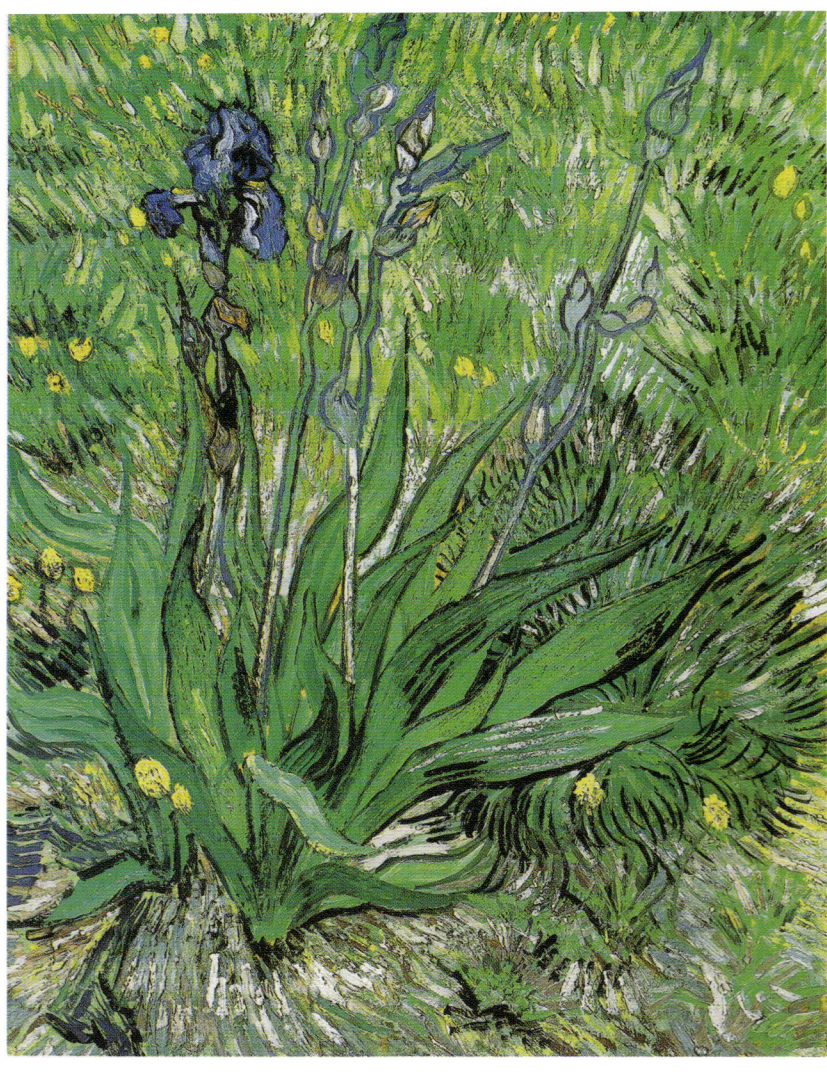

Iris (May 1889). Oil on canvas.
National Gallery of Canada, Ottawa.

This stately blue flower had already captured Vincent's imagination while he was living in Arles.

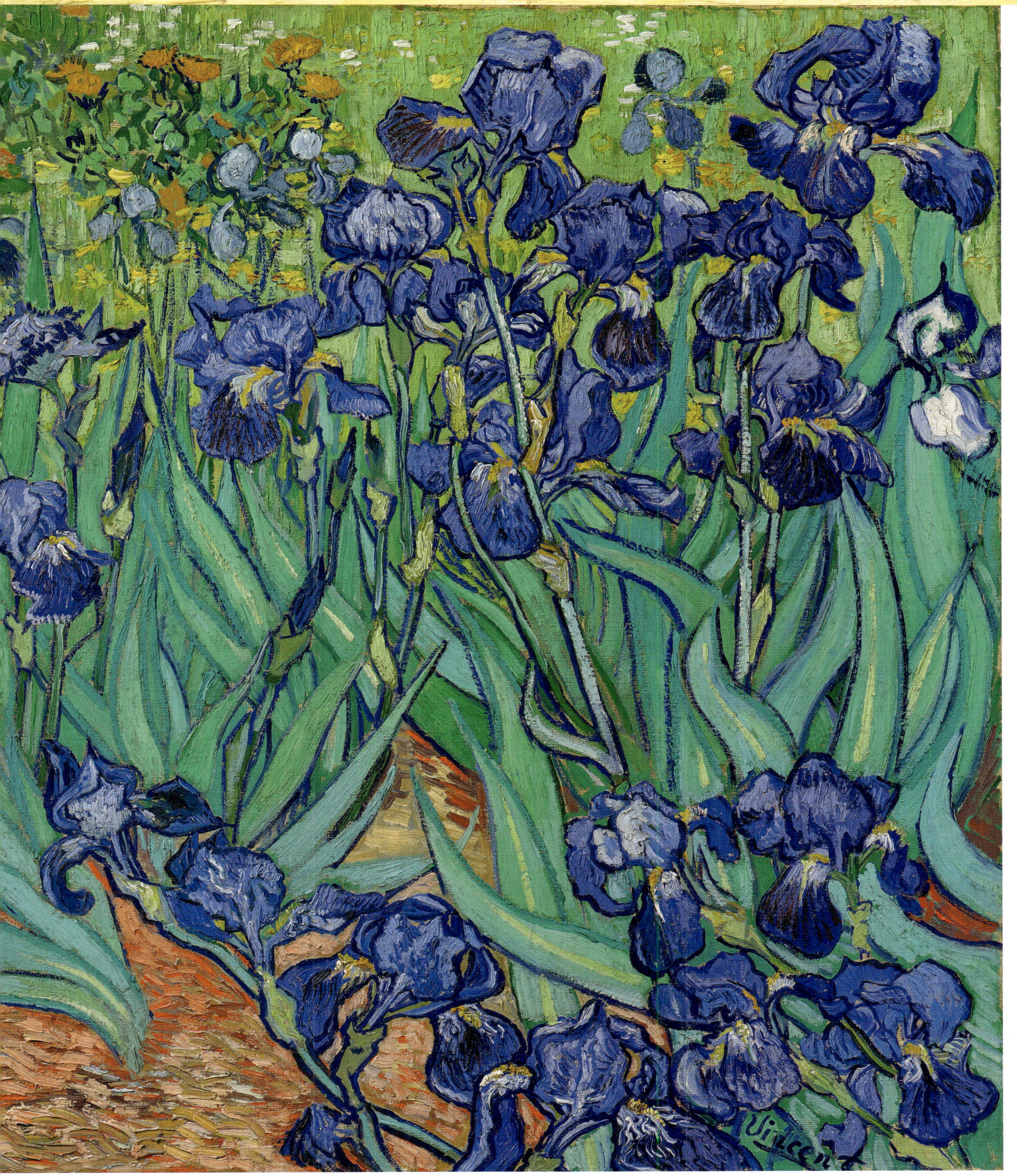

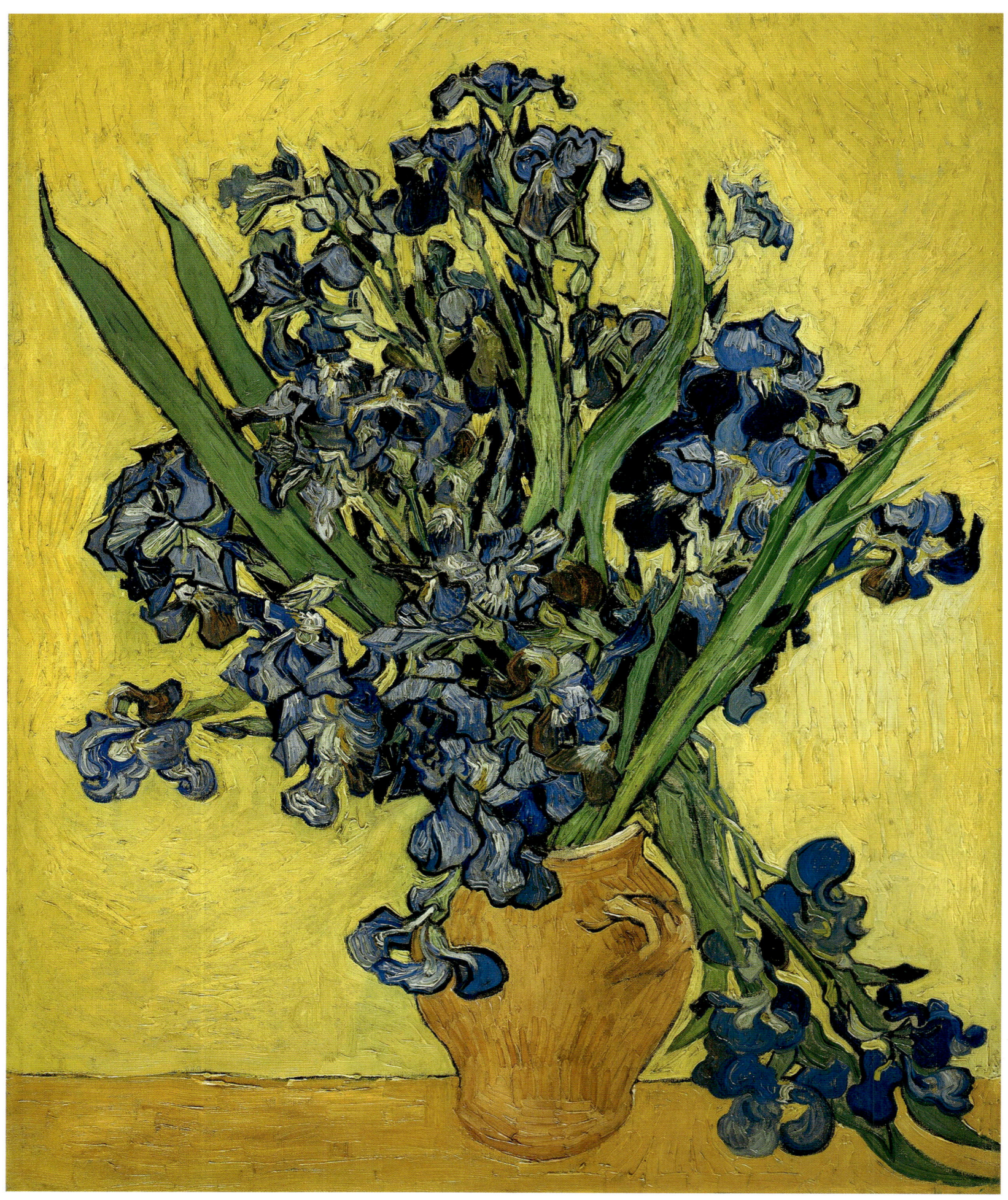

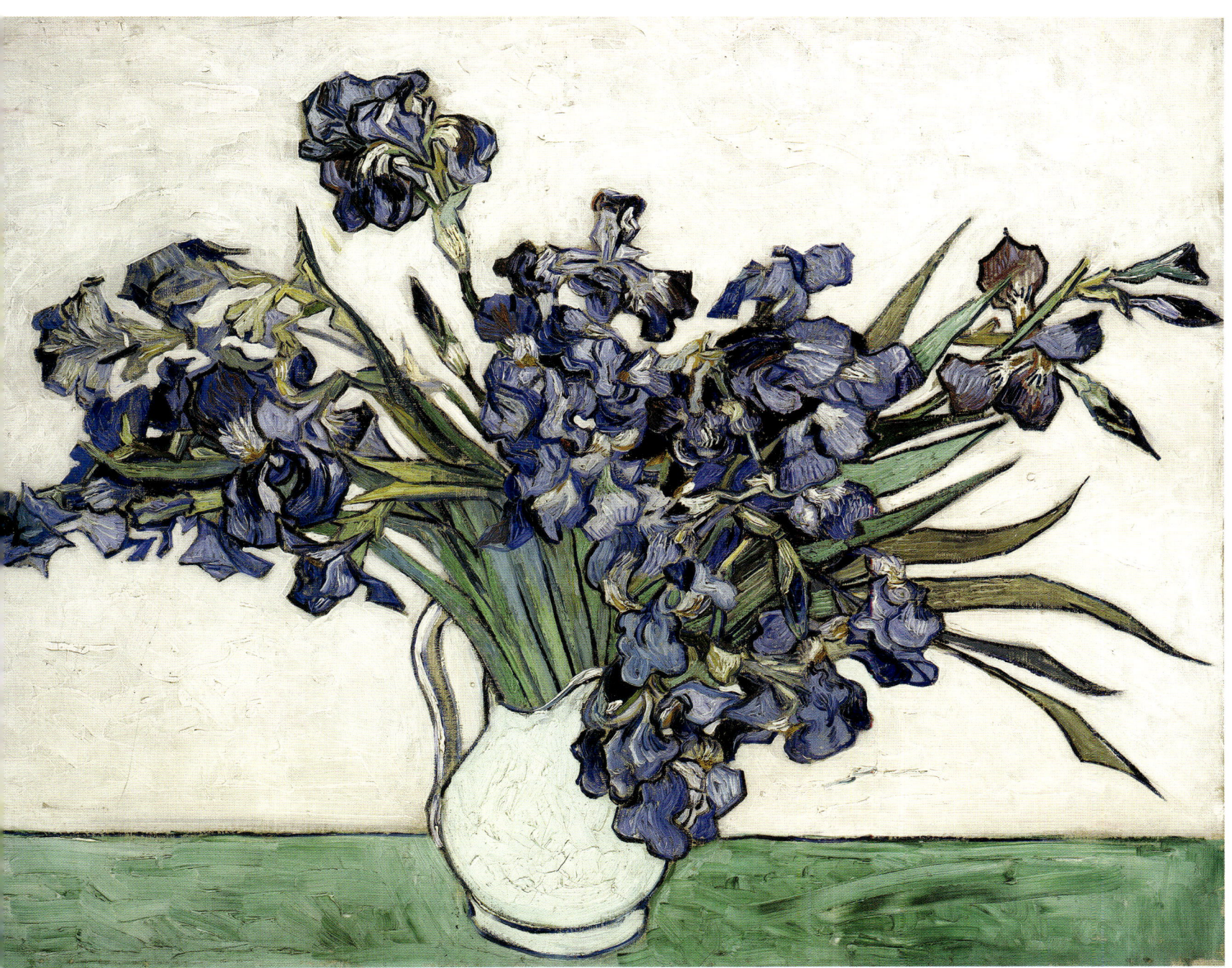

[ABOVE] *Vase with Irises*
(May 1890). Oil on canvas.
Metropolitan Museum of Art, New York.

" *The last days in Saint-Rémy I worked like a madman. Great bouquets of flowers, violet-colored irises, great bouquets of roses.*"

~ VINCENT, TO HIS SISTER WIL, 1890

[OPPOSITE PAGE] *Irises*
(May 1890). Oil on canvas.
Van Gogh Museum, Amsterdam
(Vincent van Gogh Foundation).

FLOWERS IN AUVERS

Although the landscapes produced in Auvers-sur-Oise, where Vincent spent the last days of his life, are more well-known, there are several notable still life paintings that date to this period.

[BELOW] *Still Life – Japanese Vase with Roses and Anemones* (June 1890). Oil on canvas. Musée d'Orsay, Paris.

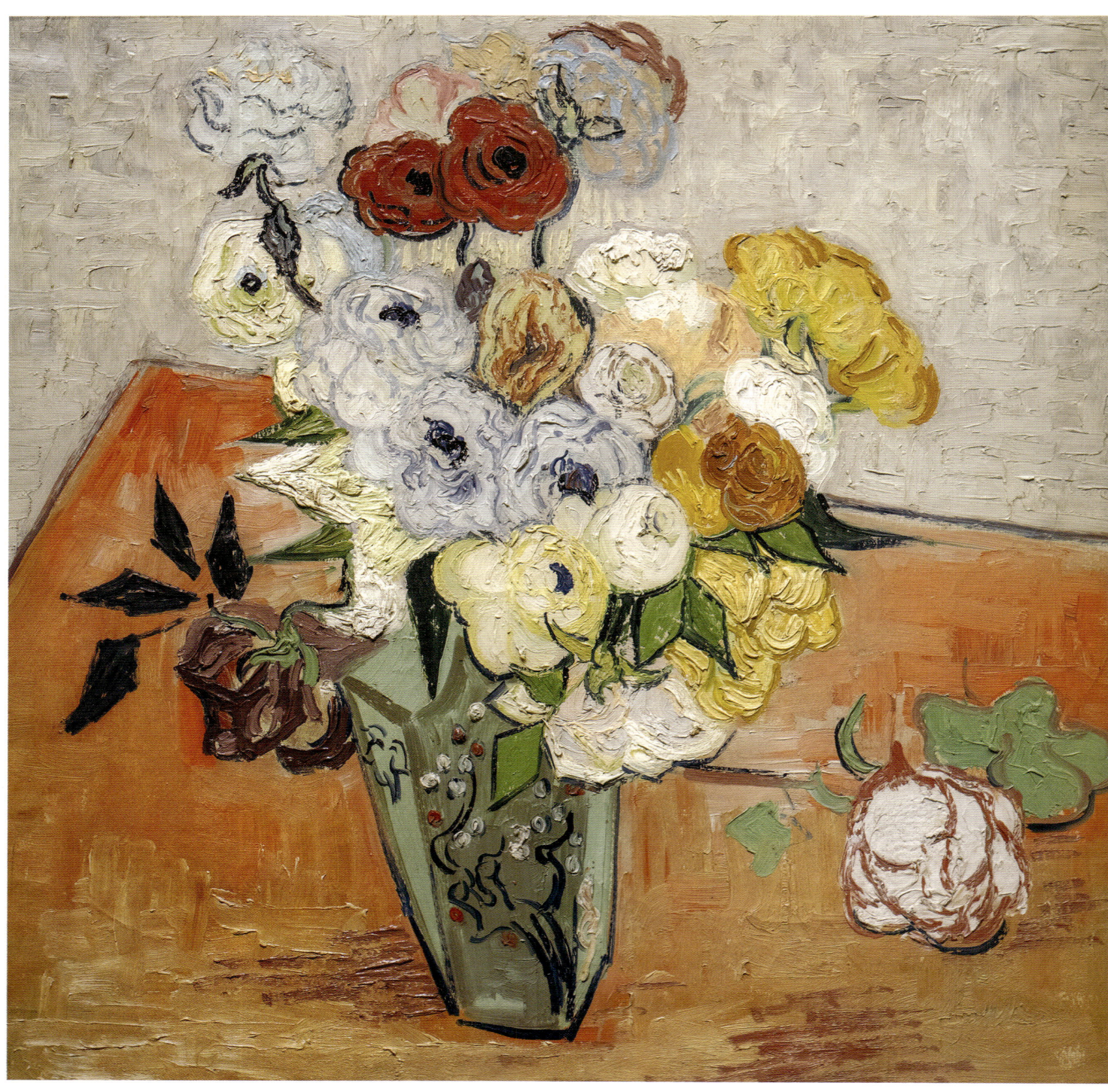

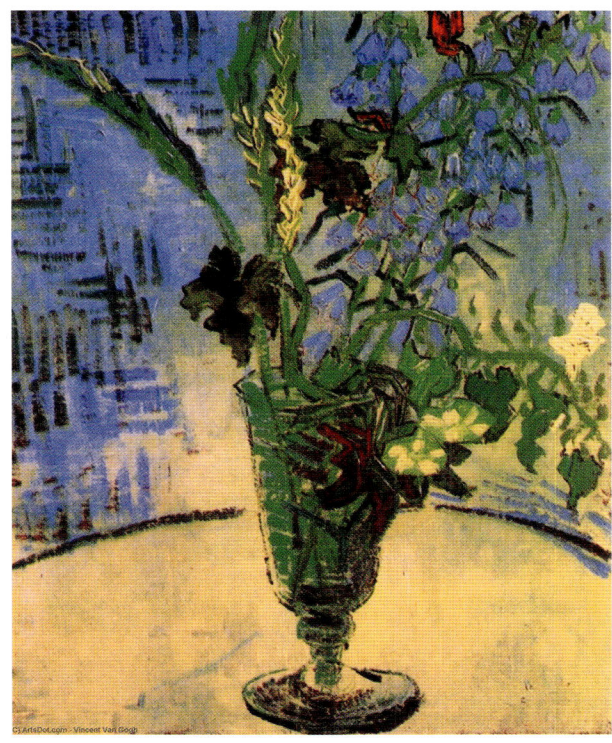

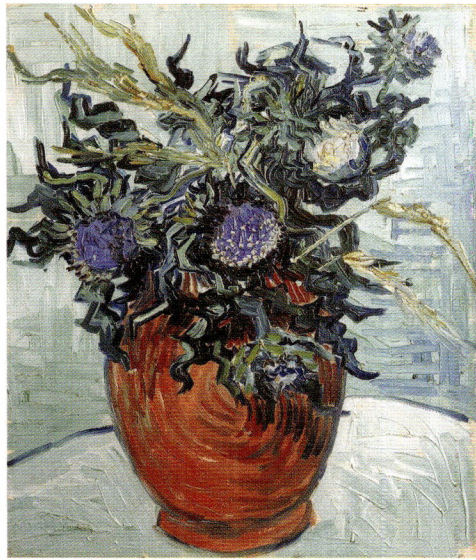

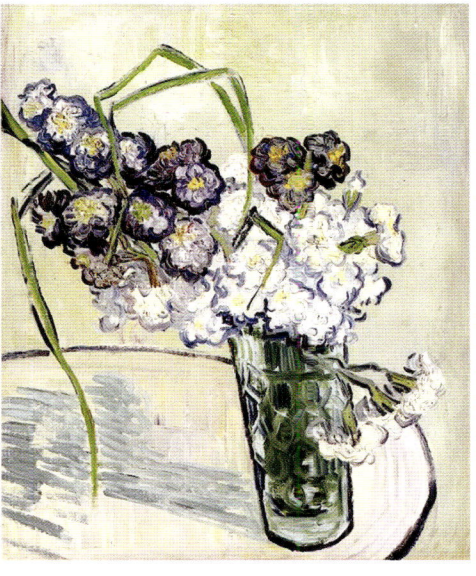

Vase with Flowers and Thistles (1890). Oil on canvas. Pola Museum of Art, Hakone, Japan.

Still Life Glass with Carnations (1890). Oil on canvas. Private collection.

Still Life Glass with Wild Flowers (1890). Oil on canvas. Private collection.

During June 1890, Vincent worked on a series of various flowers in glasses, mostly while at Paul Ferdinand Gachet's house in Auvers. Vincent was under Dr Gachet's care after he left the asylum in Saint-Rémy. There is an almost sketch-like quality to these works, which are executed with seemingly frantic, but ever evocative, brushstrokes.

"*I am working at it every morning from sunrise on, for the flowers fade so soon, and the thing is to do the whole in one rush.*"

~ VINCENT, TO HIS SISTER WIL, 1890

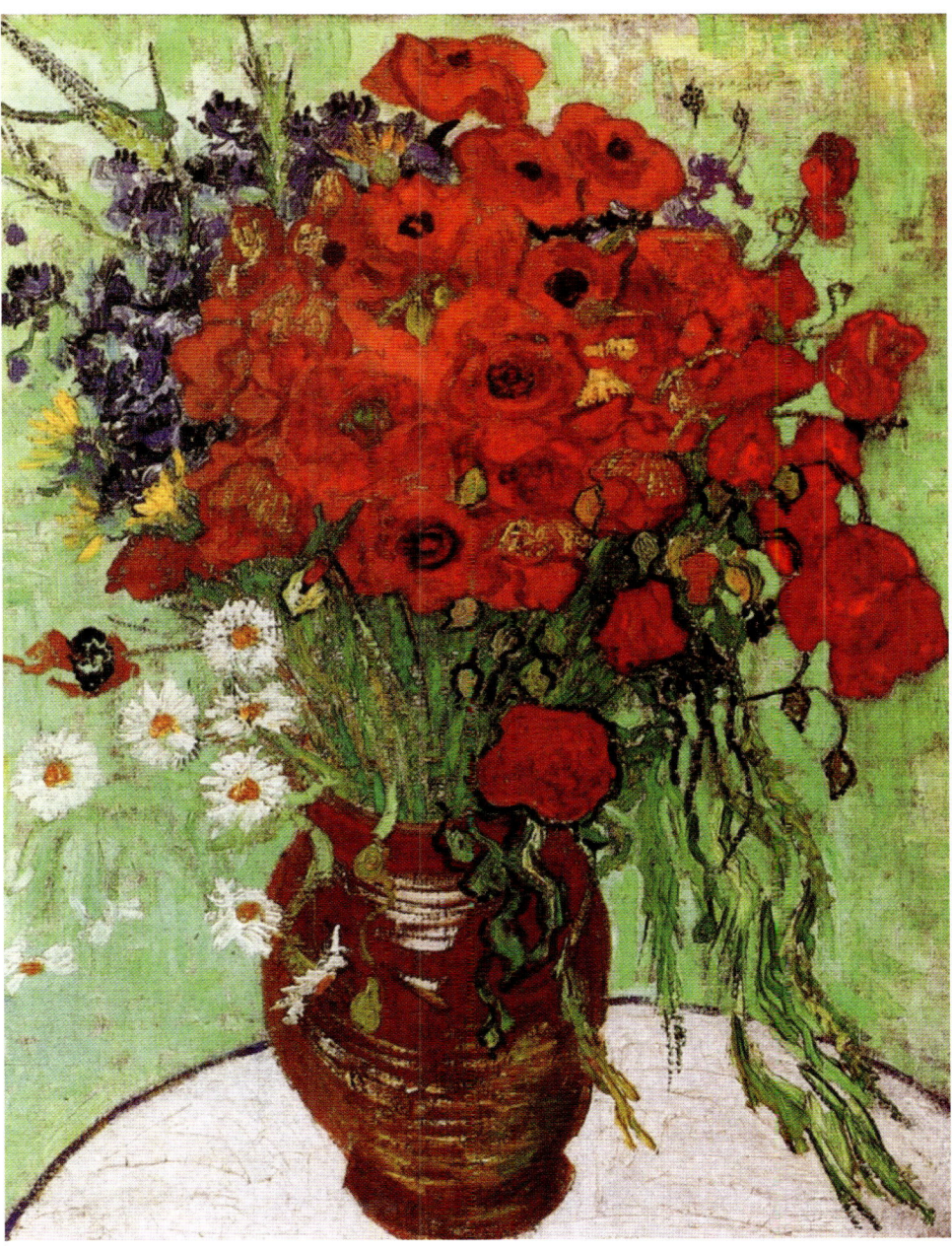

Vase with Daisies and Poppies (1890). Oil on canvas. Albright-Knox Art Gallery, Buffalo, New York.

Between the years 1886 and 1890, Vincent completed seven paintings featuring poppies.

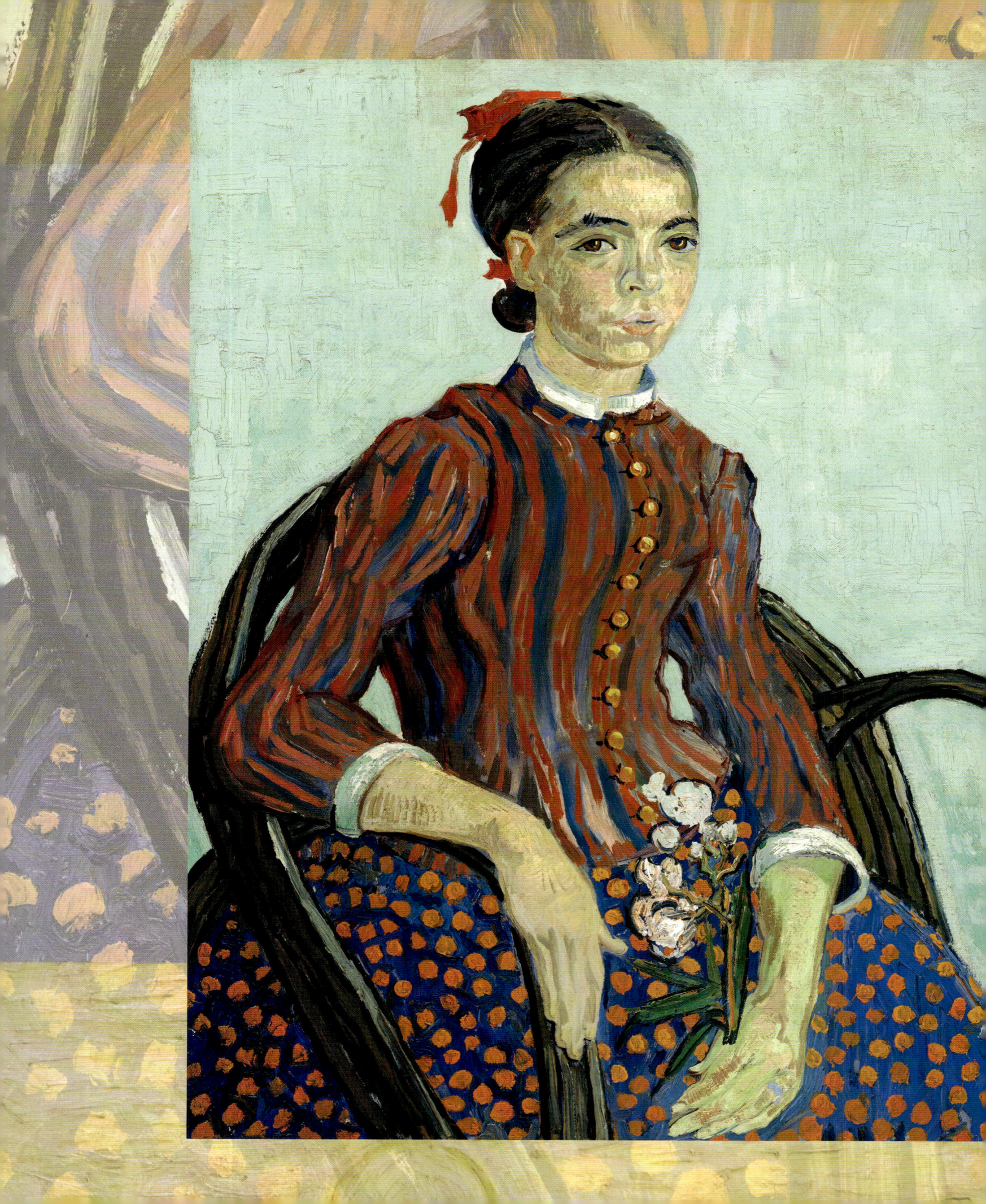

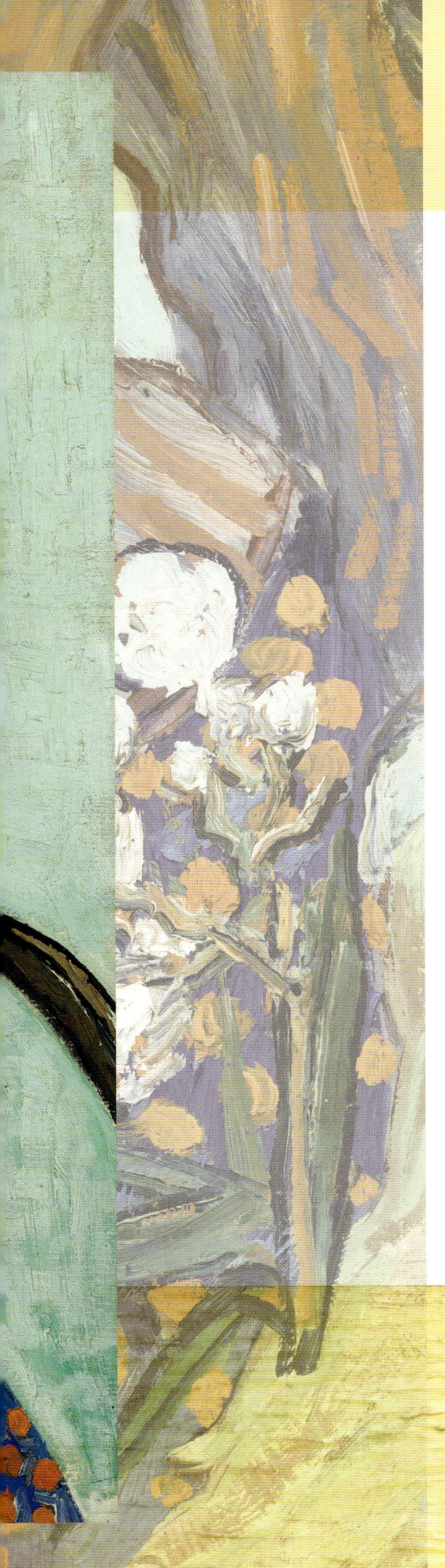

PEOPLE & PORTRAITS

ALONG WITH HIS NUMEROUS self-portraits, Vincent chose people as subjects of portraits and genre paintings. Some of his earliest works focus on the working poor and peasants—paintings and drawings executed in a dark, somber palette. His later portraits and paintings of people take on brighter, more intense tones, especially after his time in Paris and in Arles. These portraits are alive with shocking strokes of color, in almost jarring contrasts, with subjects often set in fantastical backgrounds or in front of strong layerings of solid color.

La Mousmé, or *La Mousmé, Sitting in a Cane Chair, Half-Figure* **(with a branch of oleander) (1888). Oil on canvas. National Gallery of Art, Washington, D. C.**

PEASANT LIFE

Vincent undertook a series of peasant character studies between 1881 and 1885. His first truly notable works were completed during his time in the Netherlands; these depict the working poor whom he lived amongst. From 1883 to 1885, he worked in the villages of Nieuw-Amsterdam and Nuenen, where poor soil challenged the survival of farm workers and smallholders.

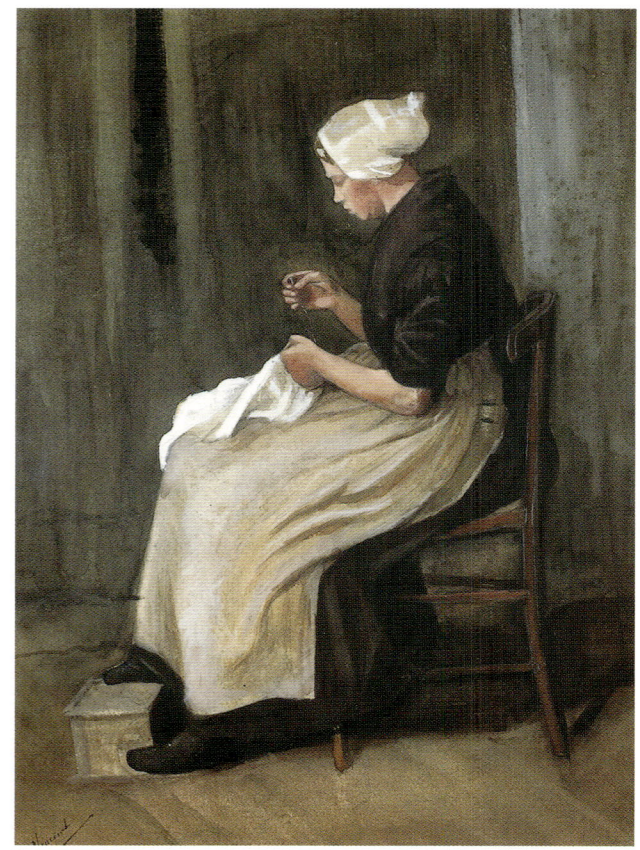

Young Scheveningen Woman Seated: Facing Left (December 1881). Watercolor. P. and N. de Boer Foundation, Amsterdam

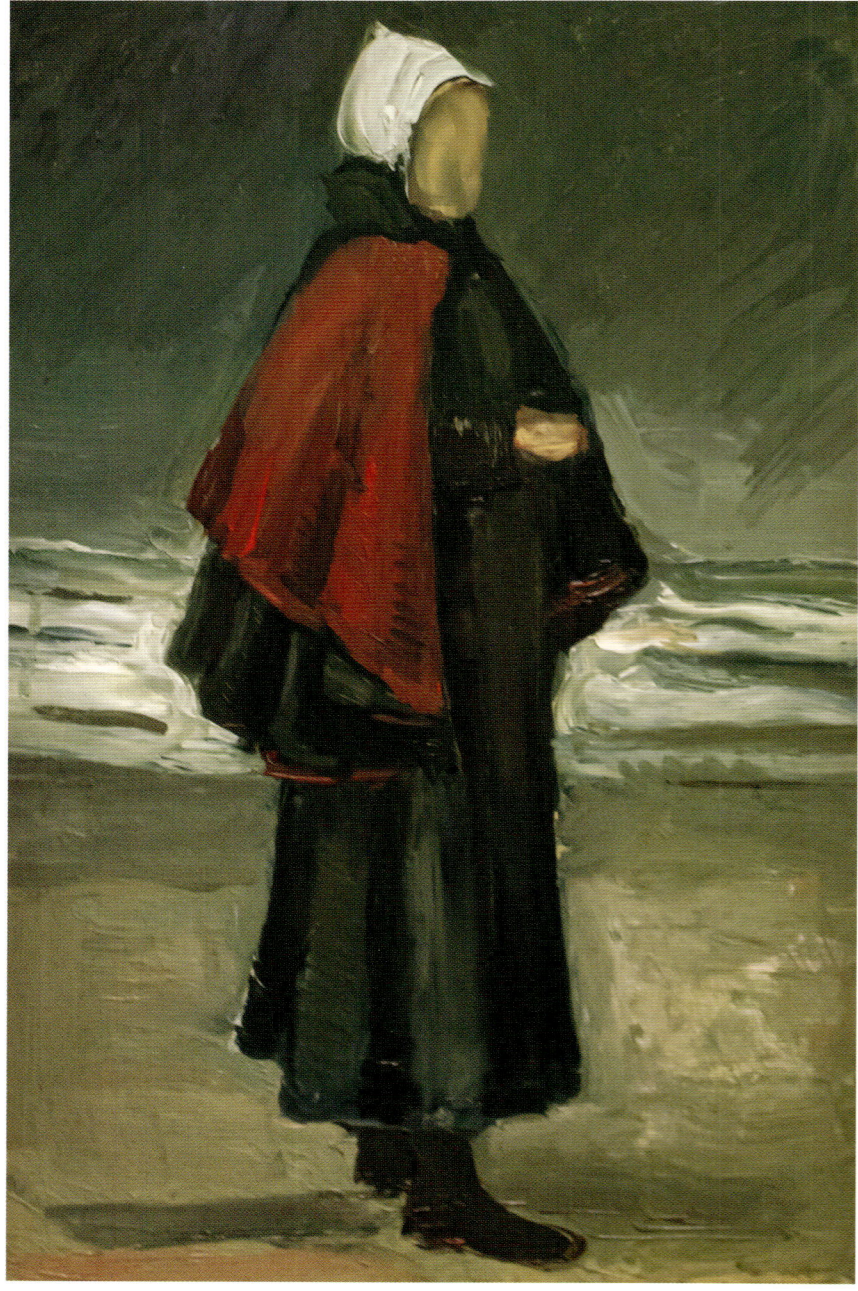

Fisherman's Wife on the Beach (early August 1882). Oil on canvas. Kröller-Müller Museum, Otterlo.

Evidence suggests that the model for this painting was Sien Hoornik, the woman Vincent lived with at the time.

[RIGHT] **Fisherman on the Beach** (1882). Oil on canvas mounted on wood. Kröller-Müller Museum, Otterlo.

[OPPOSITE PAGE] **Two Women in the Woods** (1882). Oil on canvas. Private collection.

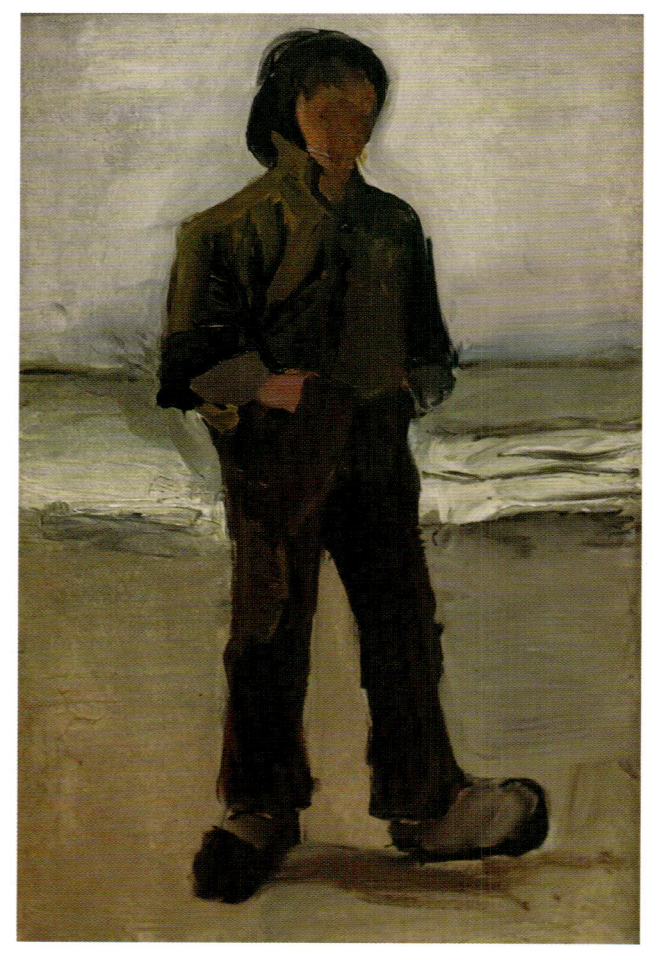

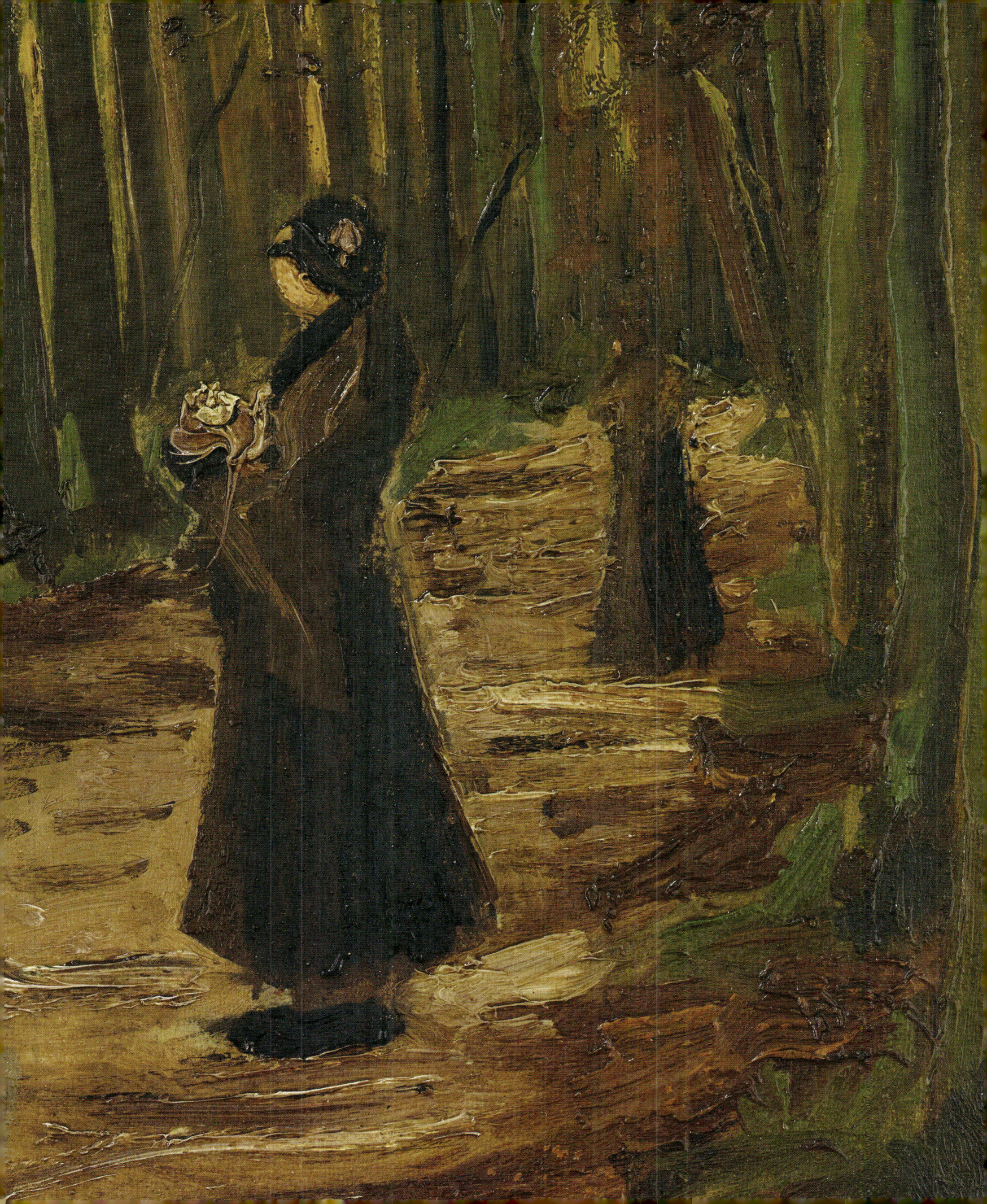

[RIGHT] *Weaver* (1884). Oil on canvas. Museum of Fine Arts, Boston.

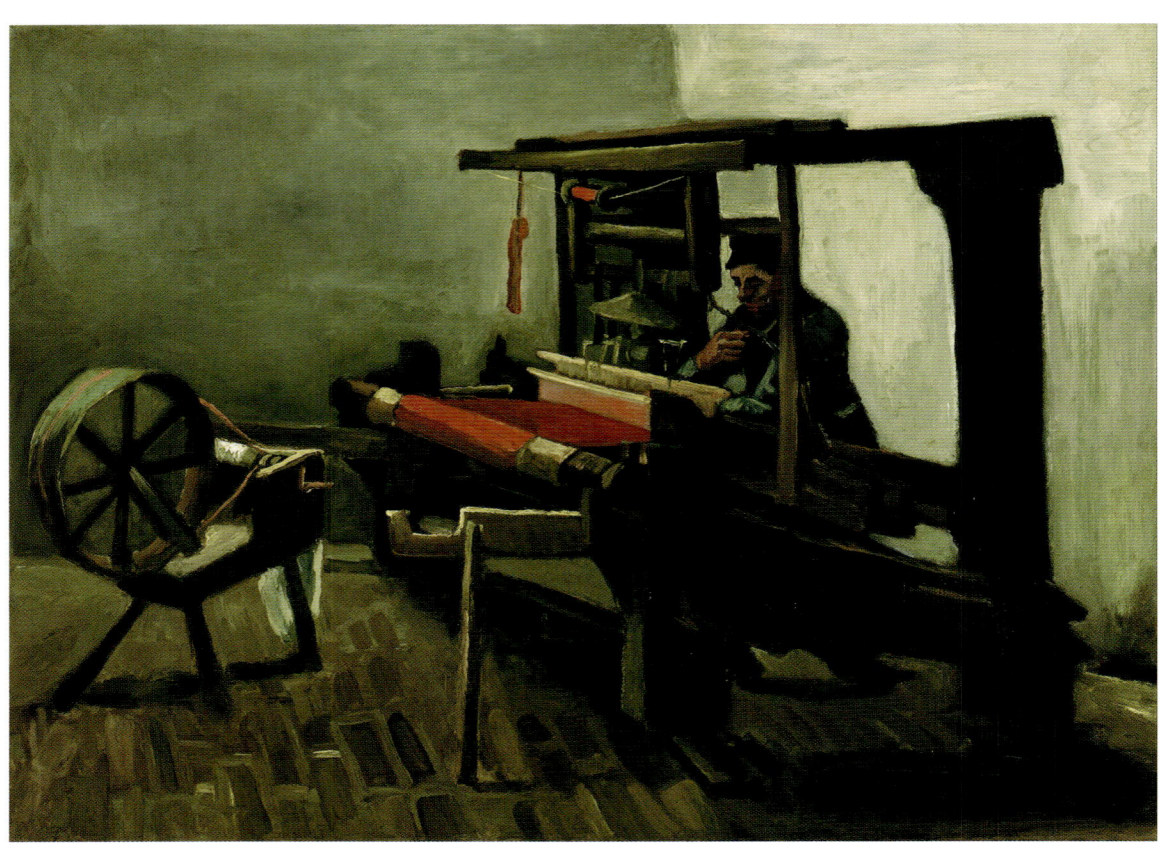

> " *A painting of peasant life should not be perfumed.*"
>
> ~VINCENT, TO THEO, APRIL 1885

[BELOW] *Weaver Facing Right* (February 1884). Oil on canvas mounted on panel. Private collection.

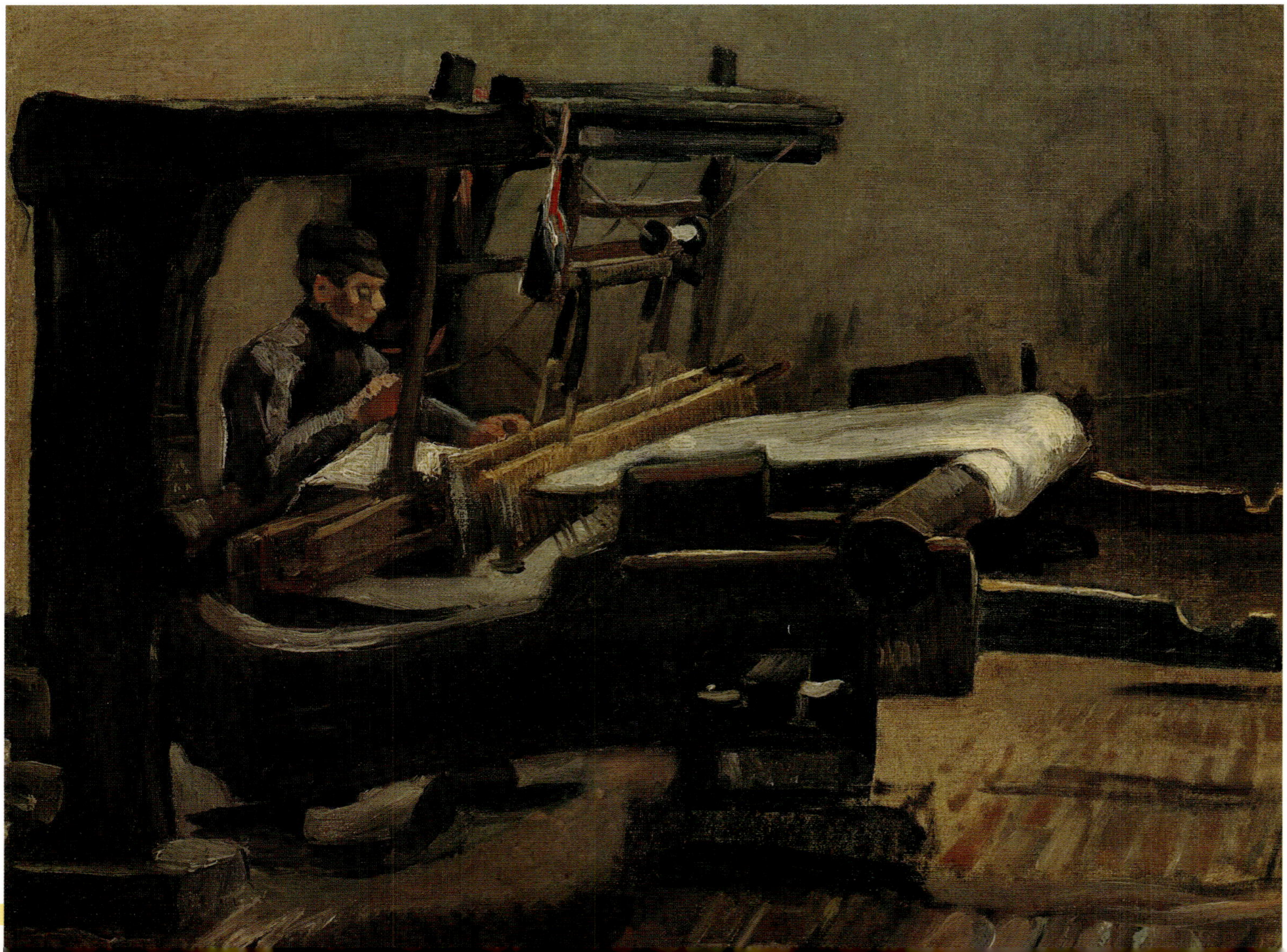

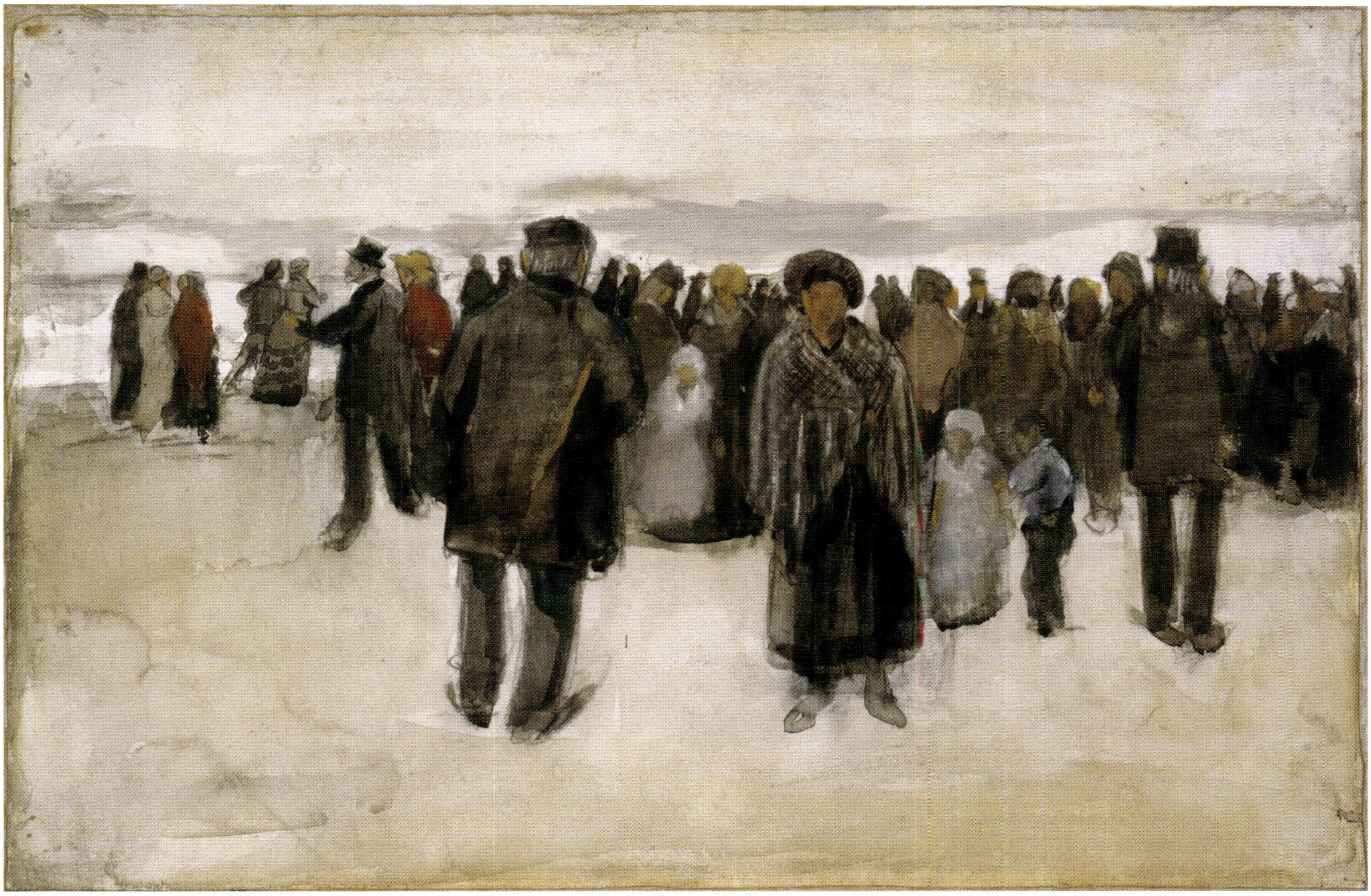

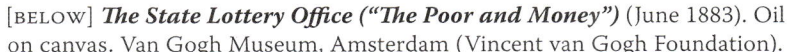

Beach at Scheveningen / People Strolling on the Beach (September 1882). Transparent and opaque watercolor with charcoal on light brown paper. Baltimore Museum of Art, The Cone Collection, formed by Dr. Claribel Cone and Miss Etta Cone of Baltimore, Maryland.

[RIGHT] *Peasant Woman Cooking by a Fireplace* (late Spring 1885). Oil on canvas. Metropolitan Museum of Art, New York.

[BELOW] *The State Lottery Office ("The Poor and Money")* (June 1883). Oil on canvas. Van Gogh Museum, Amsterdam (Vincent van Gogh Foundation).

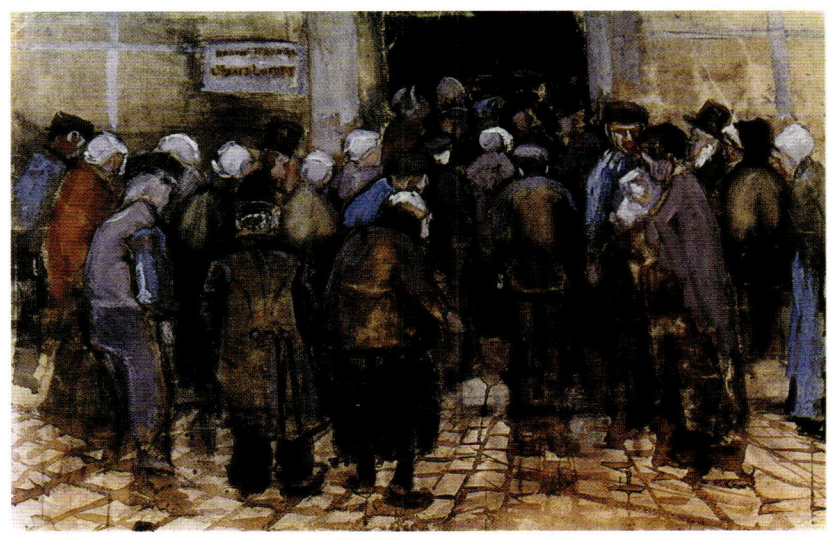

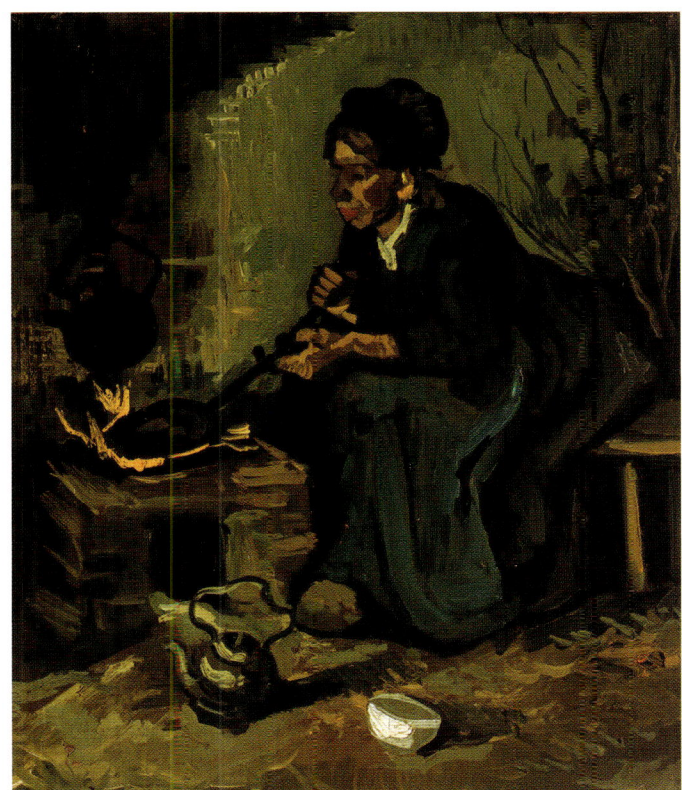

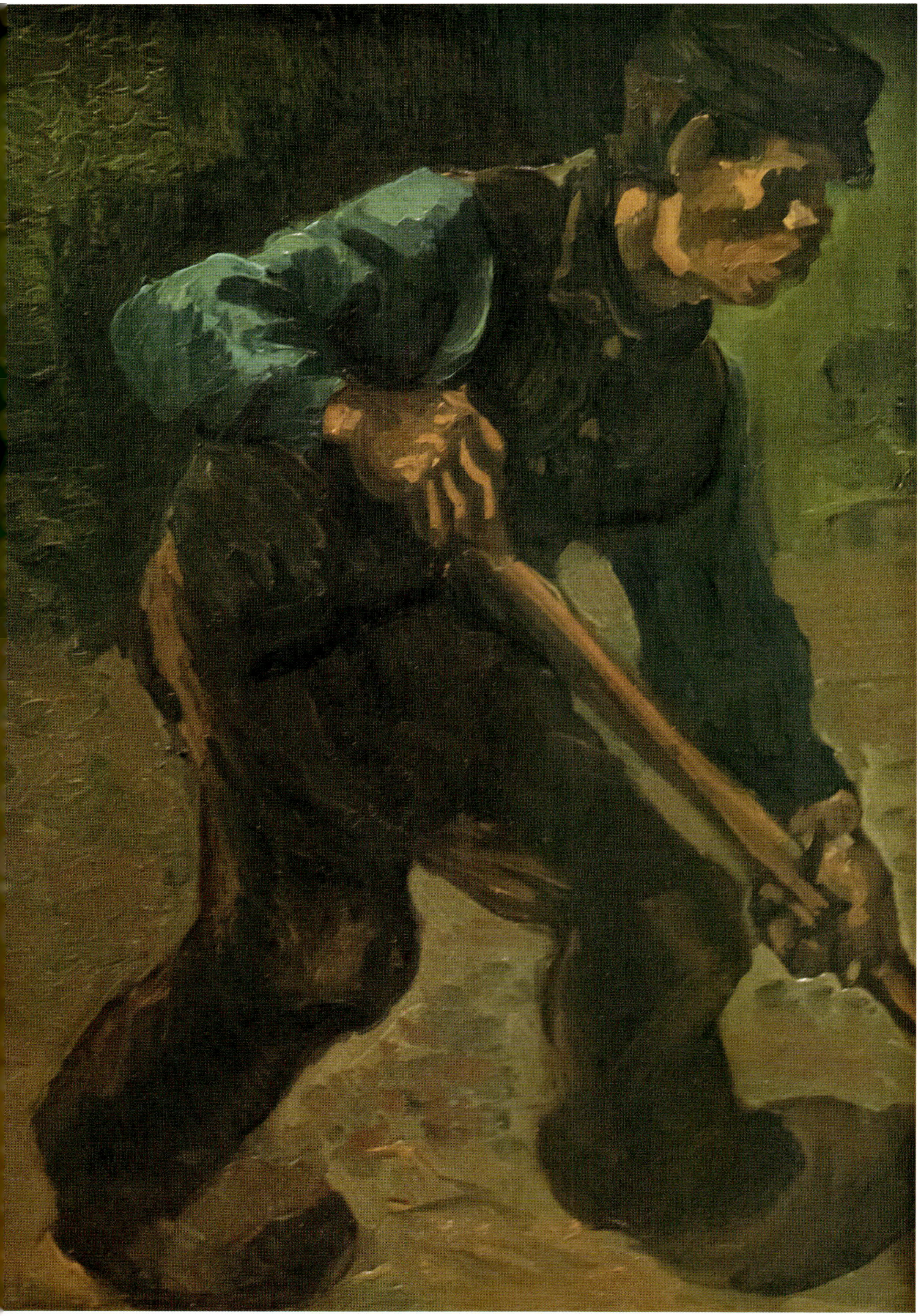

Digger (August 1885). Oil on canvas. Kröller-Müller Museum, Otterlo.

" *Personally, I am convinced that in the long run one gets better results from painting them in all their coarseness than from introducing a conventional sweetness."*

~VINCENT, TO THEO,
APRIL 1885

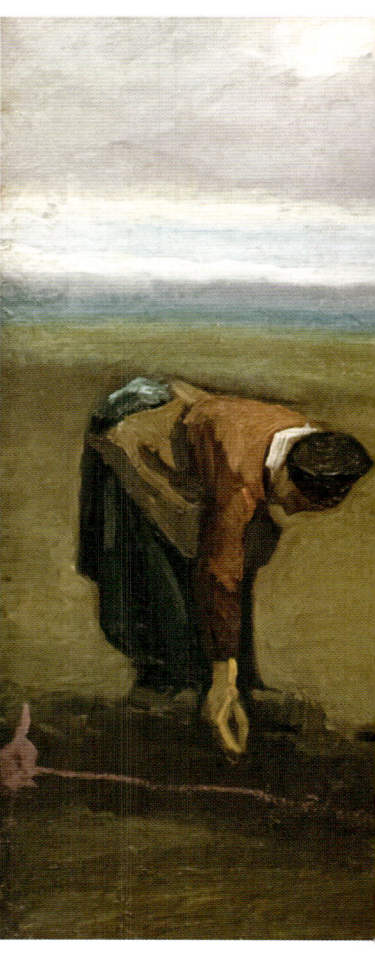

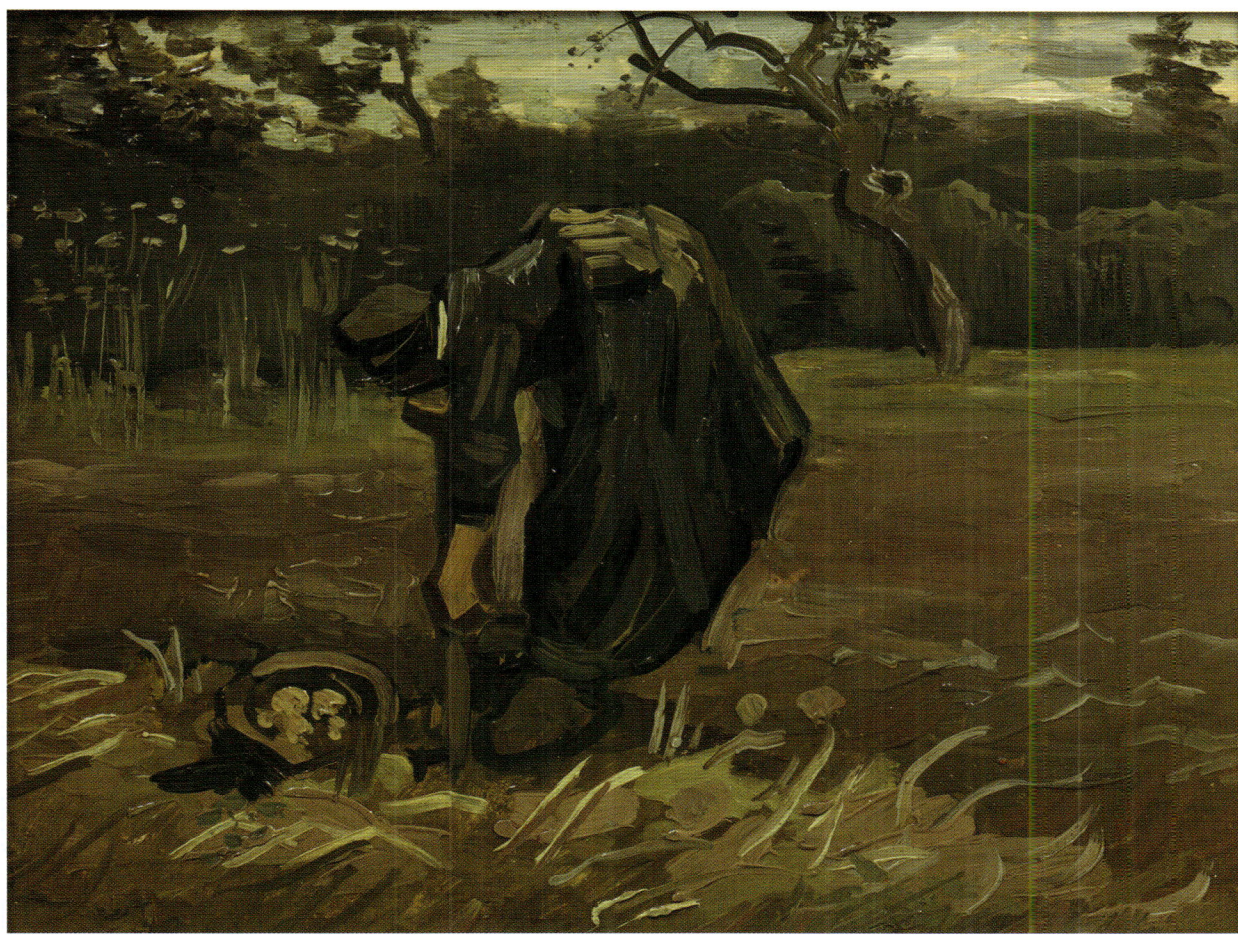

[LEFT]
***Peasant Woman,
Harvesting Potatoes***
(August 1885). Oil on
canvas mounted on panel.
Royal Museum of Fine
Arts, Antwerp.

[BELOW]
***Farmers Planting
Potatoes*** (1884).
Oil on canvas. Kröller-
Müller Museum, Otterlo.

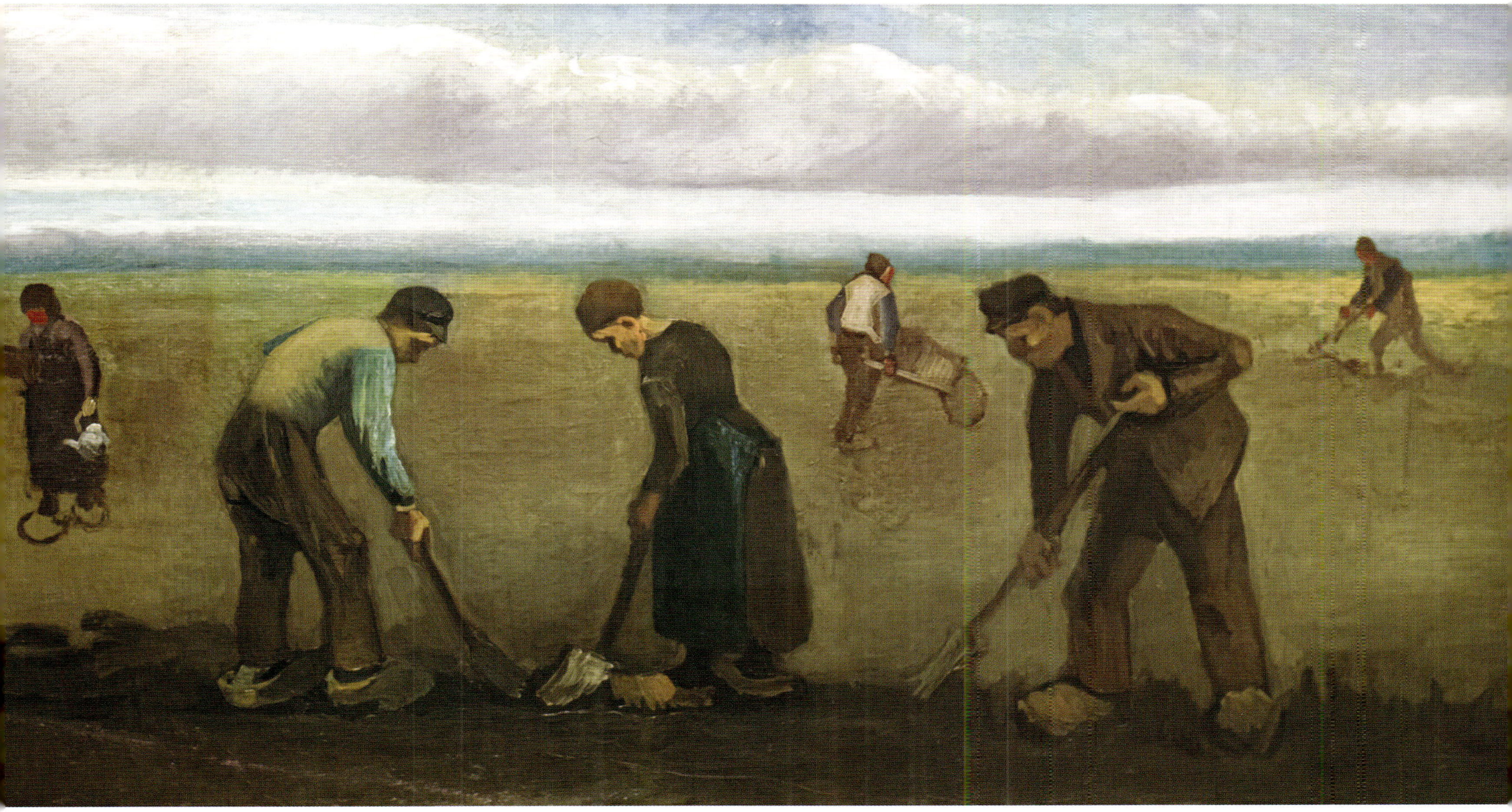

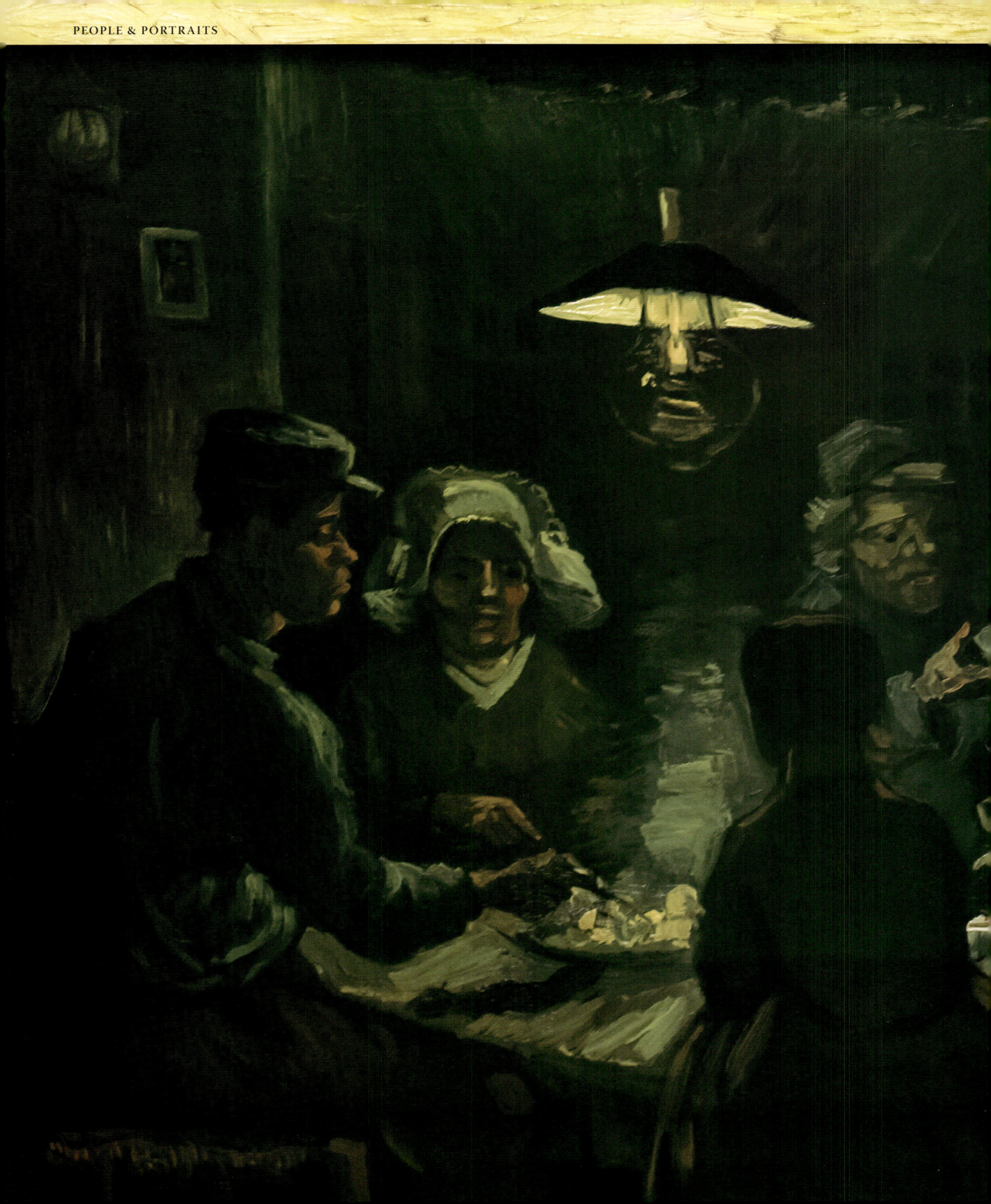

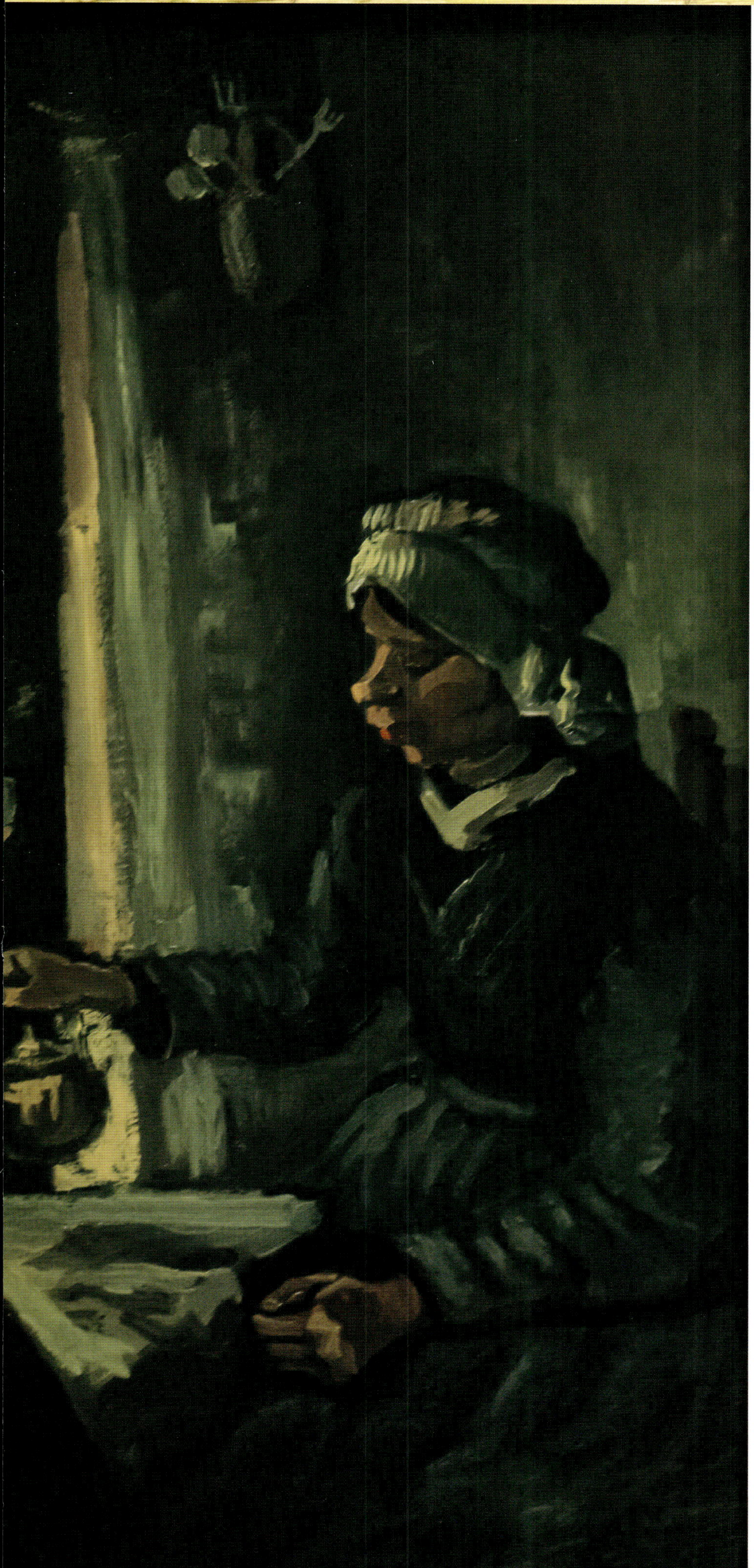

" *What I think about my own
work is that the painting of the
peasants eating potatoes that
I did in Nuenen is after all the
best thing I did.*"

~ VINCENT, IN A LETTER TO HIS SISTER WIL,
ABOUT *THE POTATO EATERS*

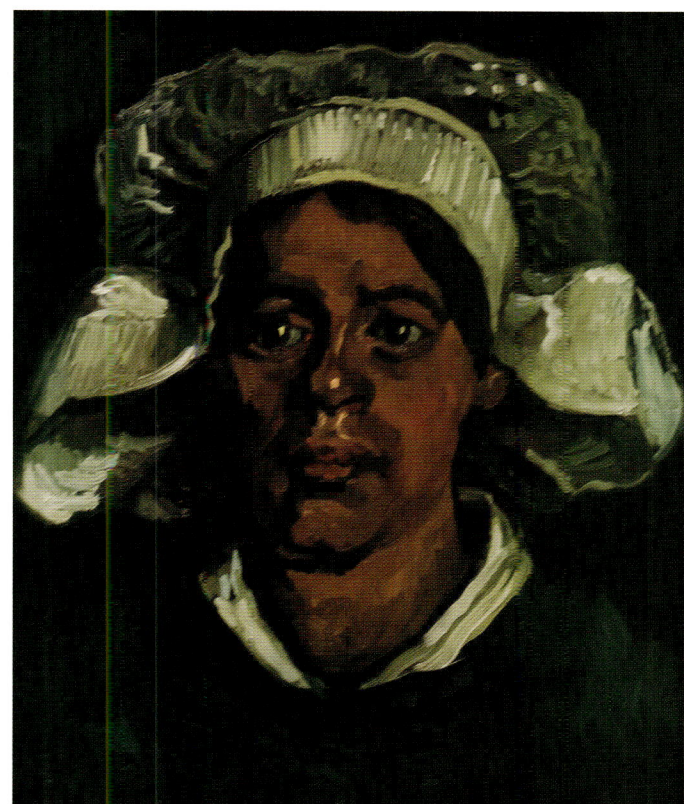

Head of a Woman Wearing a White Cap (Gordina de Groot)
(November 1884–May 1885). Oil on canvas.
Kröller-Müller Museum, Otterlo.

*Vincent made the deliberate choice of coarse and "ugly"
models for his work in Nuenen, saying he want to
depict these people in an unspoiled manner.*

PORTRAITS IN PARIS

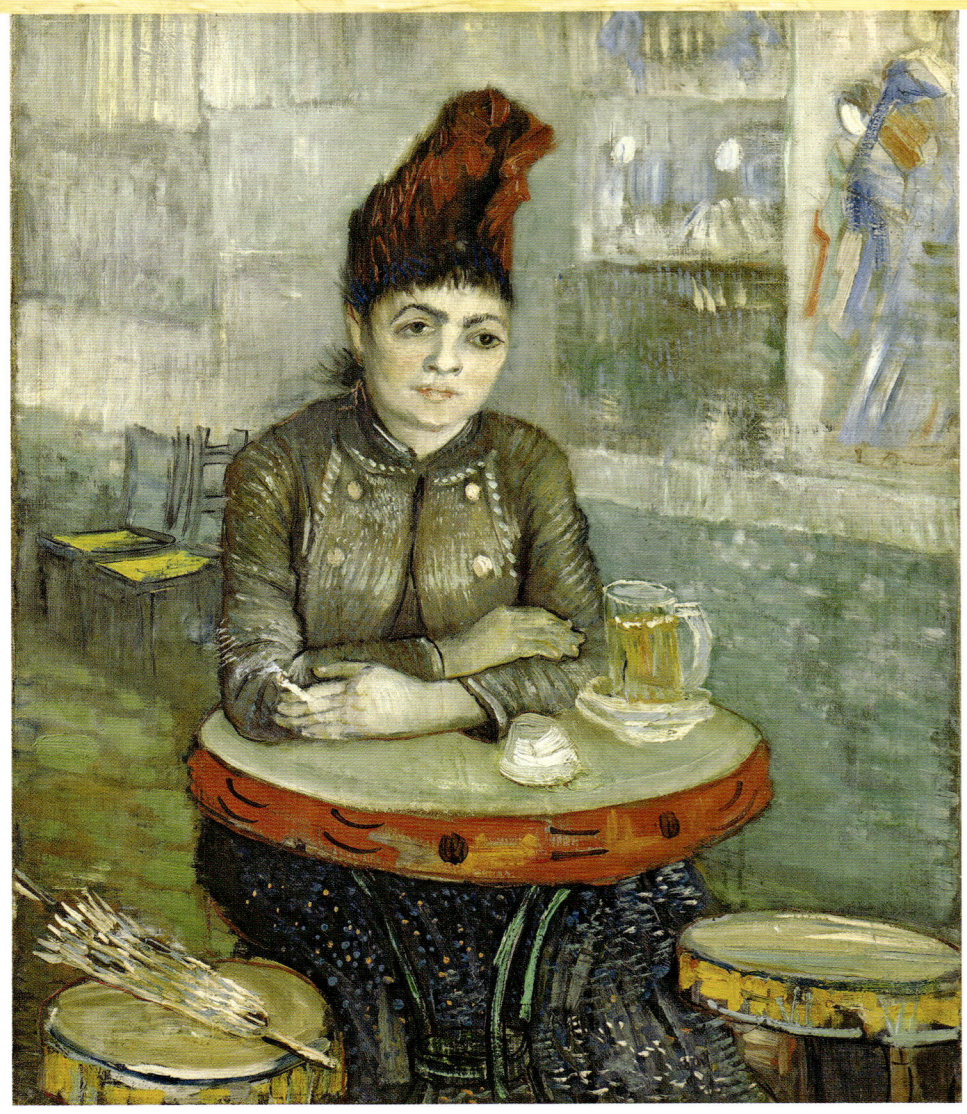

In Paris, Vincent began to paint what can truly be thought of as traditional portraits, although with a few exceptions, most of his portrait work while in the French capitol was self-portraiture. Some of the noteworthy exceptions are those of art dealer Julien Tanguy and of Agostina Segatori, who was owner of the Café du Tambourin in Montmartre, which was a favorite haunt of Parisian artists. Segatori, with whom he had a brief relationship, sat for Vincent a few times, and she is the subject of the only nudes he ever painted.

[LEFT]
In the Café: Agostina Segatori in Le Tambourin (January– March 1887). Oil on canvas. Van Gogh Museum, Amsterdam (Vincent van Gogh Foundation).

[OPPOSITE PAGE]
Italian Woman (Agostina Segatori) (1887). Oil on canvas. Musée d'Orsay, Paris.

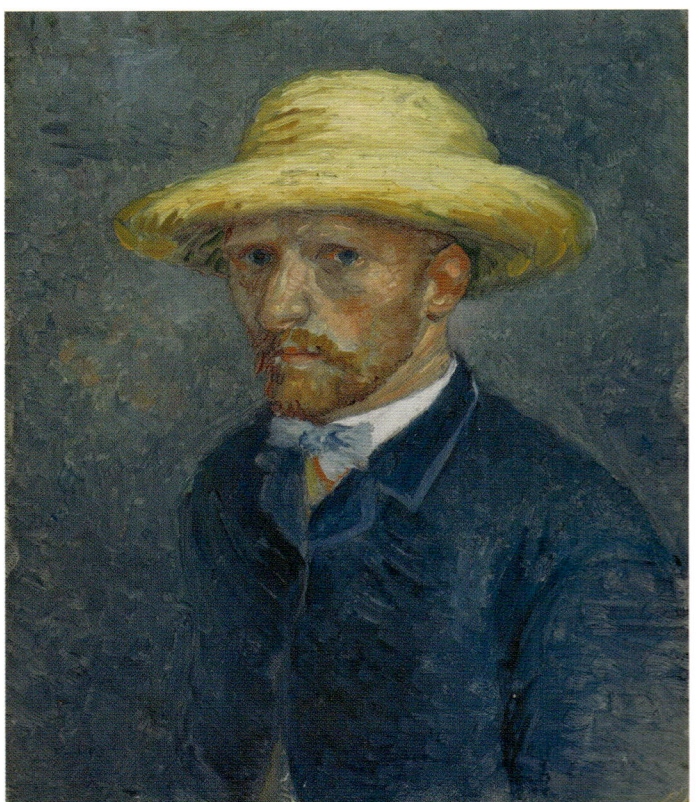

"*I cannot live without love, without a woman. I would not value life at all if there were not something infinite, something deep, something real. Every woman at every age can, if she loves and is a good woman, give a man, not the infinity of a moment, but a moment of infinity.*"

~ VINCENT, TO THEO, DECEMBER 1881

Self-Portrait, or **Portrait of Theo van Gogh** (Summer 1887). Oil on canvas. Van Gogh Museum, Amsterdam (Vincent van Gogh Foundation).

Painted in Paris in 1887, this small, detailed portrait has become a point of discussion. Long thought to be one of Vincent's many self-portraits, research published in 2011 concluded it was actually of his brother Theo, who bore a close resemblance to Vincent. The Van Gogh Museum, which owns it, has decided that no definitive evidence exists for either man as the subject, which is why the painting now has a double title.

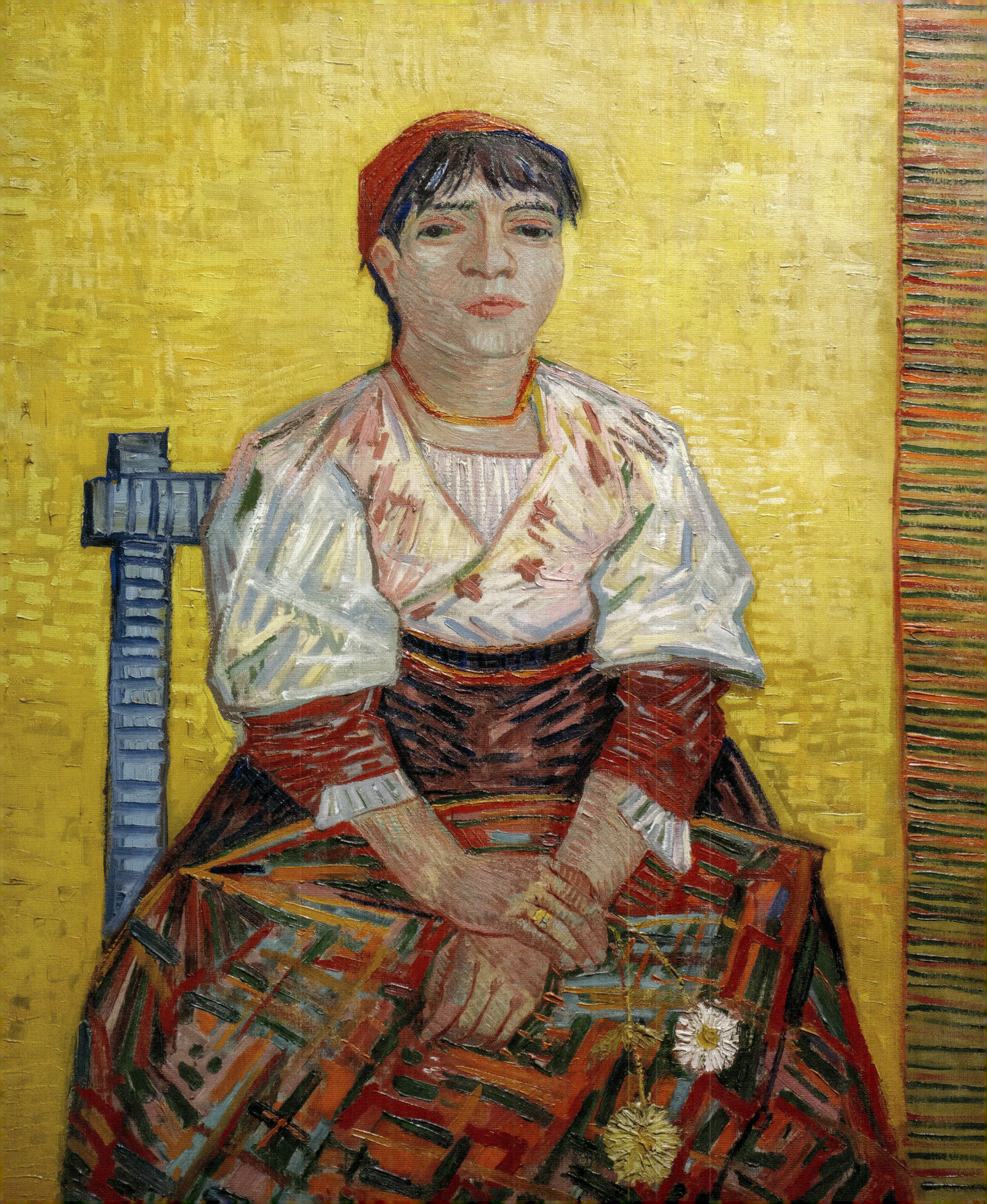

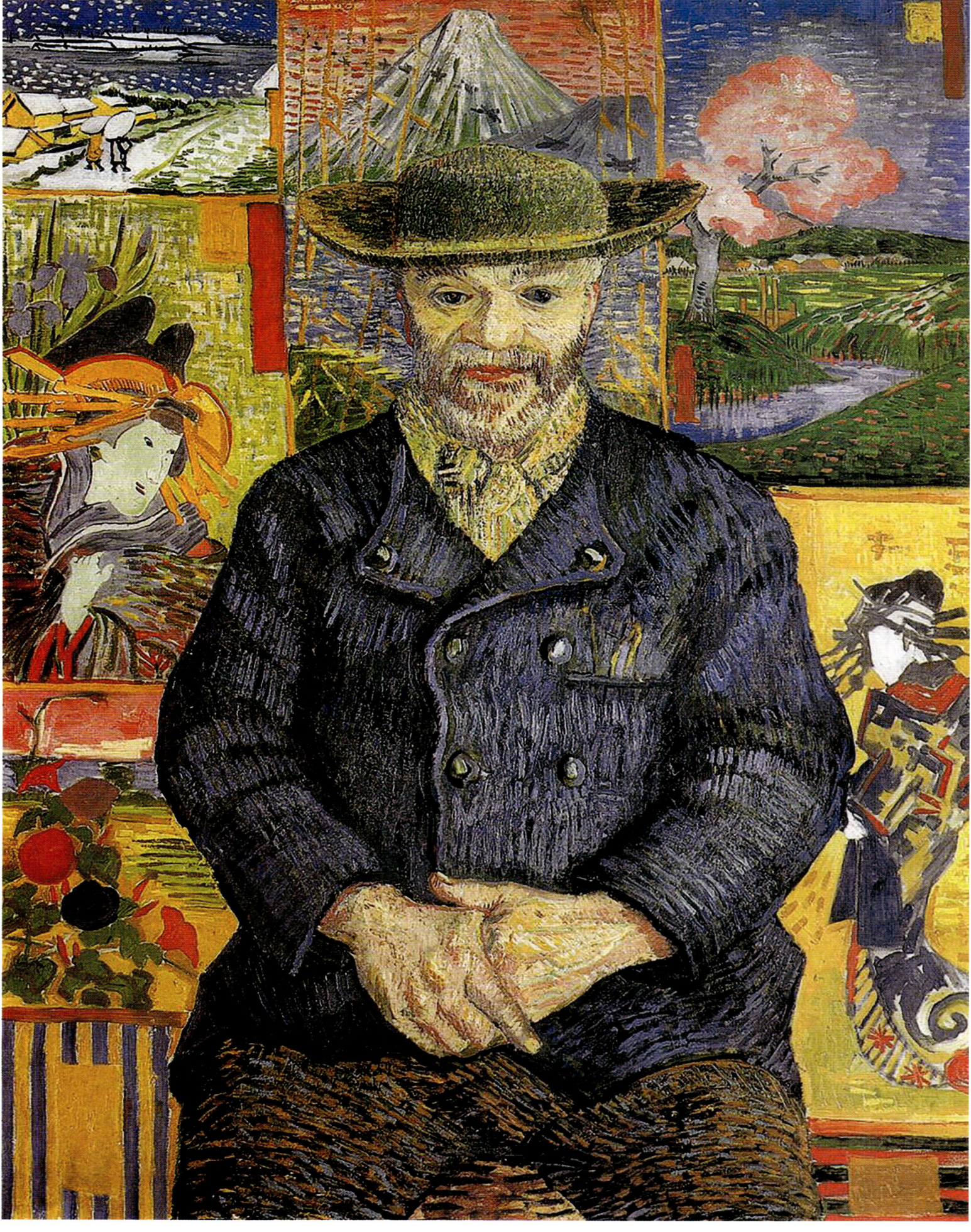

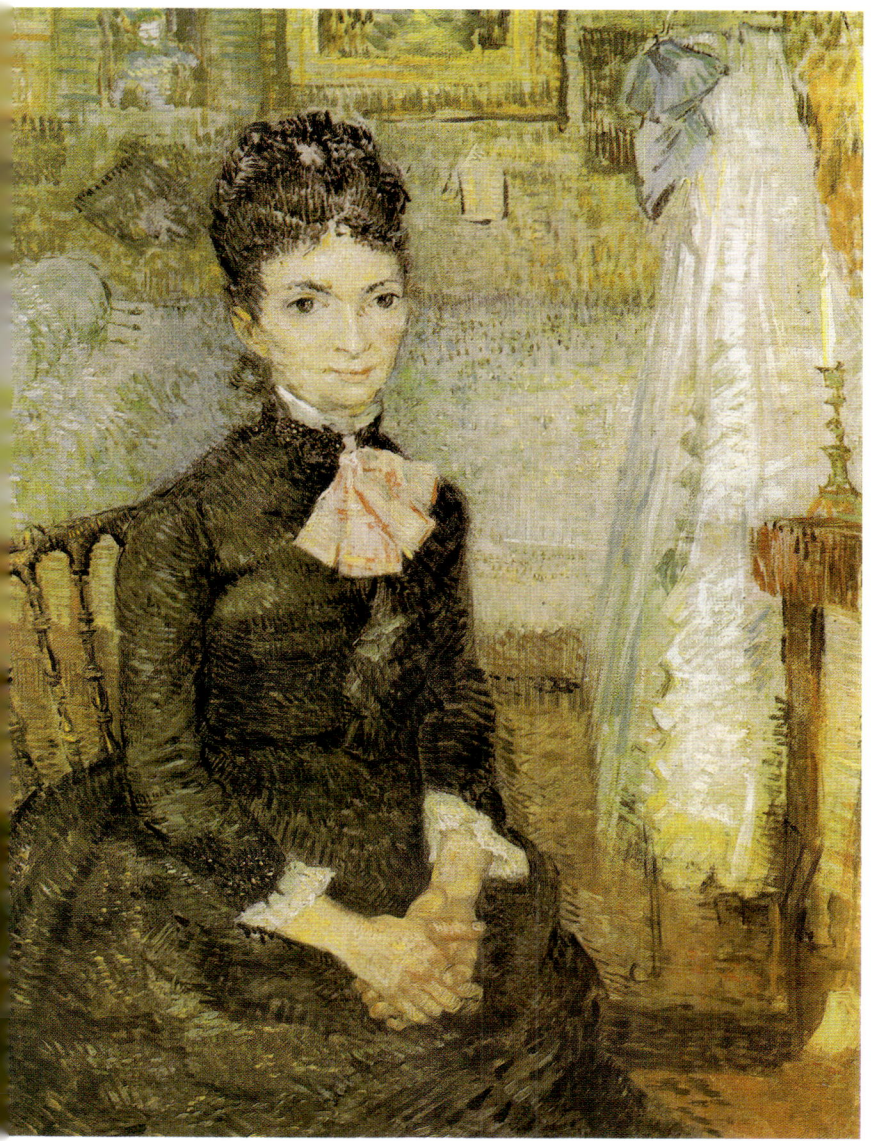

**Woman Sitting Next to a Cradle
(Portrait of Leonie Rose Davy-Charbuy)**
(Spring 1887). Oil on canvas.
Van Gogh Museum, Amsterdam (Vincent van Gogh Foundation).

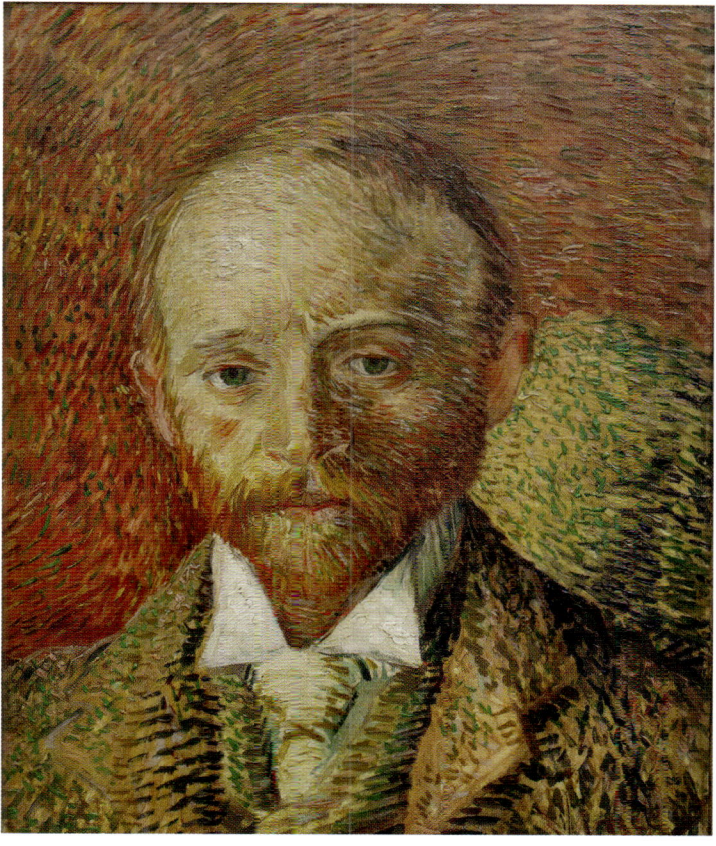

Portrait of Alexander Reid (1886–87). Oil on canvas.
Fred Jones Jr. Museum of Art, Norman, Oklahoma.

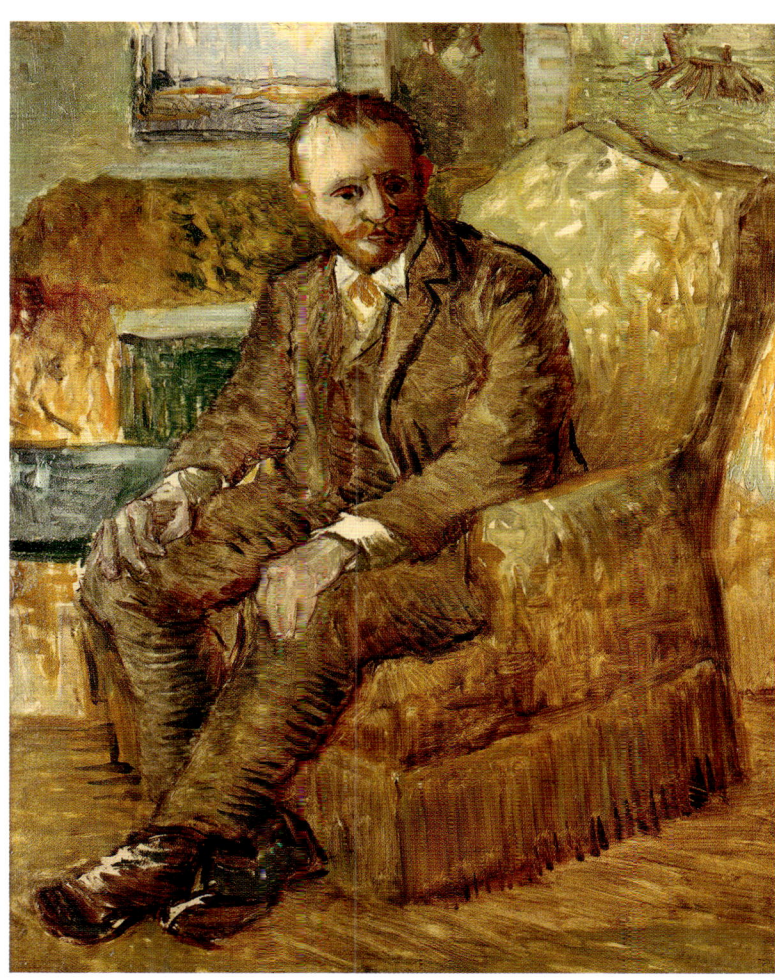

[RIGHT]
Portrait of the Art Dealer Alexander Reid (1887).
Oil on canvas. Kelvingrove Art Gallery and Museum, Glasgow.

[OPPOSITE PAGE]
Portrait of Père Tanguy (1887).
Oil on canvas. Musée Rodin, Paris.

*One of Vincent's three paintings of Julien Tanguy. Tanguy was
a Parisian art dealer, who sold art supplies, taking paintings
as payment for paints. In this portrait, the background is filled
with Vincent's Japanese prints, which Tanguy sold in his shop.*

THE PEOPLE OF ARLES

Vincent moved to Arles in southern France in 1888, and it was there that he produced some of his best work during what seems to have been one of the happiest periods of his life. His focus was on ordinary life, inspiring him to produce an extraordinary series of portraits of the local people.

> "*Painting as it is now, promises to become more subtle—more like music and less like sculpture—and above all, it promises color.*"
>
> ~ VINCENT, IN A LETTER TO THEO, AUGUST 1888

[RIGHT] **Memory of the Garden at Etten**, or **Ladies of Arles** (November 1888). Oil on canvas. Hermitage Museum, St. Petersburg.

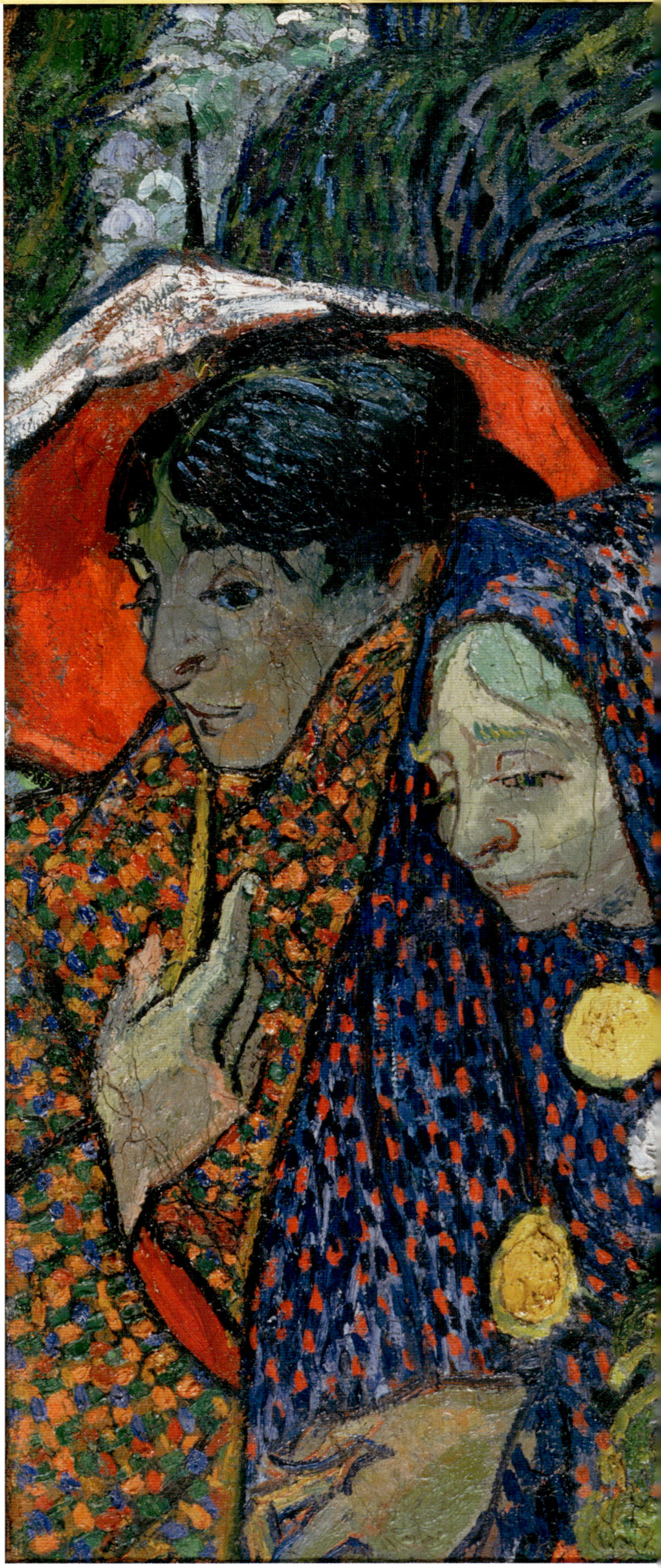

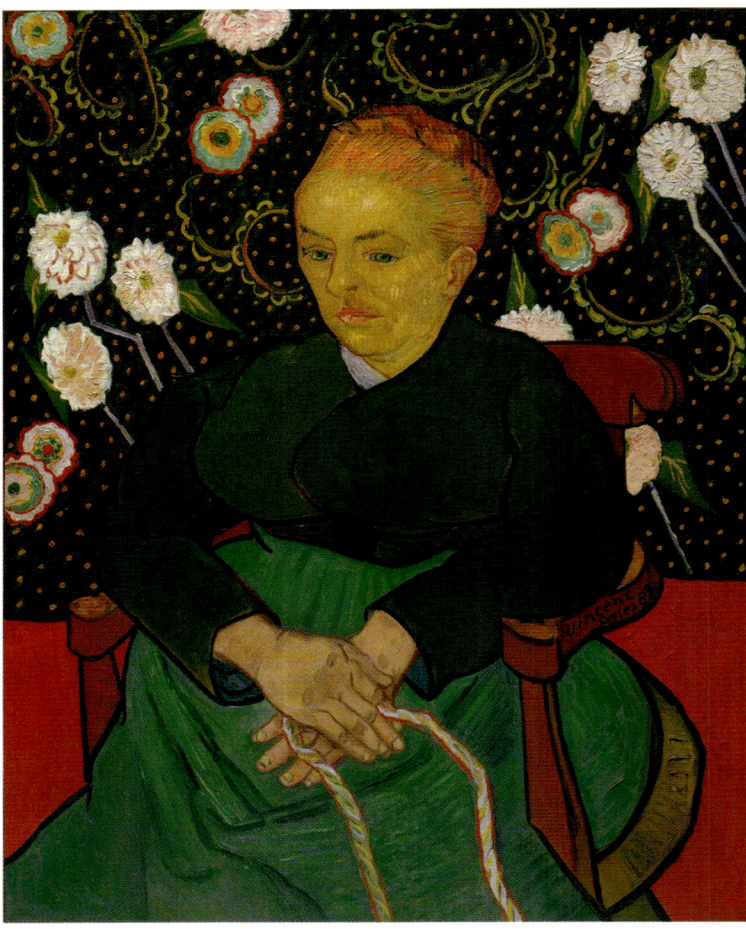

La Berceuse (Women Rocking a Cradle, Augustine-Alex Pellicot Roulin) (January 1889). Oil on canvas. Metropolitan Museum of Art, New York.

Vincent created five nearly identical versions of this painting, which depict Augustine Roulin using a string to rock an unseen cradle. In French, la berceuse means "our lullaby, or the woman rocking the cradle."

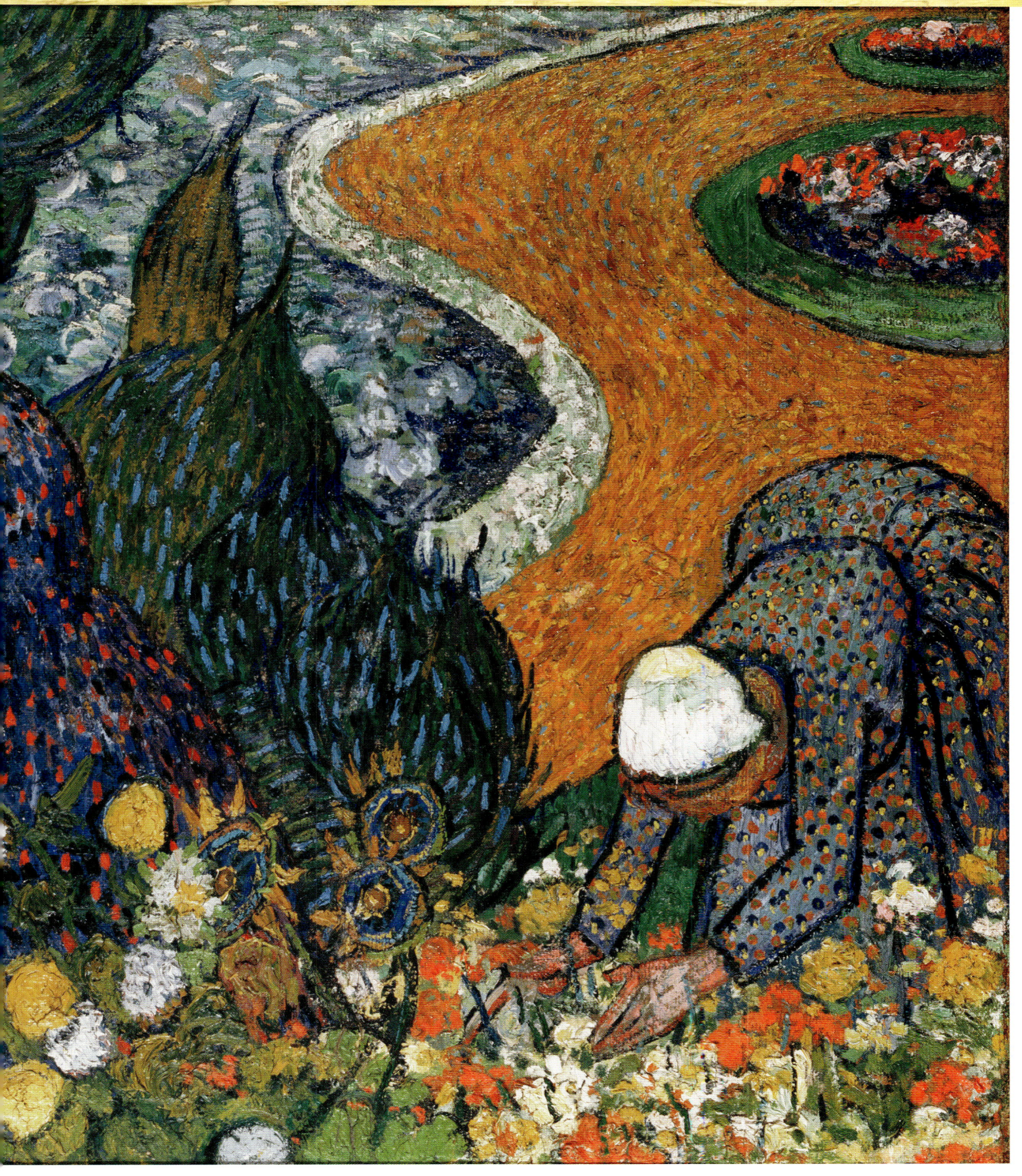

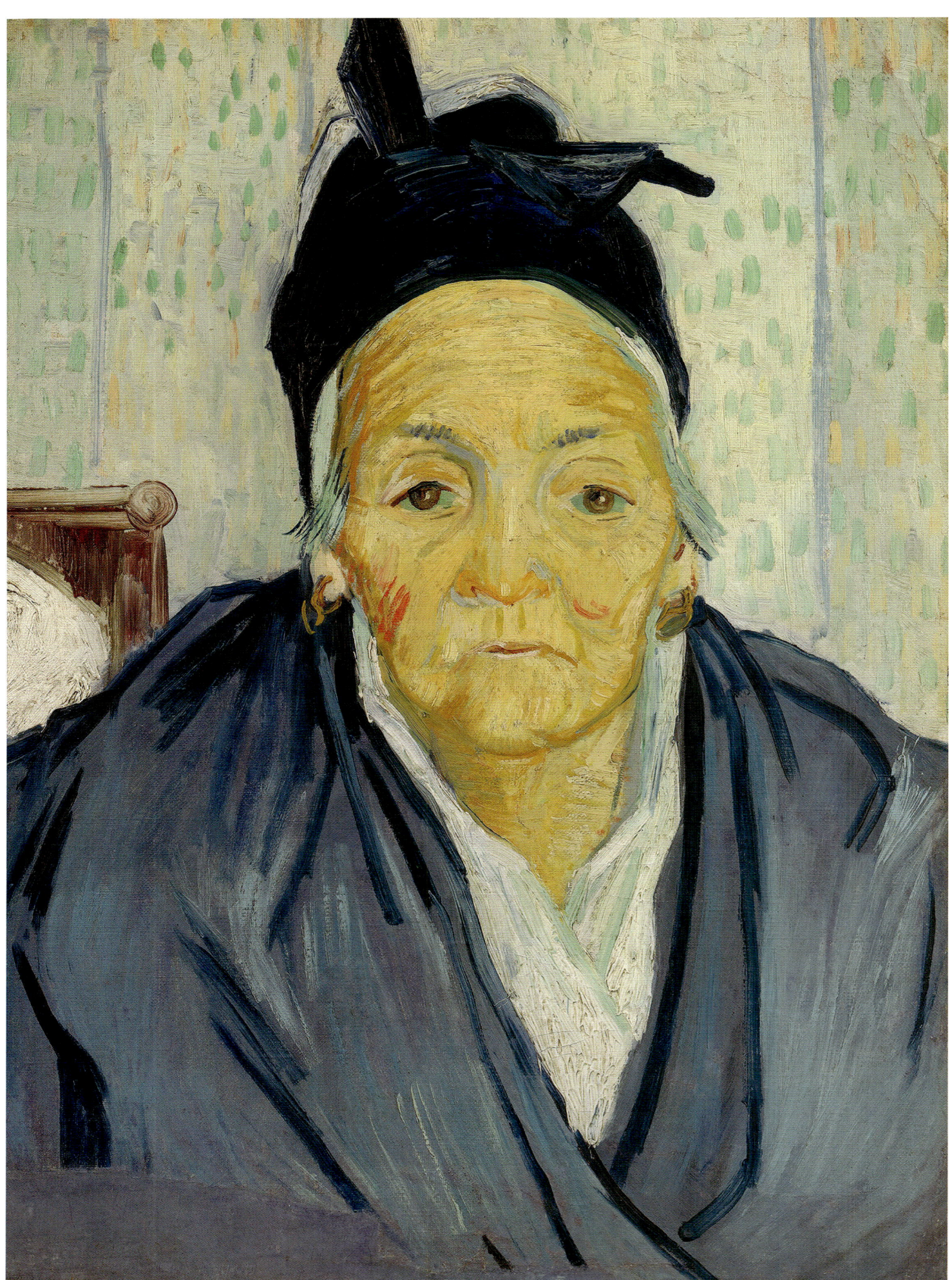

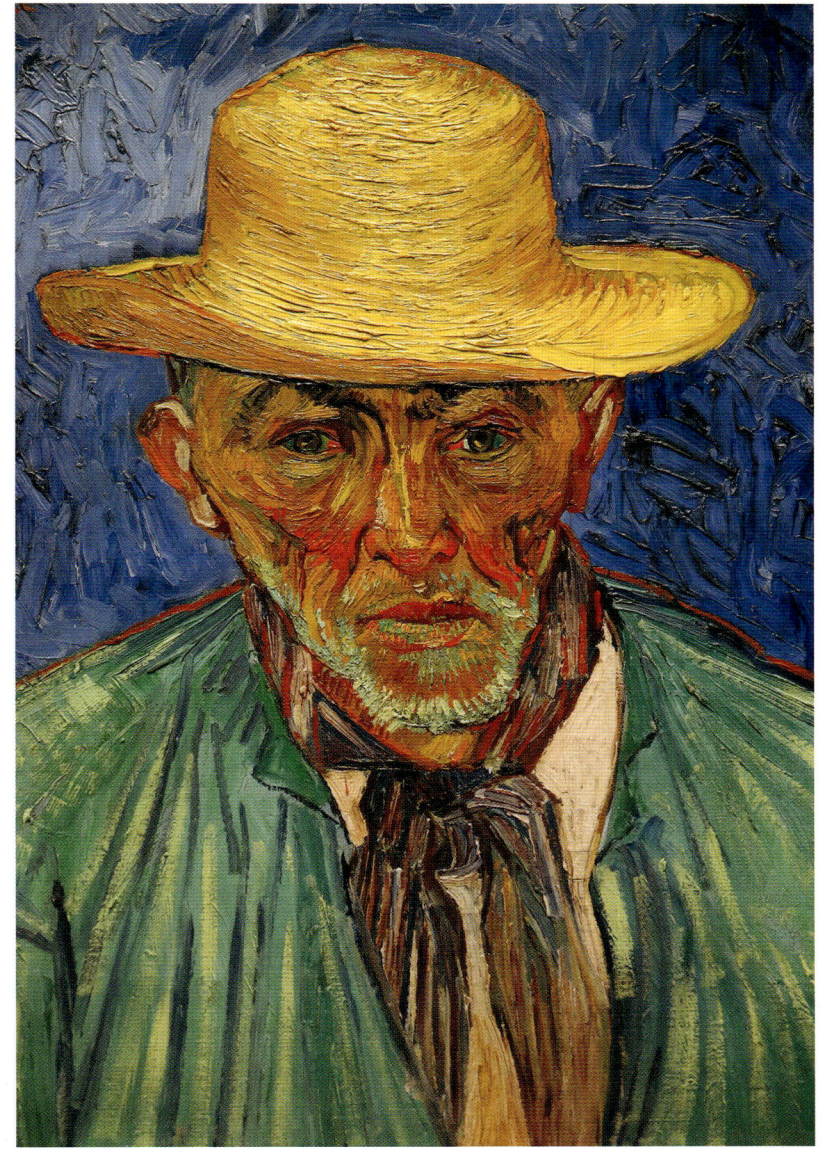

Portrait of a Peasant (Patience Escalier) (August 1888).
Oil on canvas. Norton Simon Museum, Pasadena.

" *I want to paint men and women with that something of the eternal which the halo used to symbolize, and which we try to convey by the actual radiance and vibration of our coloring."*

~ VINCENT, IN A LETTER TO THEO, DECEMBER 1889

[BELOW]
The Painter on His Way to Work (July 1888). Oil on canvas.
Believed to have been destroyed by fire in World War II.

This painting of a figure is actually a self-portrait of Vincent, showing himself walking besides the cornfields to Tarascon, a small town about 10 miles north of Arles.

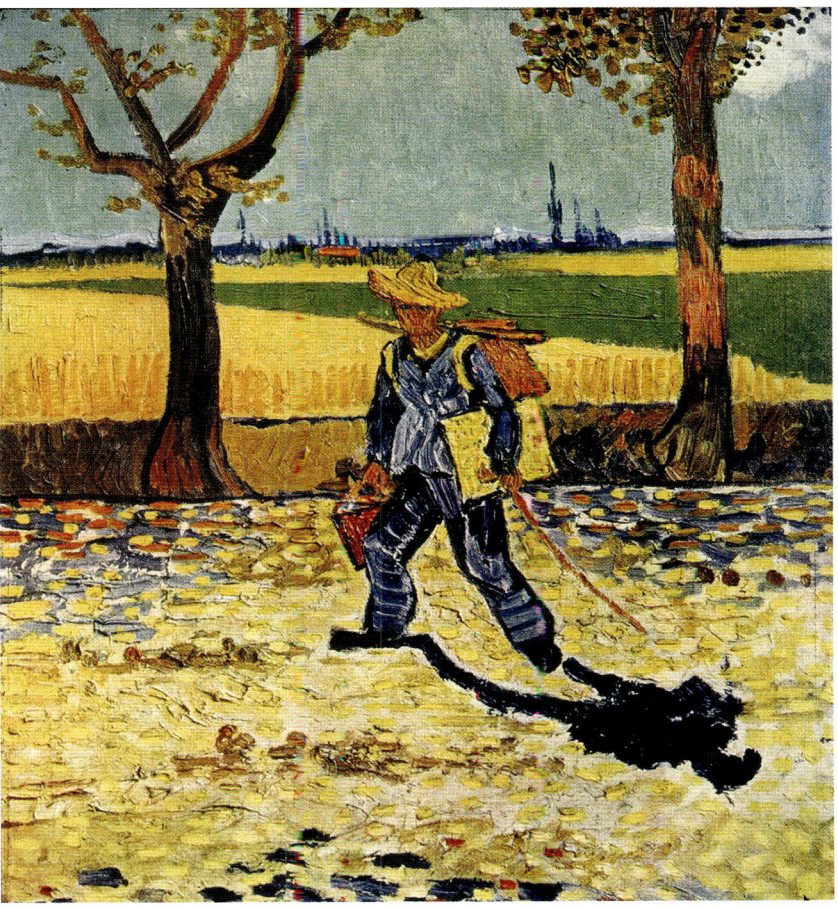

[OPPOSITE PAGE]
The Old Woman of Arles (1888). Oil on canvas. Van Gogh Museum, Amsterdam (Vincent van Gogh Foundation).

[RIGHT] *The Gardener* or *Portrait of a Young Peasant* (September 1889). Oil on canvas. National Gallery of Modern Art, Rome.

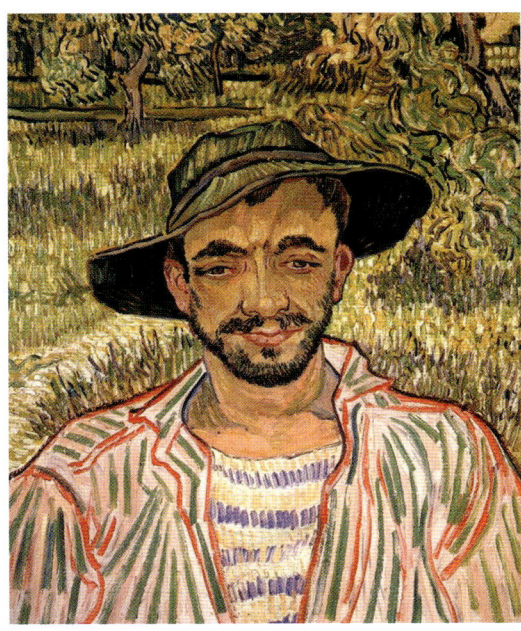

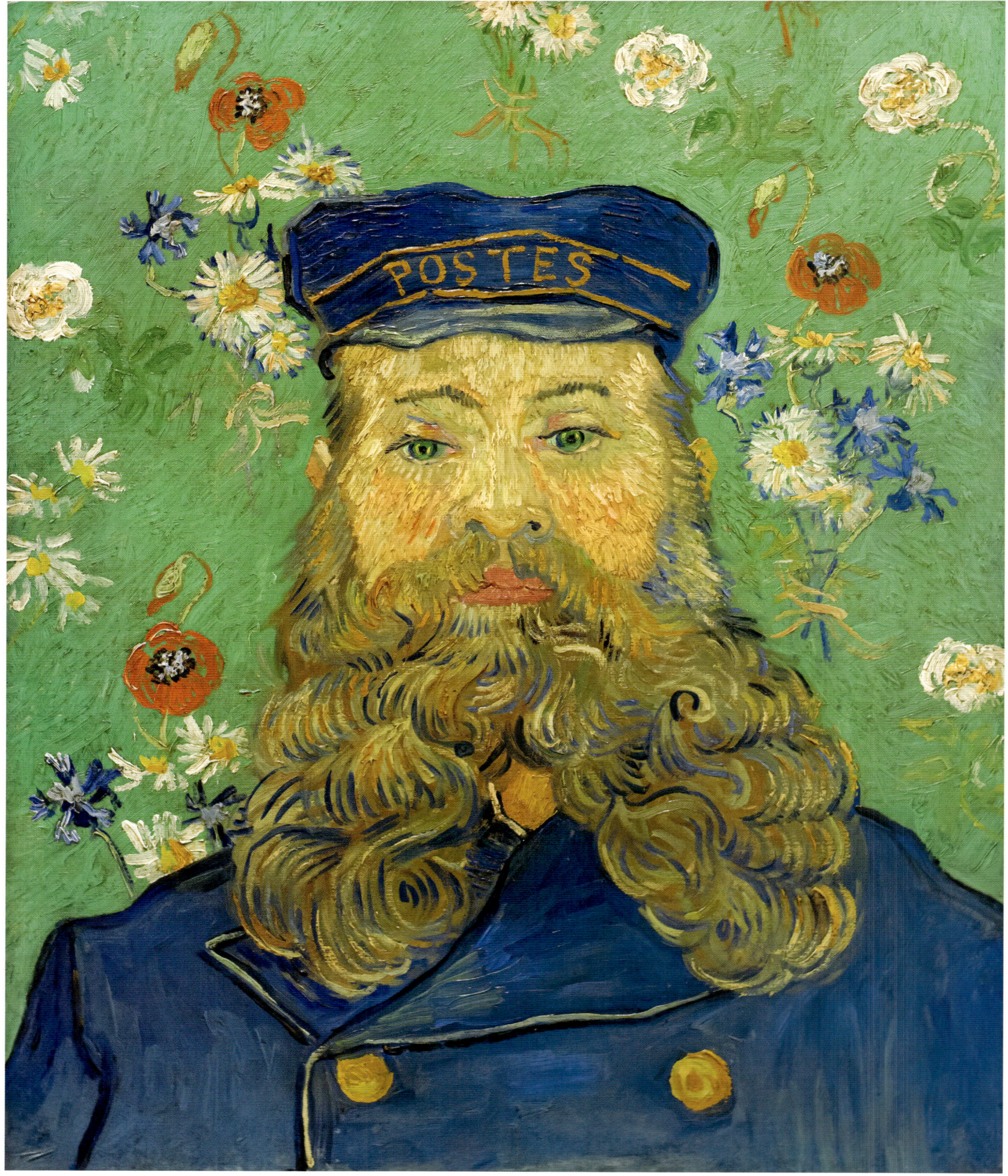

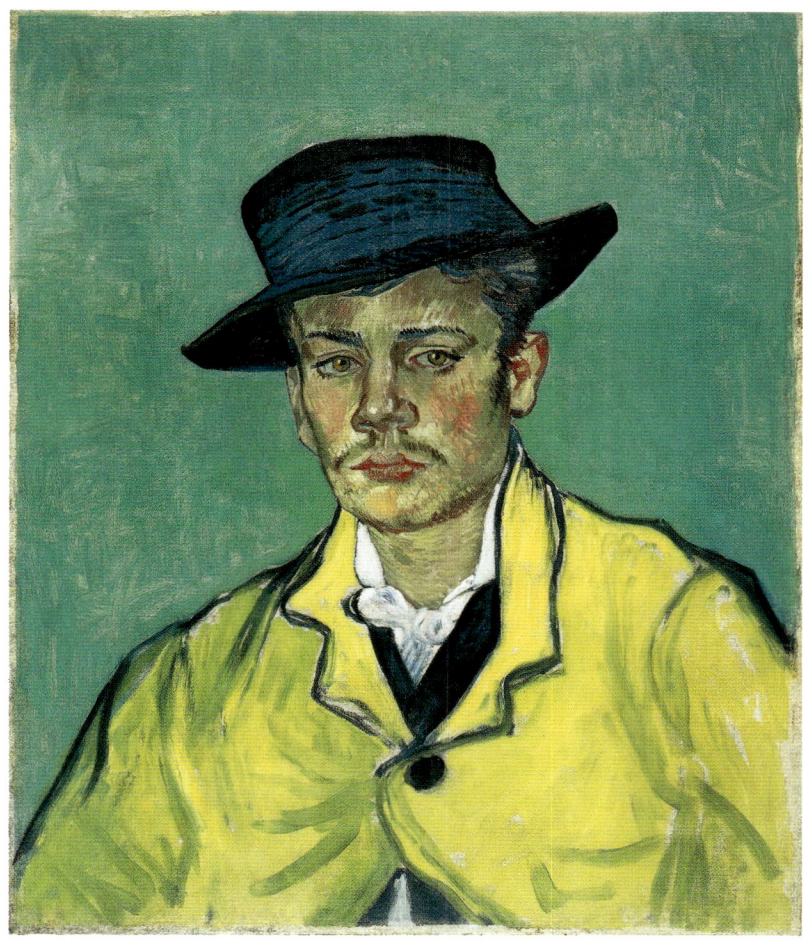

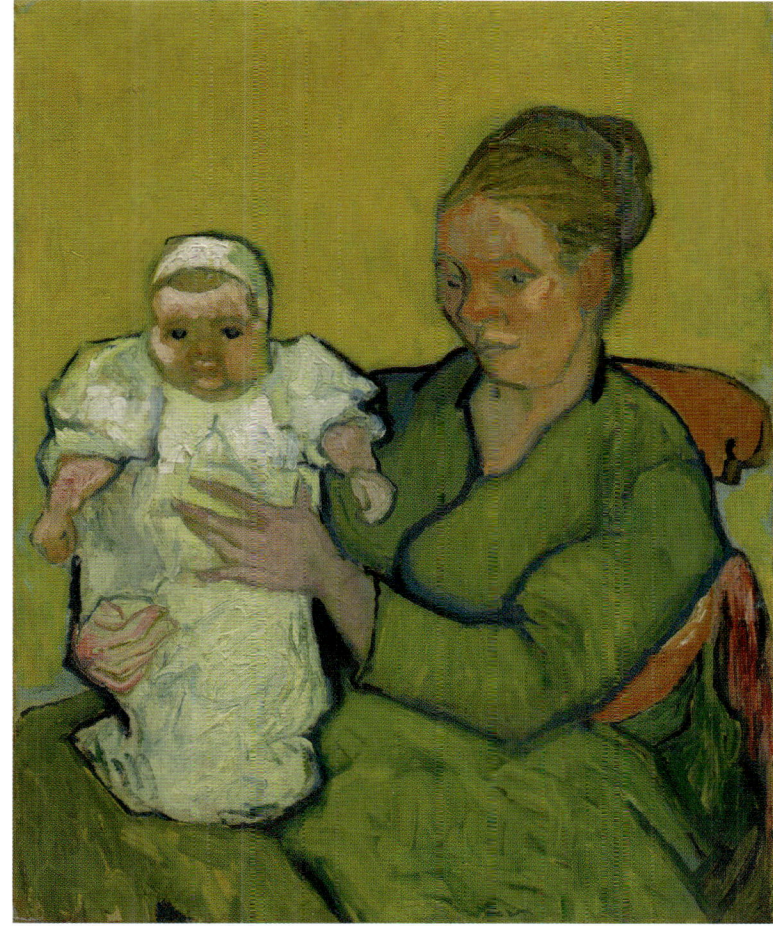

[ABOVE] ***Portrait of Armand Roulin*** (1888).
Oil on canvas. Museum Folkwang, Essen.

[ABOVE RIGHT] ***Portrait of Madame Augustine Roulin and Baby Marcelle*** (1888). Oil on canvas. The Philadelphia Museum of Art.

[RIGHT] ***Portrait of Camille Roulin*** (November 1888–December 1888). Oil on canvas. Van Gogh Museum, Amsterdam (Vincent van Gogh Foundation).

[OPPOSITE PAGE] ***Portrait of Joseph Roulin*** (April 1889).
Oil on canvas. Kröller-Müller Museum, Otterlo.

This thickly painted, colorful portrait is one of more than 20 that Vincent painted while in Arles between 1888 and 1889 of his friend Joseph Roulin, a postal worker in Arles, and his wife, Augustine, and their three children: Armand, Camille, and Marcelle.

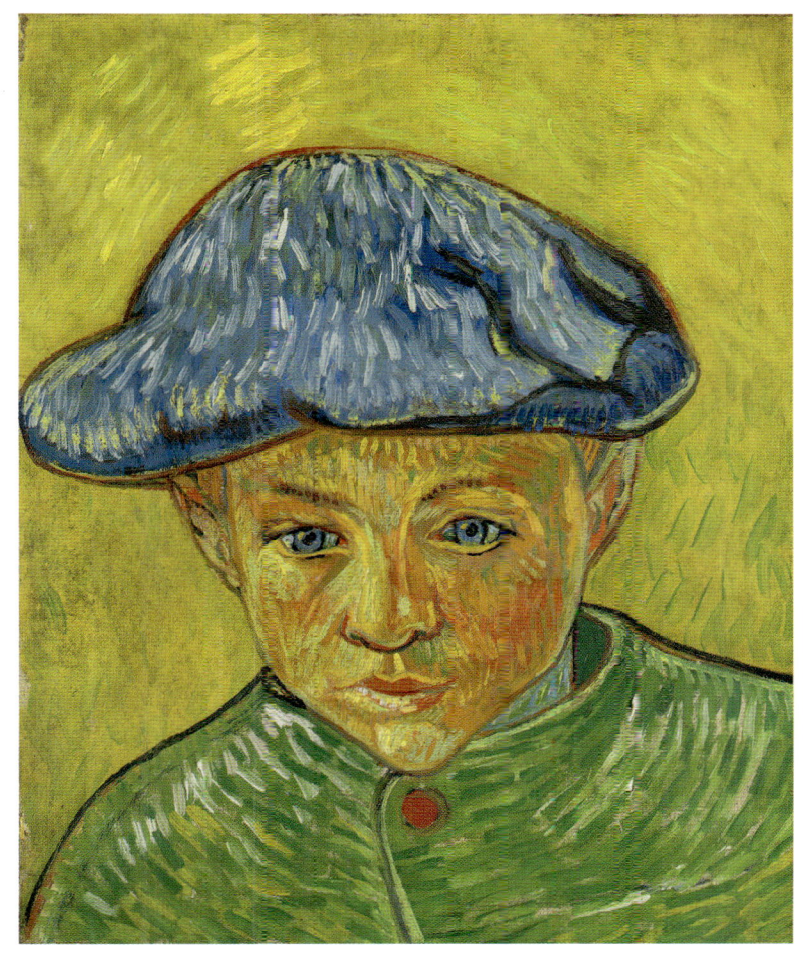

"*And if I manage to do this whole family better still, at least I shall have done something to my liking and something individual.*"

~ VINCENT, IN A LETTER TO THEO, DECEMBER 1889

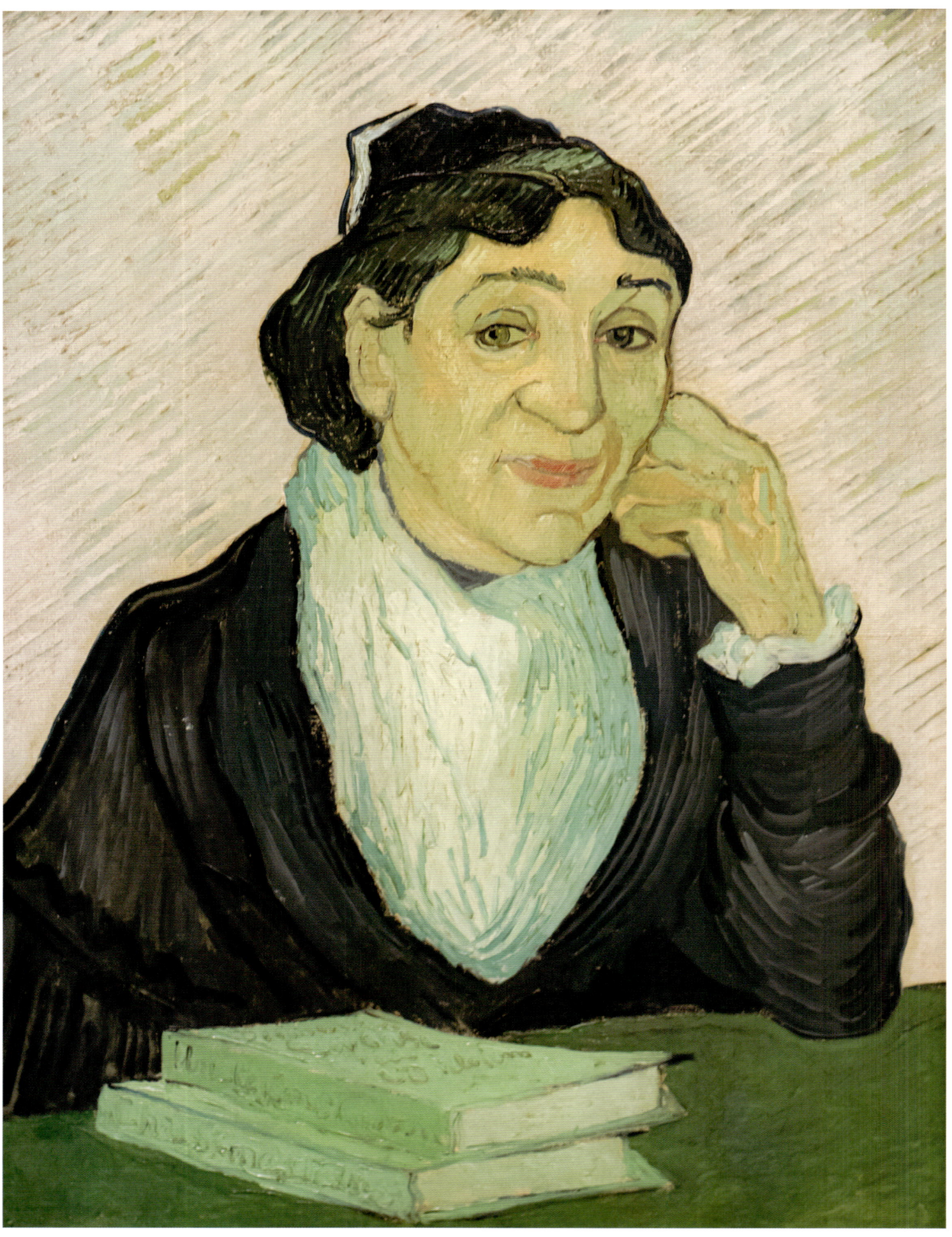

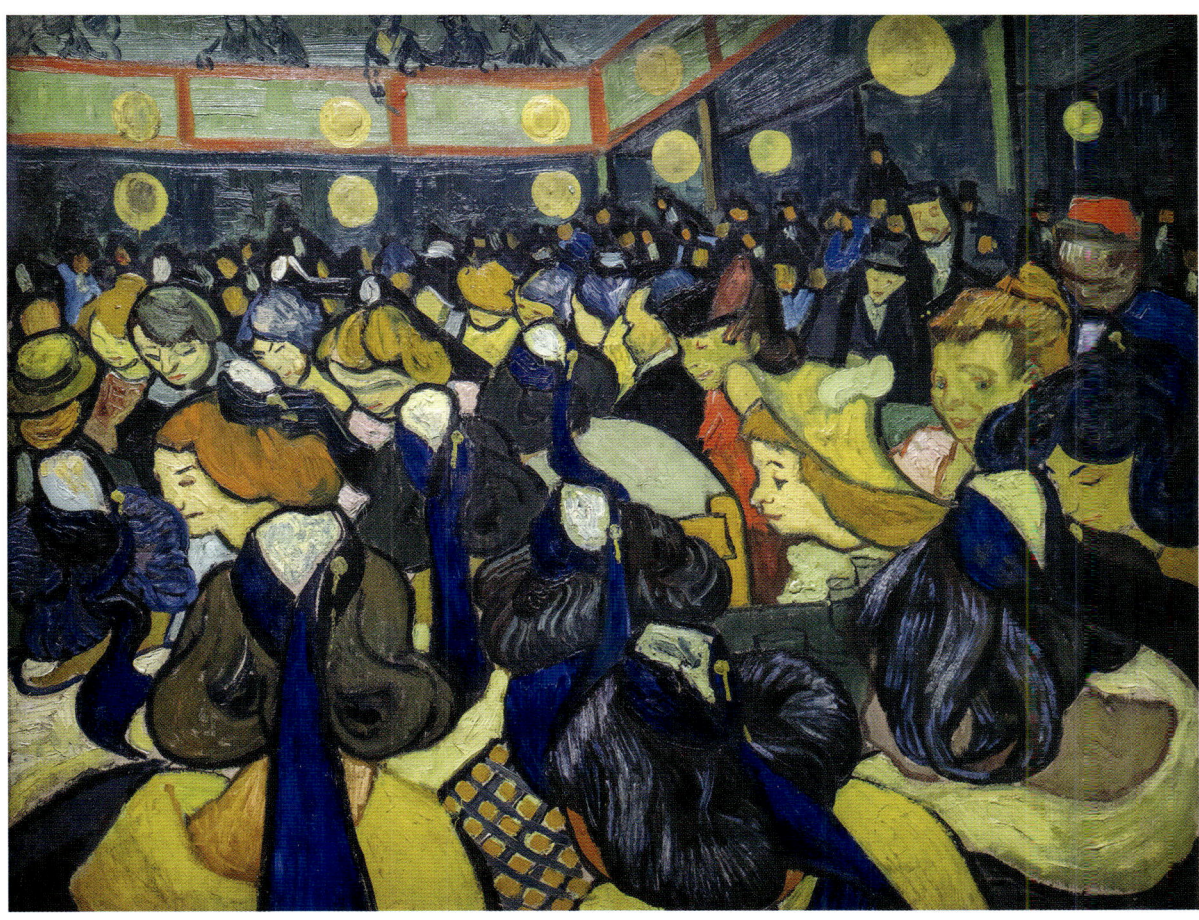

The Dance Hall in Arles (1888). Oil on canvas. Musée d'Orsay, Paris.

Depicting an evening at the Folies-Arlésiennes dance hall in Arles, this is an unusual painting: it is a combined work of Vincent and Paul Gauguin.

[BELOW] *L'Arlésienne – Madame Ginoux with Gloves and Umbrella* (November 1888). Oil on canvas. Musée d'Orsay, Paris.

Vincent did a group of portraits of Marie Julien Ginoux, who ran the Café de la Gare on the Place Lamartine in Arles (the subject of The Night Café). He executed six similar paintings: two in Arles during November 1888 (or later) and four in Saint-Rémy in February 1890. L'Arlésienne means "the woman from Arles." Madame Ginoux also sat for Paul Gauguin during his stay in Arles.

"*I've seen the canvas of Madame Ginoux. Very fine and very curious, I like it better than my drawing. Despite your ailing state you have never worked with so much balance while conserving the sensation and the interior warmth needed for a work of art, precisely in an era when art is a business regulated in advance by cold calculations.*"

~ PAUL GAUGUIN IN A LETTER TO VINCENT, JUNE 1890

[OPPOSITE PAGE] *Portrait of Madame Ginoux* (February 1890). Oil on canvas. Kröller-Müller Museum, Otterlo.

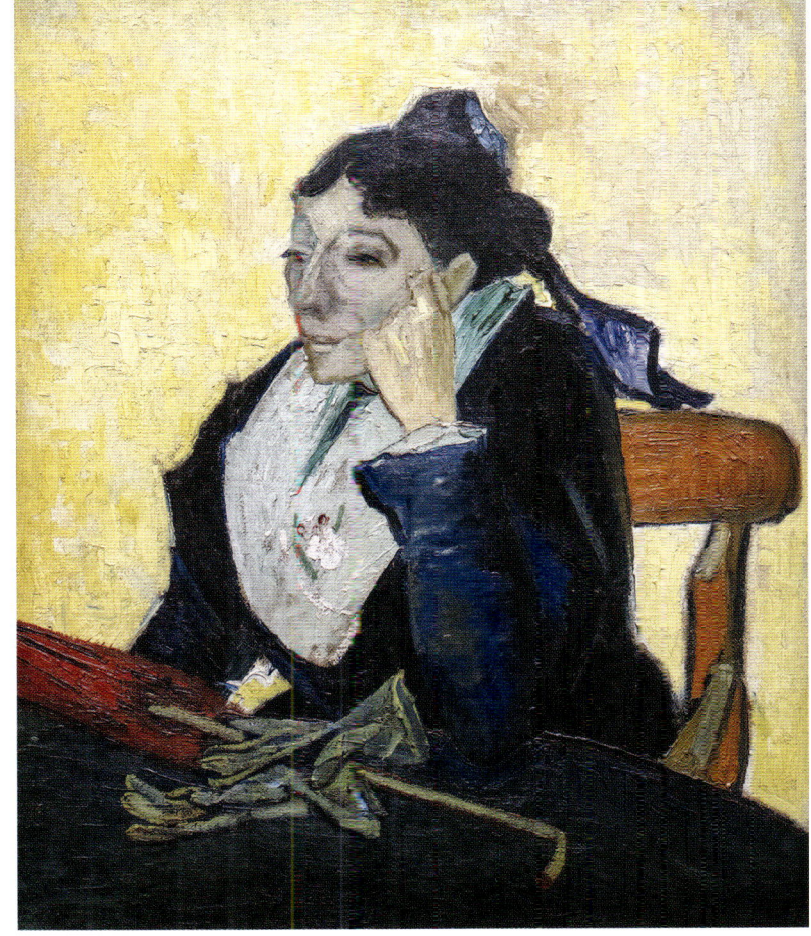

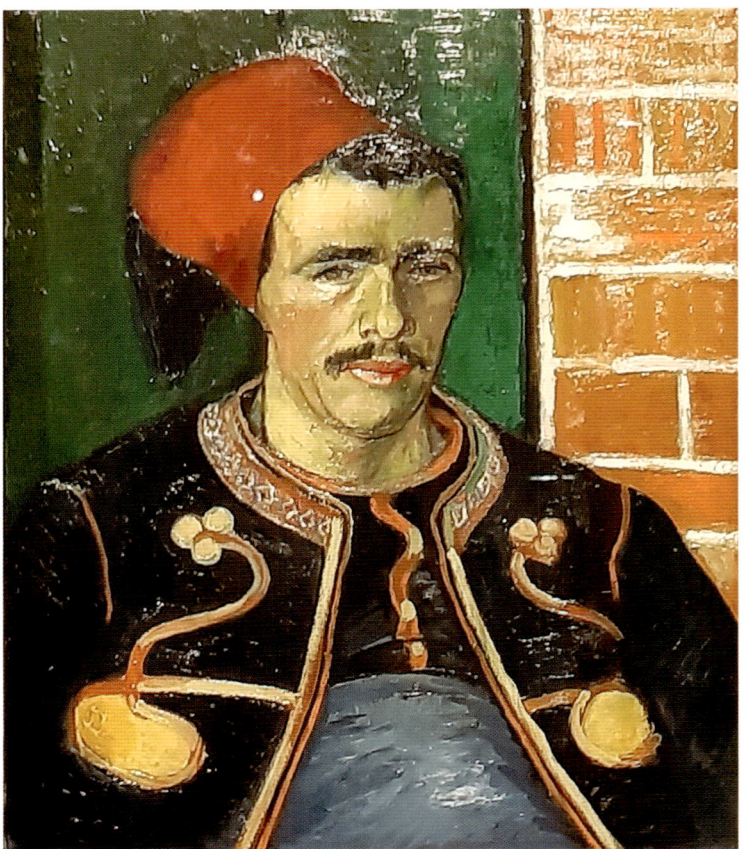

The Zouave (June 1888). Oil on canvas.
Van Gogh Museum, Amsterdam
(Vincent van Gogh Foundation).

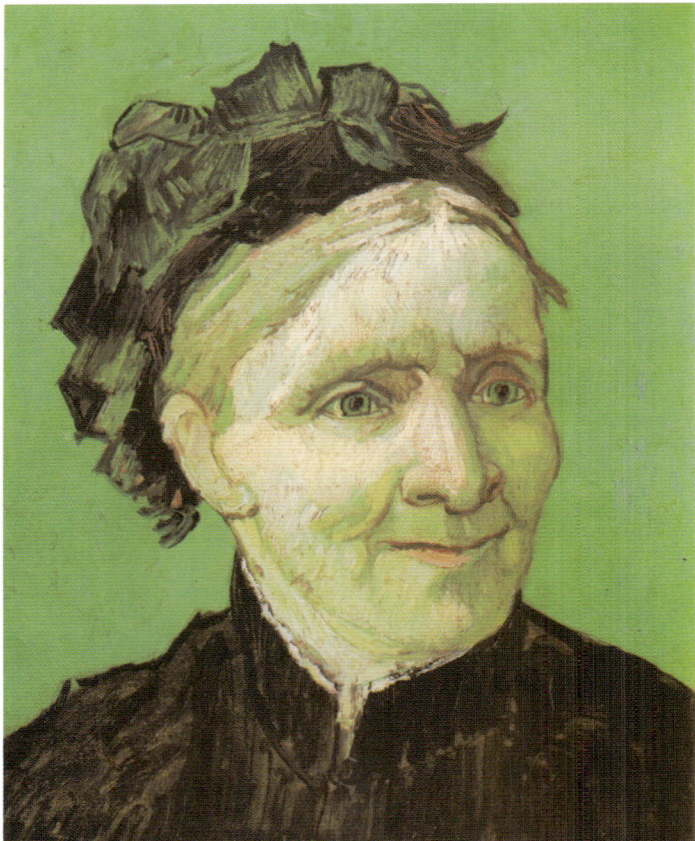

Portrait of the Artist's Mother (October 1888). Oil on canvas.
Norton Simon Museum of Art, Pasadena.

While in Arles, Vincent painted this from a black-and-white photo.

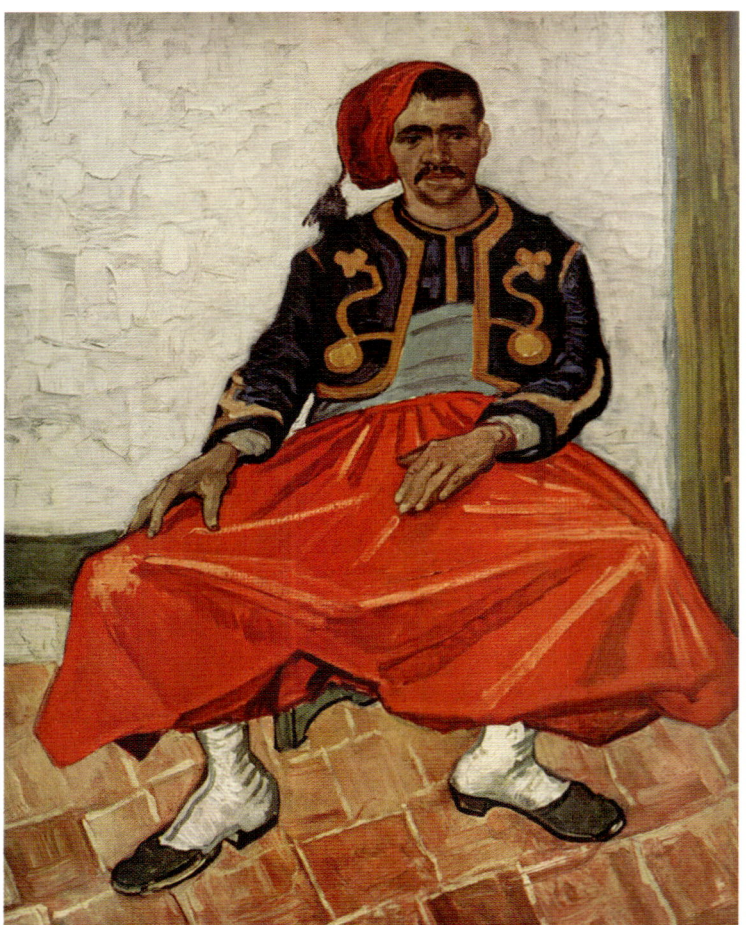

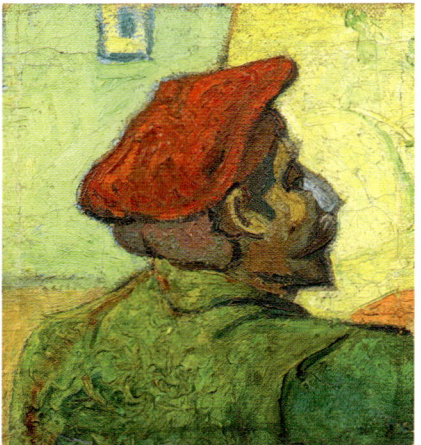

Portrait of Gauguin
(December 1888).
Oil on burlap on panel.
Van Gogh Museum,
Amsterdam (Vincent
van Gogh Foundation).

*Vincent painted his
friend Paul Gauguin
in their studio in the
Yellow House in Arles,
using inexpensive
and coarse jute cloth,
which called for a thick
layering of paint.*

[LEFT] ***The Seated Zouave***
(June 1888). Oil on canvas.
Private collection.

*In the summer of 1888, Vincent
produced several sketches and
paintings of a Zouave soldier in
Arles. He took it as a challenge
to capture the bright coloration
of the distinctive uniform, but
was ultimately displeased with
his efforts, calling the half-figure
portrait "ugly and unsuccessful."*

[OPPOSITE PAGE]
***Portrait of Doctor Félix
Rey*** (January 1889).
Oil on canvas. Pushkin
State Museum of Fine
Arts, Moscow.

*Rey was a sympathetic
attending physician at
the Arles hospital.*

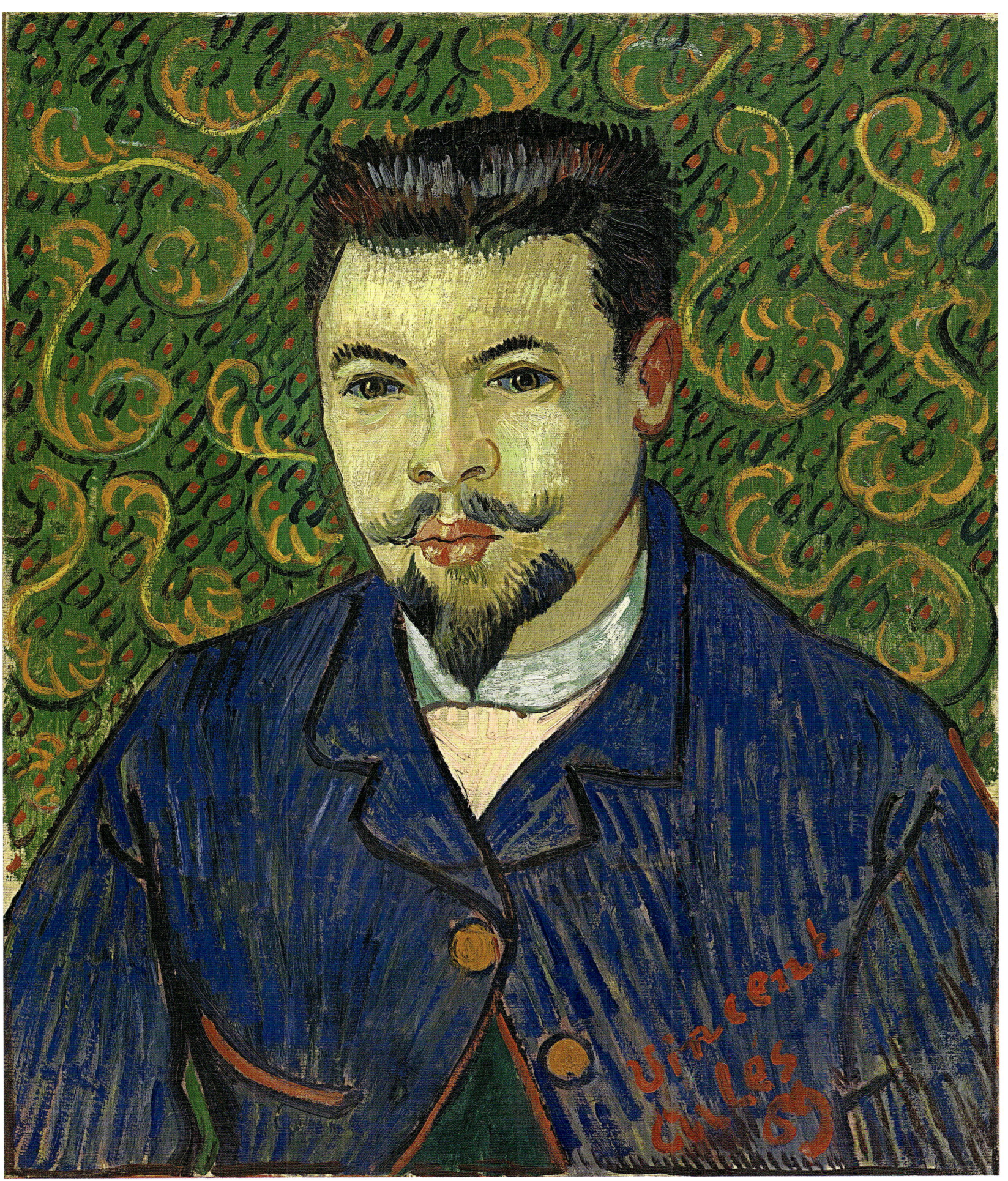

IN SAINT-RÉMY

During his stay in the asylum in Saint-Rémy, Vincent turned to other artists for inspiration, copying works of Millet and Delacroix, and he also created new versions of his older works.

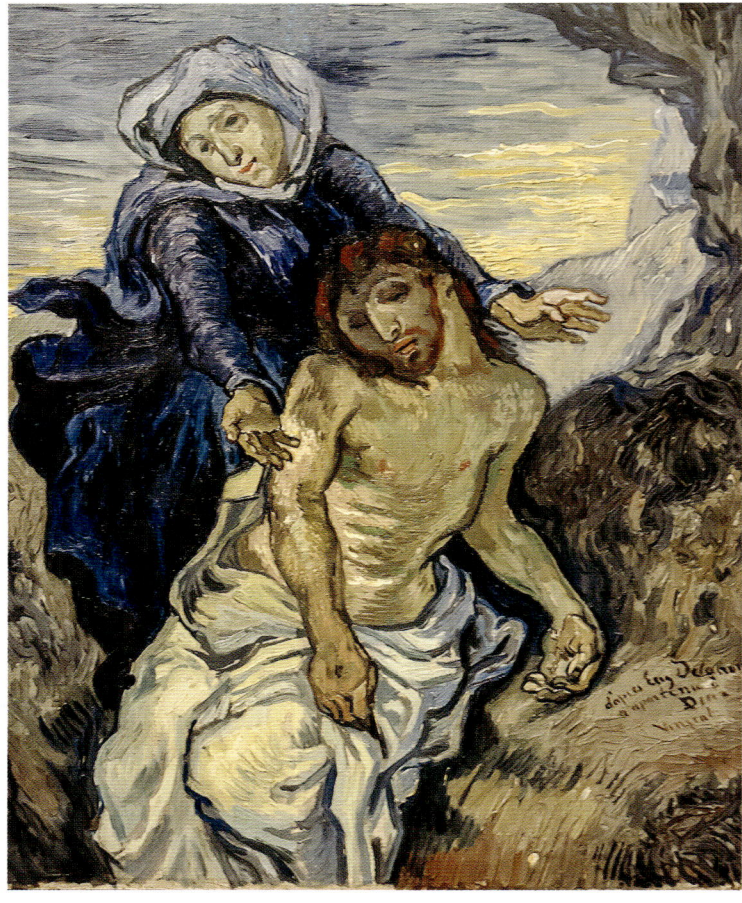

" *Today and yesterday I drew two figures of an old man with his elbows on his knees and his head in his hands. I did it of Schuitemaker once and always kept the drawing, because I wanted to do it better another time. Perhaps I'll also do a lithograph of it. What a fine sight an old working man makes, in his patched bombazine suit with his bald head."*

~ VINCENT, IN A LETTER TO THEO, NOVEMBER 1882

[LEFT] *Pietà (after Delacroix)* (November 1899). Oil on canvas. Vatican Museums, Vatican City.

Vincent was a man of profound faith, but he rarely painted religious themes. This small Pietà, *made for his sister Willemien, was inspired by a lithograph based on Eugène Delacroix's* Pietà, *and it is its mirror image. He had previously made a brighter, larger version for Theo; that painting is now displayed in the Van Gogh Museum in Amsterdam.*

[OPPOSITE PAGE] *At Eternity's Gate* (May 1890). Oil on canvas. Kröller-Müller Museum, Otterlo.

This oil painting is derived from a lithograph Vincent had based on the pencil drawing Worn Out, *which he made in 1890. These images were from a series of studies he made in 1882 of pensioner and war veteran Adrianus Jacobus Zuyderland at a local almshouse in The Hague.*

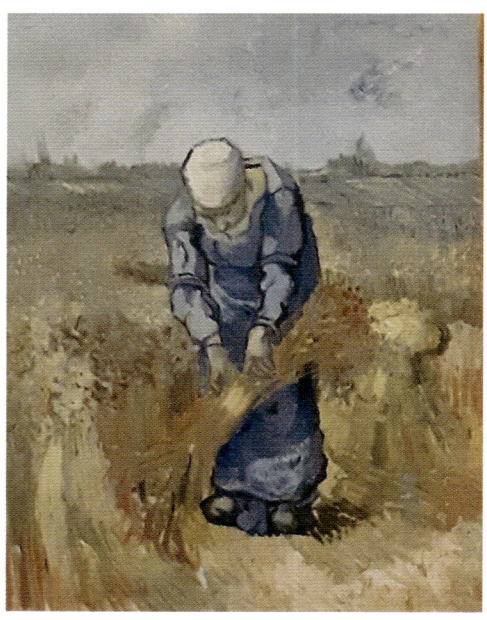

Peasant Woman Binding Sheaves (after Millet) (September 1889). Oil on canvas.

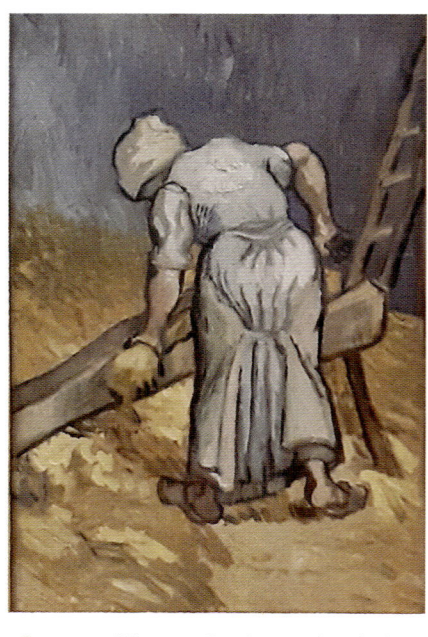

Peasant Woman Bruising Flax (after Millet) (September 1889). Oil on canvas.

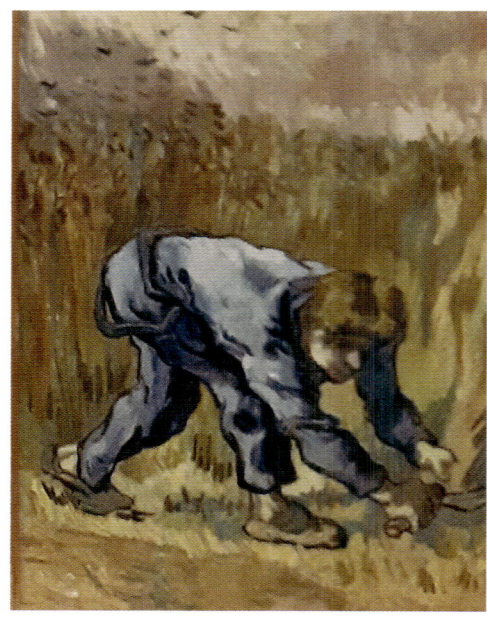

The Reaper (after Millet) (September 1889). Oil on canvas.

All of the above are displayed at the Van Gogh Museum (Vincent van Gogh Foundation) in Amsterdam.

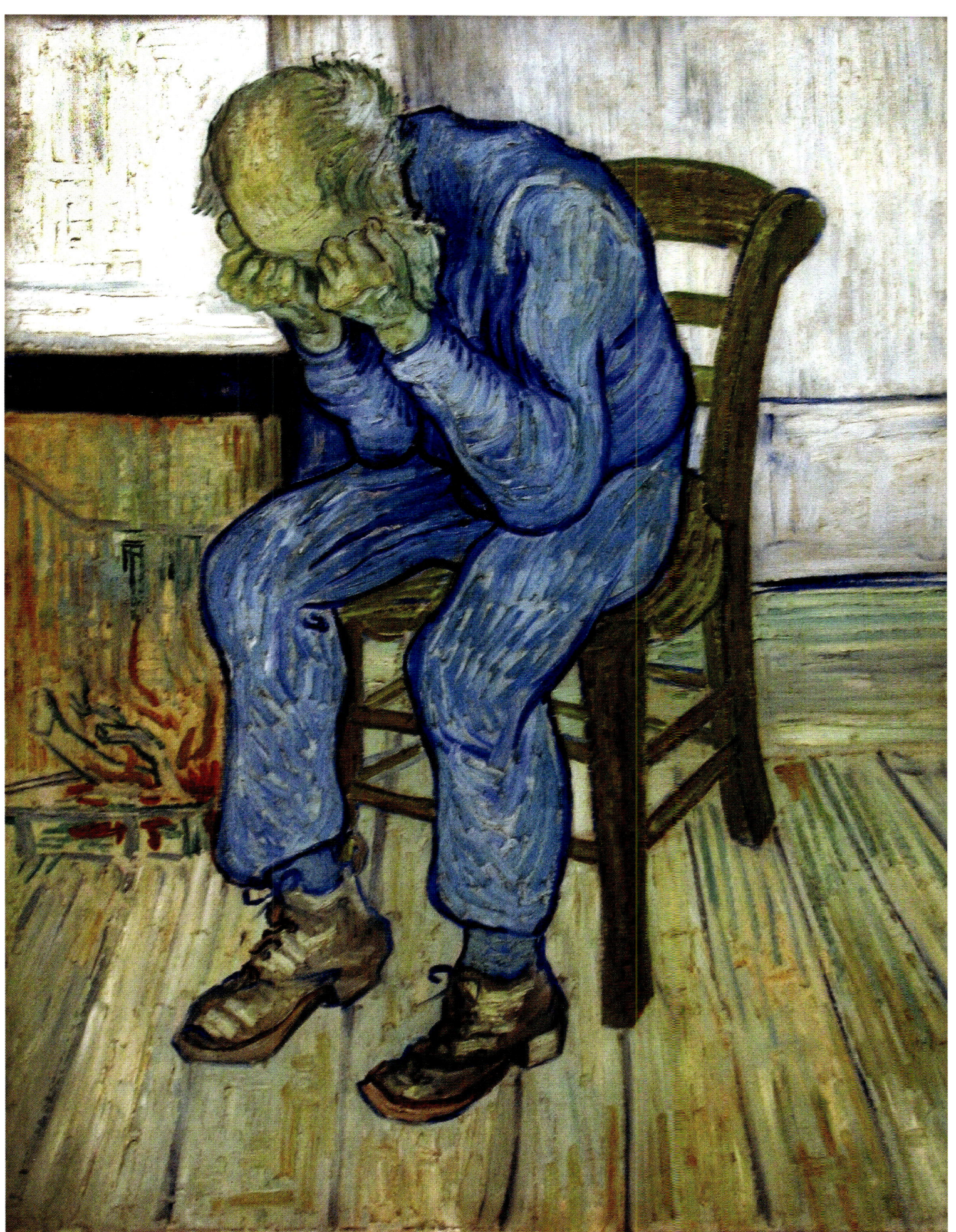

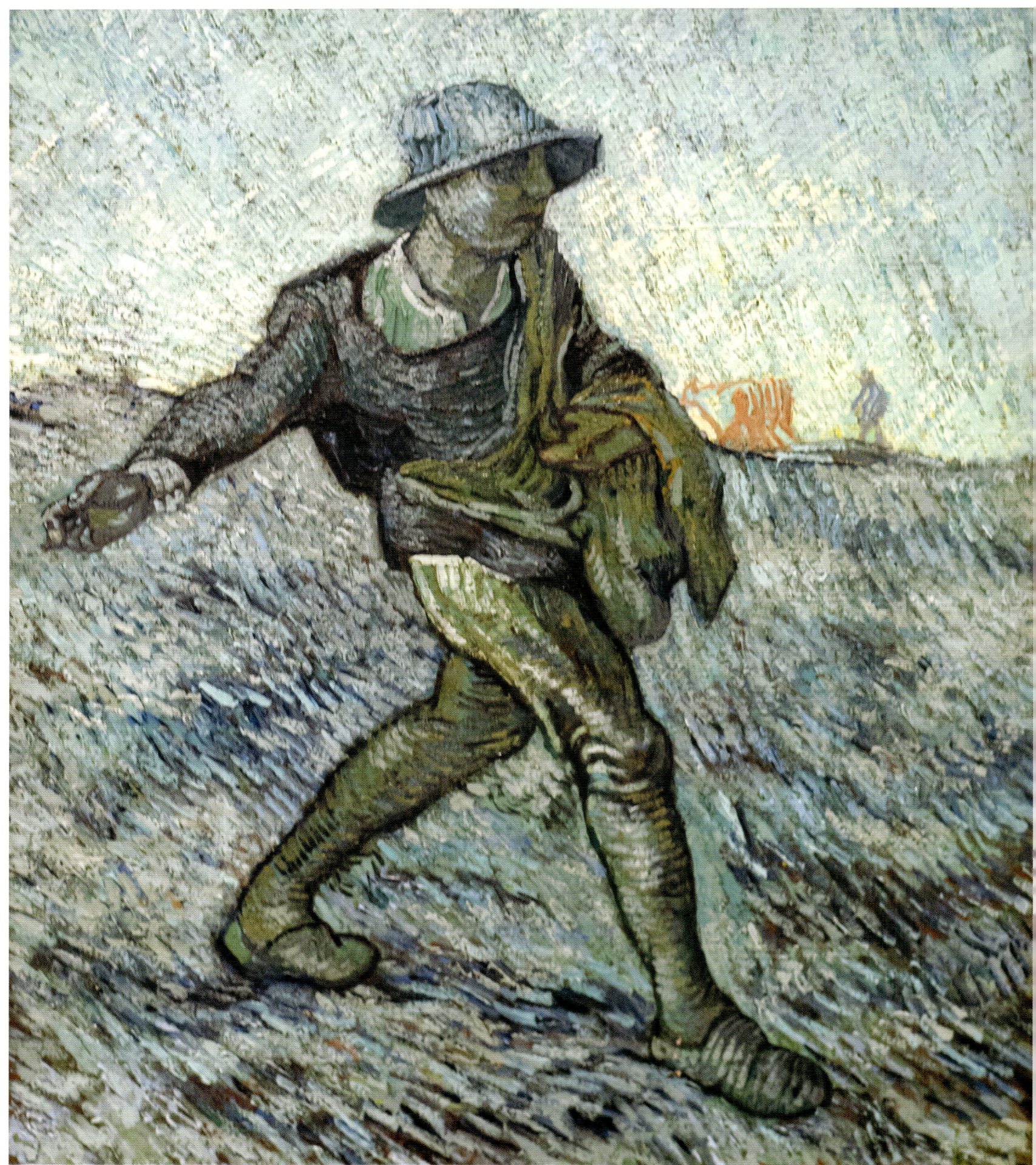

AFTER MILLET

As well as a sincere form of flattery, imitation is a tried-and-true method of improving an artist's skills. While at Saint-Rémy, Vincent began a series of 21 copies of the work of Jean-François Millet (1814–1875), whom he had long admired for the Realist painter's renditions of peasant life. Millet had been one of Vincent's inspirations for creating his own series of peasant life.

[OPPOSITE PAGE] *Sower (after Millet)* (January 1890). Oil on canvas. Kröller-Müller Museum, Otterlo.

A subject Vincent had painted many times over the years, this version of Sower *is an almost exact copy of a painting he made in 1881.*

[BELOW] *Noon – Rest from Work (after Millet)* (1890). Oil on canvas. Musée d'Orsay, Paris.

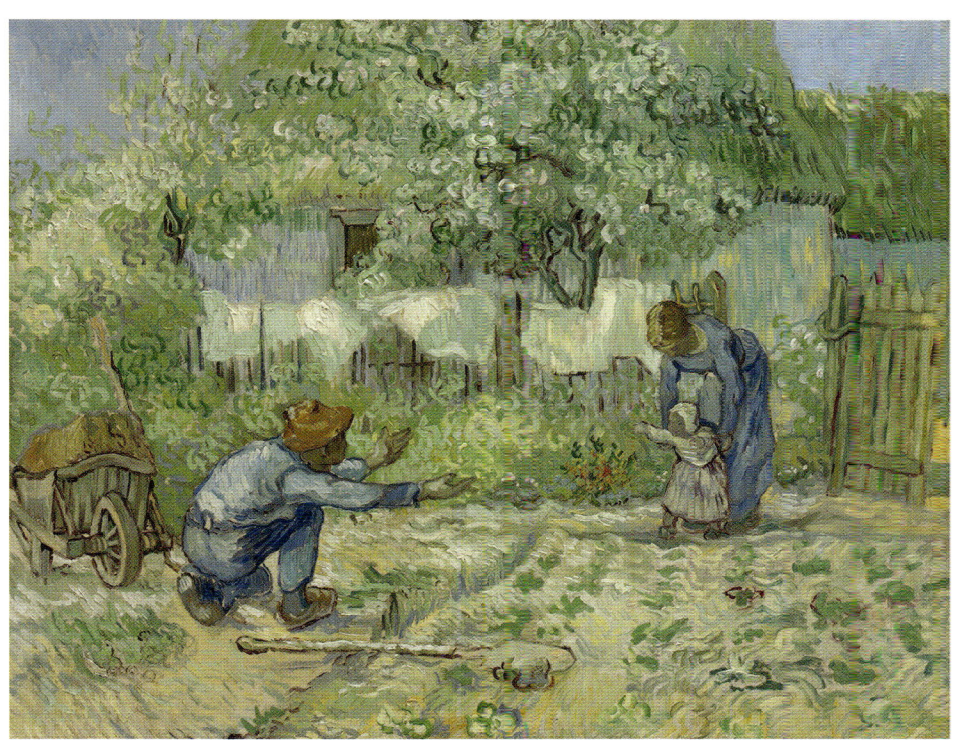

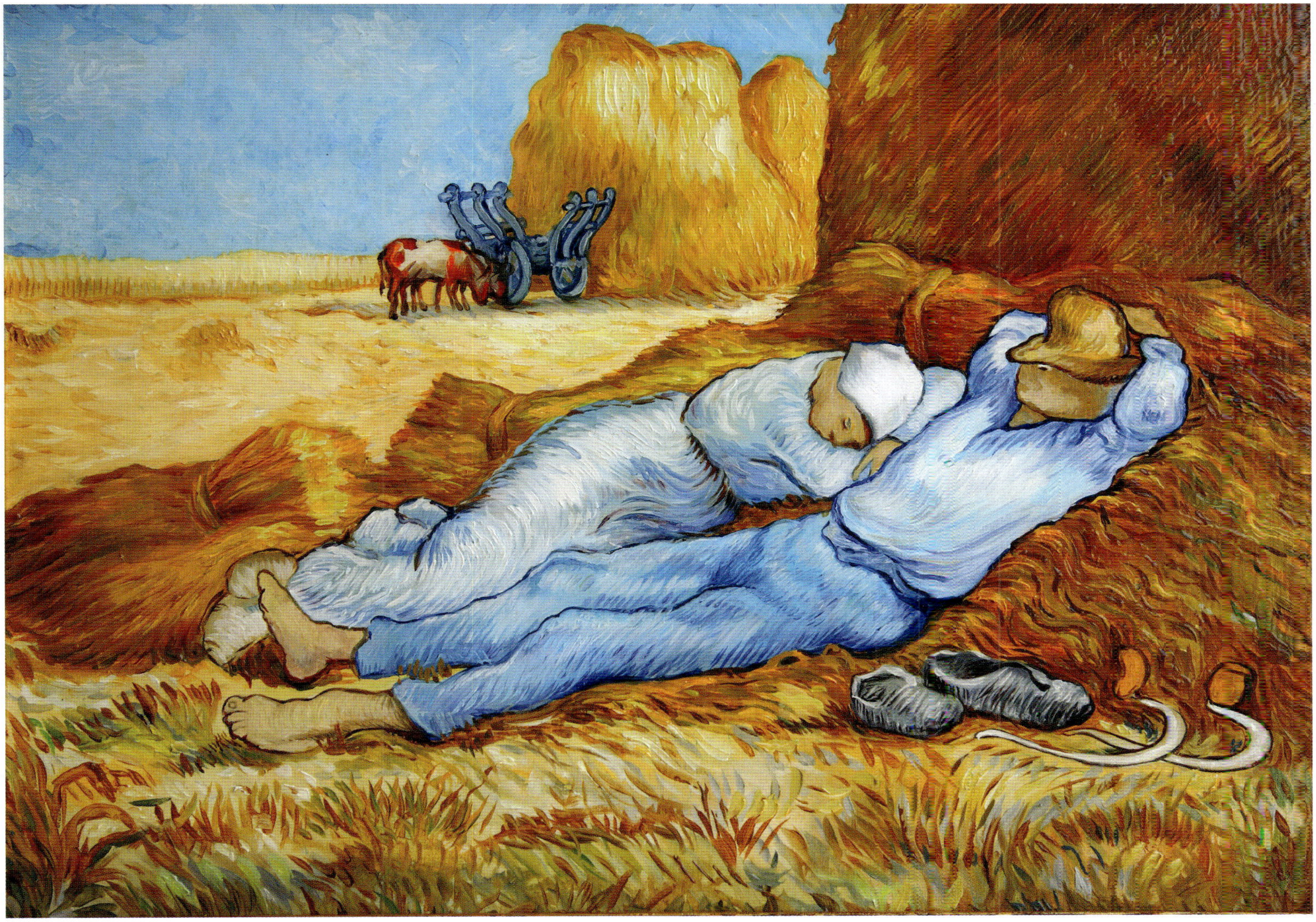

First Steps (after Millet) (1890). Oil on canvas. Metropolitan Museum of Art, New York.

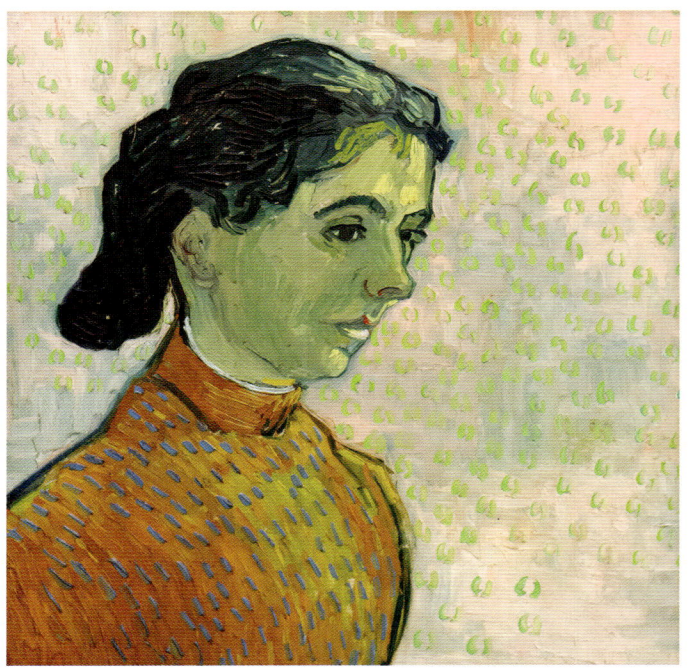

Portrait of a Young Woman (1890). Oil on canvas.
Kröller-Müller Museum, Otterlo.

THE PEOPLE
OF AUVERS

In May 1890, Vincent left the South of France to spend time in Auvers-sur-Oise and took a room at an inn owned by Arthur Ravoux. During his three months in Auvers, while under the care of Dr. Paul Ferdinand Gachet, Vincent took to painting with a renewed vigor. While there, he painted and drew a number of portraits, including ones of a local "peasant" girl, Ravoux's 13-year-old daughter Adeline, and Dr. Gachet.

"Photographic portraits wither much sooner than we ourselves do, whereas the painted portrait is a thing which is felt, done with love or respect for the human being that is portrayed."

~ VINCENT, TO HIS SISTER WIL, SEPTEMBER 1889

[OPPOSITE PAGE] ***Two Children*** (June 1890). Oil on canvas. Musée d'Orsay, Paris.

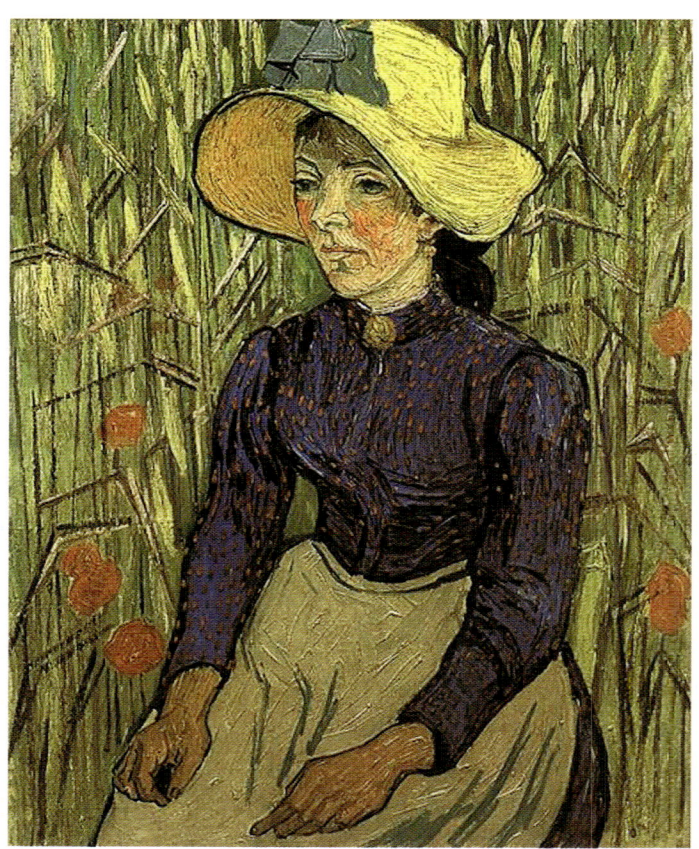

Girl in White, or ***Young Girl Standing Against a Background of Wheat*** (1890). Oil on canvas National Gallery of Art, Washington, D.C.

Peasant Woman Against a Background of Wheat, or ***Young Peasant Woman with Straw Hat*** (1890). Oil on canvas. Private collection.

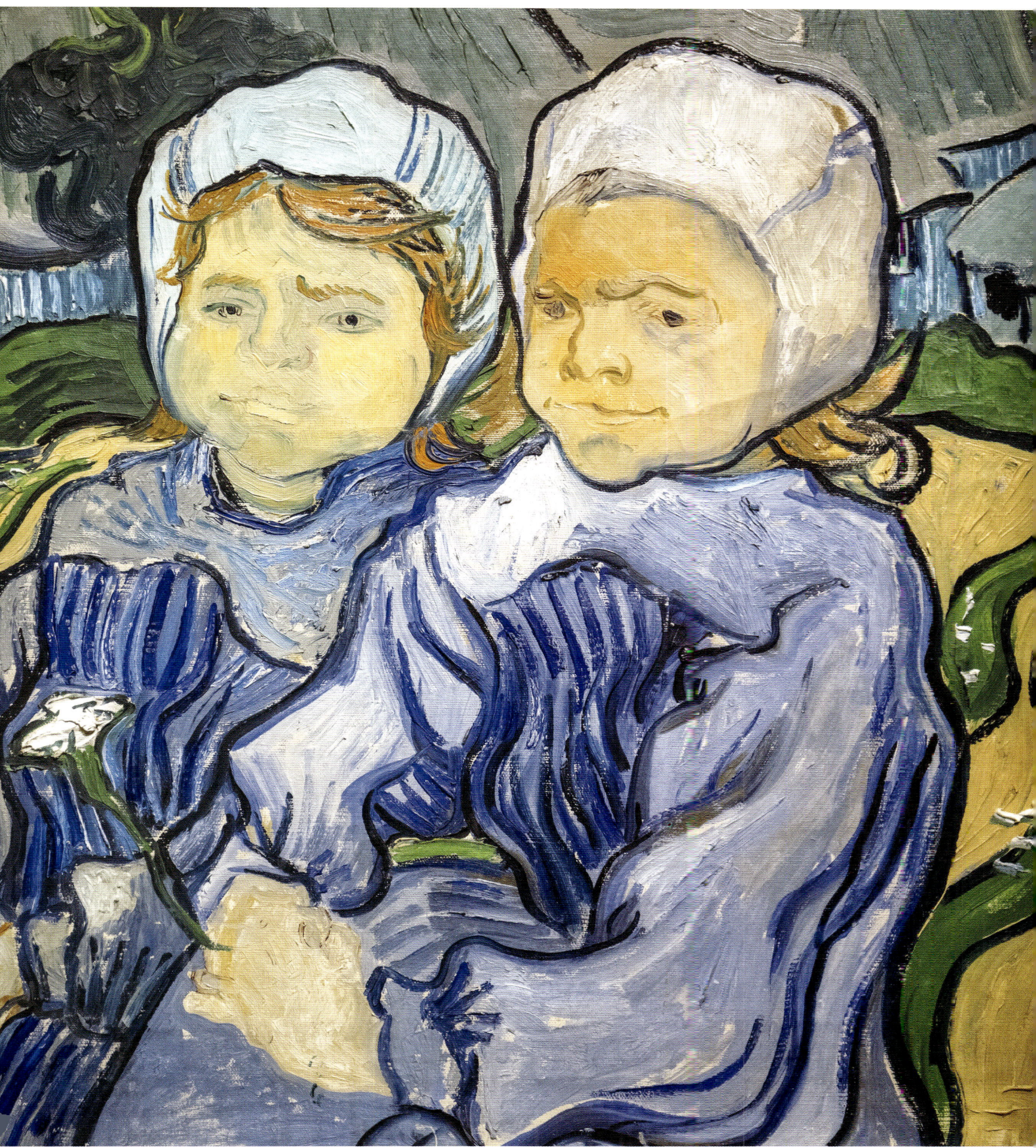

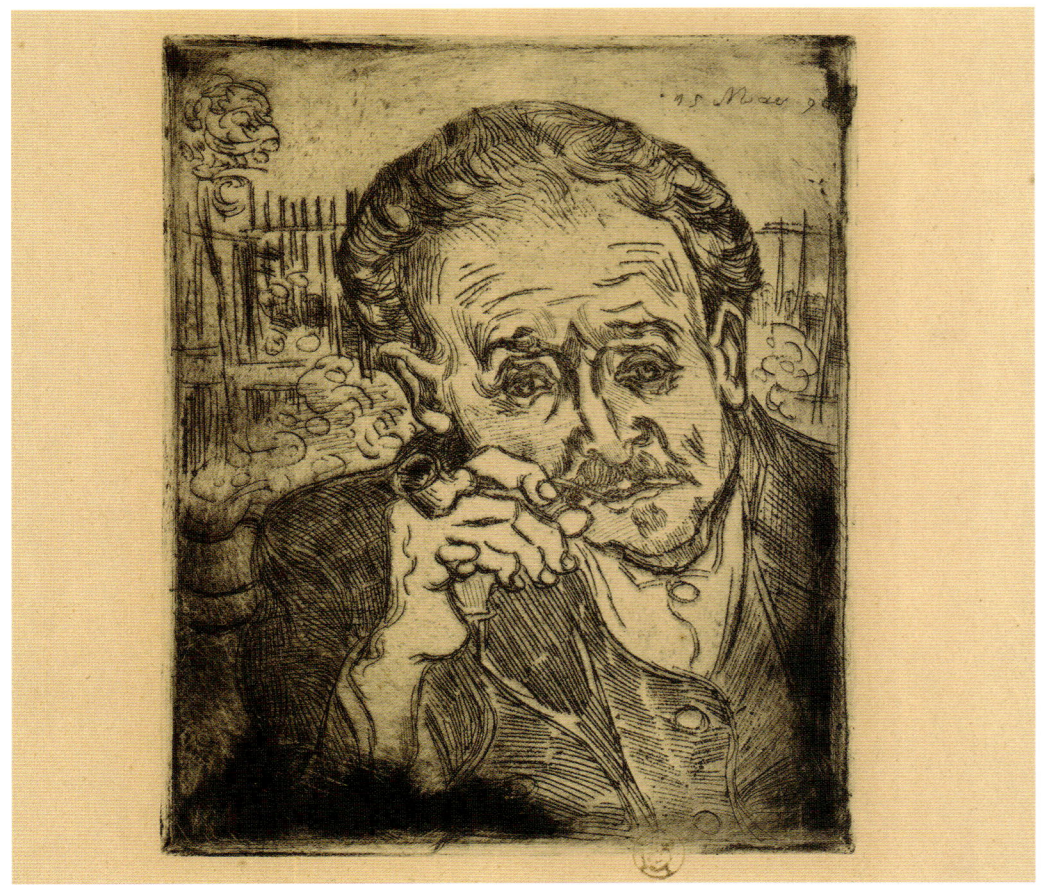

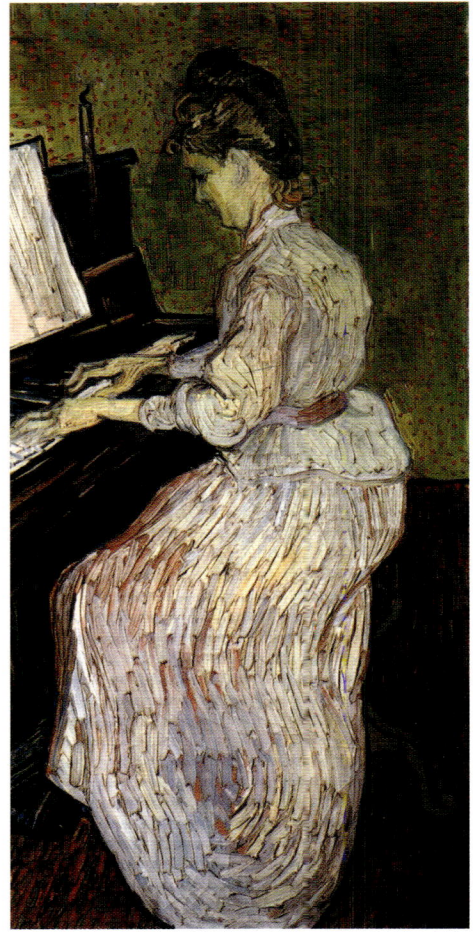

[ABOVE] *Marguerite Gachet at the Piano* (June 1890). Oil on canvas. Öffentliche Kunstsammlung, Basel.

[ABOVE LEFT] *The Man with the Pipe, Portrait of Dr. Gachet* (May 1890). Etching. Various holders.

Vincent made only one etching in his career as an artist, and he chose Paul Ferdinand Gachet as his subject. Dr. Gachet was an amateur etcher, who signed his works "Van Ryssel," and he provided Vincent with etching materials and access to his home press. It was completed just six weeks before Vincent's death.

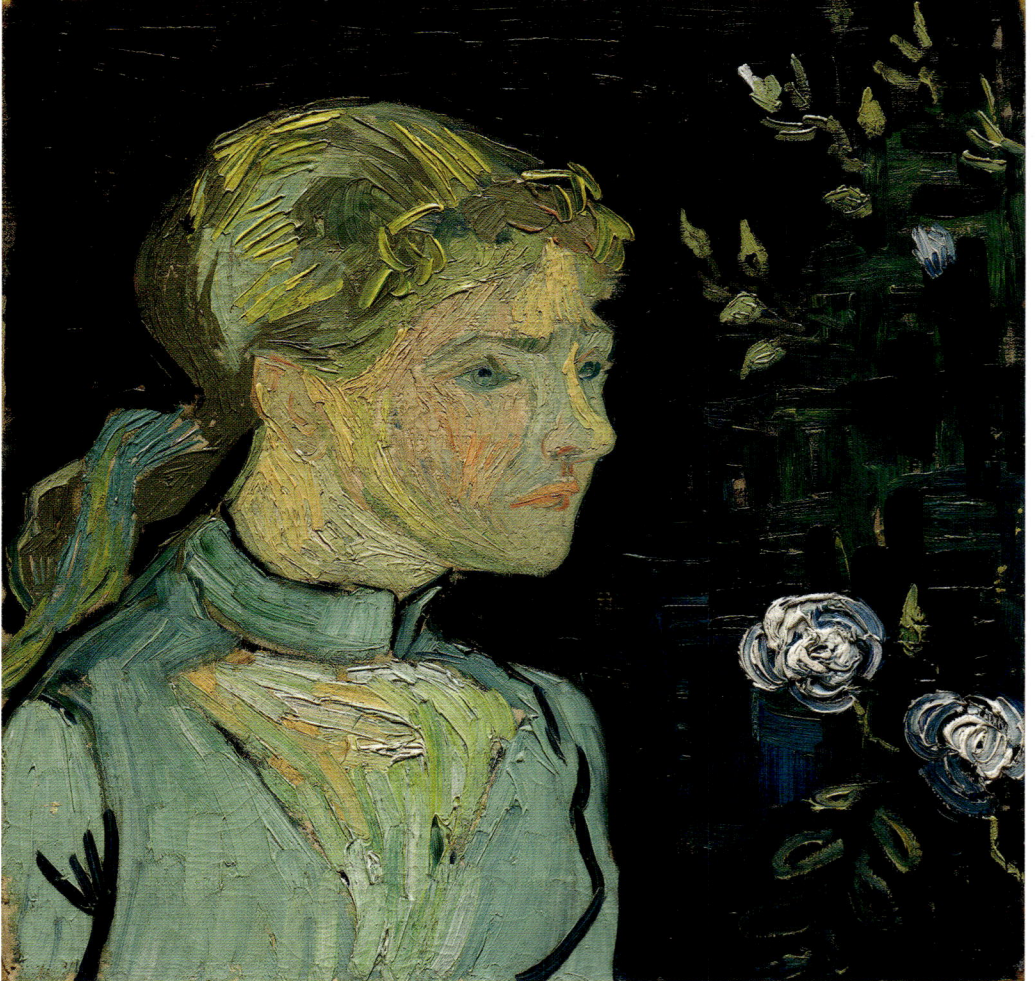

[LEFT] *Adeline Ravoux* (1890). Oil on fabric. Cleveland Museum of Art

[OPPOSITE PAGE] *Portrait of Dr. Gachet* (1890). Oil on canvas. Musée d'Orsay, Paris.

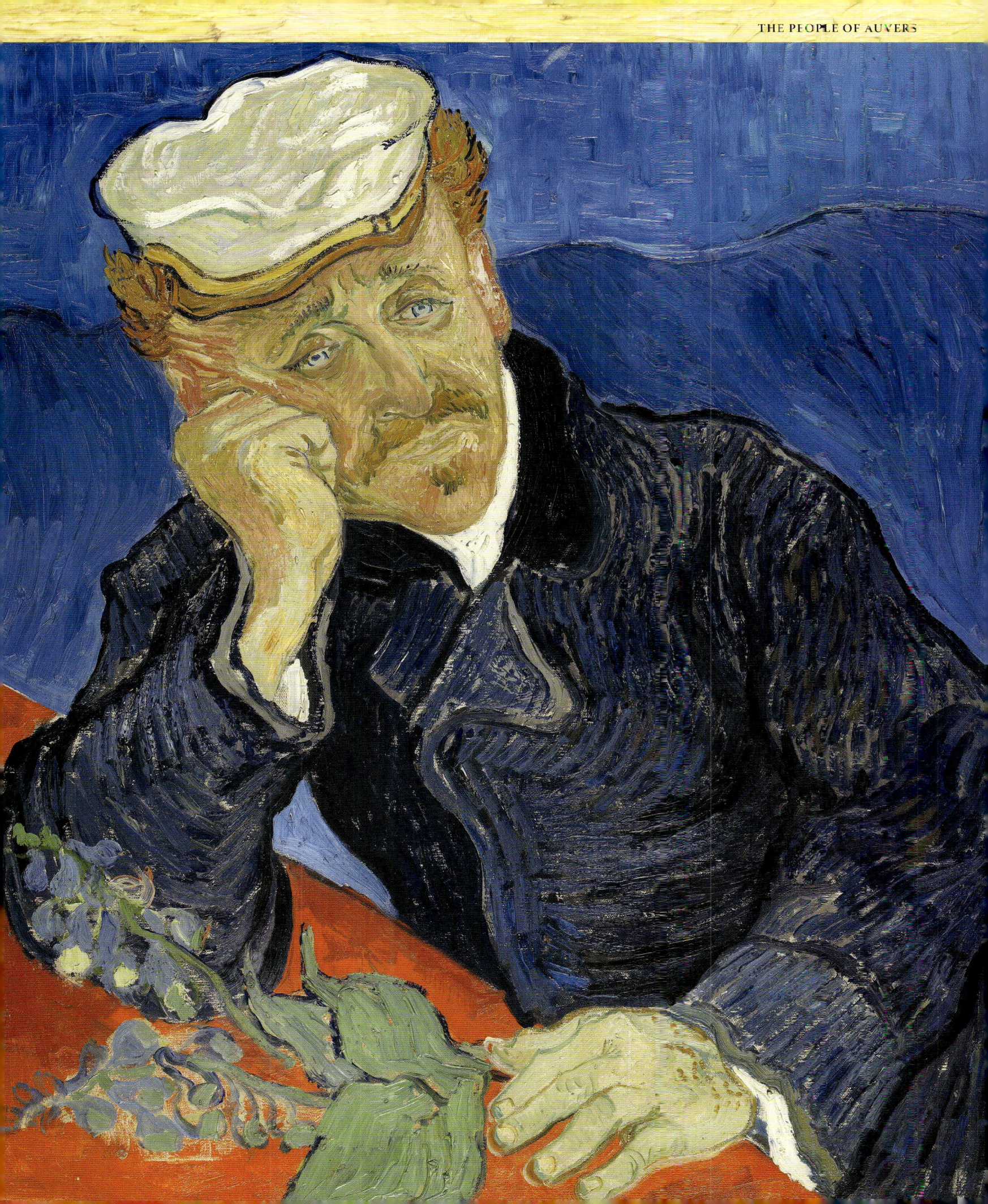

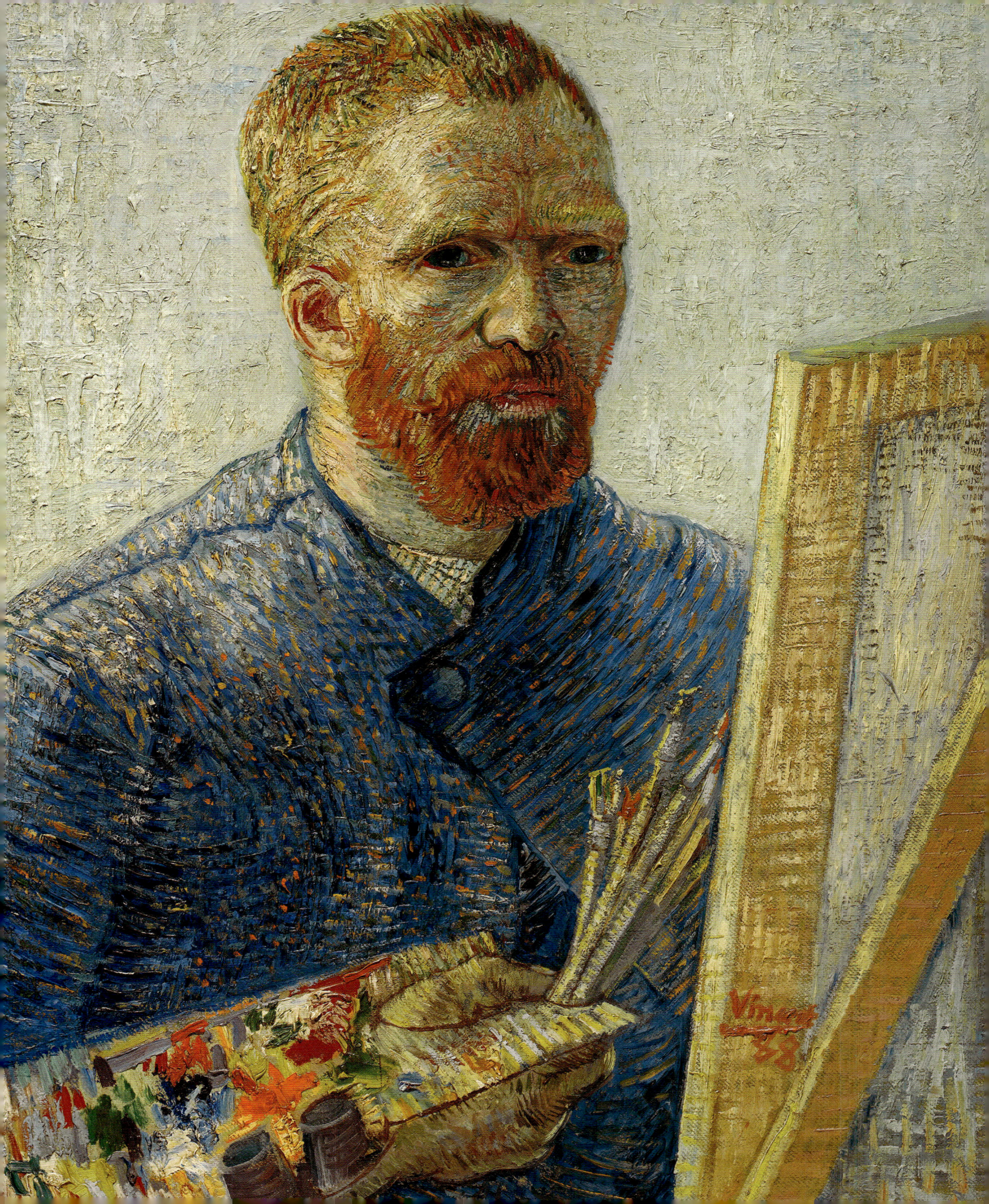

SELF-PORTRAITS

Self-portraiture is a genre Vincent repeatedly returns to—sometimes out of necessity, because he was often short of money and couldn't afford to pay a model or to persuade anyone to sit for him. He would even paint a self-portrait on the back of another painting to avoid the cost of expensive canvas. The majority of his self-portraits—more than 25 of them—were done while he was in Paris, from 1886 to 1888.

[OPPOSITE PAGE] ***Self-portrait as a Painter** (*December 1887–February 1888). Oil on canvas. Van Gogh Museum, Amsterdam (Vincent van Gogh Foundation).

This was the last work Vincent produced in Paris; the city had exhausted him both mentally and physically. He renders himself in intense, nearly unblended colors, showing himself behind his easel, with a palette and paintbrushes in hand.

" . . . wrinkles in forehead and around the mouth, stiffly wooden, a very red beard, quite unkempt and sad."

~ VAN GOGH, IN A LETTER TO HIS SISTER WIL., DESCRIBING *SELF-PORTRAIT AS A PAINTER*

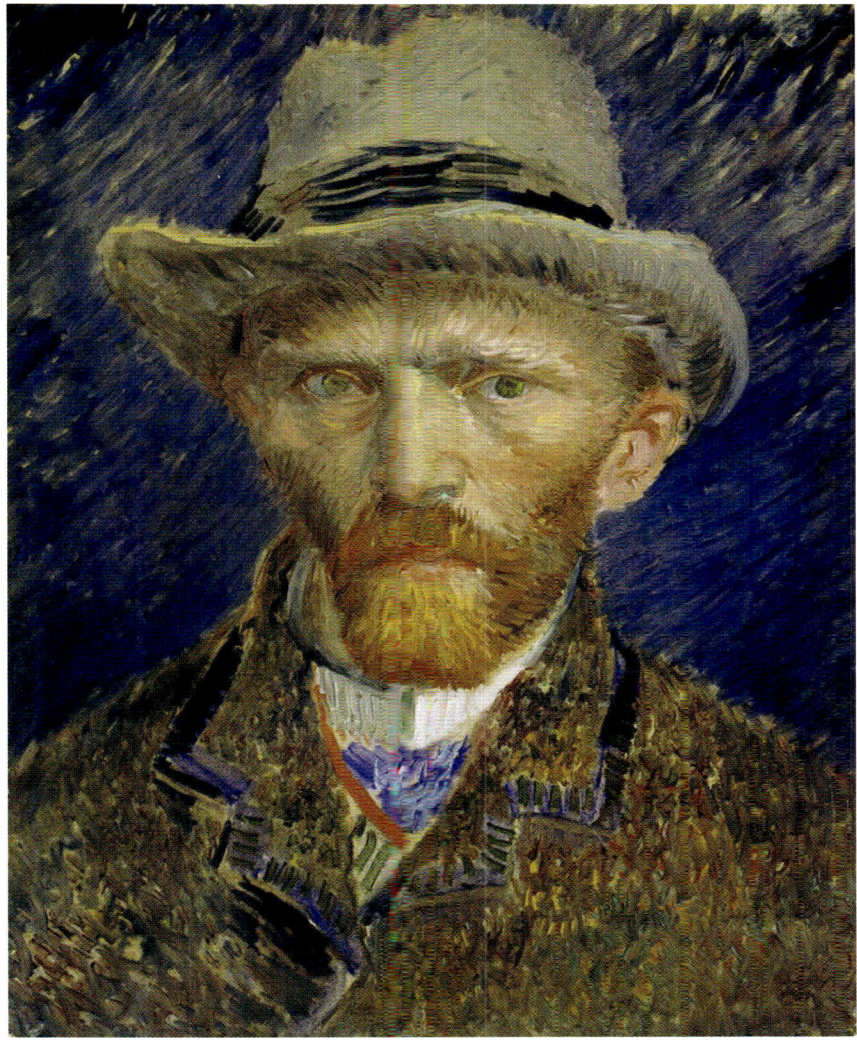

Self-Portrait with Grey Felt Hat (Winter, 1886–87). Oil on canvas. Rijksmuseum, Amsterdam.

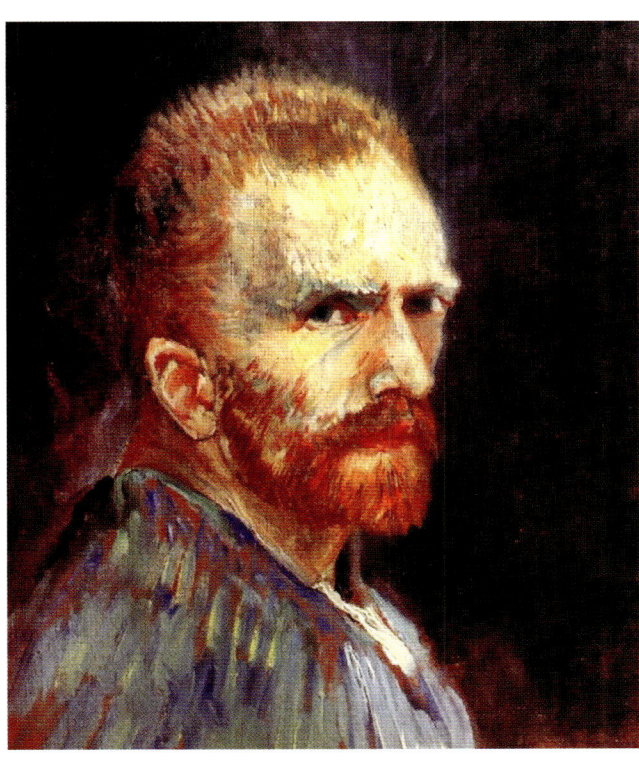

[LEFT]
Self-Portrait
(Summer, 1887). Oil on canvas. Wadsworth Atheneum, Hartford, Connecticut.

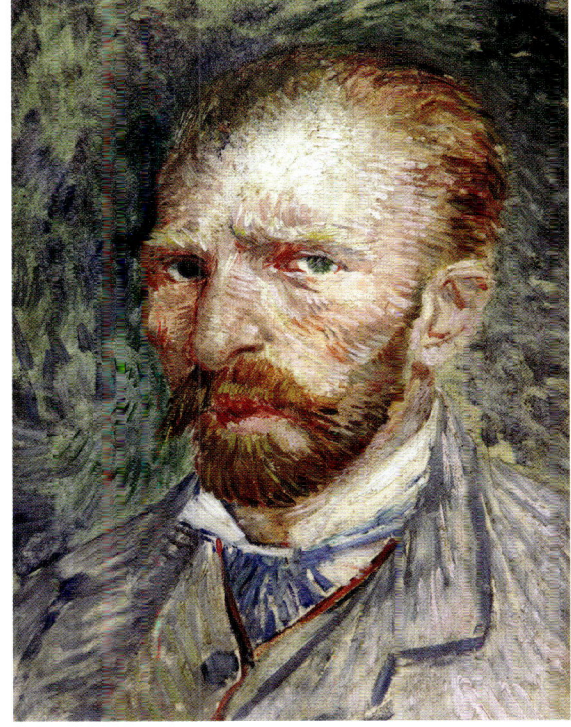

[RIGHT]
Self-Portrait (Spring, 1887). Oil on canvas. Kröller-Müller Museum, Otterlo.

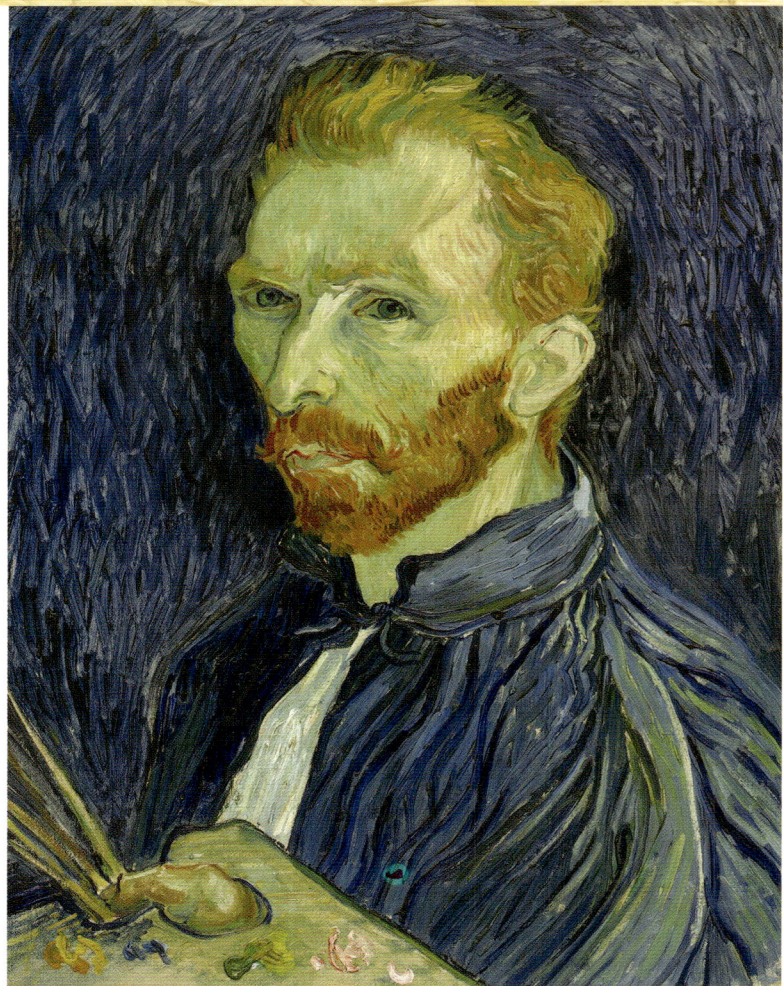

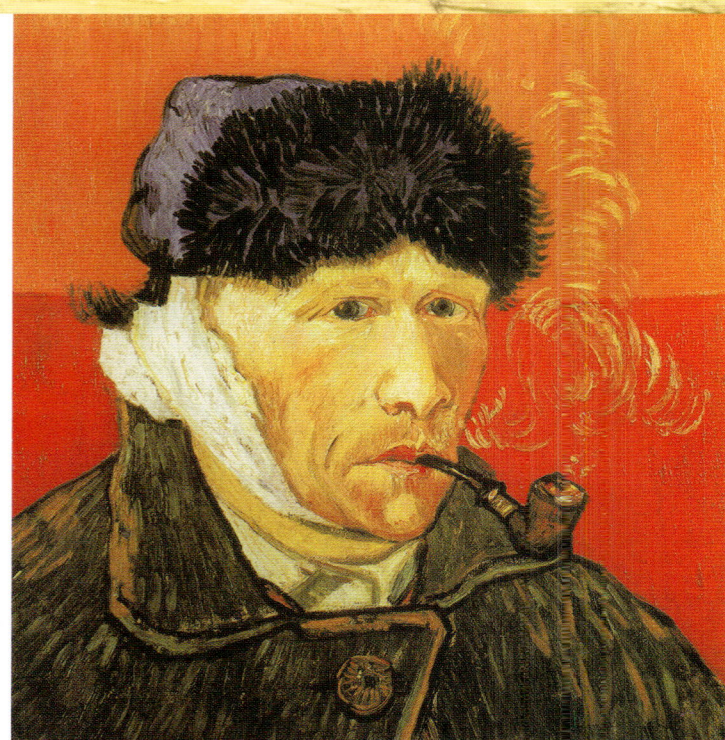

[ABOVE] *Self-Portrait with Bandaged Ear and Pipe* (January 1889). Oil on canvas. Kunsthaus Zürich.

[LEFT] *Self-Portrait* (August 1889). Oil on canvas. National Gallery of Art, Washington D.C.

[OPPOSITE PAGE] *Self-Portrait with Straw Hat* (1887). Oil on canvas. Metropolitan Museum of Art, New York.

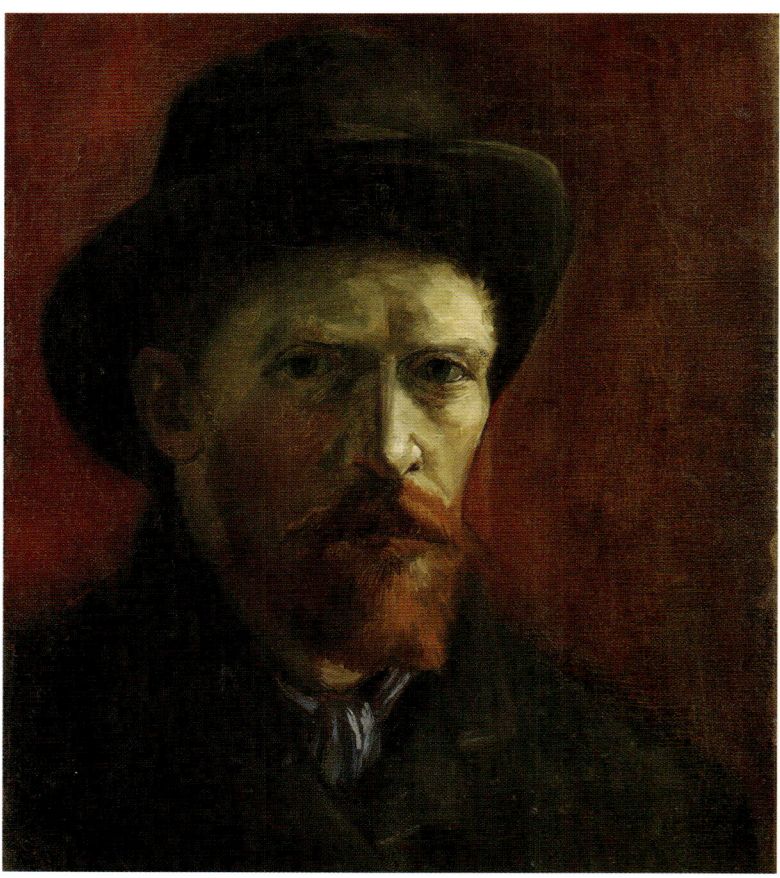

Self-Portrait with Felt Hat (December 1886). Oil on canvas. Van Gogh Museum, Amsterdam (Vincent van Gogh Foundation).

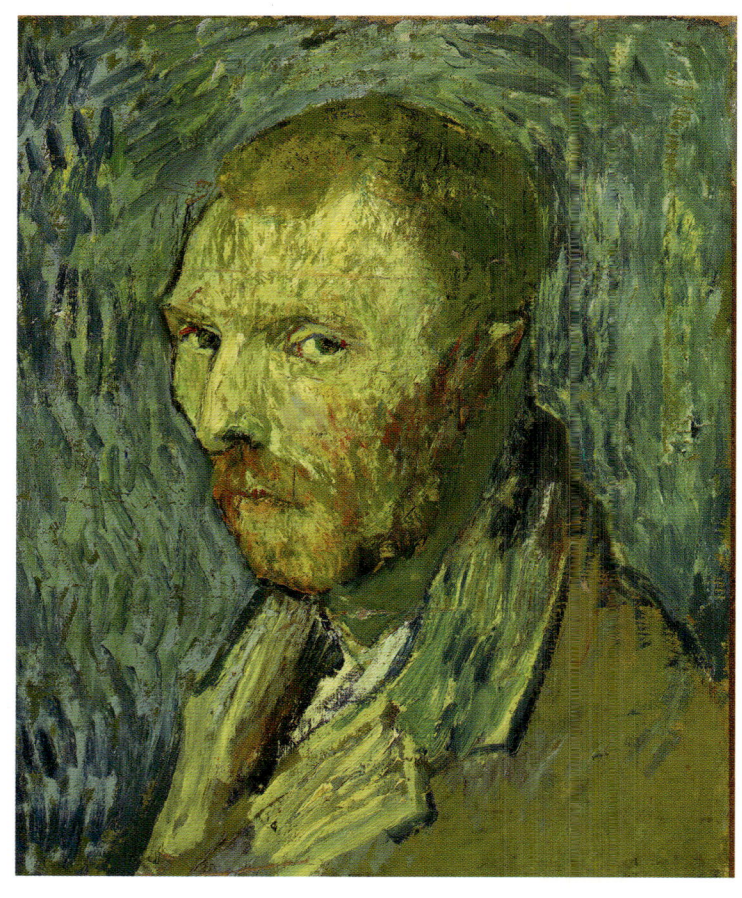

Self-Portrait (September 1889). Oil on canvas. National Gallery, Norway.

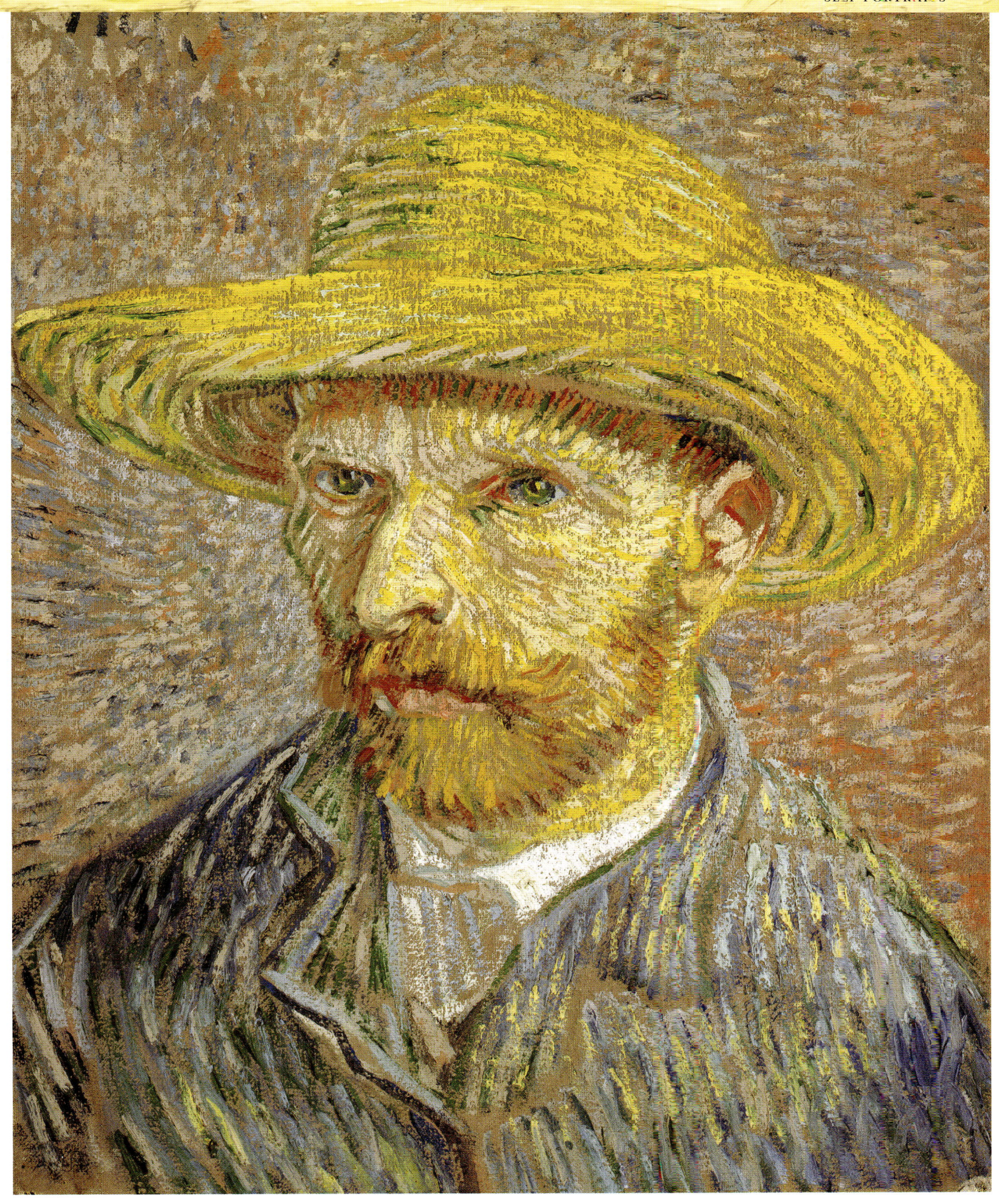

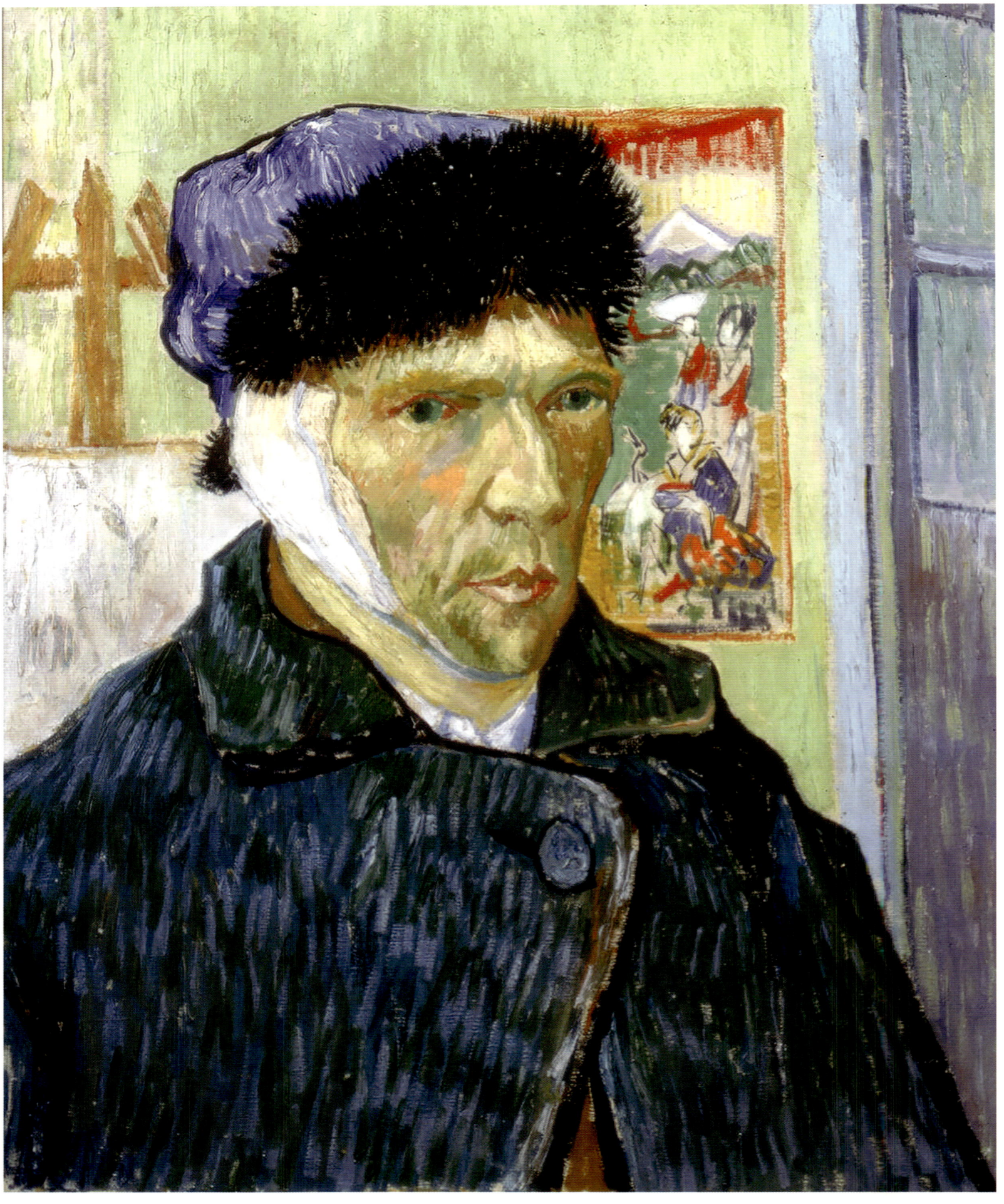

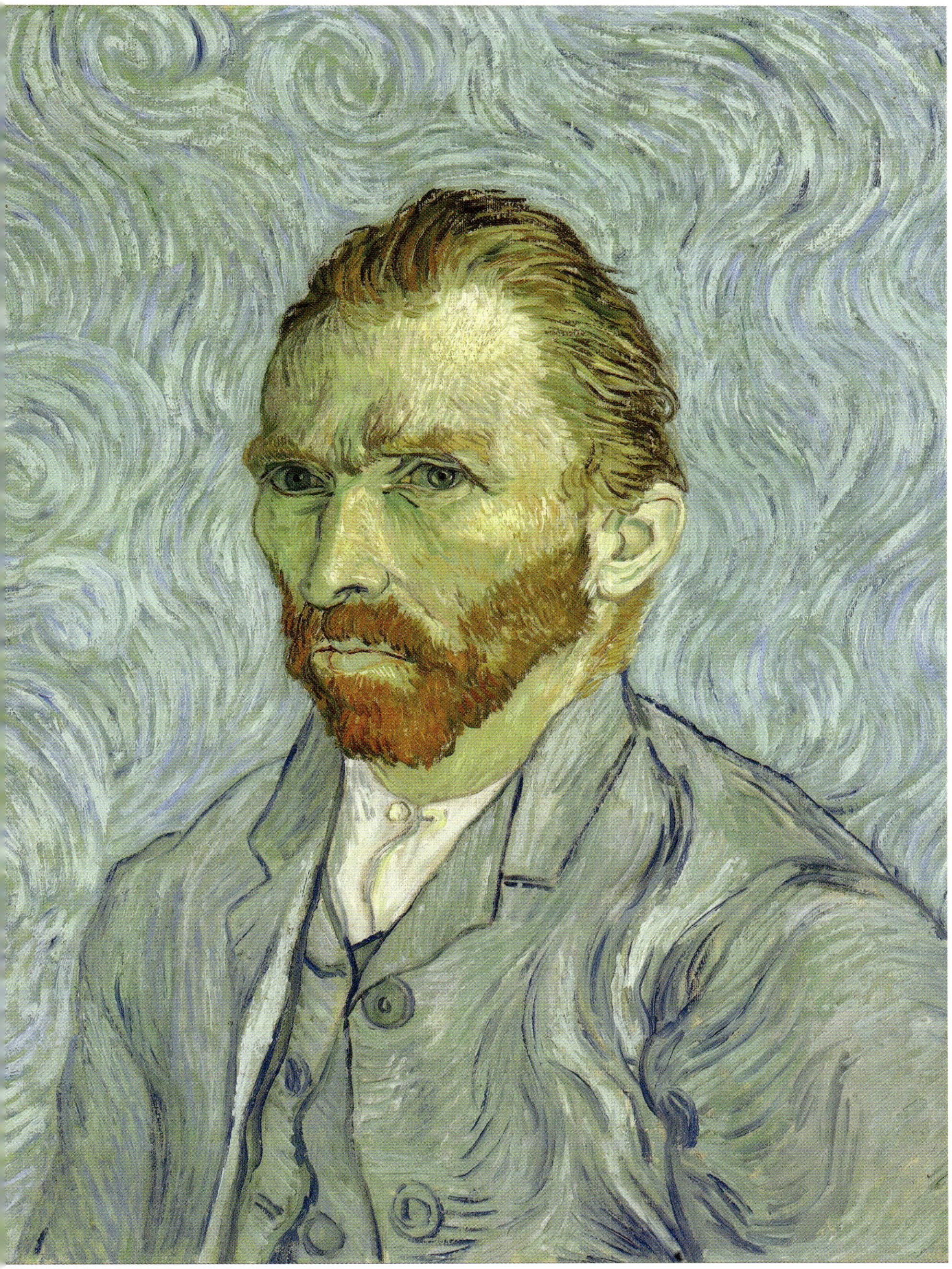

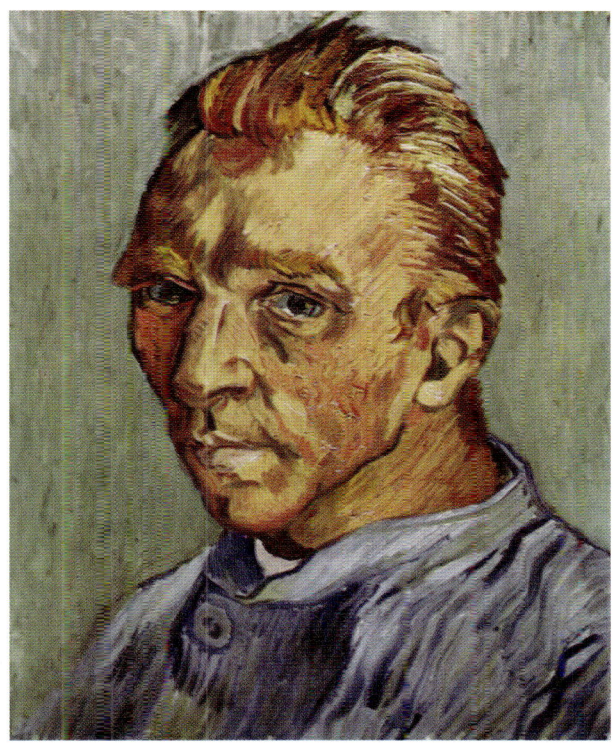

Self-Portrait without Beard (September 1889).
Oil on canvas. Private collection

*Painted after the explosive end to his co-habitation with
Gauguin, this melancholy image of Vincent is one
of the contenders for the title of "last portrait."*

Self-Portrait (September 1889). Oil on canvas. Musée d'Orsay, Paris.

*One of two works that has been speculated to be the last of Vincent's self-portraits
is often cited as his greatest. Painted just months before his death, it seems
to mirror his restless soul, with swirling brushstrokes that might seem
chaotic but are executed with masterly control.*

[OPPOSITE PAGE]
Self-Portrait with Bandaged Ear, Easel, and Japanese Print
(January 1889). Oil on canvas. Courtauld Galleries, London.

*After an argument with the artist Paul Gauguin, Vincent cut off a piece of
his ear. Shortly after his release from the hospital, he painted* Self Portrait
with Bandaged Ear, *possibly as a way of dealing with the aftermath of this
manic episode. It is unusual in that it depicts a clean-shaven Vincent.*

" *People say – and
I'm quite willing
to believe it – that
it's difficult to know
oneself – but it's
not easy to paint
oneself either.*"

~ VINCENT VAN GOGH

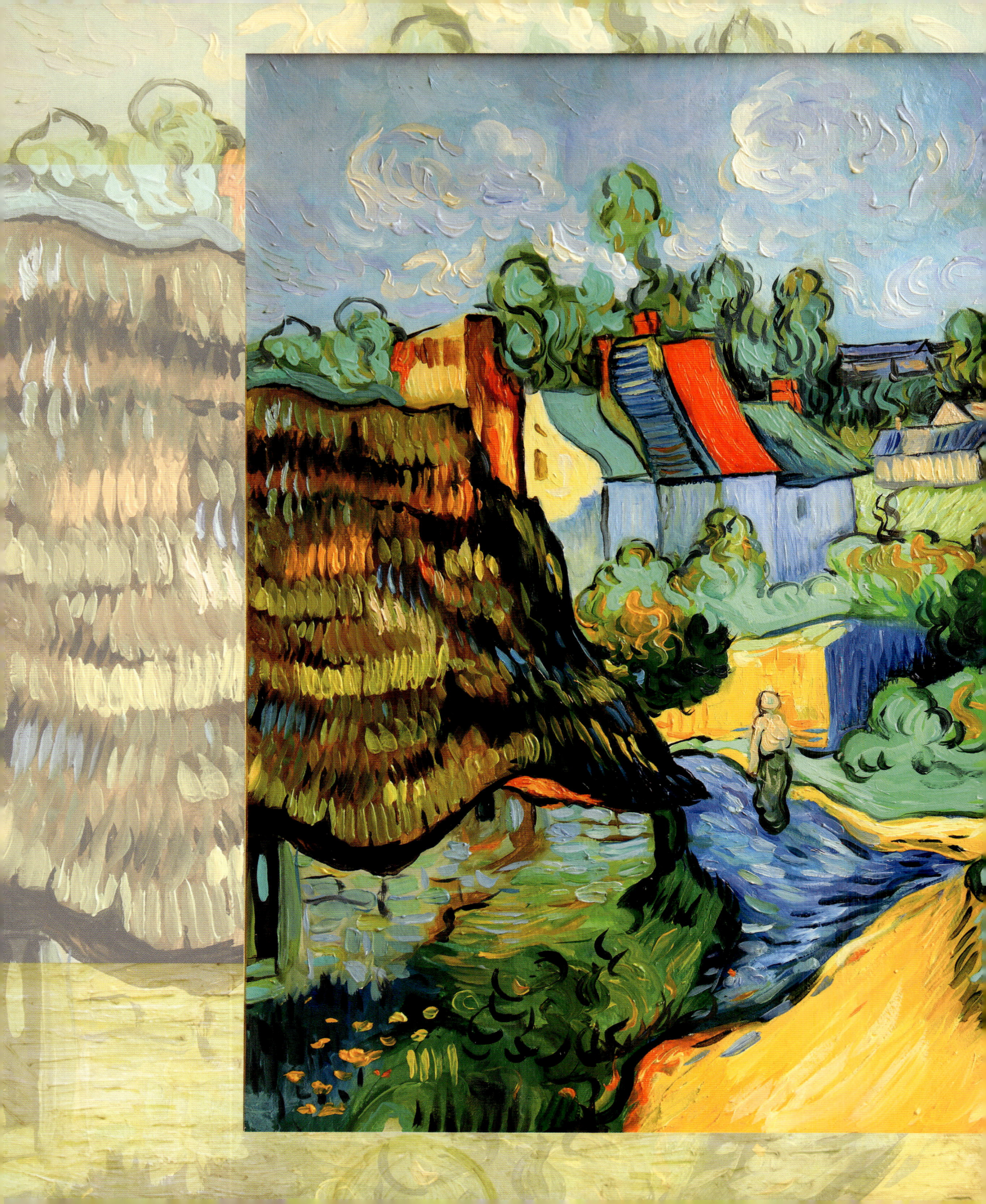

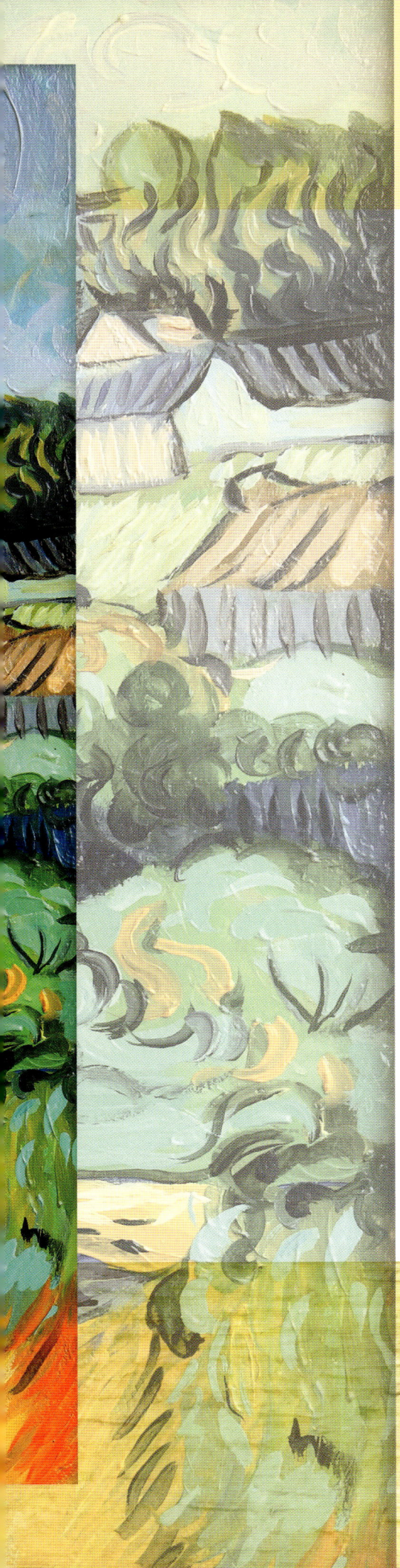

LANDSCAPES & PLACES

WHETHER IN THE UMBER tones of a dreary Dutch village or the brilliant yellows of the sun-drenched fields of Provence, Vincent found inspiration in the scenery around him, and he captured the spirit of these places in hundreds of landscape paintings. Some of his most-lauded works, such as *Starry Night* and *Wheat Field with Crows,* are brilliant examples of this venerable genre. He produced landscapes from his earliest days in the Netherlands to his final days in Auvers, transitioning from quite traditional renditions to his unique representations executed with zestful brushstrokes of vibrant color.

Houses in Auvers (1890). Oil on canvas. Museum of Fine Arts, Boston.

EARLY LANDSCAPE WORKS

Even as a child, Vincent had drawn, but 1881, when he was 28, was the true start of his life of serious artistic expression. Vincent's first forays into oil painting—what would become his medium of choice—were executed in December 1881, under the supervision of Anton Mauve, the husband of his cousin Ariëtte (Jet) Carbentus. Many of the works he produced in these early days are focused on human subjects and still lifes, yet he did execute some notable landscape paintings. Strikingly, these works appear fairly traditional, with dark and muted tones that are a far cry from the vivid colors that make his later work so remarkable.

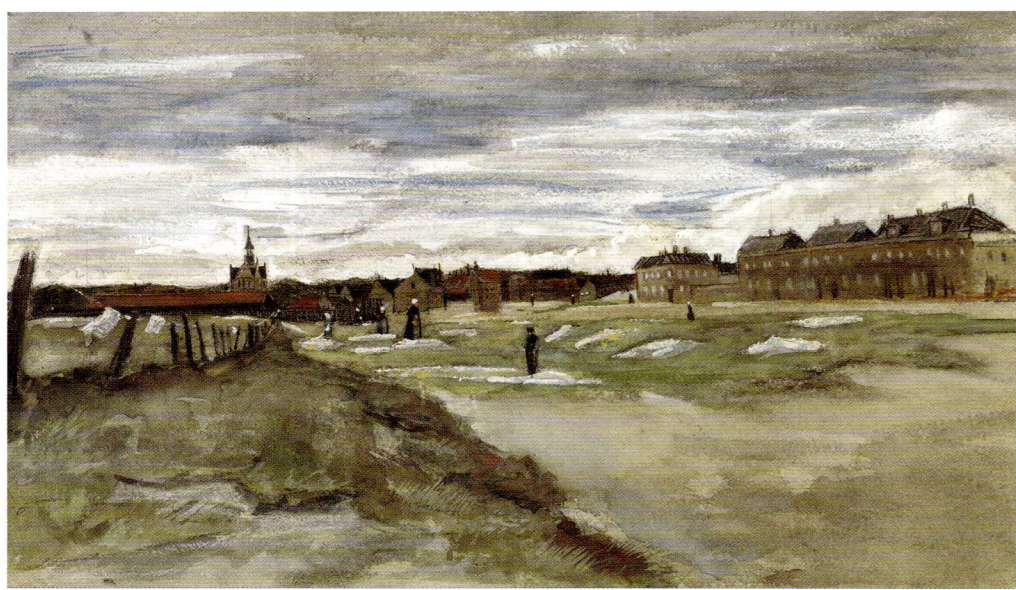

Bleaching Ground at Scheveningen (July 1882). Watercolor, heightened with white gouache. J. Paul Getty Museum, Los Angeles.

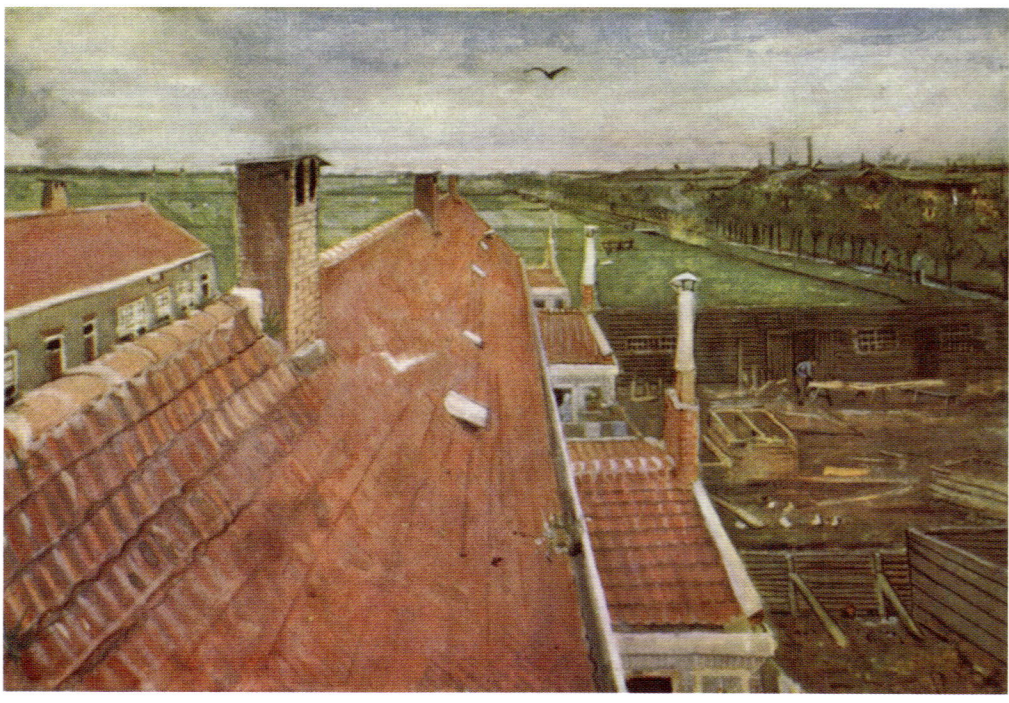

Rooftops, View from the Atelier The Hague (July 1882). Watercolor. Private collection.

Although Vincent drew and painted with watercolors while at school, few of these works survive.

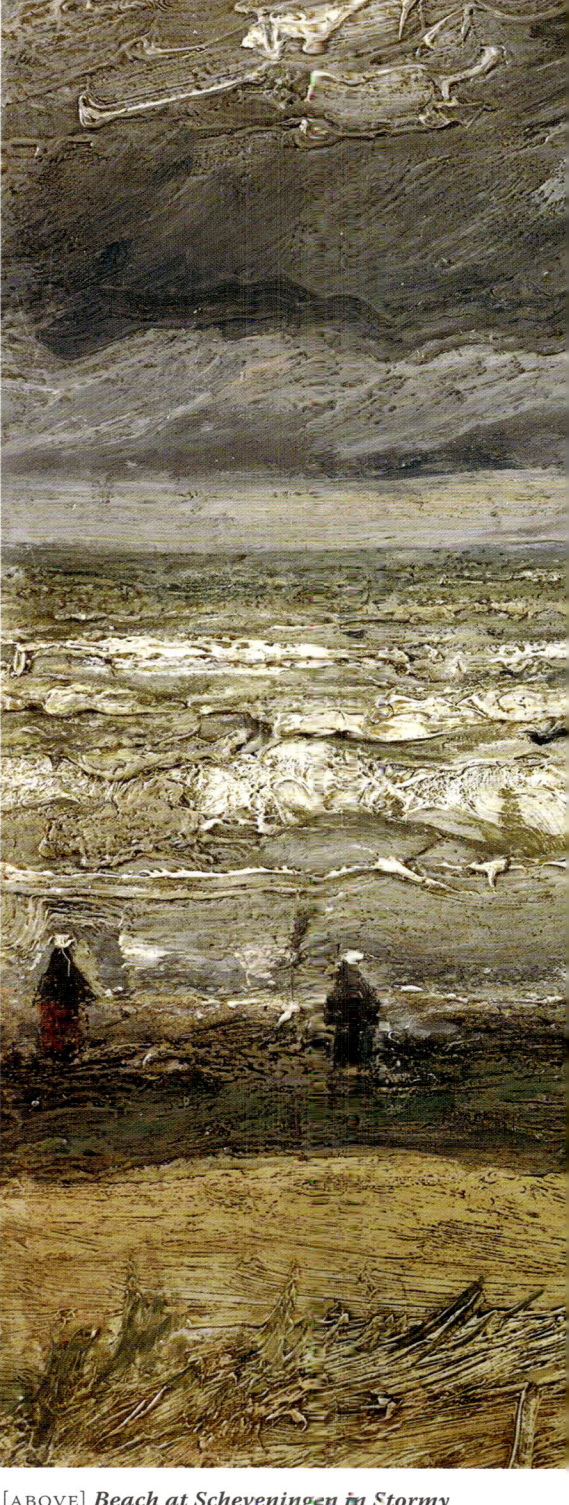

[ABOVE] ***Beach at Scheveningen in Stormy Weather*** (August 1882). Oil on canvas. Van Gogh Museum, Amsterdam (Vincent van Gogh Foundation).

Painted at Scheveningen near The Hague, Vincent's second attempt at oils was executed en plein air on an easel set up on the beach. With blustering winds whipping up sand, he had to work quickly to capture the menacing, cloud-filled sky and white-capped waves roiling in the greenish gray sea. Traces of wind-blown sand still remain embedded in its surface.

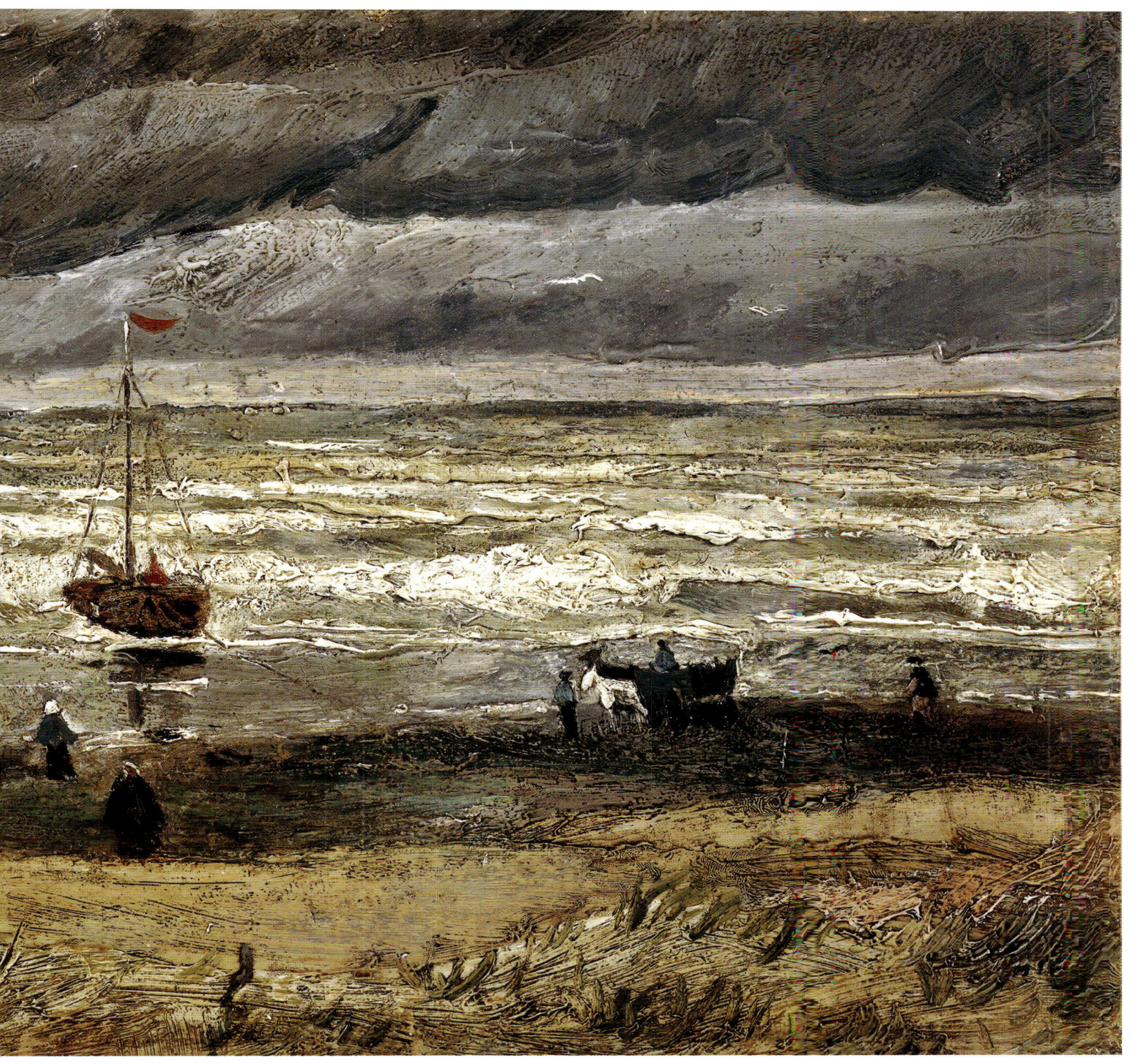

"I now consider myself to be at the beginning of the beginning of making something serious."

~ VINCENT, TO THEO, DECEMBER 1881

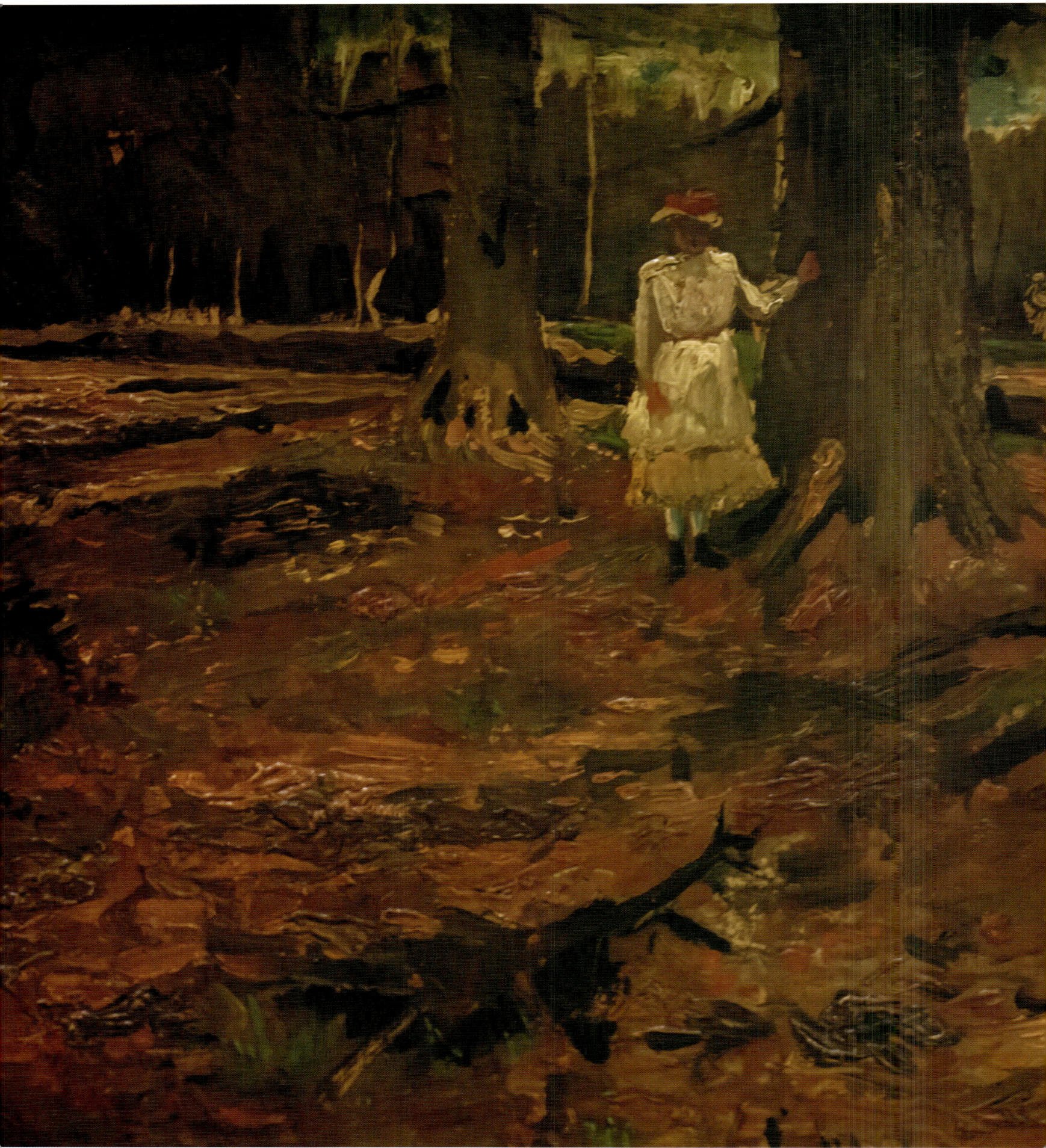

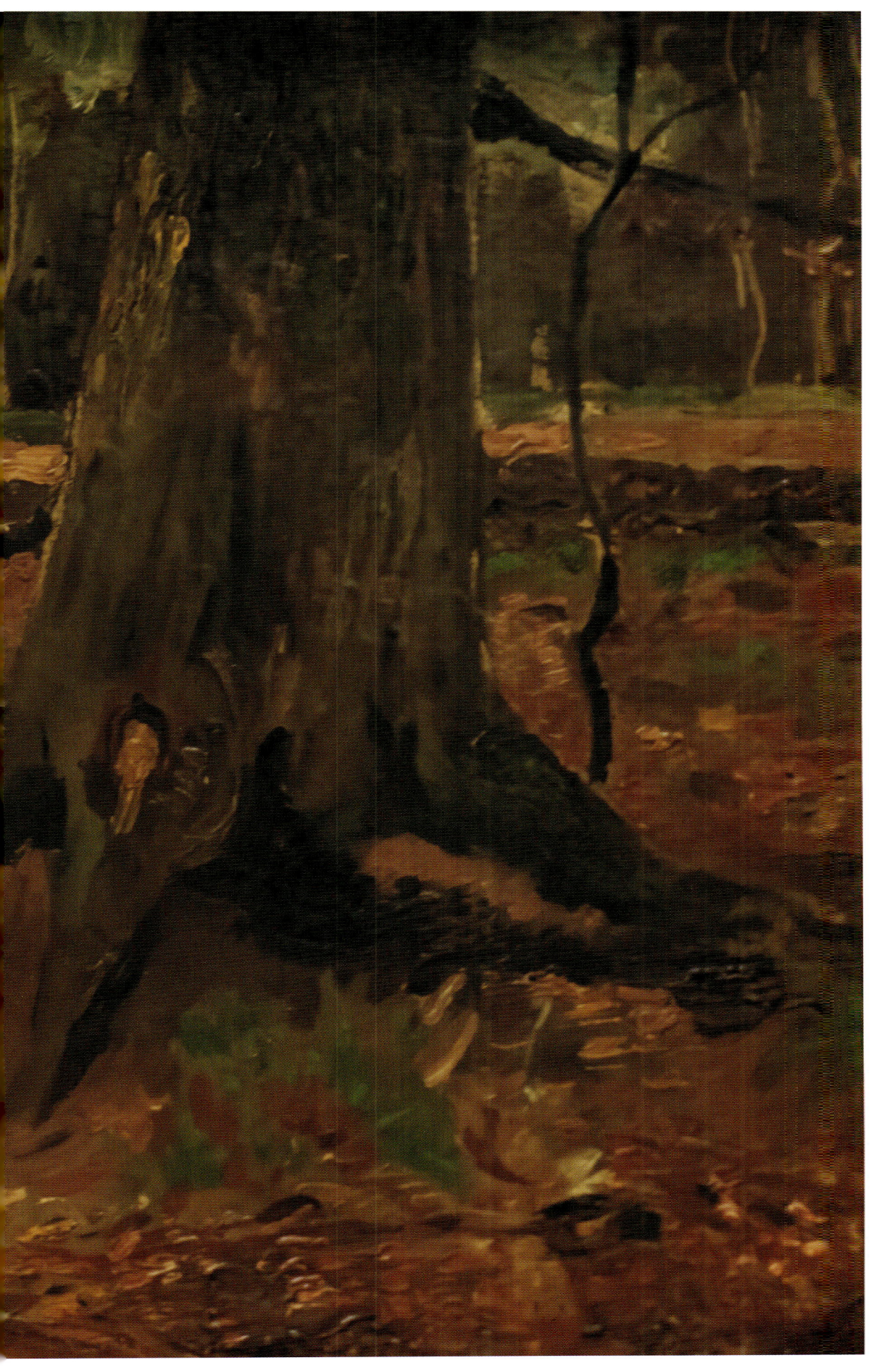

"*The other study in the wood is of some large green beech trunks on a stretch of ground covered with dry sticks, and the little figure of a girl in white. There was the great difficulty of keeping it clear, and of getting space between the trunks standing at different distances . . . to make it so that one can breathe and walk around in it, and to make you smell the fragrance of the wood.*"

~ VINCENT, DESCRIBING
GIRL IN WHITE IN THE WOODS,
TO HIS BROTHER THEO,
AUGUST 1882

Girl in White in the Woods
(1882). Oil on canvas. Kröller-Müller Museum, Otterlo.

IN NUENEN

In December 1883, Vincent traveled to his parents' home in Nuenen. He lived and worked in Nuenen from 1883 to 1885, and he captured in paint at least 14 locations in this village in the Dutch province of North Brabant.

The Cottage (May 1885). Oil on canvas. Van Gogh Museum, Amsterdam (Vincent van Gogh Foundation).

The De Groots, who were the subjects of The Potato Eaters, *shared this home with another family.*

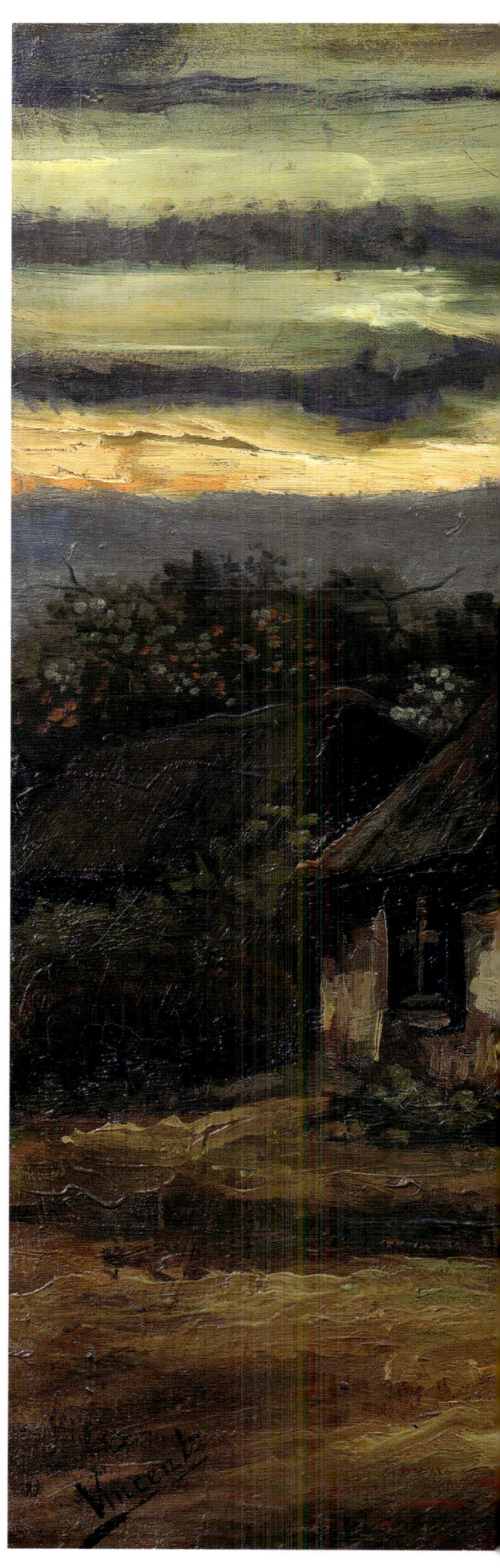

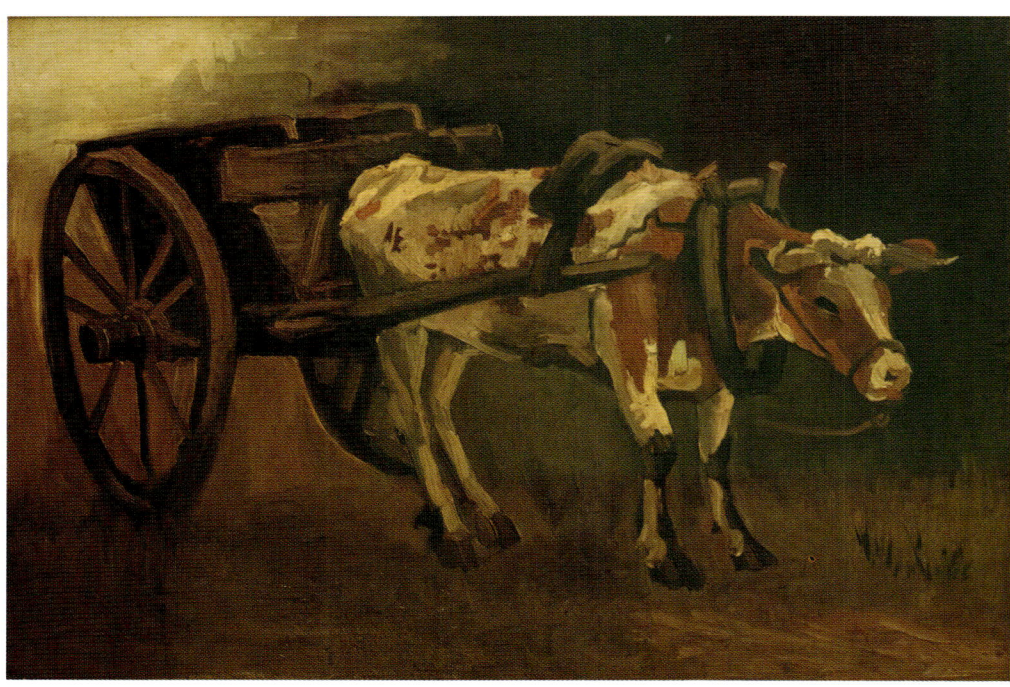

Cart with Reddish-Brown Ox (July 1884). Oil on canvas. Kröller-Müller Museum, Otterlo.

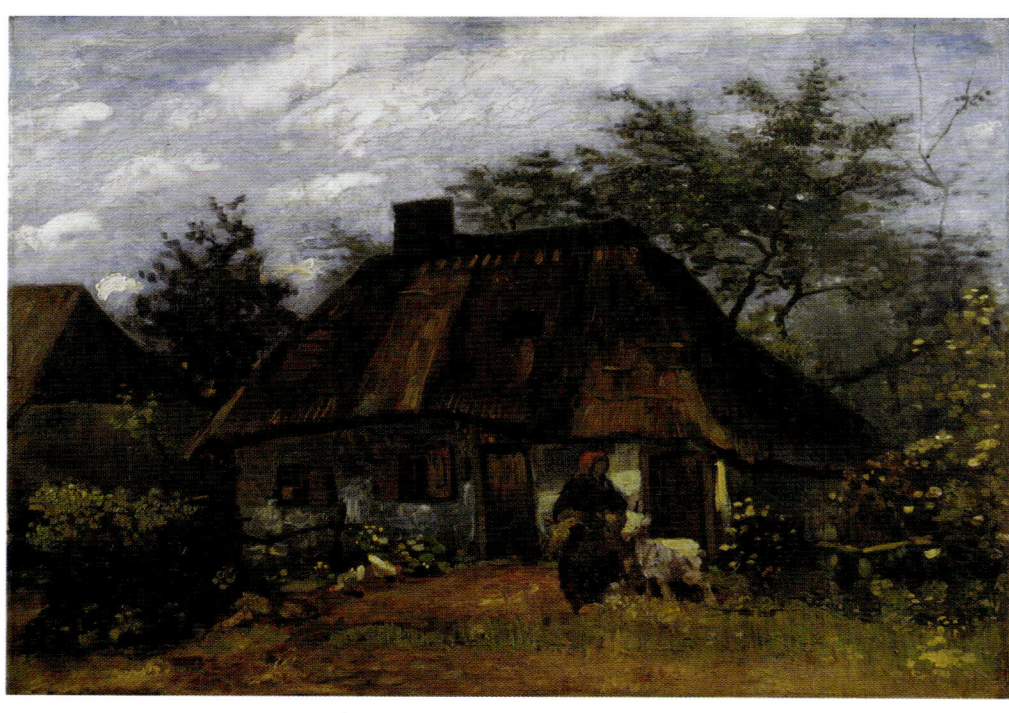

Farmhouse in Nuenen ("The Peasants' Churchyard") (June–July 1885). Oil on canvas. Eigentum Städelscher Museums-Verein e.V.

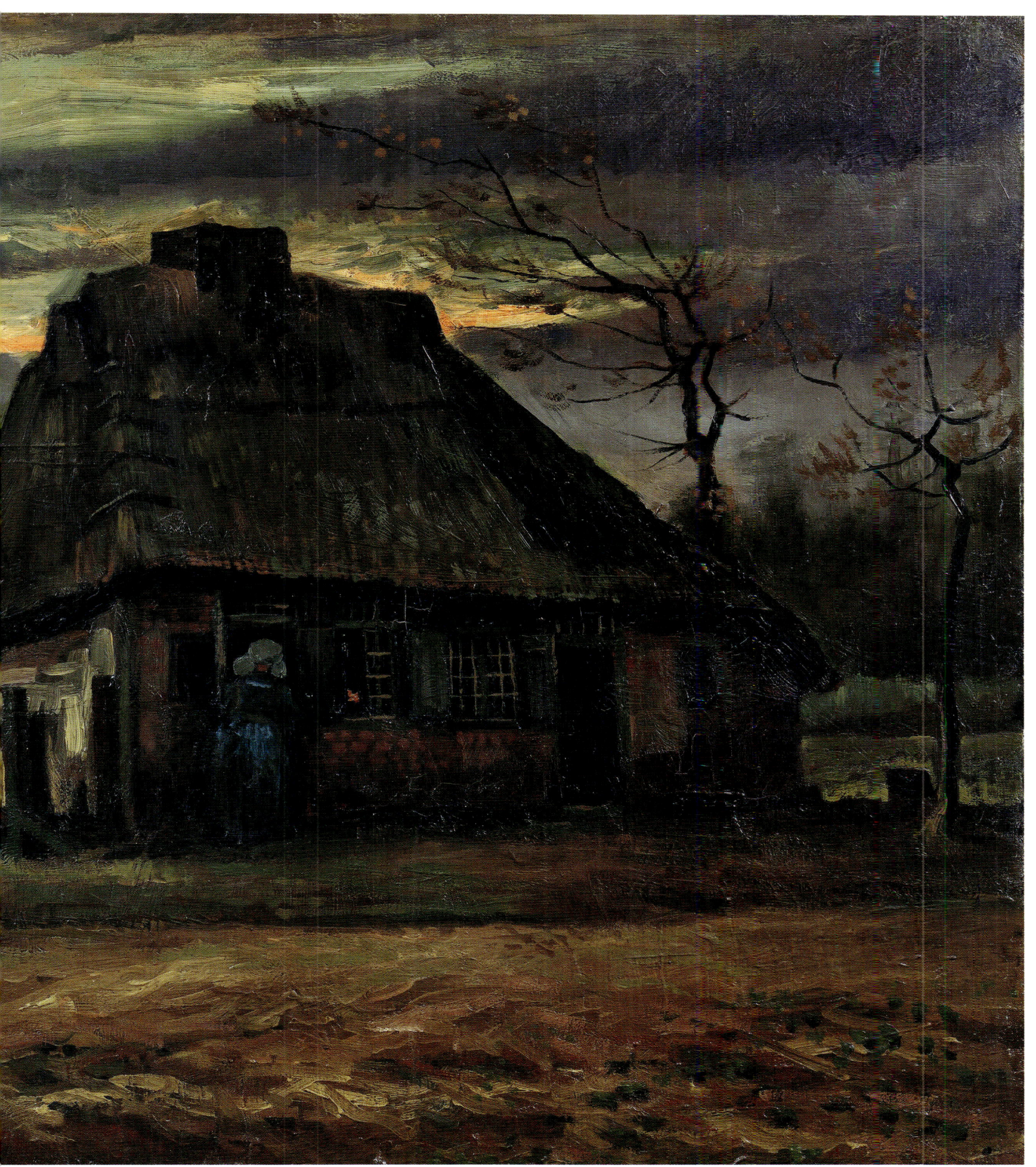

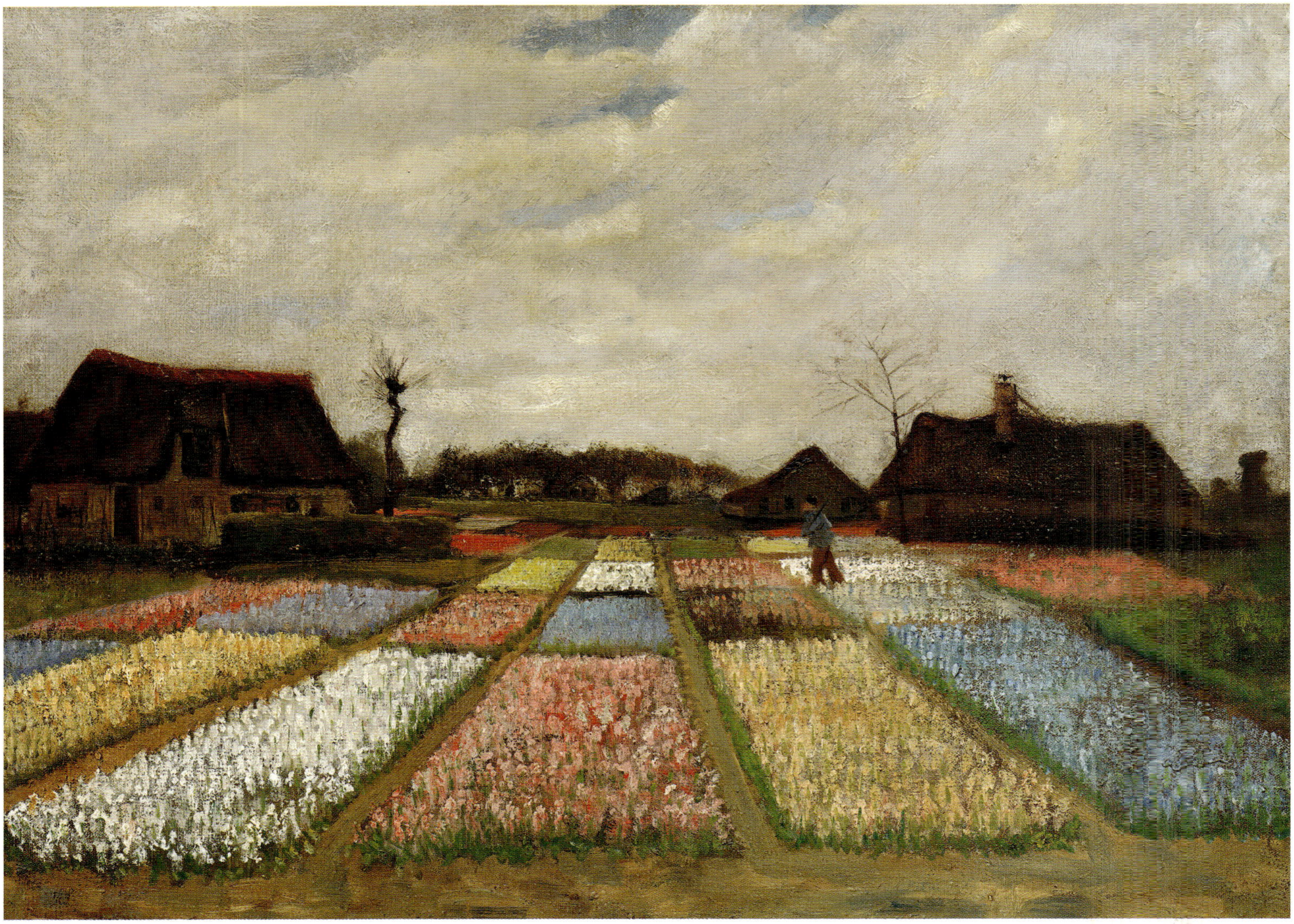

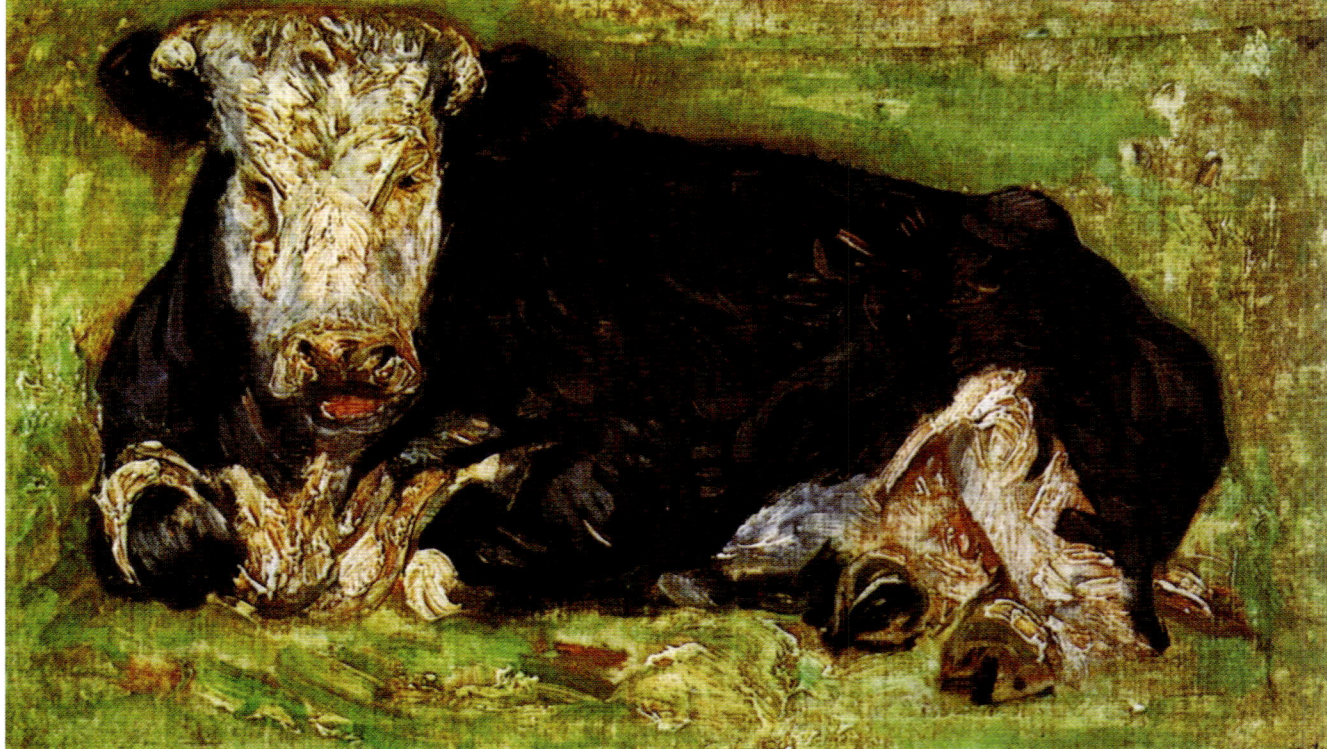

ABOVE
**The Bulb
Fields** (1883).
Oil on canvas
mounted on
wood. National
Gallery of Art,
Washington,
D.C.

*Vincent produced
his first garden
painting,* Bulb
Fields *(also known
as* Flower Beds
in Holland) *in his
second year in
The Hague.*

LEFT
The Lying Cow
(August 1883).
Oil on canvas.
Private collection.

" Though I am often in the depths of misery, there is still calmness, pure harmony and music inside me. I see paintings or drawings in the poorest cottages, in the dirtiest corners. And my mind is driven towards these things with an irresistible momentum."

~ VINCENT, TO THEO, JULY 1882

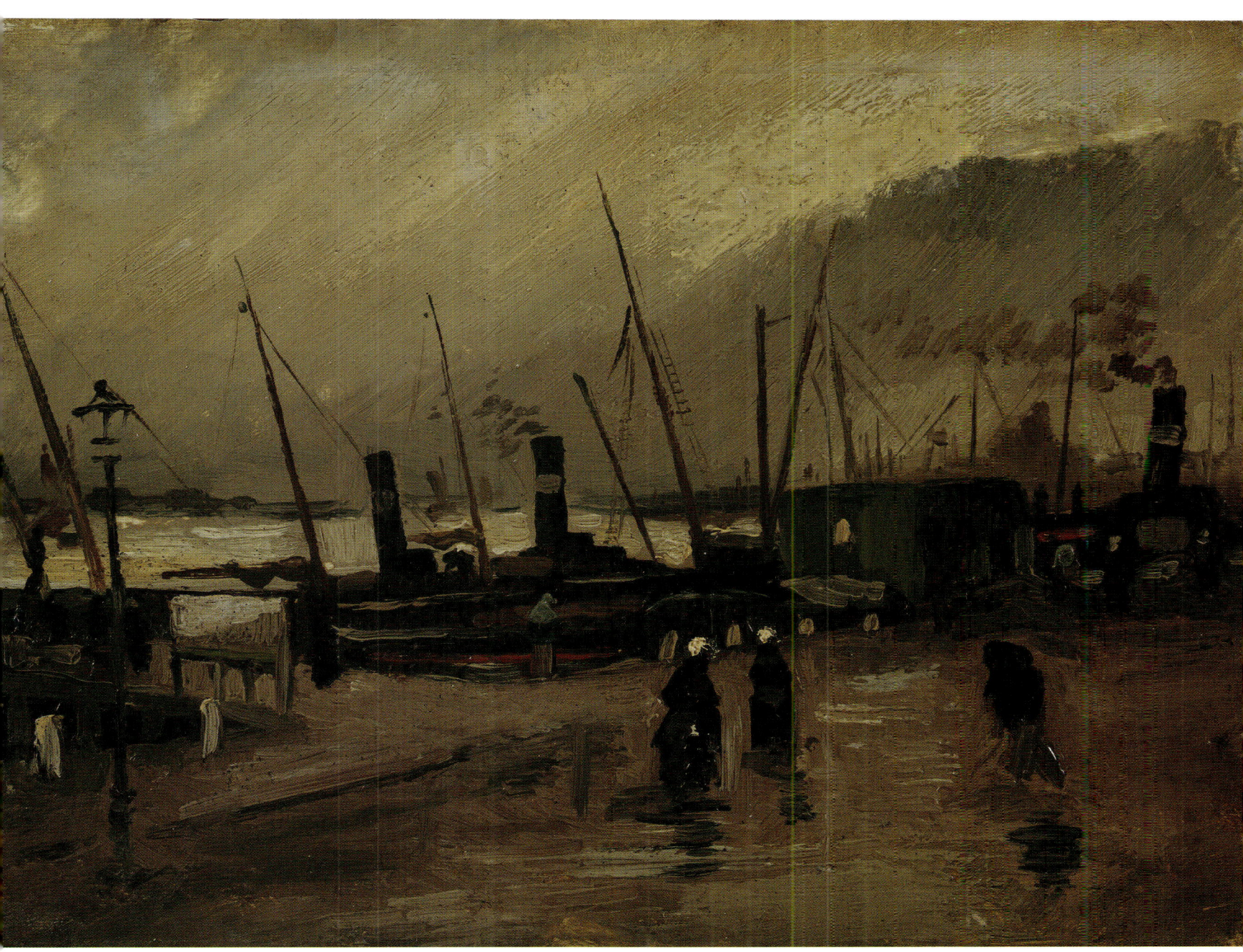

The De Ruijterkade in Amsterdam (1885). Oil on canvas. Van Gogh Museum, Amsterdam (Vincent van Gogh Foundation).

In 1885, on his final visit to Amsterdam, Vincent went to the newly opened Rijksmuseum with his friend Anton Kerssemakers.

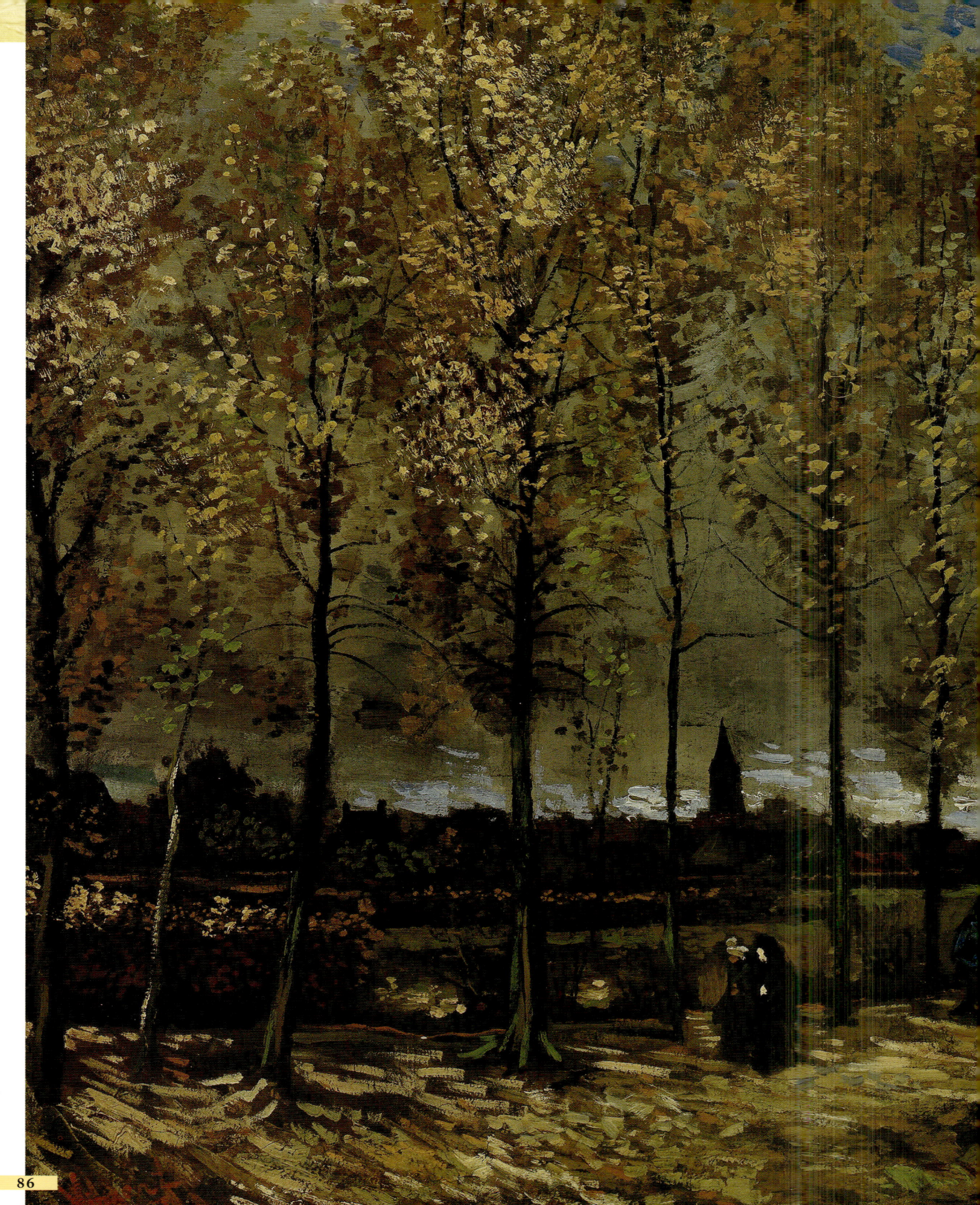

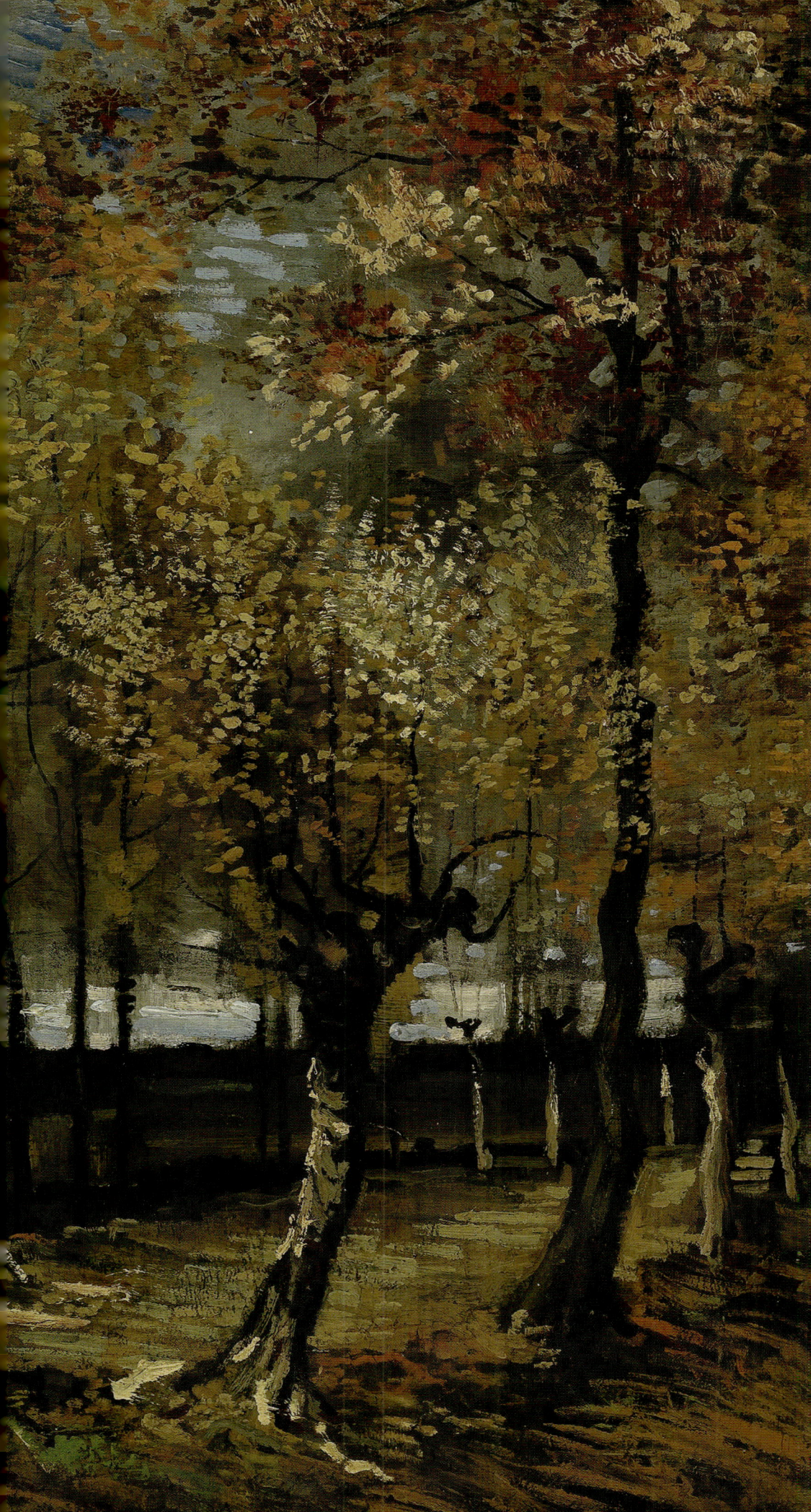

Poplars Near Nuenen (October 1884 or November 1885). Oil on canvas. The Museum Boijmans Van Beuningen, Rotterdam.

Vincent first painted this scene in the dark tones that characterize his early landscapes. There are indications, however, that he reworked the painting two years later, in 1886, with brighter colors.

" *The last thing I made is a rather large study of an avenue of poplars with the yellow autumn leaves, where the sun makes glittering patches here and there on the fallen leaves on the ground, which are interspersed with the long shadows cast by the trunks. At the end of the road a peasant cottage, and the blue sky above it between the autumn leaves.*"

~ VINCENT, IN A LETTER
TO THEO, OCTOBER 1884

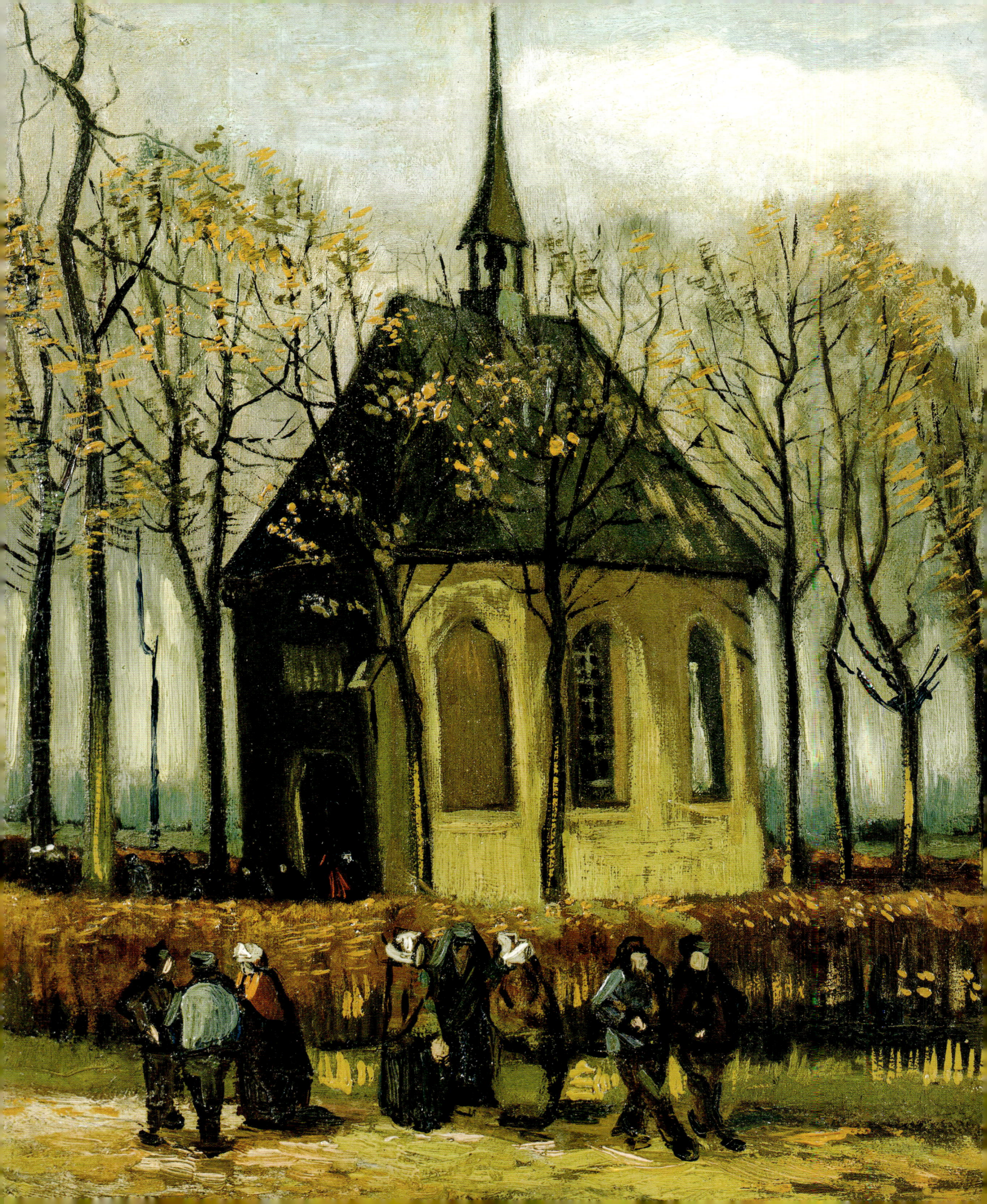

[OPPOSITE PAGE] ***Congregation Leaving the Reformed Church in Nuenen*** (January–February 1884). Oil on canvas. Van Gogh Museum, Amsterdam (Vincent van Gogh Foundation).

Vincent painted the Dutch Reformed Church in Nuenen, where his father was pastor, in January or February 1884, for his bedridden mother, showing it surrounded by a hedge and bare trees. Evidence suggests that he amended it, probably in late 1885, to add a congregation in mourning clothes to commemorate his father, who had died in March 1885.

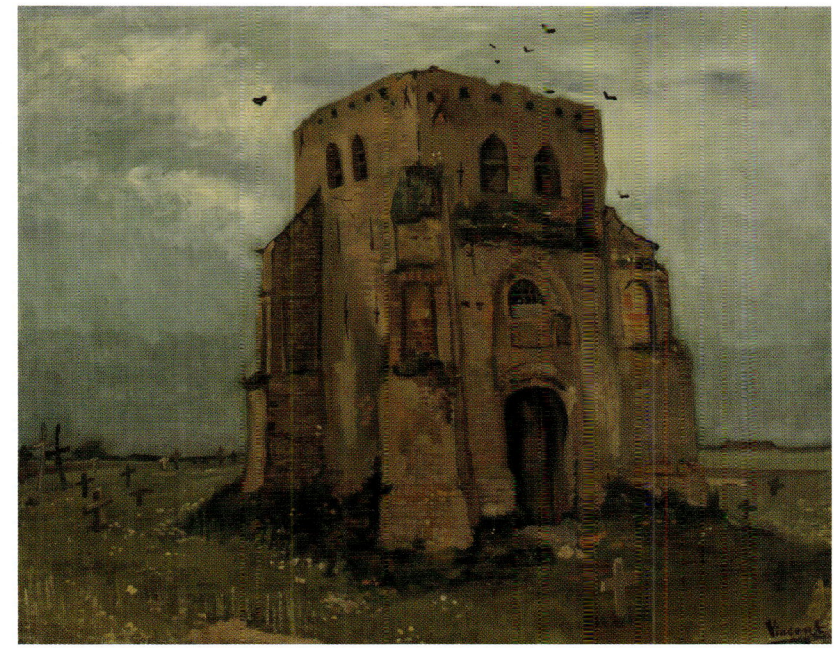

[RIGHT] ***The Old Church Tower at Nuenen ("The Peasants' Churchyard")*** (May–June 1885). Oil on canvas. Van Gogh Museum, Amsterdam (Vincent van Gogh Foundation).

While Vincent was in Nuenen, the Old Church Tower was just a crumbling ruin of a 12th-century Romanesque church. Its spire was demolished before his early watercolors of it could be developed into oil paintings, and during his stay, the entire building was demolished.

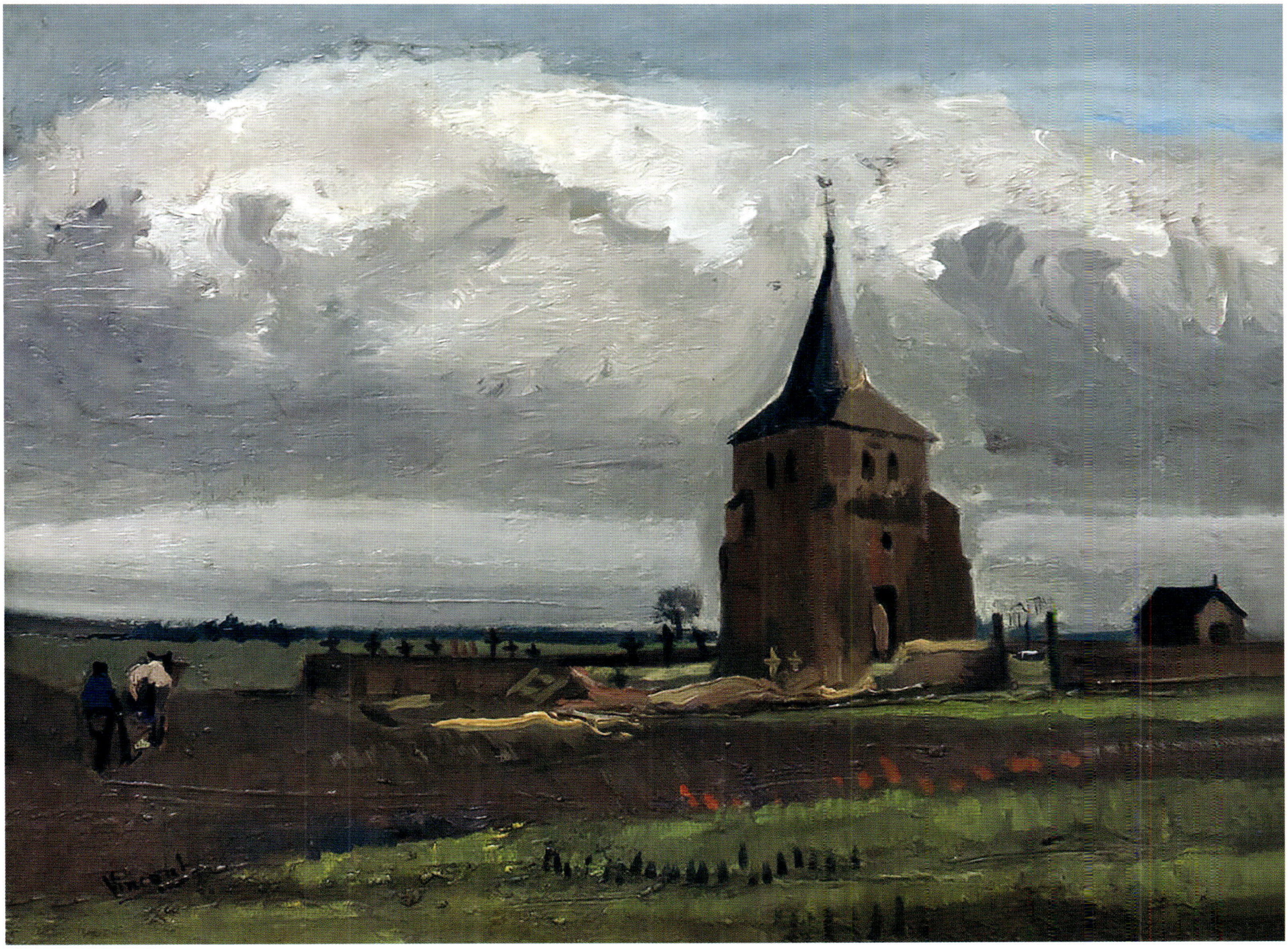

The Old Cemetery-Tower in Nuenen with Plowing Farmers (February 1884). Oil on canvas. Kröller-Müller Museum, Otterlo.

The Vicarage at Nuenen (September–October 1885). Oil on canvas. Van Gogh Museum, Amsterdam (Vincent van Gogh Foundation).

This house depicted here is the vicarage in which Vincent's parents lived in Nuenen. The building is still standing.

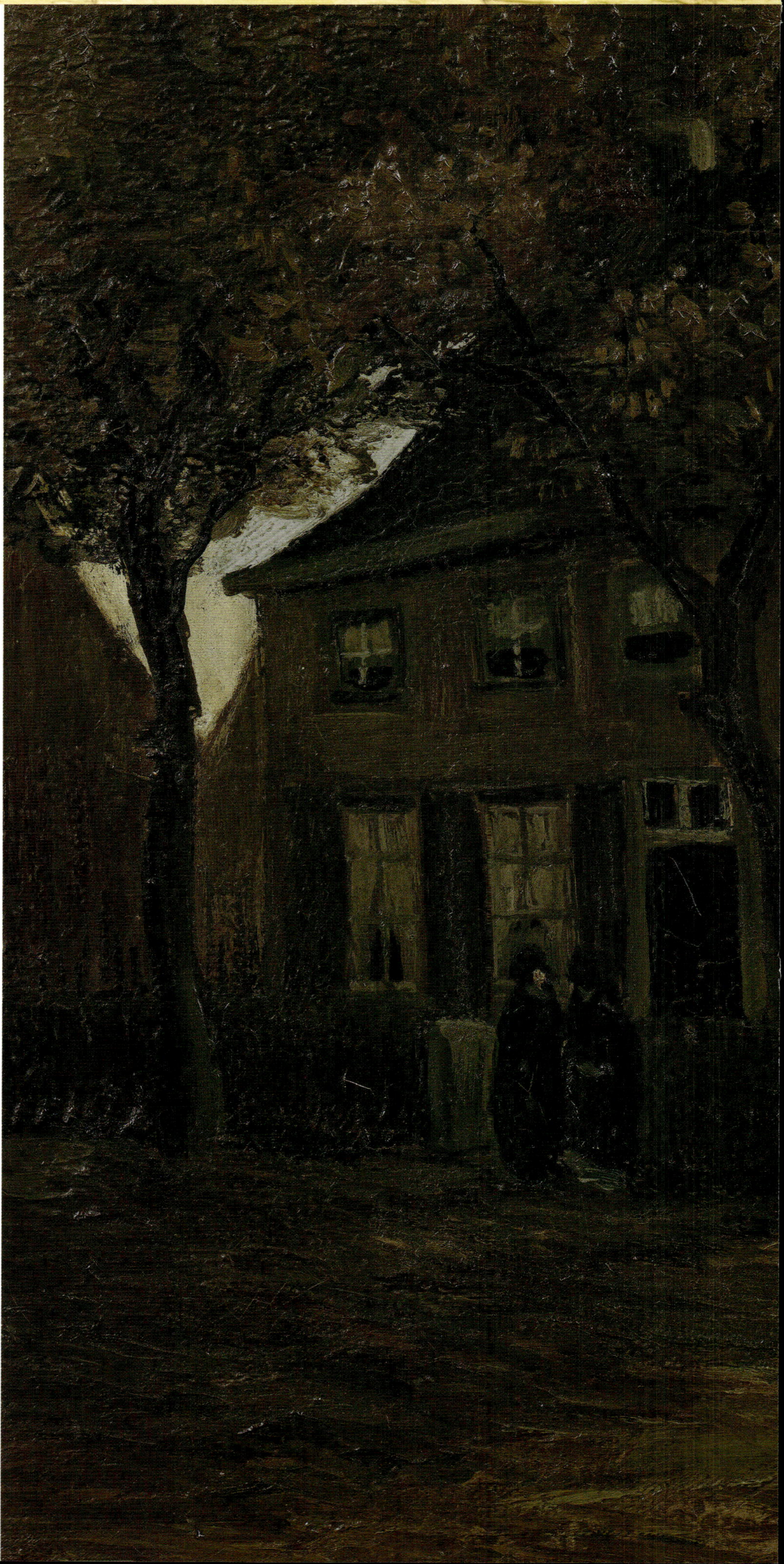

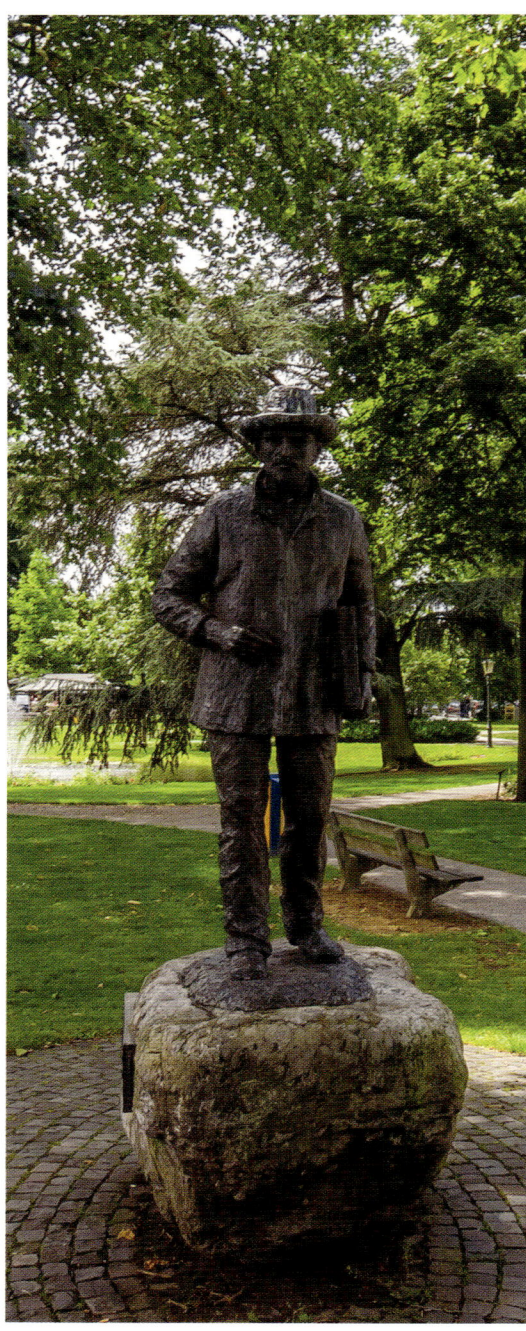

Van Gogh Statue in Nuenen Central Park

In 1984, a statue of Van Gogh, based on his Self-Portrait in a Gray Hat, was erected in Nuenen Central Park to mark the centenary of his stay in the town, from 1883 to 1885. The sculpture was commissioned by the Nuenen — 100 Years of Van Gogh Foundation and was created by the Dutch artist Klaas van Rosmalen.

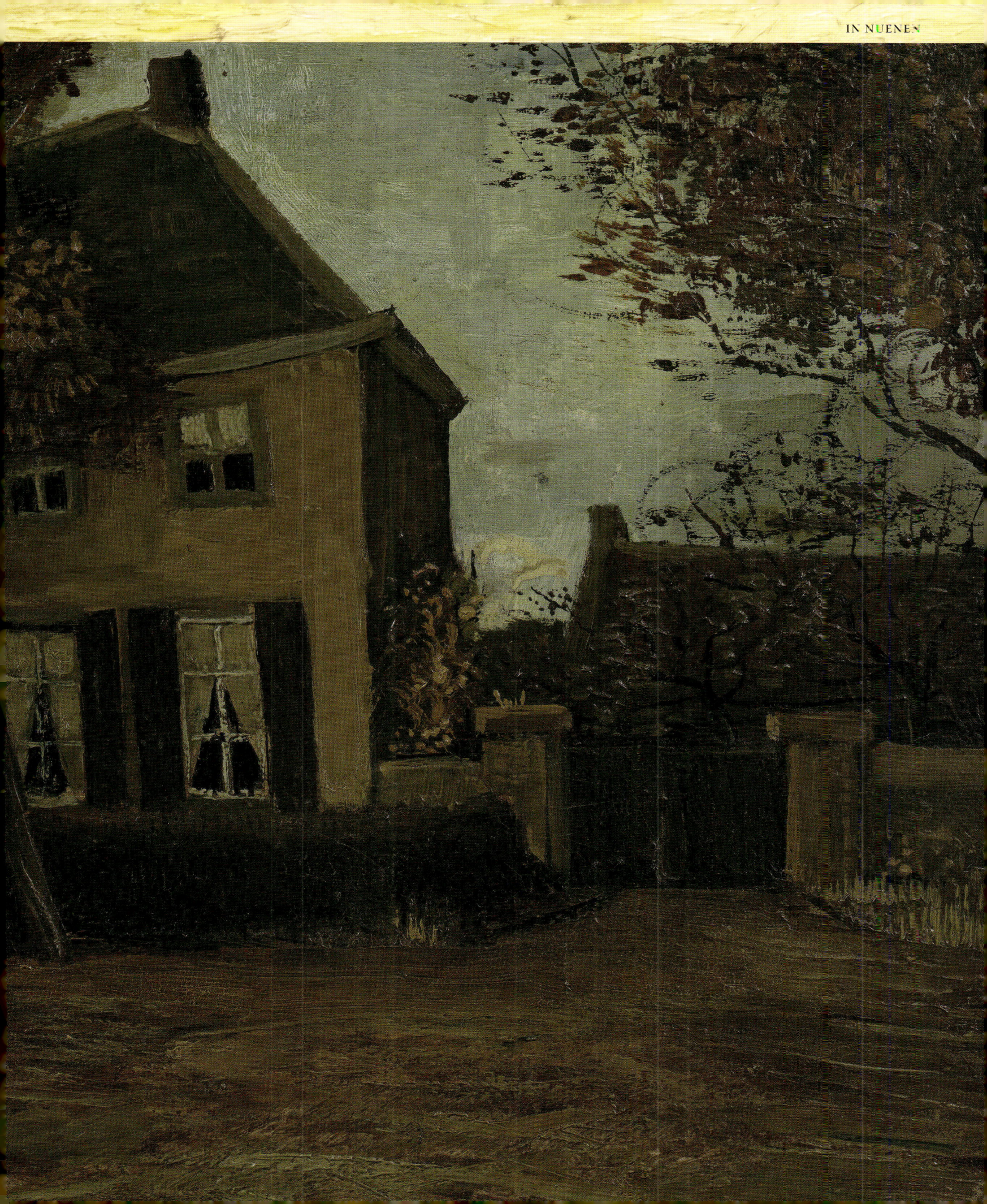

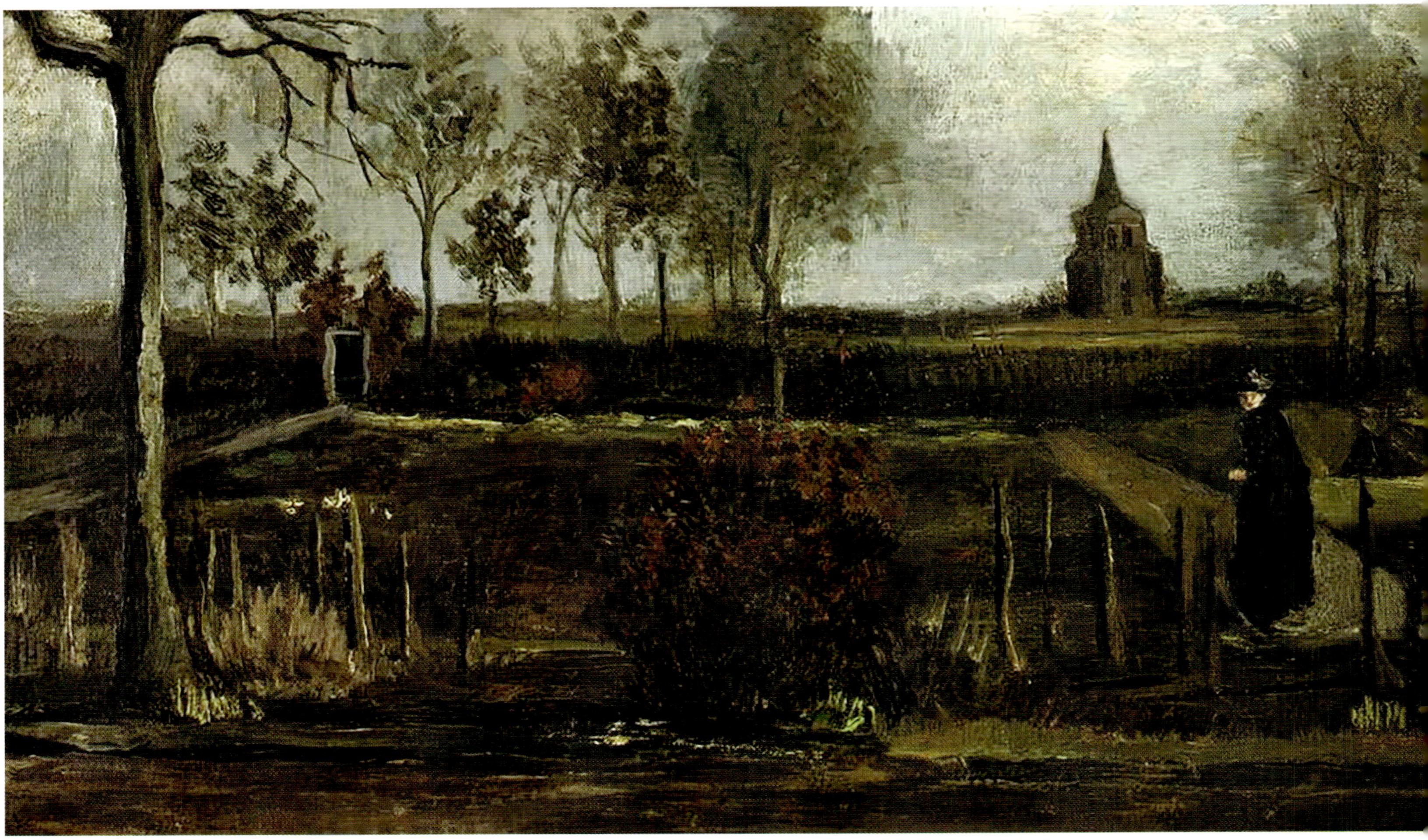

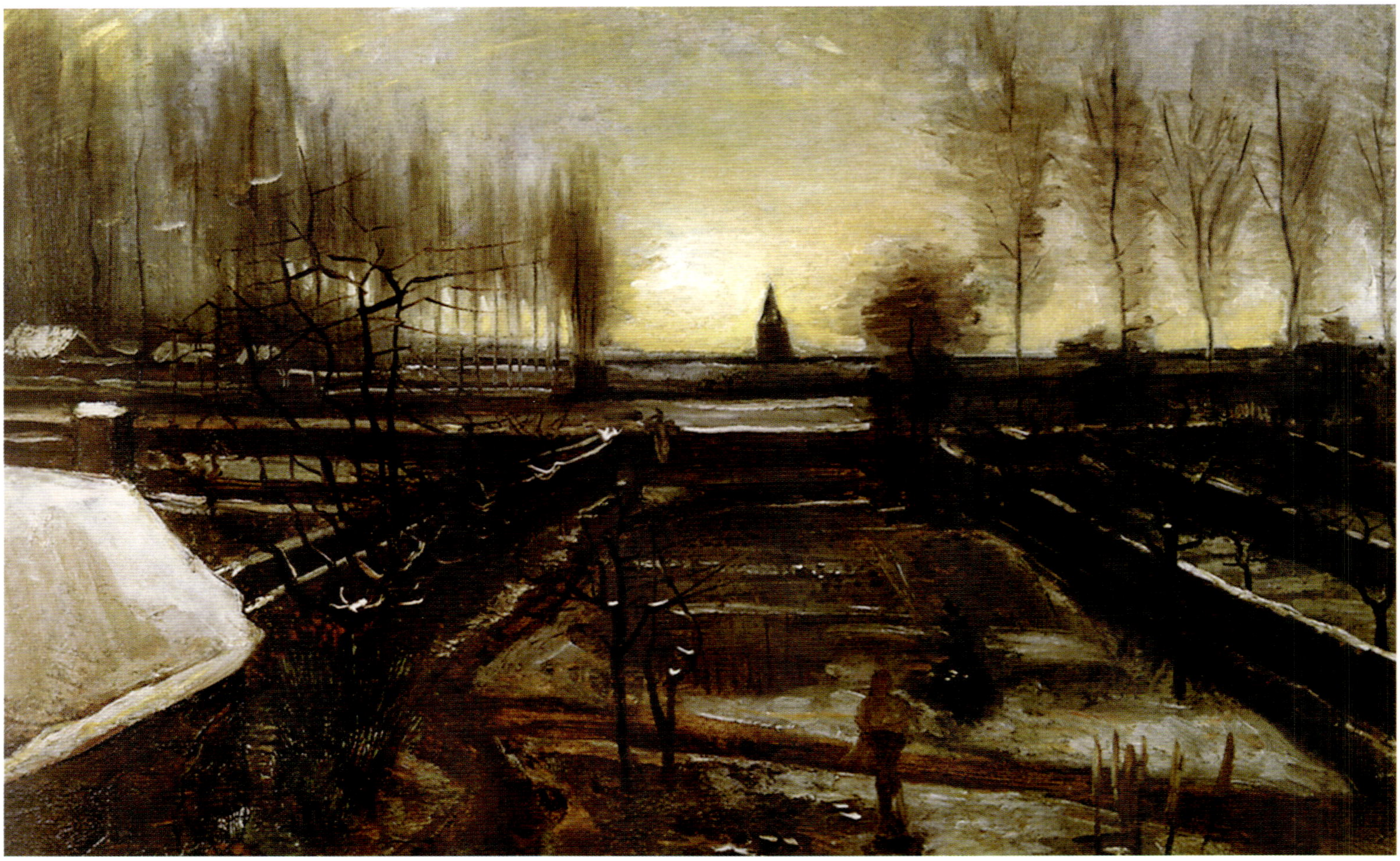

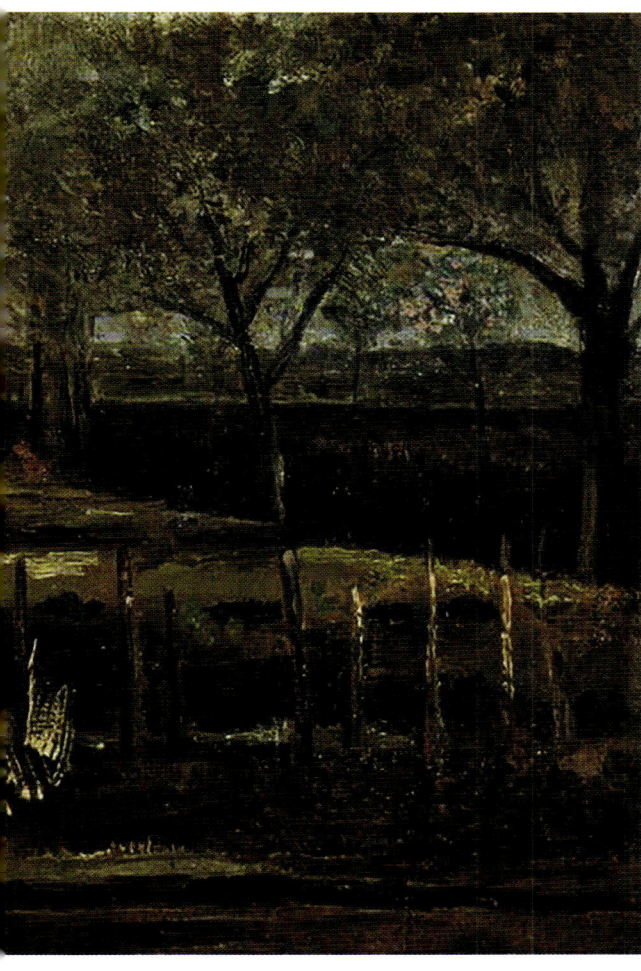

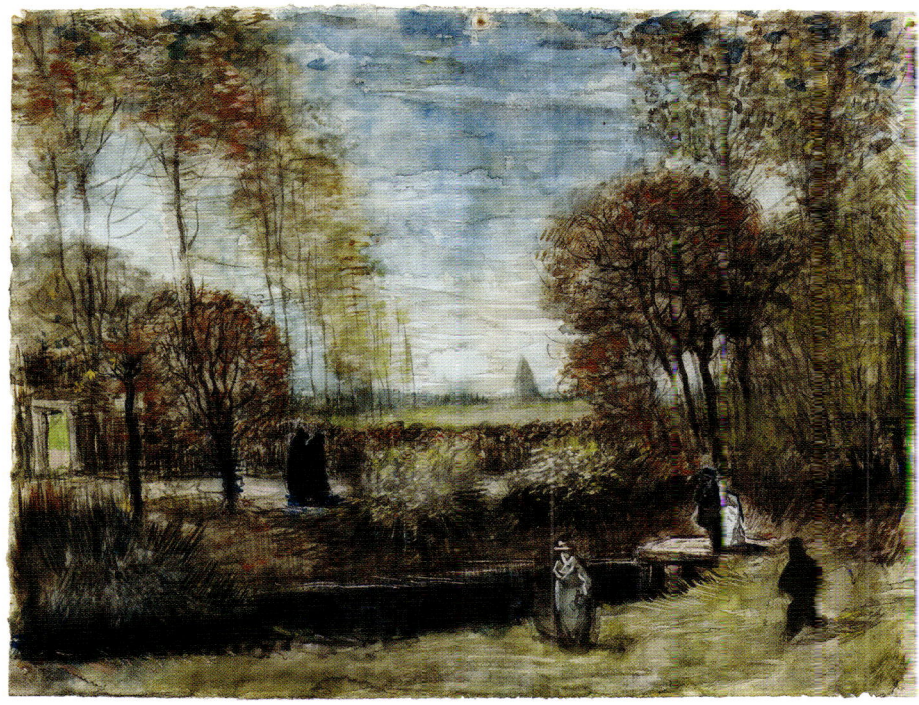

[ABOVE] *The Parsonage Garden at Nuenen* (May 1884). Oil on paper. Owned by Groninger Museum, Groningen.

The location of this painting is now unknown —it was stolen from the Singer Laren Museum on March 30, 2020.

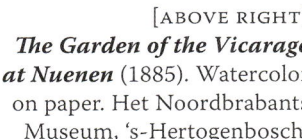

[ABOVE RIGHT] *The Garden of the Vicarage at Nuenen* (1885). Watercolor on paper. Het Noordbrabants Museum, 's-Hertogenbosch.

[RIGHT] *The Parsonage Garden at Nuenen in Winter* (1884). Pen and brown ink with lead white on paper. Museum of Fine Arts, Budapest.

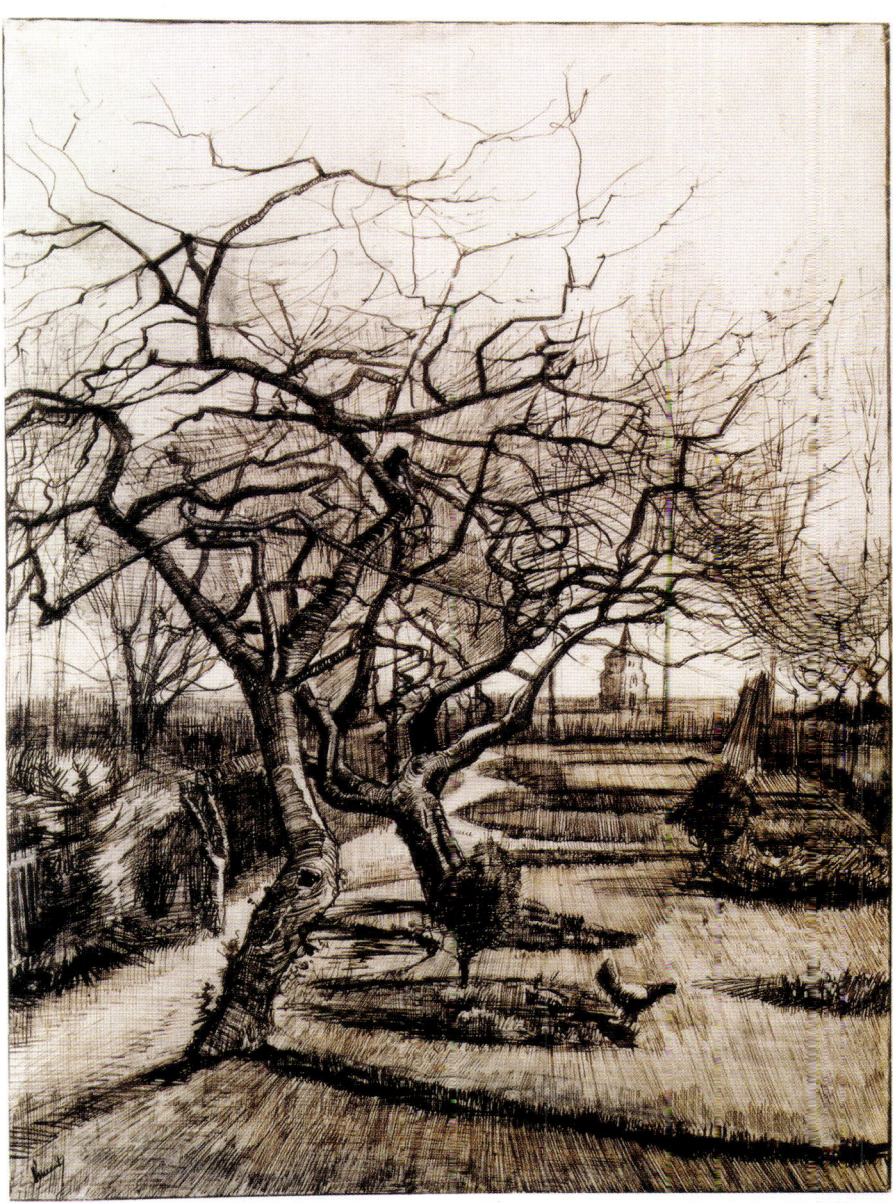

[OPPOSITE PAGE] *The Parsonage Garden in Nuenen in the Snow* (January 1885). Oil on canvas on panel. Armand Hammer Museum of Art, Los Angeles.

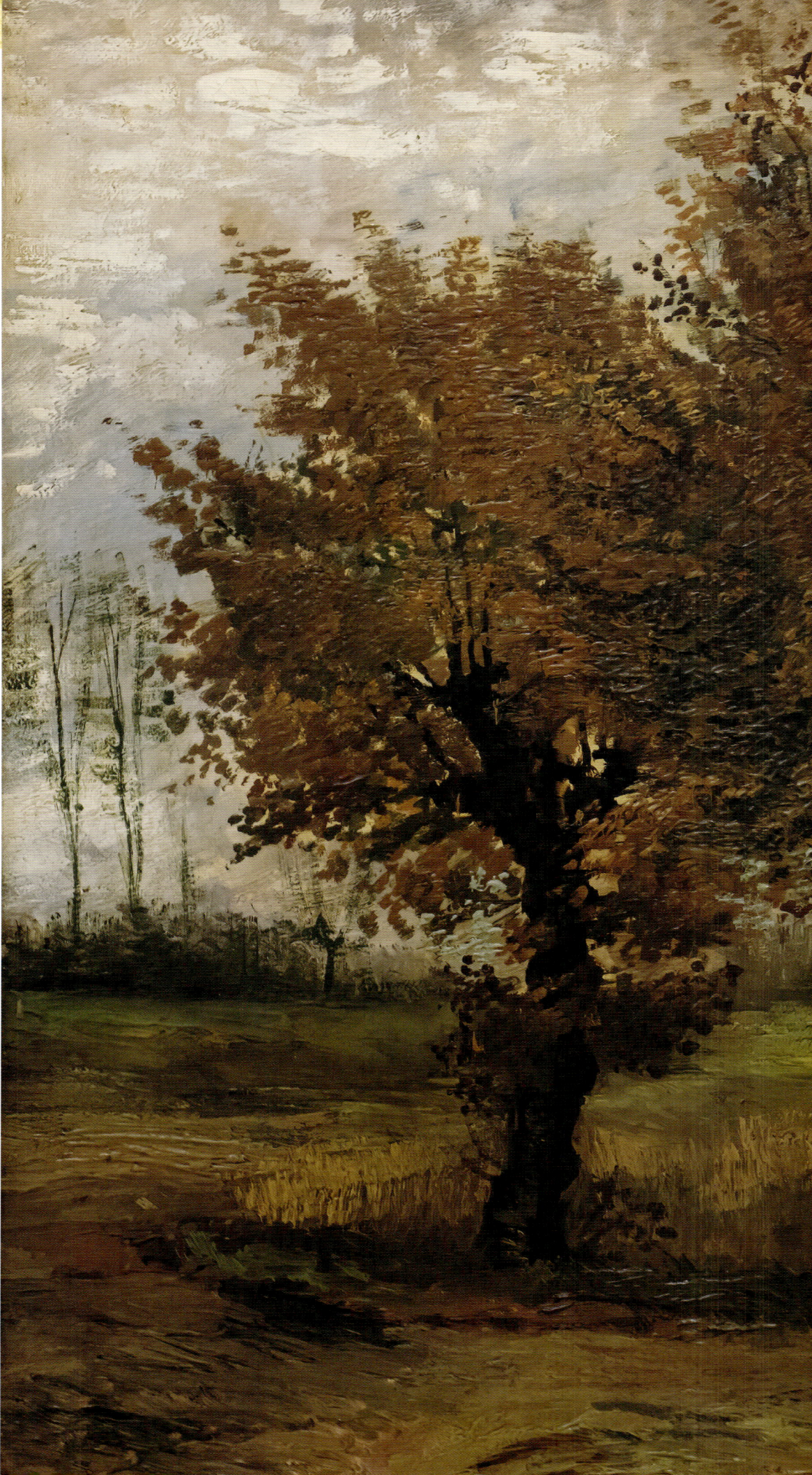

Autumn Landscape with Four Trees (November 1885). Oil on canvas. Kröller-Müller Museum, Otterlo.

This painting demonstrates Vincent's focus on improving his technique after reading French art Theorist Charles Blanc's Theory of the "law of simultaneous contrast," meaning colors can reinforce or diminish one another, depending on the combinations in which they are applied.

"*I've just kept on ceaselessly painting in order to learn painting.*"

~ VINCENT, TO HIS BROTHER THEO, NOVEMBER 1885

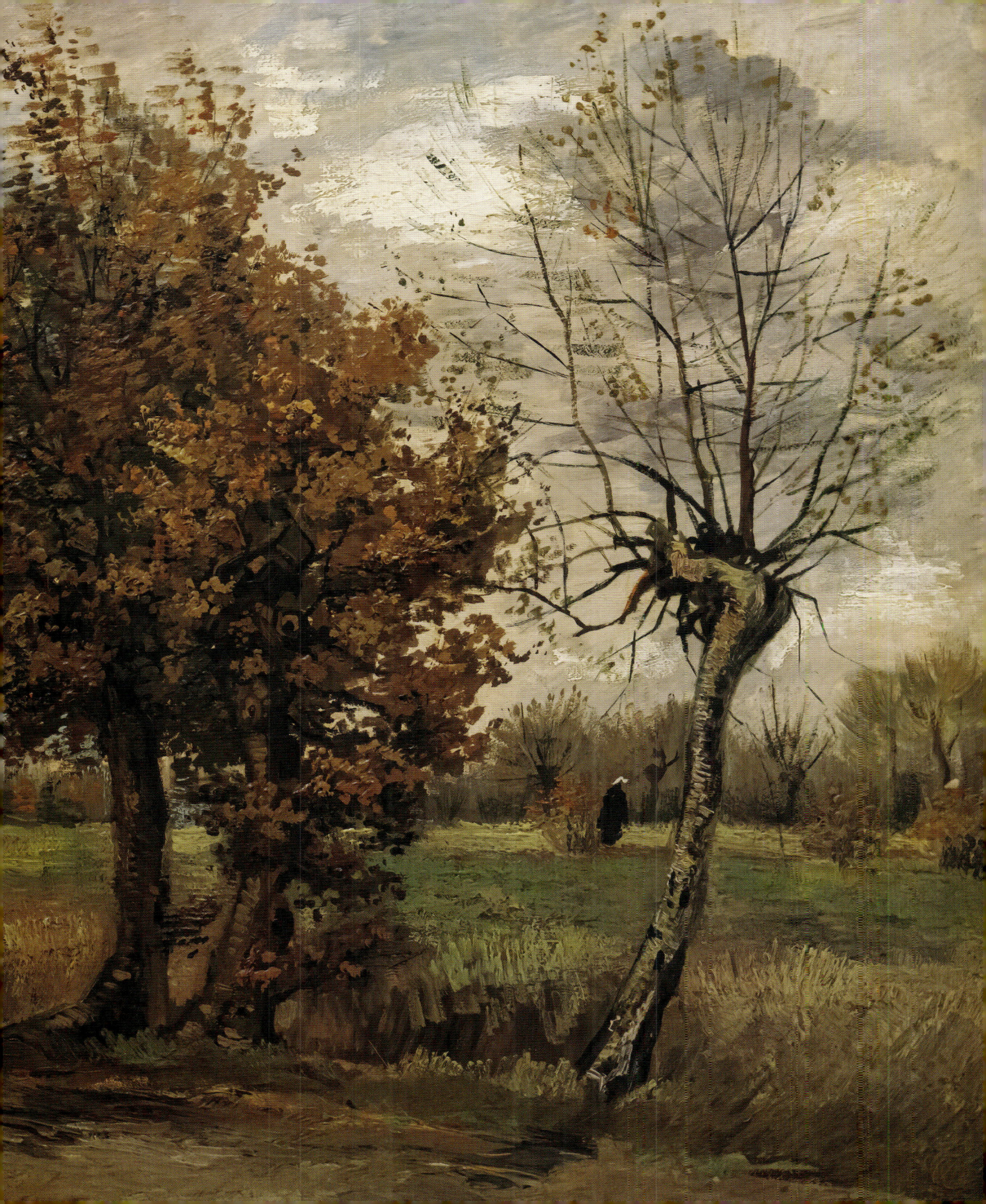

IN PARIS

Between March 1886 and February 1888, Vincent lived with his brother Theo in the north of Paris: first in rue de Laval, then in rue Lepic from June 1886. His work during this period shows influences of the Impressionists painters, lightening his palette, but retaining his more idiosyncratic techniques.

[RIGHT]
The Restaurant de la Sirène in Asnières (1887).
Oil on canvas. Musée d'Orsay, Paris.

Vincent chose the popular restaurant de la Sirène as a subject of this painting. Asnières, originally a rural area that took its name from the Latin for "donkey," was in the northwest of Paris, a neighborhood swallowed by the burgeoning Parisian suburbs. Showing signs of the influence of Impressionism, the painting's rich colors are enhanced by white brushstrokes in parallel hatching.

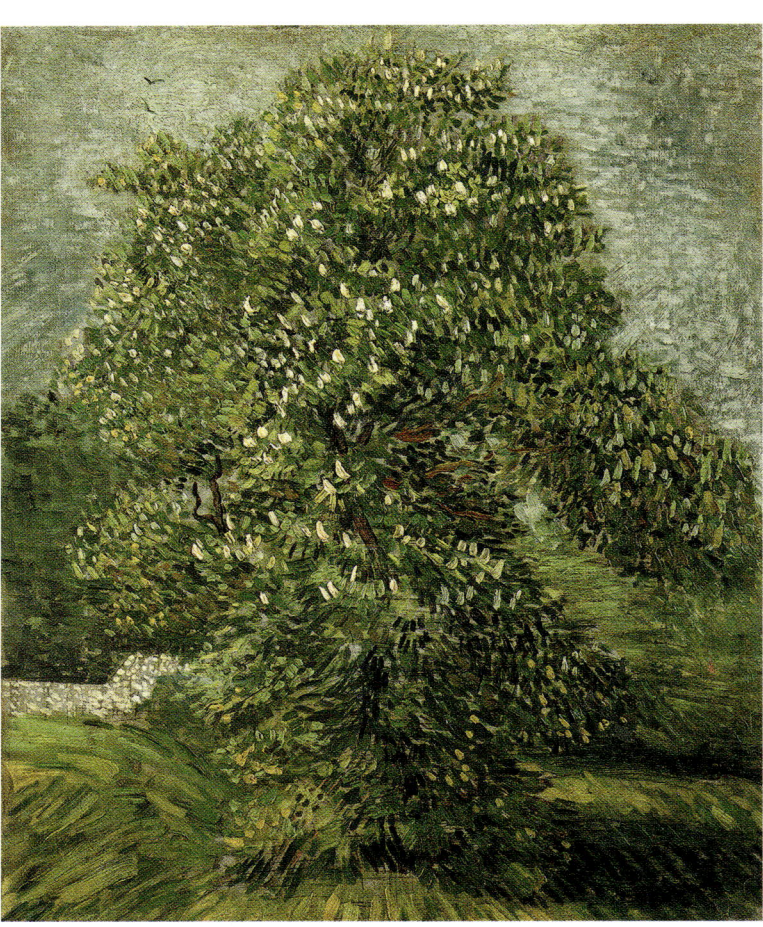

Horse Chestnut Tree in Blossom (May 1887).
Oil on canvas. Van Gogh Museum, Amsterdam
(Vincent van Gogh Foundation).

Research has revealed that this picture was painted on top of a previous one.

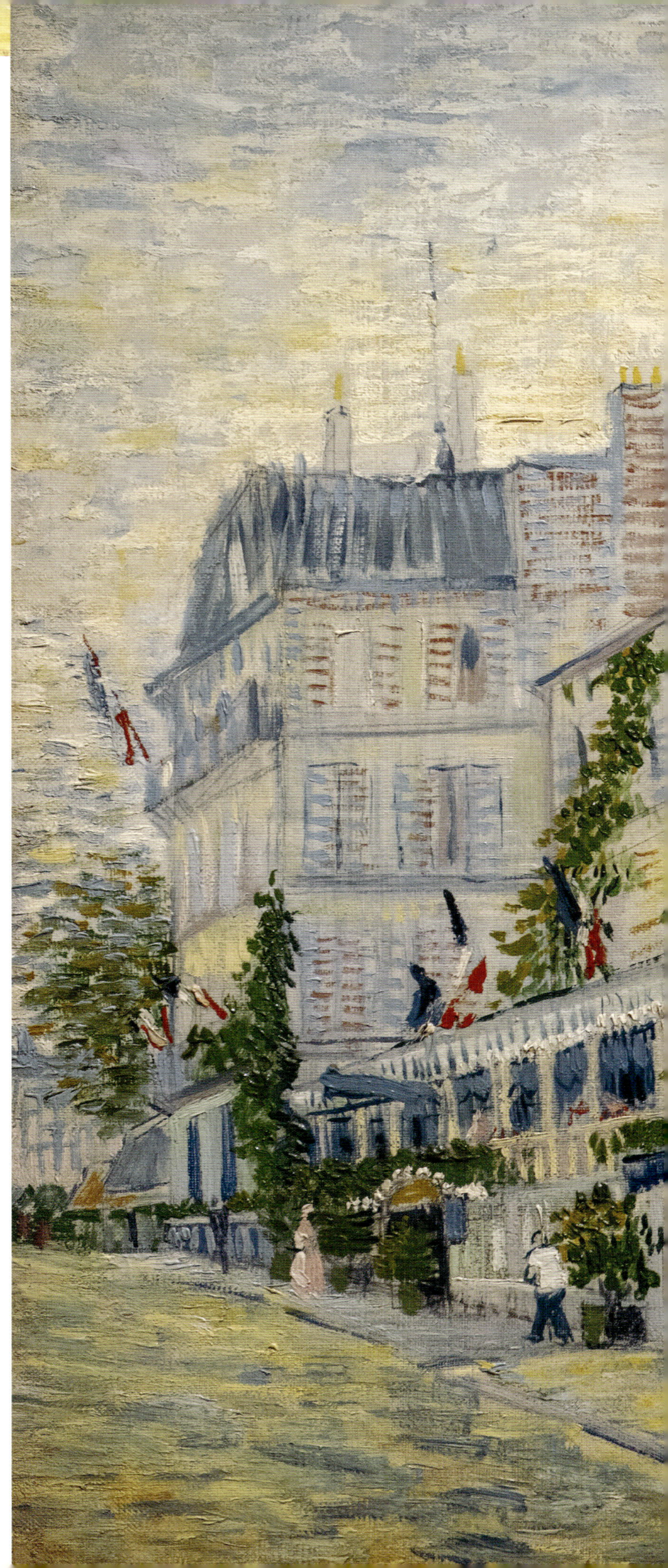

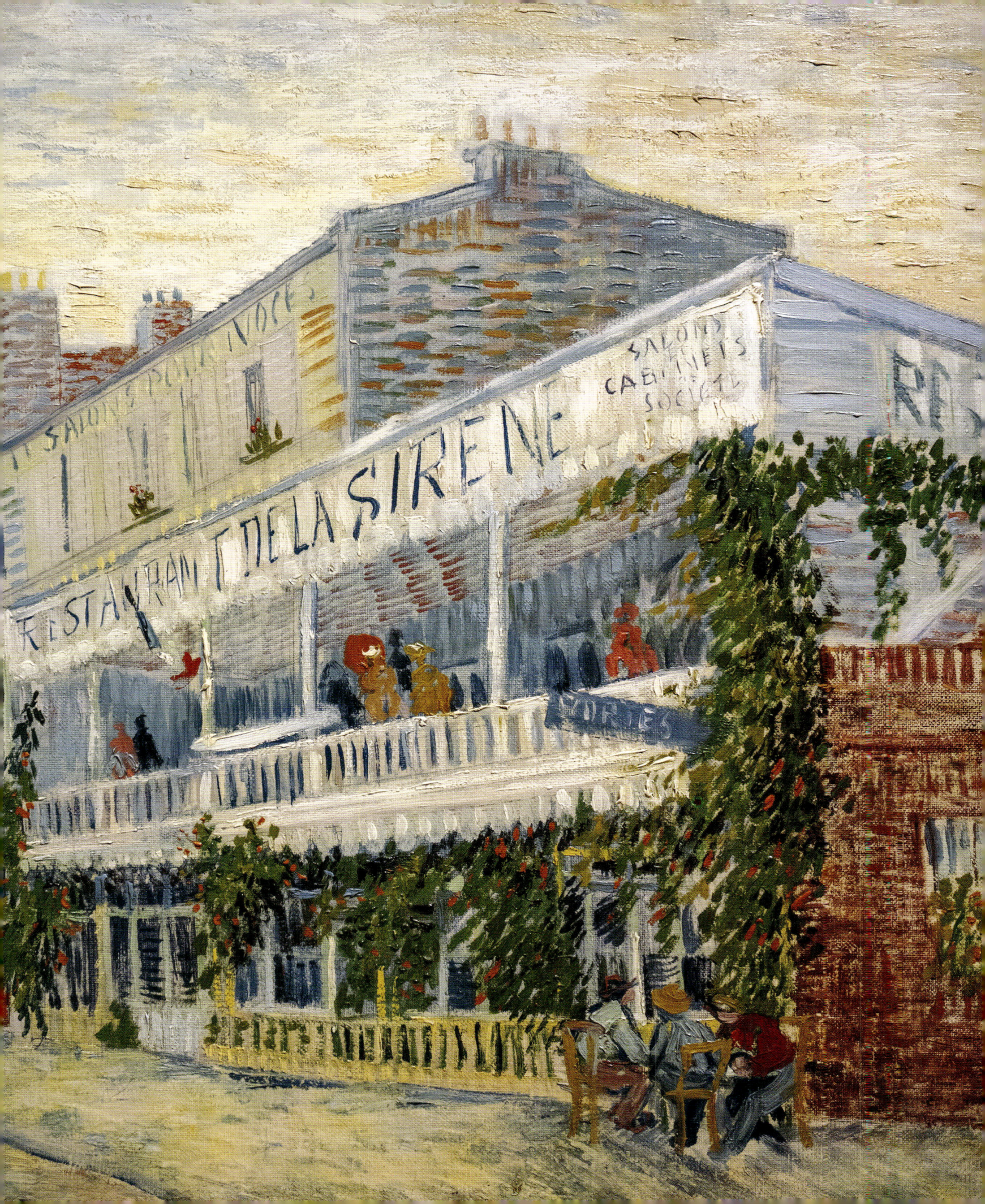

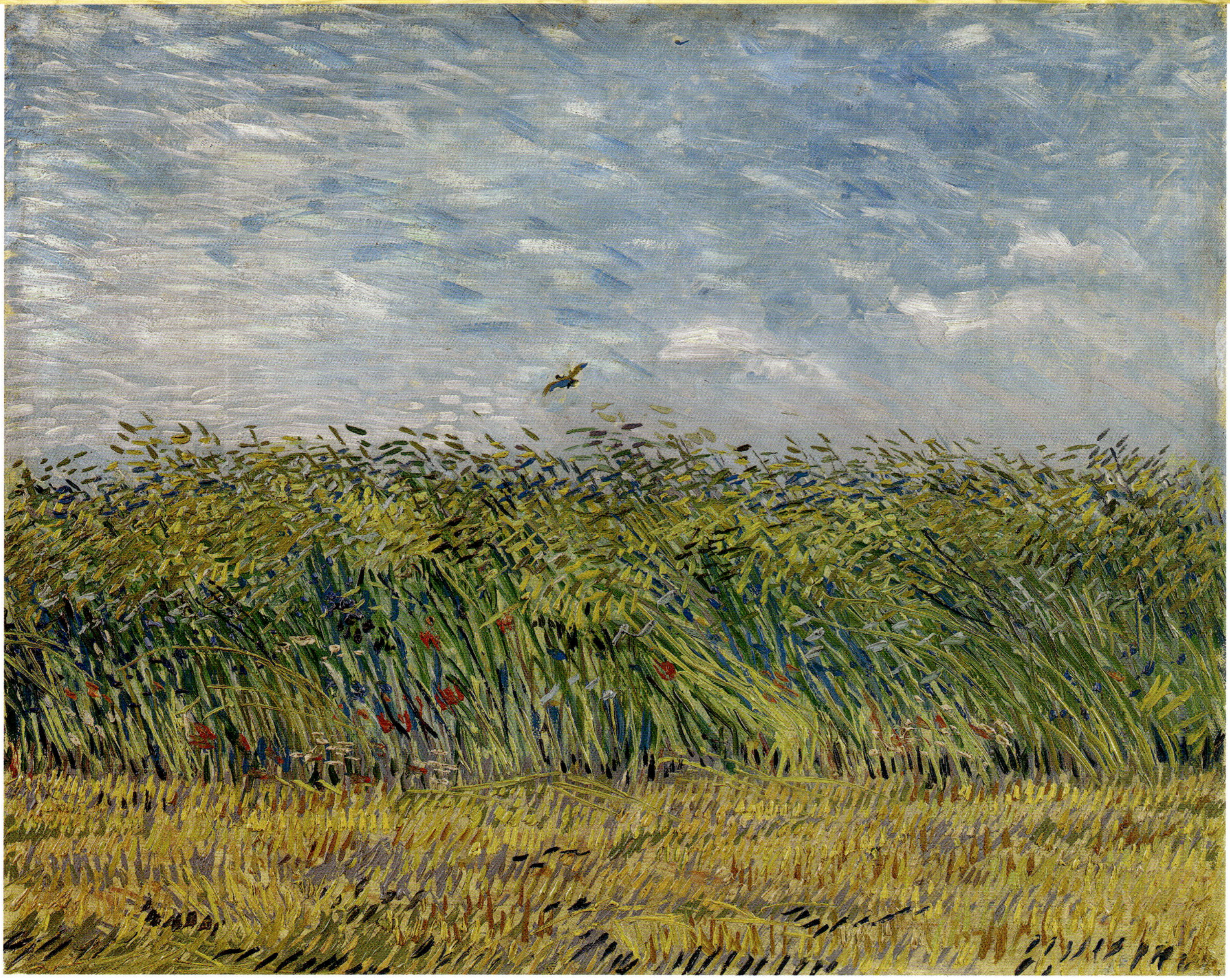

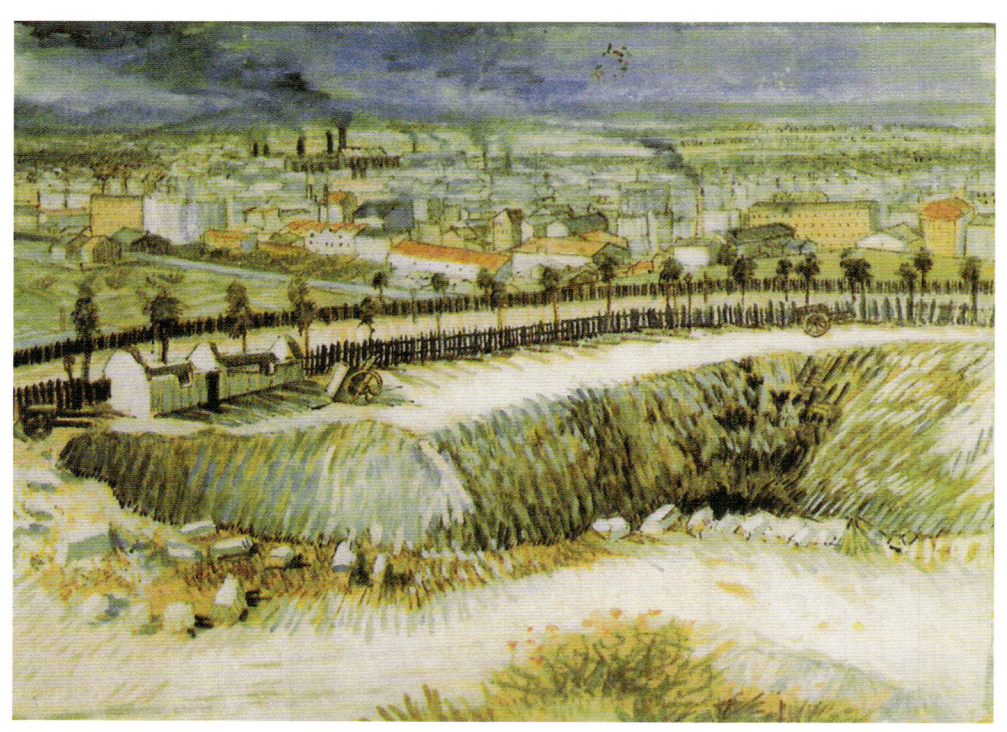

"*There is but one Paris and however hard living may be here, and if it became worse and harder even—the French air clears up the brain and does good —a world of good.*"

[OPPOSITE PAGE TOP]
Wheat Field with a Lark (Summer 1887).
Oil on canvas. Van Gogh Museum, Amsterdam
(Vincent van Gogh Foundation).

[OPPOSITE PAGE BOTTOM]
Outskirts of Paris near Montmartre (1887).
Watercolor. Stedelijk Museum, Amsterdam.

[RIGHT]
On the outskirts of Paris (Spring 1887).
Oil on canvas. Private collection.

[BELOW]
By the Seine (May–July 1887). Oil on
canvas. Van Gogh Museum, Amsterdam
(Vincent van Gogh Foundation).

*During his Paris days, Vincent spent much
time wandering the area with a field easel
and painting materials with him. He first
sketched this spot in the river Seine in pencil,
and the lines are still visible in the painting.*

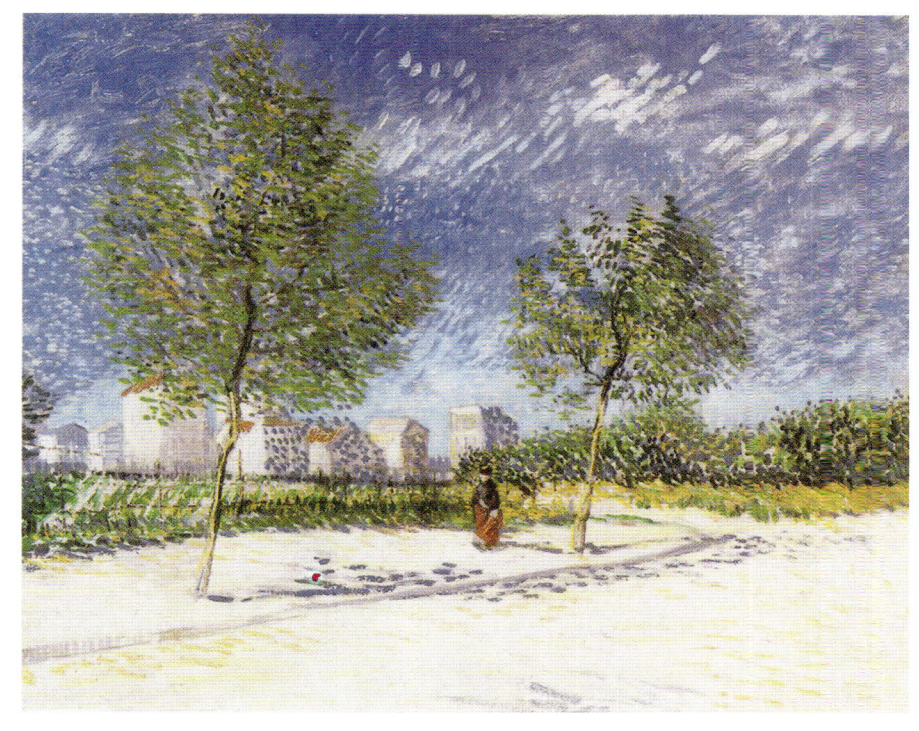

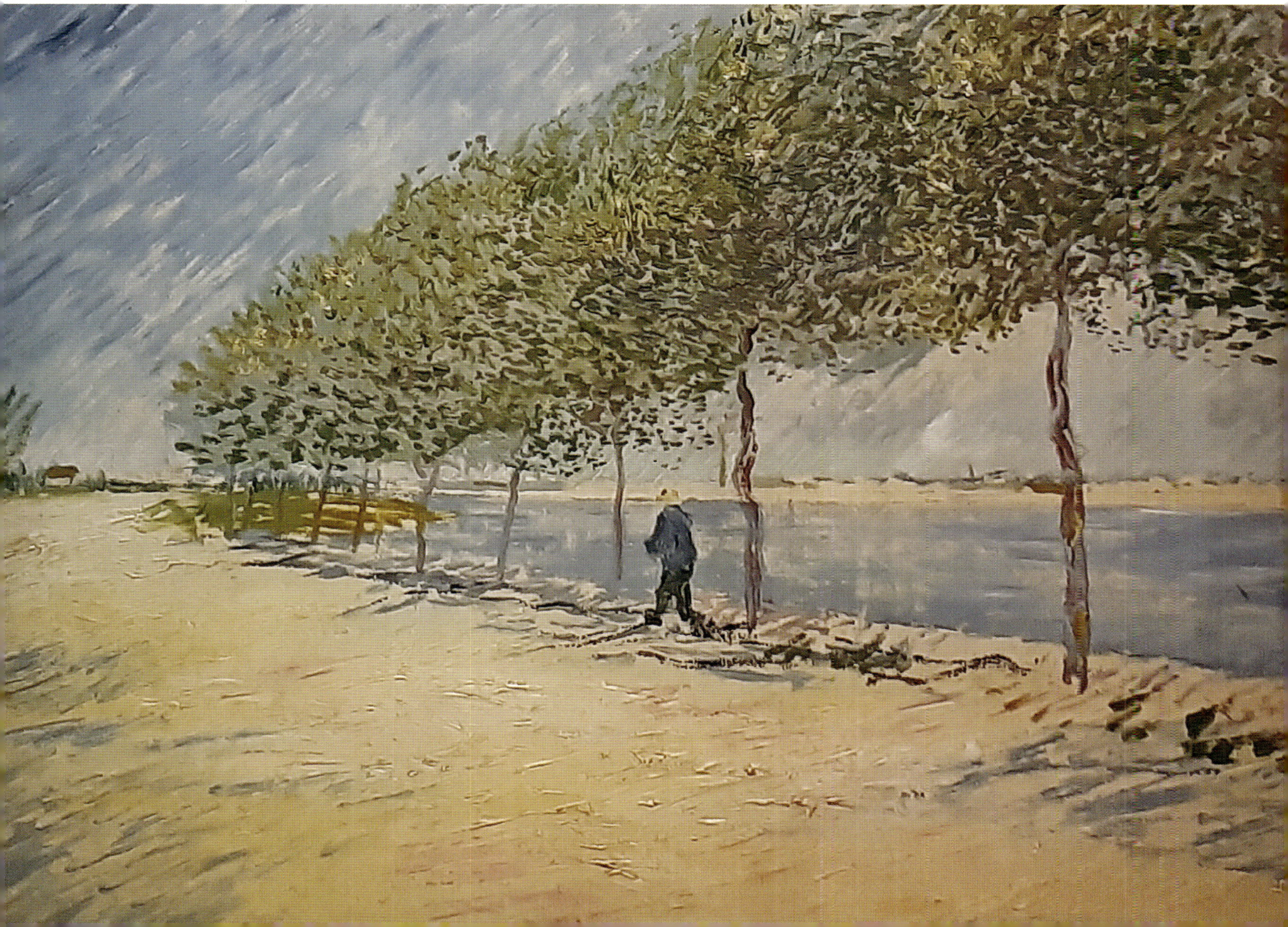

LIFE IN MONTMARTRE

Perched on the top of a small hill in the 18th arrondissement, the Parisian district of Montmartre brings to mind the vibrant artists' enclave of the 19th century. It is no surprise that Vincent and his brother Theo shared an apartment at the foot of the hill of Montmartre. One of the district's landmarks, the Moulin de la Galette, was the site of a dance hall and terrace and was a favorite with painters, such as Renoir, who immortalized it in *Bal du moulin de la Galette* in 1876. Vincent, too, chose this site as a subject, completing several paintings of the windmill. These windmill paintings are a subset of what has become known as the Montmartre series.

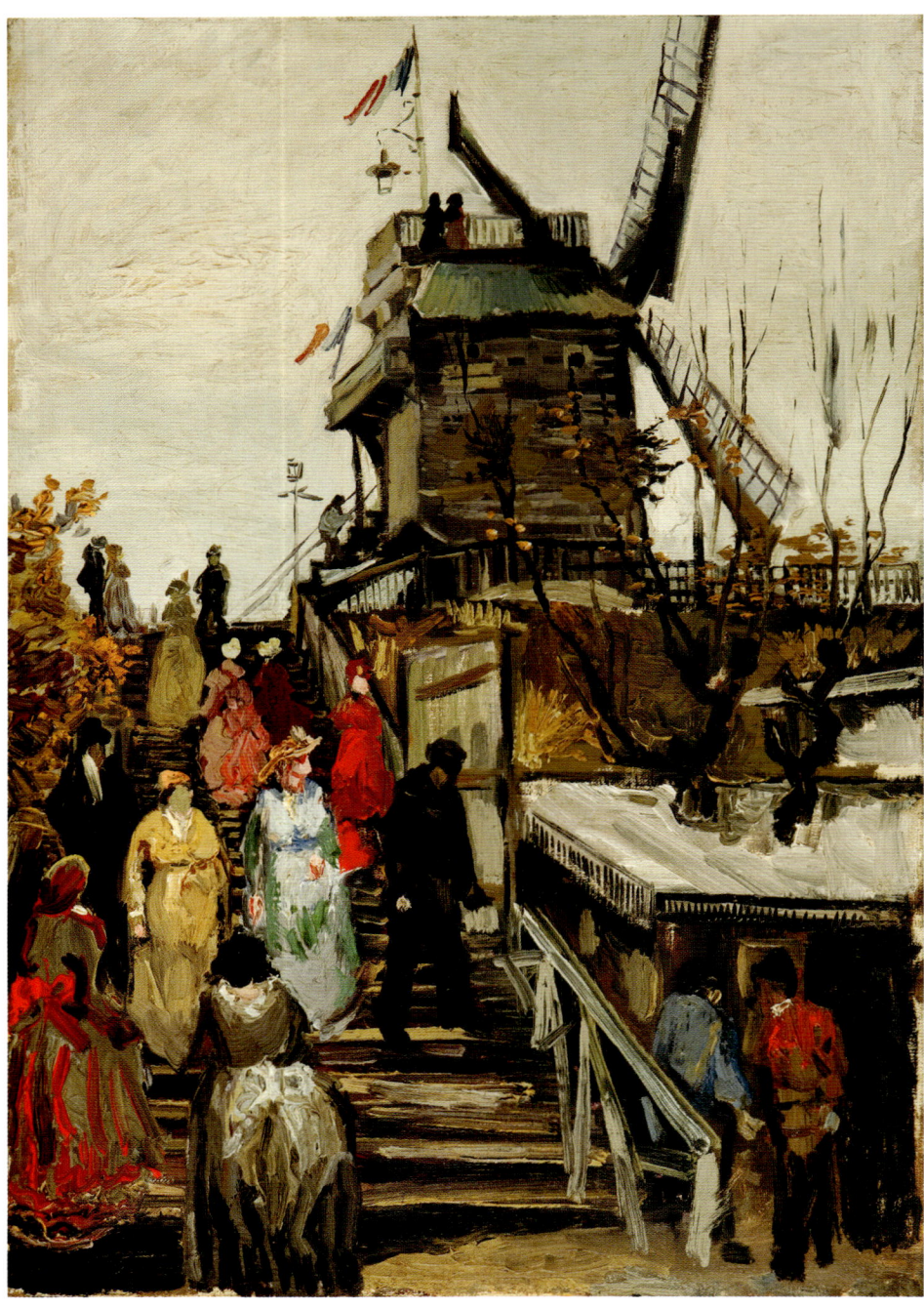

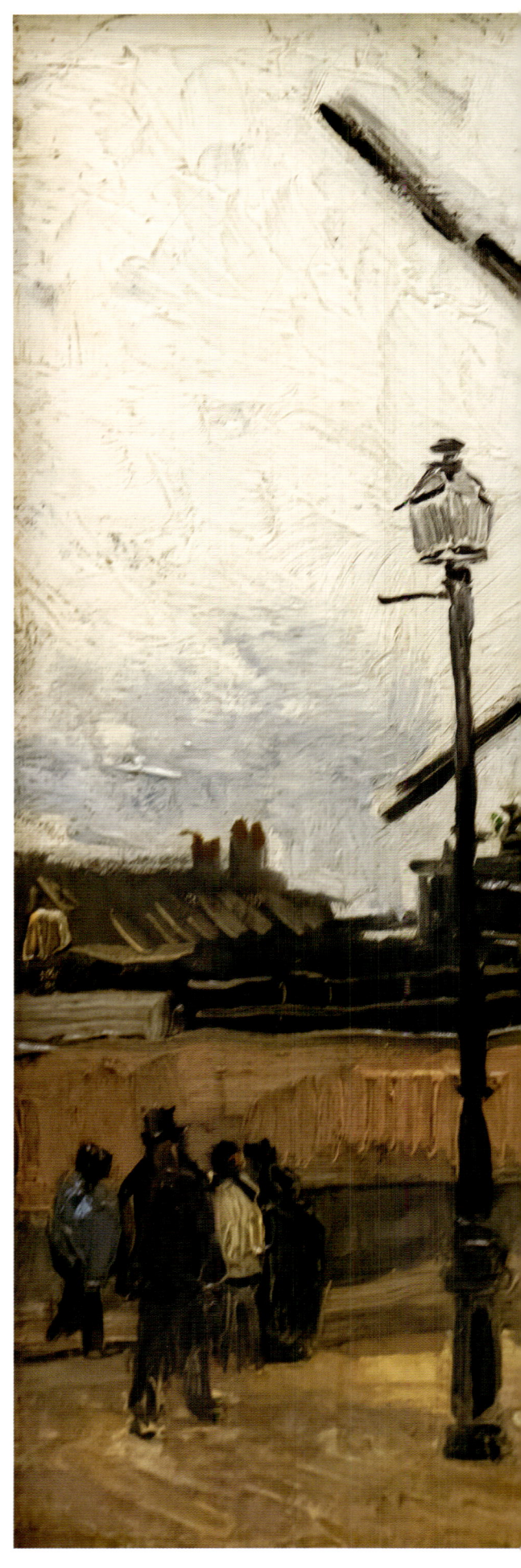

[ABOVE]
The Blute-Fin Mill (Summer 1886).
Oil on canvas. Museum de Fundatie,
Zwolle, Netherlands.

[RIGHT]
Le Moulin de la Galette
(1886). Oil on canvas.
Neue Nationalgalerie, Berlin.

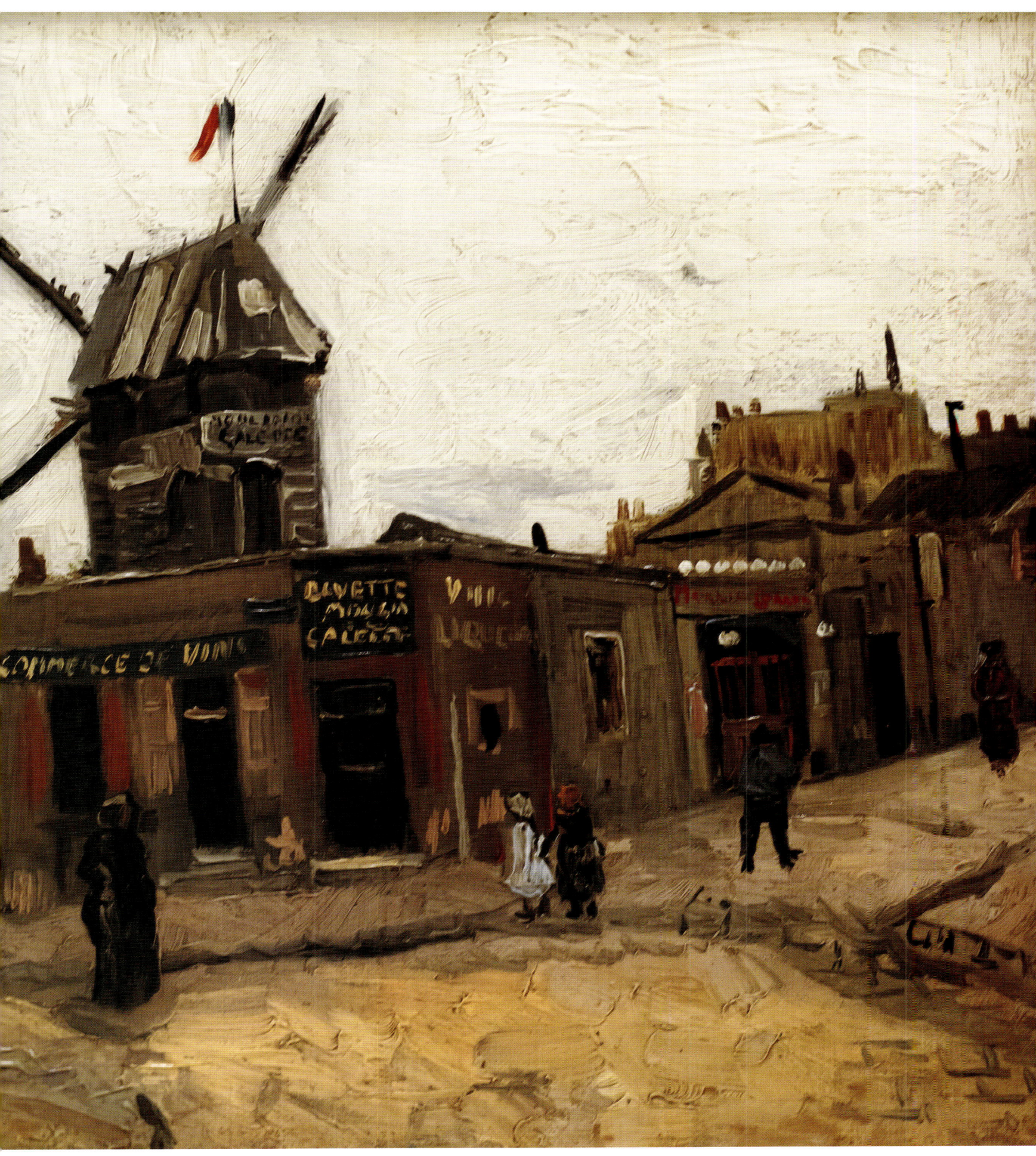

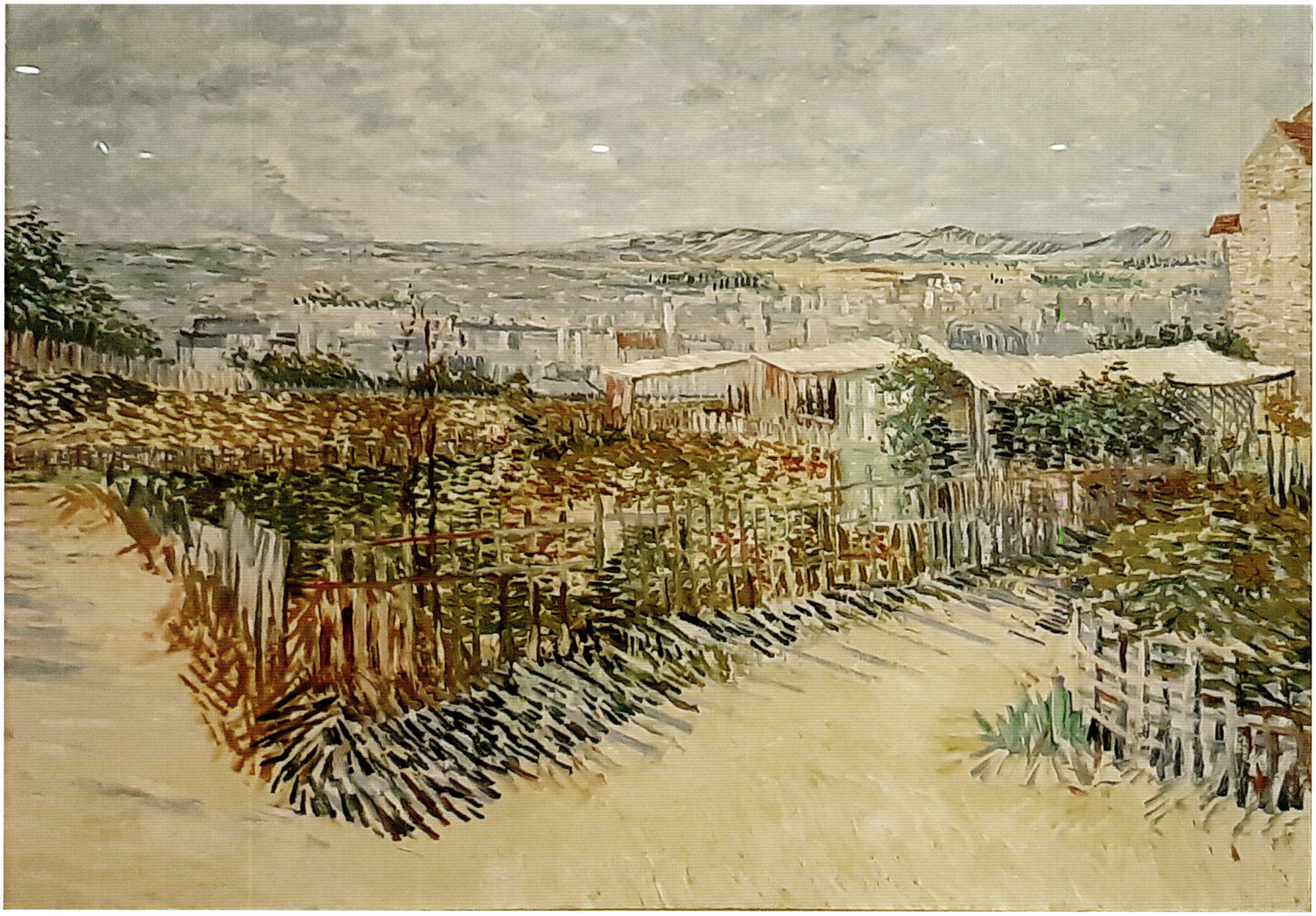

Montmartre: Behind the Moulin de la Galette. (July 1887). Oil on canvas. Van Gogh Museum, Amsterdam (Vincent van Gogh Foundation).

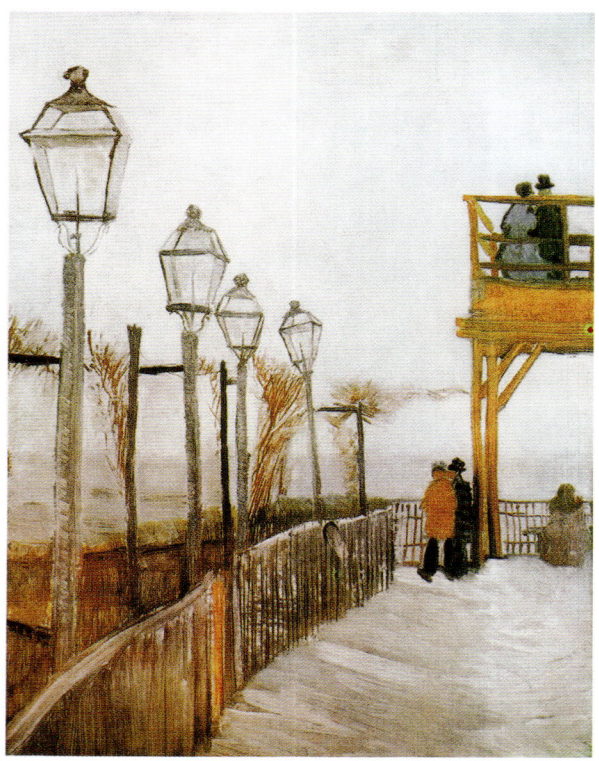

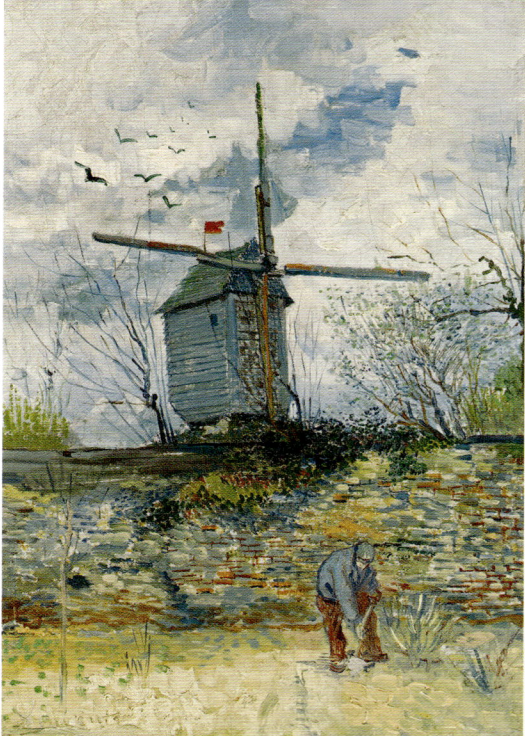

[FAR LEFT]
Terrace and Observation Deck at the Moulin de Blute-Fin (1886). Art Institute of Chicago.

Le Moulin de la Galette was also known as the Blute-Fin Windmill.

[LEFT]
Le Moulin de la Galette (Autumn 1886). Oil on canvas. Private collection.

[OPPOSITE PAGE]
Le Moulin de la Galette (The Blute-Fin Windmill, Montmartre) (Summer 1886). Oil on canvas. Kelvingrove Art Gallery and Museum, Glasgow.

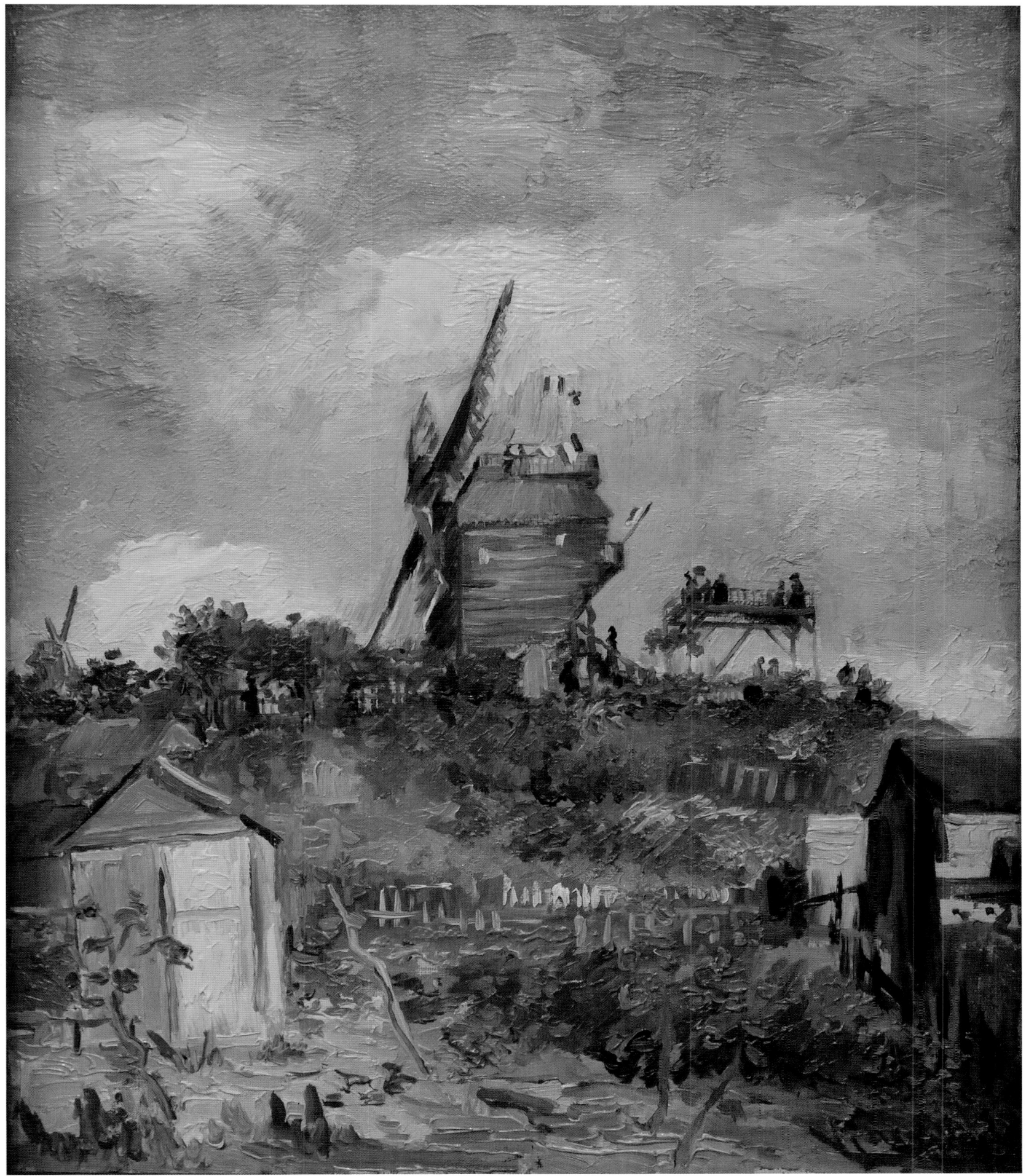

[RIGHT] *Terrace of a Cafe on Montmartre (La Guinguette)* (1886). Oil on canvas. Musée d'Orsay, Paris.

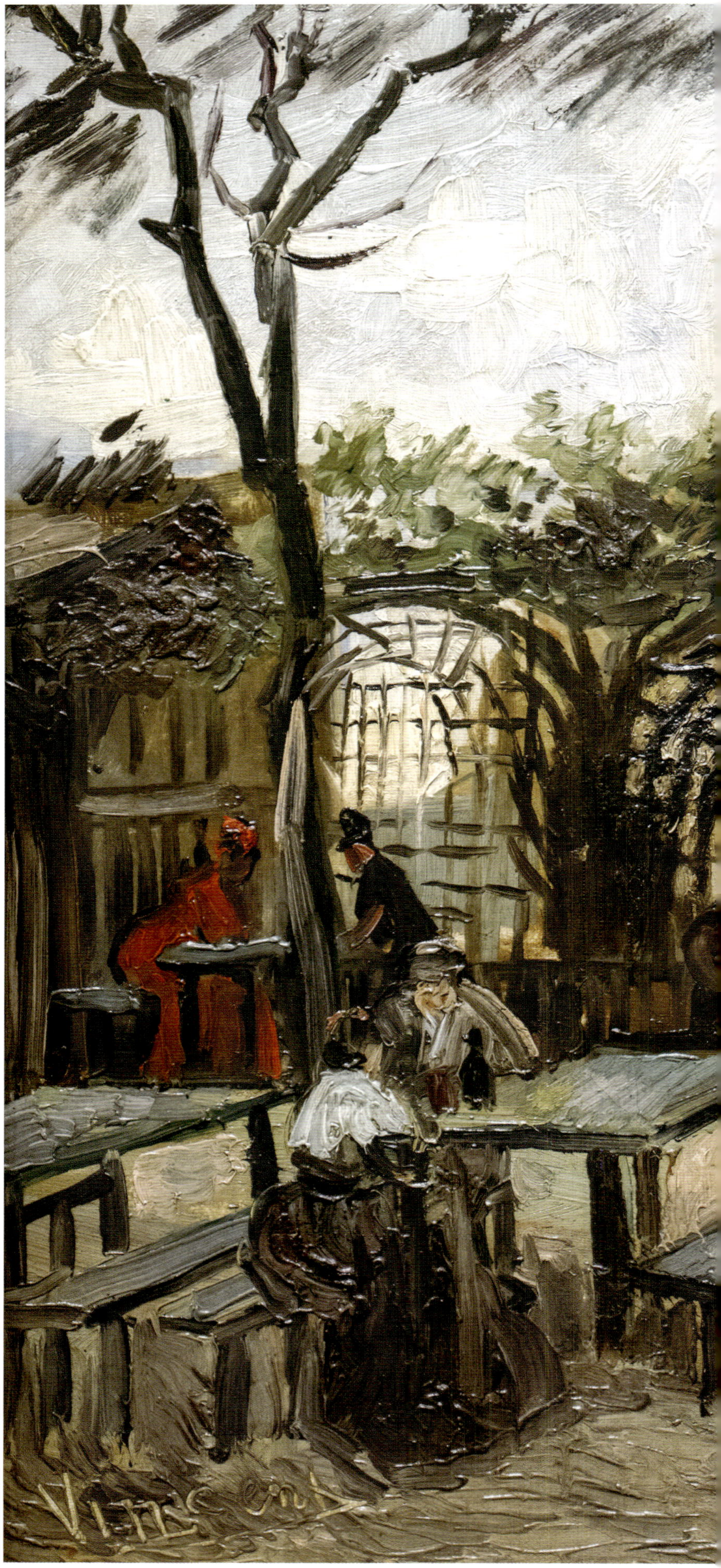

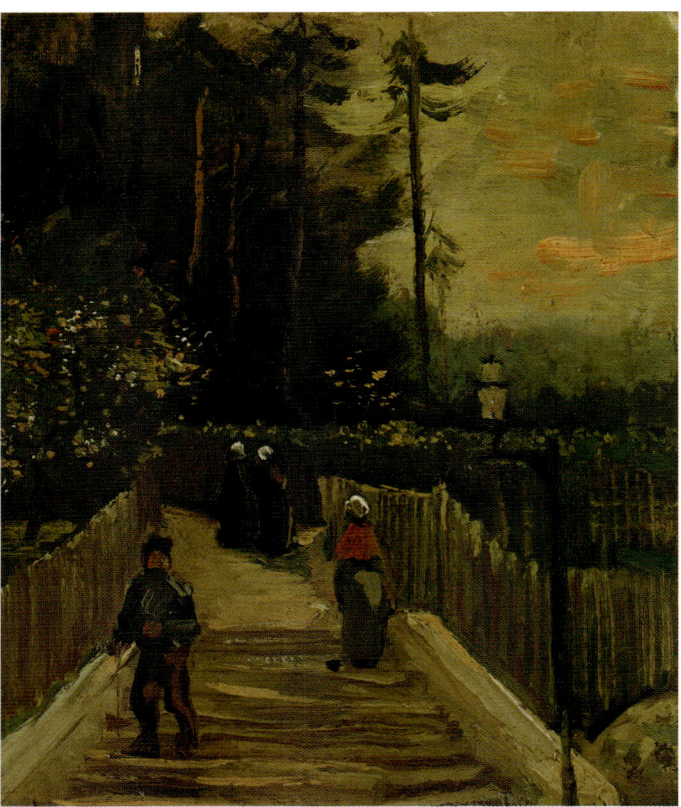

Sloping Path in Montmartre (1886). Oil on canvas. Van Gogh Museum, Amsterdam (Vincent van Gogh Foundation).

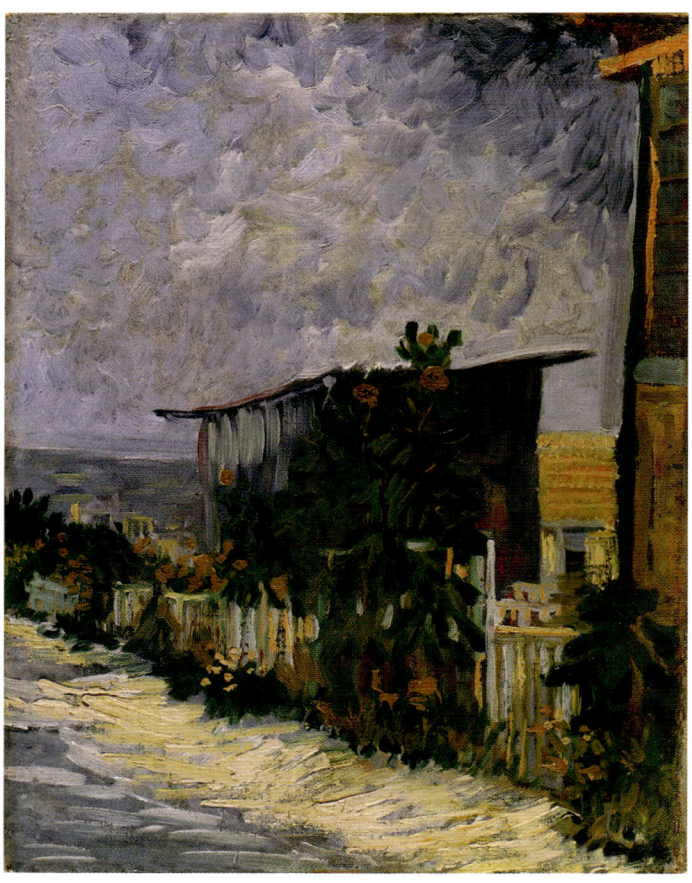

Shelter on Montmartre (1886). Oil on canvas. Fine Arts Museums of San Francisco.

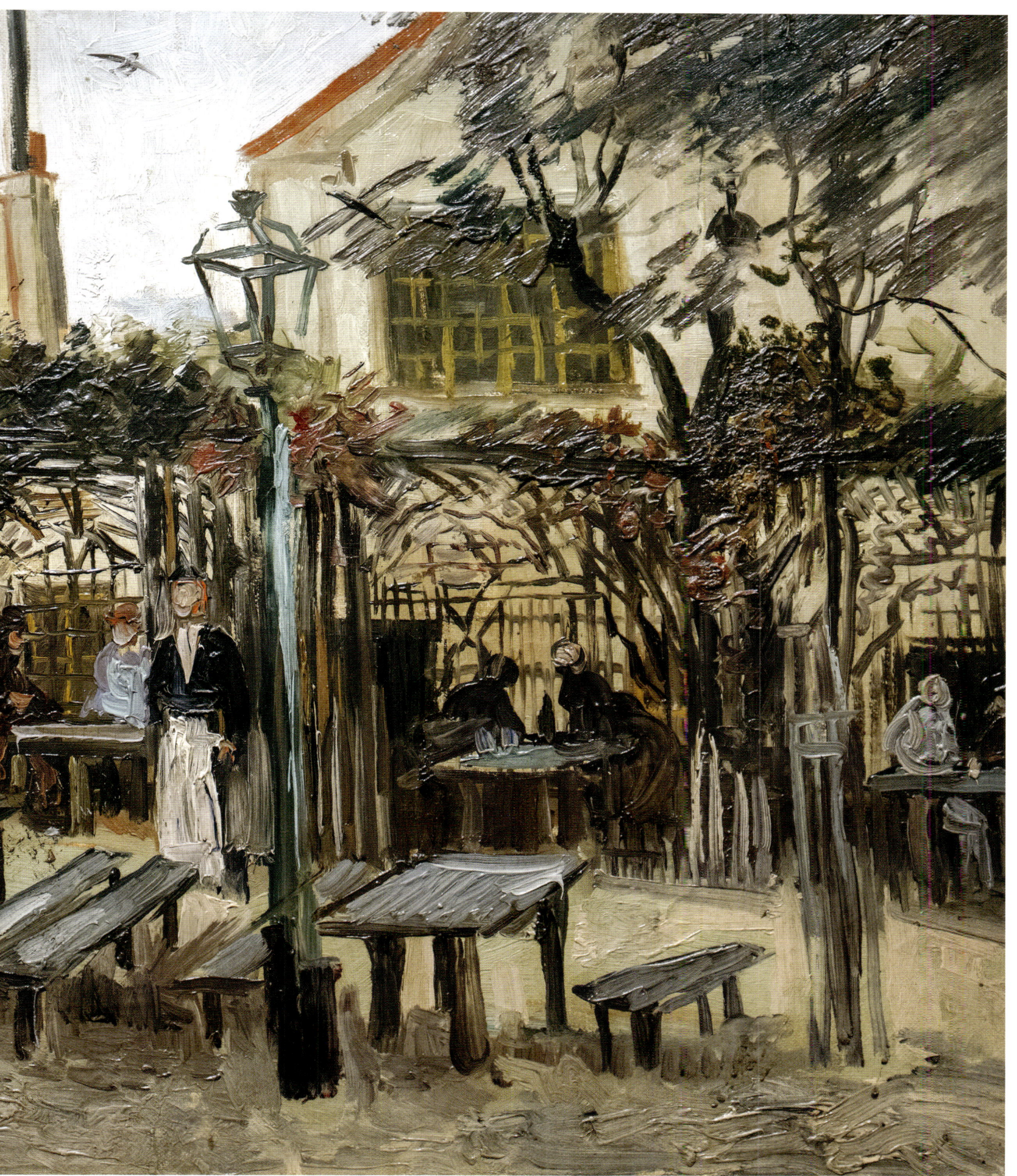

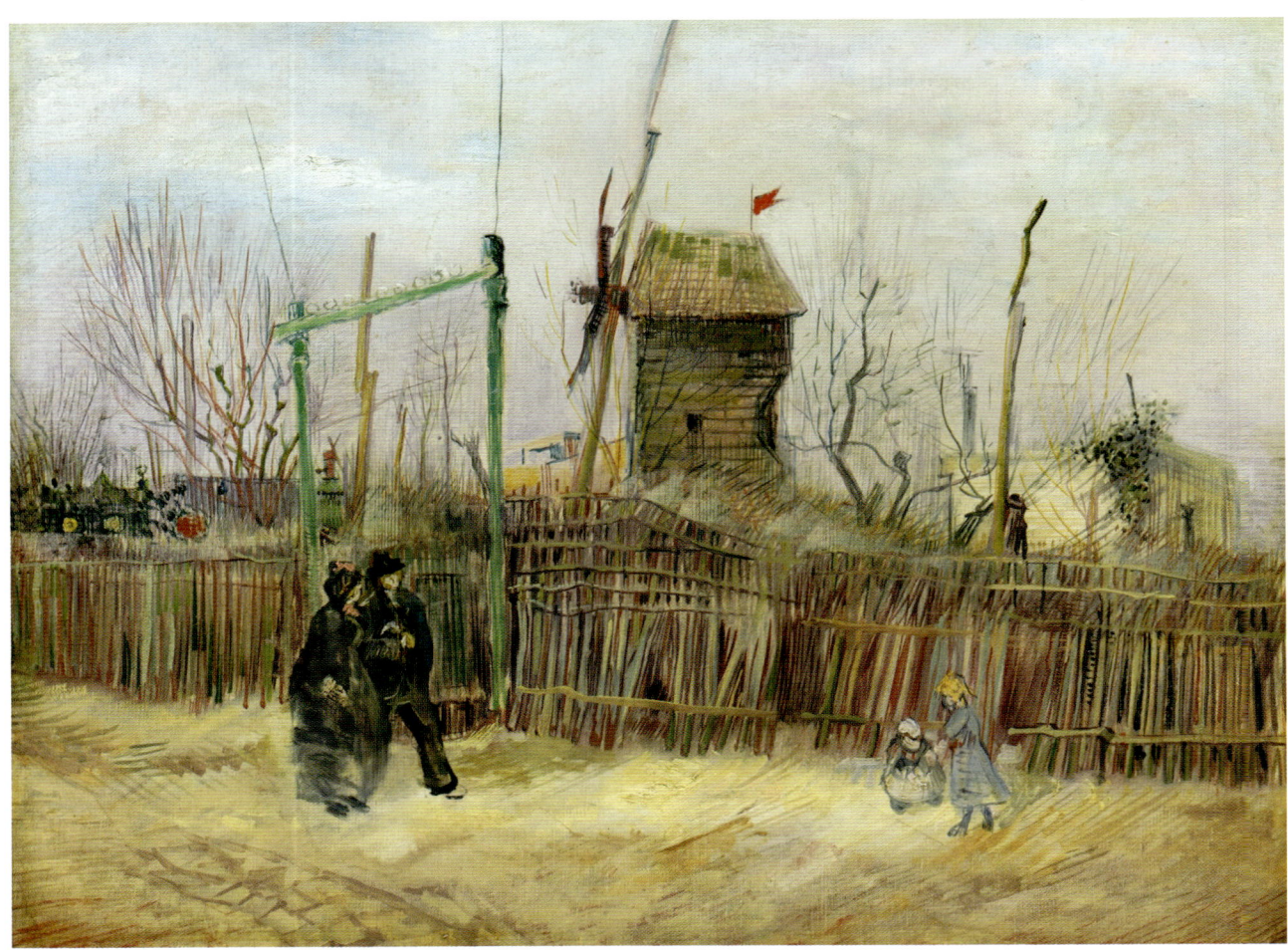

[LEFT]
Street Scene in Montmartre (1887). Oil on canvas. Private collection.

[BELOW]
View of Paris from Montmartre (1886). Oil on canvas. Kunstmuseum Basel, Switzerland.

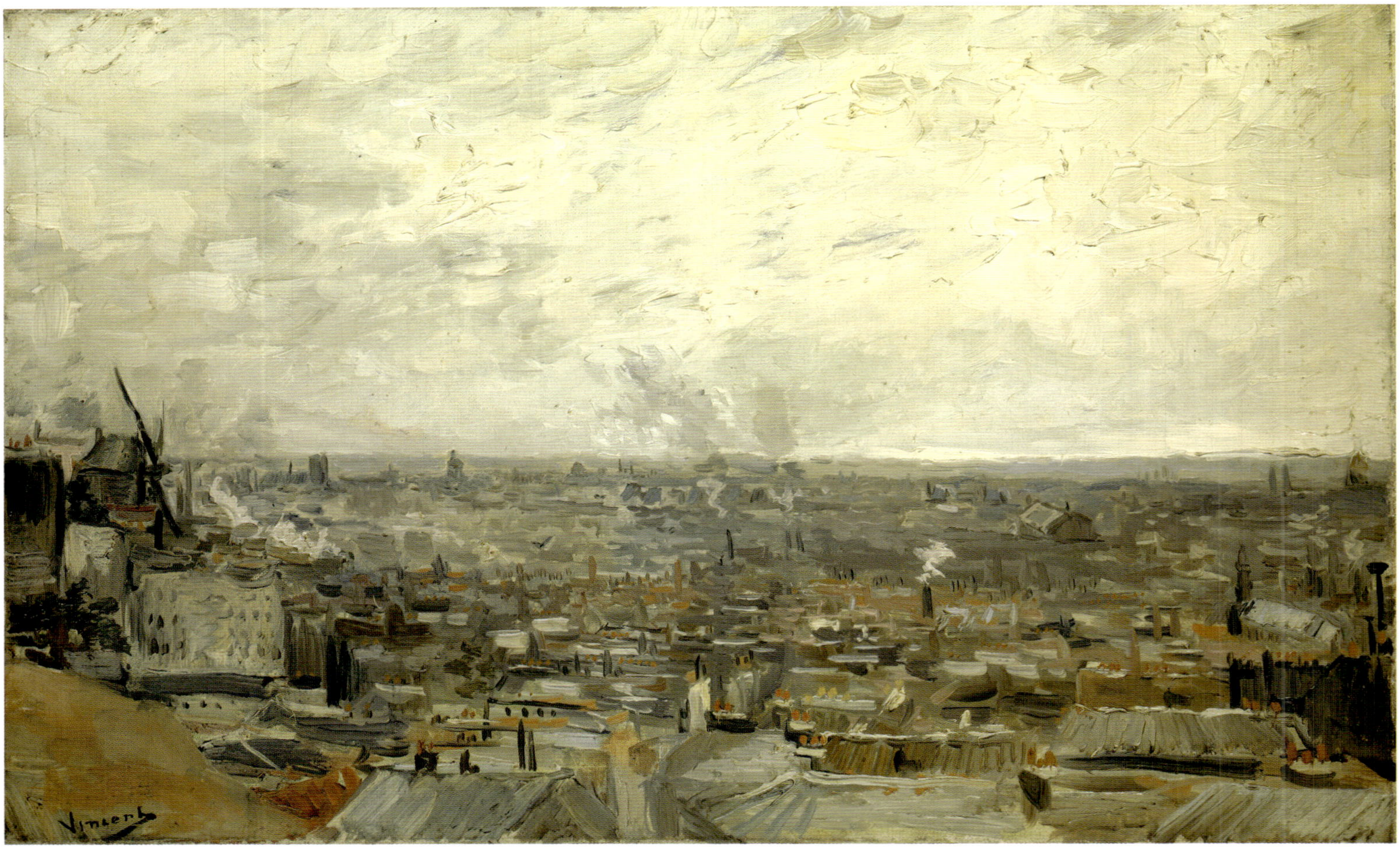

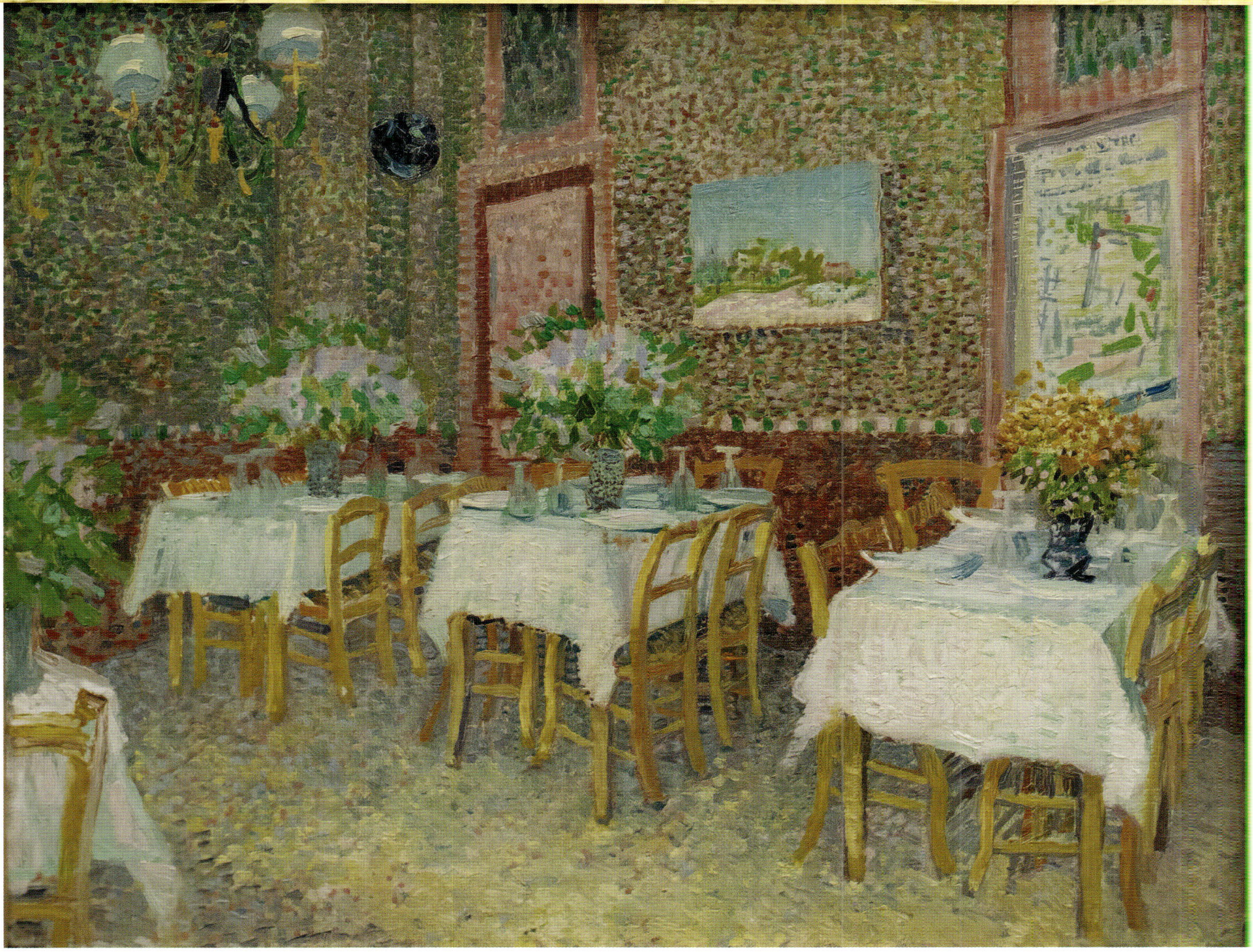

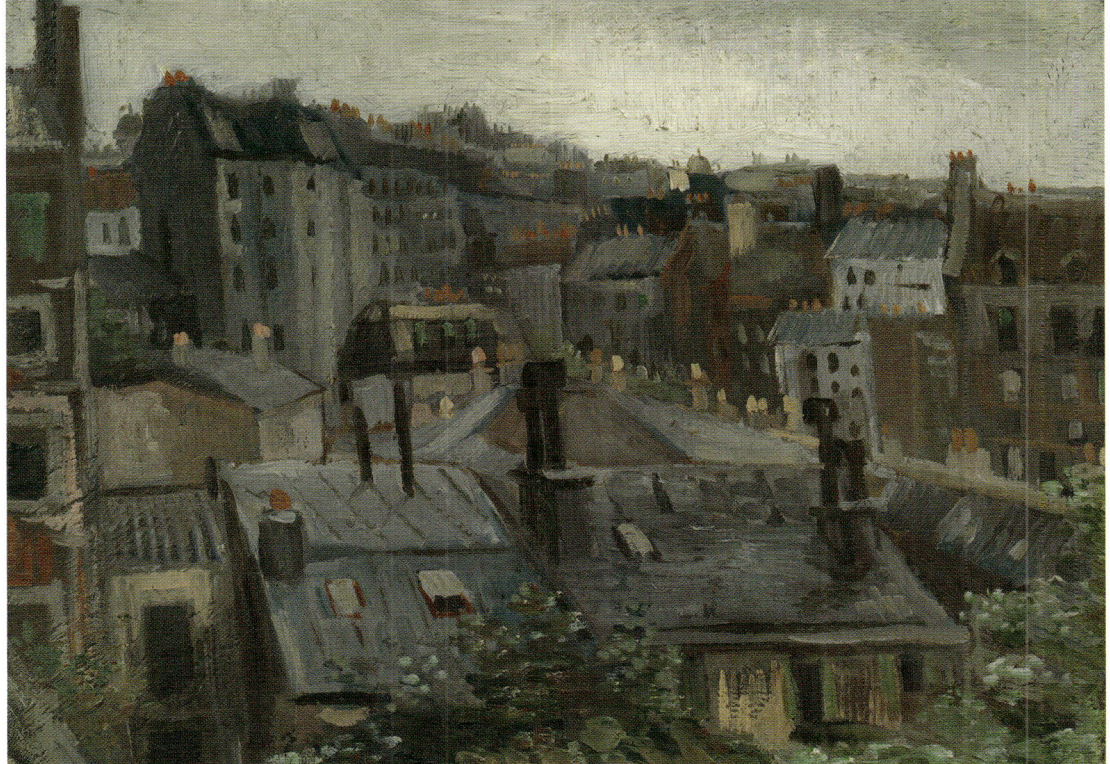

[ABOVE]
Interior of a Restaurant
(Summer 1887). Oil on canvas.
Kröller-Müller Museum, Otterlo.

Vincent applies a stippling technique in his own distinctive manner, but this is his most Pointillist work. Much of the background is rendered in dots, but the tables and chairs are rendered in long brushstrokes. He also created the suggestion of shadows from gradations of color, a Realist technique not consistent with Pointillism.

[LEFT]
View of the Roofs of Paris
(1886). Oil on canvas.
Van Gogh Museum, Amsterdam
(Vincent van Gogh Foundation).

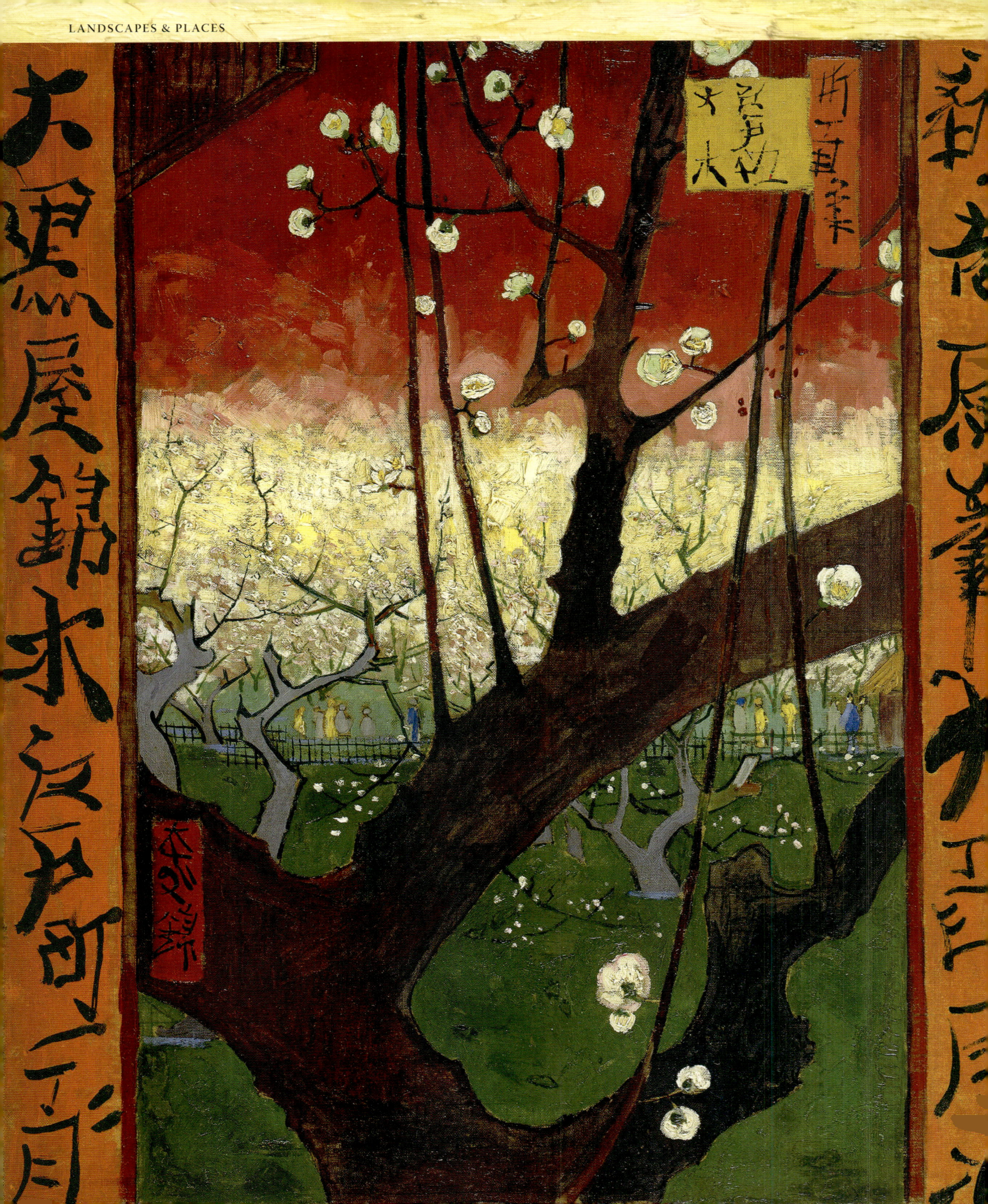

JAPONAISE SERIES

Vincent's interest in Japan and Japanese prints came to fruition in three paintings he completed in the autumn of 1887. Using images from a collection of Japanese art he shared with his brother Theo, he closely followed the compositions of the originals, but added his own unique touches that save them from being mundane copies.

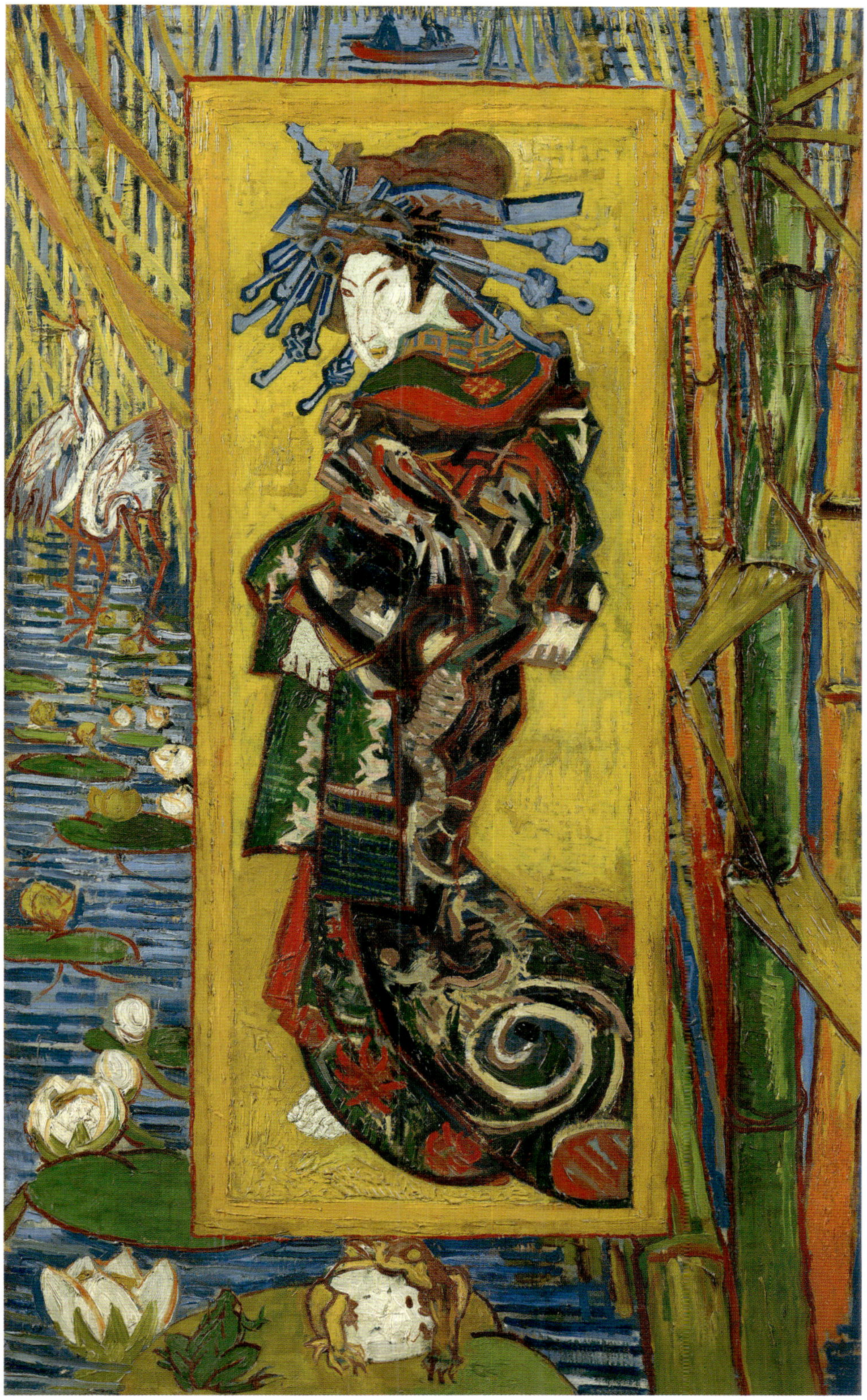

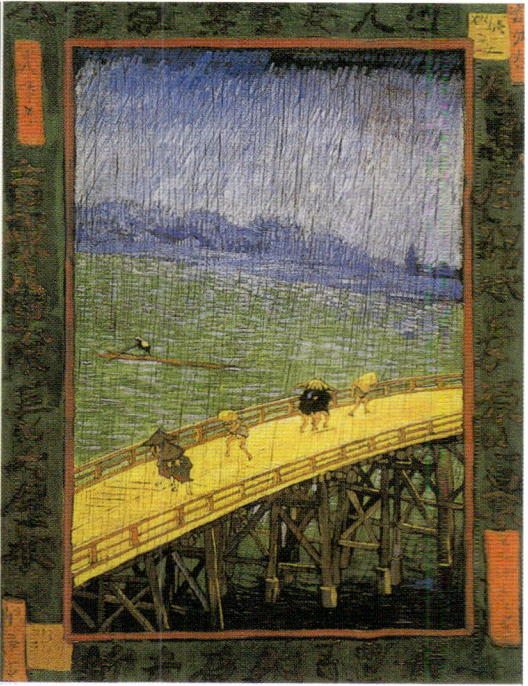

Bridge in the Rain: after Hiroshige
(October–November 1887). Oil on canvas.
Van Gogh Museum, Amsterdam
(Vincent van Gogh Foundation).

This was Vincent's take on the woodblock print Sudden Shower Over Shin-Ohashi Bridge and Atake *(1857) by Japanese* ukiyo-e *artist Hiroshige (1797–1858).*

[LEFT]
Courtesan: after Eisen (October–November 1887). Oil on canvas. Van Gogh Museum, Amsterdam (Vincent van Gogh Foundation).

Vincent based this on the cover of Paris Illustré *done by the Japanese artist Kesai Eisen (1790–1848).*

"And we wouldn't be able to study Japanese art, it seems to me, without becoming much happier and more cheerful, and it makes us return to nature, despite our education and our work in a world of convention."

~ VINCENT, TO THEO, SEPTEMBER 1888

[OPPOSITE PAGE] ***Flowering plum orchard: after Hiroshige*** (October–November 1887). Oil on canvas. Van Gogh Museum, Amsterdam (Vincent van Gogh Foundation).

Vincent closely followed the composition of Hiroshige's woodblock print The Plum Garden in Kameido *(1857), but did not stick to the original's color palette.*

IN ARLES

In February 1888, Vincent arrived in Arles, heralding the start of the period of his highest artistic growth. During the 15 months he spent in this ancient Provençal town, he produced some of his landmark works, inspired by the local people and by the countryside scenery of wheat fields and orchards bathed in the luminous light and colors only found in the South of France. It was here he truly developed the expressive painting style that he is known for, using bright, bold hues and dynamic brushstrokes of thickly laid-on paint.

[RIGHT]
Farmhouse in Provence (June 1888). Oil on canvas. National Gallery of Art, Washington, D.C.

[BELOW]
The Avenue in Arles (1888). Oil on canvas. Pomeranian State Museum, Greifswald, Germany.

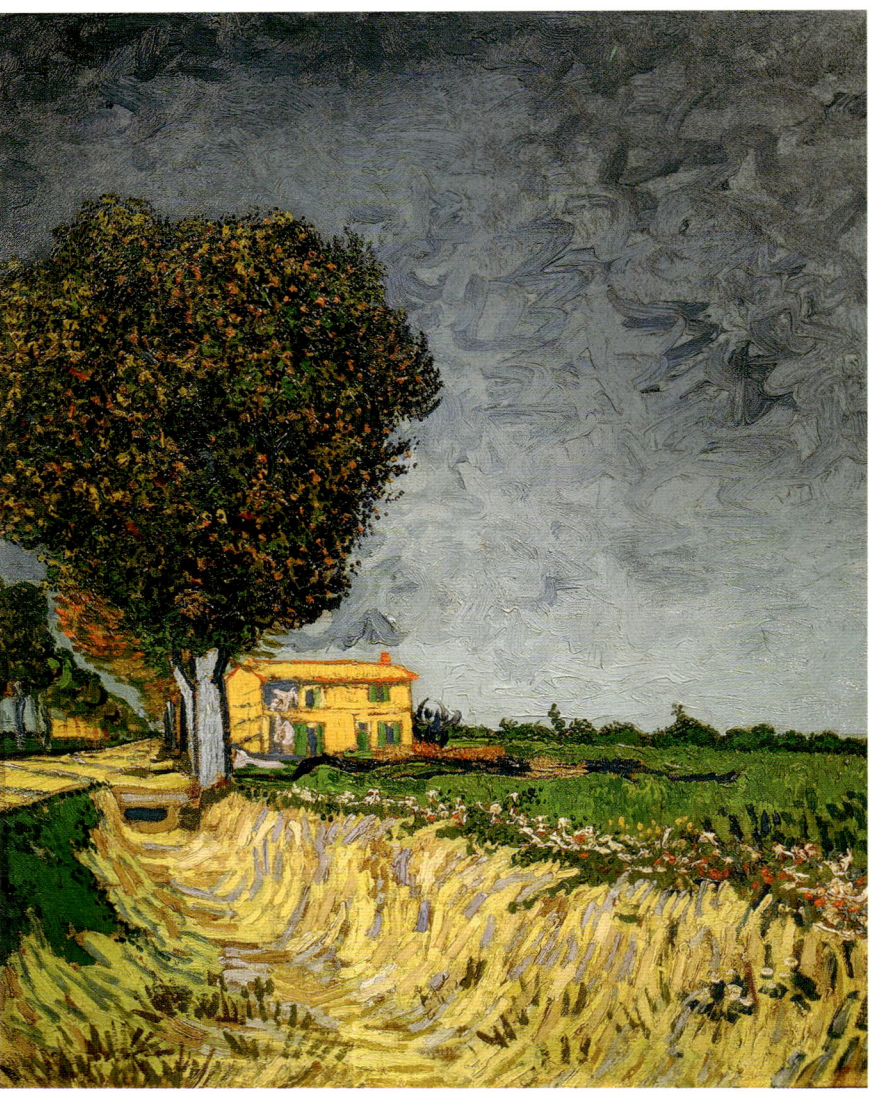

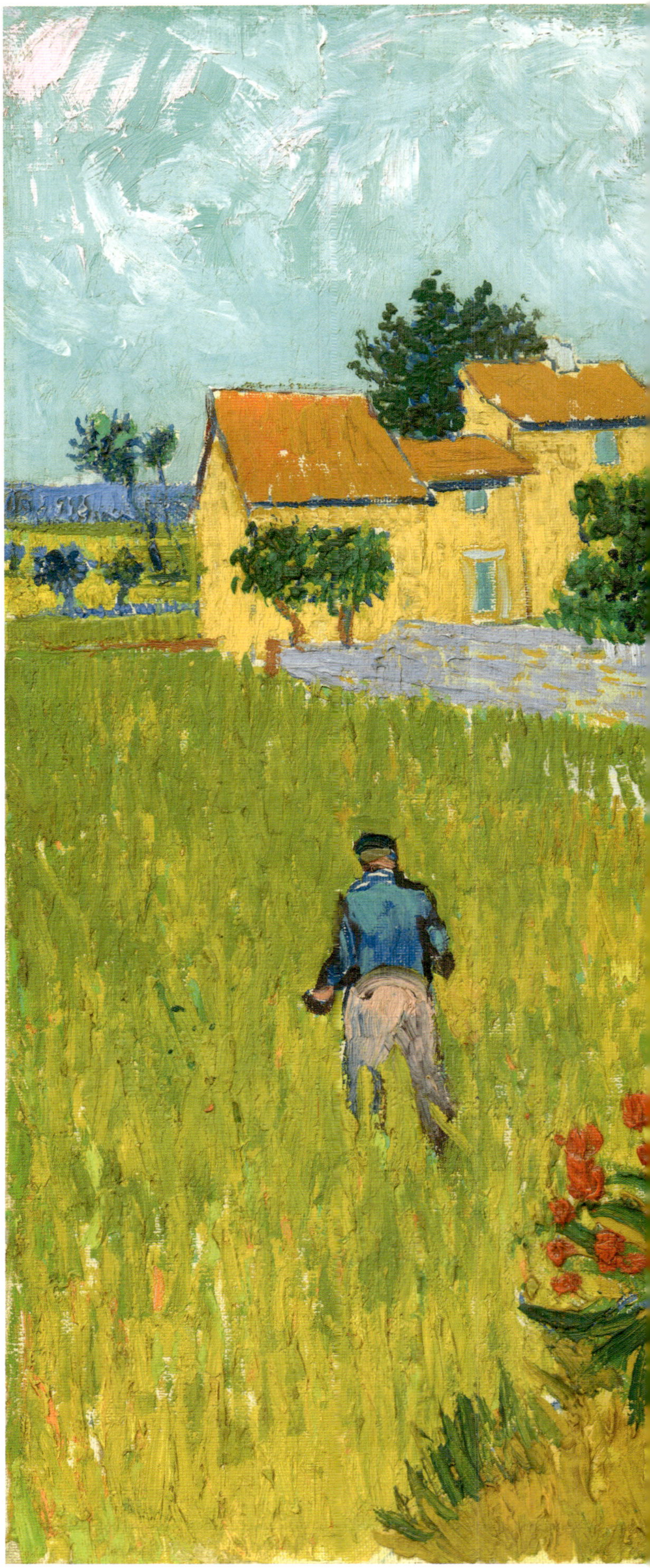

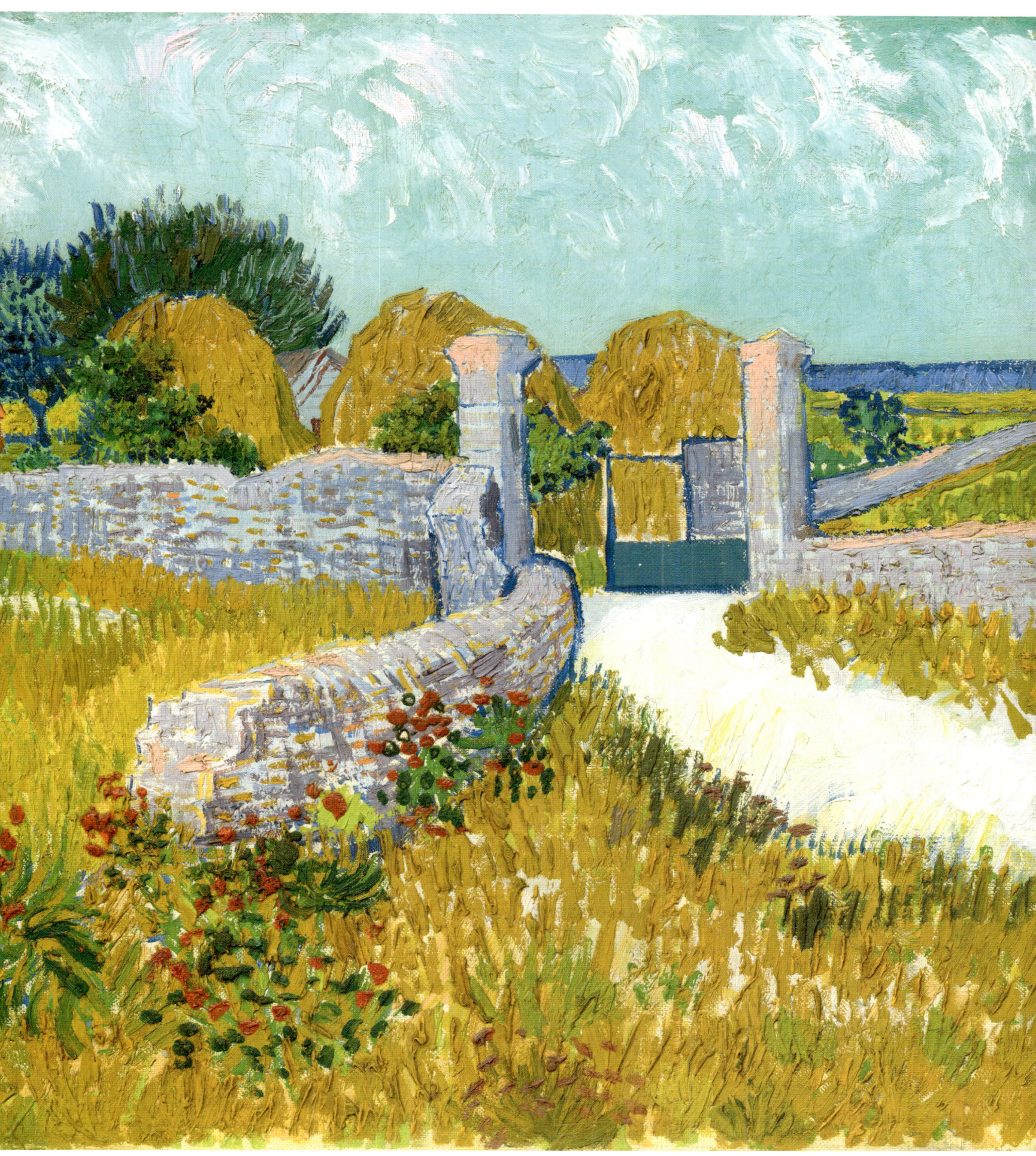

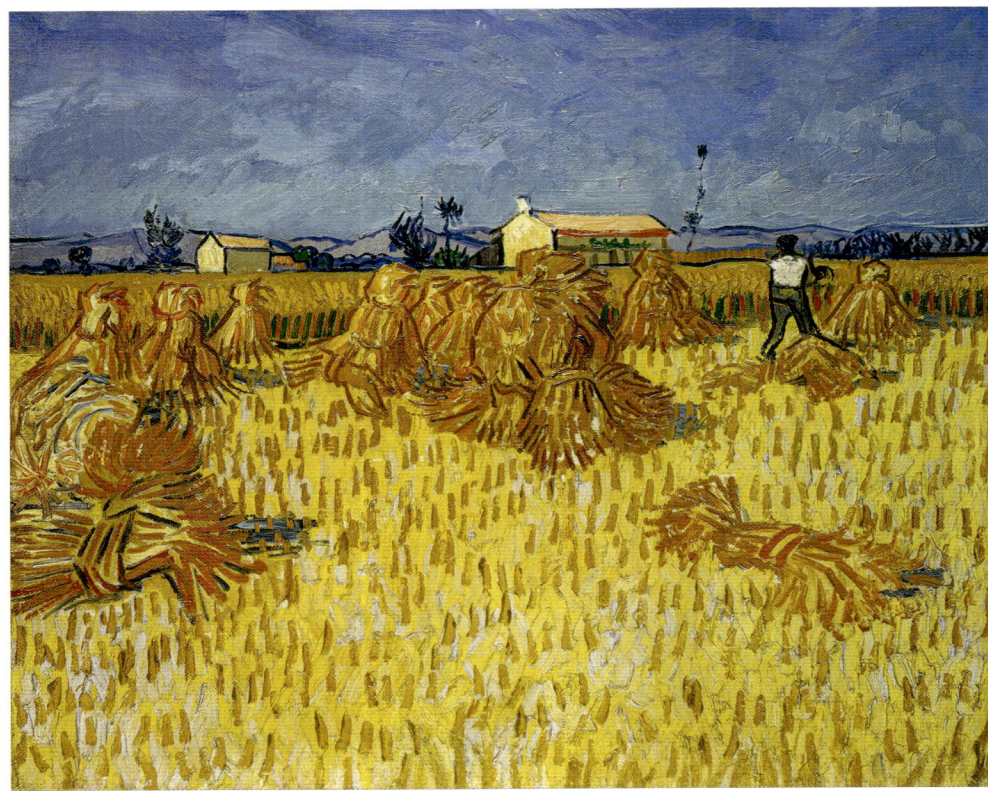

Corn Harvest in Provence (June 1888). Oil on canvas. Israel Museum, Jerusalem.

[RIGHT]
The Sower
(June 1888).
Oil on canvas.
Kröller-Müller
Museum, Otterlo.

[BELOW]
Haystacks in Provence
(June 1888). Oil on canvas.
Kröller-Müller Museum, Otterlo.

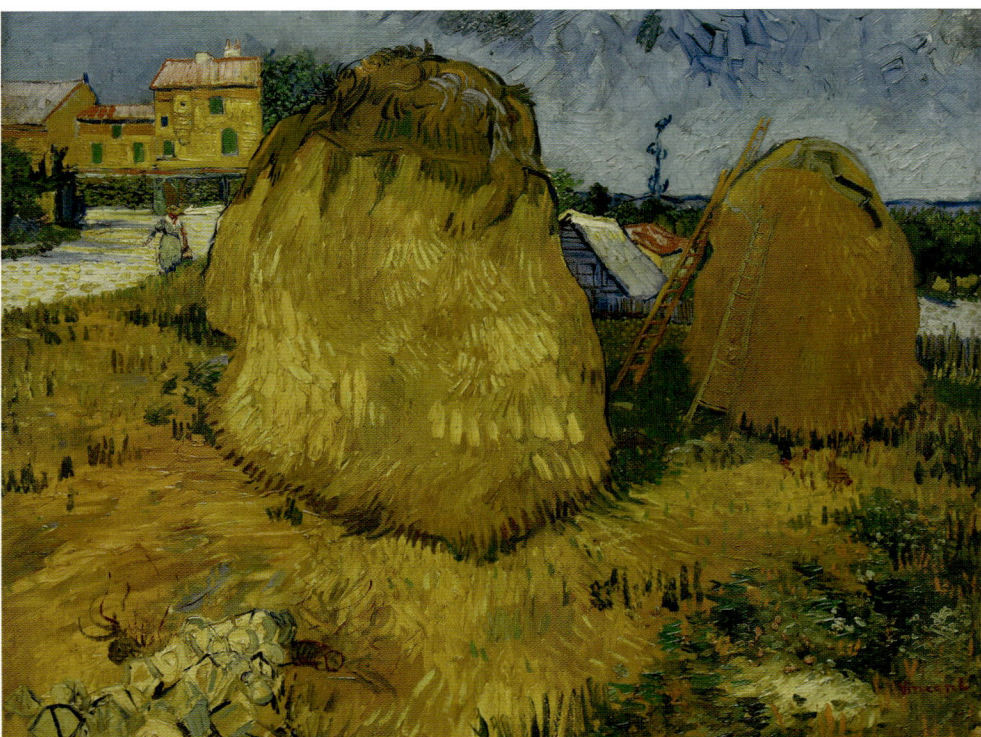

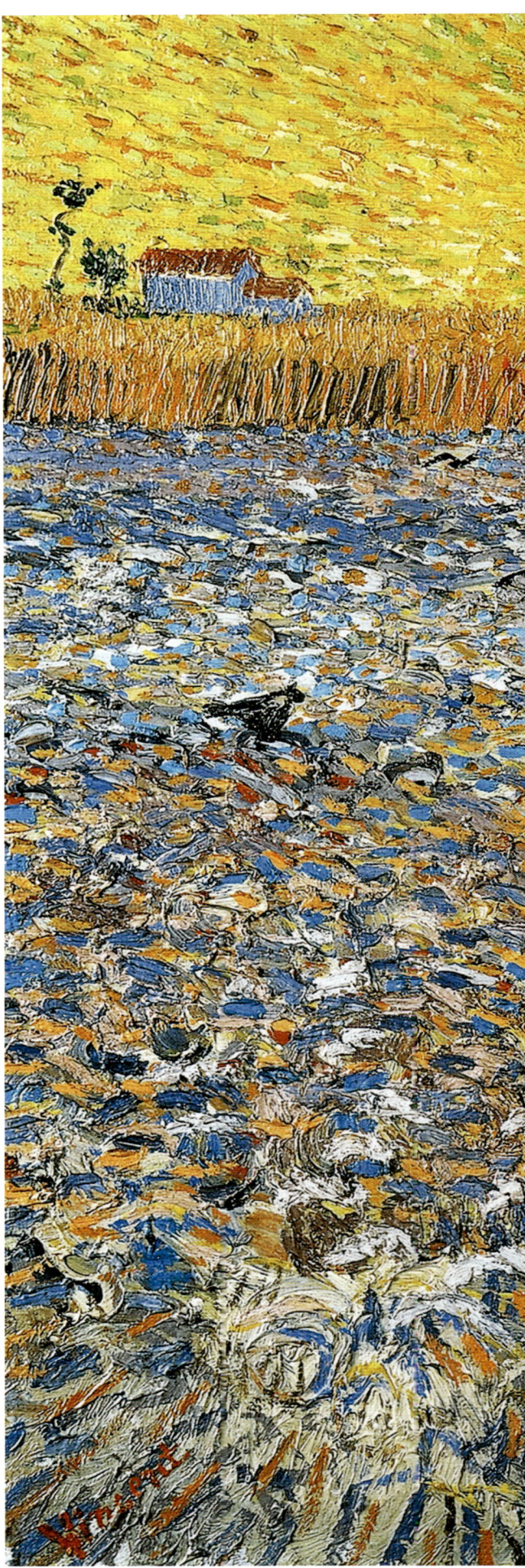

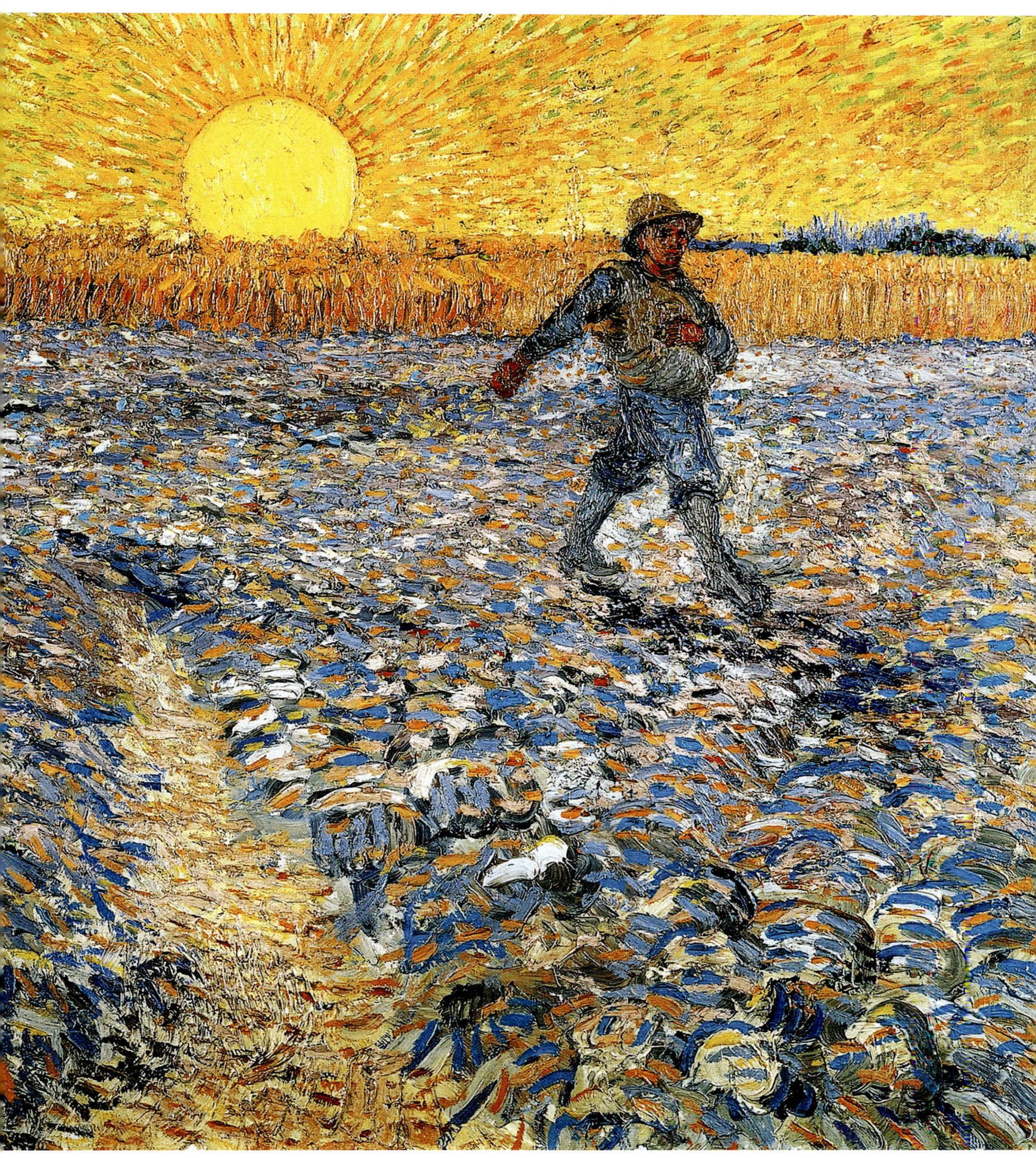

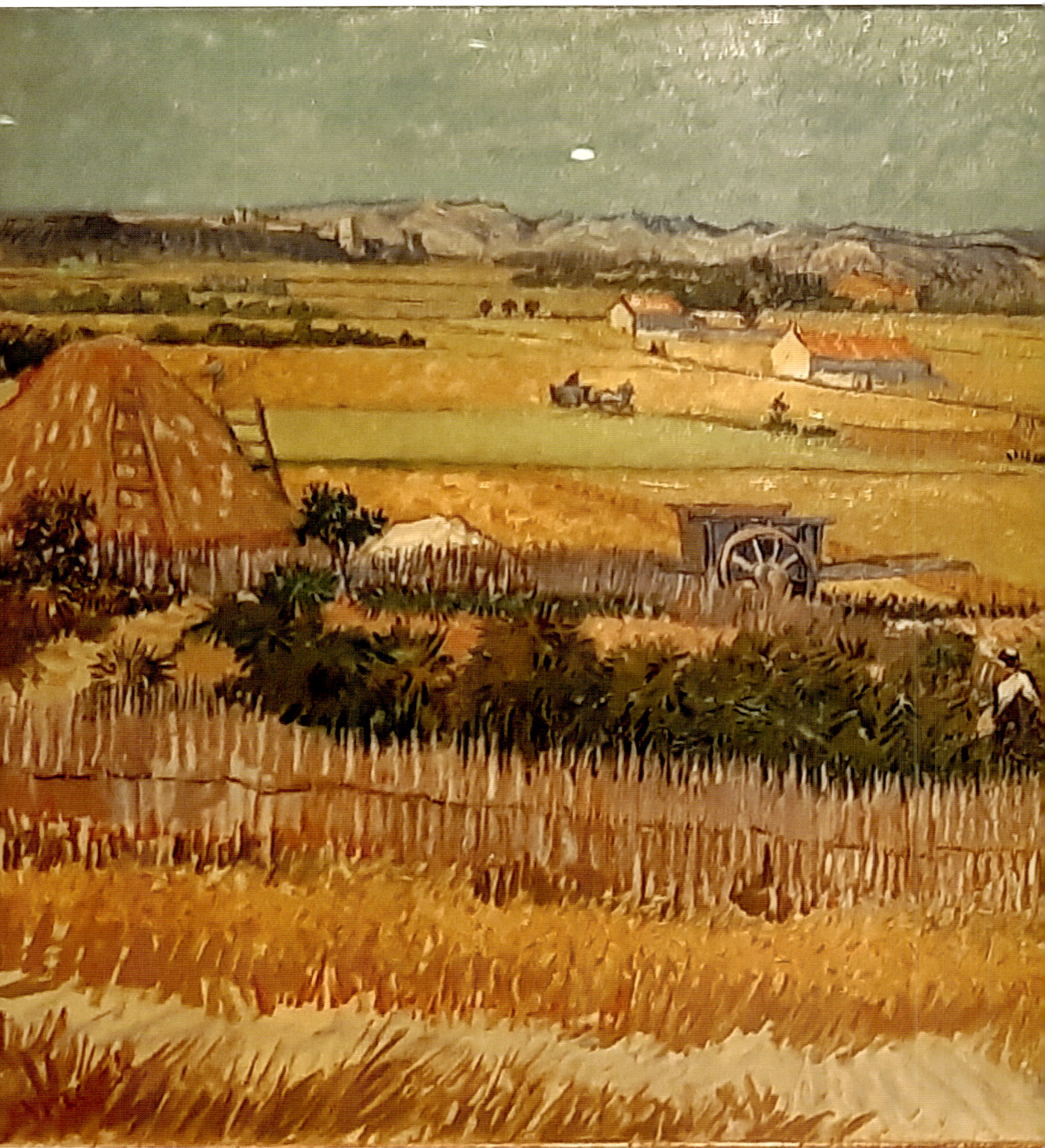

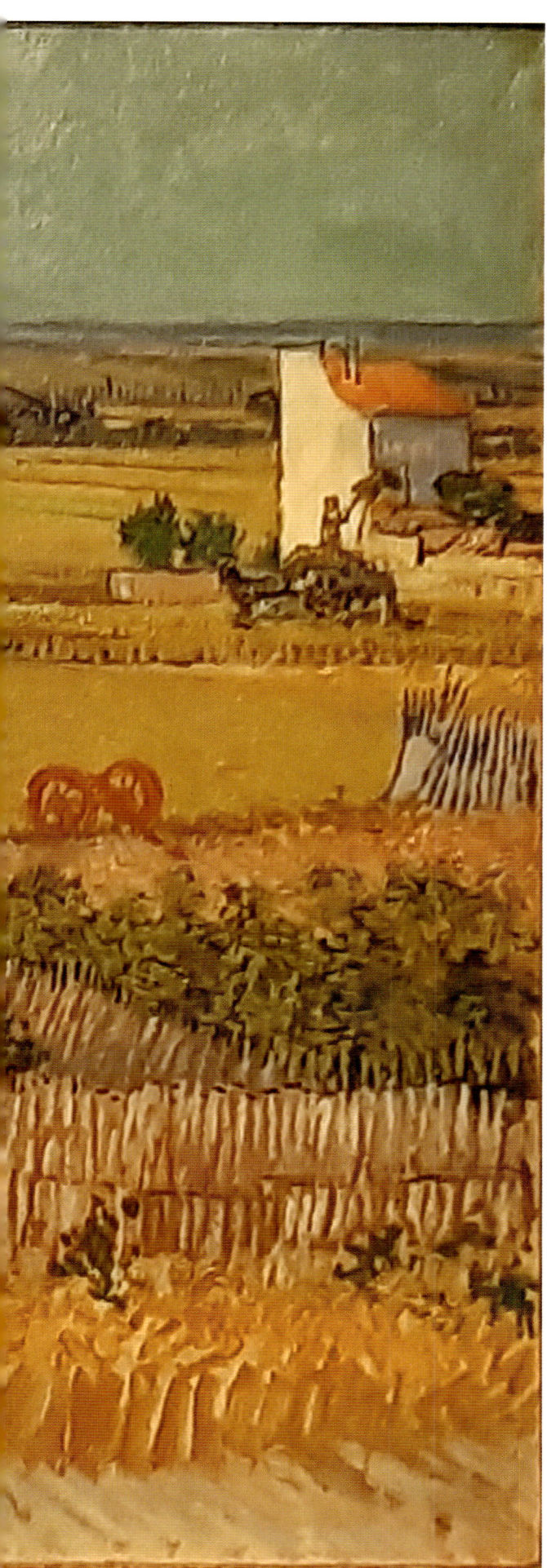

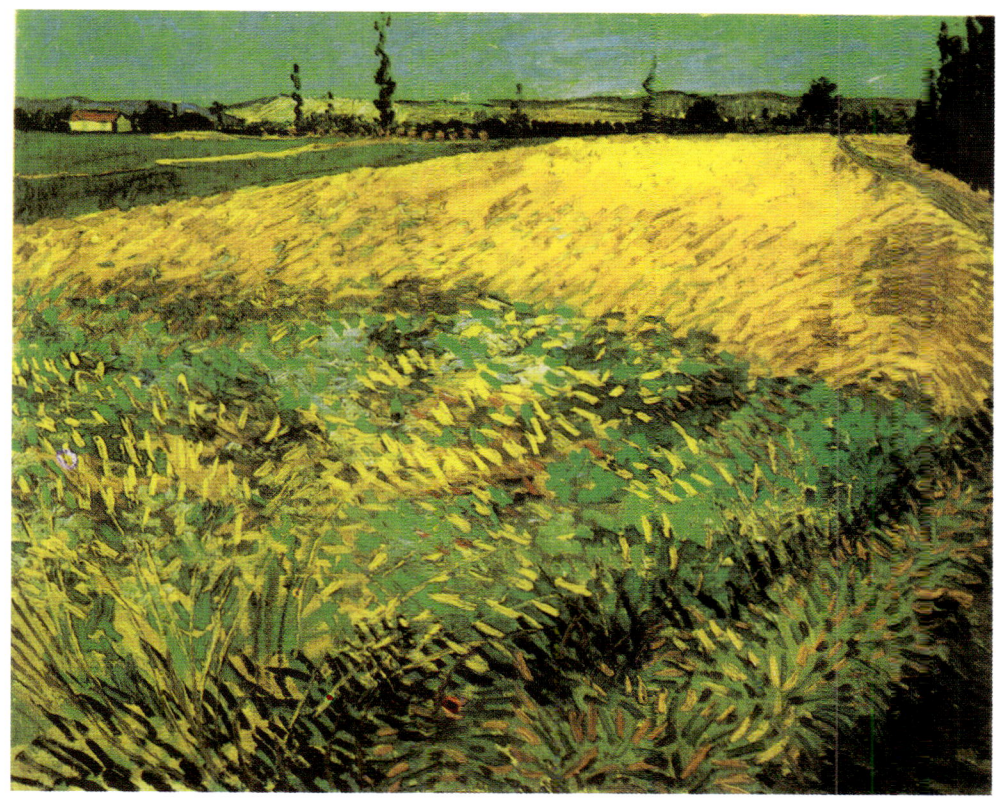

[ABOVE]
Wheat Field with the Alpilles Foothills in the Background (June, 1888). Oil on canvas on cardboard. Van Gogh Museum, Amsterdam (Vincent van Gogh Foundation).

[LEFT]
Harvest at La Crau, with Montmajour in the Background (June, 1888). Oil on canvas. Van Gogh Museum, Amsterdam (Vincent van Gogh Foundation).

[BELOW]
Encampment of Gypsies with Caravans (August, 1888). Oil on canvas. Musée d'Orsay, Paris.

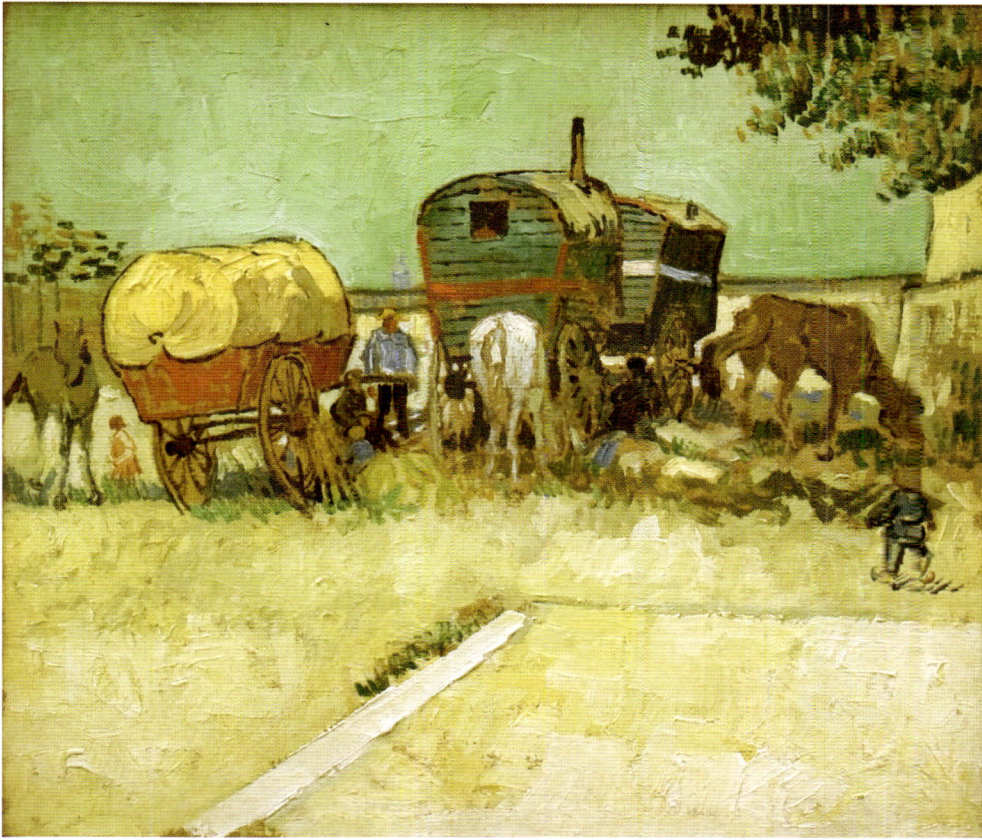

" *The uglier, older, meaner, iller, poorer I get, the more I wish to take my revenge by doing brilliant color, well arranged, resplendent.*"

~ VINCENT TO HIS SISTER WIL, 1888

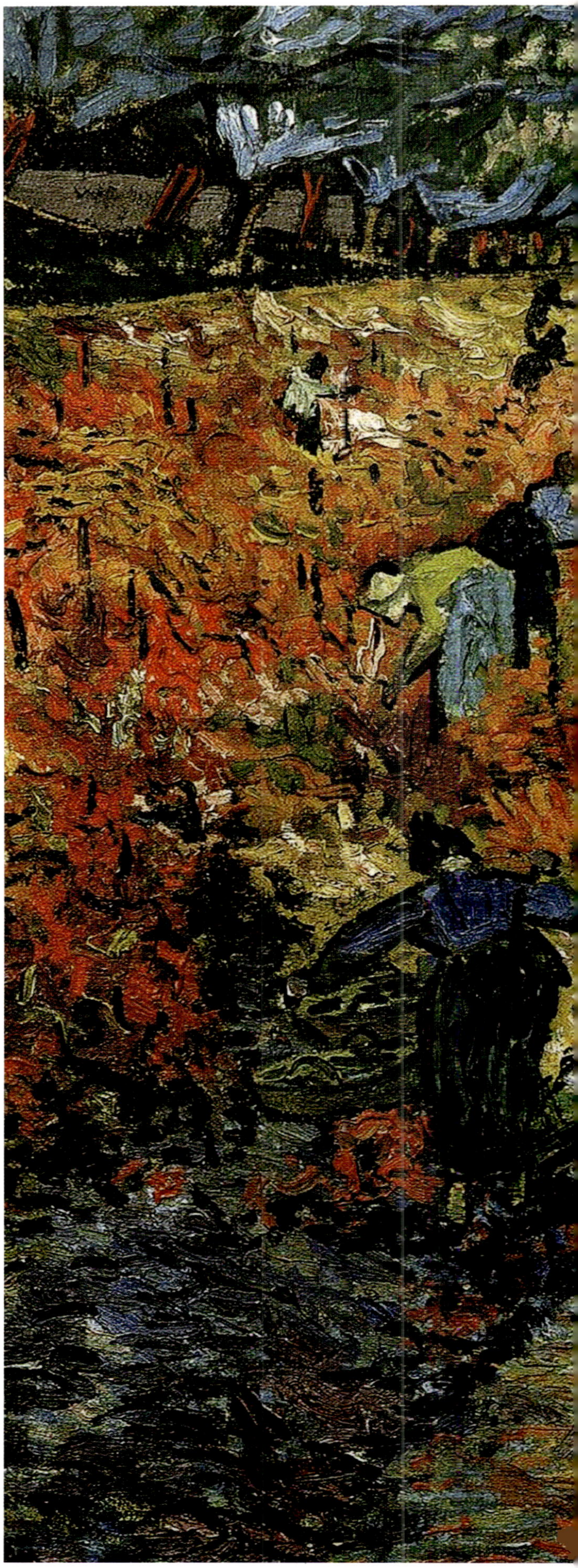

[RIGHT]
Red Vineyards at Arles
(1888). Oil on canvas. Pushkin
Museum, Moscow.

[BELOW]
Pollard Willows at Sunset (March 1888). Oil on
canvas on cardboard. Kröller-Müller Museum, Otterlo.

*Painted during an early-spring sunset, just as the
willows have begun to sprout leaves, this painting is
alive with intense yellows, oranges, reds, and blues.*

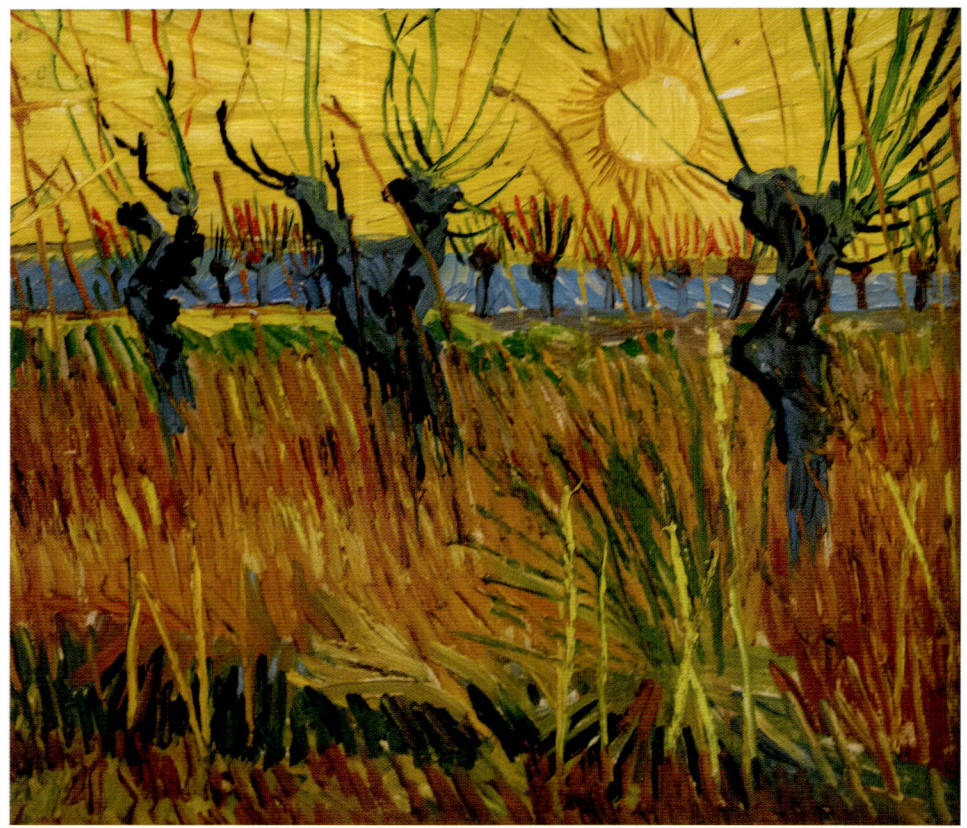

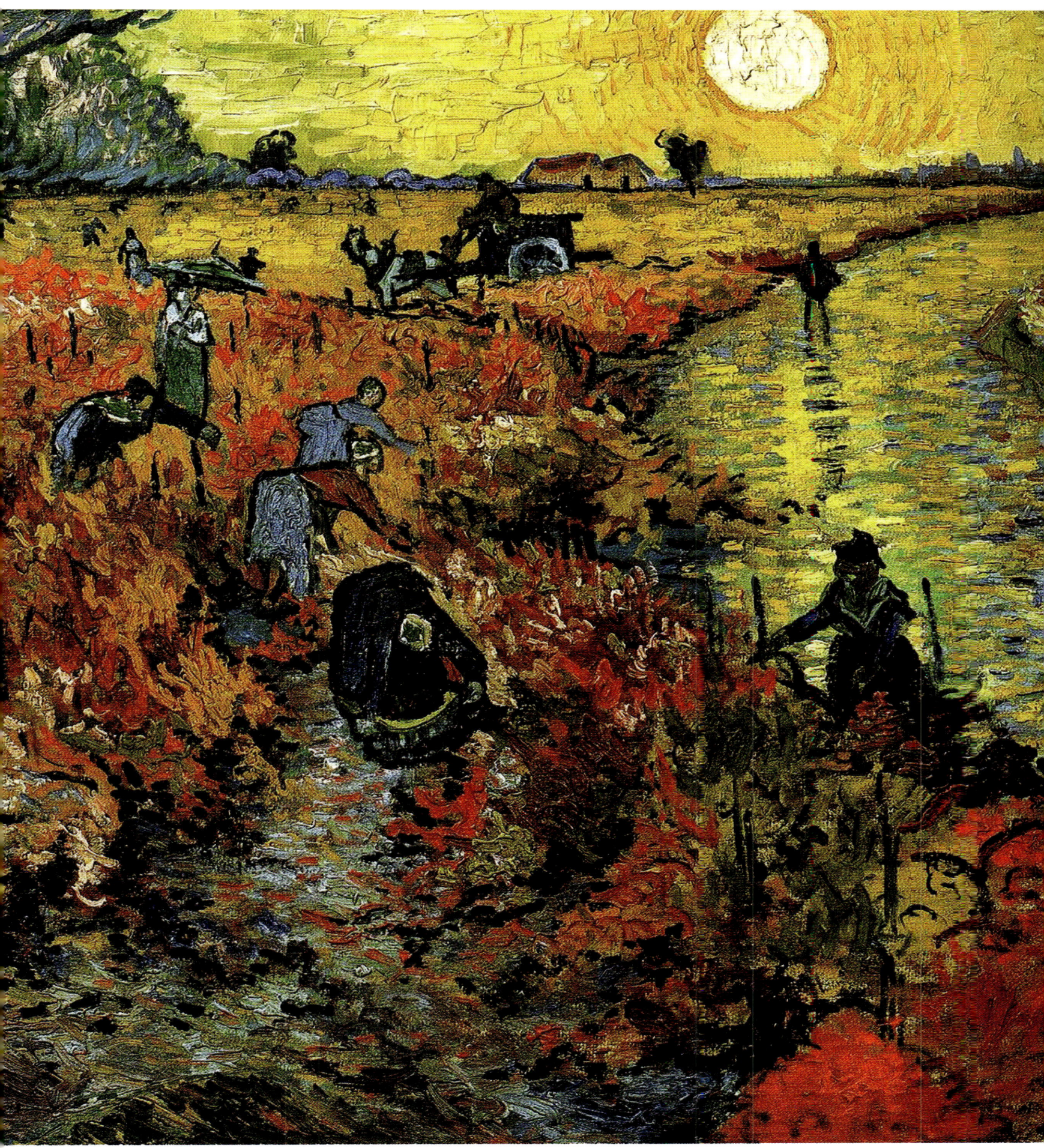

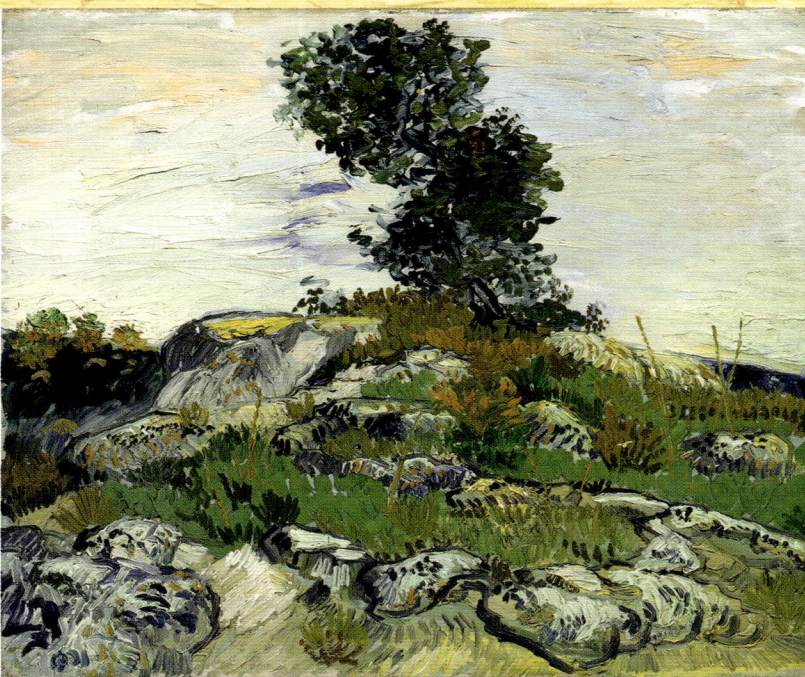

The Rocks with Oak Tree (1888). Oil on canvas. Museum of Fine Arts, Houston.

[RIGHT] *Sunset at Montmajour* (1888). Oil on canvas.
Van Gogh Museum, Amsterdam (Vincent van Gogh Foundation).

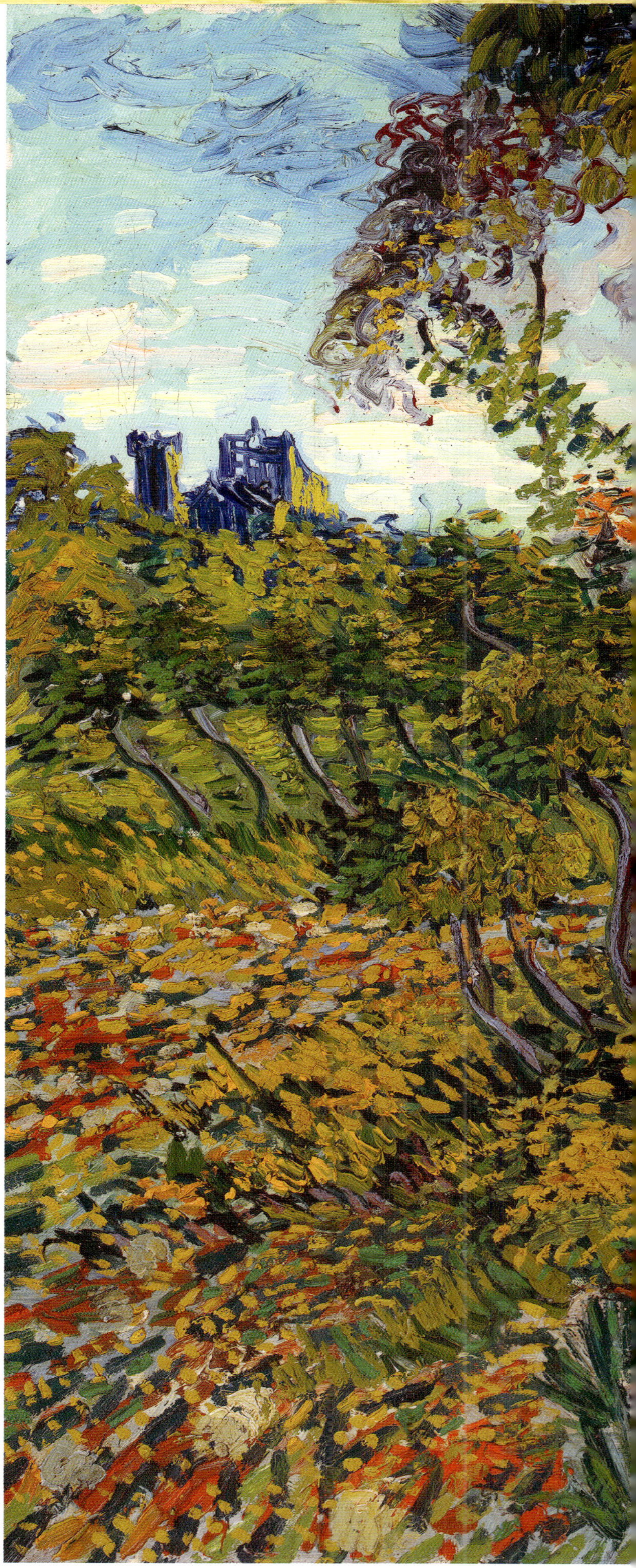

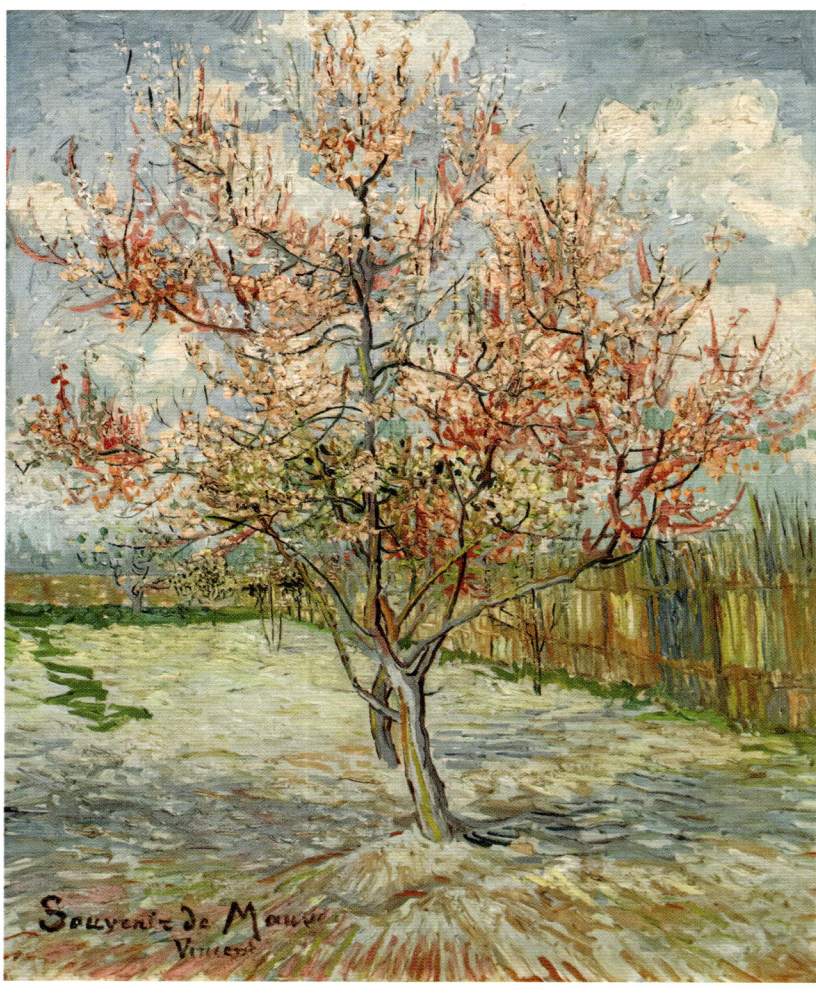

Pink Peach Tree in Blossom (Reminiscence of Mauve)
(March 1888). Oil on canvas. Kröller-Müller Museum, Otterlo.

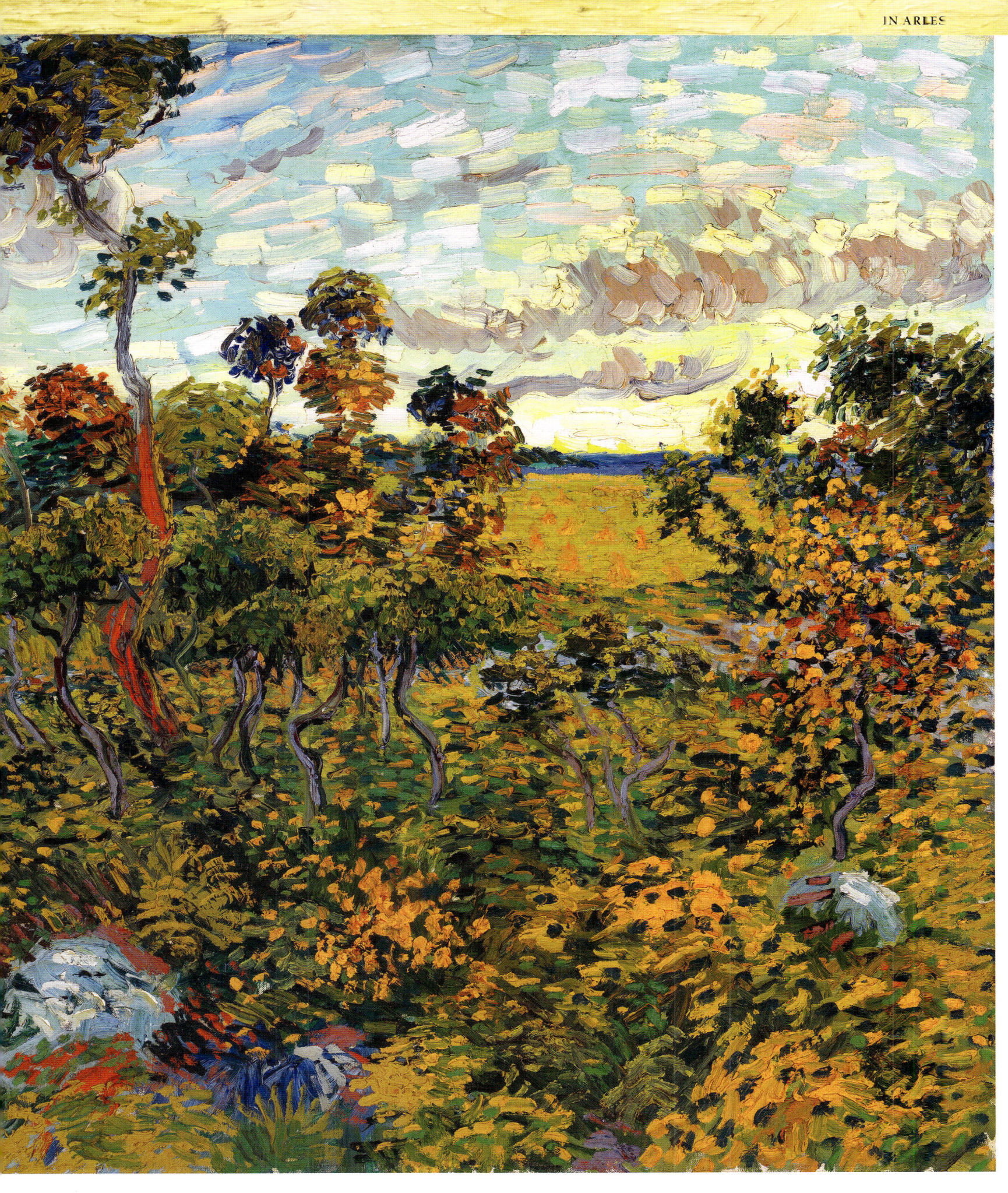

"*Under the blue sky, the orange, yellow, red patches of flowers take on an amazing brilliance, and in the limpid air there's something happier and more suggestive of love than in the north.*"

~ VINCENT IN A LETTER TO HIS BROTHER THEO IN THE SUMMER OF 1888

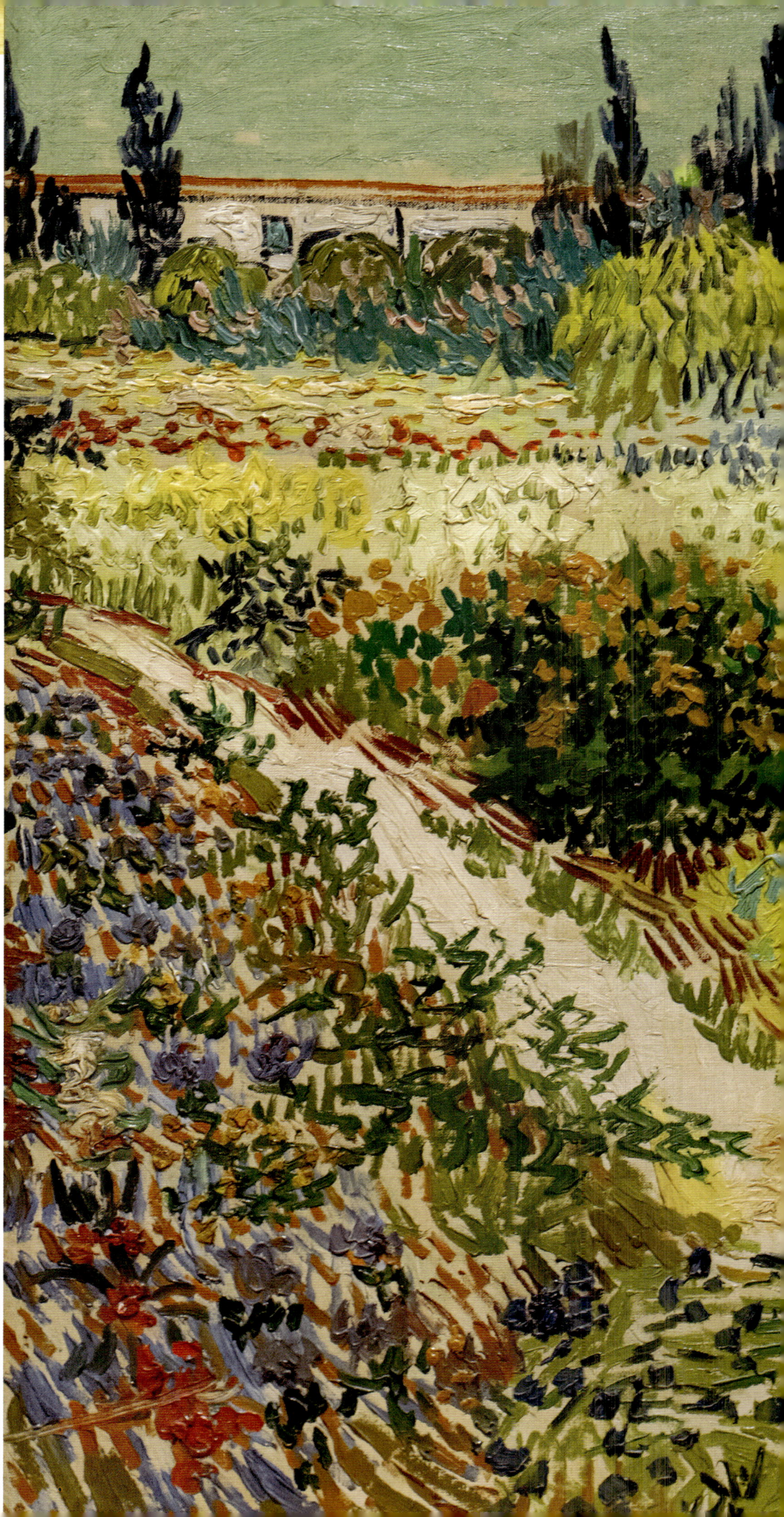

[RIGHT] **Garden at Arles** or **Flowering Garden with Path** (July 1888). Oil on canvas. Kunstmuseum, The Hague.

In one of two paintings Vincent made of the garden at Arles in July 1888, he applied short color-laden brushstrokes, experimenting with the Pointillist technique of his friends Paul Signac and of Georges Seurat.

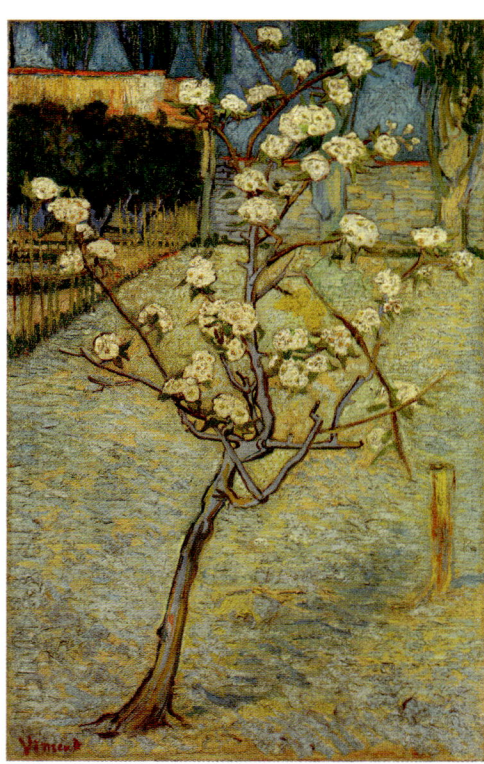

Blossoming Pear Tree (April, 1888). Oil on canvas. Van Gogh Museum, Amsterdam (Vincent van Gogh Foundation).

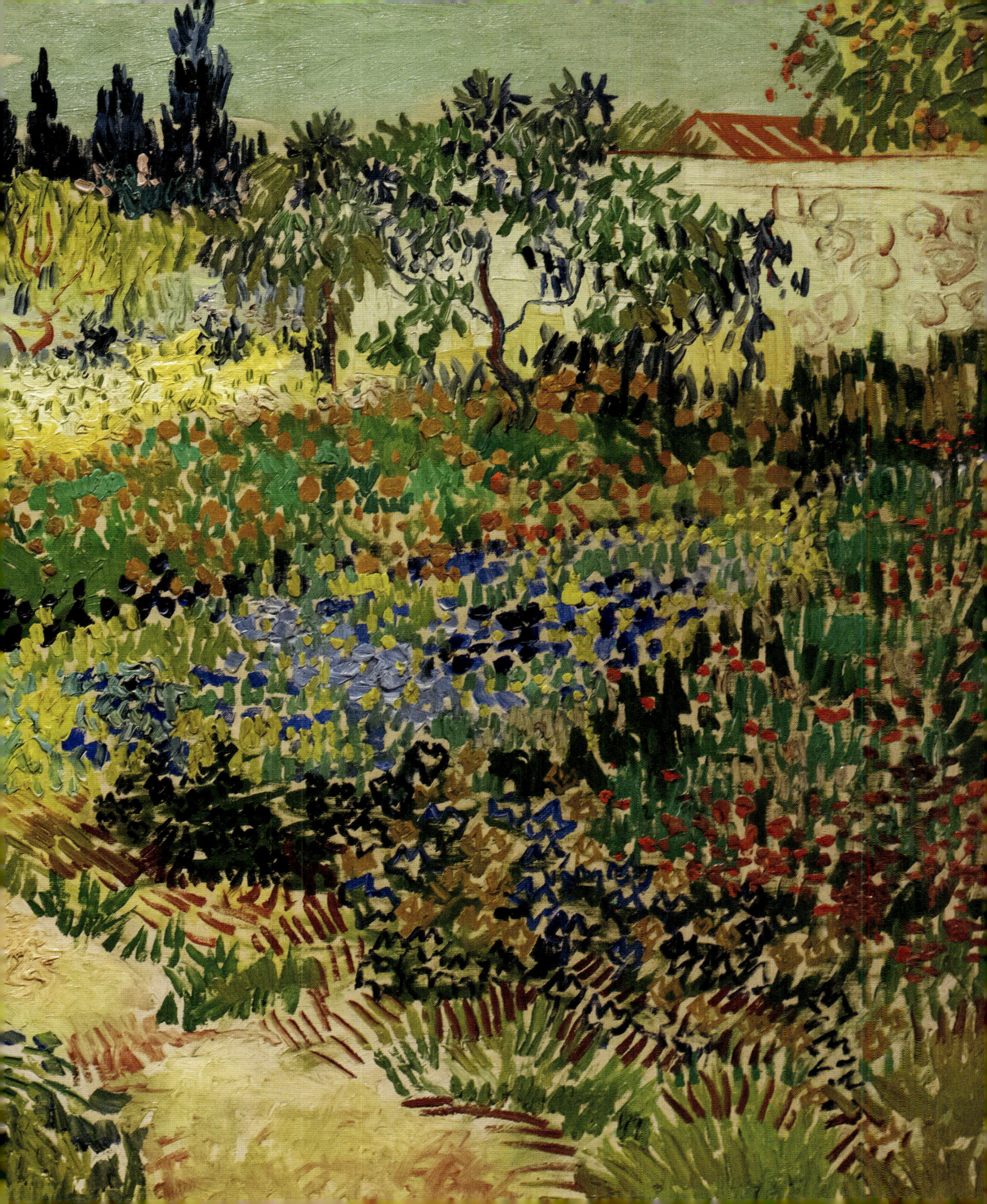

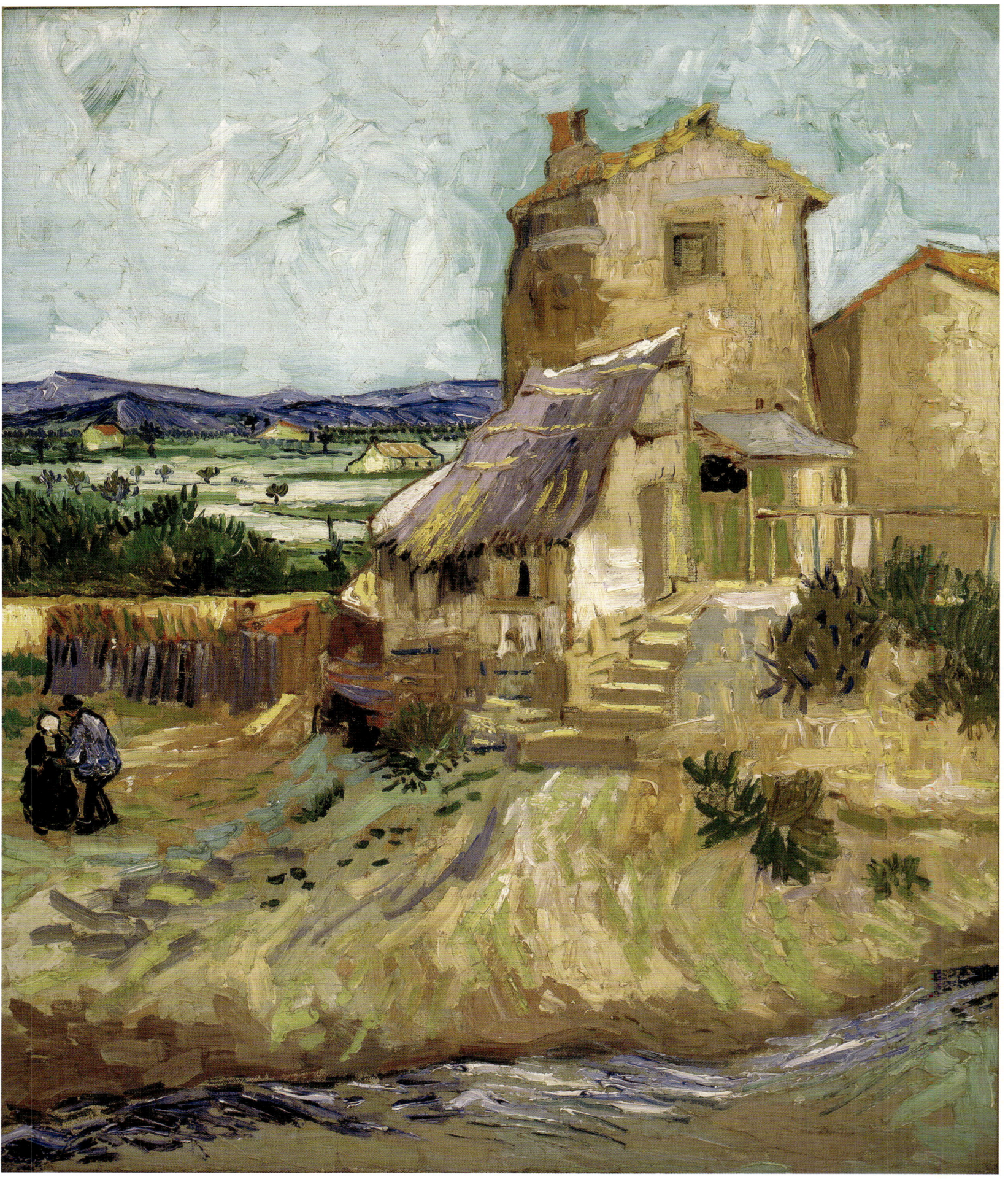

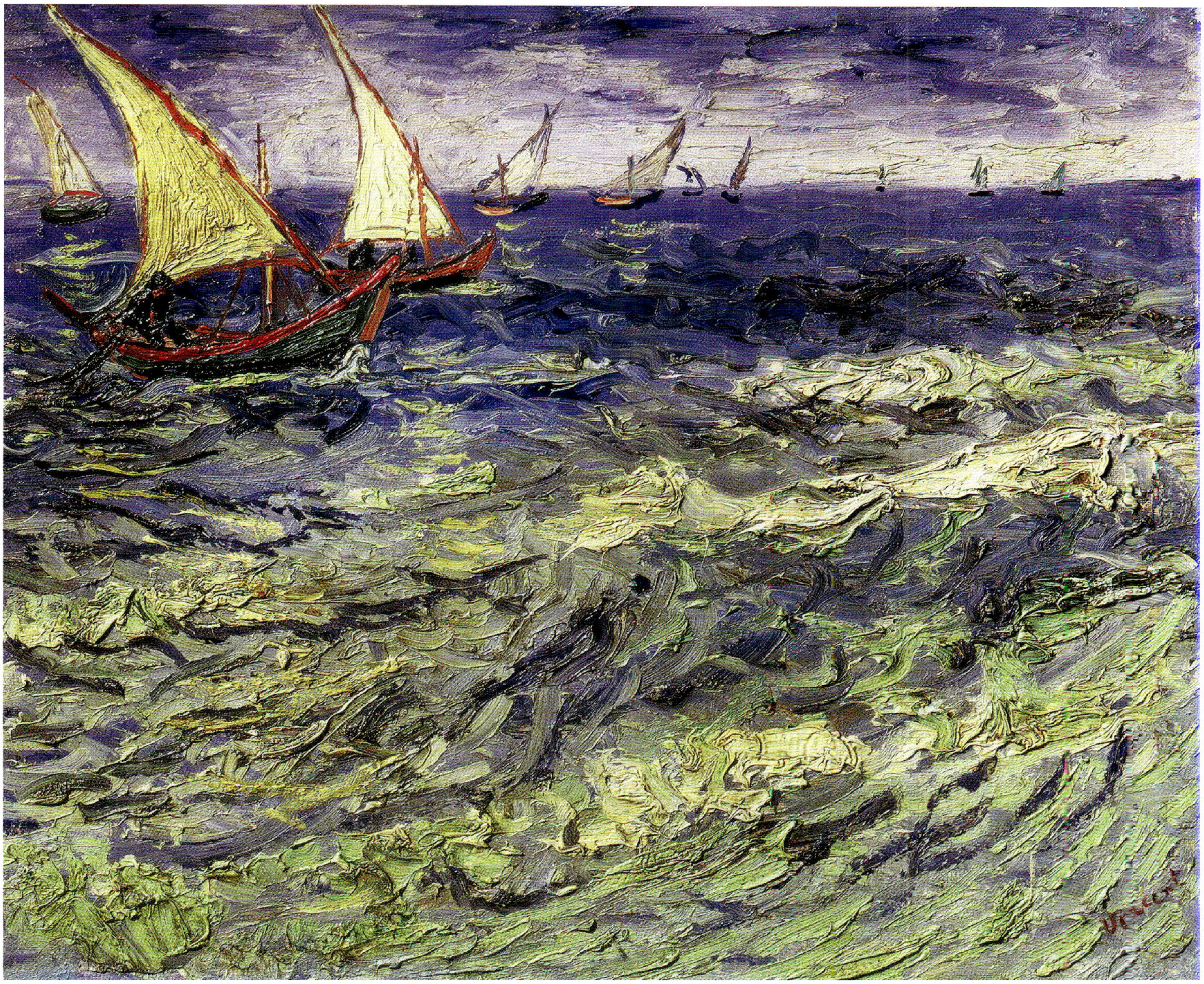

[OPPOSITE PAGE]
The Old Mill
(September 1888). Oil on canvas. Albright-Knox Art Gallery, Buffalo, New York.

[ABOVE]
Fishing Boats in Sea
(1888). Oil on canvas. Pushkin Museum, Moscow.

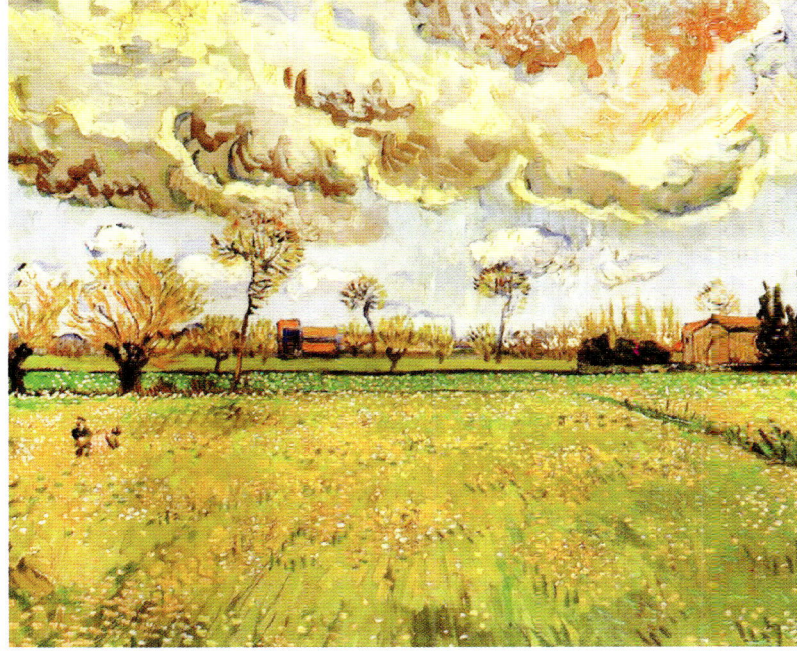

[RIGHT] **Landscape Under a Stormy Sky**
(May 1888). Oil on canvas. Private collection.

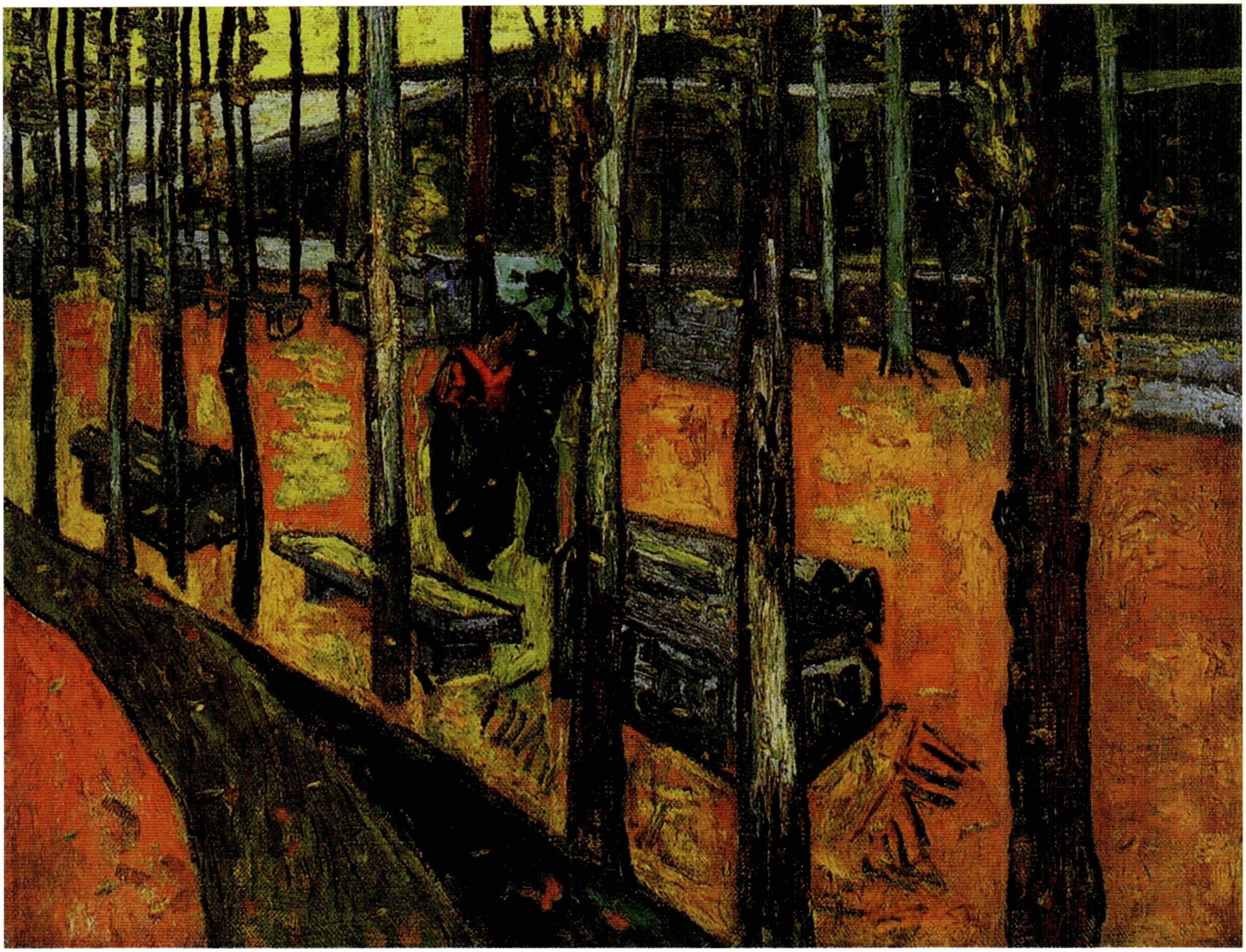

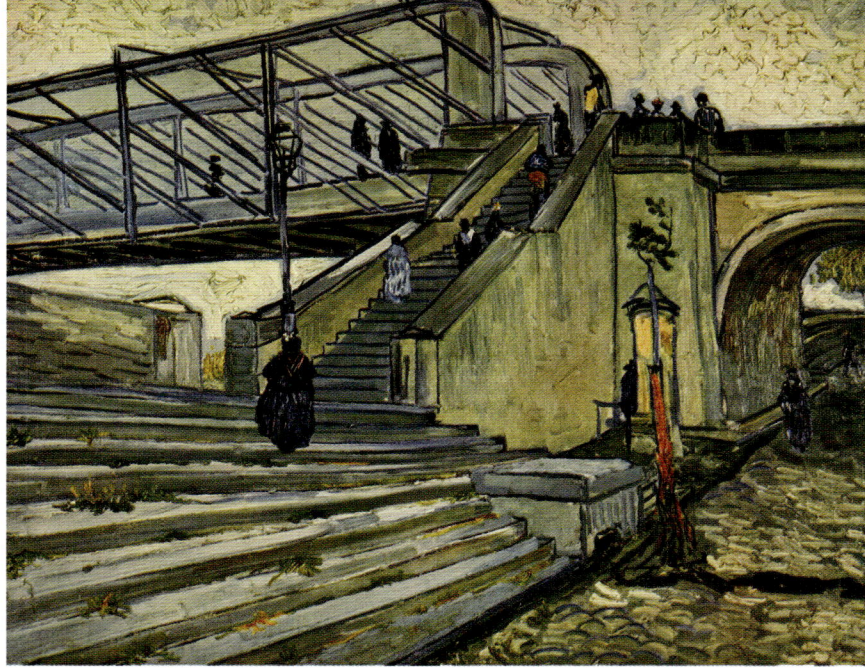

[ABOVE]
Les Alyscamps
(November 1888).
Oil on canvas.
Collection Niarchos.

[OPPOSITE PAGE]
Les Alyscamps (late October
1888). Oil on canvas. Basil and
Elise Goulandris Museum of
Contemporary Art, Athens.

[LEFT]
**The Trinquetaille
Bridge** (October
1888). Oil on canvas.
Private collection.

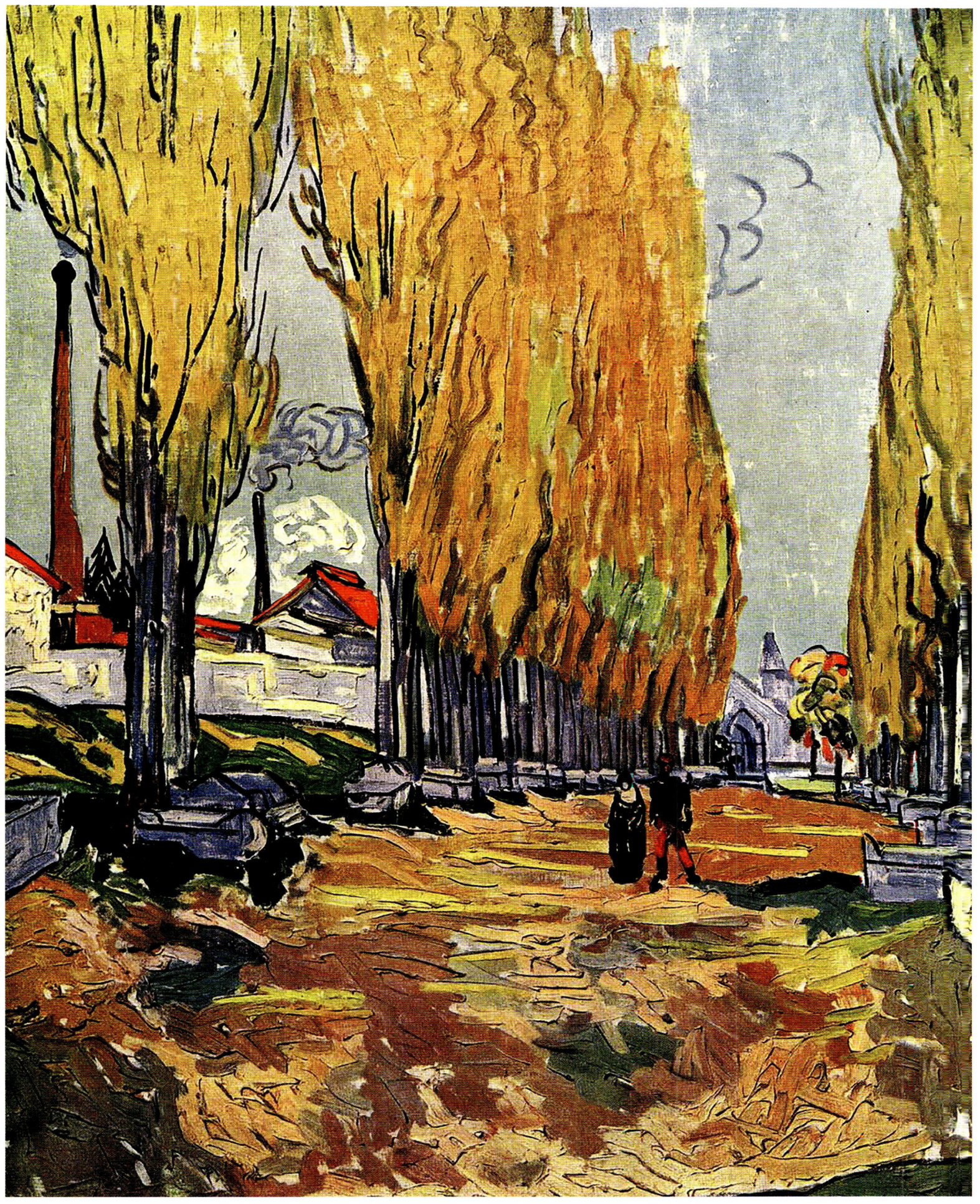

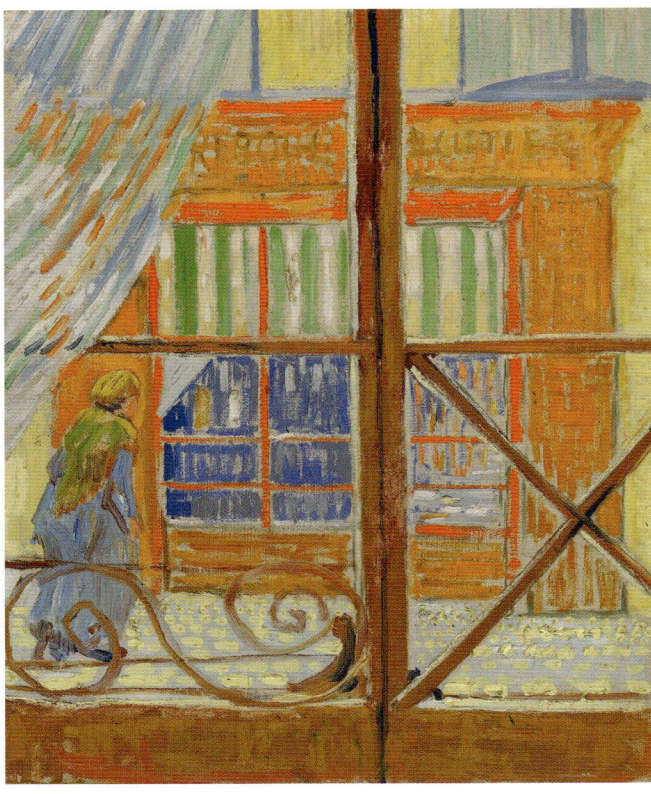

A Pork-Butcher's Shop Seen from a Window (1888).
Oil on canvas. Van Gogh Museum, Amsterdam
(Vincent van Gogh Foundation).

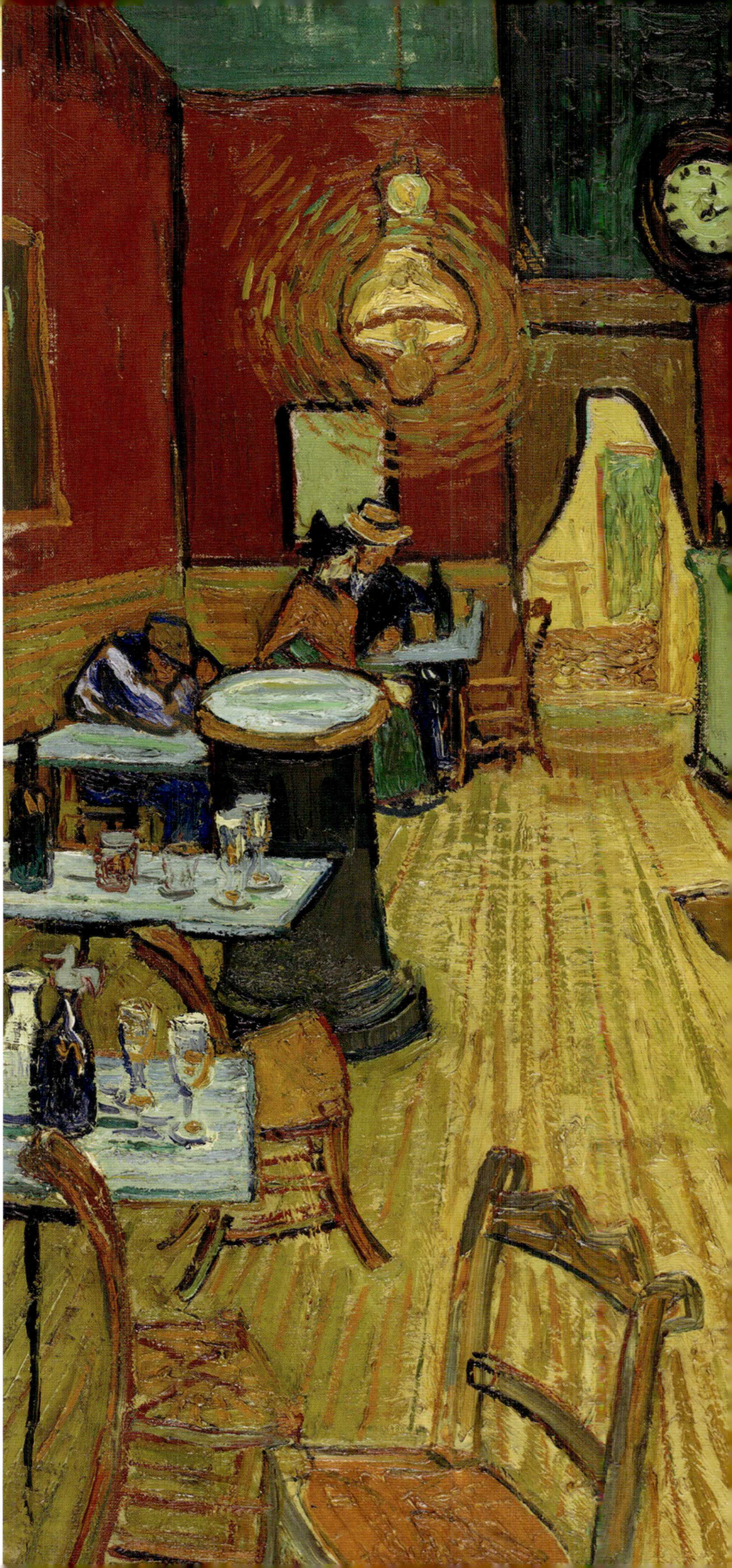

[RIGHT]
***The Night Café in the
Place Lamartine in Arles***
(September 1888). Oil on canvas.
Yale University Art Gallery,
New Haven, Connecticut.

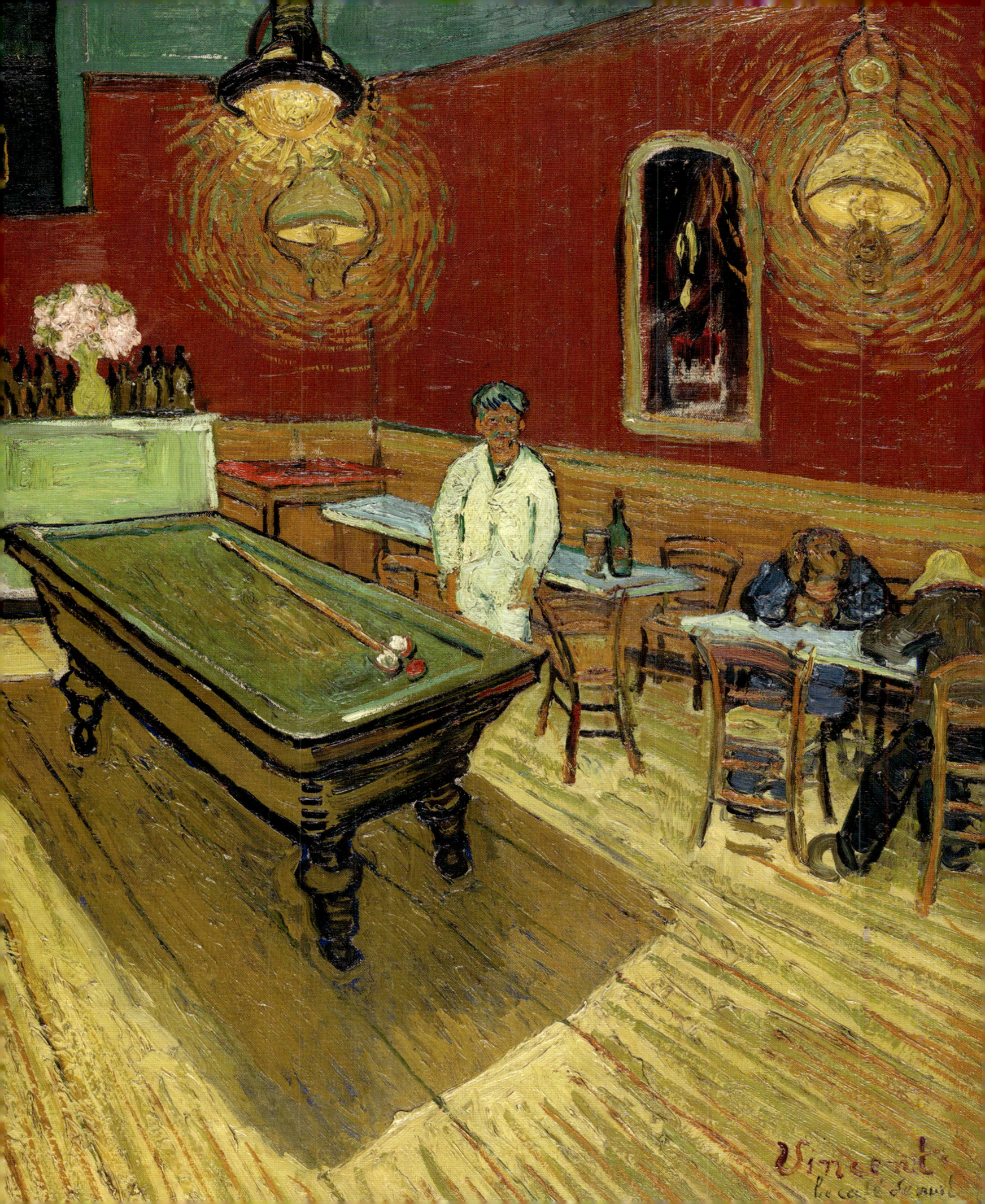

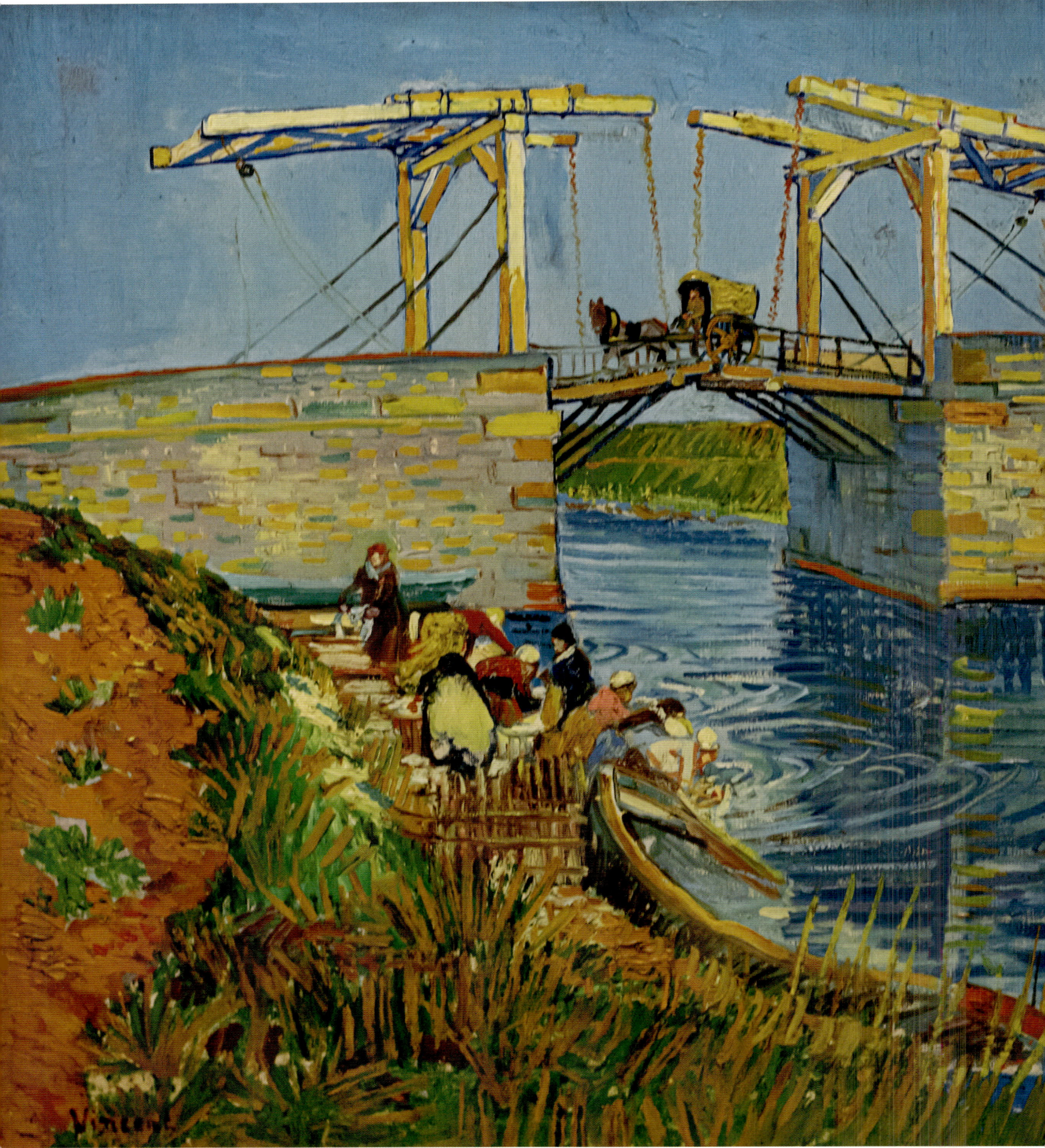

THE LANGLOIS BRIDGE

Vincent found in the Langlois Bridge a worthy subject, producing four oil paintings, one watercolor and four drawings of this structure in Arles. This crawbridge on a canal reminded him of the sights in his homeland of the Netherlands. The reconstructed Langlois Bridge is now named Pont Van-Gogh in his honor.

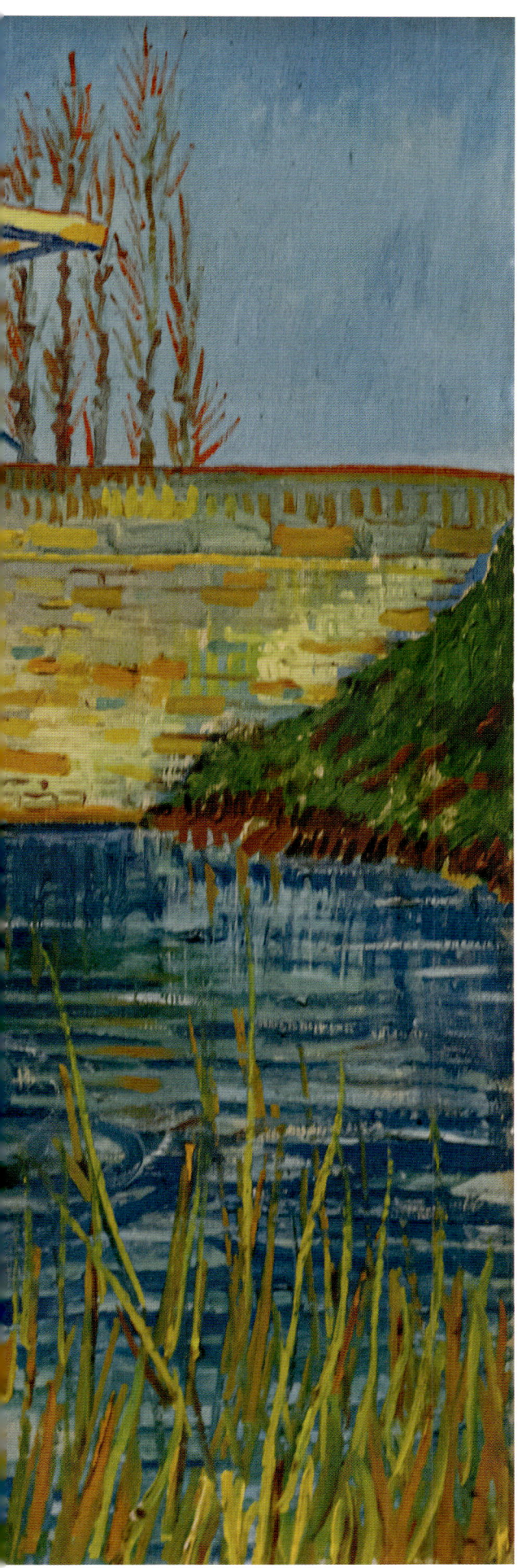

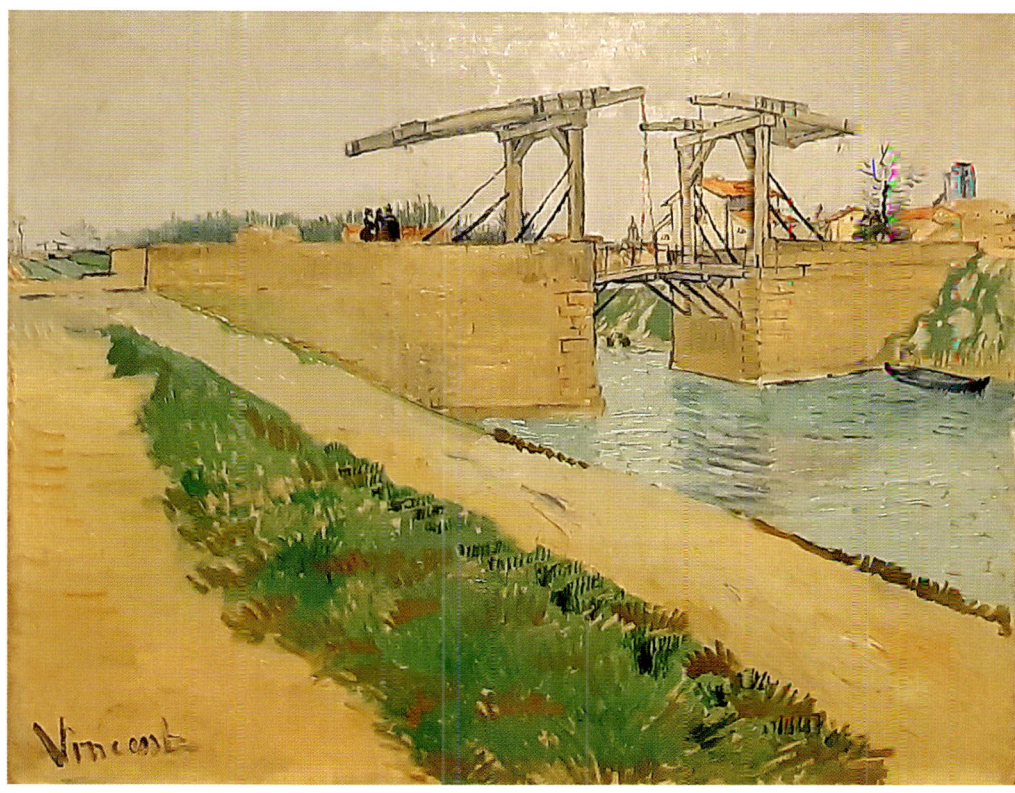

The Langlois Bridge at Arles with Road Alongside the Canal (March 1888). Oil on canvas. Van Gogh Museum, Amsterdam (Vincent van Gogh Foundation)

[LEFT]
The Langlois Bridge at Arles with Women Washing (March 1888). Oil on canvas. Kröller-Müller Museum, Otterlo.

[RIGHT]
The Gleize Bridge over the Vigueirat Canal (March, 1888). Oil on canvas. Pola Museum of Art, Hakone, Japan.

Vincent painted another Arles bridge, where washerwomen kneel alongside the canal bank.

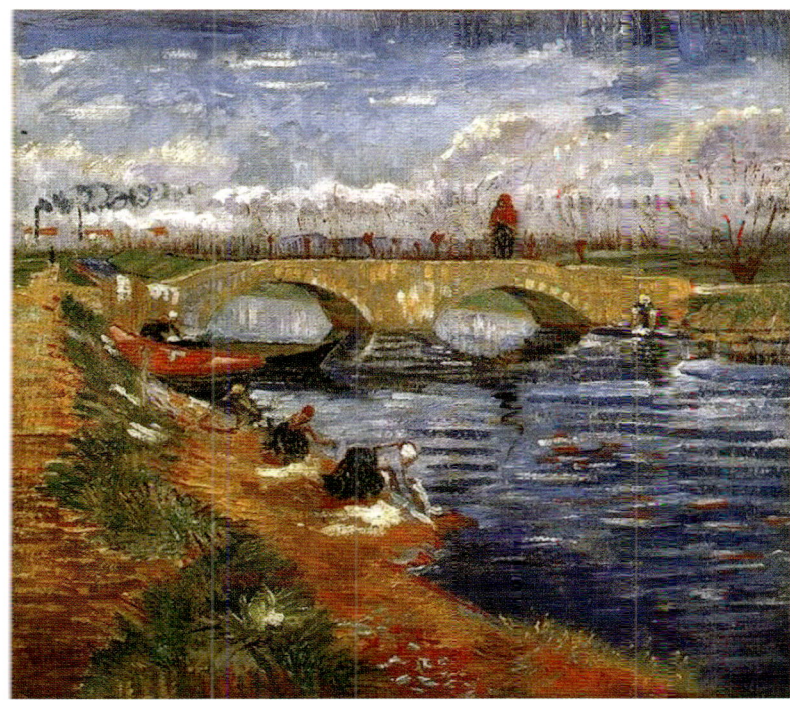

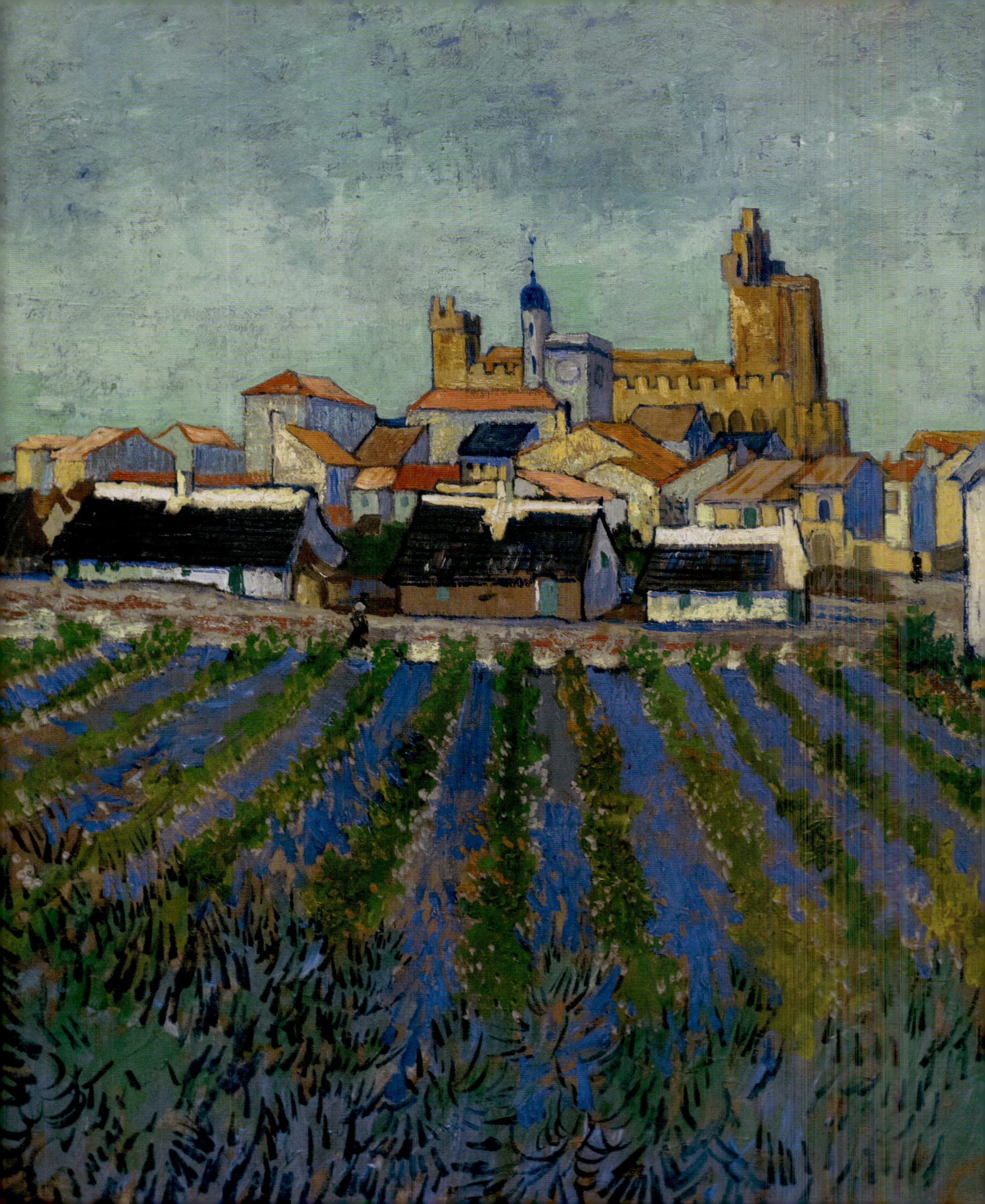

SAINTES-MARIES-DE-LA-MER

During his time in Arles, Vincent took a stagecoach trip to Saintes-Maries-de-la-Mer on the Mediterranean Sea. While staying in the fishing village, he made several paintings of the seaside and town.

[OPPOSITE PAGE] *View of Saintes-Maries-de-la-Mer* (June 1888). Oil on canvas. Kröller-Müller Museum, Otterlo.

[RIGHT] *Three White Cottages in Saintes-Maries* (June 1888). Oil on canvas. Kunsthaus Zürich.

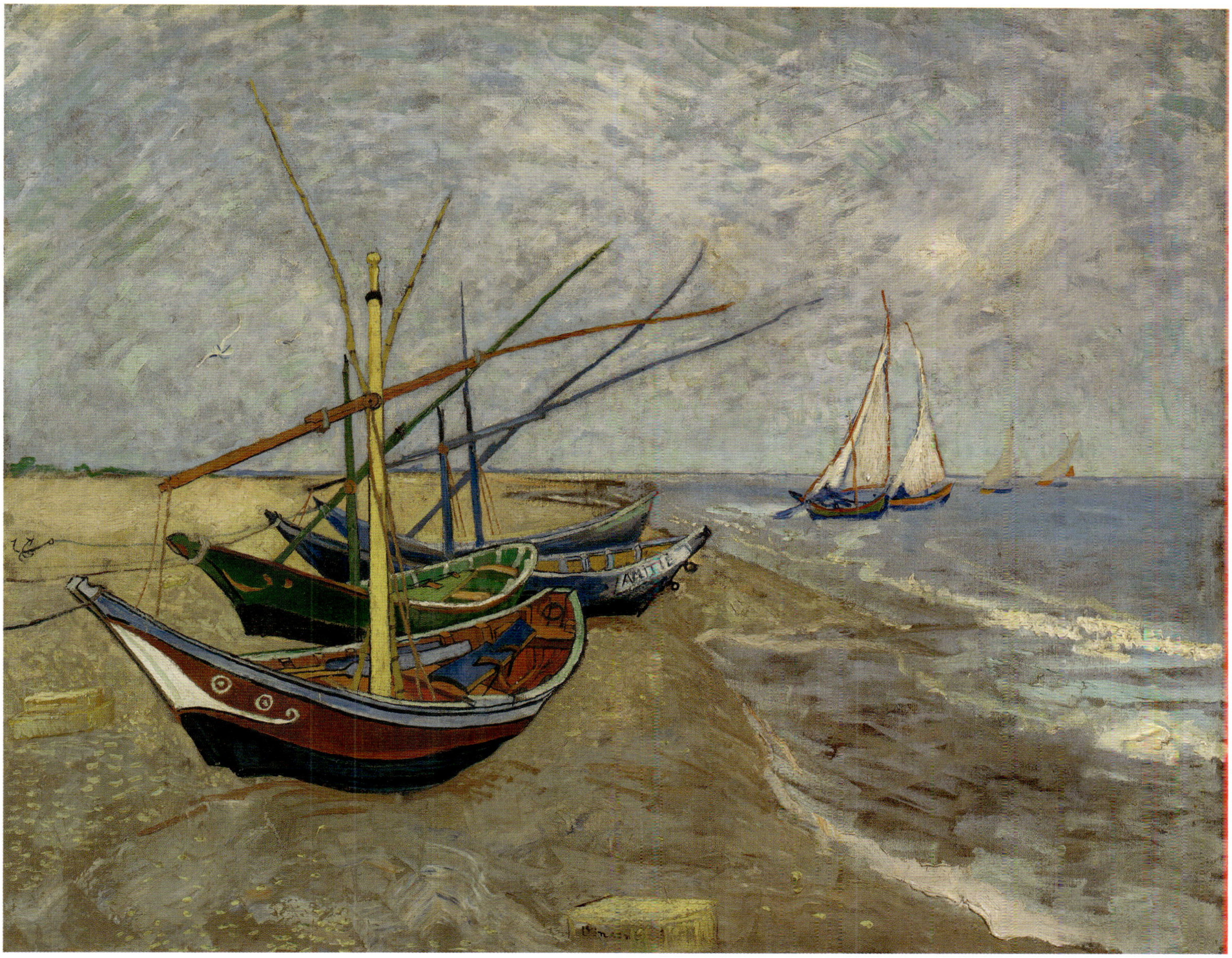

[BELOW] *Fishing Boats on the Beach at Les Saintes-Maries-de-la-Mer* (June 1888). Oil on canvas. Van Gogh Museum, Amsterdam (Vincent van Gogh Foundation).

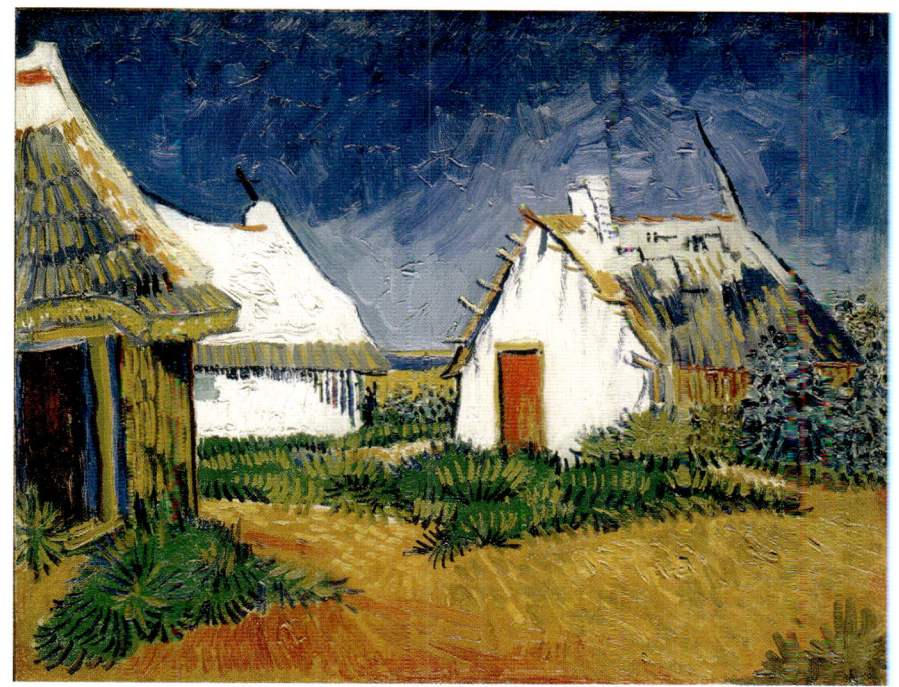

THE YELLOW HOUSE

In May 1888, Vincent rented studio space in a yellow stucco-faced building on the Place Lamartine, before completely moving in in September. He nicknamed it the "Yellow House" and painted to fill it with colorful works. His hope was to turn the house into a collective workspace—the "Studio of the South"—with other artists coming there to live and work. In October, Paul Gauguin took up Vincent's offer, and the two worked harmoniously before a disastrous split in December saw Vincent cutting off part of his ear and Paul heading back to Paris. Vincent was hospitalized in early January 1889, but by February he had suffered another breakdown. His stay in Arles was now provoking his neighbors, who saw him as dangerous. He was sent back to the Arles hospital. These bouts of mental illness put an end to any of his hope for a Studio of the South. In May 1889, he left Arles for Saint-Rémy, voluntarily committing himself to the Saint-Paul de Mausole asylum.

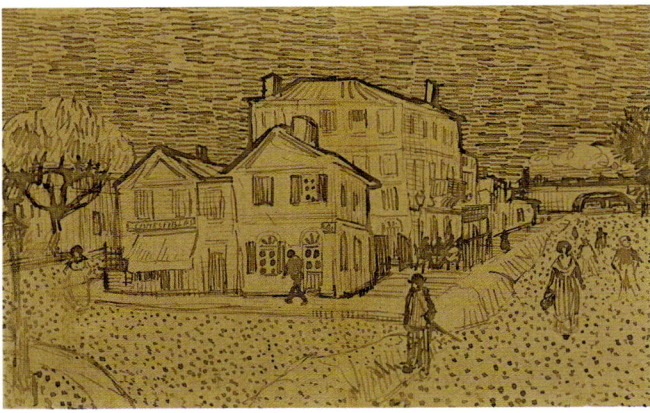

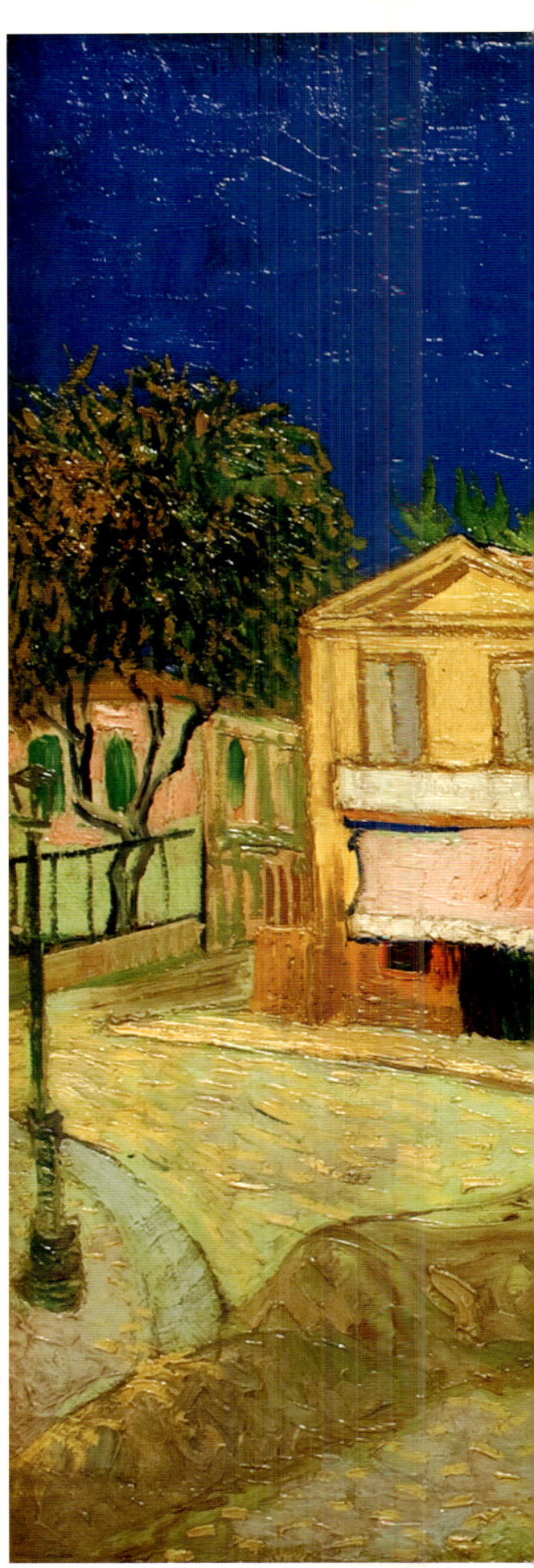

The Yellow House (September 1888). Ink on paper. Private collection.

Van Gogh included this sketch of the Yellow House in a letter to Theo.

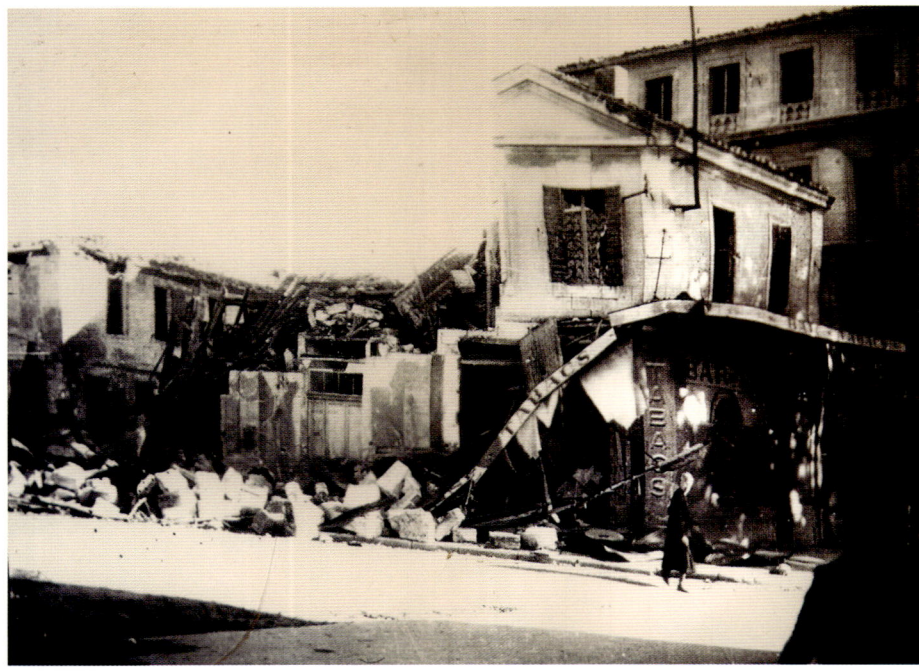

The demolished Yellow House after the bombing raid on Arles on June 25, 1944.

Many of the sites in Van Gogh's works were destroyed by Allied bombing in World War II. Today, the Yellow House site is a mecca for painters and fans.

[RIGHT] *The Yellow House (The Street)* (September 1888). Oil on canvas. Van Gogh Museum, Amsterdam (Vincent van Gogh Foundation).

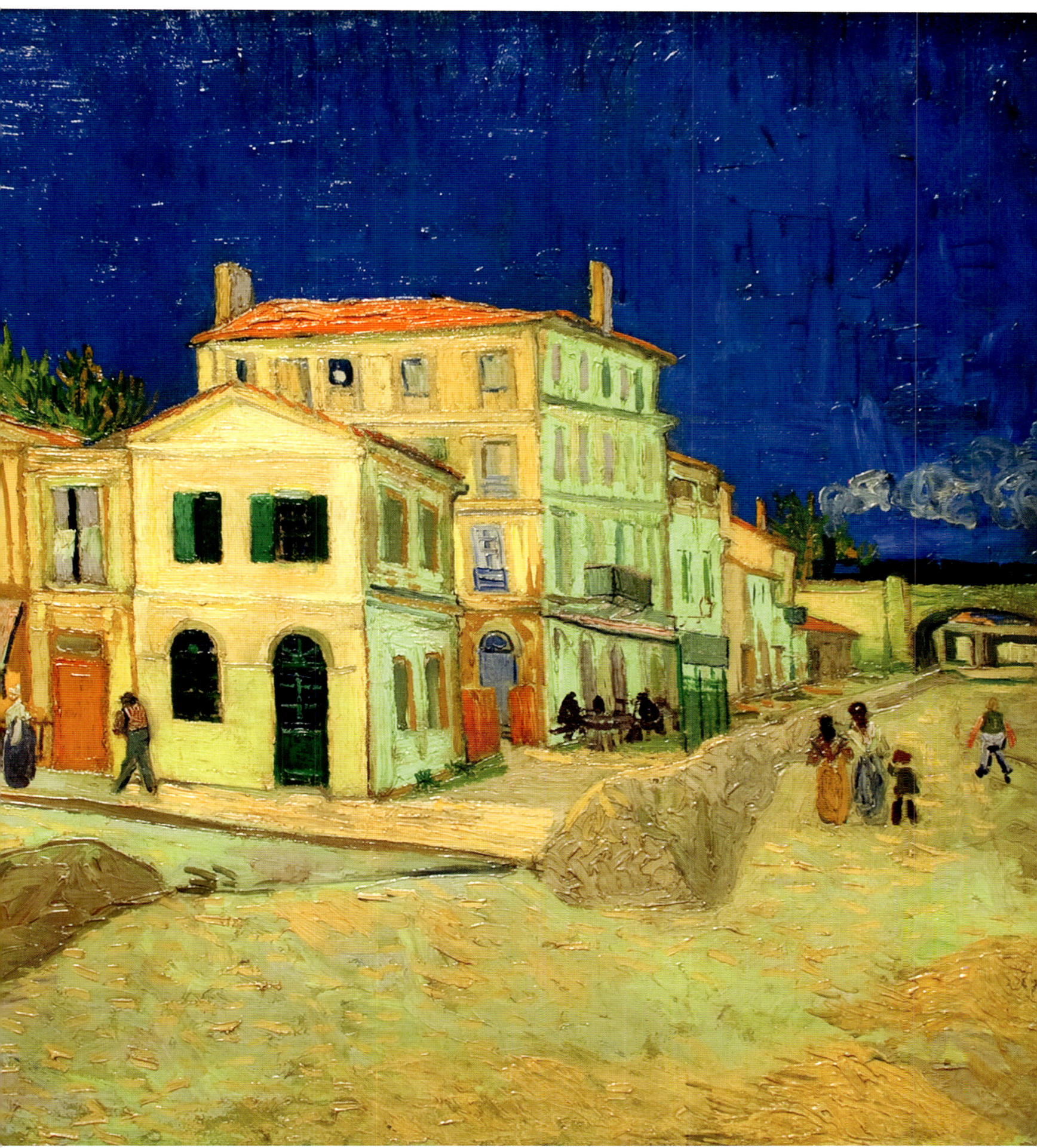

"*I try more and more to be myself, caring relatively little whether people approve or disapprove.*"

~ VINCENT

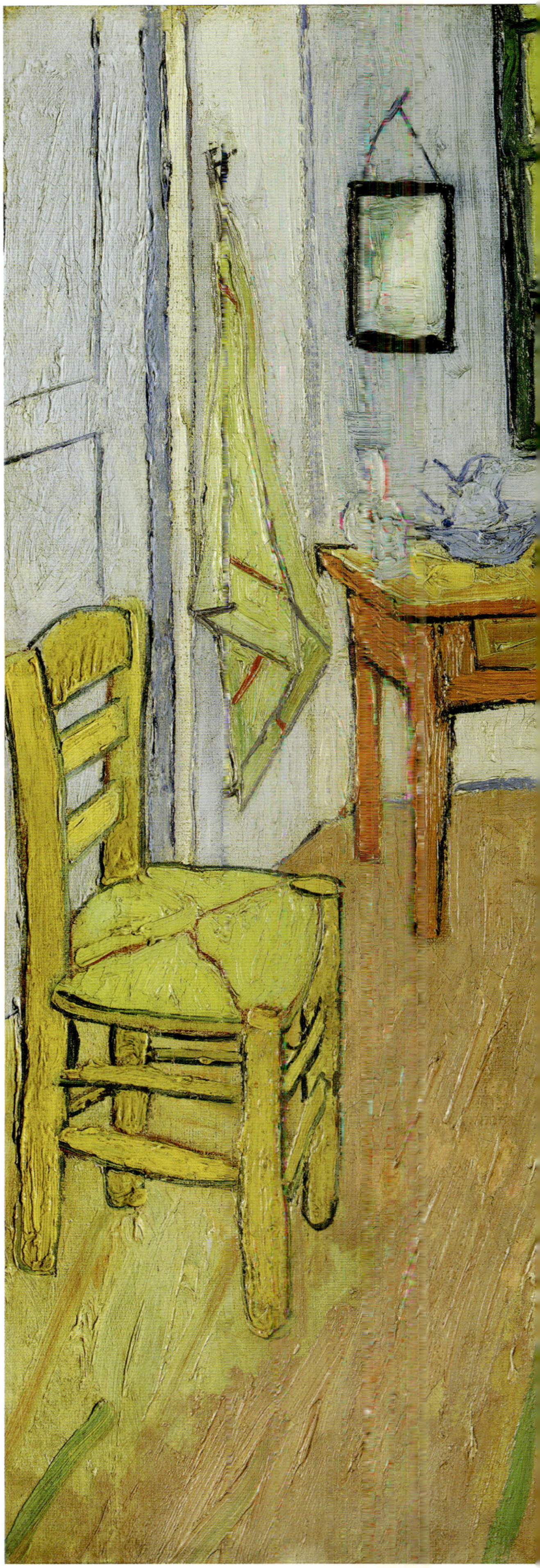

[RIGHT] **The Bedroom** (first version, 1888).
Oil on canvas. Van Gogh Museum, Amsterdam (Vincent van Gogh Foundation).

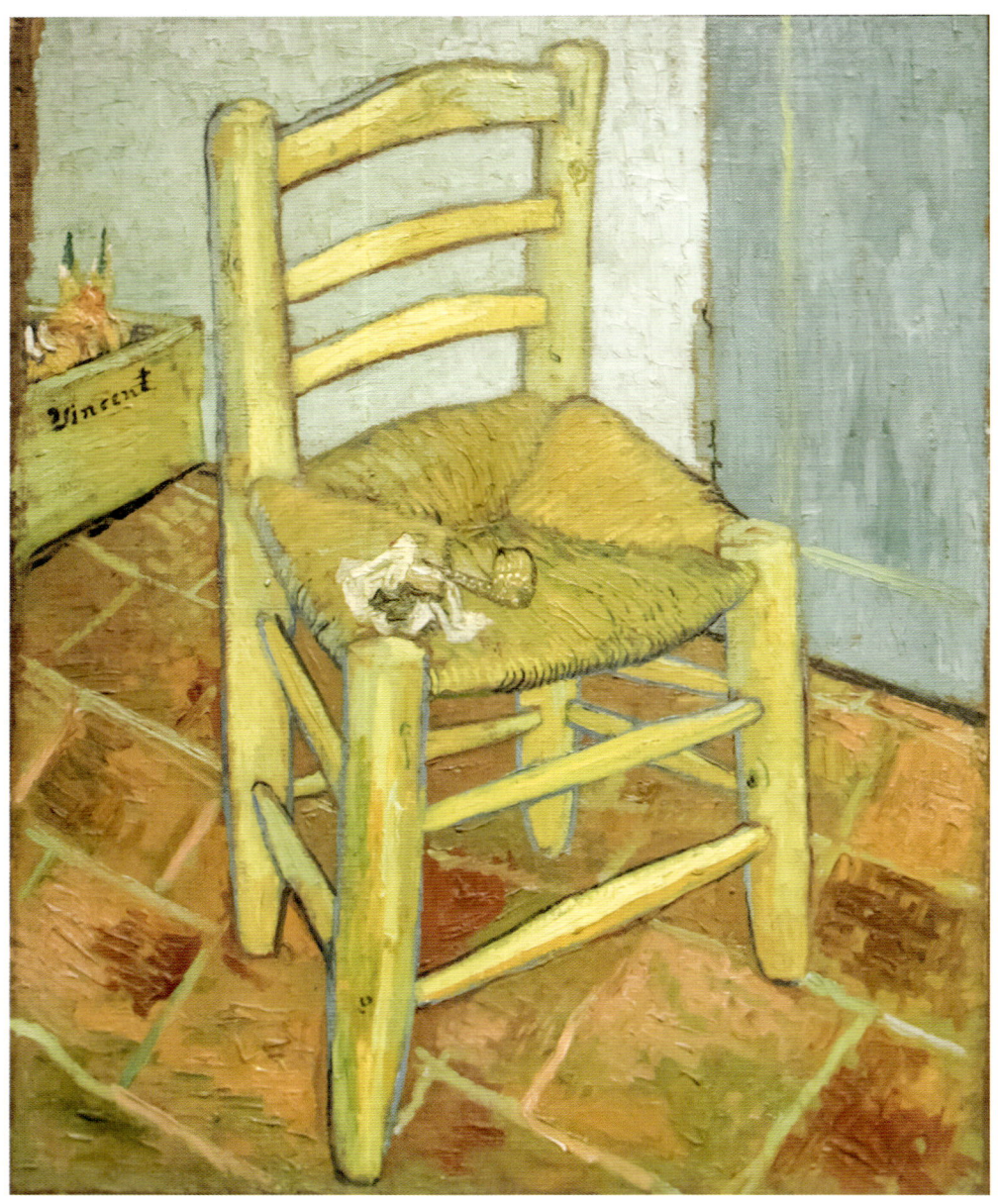

Vincent's Chair with His Pipe (December, 1888). Oil on canvas. National Gallery, London.

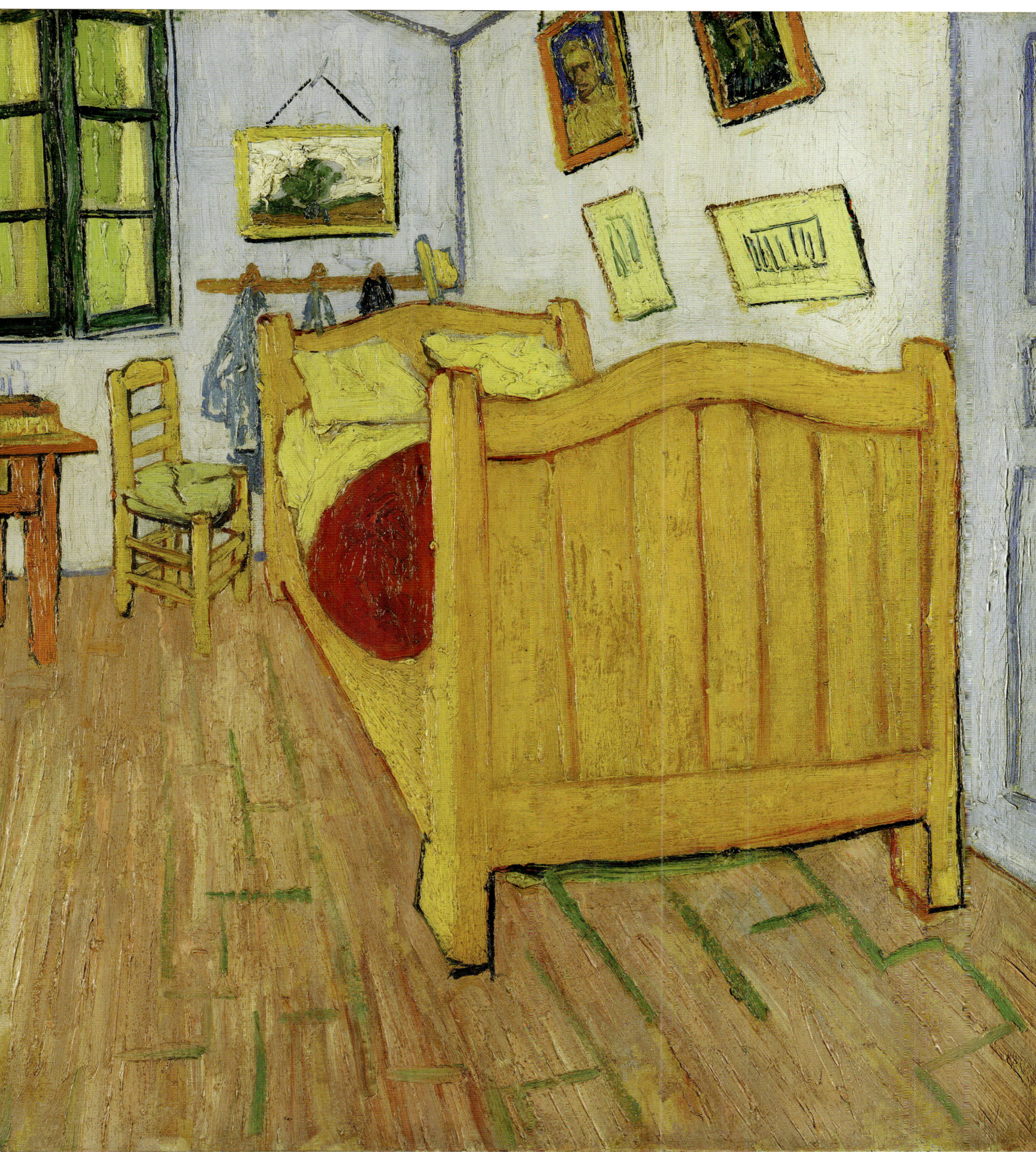

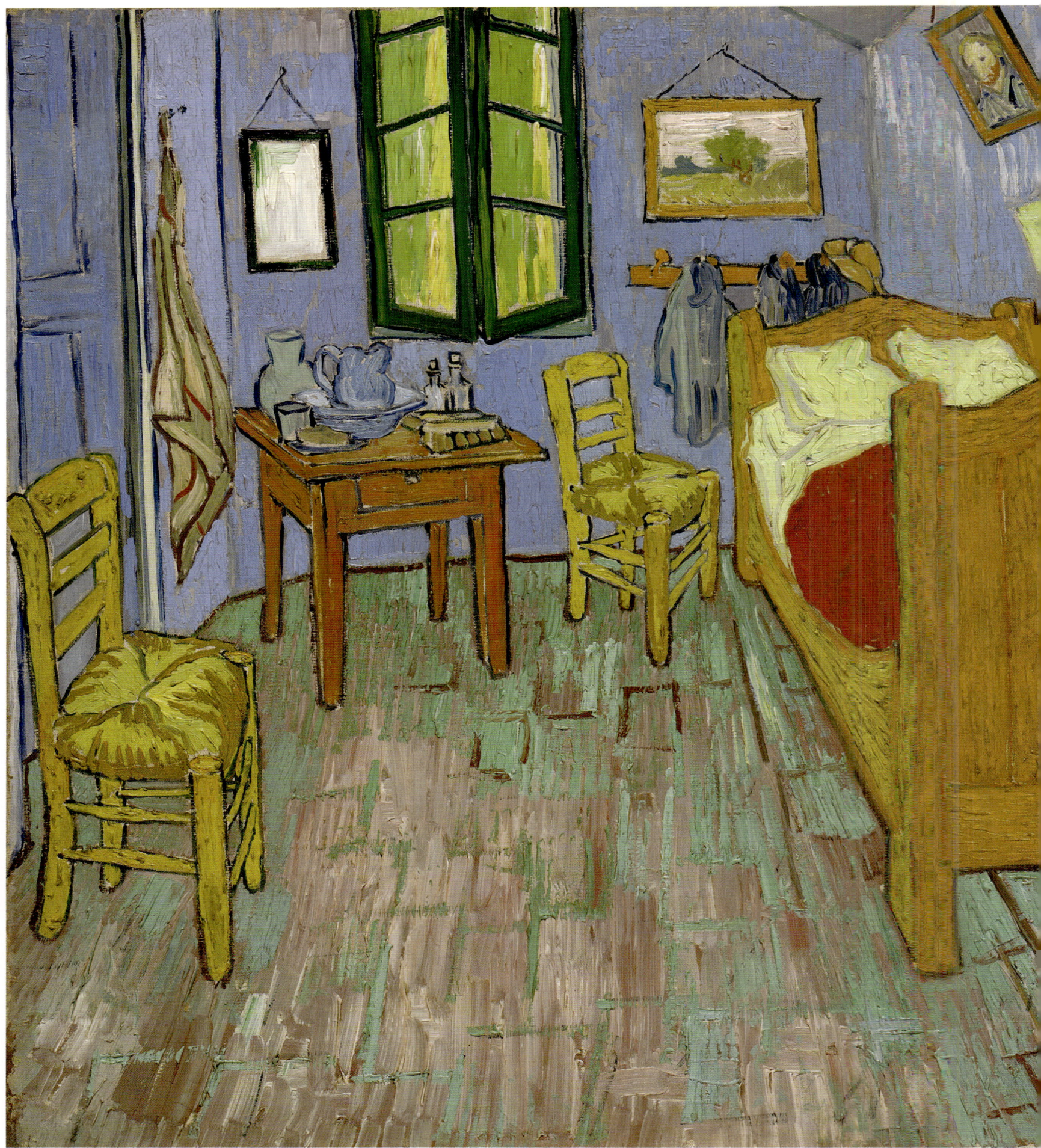

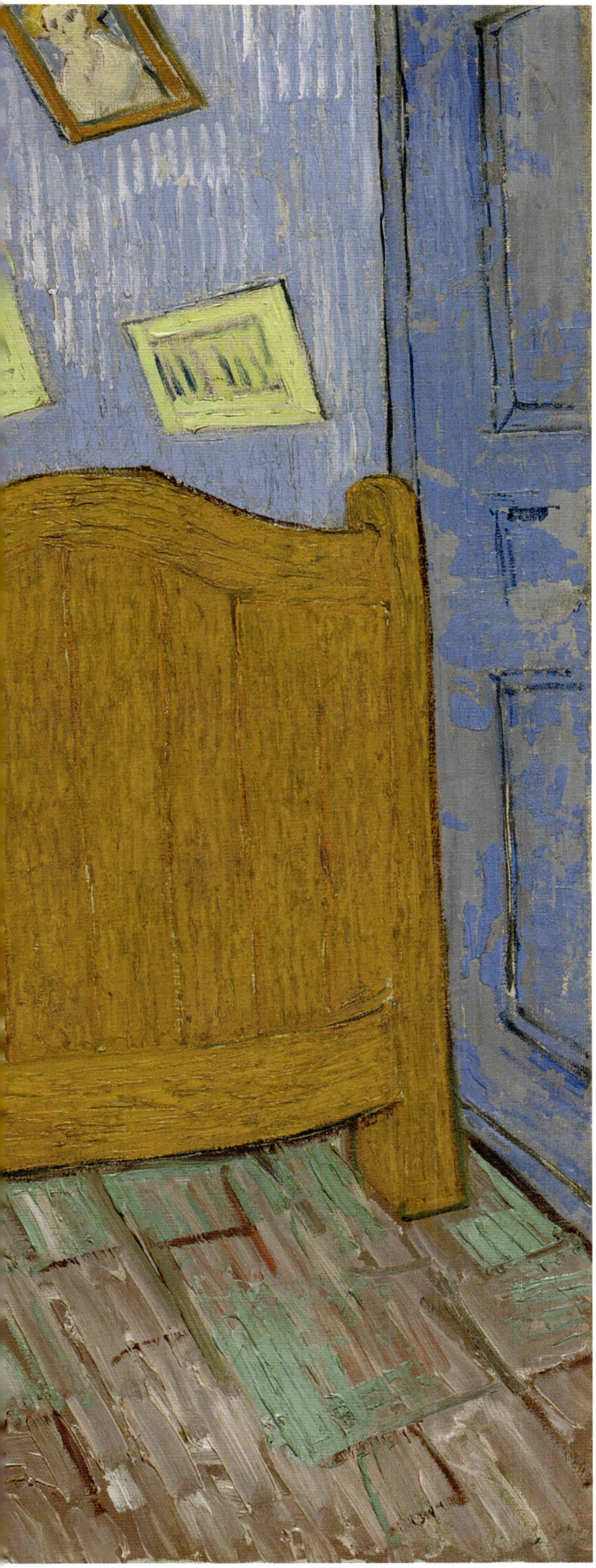

[LEFT] *The Bedroom* (second version, September 1889).
Oil on canvas. The Art Institute of Chicago.

In summer 1889, Vincent set about to redo some of what he considered his best work in "réductions," or smaller versions, for his mother and his sister Wil. He painted two new versions of The Bedroom, and although they are quite similar to the first, they are not exact copies.

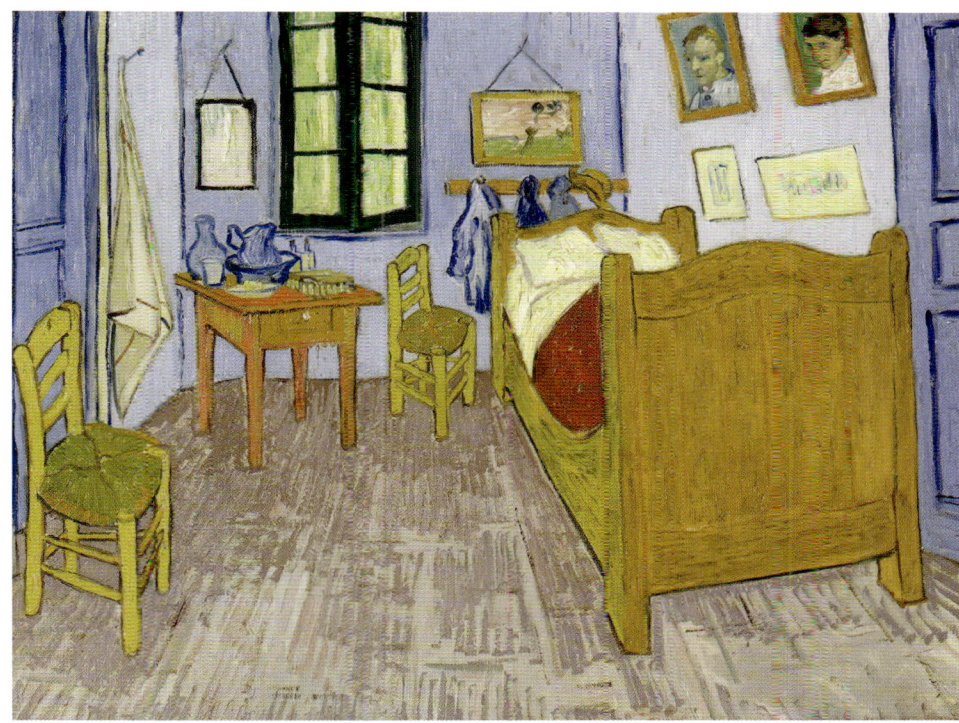

The Bedroom (third version, September 1889).
Oil on canvas. Musée d'Orsay, Paris

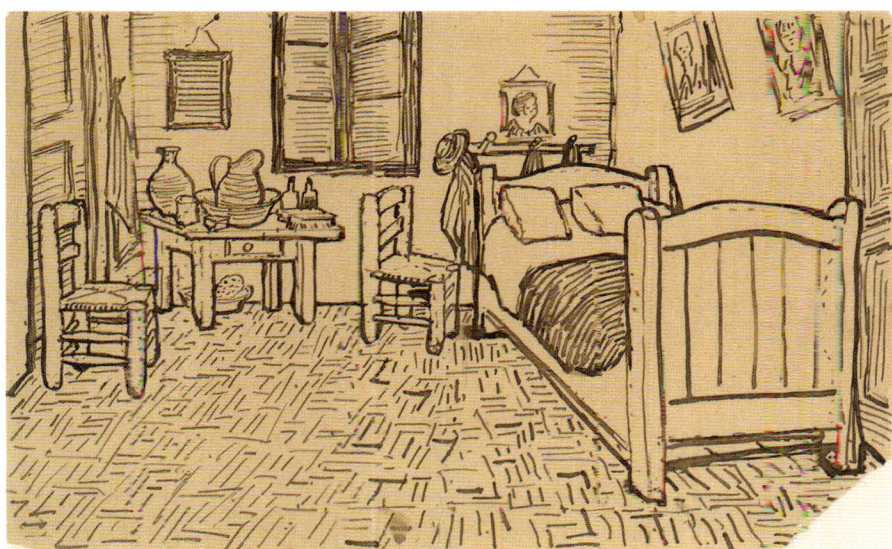

Vincent's Bedroom in Arles (October 1888). Pen and India ink on paper.
Van Gogh Museum, Amsterdam (Vincent van Gogh Foundation).

Vincent included this sketch in a letter to Theo.

"*It is a study of his armchair of dark, red-brown wood, the seat of greenish straw, and in the absent person's place a lighted candlestick and some modern novels.*"

~ VINCENT, IN A LETTER TO ALBERT AURIER

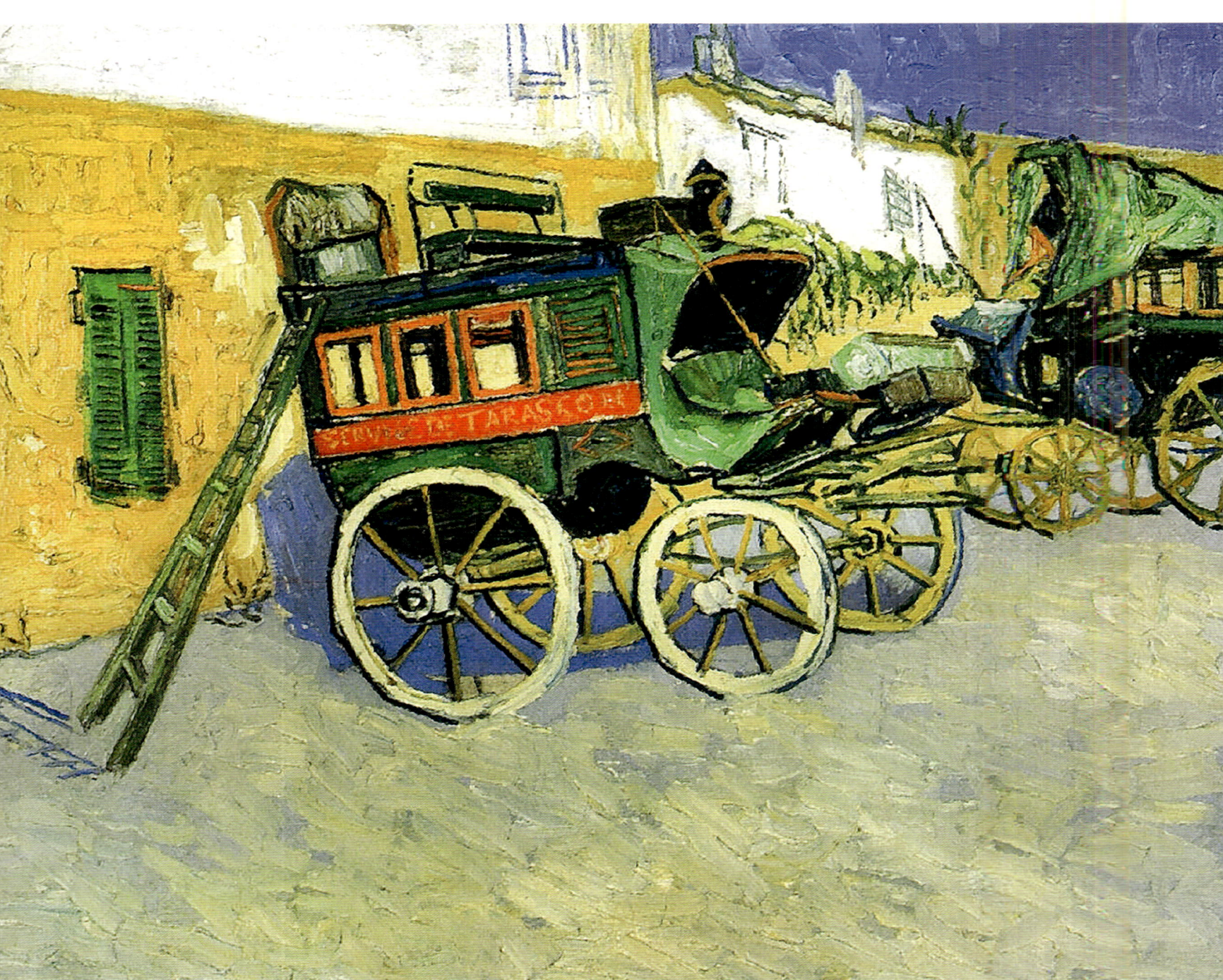

[ABOVE]
The Tarascon Diligence (October 1888). Oil on canvas. The Art Museum, Princeton, New Jersey.

This painting is part of the Décoration for the Yellow House, Vincent's main project in Arles, which he worked on from August 1888 until his breakdown the day before Christmas of that year.

[OPPOSITE PAGE]
Paul Gauguin's Armchair (December 1888). Oil on canvas. Van Gogh Museum, Amsterdam (Vincent van Gogh Foundation).

This chair, which Paul Gauguin used during his stay at the Yellow House in Arles, served as a kind of portrait of Vincent's estranged fiend.

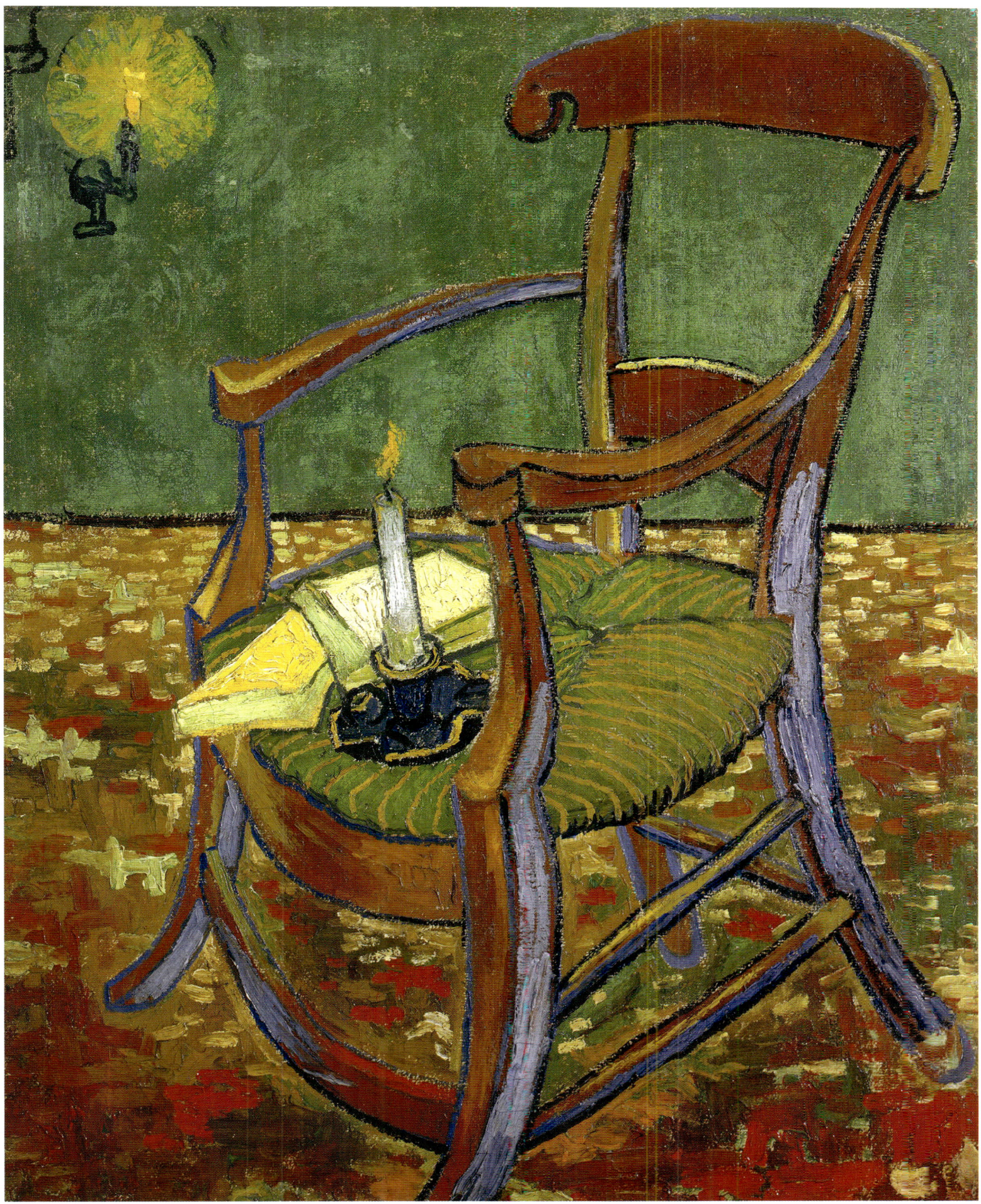

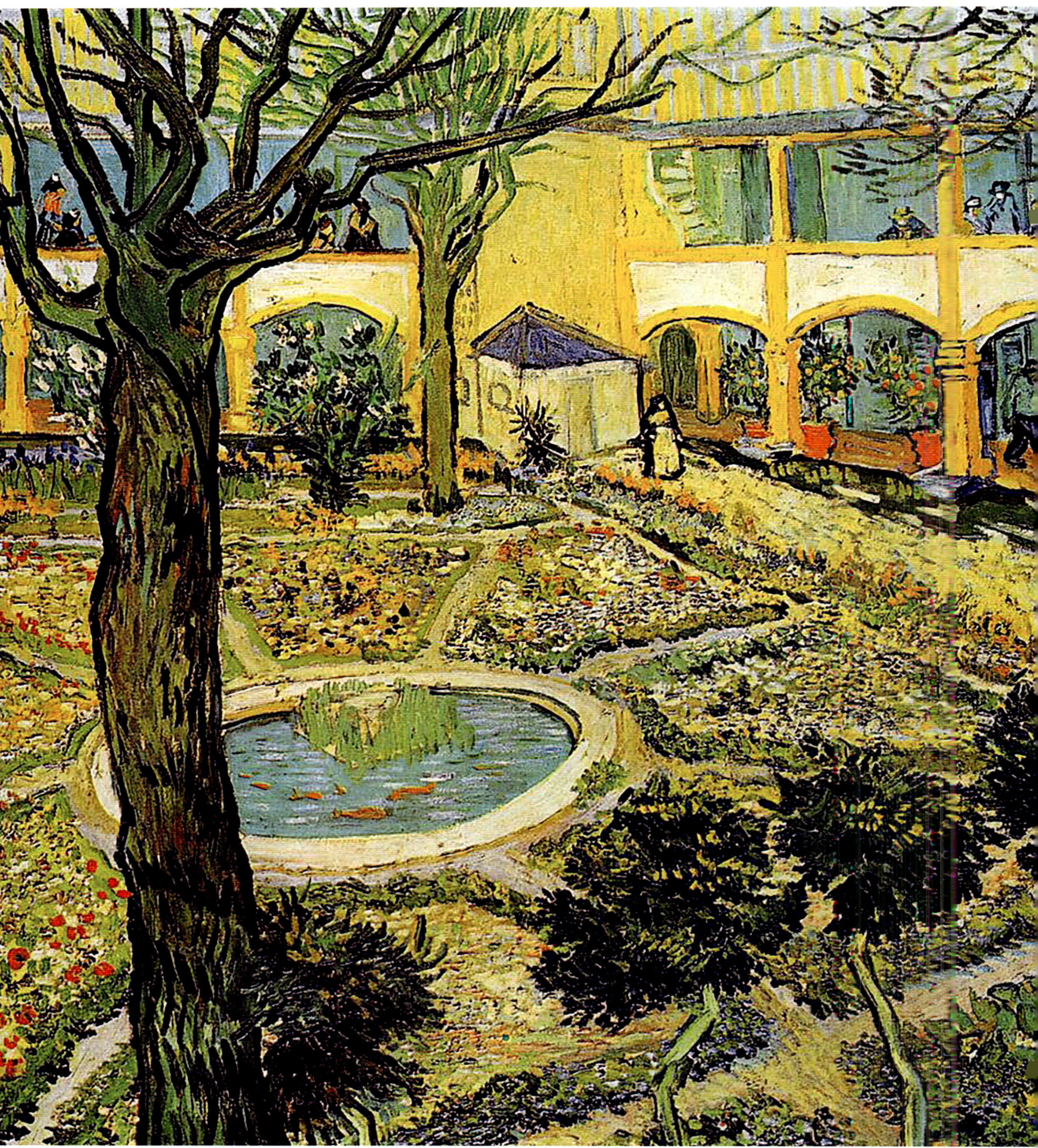

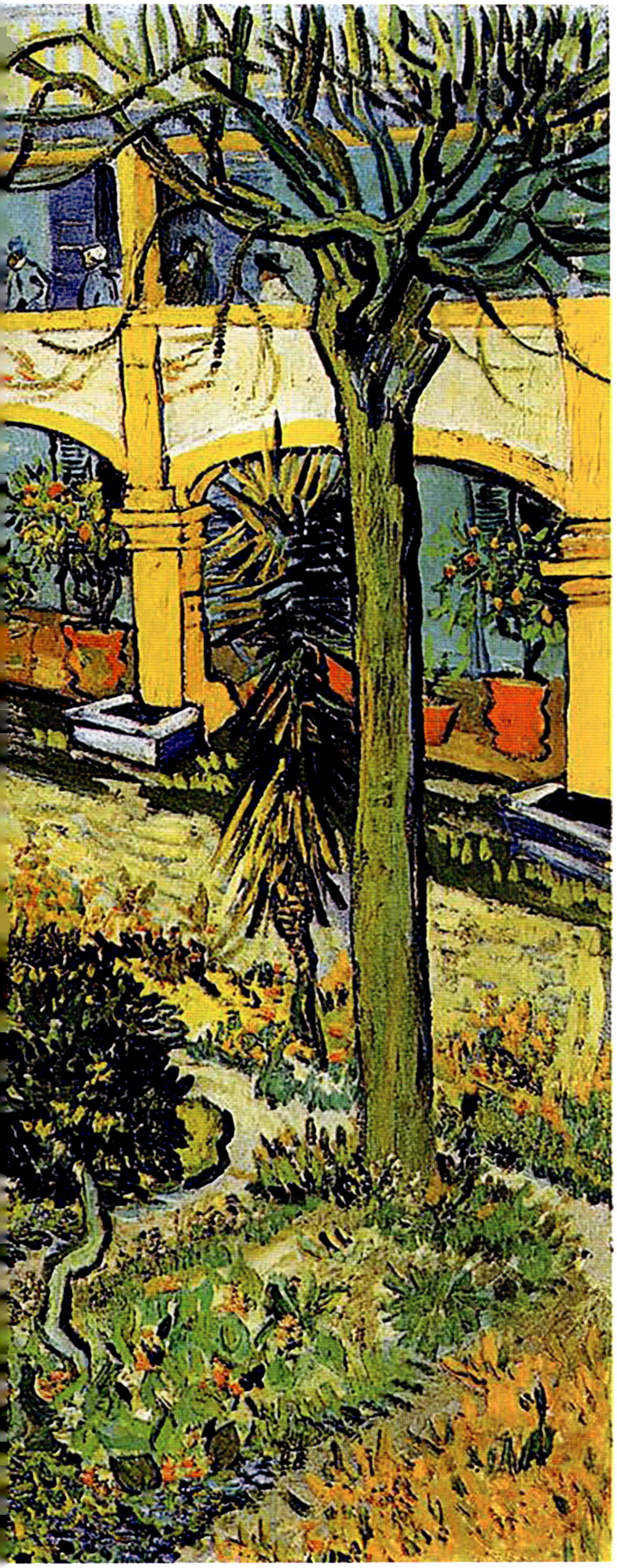

IN THE ARLES HOSPITAL

Vincent painted three works of the Arles hospital: *Arles: Ward in the Hospital in Arles, Garden of the Hospital in Arles,* and *Portrait of Doctor Félix Rey,* who had treated him there. The Old Hospital of Arles, also known as Hôtel-Dieu-Saint-Espirit, was built in the 16th and 17th centuries. The courtyard of the former Arles hospital is now called Espace Van Gogh in Vincent's honor.

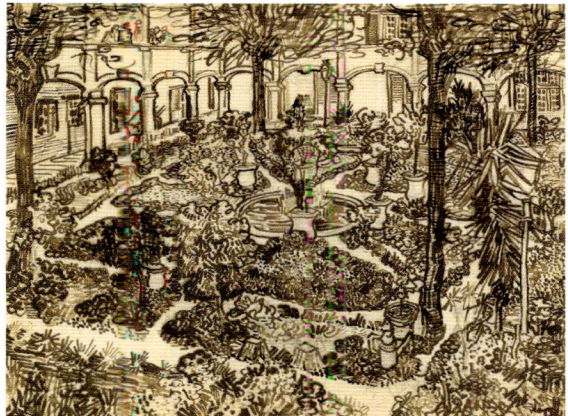

Garden of the Hospital (May 1889). Pencil, reed-pen and pen, brush, and ink on paper. Van Gogh Museum, Amsterdam (Vincent van Gogh Foundation).

This courtyard was Vincent's view during his months at the hospital in Arles.

[LEFT]
Garden of the Hospital in Arles
(April 1889). Oil on canvas. Winterthur Museum, Delaware (Oskar Reinhart Collection 'Am Römerholz').

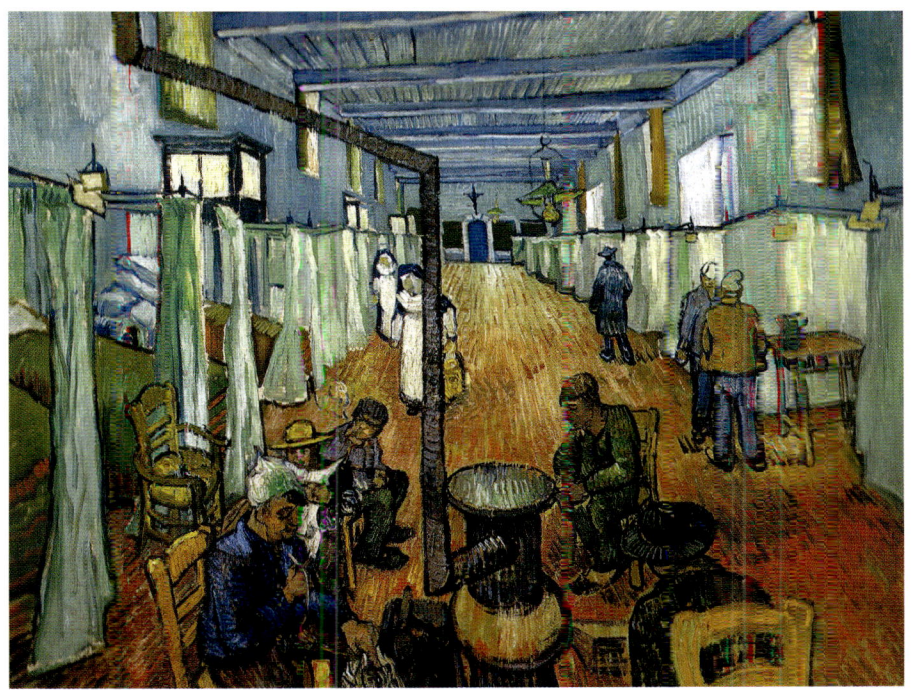

Ward in the Hospital in Arles (April, 1889). Oil on canvas Winterthur Museum, Delaware (Oskar Reinhart Collection 'Am Römerholz').

This painting of the fever ward at the Arles Hospital was finished in late 1889, some months after he had left the facility

AT SAINT-PAUL DE MAUSOLE IN SAINT-RÉMY

On May 8, 1889, Vincent allowed himself to be committed to Saint-Paul de Mausole, a psychiatric asylum in Saint-Rémy de Provence, just outside Arles, and began a near-year-long stay. He did not give up his art while hospitalized, and in between bouts of psychoses, he painted and drew, drawing inspiration from the asylum's garden and its hilly surrounding landscape of wheat fields, olive groves, and cypress trees. It was amid the arresting scenery of Saint-Rémy that he created some of his most famous works.

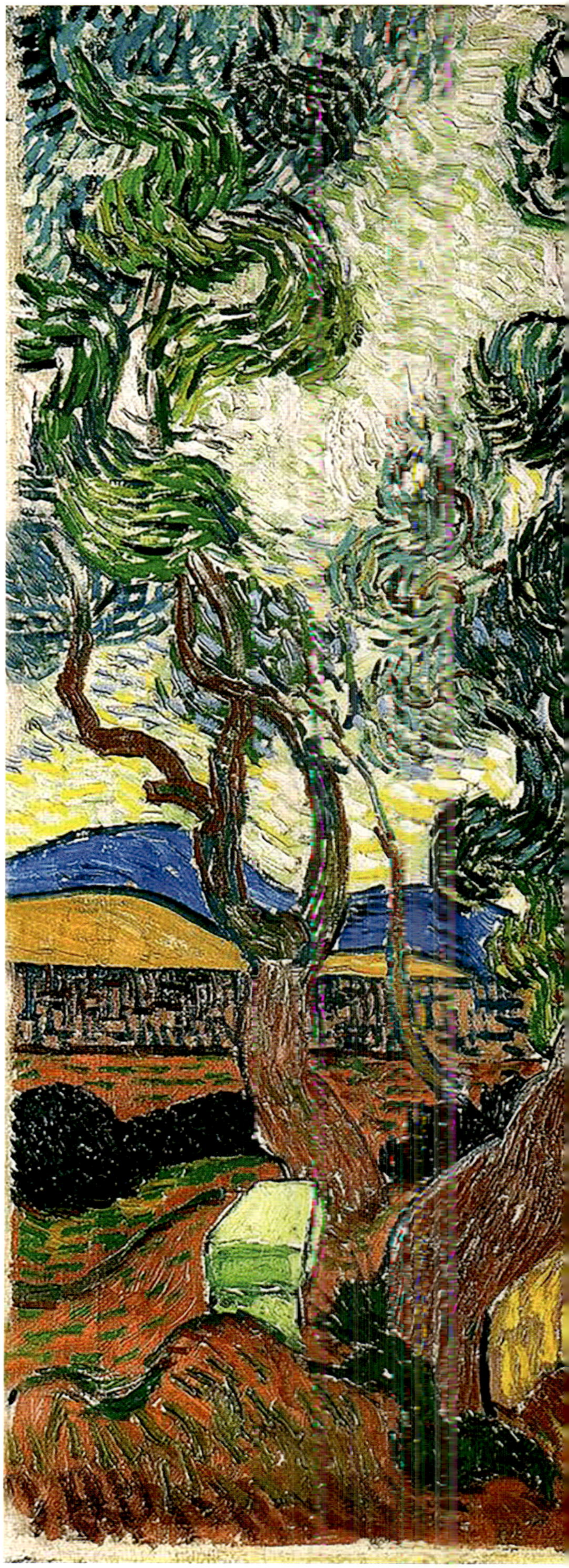

[RIGHT]
The Garden of Saint-Paul Hospital (December 1889). painting. Oil on canvas. Van Gogh Museum, Amsterdam (Vincent van Gogh Foundation).

[BELOW]
The Garden of Saint-Paul Hospital (May 1889). Oil on canvas. Kröller-Müller Museum, Otterlo.

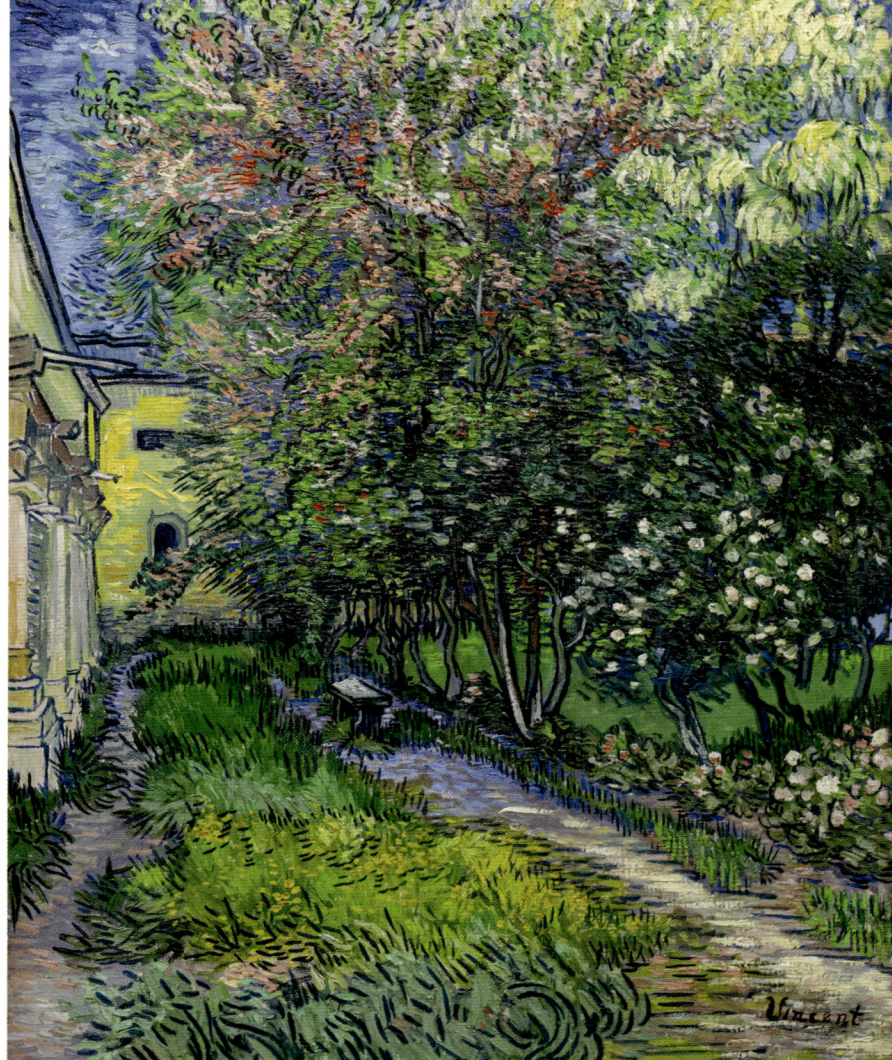

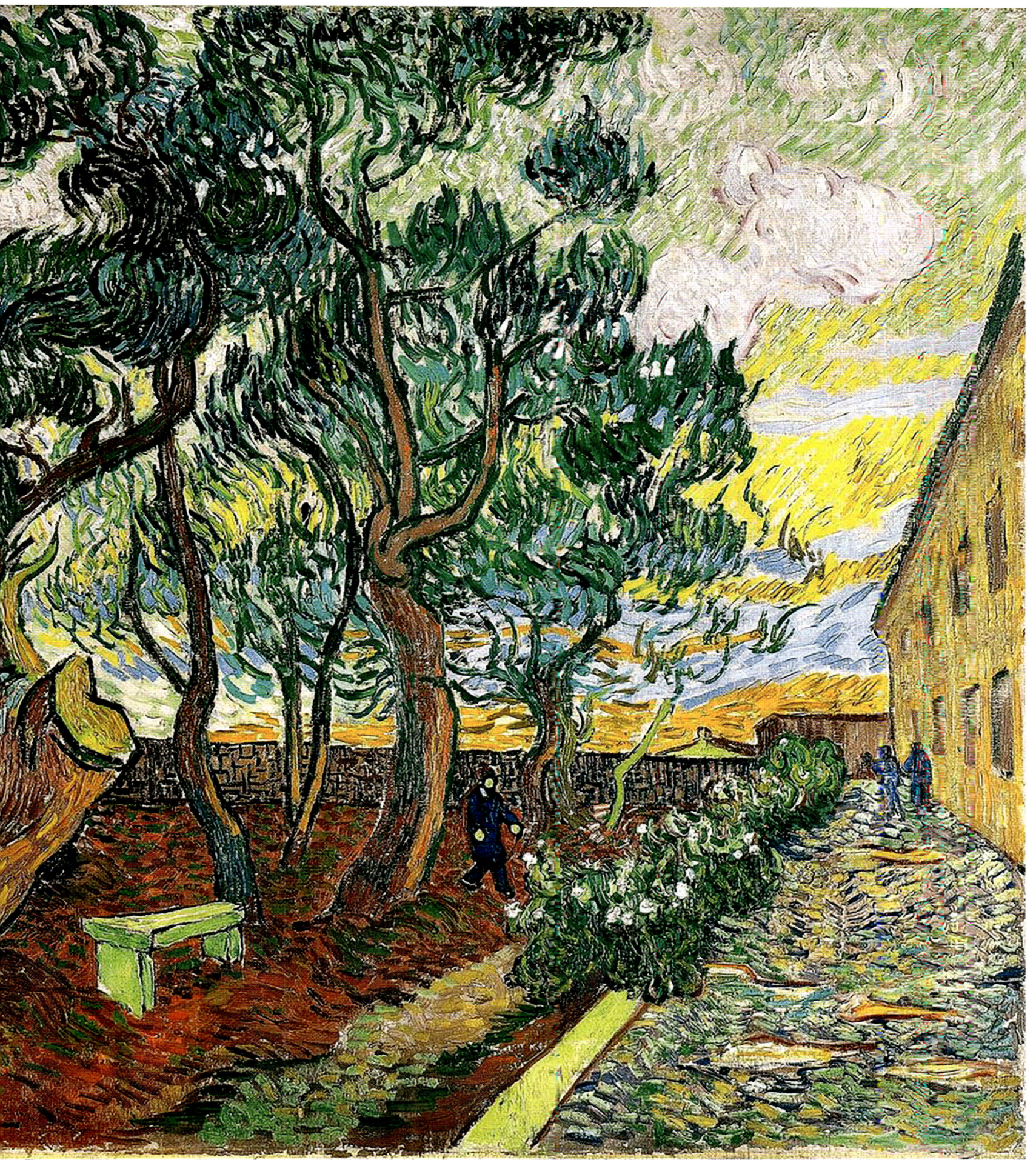

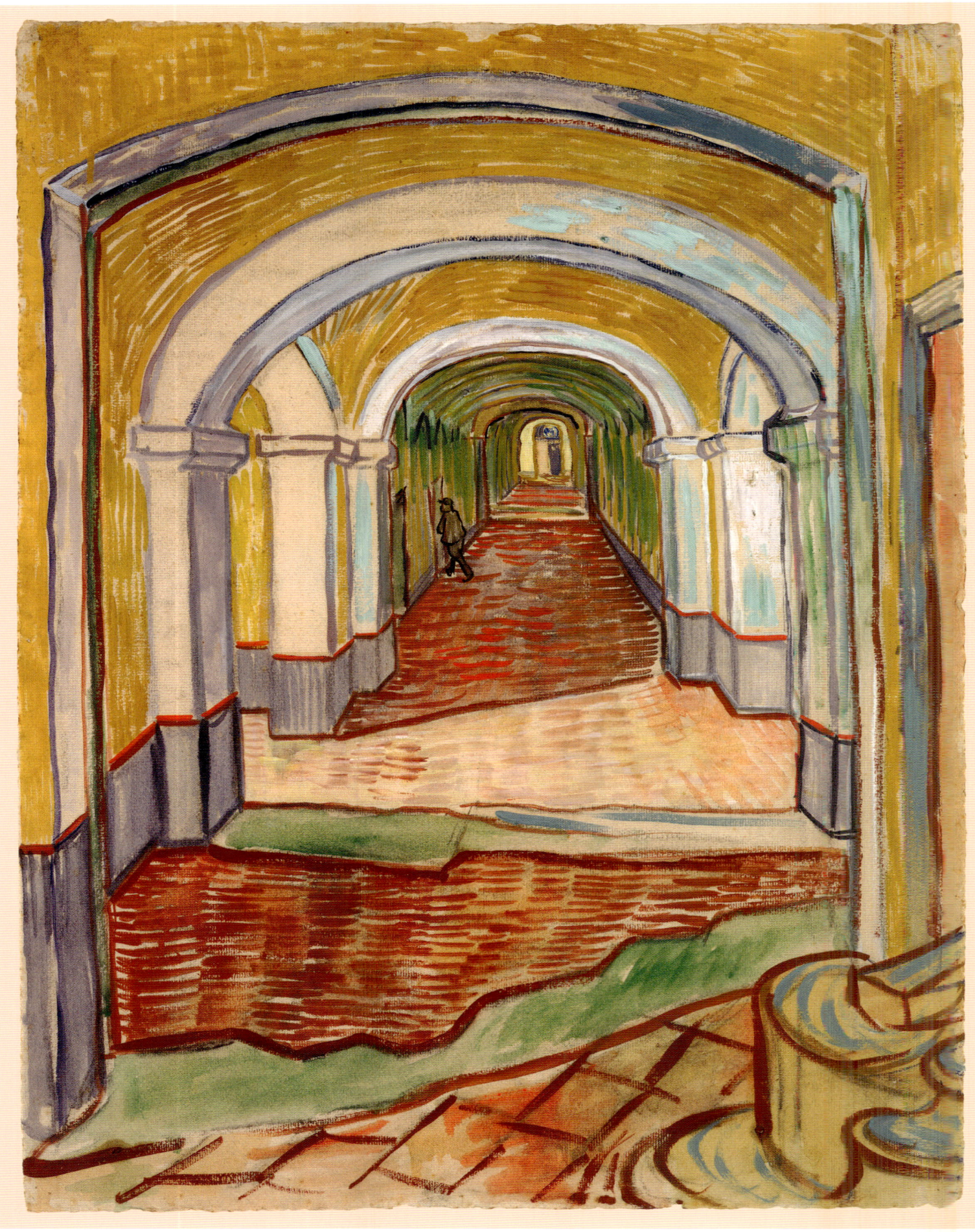

[OPPOSITE PAGE]
Corridor in the Asylum
(September 1889). Oil
on canvas. Metropolitan
Museum of Art, New York.

*Vincent painted this
haunting image of a lonely
corridor stretching into
the distance in the Saint-
Paul hospital. Despite the
bleakness of this view, it was
here he found the inspiration
to paint such masterpieces
as* Irises *and* Starry Night, *as
well as his* Wheat Field *and*
Olive Grove *series.*

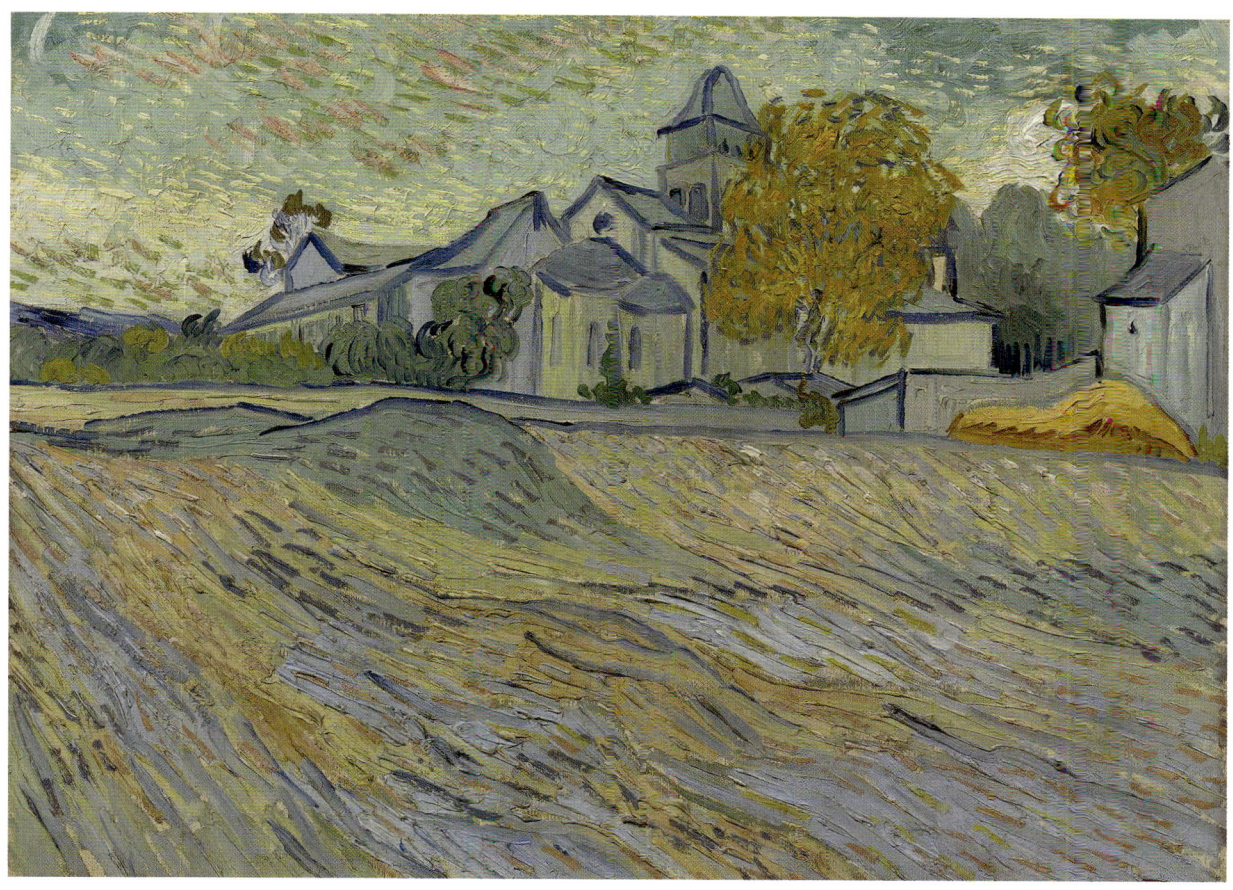

[ABOVE]
*View of the
Asylum and
Chapel of
Saint-Rémy*
(Autumn
1889). Oil on
canvas. Private
collection.

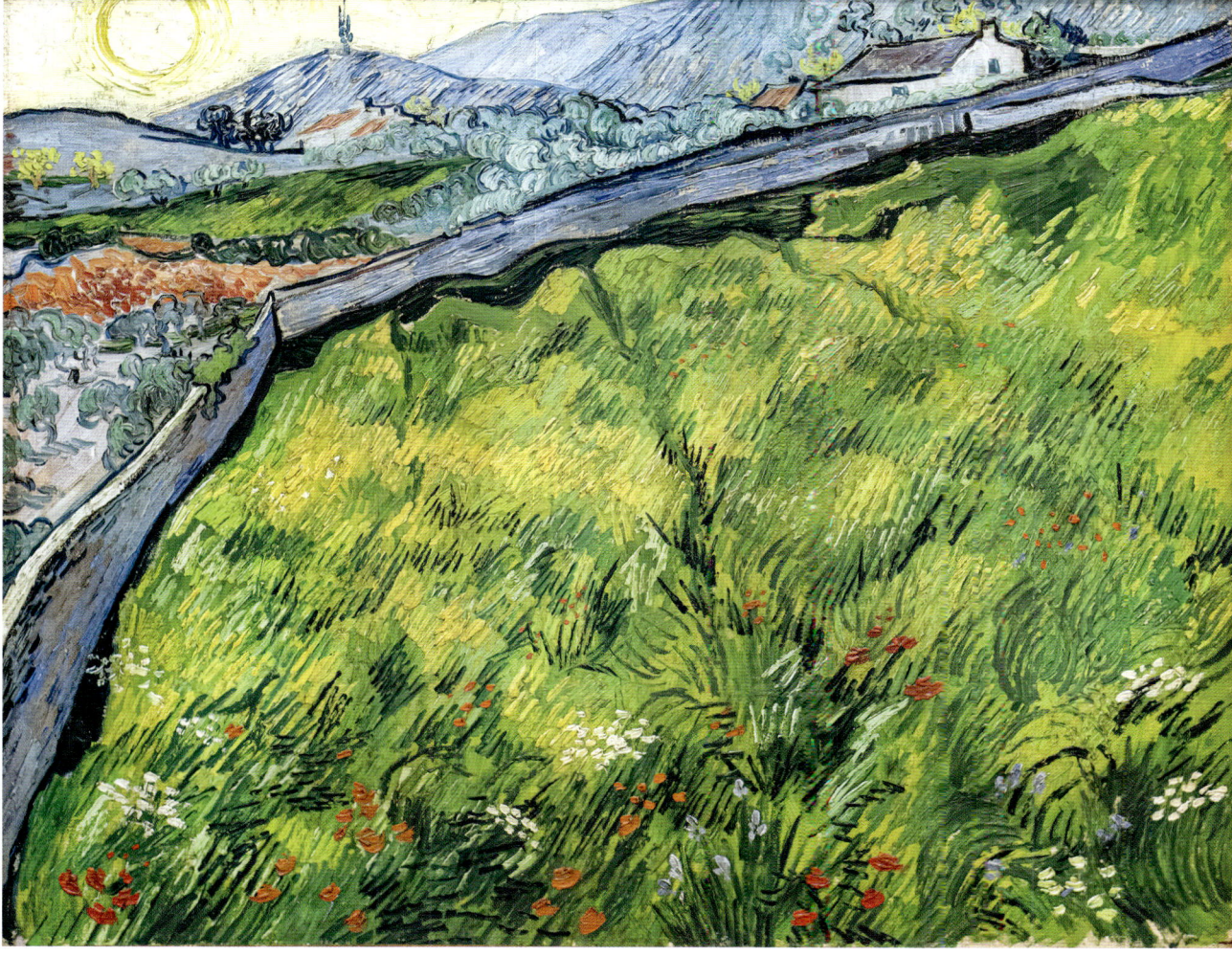

[LEFT]
*Field of Spring
Wheat at Sunrise*
(May–June, 1889).
Oil on canvas.
Kröller-Müller
Museum, Otterlo.

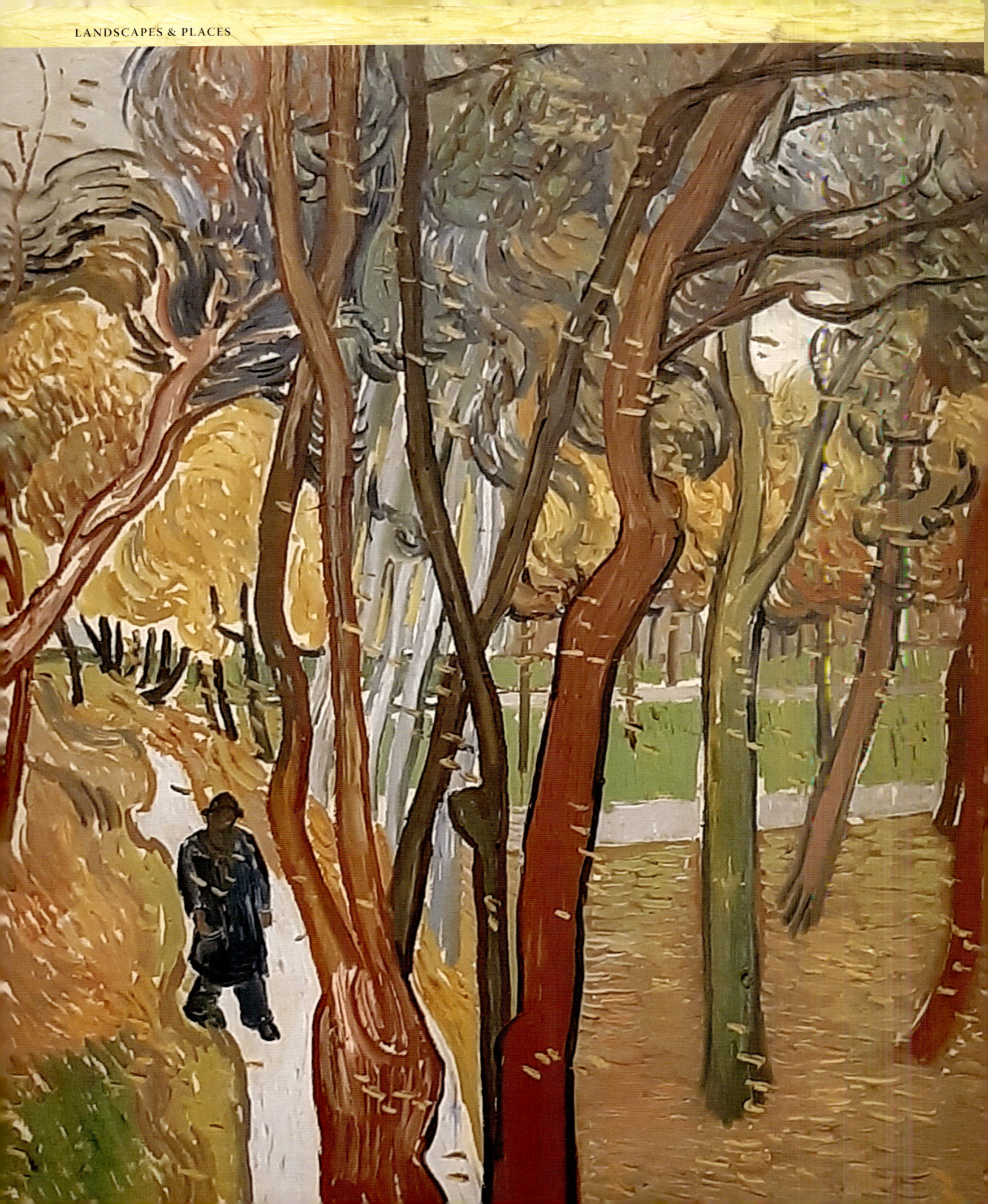

[OPPOSITE PAGE] ***The Garden of Saint Paul's Hospital ("Leaf-Fall")*** (October 1889).
Oil on canvas. Van Gogh Museum, Amsterdam (Vincent van Gogh Foundation).

During his first two months at Saint Paul's, Vincent remained indoors, fearing another attack, but he did begin to work outdoors in October. He most likely painted this in or near the garden of the hospital. From a high vantage point, it shows a lonely walker amid a swirl of leaves created by tall trees with bare trunks and dense crowns. The red-brown trees in the foreground seem to split the canvas in two.

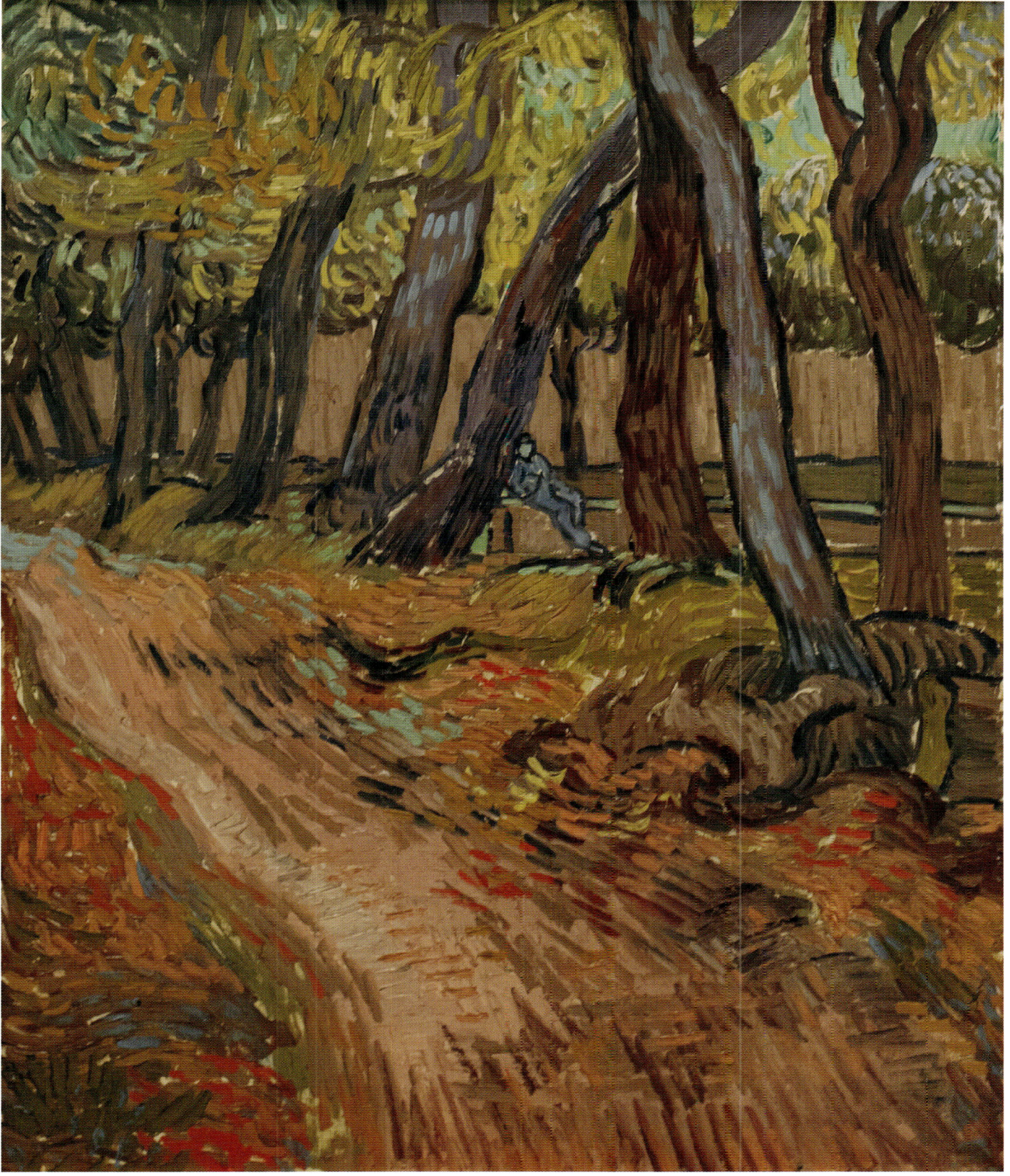

Path in the Garden of the Asylum (November 1889). Oil on canvas. Kröller-Müller Museum, Otterlo.

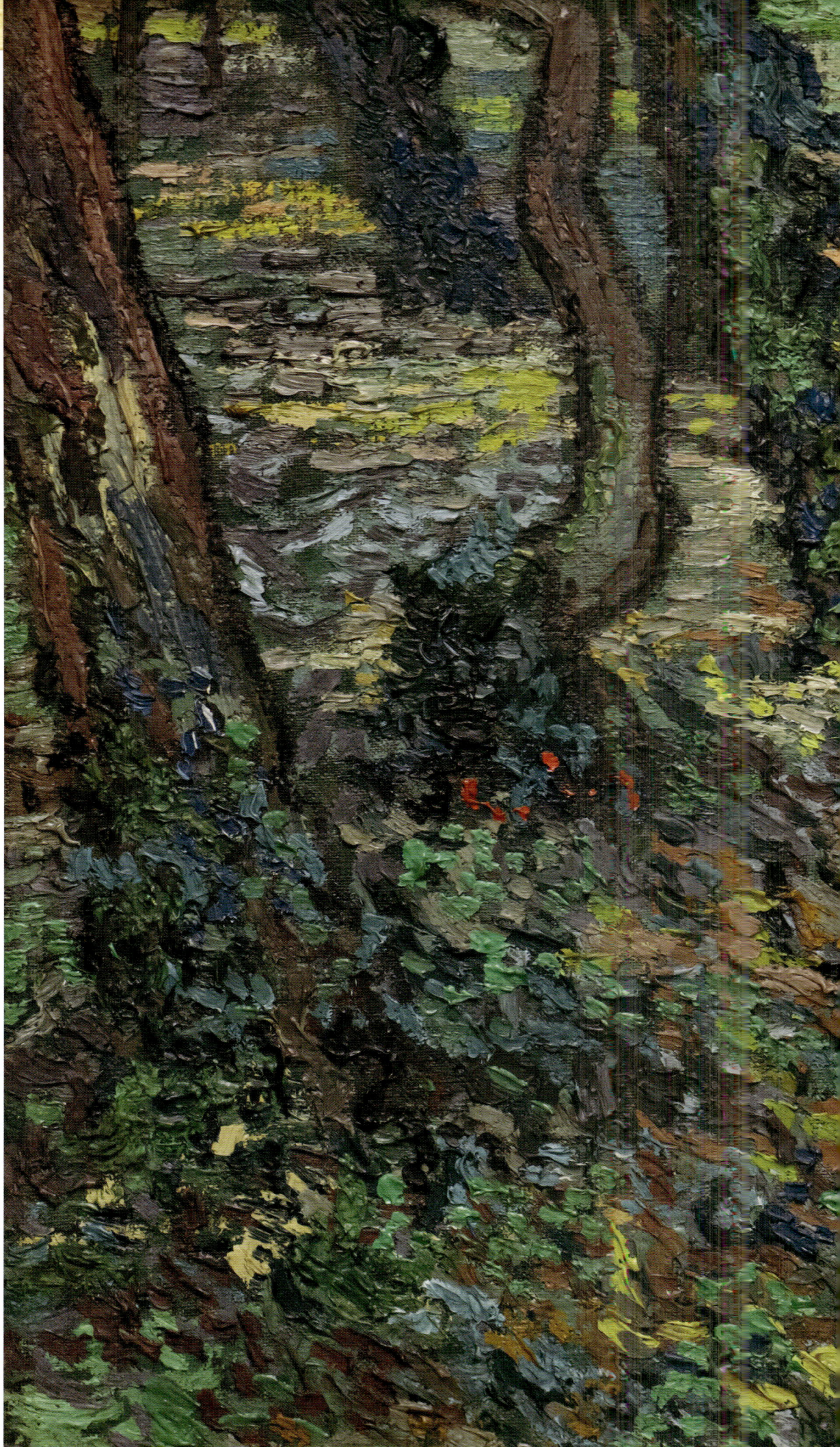

" They all come to see when I'm working in the garden, and I can assure you are more discreet and more polite to leave me in peace than, for example, the good citizens of Arles."

~ VINCENT, ON THE HABIT
OF OTHER SAINT-PAUL
RESIDENTS WATCHING
HIM PAINT OUTDOORS

Tree Trunks with Ivy
(July 1889). Oil on canvas.
Kröller Müller Museum, Otterlo.

Here, Vincent uses thick impasto to capture the sous-bois, *or undergrowth of vegetation on the forest floor. He called the* sous-bois *motif the "eternal nests of greenery for lovers."*

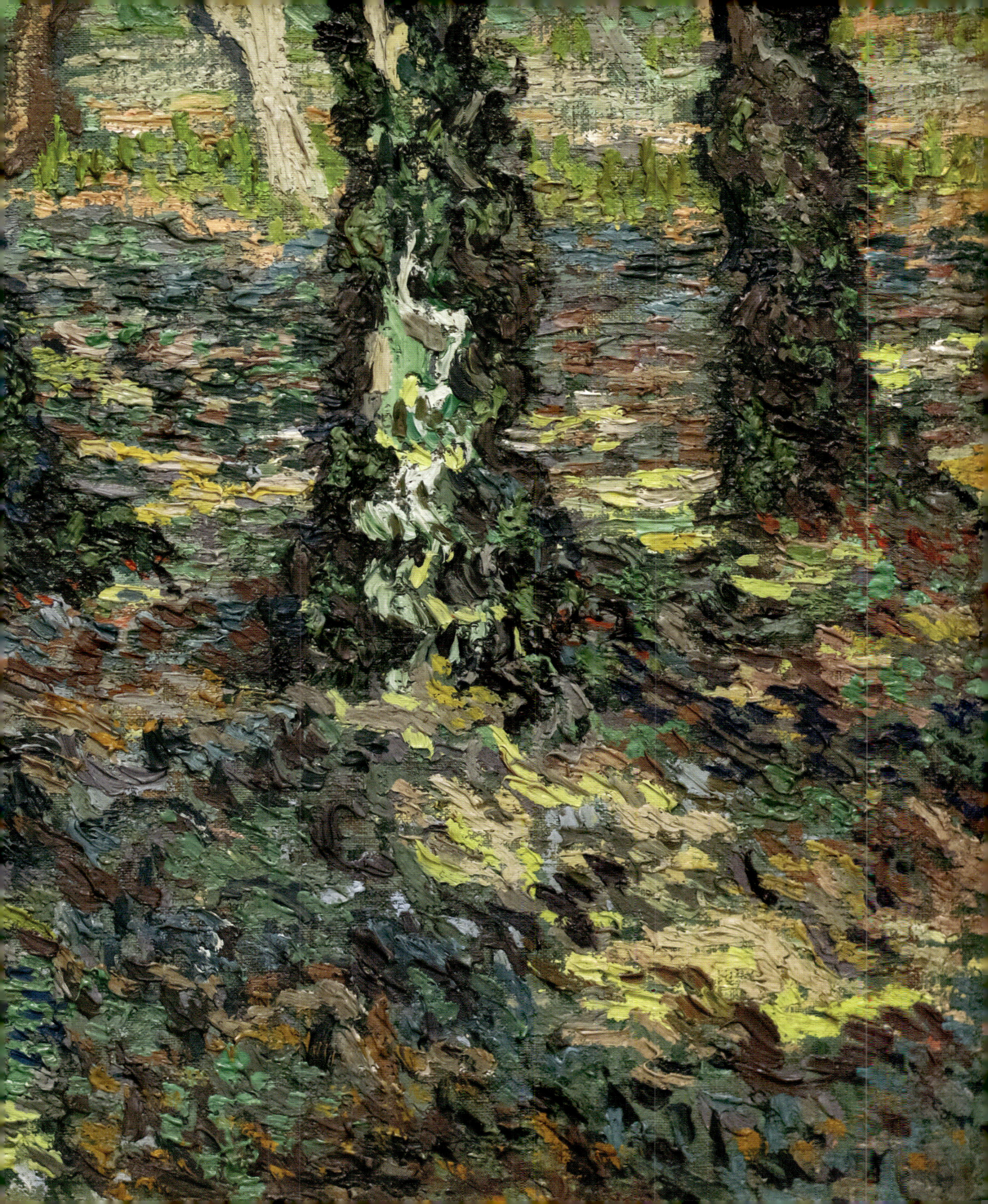

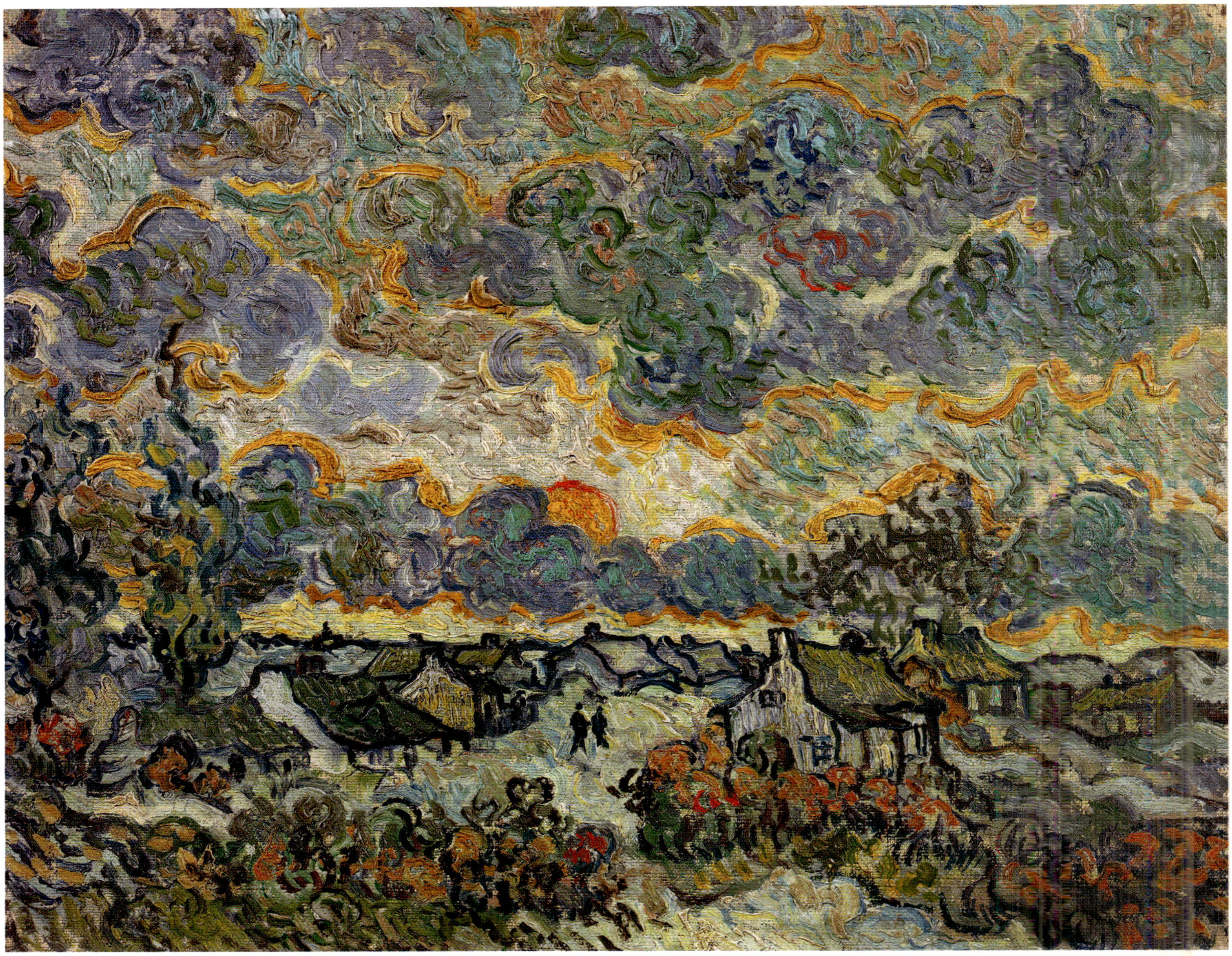

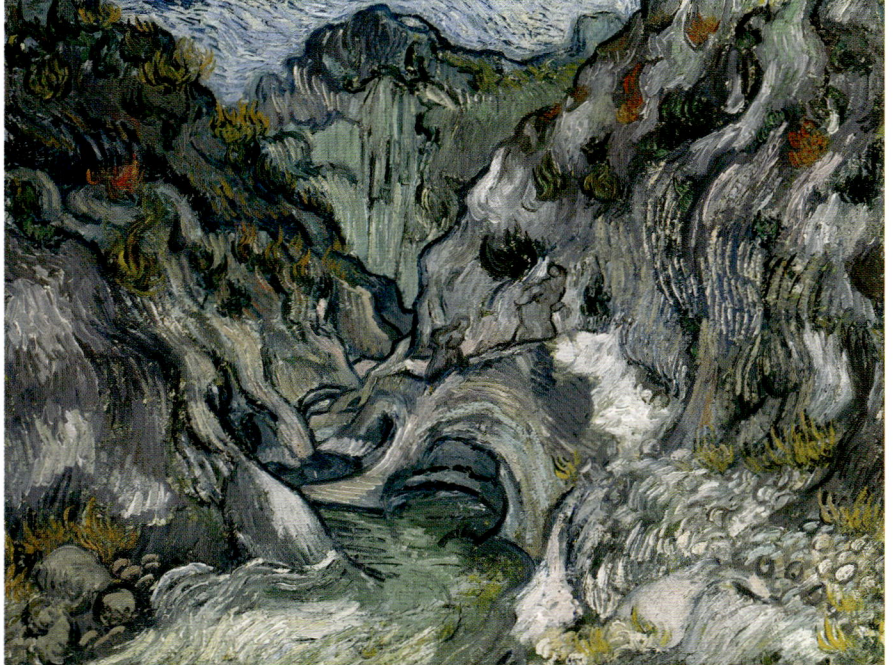

[ABOVE]
Cottages and Cypresses: Reminiscence of the North
(March–April 1890). Oil on canvas on panel. Van Gogh
Museum, Amsterdam (Vincent van Gogh Foundation).

[LEFT]
Les Peiroulets Ravine (December, 1889)
Oil on canvas. Kröller-Müller Museum, Otterlo.

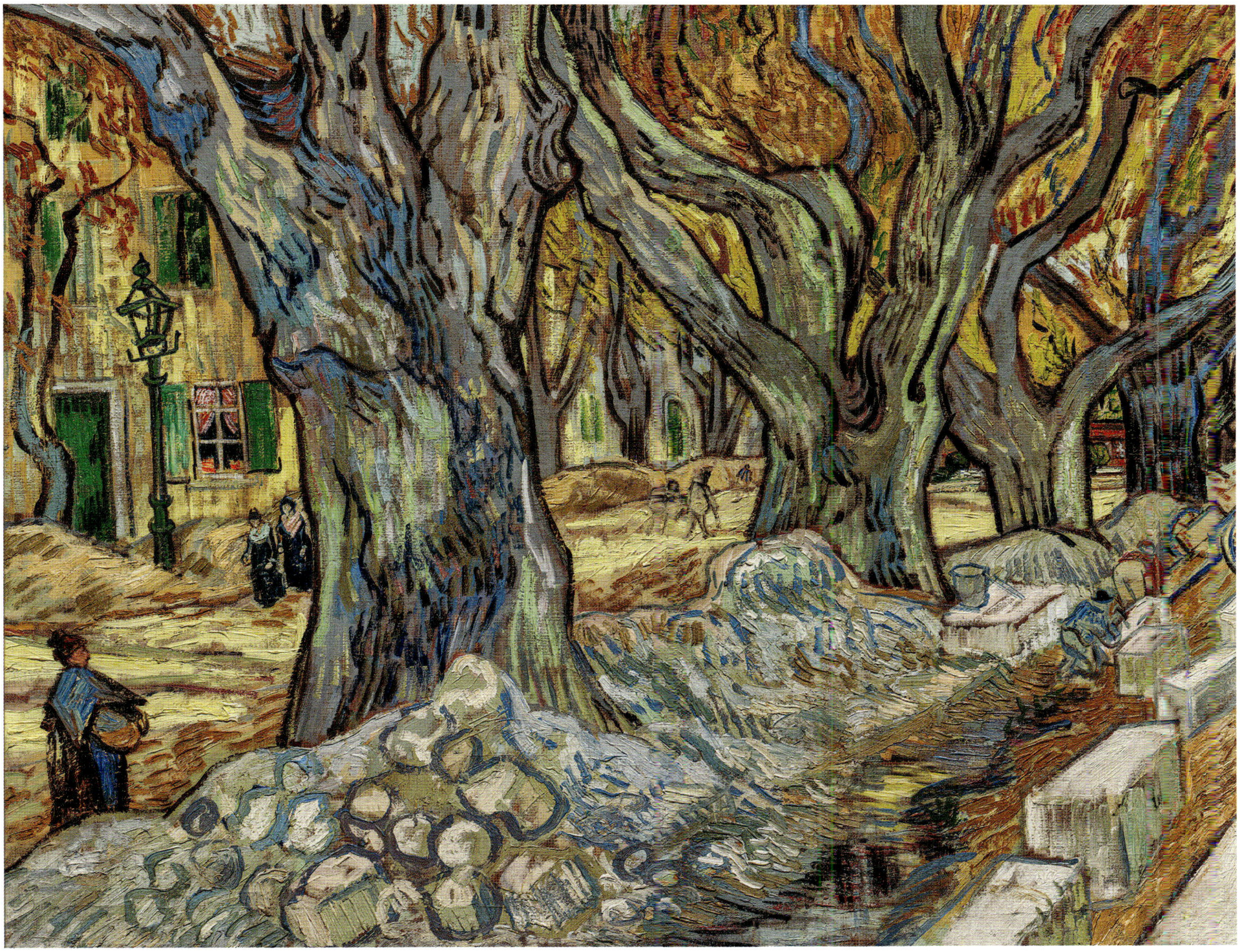

The Road Menders (November 1889). Oil on canvas. The Phillips Collection, Washington, D.C.

"*The last study I have done is a view of the village, where they were at work – under some enormous plane trees – repairing the pavements. So there are heaps of sand, stones and gigantic trunks – the leaves yellowing and here and there you get a glimpse of a house front and small figures.*"

~ VINCENT, TO THEO, DECEMBER 1889

The Road Menders (November 1889). Oil on canvas. Cleveland Museum of Art.

Vincent painted two versions of The Road Menders, *which show the repaving of the Cours de l'Est in Saint-Rémy. The first he executed* en plein air, *and shortly after he created the Phillips version in the studio.*

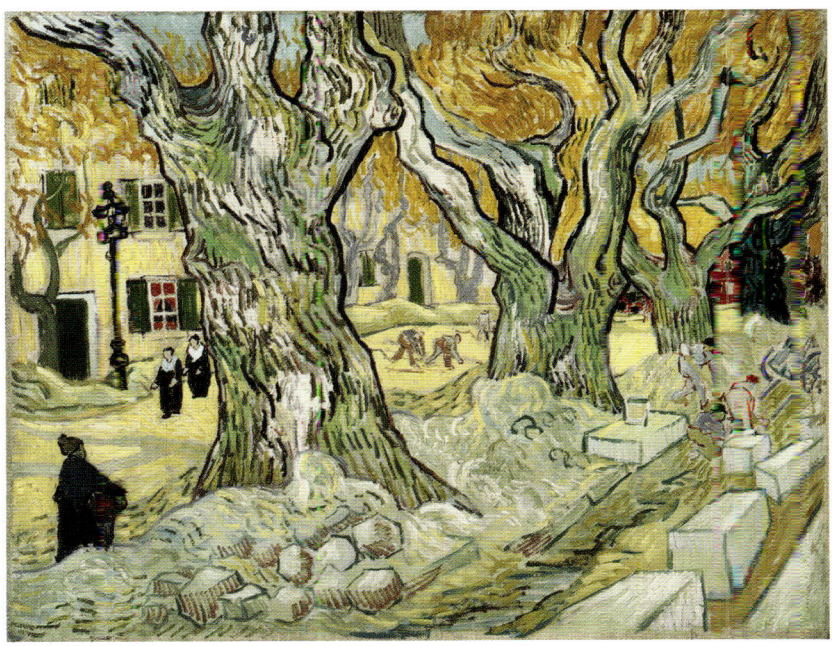

TREES AND ORCHARDS

While in Arles in 1888, Vincent made a series of paintings of flowering trees, which he found both aesthetically pleasing and spiritually renewing. He took to the subject with zeal, completing about 14 of them before he left Arles. He would return to the theme of trees—solitary and in groves—while in Saint-Rémy the following year, and again in his final days in Auvers.

"In trees, I see expression and soul."

~ VINCENT

[RIGHT] **The Olive Trees with Yellow Sky and Sun** (November 1889). Oil on canvas. The Minneapolis Institute of Arts.

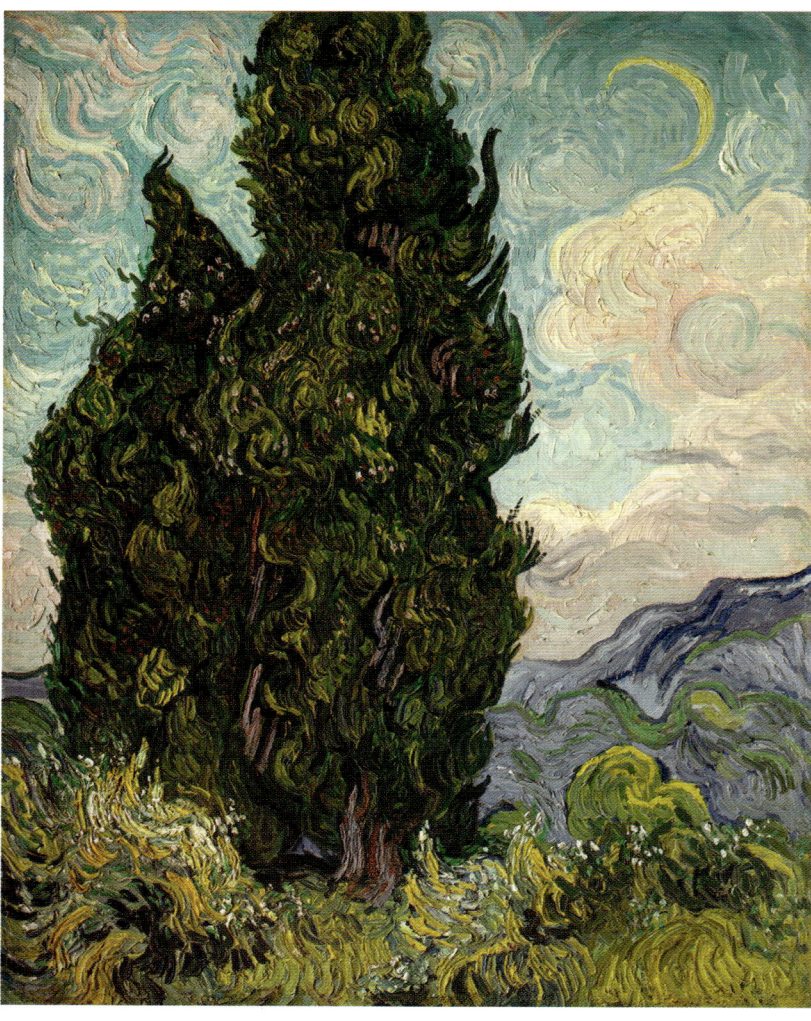

Cypresses (June 1889). Oil on canvas.
Metropolitan Museum of Art, New York.

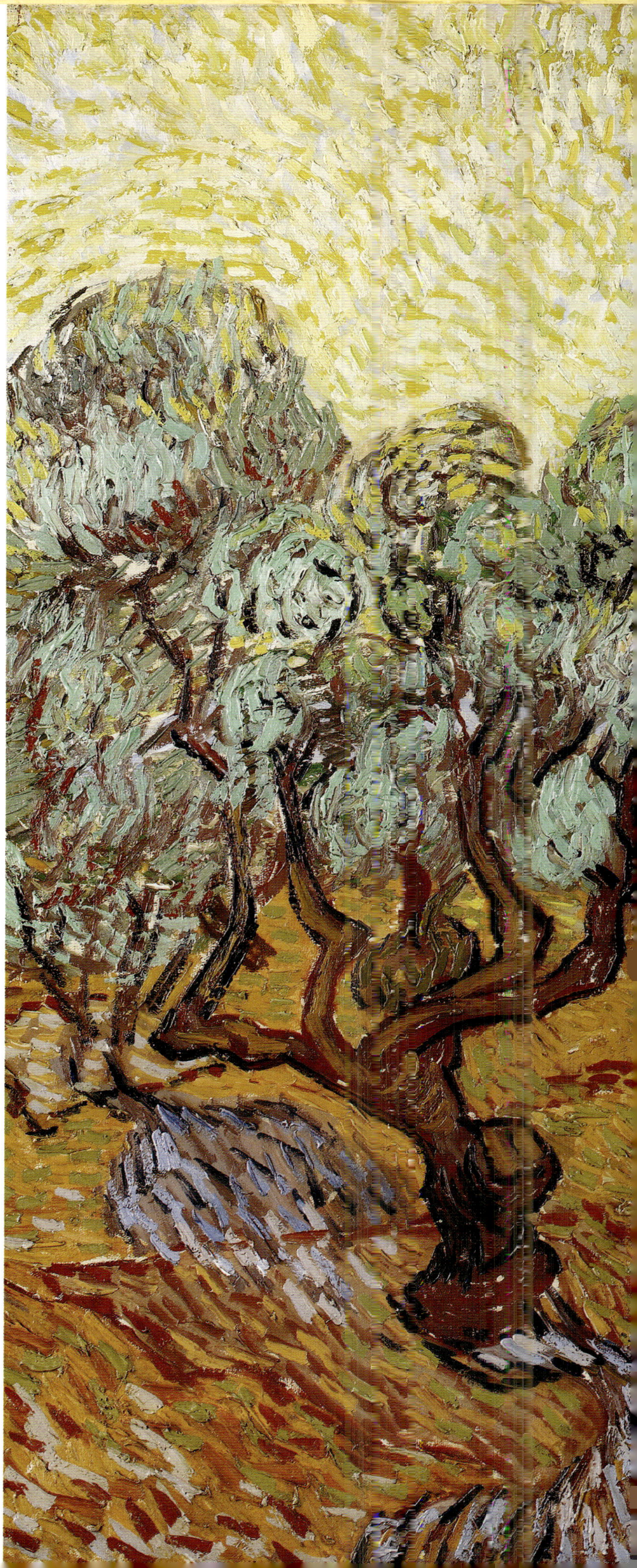

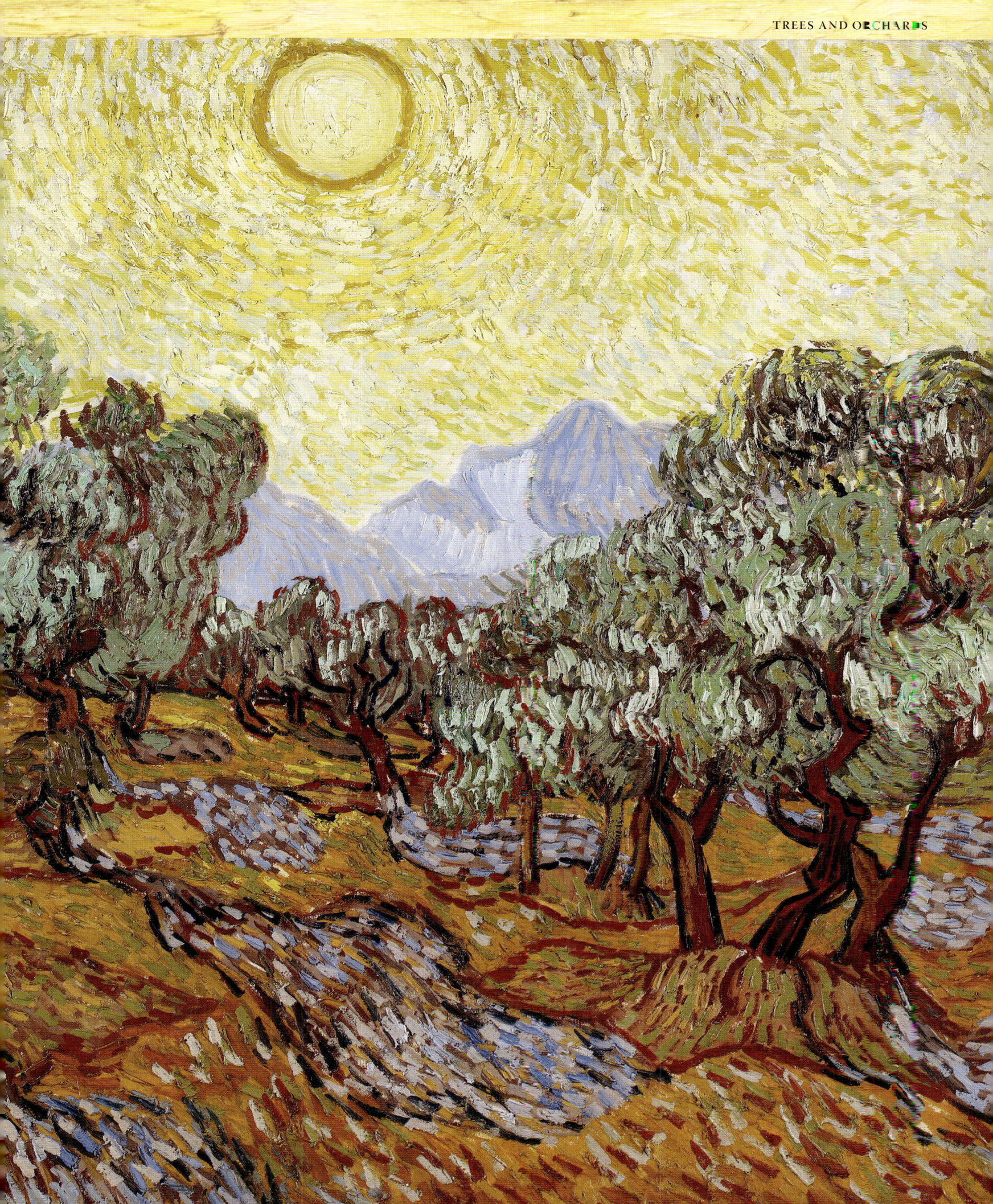

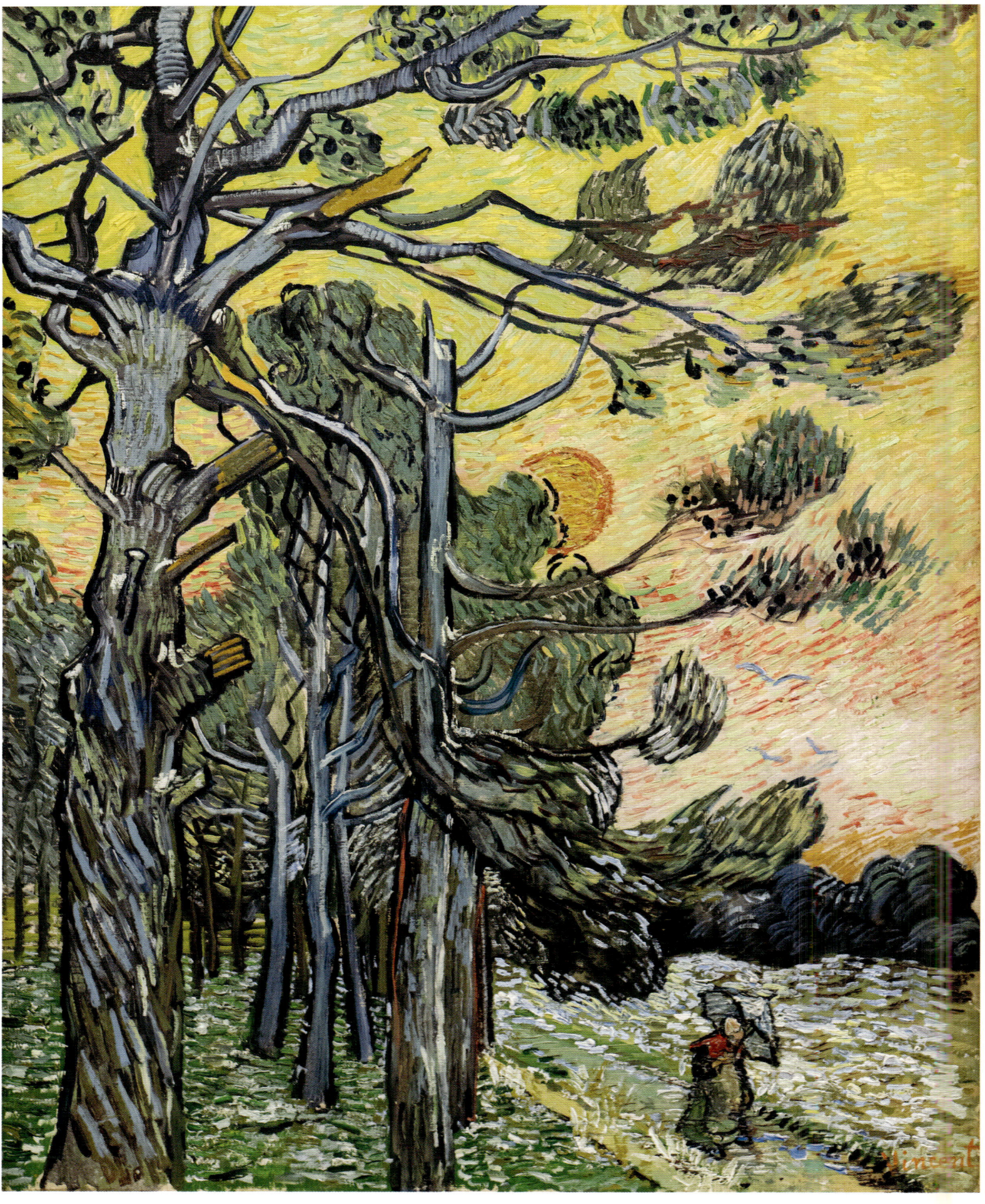

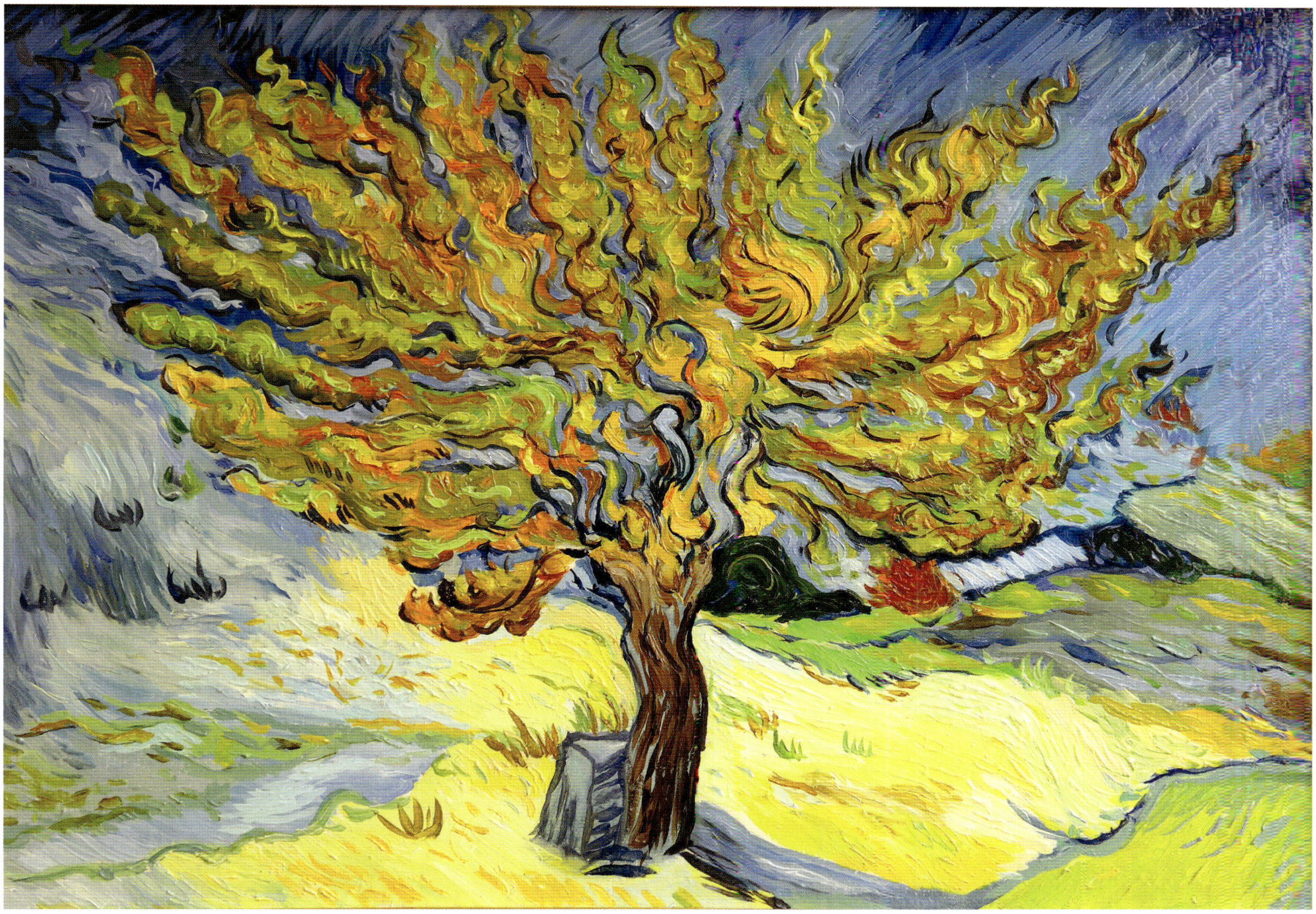

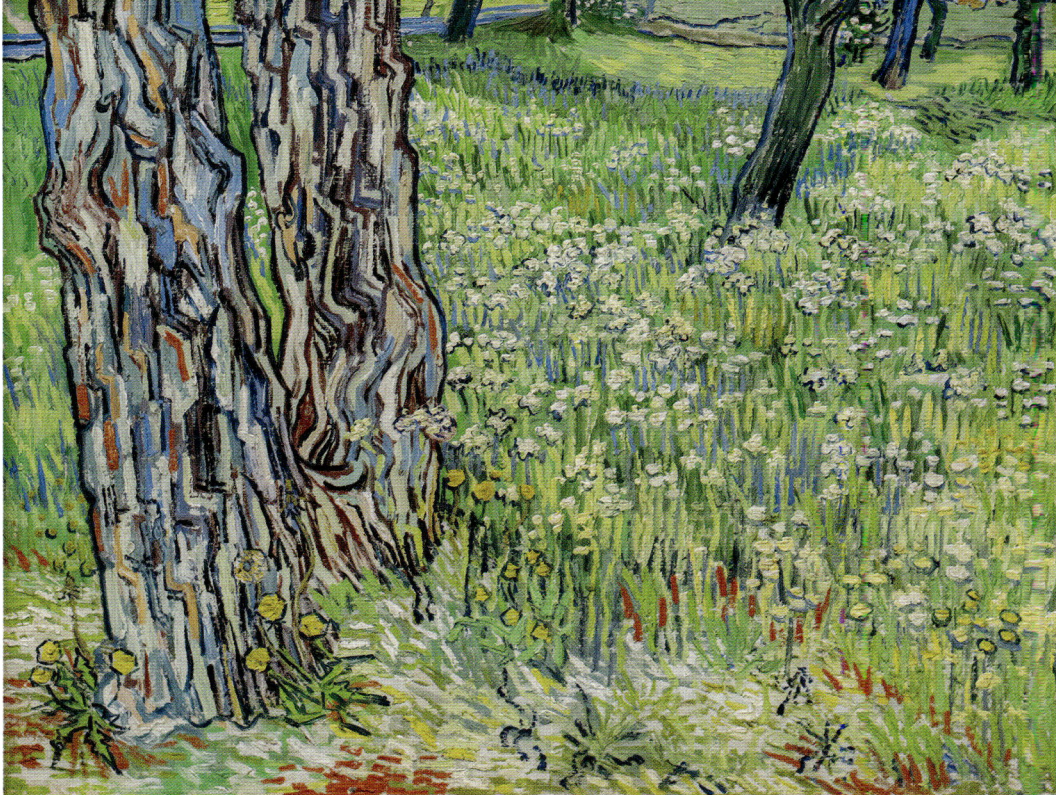

[ABOVE]
Mulberry Tree
(October 1889).
Oil on canvas.
The Norton Simon
Museum of Art, Pasadena.

[LEFT]
Tree Trunks in the Grass
(late April 1890). Oil on canvas.
Kröller-Müller Museum, Otterlo

[OPPOSITE PAGE]
*Pine Trees against a Red Sky
with Setting Sun* (November,
1889). Oil on canvas. Kröller-
Müller Museum, Otterlo.

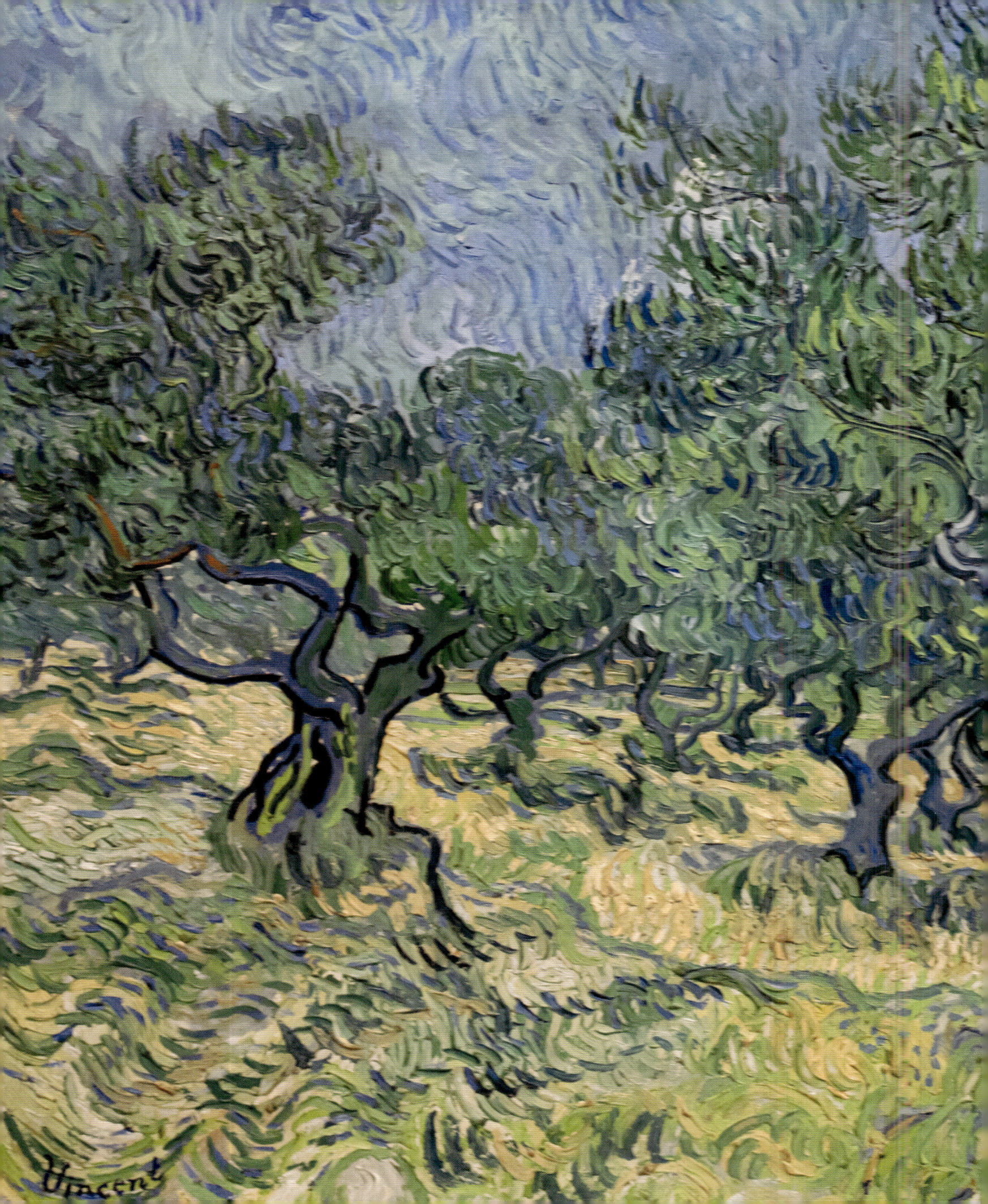

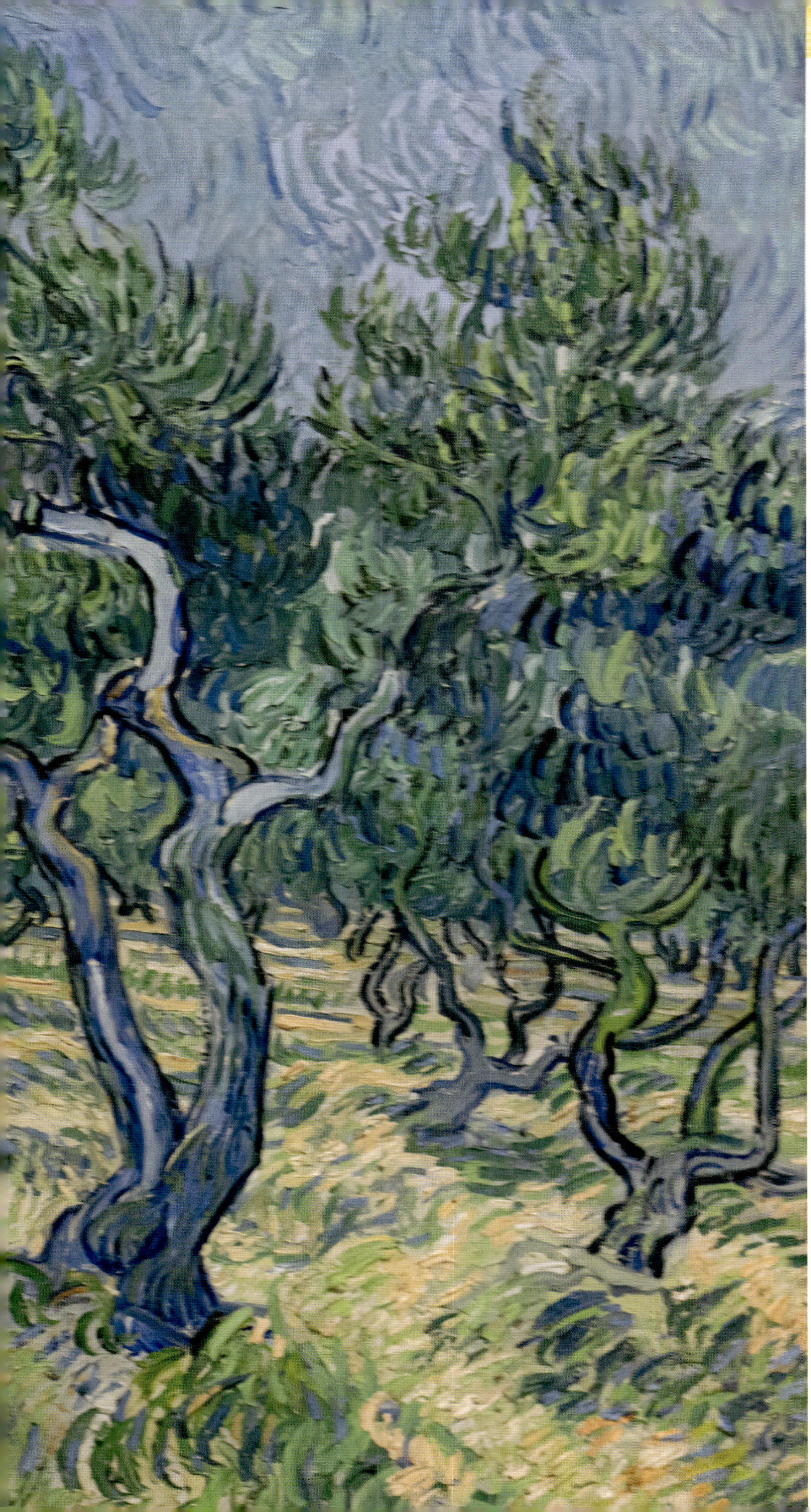

[LEFT] *Olive Trees* (mid-June 1889). Oil on canvas. Kröller-Müller Museum, Otterlo.

"*Yesterday I drew a very large, rather rare night moth there which is called the death's head, its coloration astonishingly distinguished: black, gray, white, shaded, and with glints of carmine or vaguely tending towards olive green; it's very big. To paint it I would have had to kill it, and that would have been a shame since the animal was so beautiful.*"

~ VINCENT, TO THEO, MAY 1889

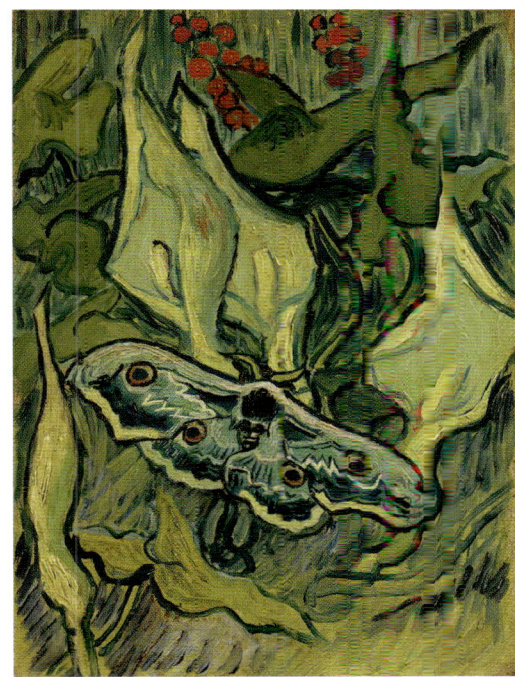

Great Peacock Moth (May 1889). Oil on canvas. Van Gogh Museum, Amsterdam (Vincent van Gogh Foundation)

In his wanderings, Vincent came upon this peacock moth (which he called a death's head). He later painted it from his drawing.

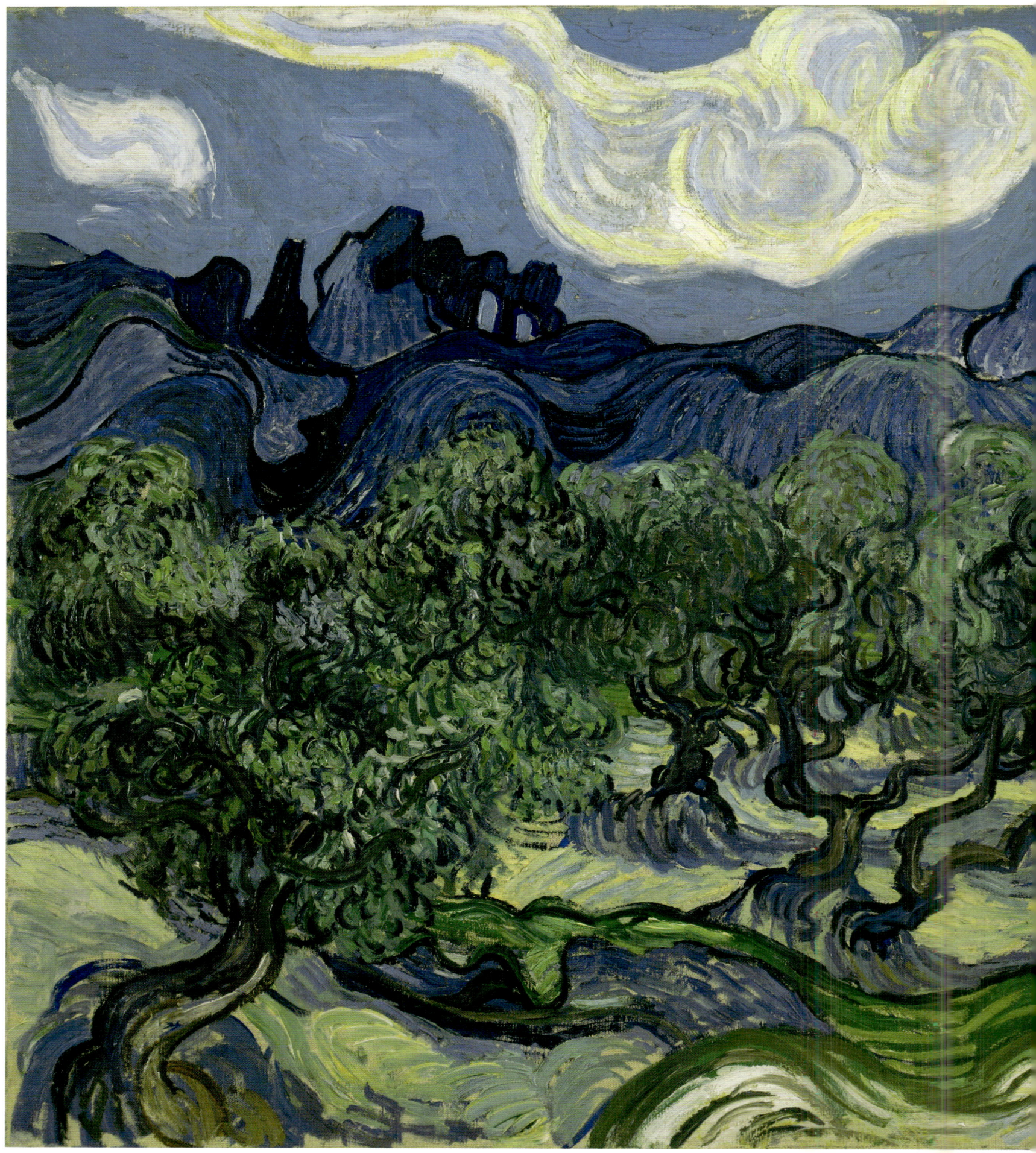

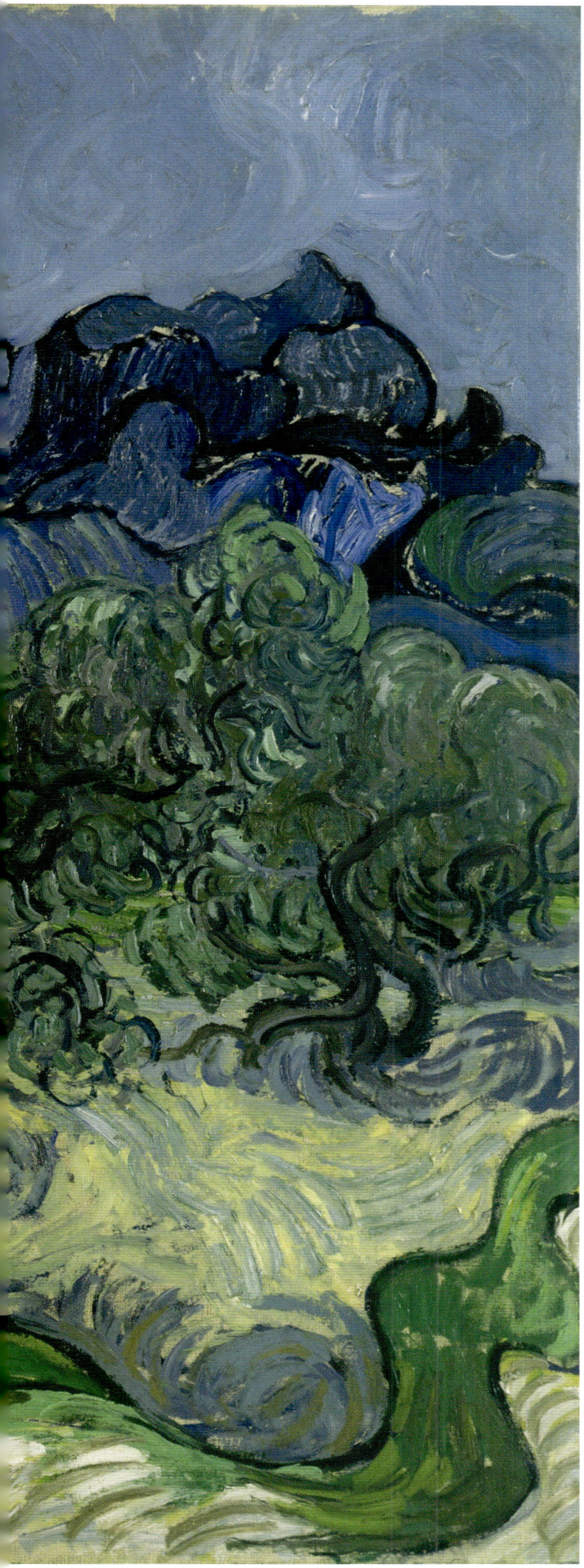

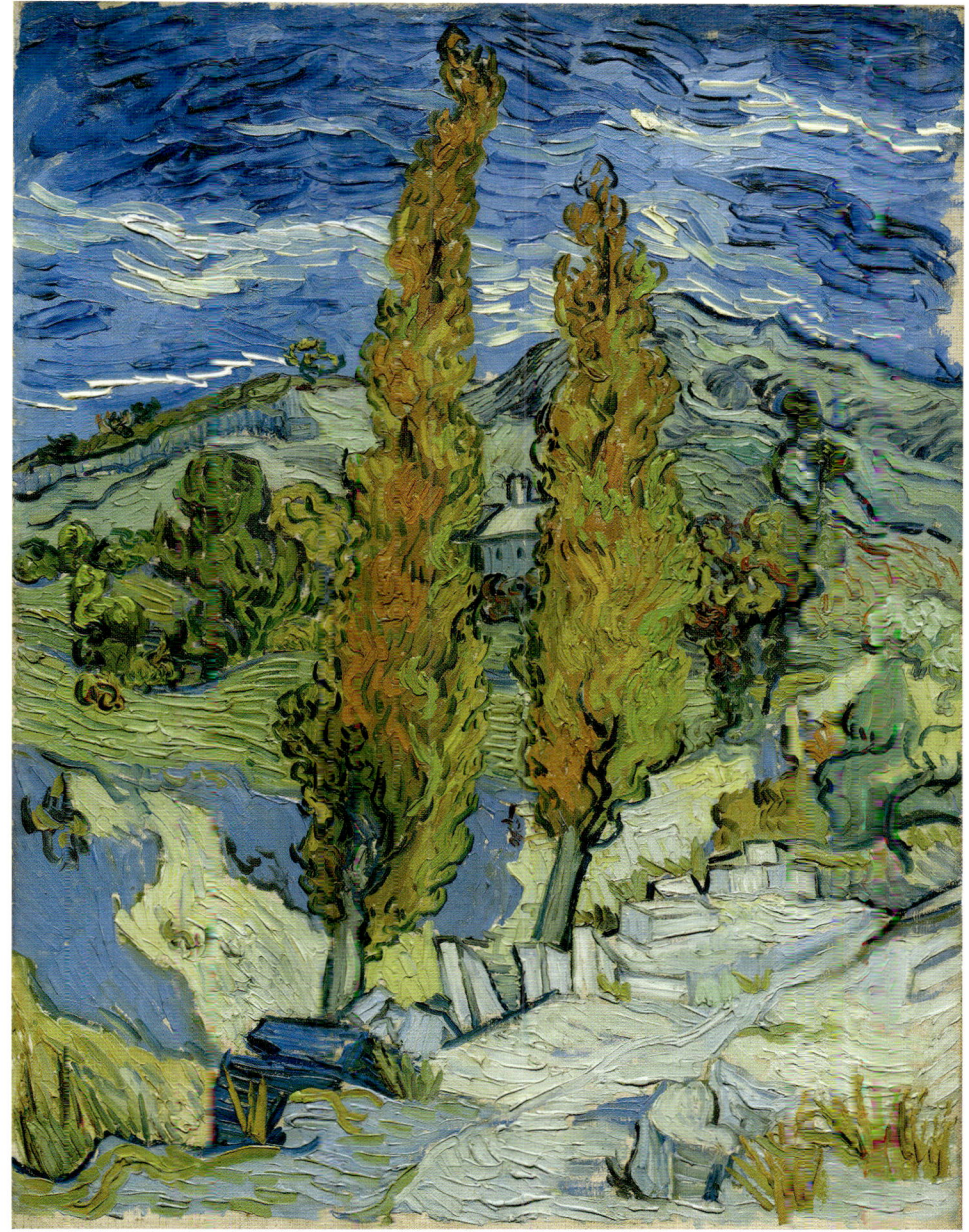

Olive Trees with the Alpilles in the Background (June 1889).
Oil on canvas. Museum of Modern Art, New York.

[LEFT]
Olive Trees with the Alpilles in the Background (June 1889).
Oil on canvas. Museum of Modern Art, New York.

Vincent depicts with charged, swirling brushstrokes this stand of twisting olive trees set in an undulating landscape and against a turbulent, cloudy sky.

WHEAT FIELDS AND CYPRESSES

These paintings were inspired by Vincent's view toward the Alpilles from his window at Saint-Paul de Mausole, where they were later exhibited. Vincent expressed a lifelong fascination with wheat fields, and he had begun painting them back in Nuenen. He found ones in Paris and in Arles to paint before he came upon the Saint-Rémy fields.

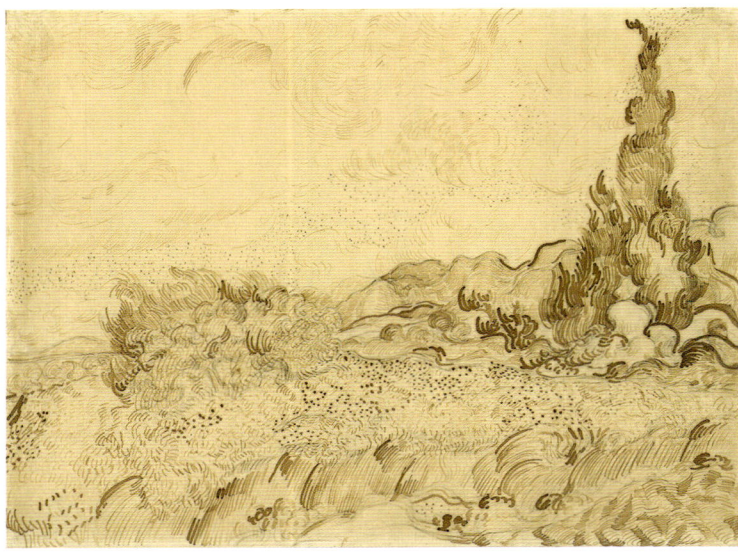

Study for **Wheat Field with Cypresses** (June 1889). Reed-pen on paper. Van Gogh Museum, Amsterdam (Vincent van Gogh Foundation).

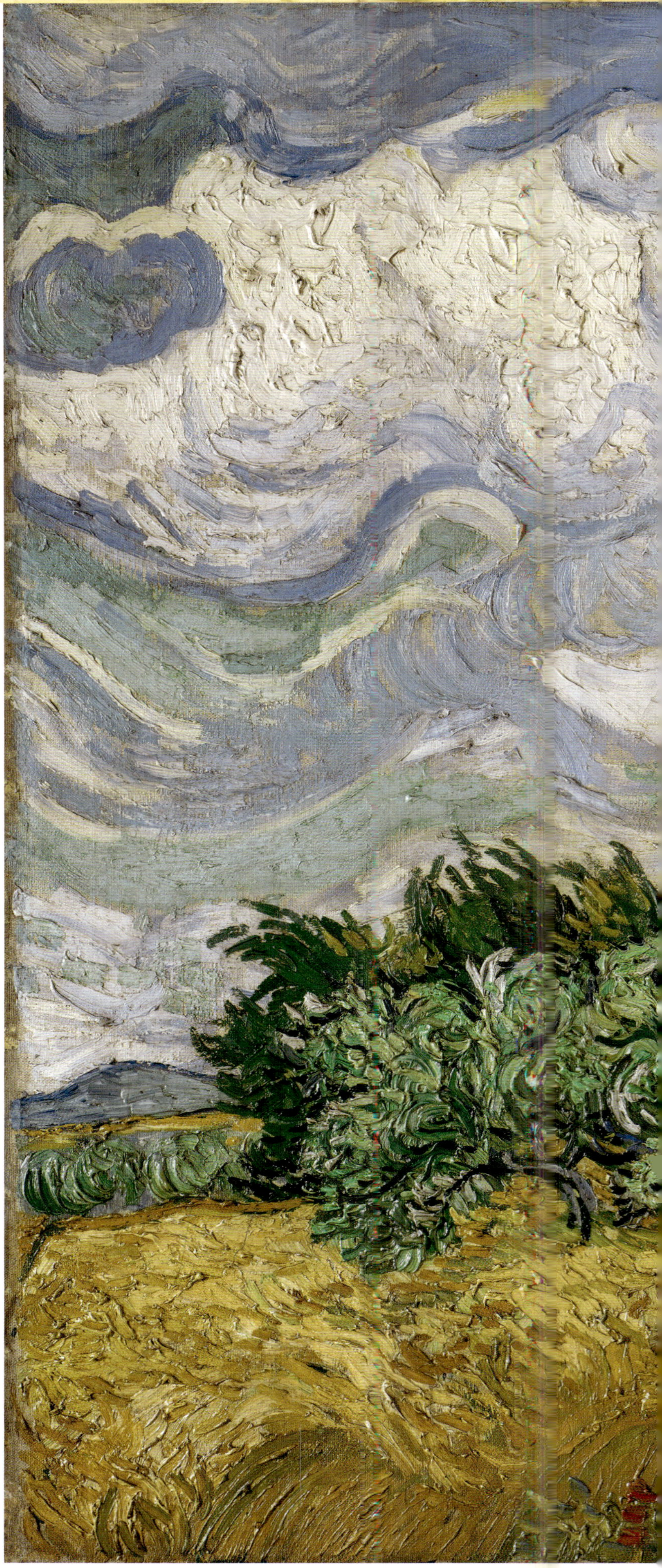

[RIGHT]
Wheat Field with Cypresses
(July 1889). Oil on canvas.
Metropolitan Museum of Art, New York.

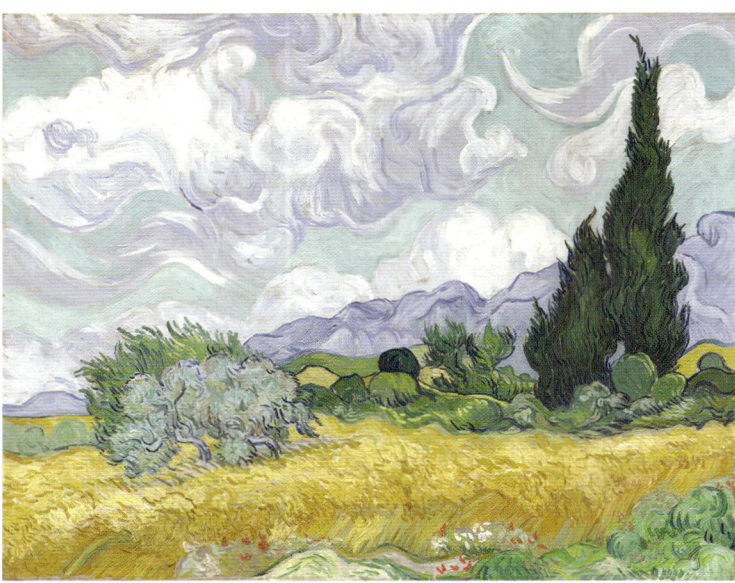

Wheat Field with Cypresses (September 1889).
Oil on canvas. National Gallery, London.

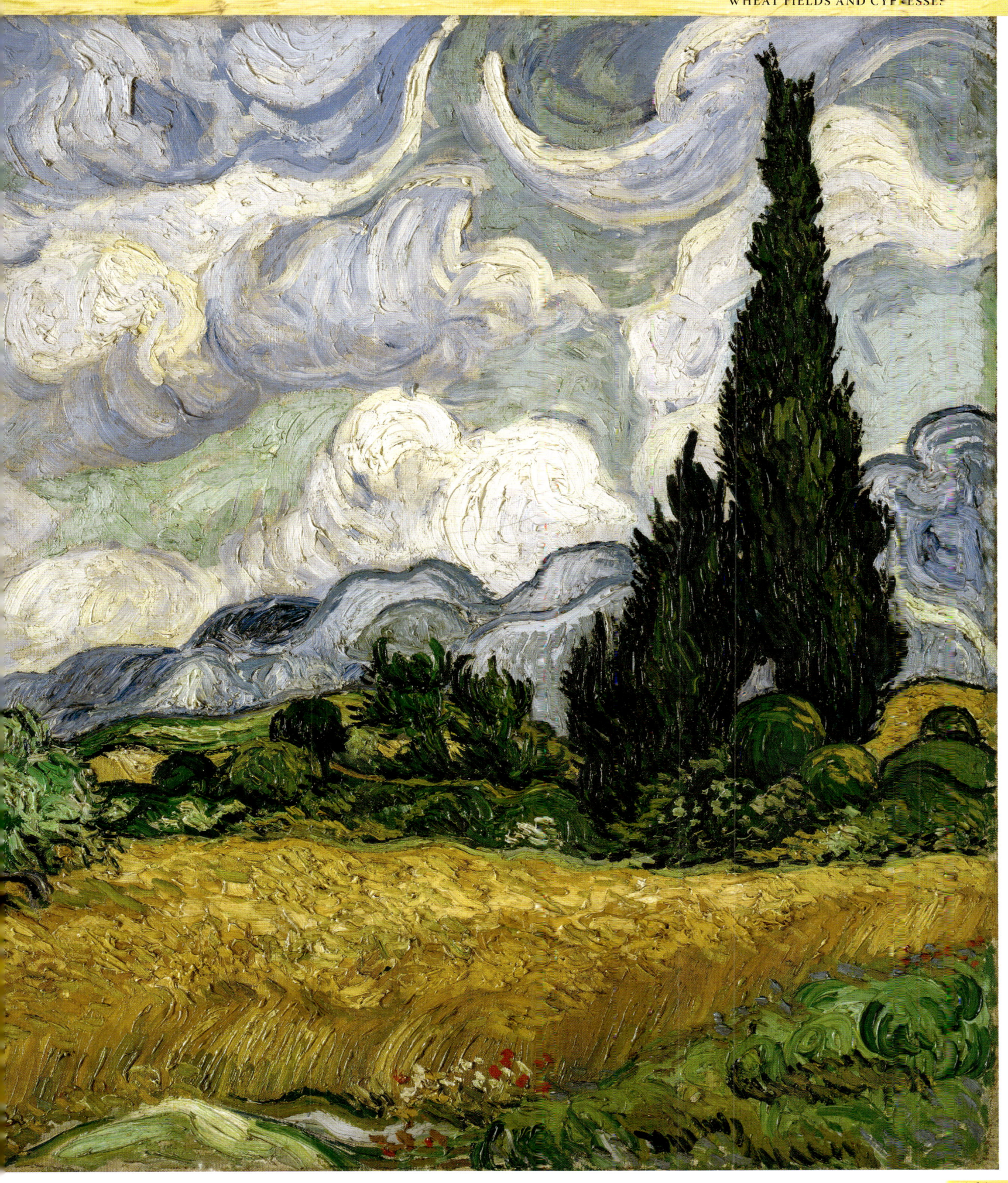

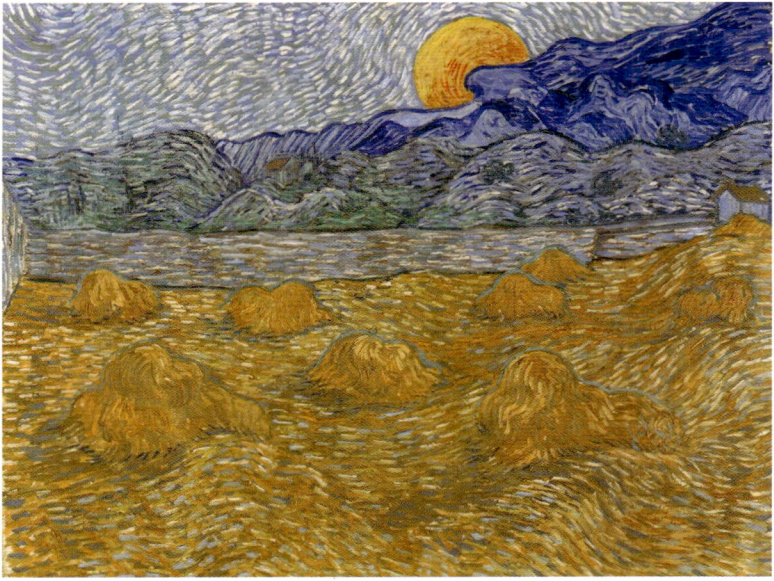

Landscape with Wheat Sheaves and Rising Moon (July 1889).
Oil on canvas. Kröller-Müller Museum, Otterlo.

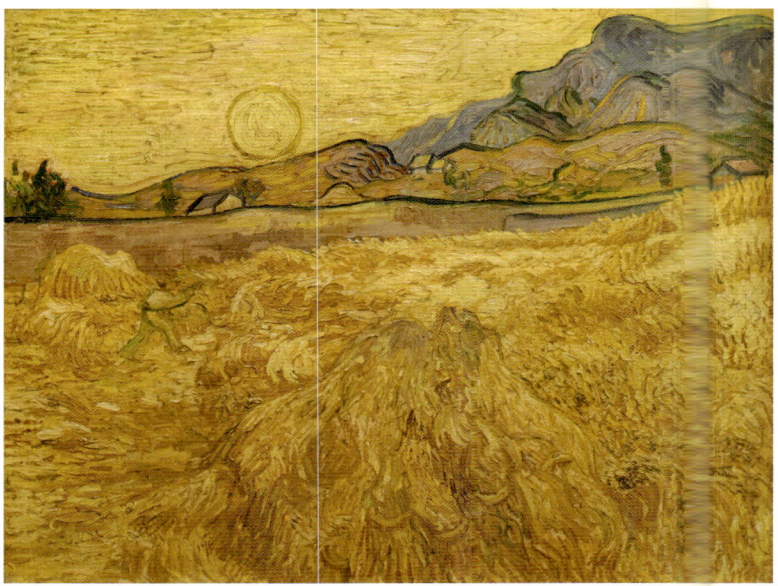

Wheat Field with Reaper and Sun (late June 1889).
Oil on canvas. Kröller-Müller Museum, Otterlo.

[BELOW] *Rain or Enclosed Wheat Field in the Rain*
(November 1889). Oil on canvas. Philadelphia Museum of Art.

[opposite page] *Wheat Field with Reaper* (September 1889) ⬚ on
canvas. Van Gogh Museum, Amsterdam (Vincent van Gogh Foundation).

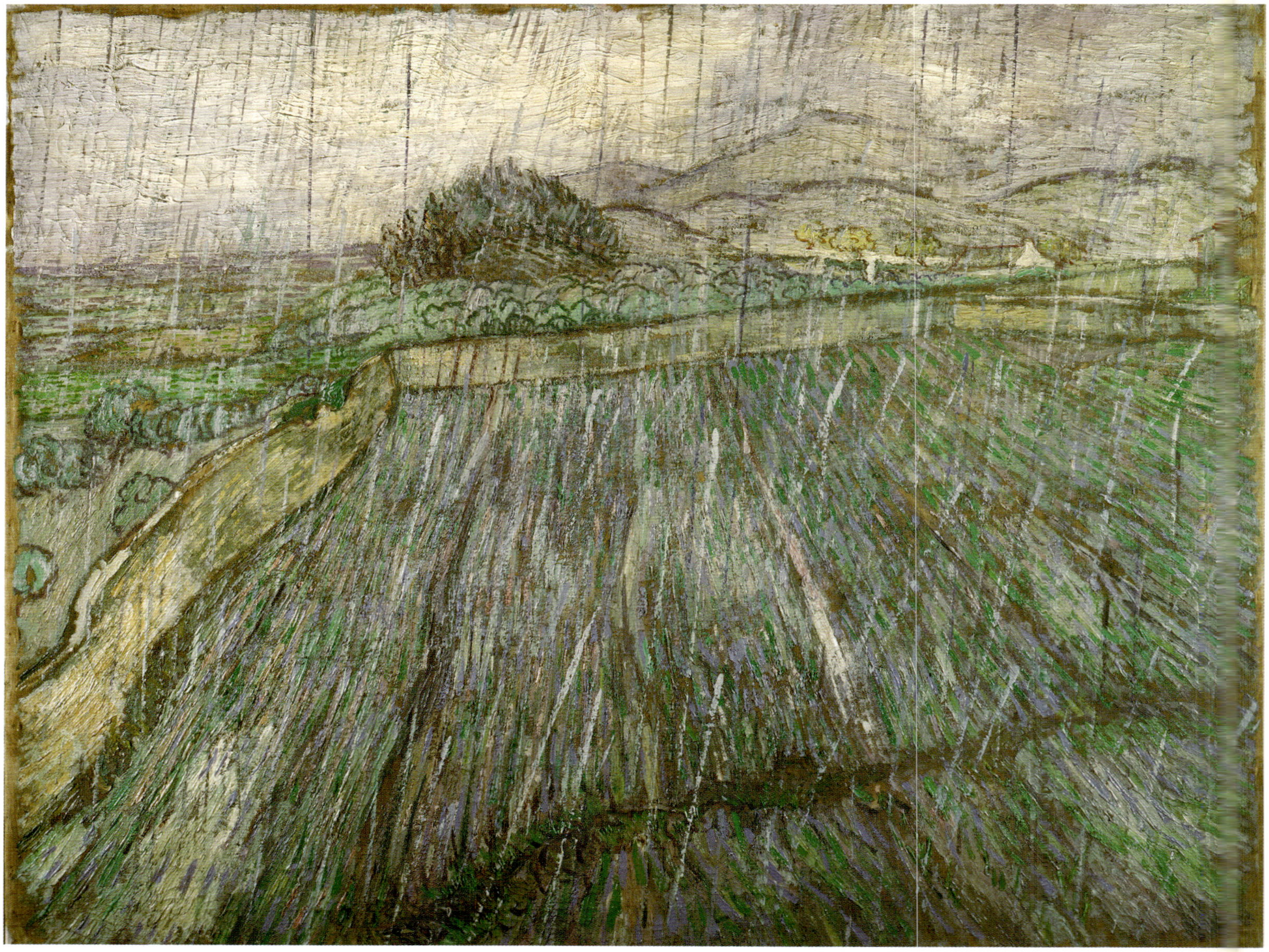

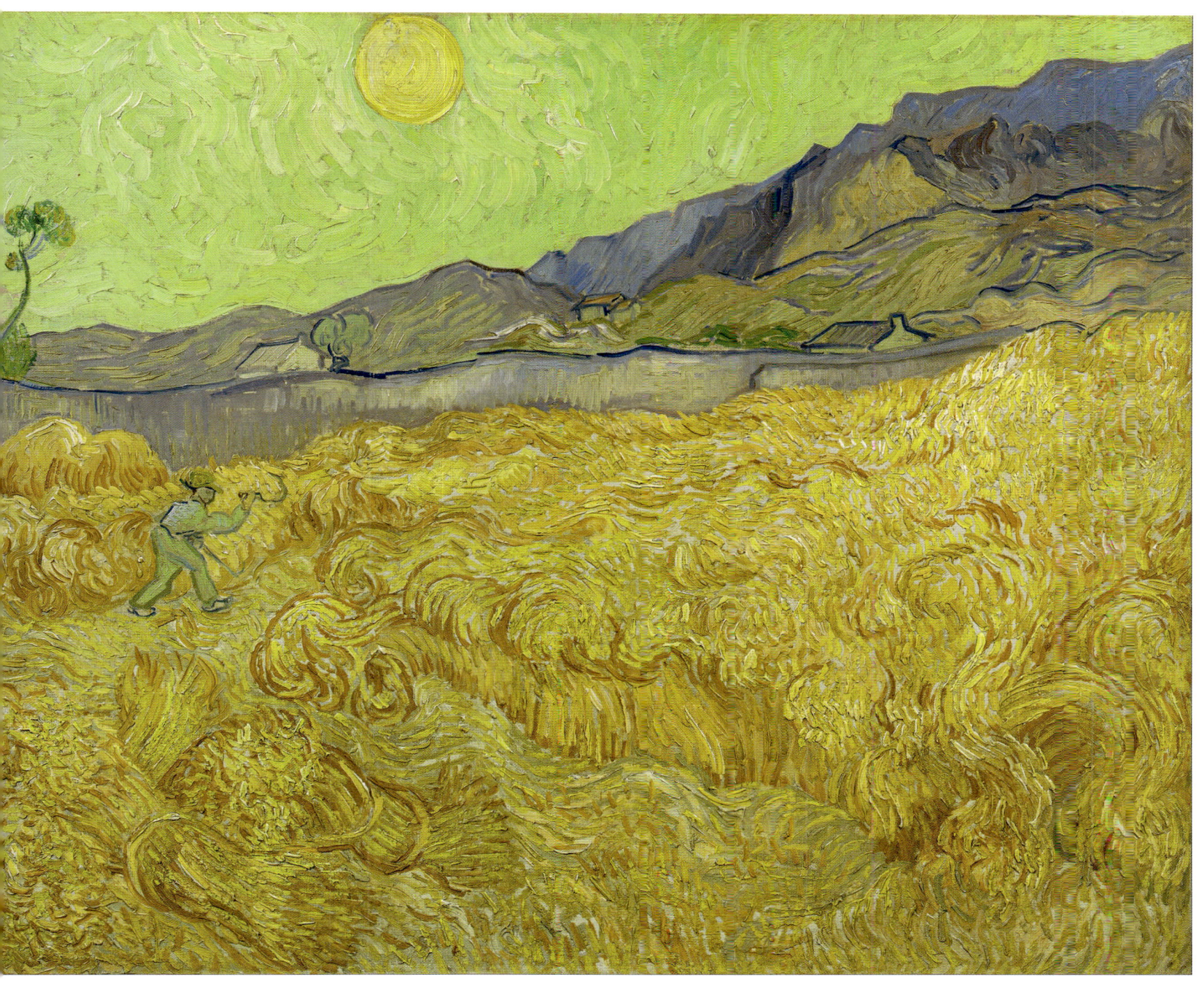

"*A reaper, the study is all yellow, terribly thickly impasted, but the subject was beautiful and simple. I then saw in this reaper – a vague figure struggling like a devil in the full heat of the day to reach the end of his toil – I then saw the image of death in it, in this sense that humanity would be the wheat being reaped. . . . But in this death nothing sad, it takes place in broad daylight with a sun that floods everything with a light of fine gold.*"

~ VINCENT, TO THEO, SEPTEMBER 1889

NIGHT SKIES

With blotches of cadmium and zinc yellows surrounded by umbras of lead white scattered across a field of vibrant cobalt, Prussian, and ultramarine blues, Vincent captured night skies twinkling with stars. In one of his most famous paintings, the iconic *The Starry Night*, he uses these colors in turbulent swirls to create an almost menacing feeling. Along with other starry sky paintings, including *Starry Night Over the Rhône*, it makes up a visually stark series that stands in counterpoint to his works that celebrate the blazing Provençal sun.

"For my part I know nothing with any certainty, but the sight of the stars makes me dream."

~ VINCENT

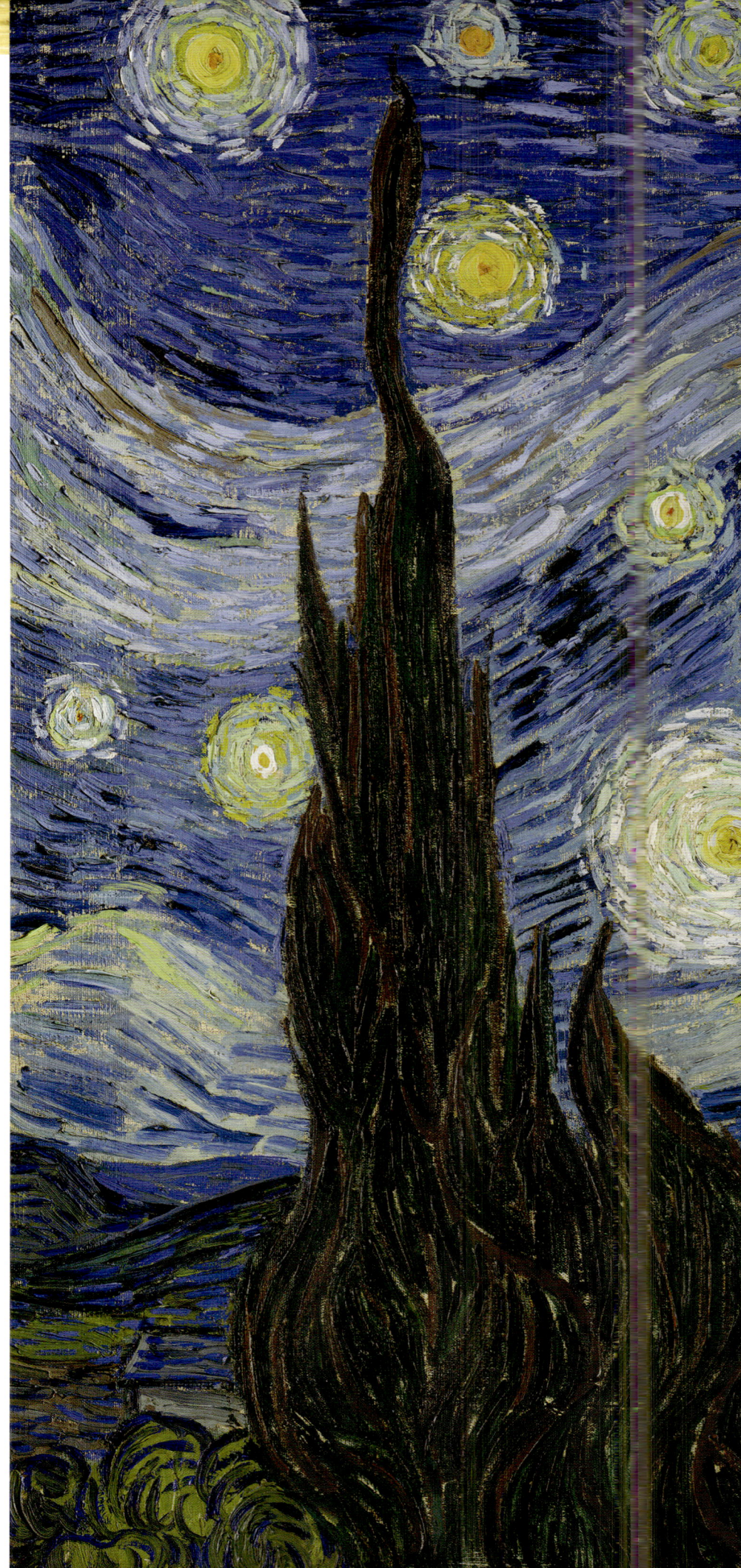

The Starry Night
(June 1889).
Oil on canvas.
Museum of Modern
Art, New York.

Surely van Gogh's magnum opus is the now-renowned The Starry Night. *In this painting, he depicts Saint-Rémy-de-Provence as seen from his asylum room. There is an almost end-of-the world feel to the night sky, in which meteoric stars shine amid a turbulent, swirling atmosphere.*

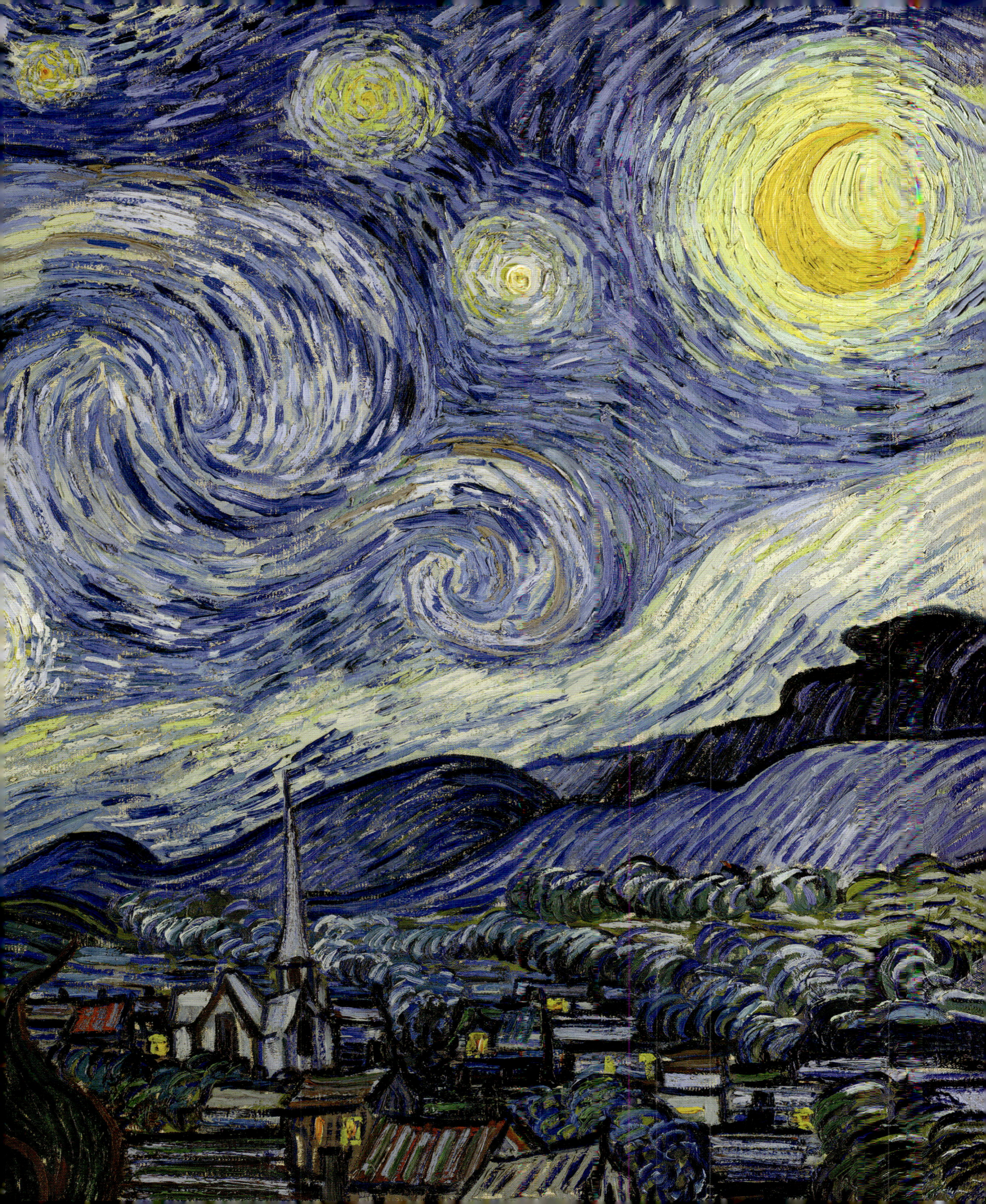

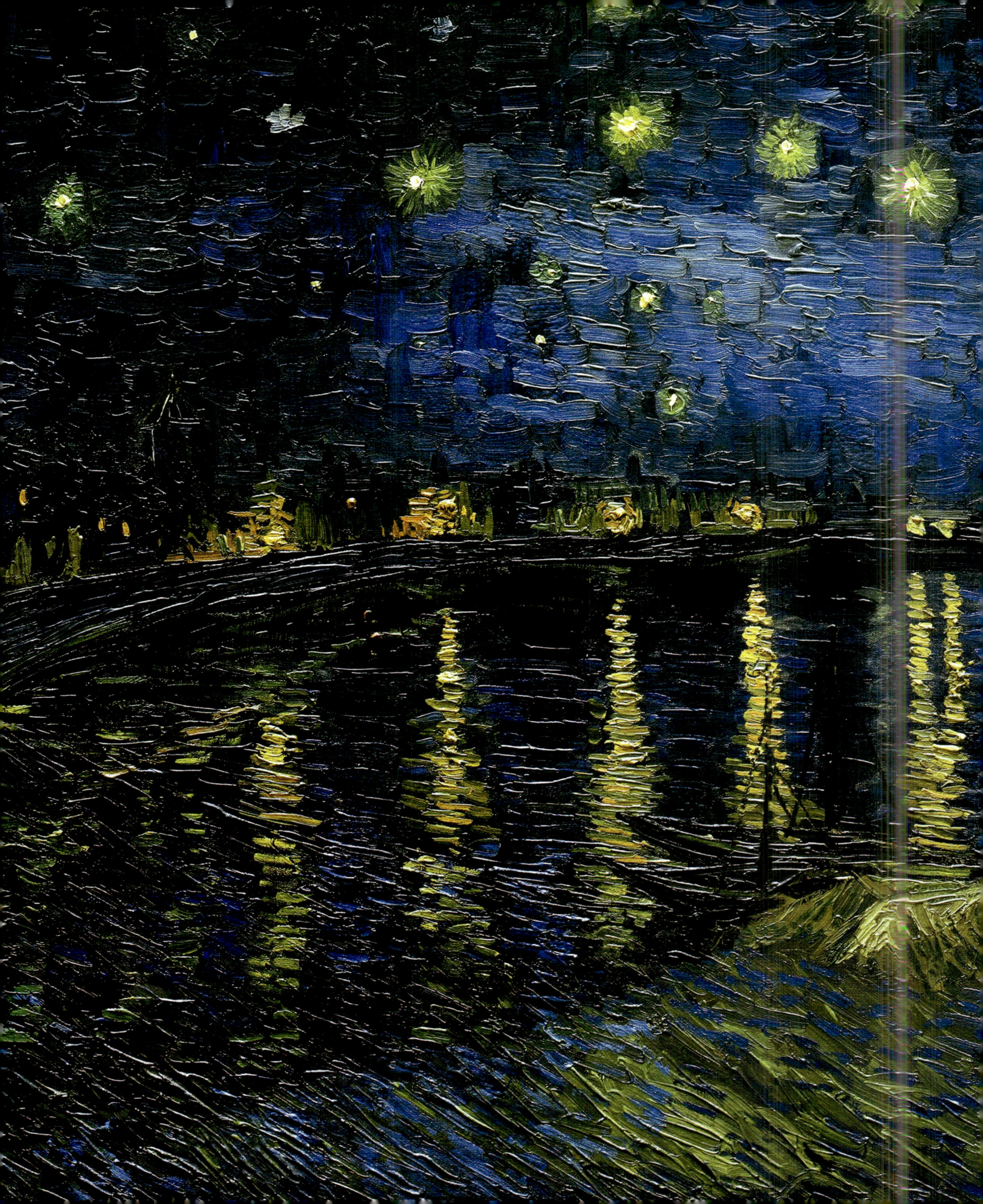

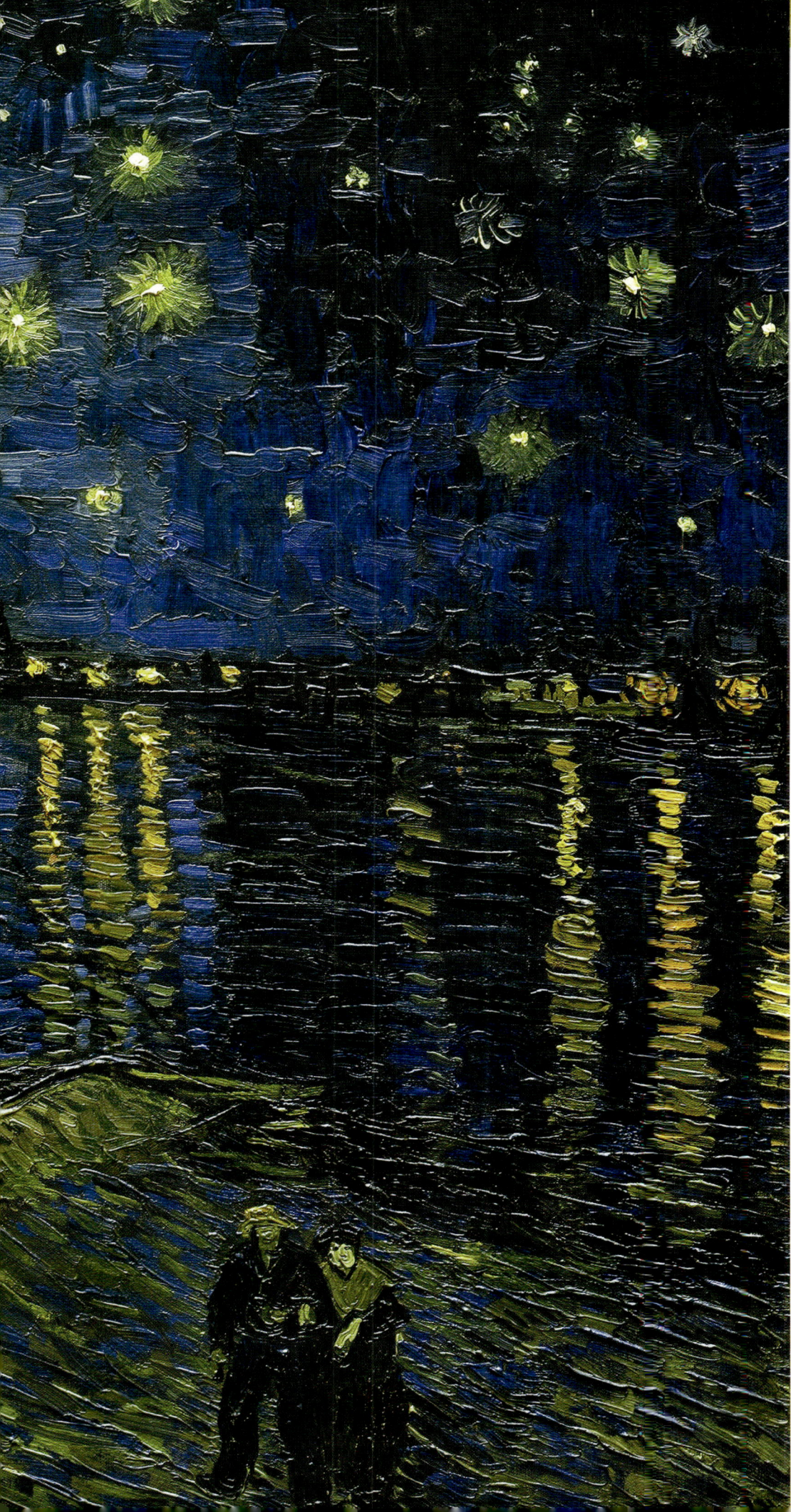

"At present I absolutely want to paint a starry sky. It often seems to me that night is still more richly colored than the day; having hues of the most intense violets, blues and greens. If only you pay attention to it you will see that certain stars are lemon-yellow, others pink or a green, blue and forget-me-not brilliance. And without my expatiating on this theme it is obvious that putting little white dots on the blue-black is not enough to paint a starry sky."

~ VINCENT, IN A LETTER
TO HIS SISTER WIL, SEPTEMBER 1888

Starry Night Over the Rhône
(September 1888). Oil on canvas.
Musée d'Orsay, Paris.

Painted from a spot on the bank of a river that was only a minute or two's walk from the Yellow House, Starry Night Over the Rhône explores the effects of starlight and artificial light on the inky waters of the river. In it, Vincent shows two lovers strolling near the river under the vast starlit sky.

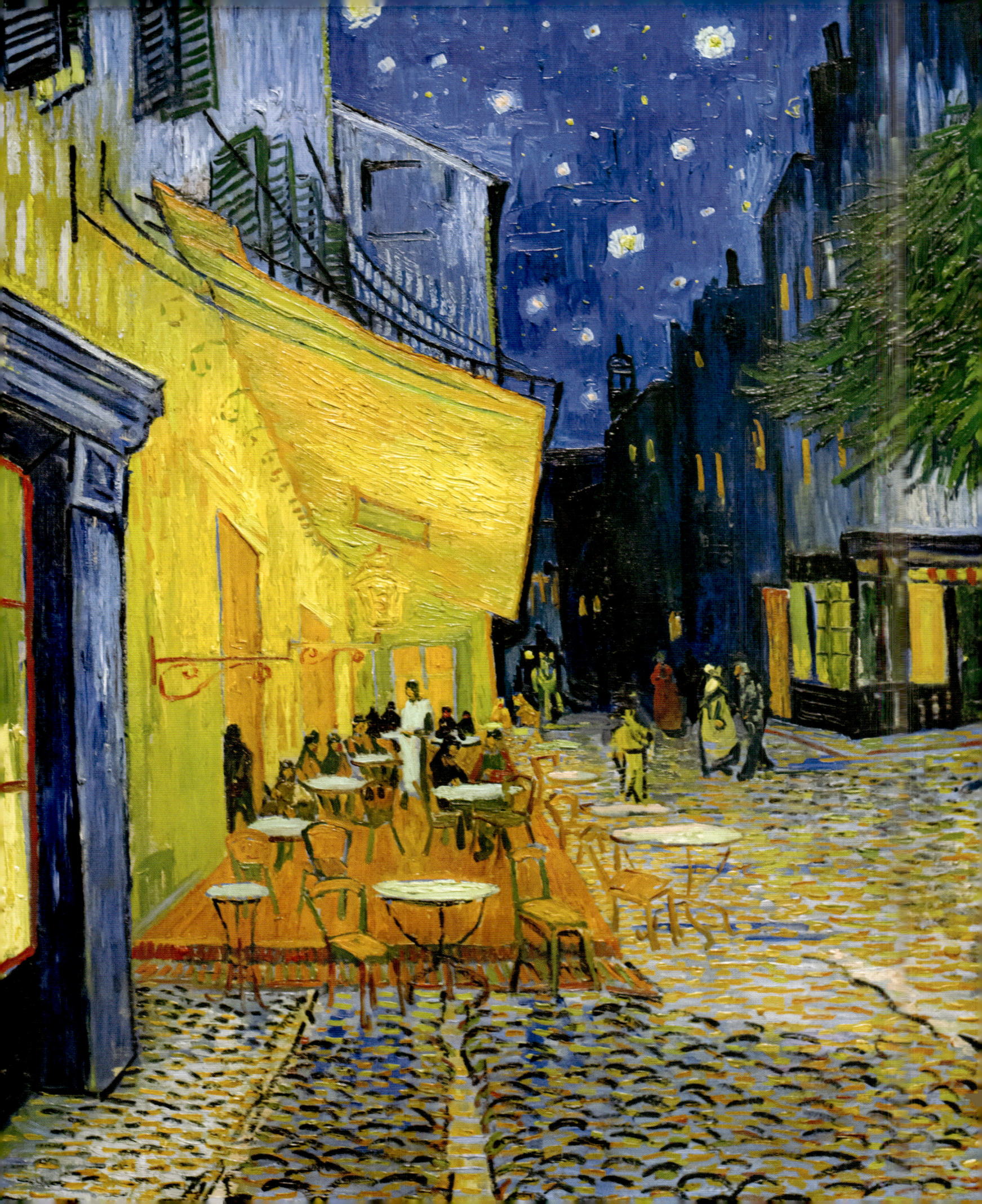

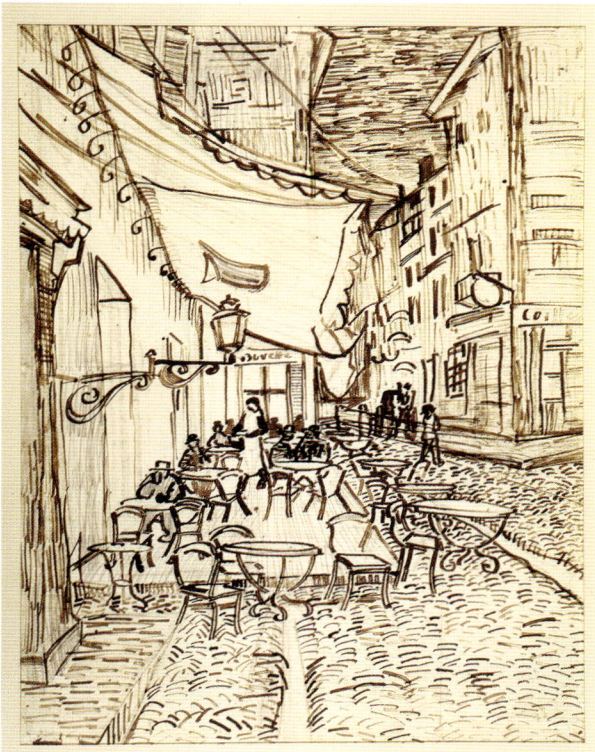

Study for **Café Terrace at Night** (September 1888).
Chalk, Reed-pen, India ink, and graphite on laid paper.
Dallas Museum of Art.

[OPPOSITE PAGE] **Café Terrace at Night** (1888).
Oil on canvas. Kröller-Müller Museum, Otterlo.

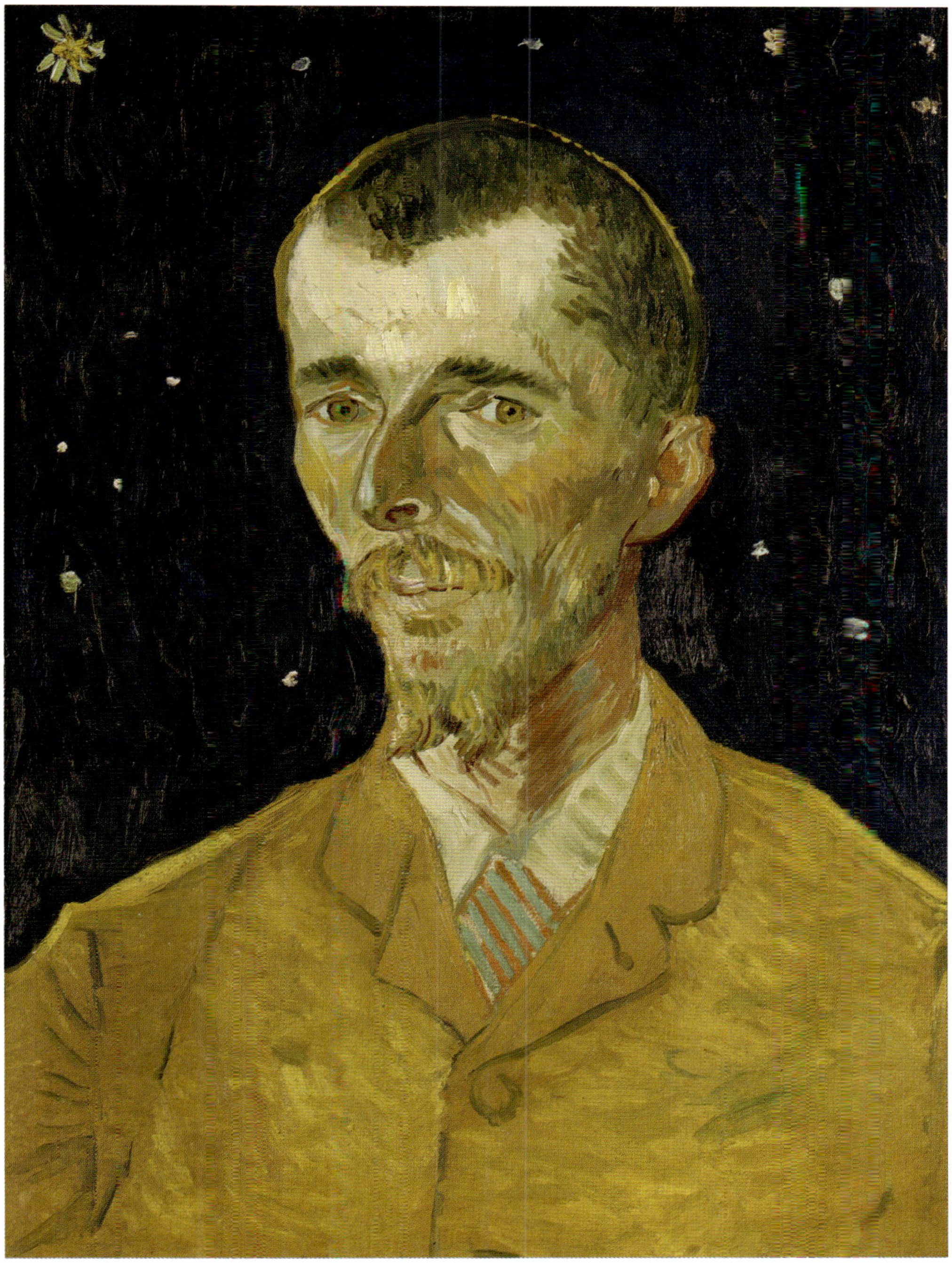

[RIGHT]
Portrait of Eugène Boch (1888).
Oil on canvas. Musée d'Orsay, Paris.

*In this portrait of Belgian painter Eugène
Boch, Vincent chose to replace a shabby
background with a starry night sky.*

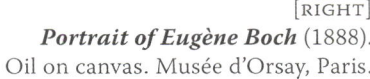

"*Behind his head, instead of painting the ordinary wall of this shabby
apartment, I will paint infinity, I will do a simple background of the richest blue,
the most intense blue that I can create, and through this simple combination
of the bright head against this rich, blue background, I will obtain a mysterious
effect, like a star in the depths of an azure sky.*"

~ VINCENT, DESCRIBING HIS PAINTING OF EUGÈNE BOCH, IN A LETTER TO THEO

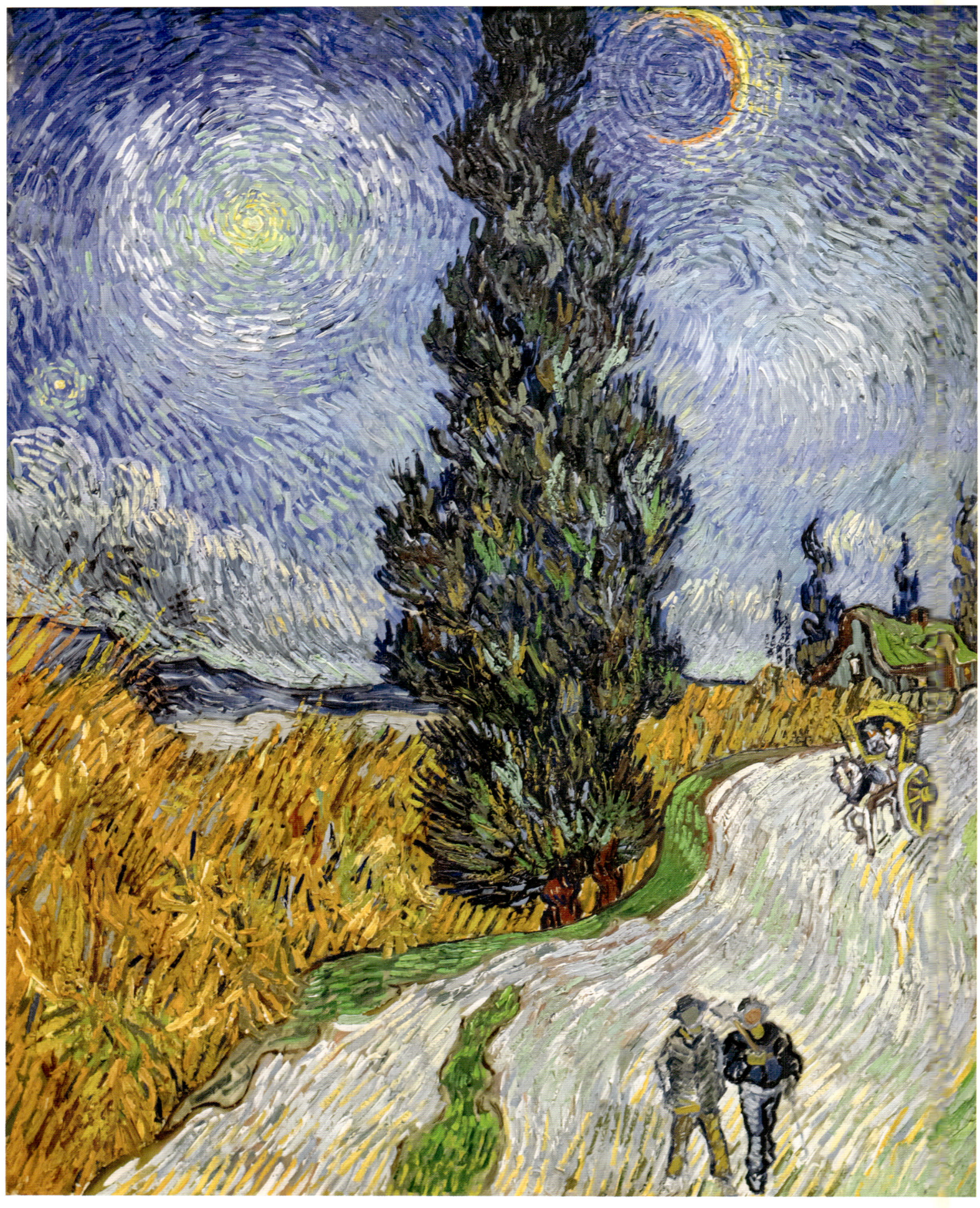

[OPPOSITE PAGE] ***Road with Cypress and Star*** (May 1890).
Oil on canvas. Kröller-Müller Museum, Otterlo.

Shortly before leaving the hospital, Vincent painted what appears to be a sky at dusk or early evening with the moon and sun shining over a lone cypress, creating the landscape from his imagination and not from any view he could see from his window. In a letter to Paul Gauguin, he refers to it as a "last attempt" at a star painting.

[BELOW]
Landscape with Couple Walking and Crescent Moon (May 1890). Oil on canvas. Museu de Arte de Sao Paulo.

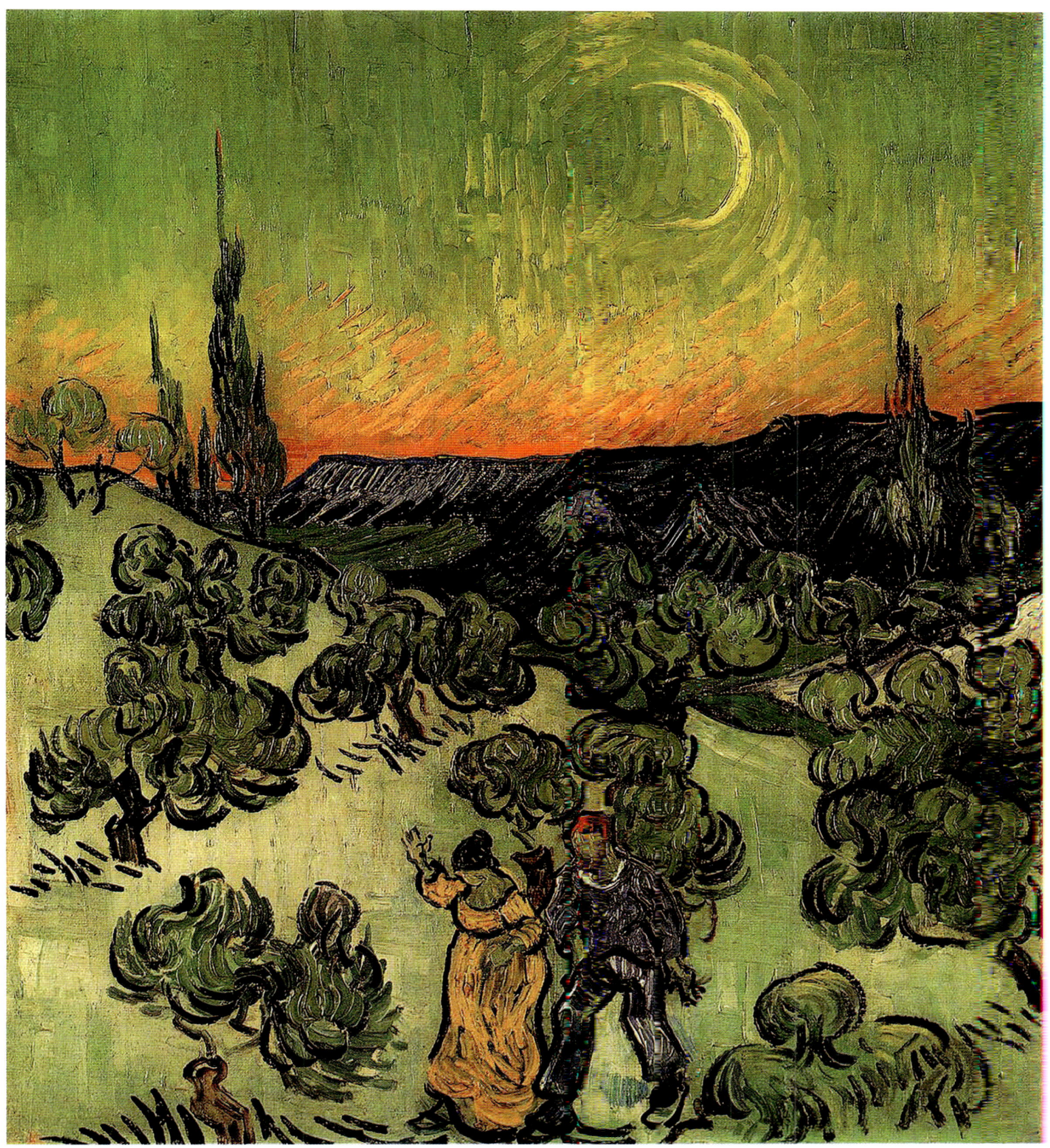

LAST DAYS IN AUVERS

Vincent spent the final days of his life in Auvers, a village just north of Paris. He thought of his move as a homecoming; here he might find peace amid the soothing cool greens and blues found in the north of France after the stirring hot reds and yellows of the south. He was productive here, painting the Romanesque church, the town hall, thatched-roof houses, and the surrounding landscape. From his arrival in late May 1890 to his death on July 29, he produced about 70 paintings, more than one per day, as well as numerous drawings.

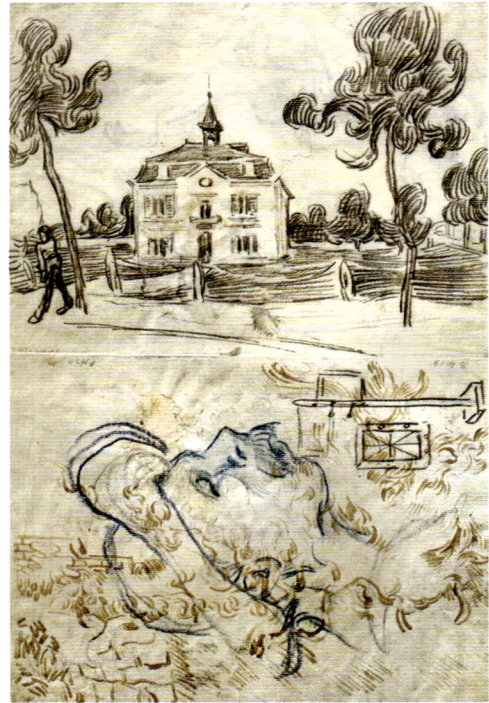

[OPPOSITE PAGE]
The Church in Auvers (June 1890). Oil on canvas. Musée d'Orsay, Paris.

[LEFT]
Auvers Town Hall and Head of a Man (June–July 1890). Chalk on paper. Van Gogh Museum, Amsterdam (Vincent van Gogh Foundation).

[BELOW]
Auvers Town Hall on 14 July 1890 (July 1890). Oil on canvas. Private collection.

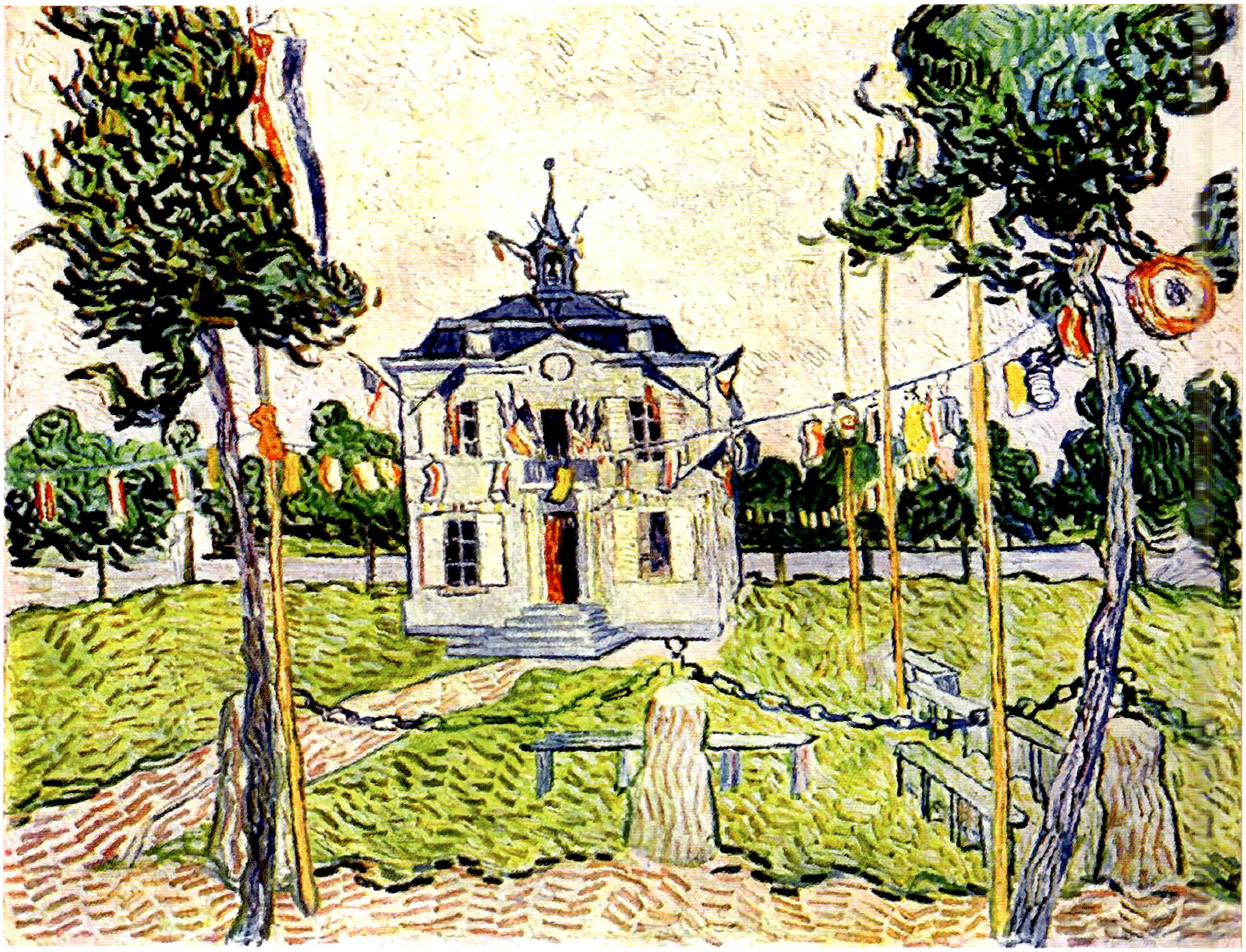

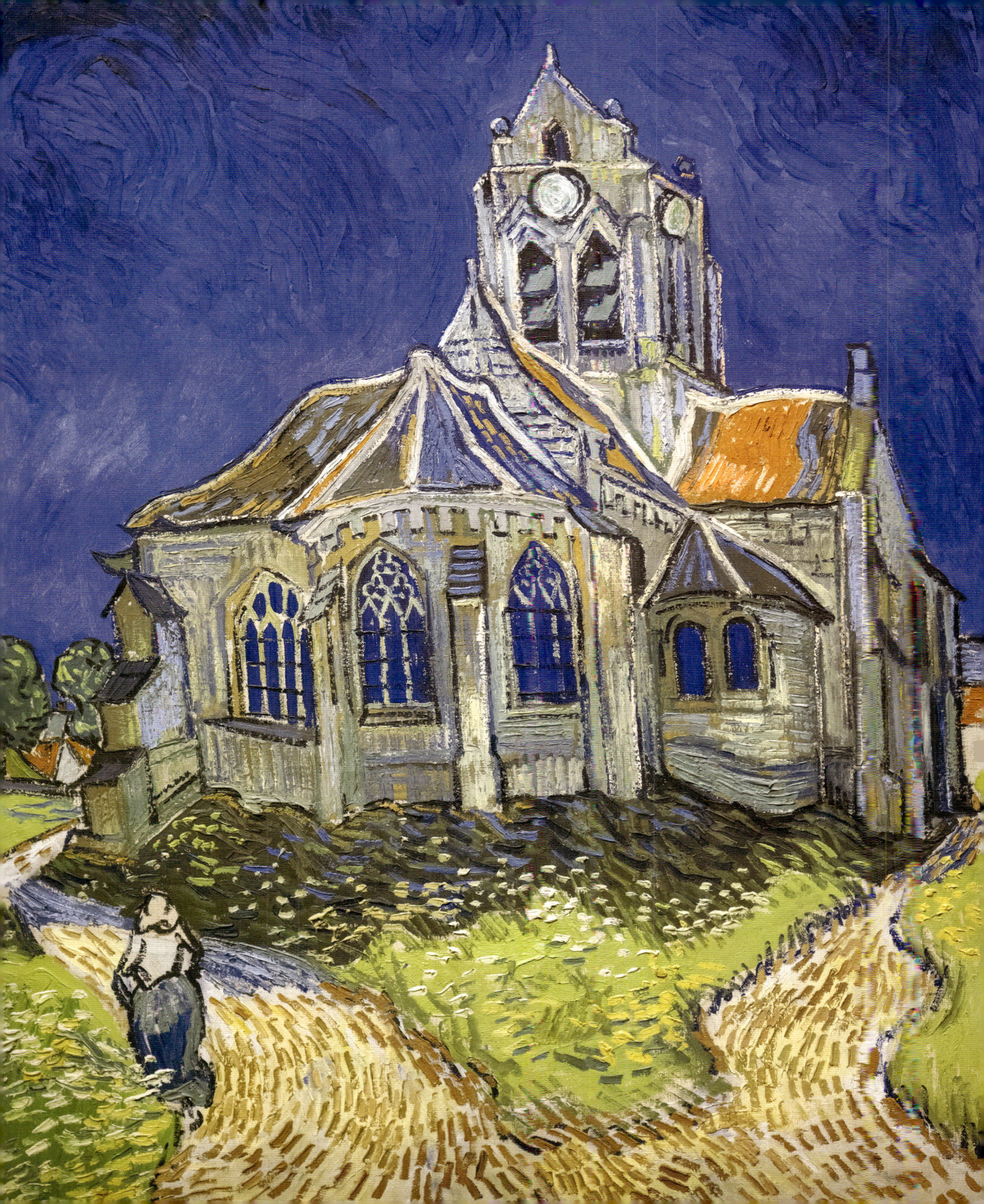

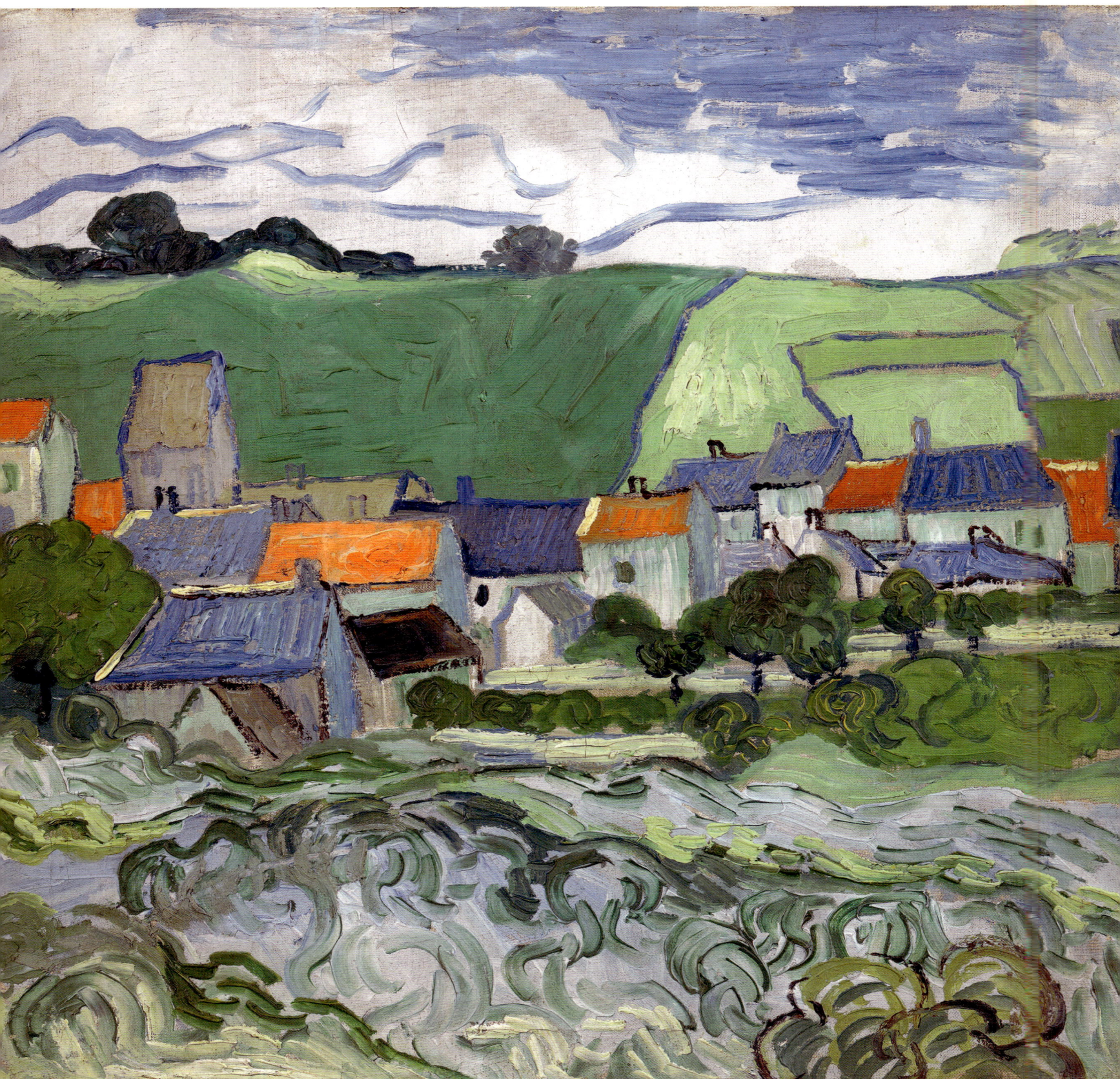

View of Auvers (May–June 1890).
Oil on canvas. Van Gogh Museum,
Amsterdam (Vincent van Gogh Foundation).

"*Auvers is really beautiful – among other things many old thatched roofs, which are becoming rare.*"

~ VINCENT, TO THEO AND JO, MAY 1890

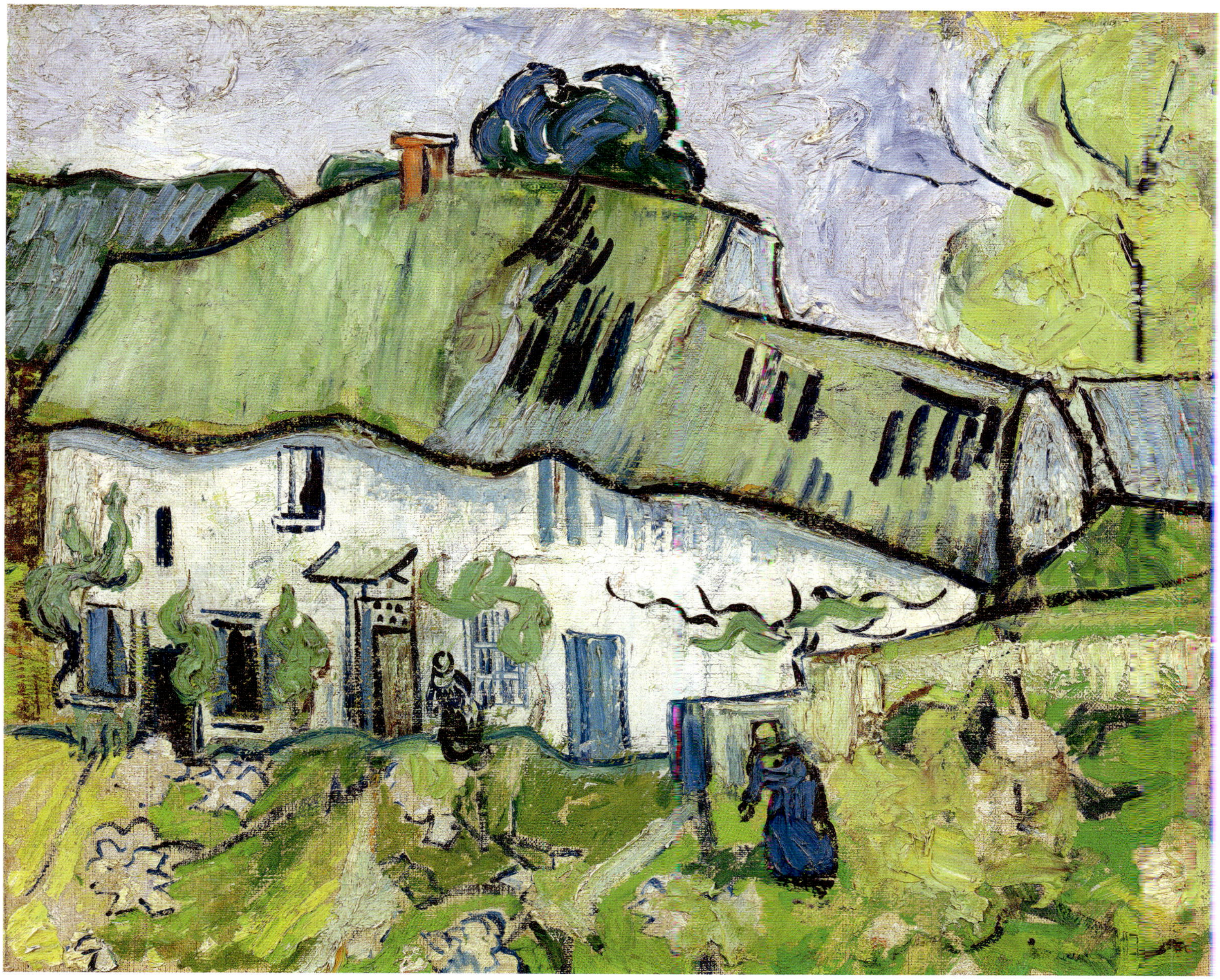

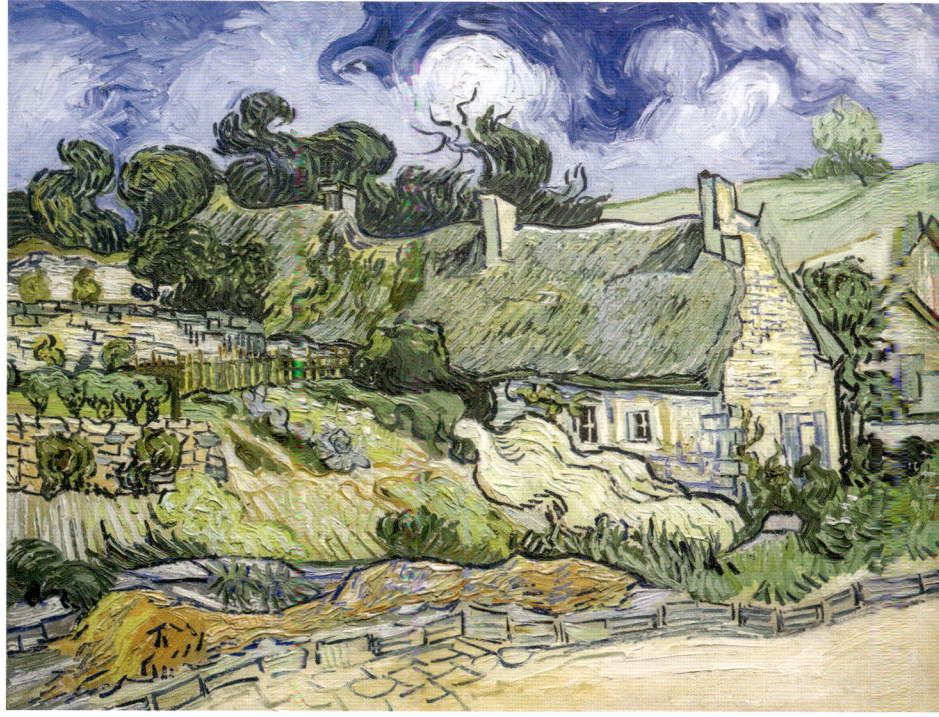

[ABOVE]
Farmhouse with Two Figures (May–June 1890). Oil on canvas. Van Gogh Museum, Amsterdam (Vincent van Gogh Foundation).

[RIGHT]
Thatched Cottages at Cordeville (June 1890). Oil on canvas. Musée d'Orsay, Paris.

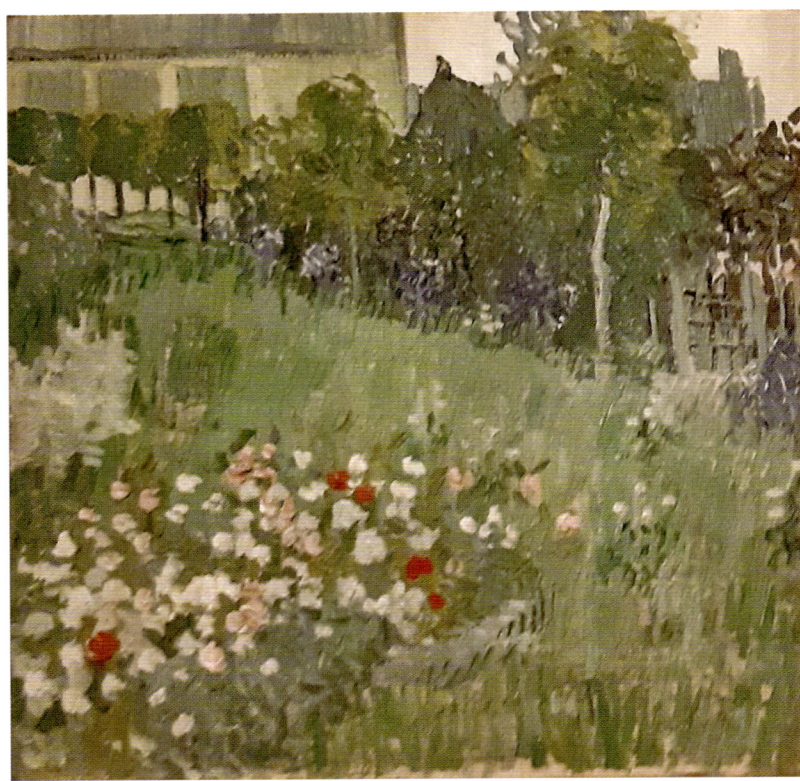

Daubigny's Garden (June 1890). Oil on canvas.
Van Gogh Museum, Amsterdam (Vincent van Gogh Foundation).

*A lifelong admirer of Charles-François Daubigny, Vincent sought out the
landscape painter's home in Auvers. This is the first painting of the garden
there, and with no canvas at hand, he painted on a red-and-white striped tea
towel covered with a bright pink ground layer of lead white pigment mixed
with red. He later made two larger versions on canvas.*

[RIGHT] ***Marguerite Gachet in the Garden***
(June 1890). Oil on canvas. Musée d'Orsay, Paris.

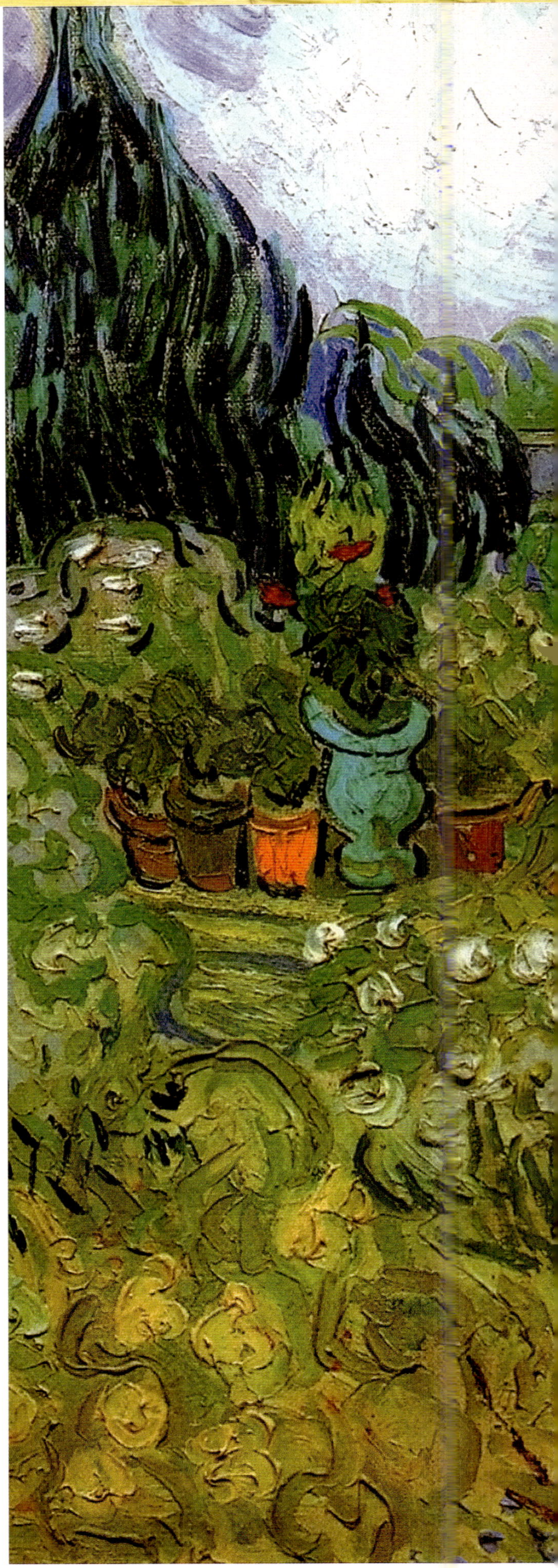

[BELOW] ***Garden in Auvers*** (June–July, 1890). Oil on canvas. Private collection.

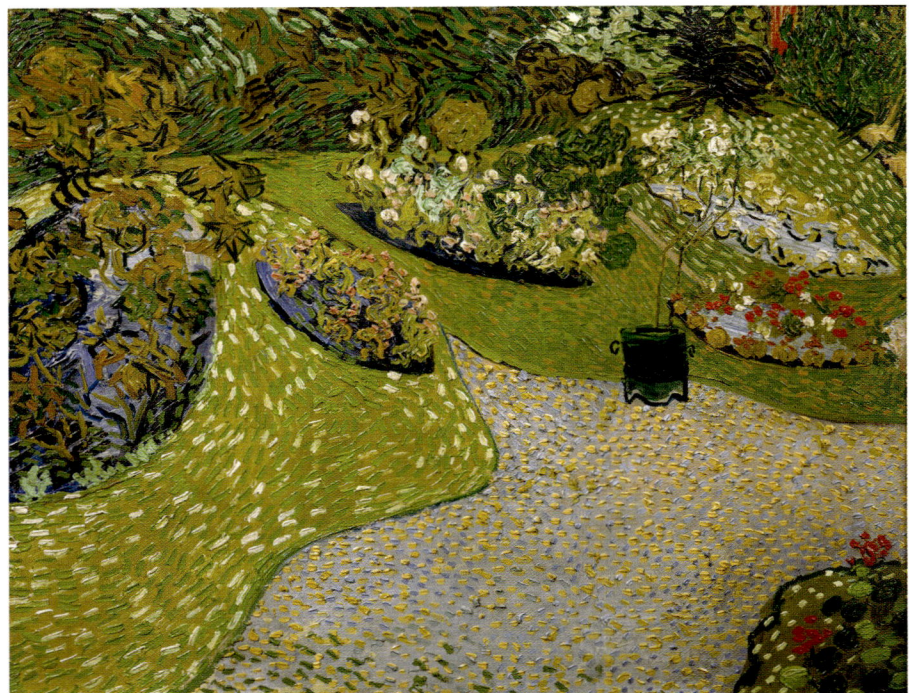

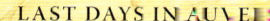

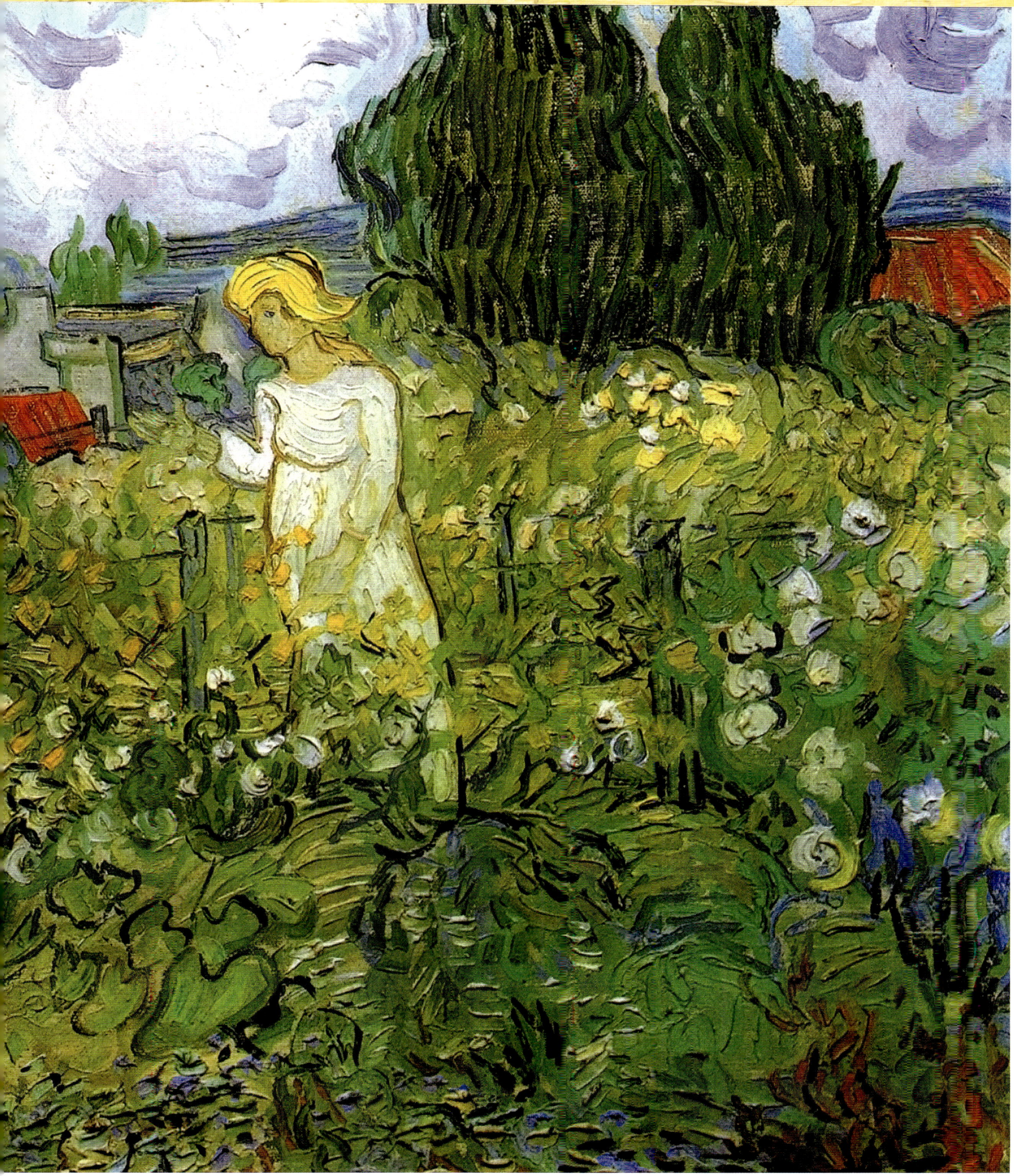

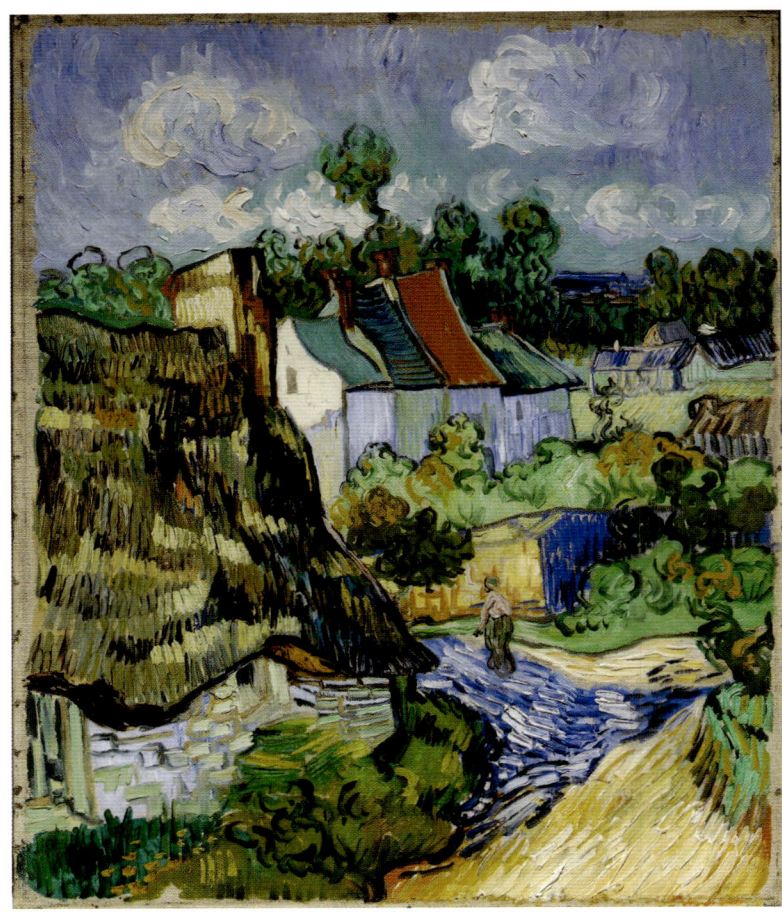

Houses in Auvers (May, 1890). Oil on canvas.
Museum of Fine Arts, Boston.

"*I'd hope, then, that in doing a few canvases of that really seriously, there would be a chance of recouping some of the costs of my stay – for really it's gravely beautiful, it's the heart of the countryside, distinctive and picturesque.*"

~ VINCENT, TO THEO AND JO, MAY 1890

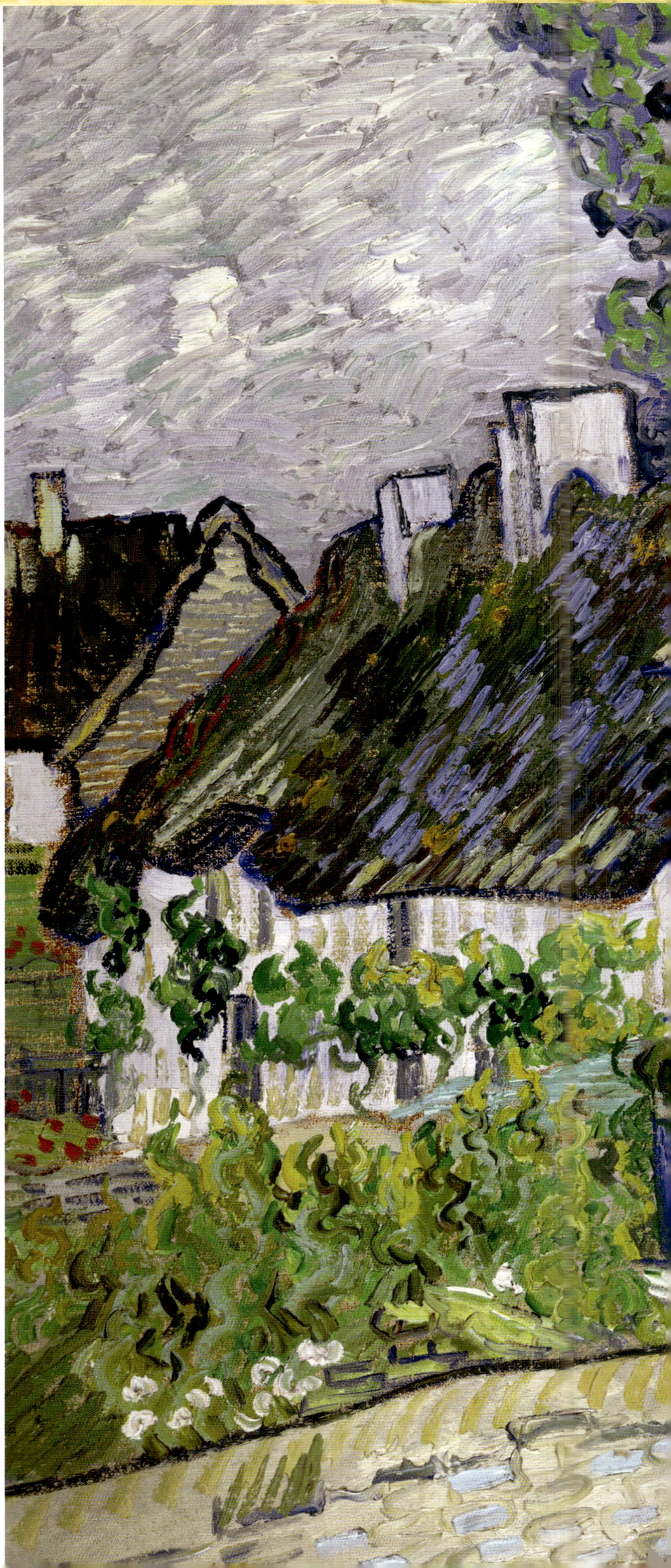

[RIGHT]
Houses in Auvers (June, 1890).
Oil on canvas. The Toledo
Museum of Art, Ohio.

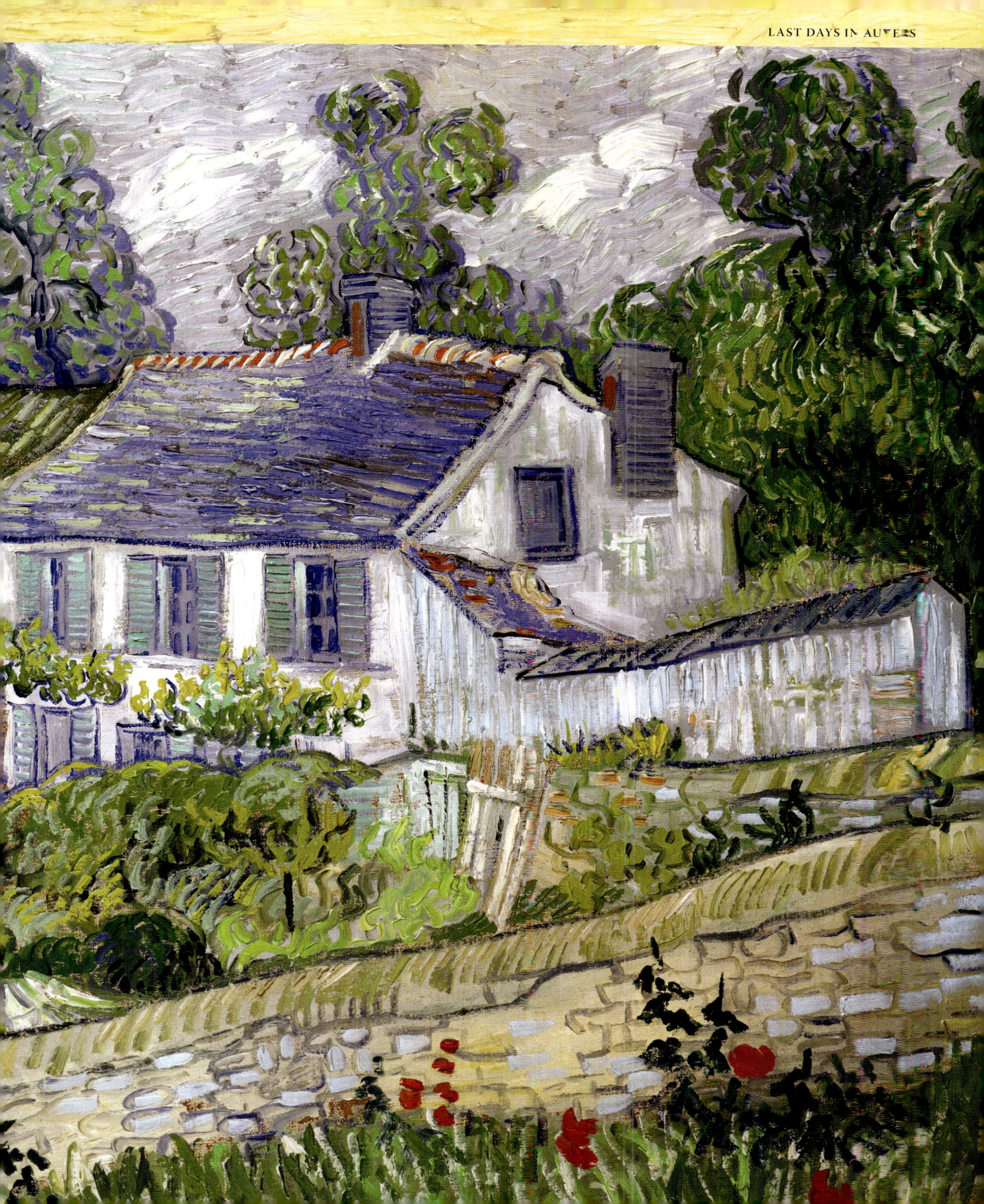

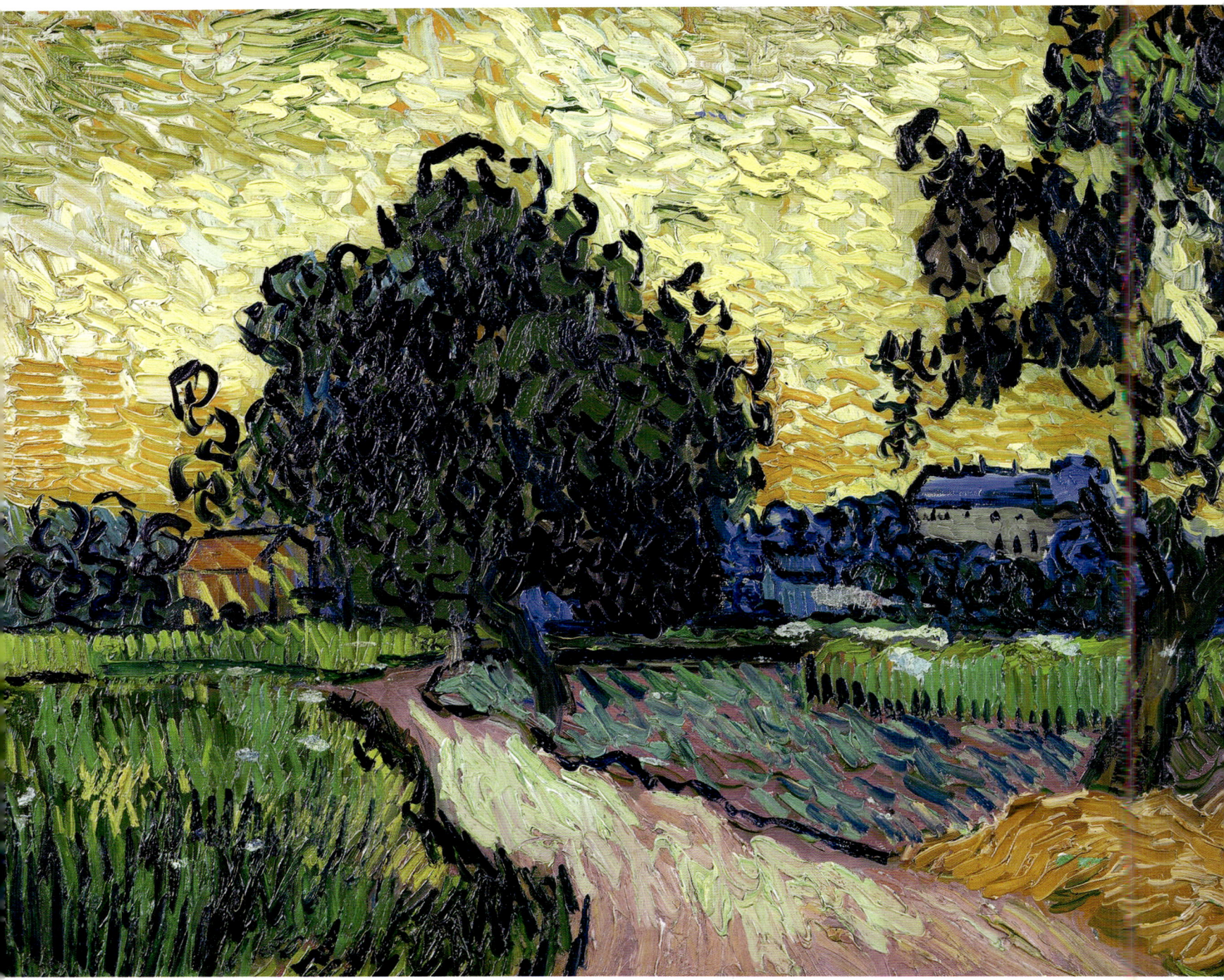

Landscape with the Chateau of Auvers at Sunset (June 1890). Oil on canvas.
Van Gogh Museum, Amsterdam (Vincent van Gogh Foundation).

One of Vincent's vibrant double-square paintings, this landscape is notable for its striking yellow sky.

> *"Lastly, an evening effect – two pear trees quite black against a yellowing sky, with some wheat, and in the violet background the château surrounded by somber greenery."*

~ VINCENT, TO THEO AND JO, JULY 1890

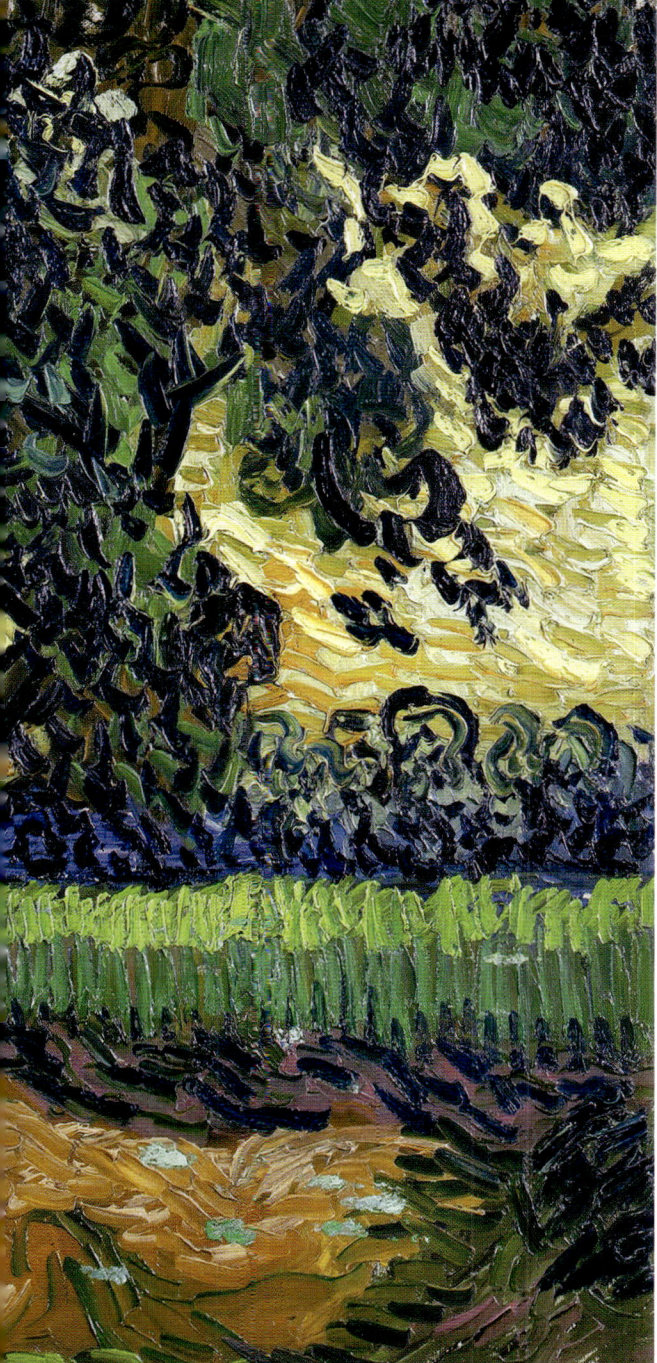

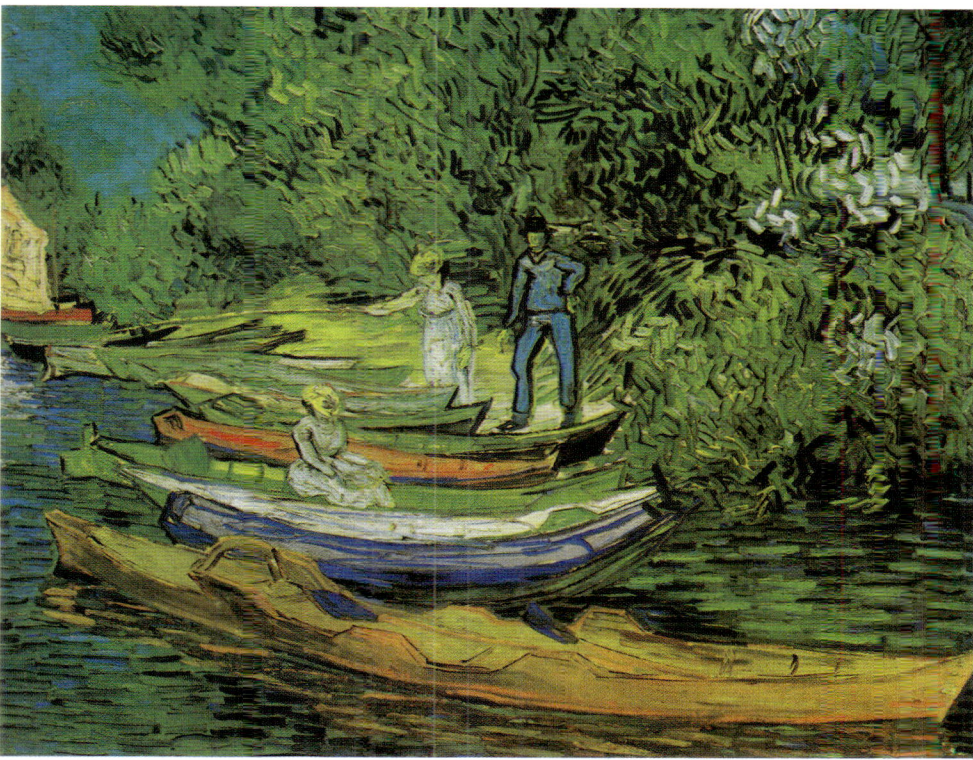

[ABOVE RIGHT]
Bank of the Oise at Auvers
(July 1890). Oil on canvas.
The Detroit Institute of Arts.

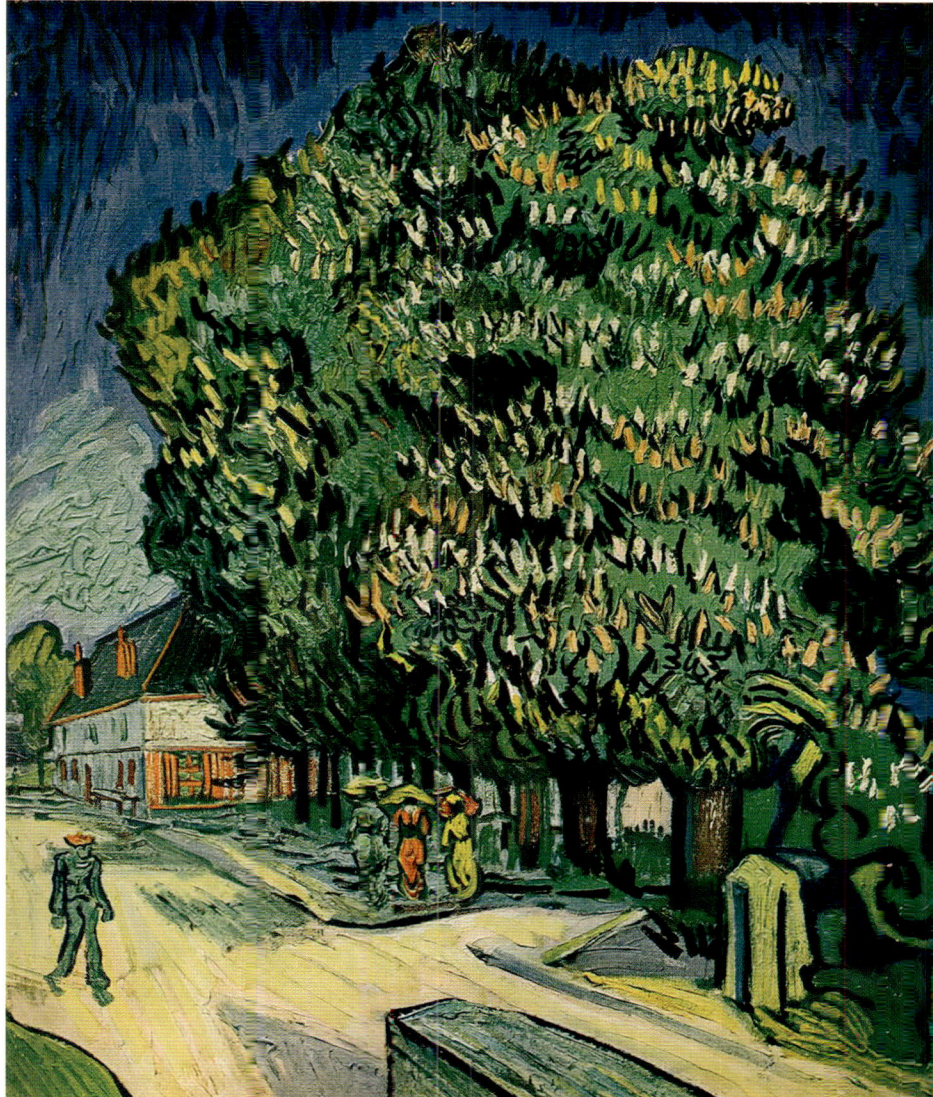

[RIGHT]
Chestnut Trees in Blossom
(May 1890). Oil on canvas.
Private collection.

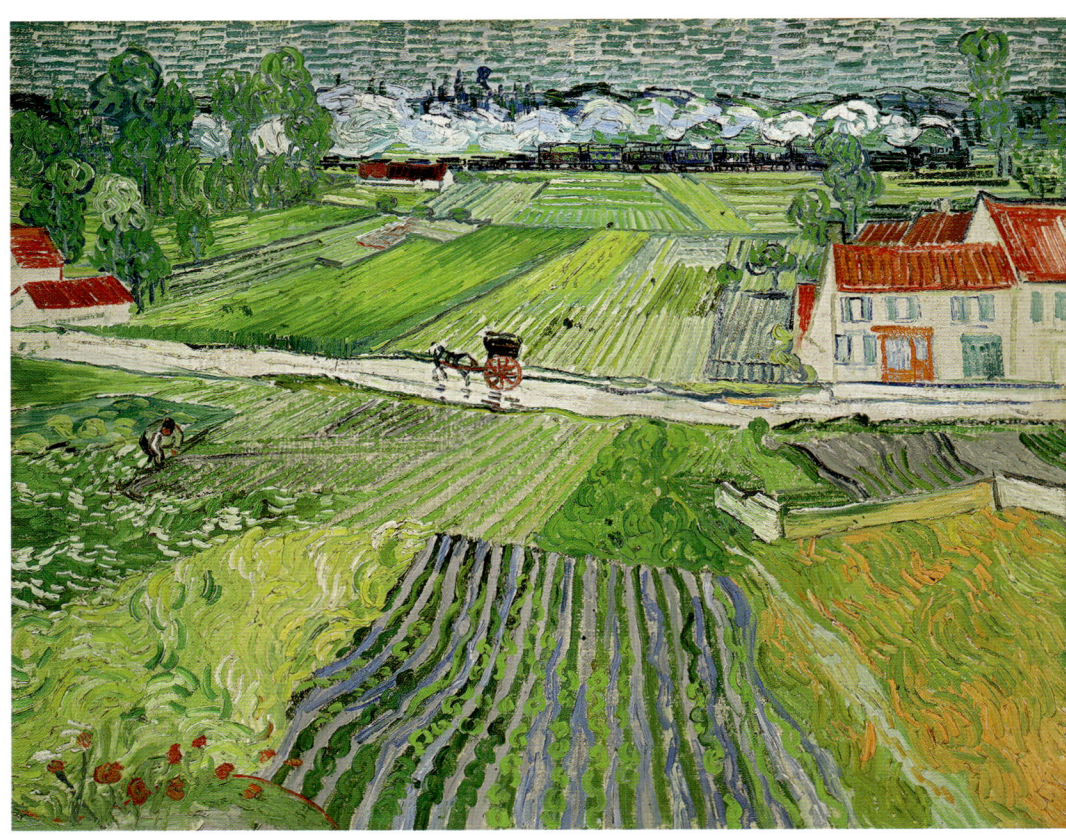

Landscape with Carriage and Train in the Background
(June 1890). Oil on canvas. Pushkin Museum, Moscow.

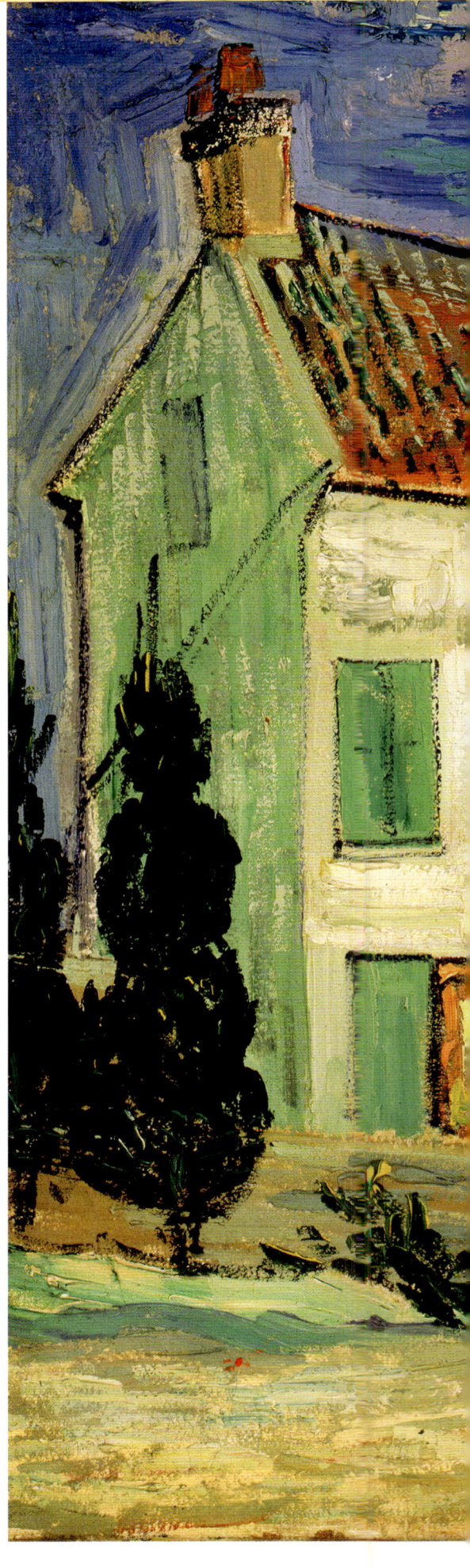

[RIGHT]
The White House at Night (June 1890). Oil on canvas. Hermitage Museum, St. Petersburg.

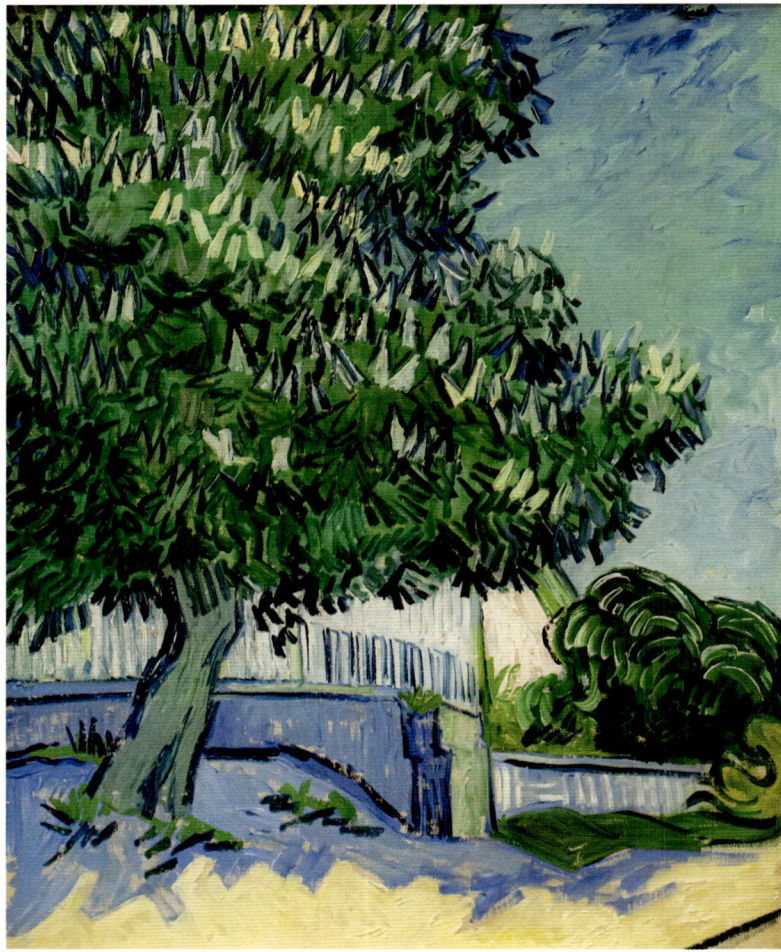

[LEFT]
Chestnut Tree in Blossom (May 1890). Oil on canvas. Kröller-Müller Museum, Otterlo.

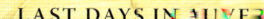

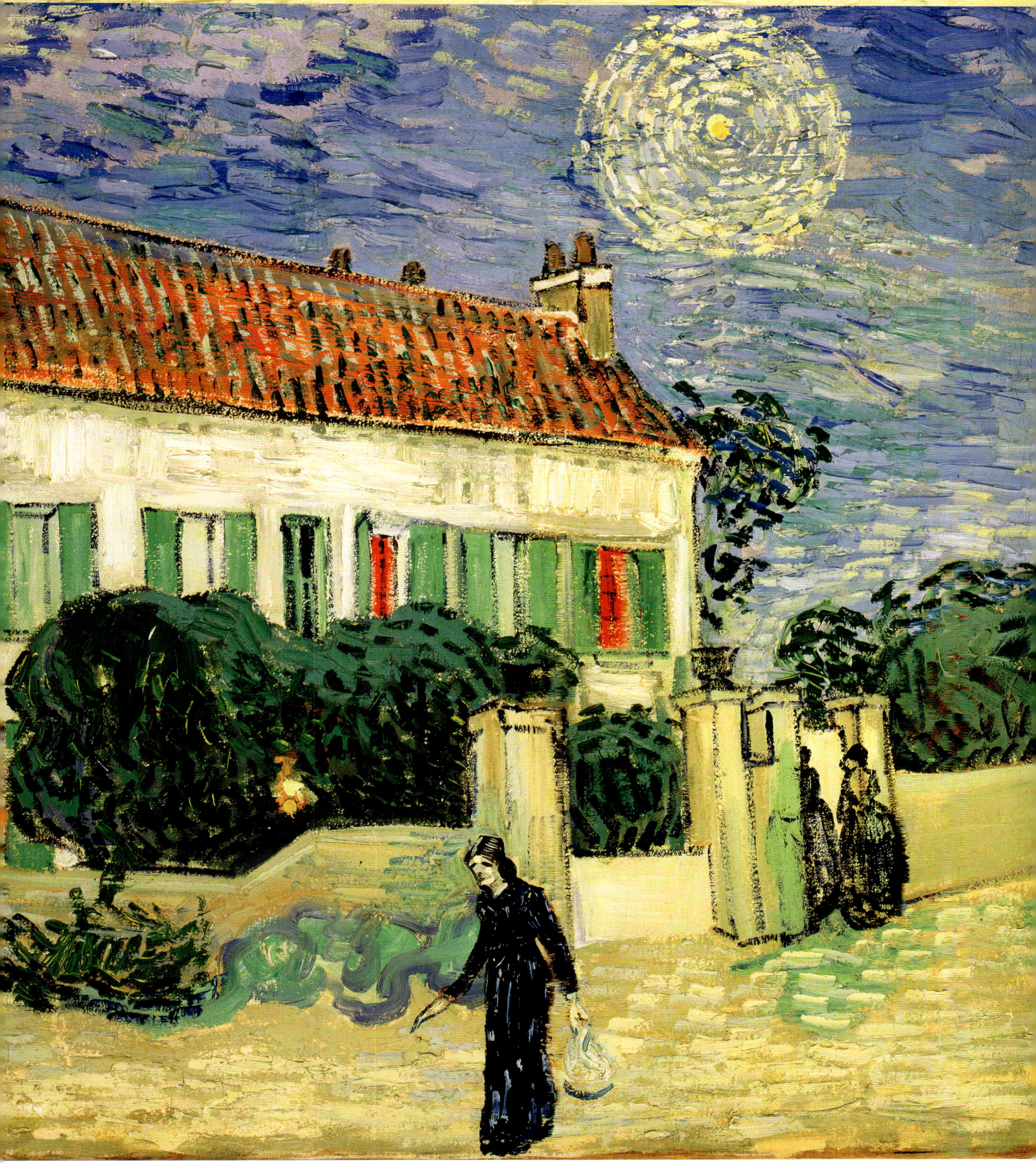

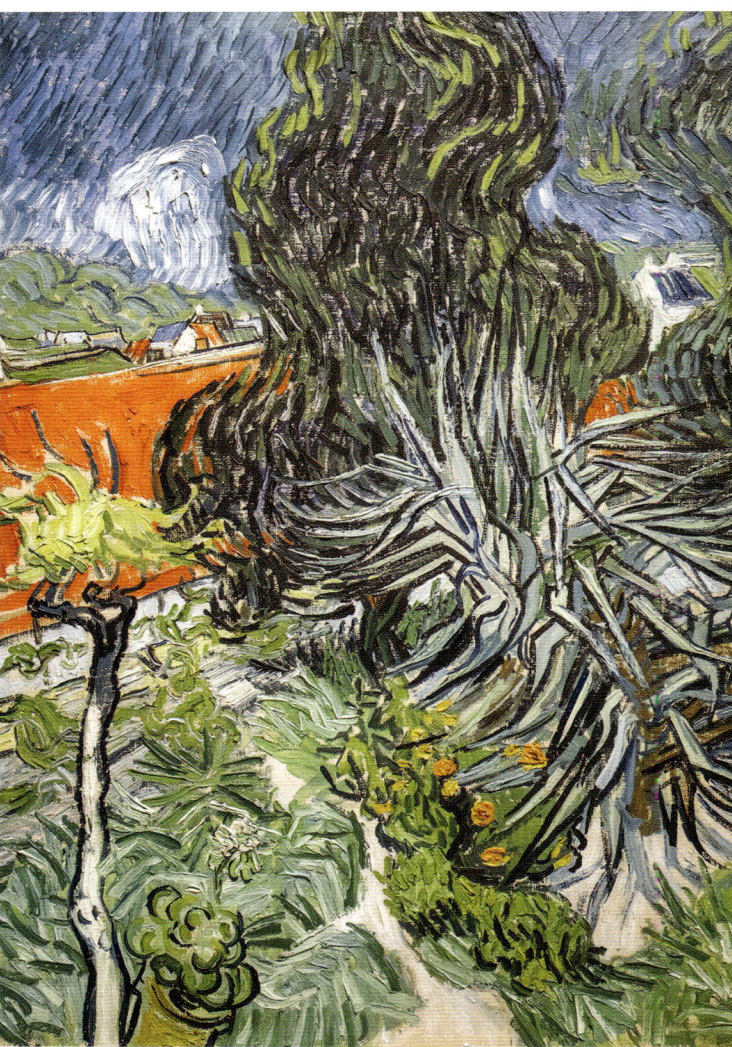

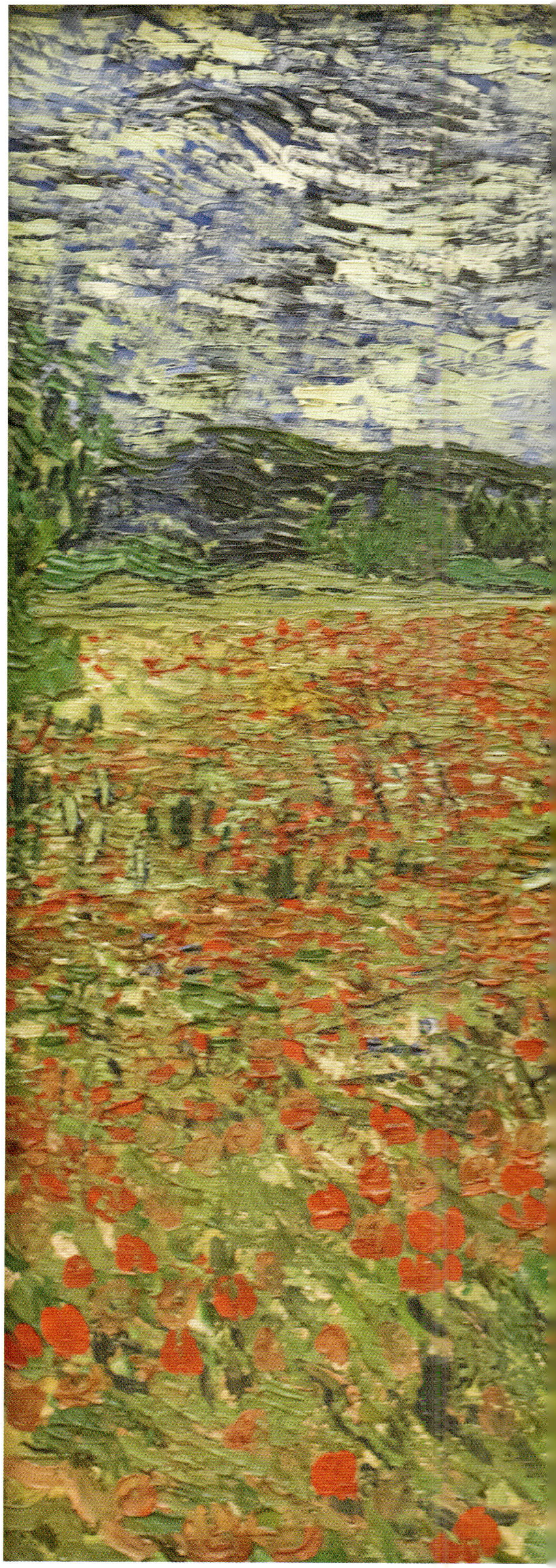

[RIGHT]
Field with Poppies
(June 1890).
Oil on canvas.
Kunstmuseum Den
Haag, The Hague.

[LEFT]
*Doctor Gachet's
Garden in Auvers*
(May 1890). Oil
on canvas. Musée
d'Orsay, Paris.

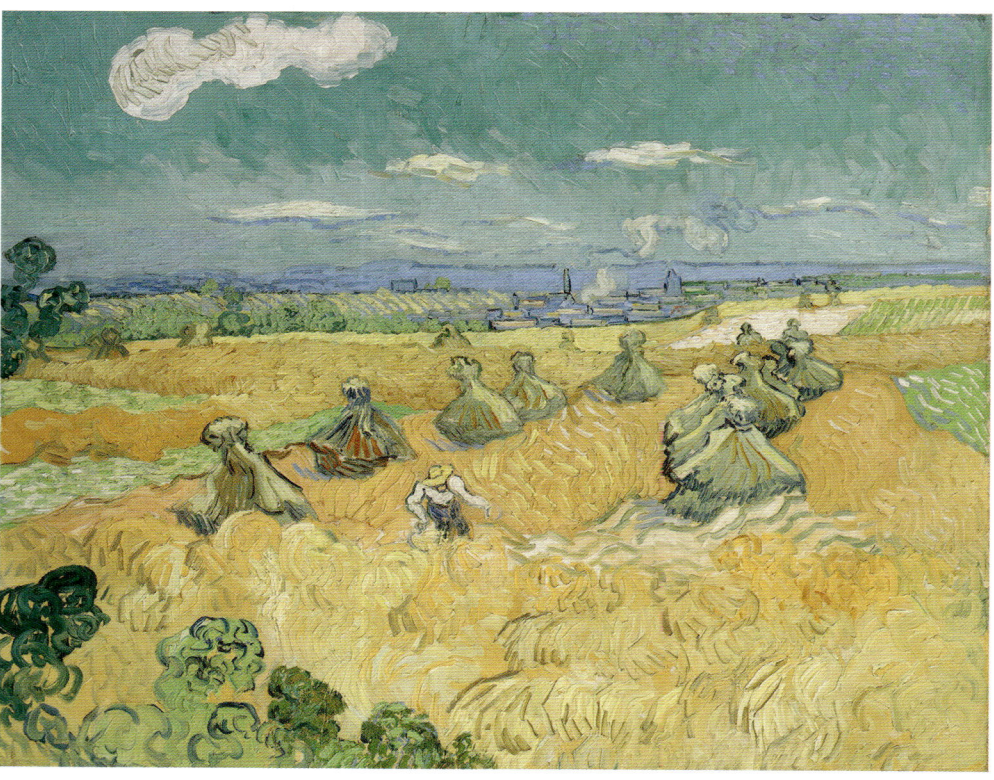

Wheat Stacks with Reaper (July 1890). Oil on canvas.
Toledo Museum of Art, Ohio (Gift of Edward Drummond Libbey).

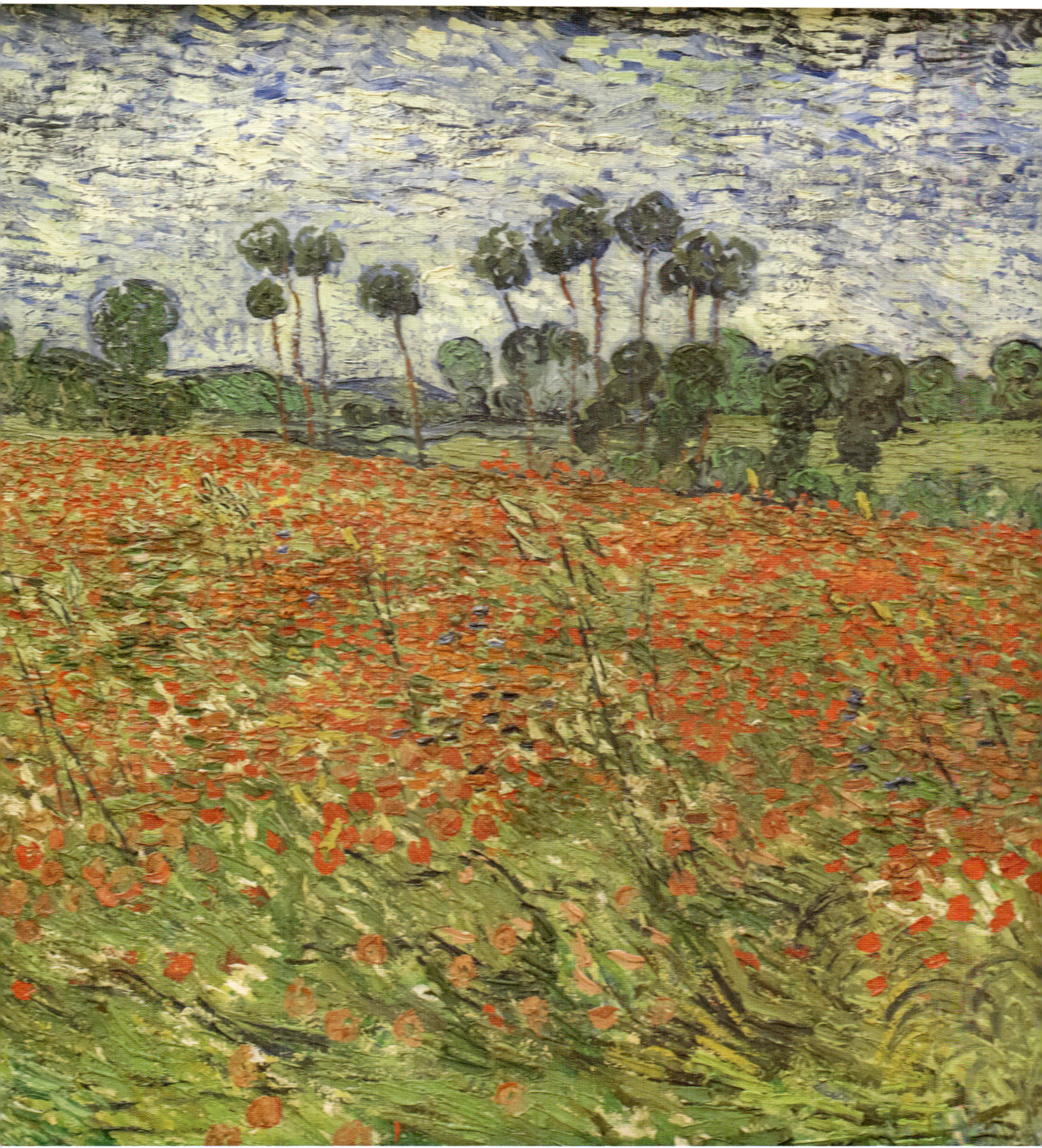

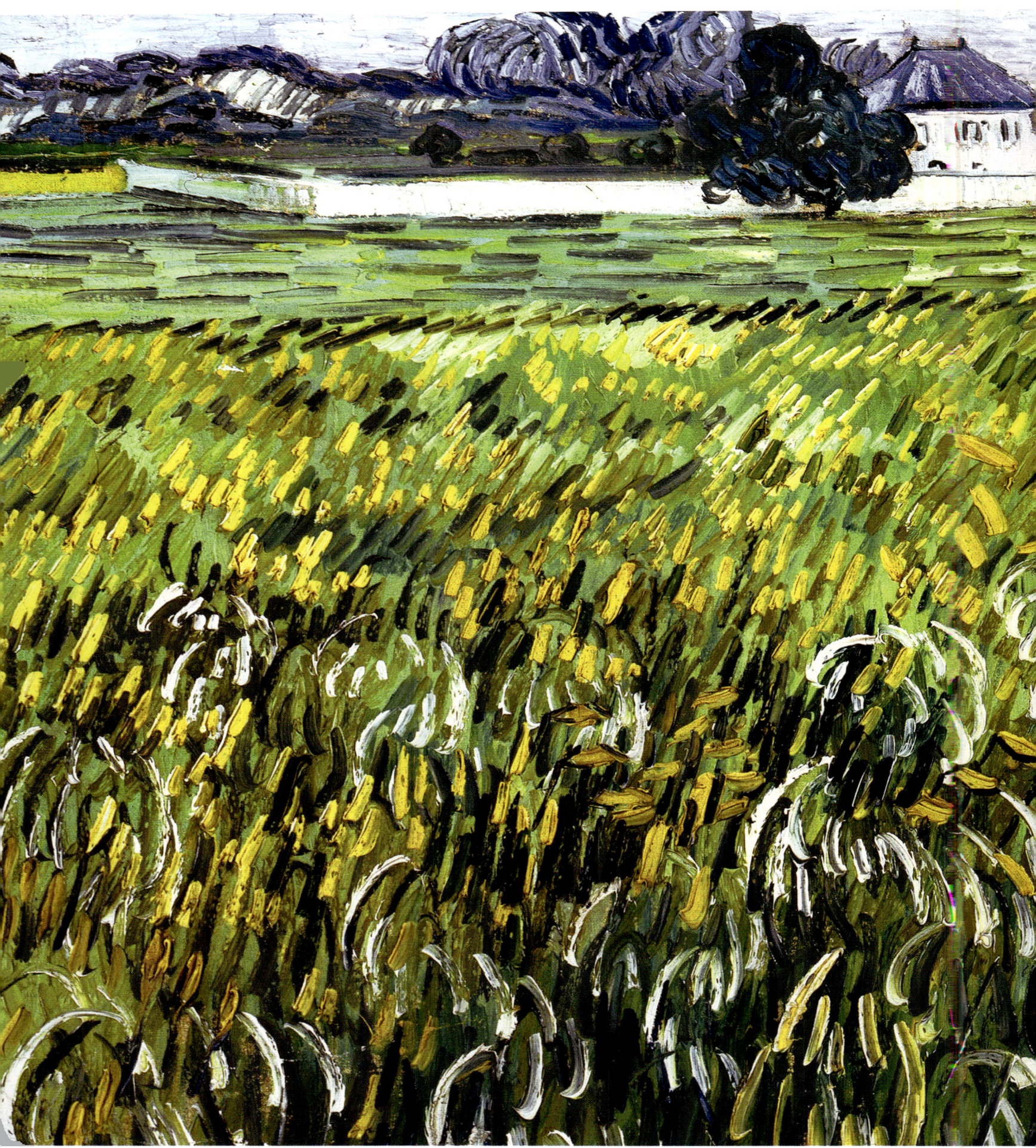

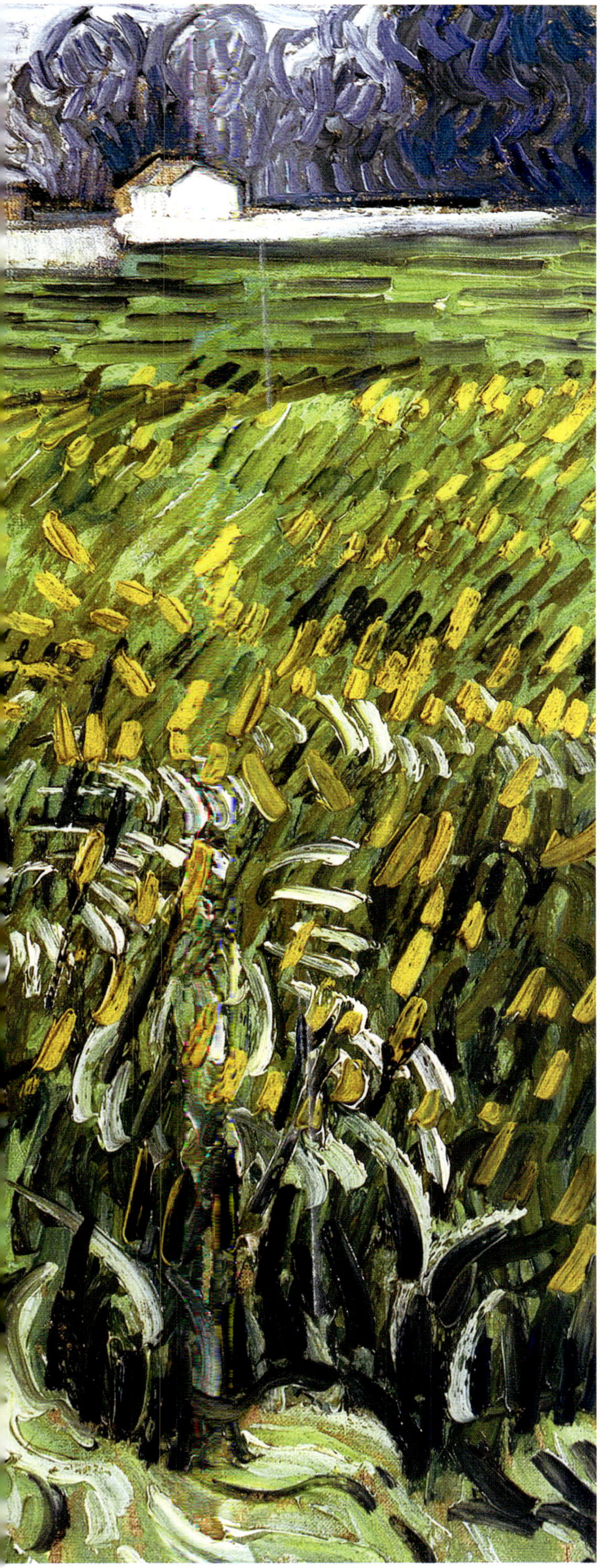

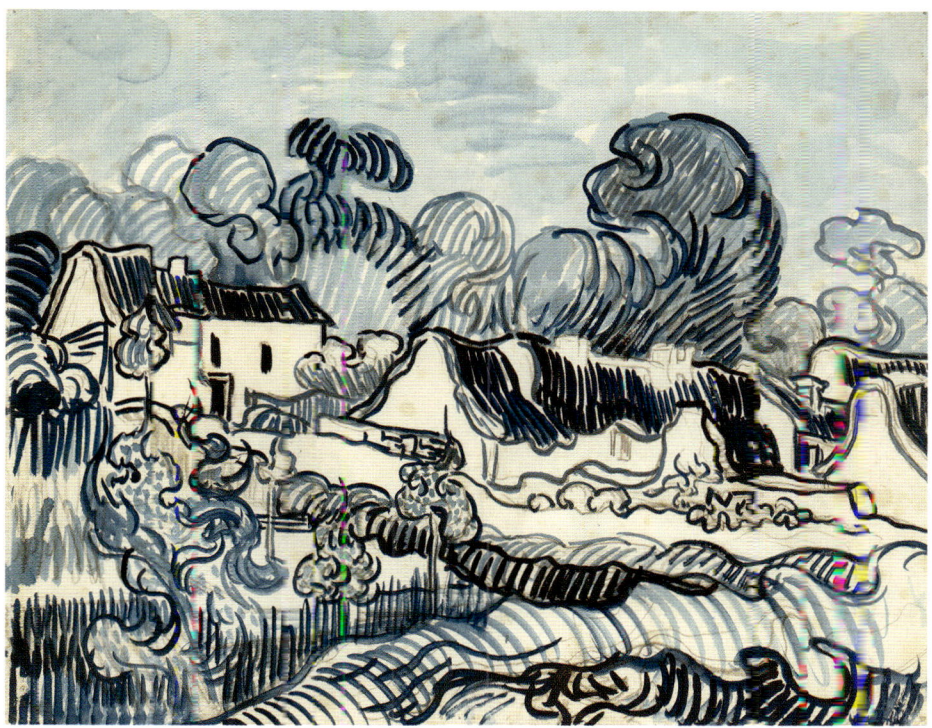

The Landscape With Houses (c. May 1890). Pencil, brush and oil paint, and watercolor on paper. Van Gogh Museum, Amsterdam (Vincent van Gogh Foundation).

[LEFT]
The Wheat Field At Auvers with White House (June 1890).
Oil on canvas. The Phillips Collection, Washington, D.C.

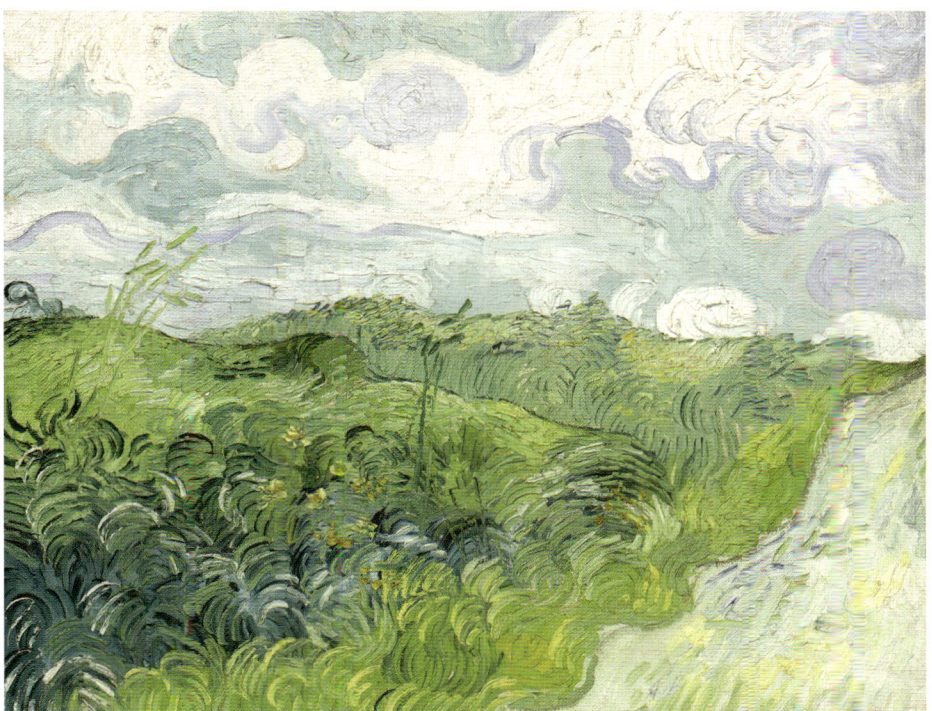

Green Wheat Fields, Auvers (1890).
Oil on canvas. National Gallery of Art, Washington, D.C

*Painted in the last months of his life, this canvas shows another
of his preferred subjects executed with broad, almost calligraphic brushstrokes*

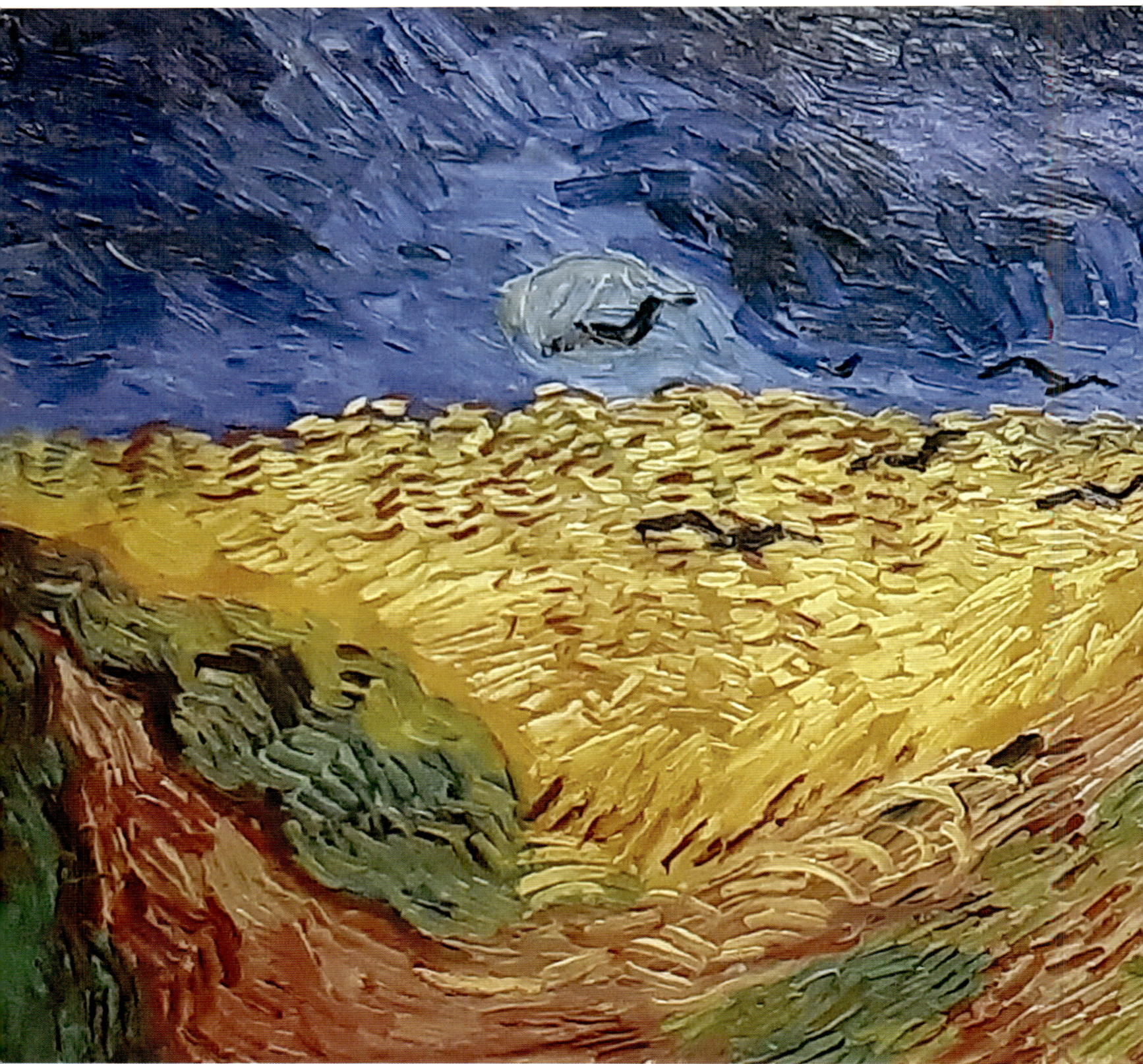

"*Returning there, I set to work. The brush almost fell from my hands …
I had no difficulty in expressing sadness and extreme solitude.*"

VINCENT, WRITING OF THIS PICTURE SHORTLY BEFORE HIS SUICIDE.

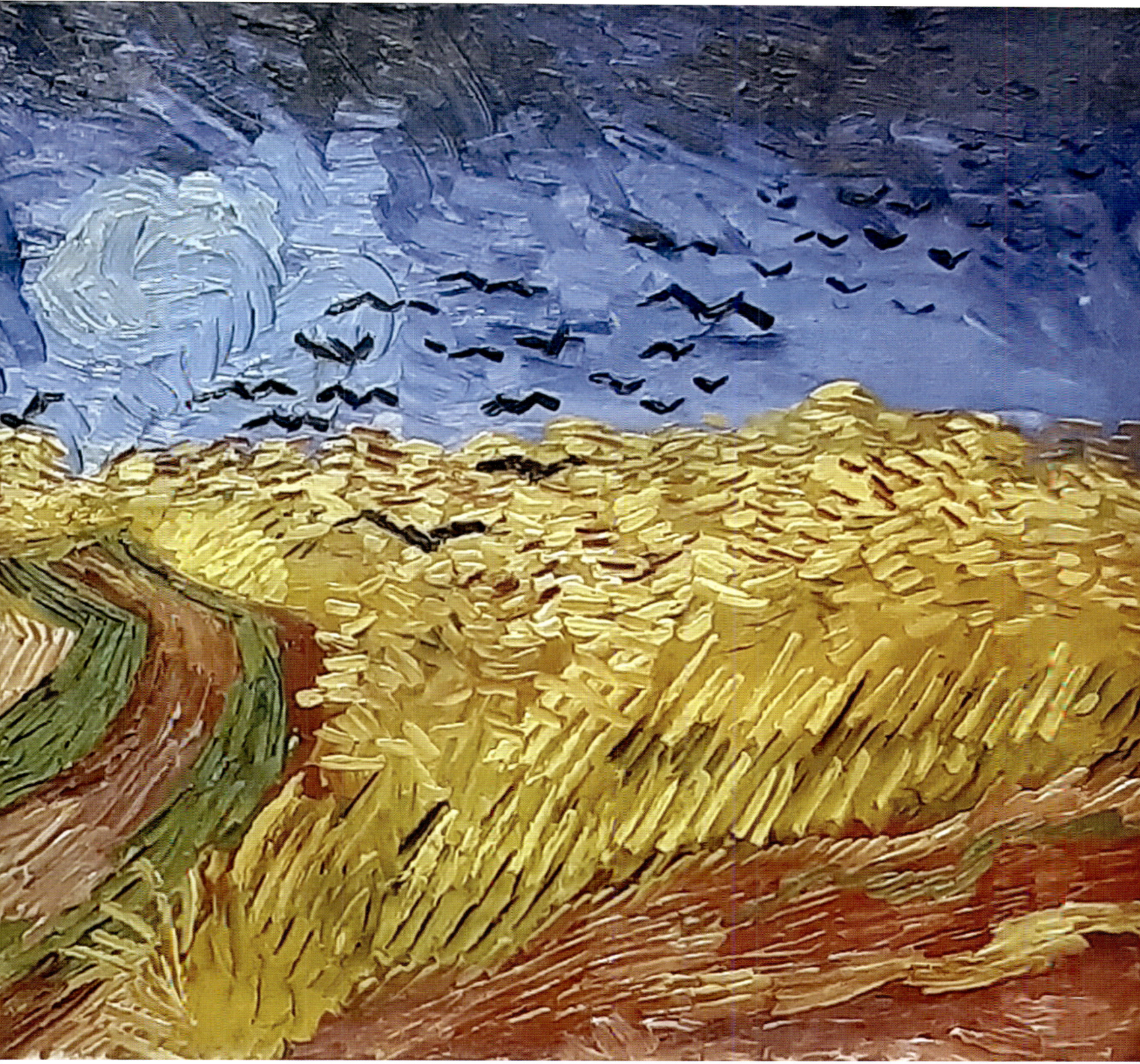

Wheat Field with Crows (July 1890). Oil on canvas.
Van Gogh Museum, Amsterdam (Vincent van Gogh Foundation).

One of Vincent's most famous paintings, Wheat Field with Crows was executed in the last weeks of the artist's life. It is a subject he re-created from his memories of the North as he plunged deeper into depression, and it has garnered much speculation and contention. One of two works that scholars debate over as his last, some think this is a sort of "suicide note." (He shot himself in the very wheat fields he had repeatedly painted). It is a disquieting image for the viewer, with the inversion of a sharply delineated horizon above a turbulent blue sky leading the eye downward over the yellow wheat field to three converging paths, while a flock of menacing black crows swoops forward toward the viewer.

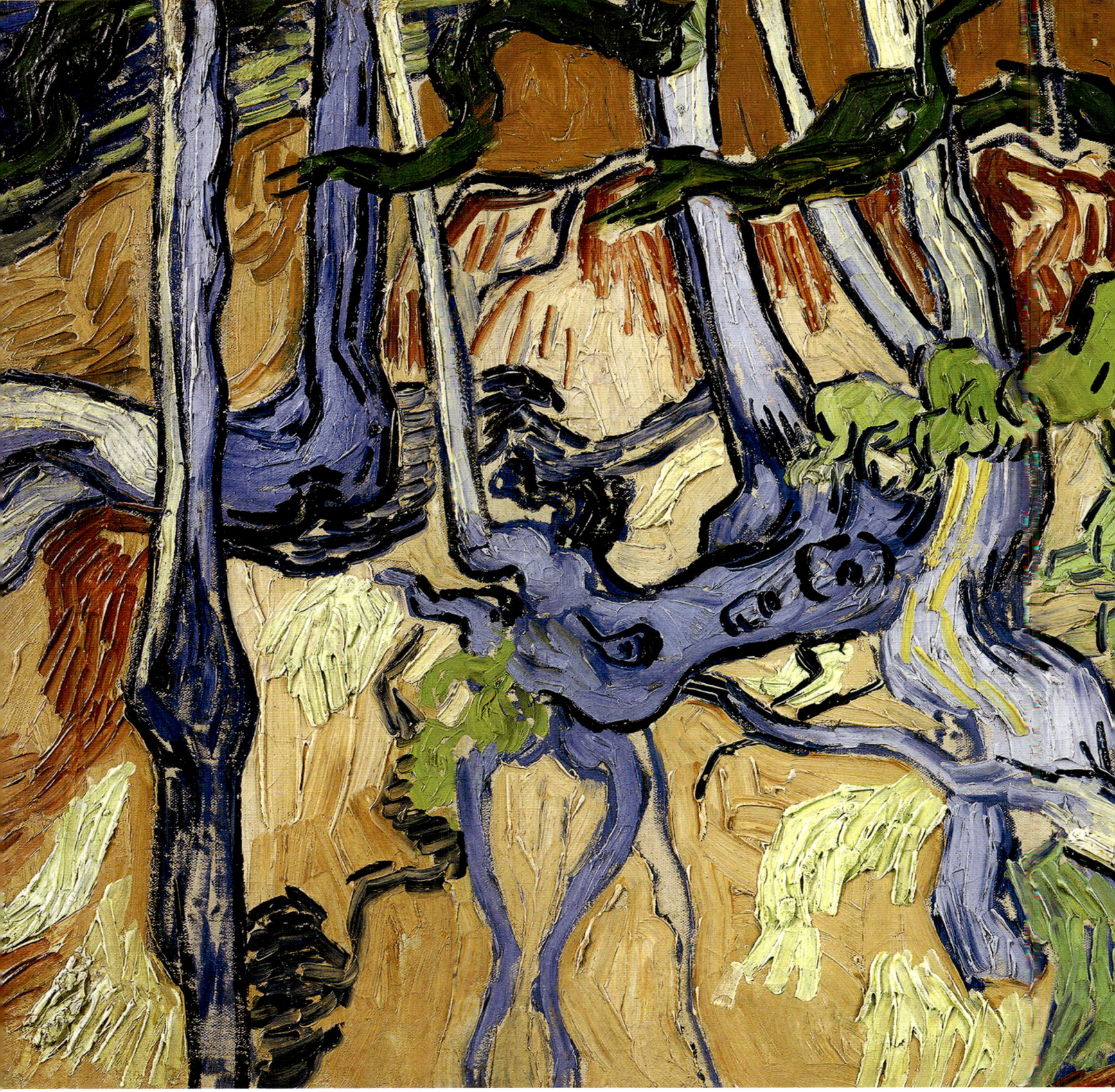

Tree Roots (July 1890). Oil on canvas.
Van Gogh Museum, Amsterdam (Vincent van Gogh Foundation).

*During his final months Vincent chose to paint on double-square canvases, which
are a combination of two 50-by-100-centimeter canvases, resulting in elongated
rectangles, such as* Tree Roots *and the more famous* Wheat Field with Crows.
*Wouter van der Veen, the scientific director of the Institut Van Gogh, believes
Vincent might have been working on this painting just hours before his suicide.*

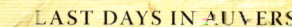

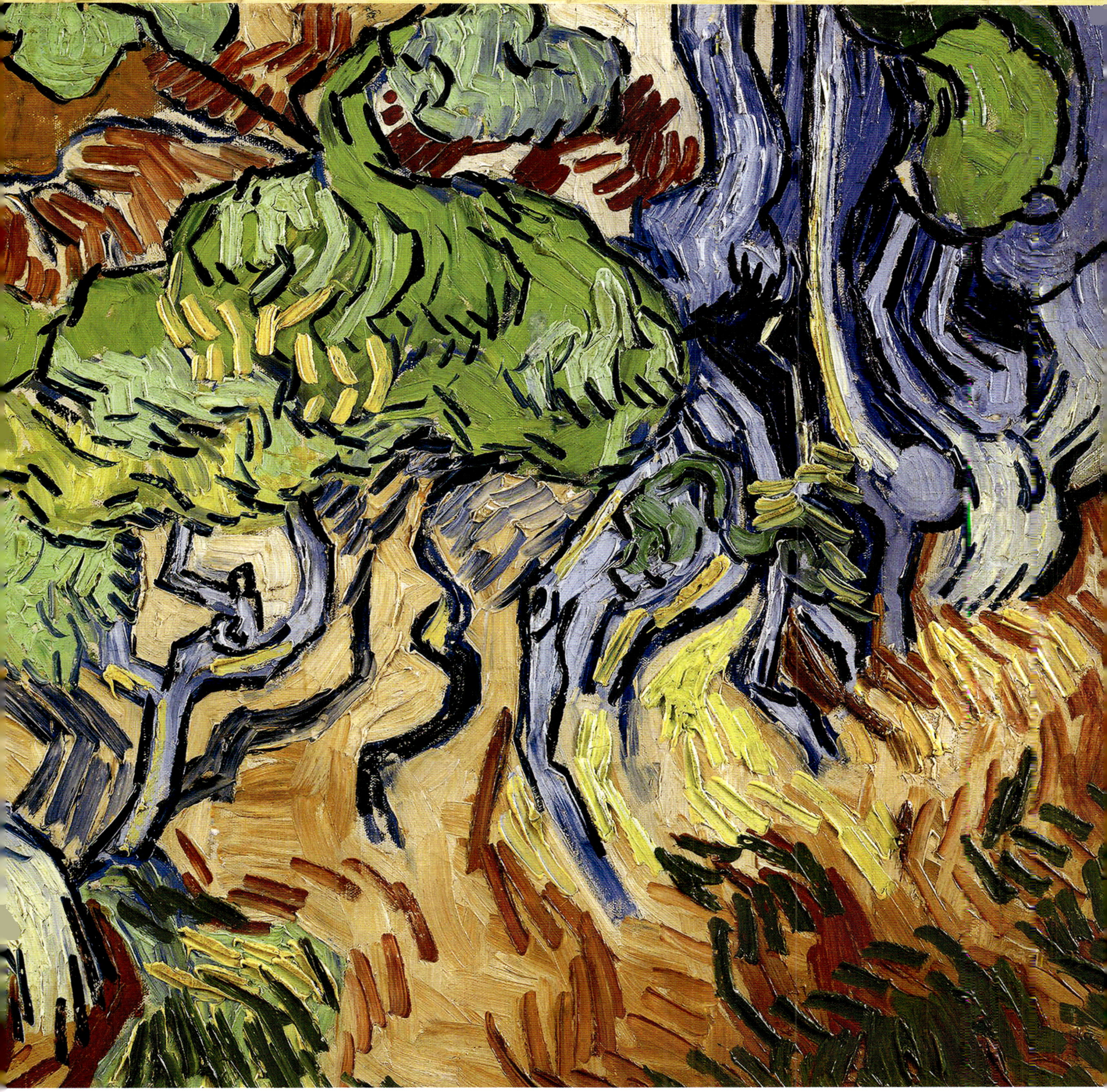

“ *The sadness will last forever.*”

~ VINCENT'S LAST WORDS, ACCORDING TO HIS BROTHER THEO

IMAGE CREDITS

All works are in the public domain, but the publisher and author would like to acknowledge the many museums that display the works of the artist. They would also like to acknowledge the following photographers for their photos of the artwork.

KEY

AL = Alamy Stock Photo
DT = Dreamstime.com
GAP = Google Art Project
SS = Shutterstock.com

t = top   b = bottom   r = right   l = left

Cover: Mrreporter/DT
Table of Contents: Google Art Project
Introduction: Rjcvanhees/DT
Background: Rjcvanhees/DT

STILL LIFE & FLOWER PAINTINGS

6 Artefact/AL; 10 PAINTING/AL; 11t Peter Barritt/AL; 11b Mrreporter /DT; 12t GAP; 12b Tarlaczzoltan /DT; 13t Tarlaczzoltan /DT; 13bl Mrreporter /DT; 14 Art Collection 2/AL; 15l Mrreporter / DT; 16t Everett Collection/SS; 17 Niday Picture Library/AL; 18 Wisconsinart /DT; 19 Mrreporter /DT; 20b Mrreporter /DT; 21 incamerastock/AL; 22–23 Rjcvanhees / DT; 24r incamerastock/AL; 25 Photo 12/ AL; 26 Archivart/AL; 29 Giorgio65 /DT; 32¬–33 Giorgio65 /DT; 34 Mrreporter /DT; 35 Mrreporter /DT; 36 Wisconsinart /DT

PEOPLE & PORTRAITS

40l Rjcvanhees/DT; 40br Rjcvanhees/DT; 42 GAP; 44 Rjcvanhees/DT; 44–45 Rjcvanhees/ DT; 45t Hugo Maertens; 46-47 Rob van Hees/ DT; 47 Rjcvanhees/DT; 49 Wisconsinart/ DT; 50 Bill Waterson/AL; 54 Mrreporter/DT; 55tl Pascaldeloche/DT; 56 Rjcvanhees/DT; 57br Maurice Tromp; 58 Rjcvanhees/DT; 59t Wisconsinart/DT; 59b Wisconsinart/DT; 60tl Tarlaczzoltan/DT; 60br Art Library/AL; 61 GAP; 62t Marsana/DT; 62bl–br Tarlaczzoltan/ DT; 63 Mrreporter/DT; 64 Rjcvanhees/DT; 65t Everett Collection/ SS; 65b Edwardgerges/DT; 66tl Rjcvanhees/DT; 66br Wisconsinart/DT; 67 Historic Images/AL; 68tl Hyla Skopitz; 68bl Cleveland Museum of Art/Howard Agriesti; 71tr Archivart/AL; 71bl PAINTING/AL; 71br Peter van Evert/AL; 72tl Everett Collection/ SS; 72bl Maurice Tromp; 72br Mrreporter/ DT; 73 Giorgio65/DT; 74 Archivart/AL; 75l Mrreporter/DT

LANDSCAPES & PLACES

76 Edwardgerges/DT; 78t GAP; 78–79 Mrreporter/DT; 80–81 Rjcvanhees/DT; 82t Rjcvanhees/DT; 82–83 Mrreporter/DT; 84t Mrreporter/DT; 84b Mrreporter/DT; 85 Maurice Tromp; 86–87 Heritage Image Partnership Ltd /AL; 88 incamerastock/ AL; 89b Peter Barritt/AL; 90 Hoexema/ DT; 90–91 Artefact/AL; 92t Bill Waterson/ AL; 92b Pictures Now/AL; 93t Album/ AL; 93b World History Archive/AL; 94–95 Rjcvanhees/DT; 96 FabioConcetta/DT; 96–97 Wisconsinart/DT; 98t Giorgio65/DT; 99b Tarlaczzoltan/DT; 100–101 Rjcvanhees/DT; 102t Tarlaczzoltan/DT; 104t Maurice Tromp; 104–105 Wisconsinart/DT; 107t Rjcvanhees/ DT; 107b Maurice Tromp; 108 Mrreporter/DT; 109l Mrreporter/DT; 110 Mrreporter/DT; 112t Giorgio65/DT; 112–113 Mrreporter/DT; 114–115 Tarlaczzoltan/DT; 116 Rjcvanhees/DT; 116–117 Mrreporter/DT; 118t Mrreporter/DT; 118b Rjcvanhees/DT; 118–119 Mrreporter/DT; 120–121 Rjcvanhees/DT; 122 Giorgio65/DT; 123t Mrreporter/DT; 123b PAINTING/AL; 124t Universal Images Group North America LLC/AL; 125 Universal Images Group North America LLC/AL; 126 FAMOUS PAINTINGS/ AL; 126–127 Mrreporter/DT; 128–129 Rjcvanhees/DT; 129t Tarlaczzoltan/DT; 129b Art Collection 2/AL; 130 Rjcvanhees/DT;

131b Maurice Tromp; 132bl Peter Horree /AL; 132–133 FineArt /AL; 134 Karaul/DT; 134–135 Mrreporter/DT; 136–137 Mikolaj64/DT; 138 PAINTING /AL; 139 Mrreporter/DT; 140–141 Artefact /AL; 142 Rjcvanhees/DT; 142–143 incamerastock /AL; 145b Rjcvanhees/DT; 146 Tarlaczzoltan/DT; 147 Rjcvanhees/DT; 148–149 Rjcvanhees/DT; 150t Mrreporter/DT; 151t YUNUSI/DT; 152–153 Mrreporter/DT; 154 Rjcvanhees/DT; 155t Edwardgerges/DT; 155b Rjcvanhees/DT; 156–157 Rjcvanhees/DT; 159 Giorgio65/DT; 160–161Giorgio65/DT; 162tr Rjcvanhees/DT; 162b GAP; 163 Giorgio65/DT; 164–165 Giorgio65/DT; 166–167 Mrreporter/ DT; 168 Rjcvanhees/DT; 170 Rjcvanhees/DT; 171 Artefact /AL; 172t Peter Horree /AL; 172b PAINTING /AL; 174 Mrreporter/DT; 173 Wisconsinart/DT; 175t Mrreporter/DT; 175b Wisconsinart/DT; 176t Tarlaczzoltan/DT; 176–177 Mrreporter/DT; 178–179 Mrreporter/ DT; 180–181 Mrreporter/DT; 181b The Print Collector /AL; 182t Mrreporter/DT; 182b Rjcvanhees/DT; 182–183 Mrreporter/DT; 184t Wisconsinart/DT; 184–185 Rjcvanhees/DT; 186–187 Mrreporter/DT; 187t Mrreporter/ DT; 187b Everett Collection/SS; 188–189 Tarlaczzoltan/DT; 190–191 Mrreporter/DT; 192 Tarlaczzoltan/DT

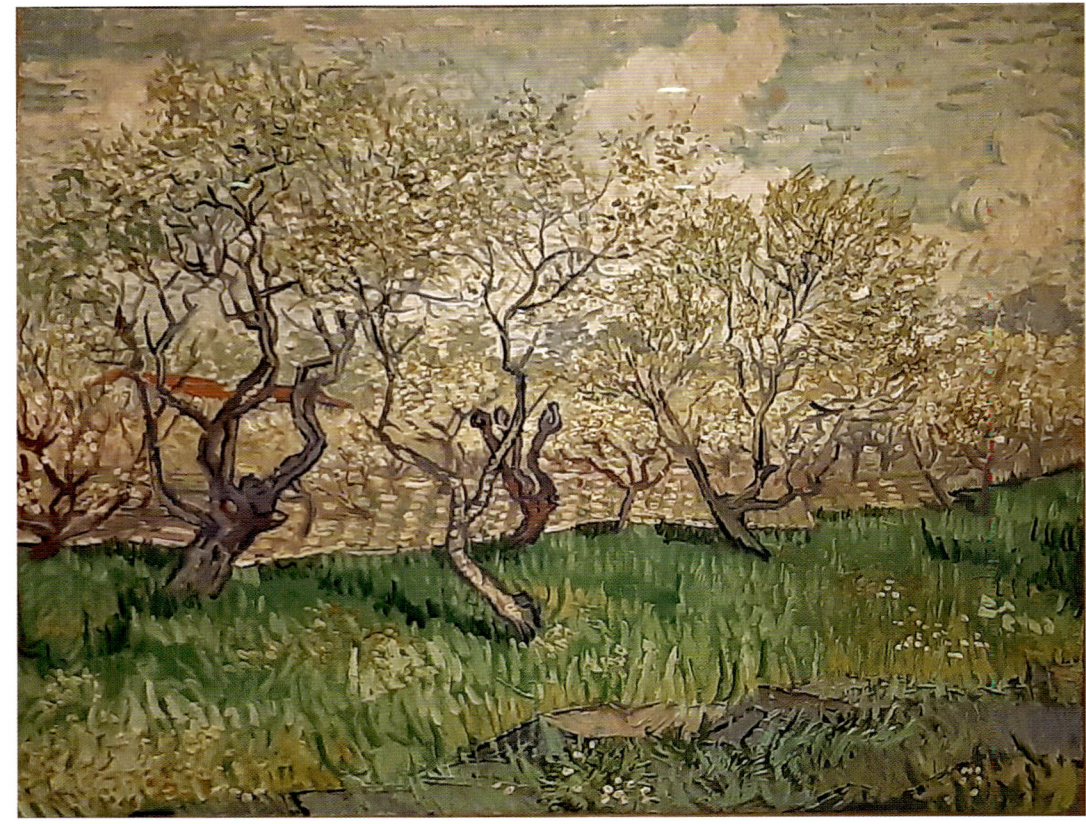

Orchard in Blossom (April 1888). Oil on canvas.
Van Gogh Museum, Amsterdam (Vincent van Gogh Foundation).